THE LETTERS OF QUE[...]
FROM HER MAJESTY'S [...]
THE YEARS 1837 AND [...]

Queen of Great

J

J

ᴚꓚ

THE LETTERS OF QUEEN VICTORIA : A SELECTION FROM HER MAJESTY'S CORRESPONDENCE BETWEEN THE YEARS 1837 AND 1861 : VOLUME 1, 1837-1843

Published by Wallachia Publishers

New York City, NY

First published circa 1901

Copyright © Wallachia Publishers, 2015

All rights reserved

ABOUT WALLACHIA PUBLISHERS

Wallachia Publishers mission is to publish the world's finest European history texts. More information on our recent publications and catalog can be found on our website.

Links to: Volume II: Volume III

QUEEN VICTORIA RECEIVING THE NEWS OF HER ACCESSION TO THE THRONE, JUNE 20, 1837
From the picture by H. T. Wells, R.A., at Buckingham Palace
Frontispiece, Vol. I.

PREFACE

Entrusted by His Majesty the King with the duty of making a selection from Queen Victoria's correspondence, we think it well to describe briefly the nature of the documents which we have been privileged to examine, as well as to indicate the principles which have guided us throughout. It has been a task of no ordinary difficulty. Her Majesty Queen Victoria dealt with her papers, from the first, in a most methodical manner; she formed the habit in early days of preserving her private letters, and after her accession to the Throne all her official papers were similarly treated, and bound in volumes. The Prince Consort instituted an elaborate system of classification, annotating and even indexing many of the documents with his own hand. The result is that the collected papers form what is probably the most extraordinary series of State documents in the world. The papers which deal with the Queen's life up to the year 1861 have been bound in chronological order, and comprise between five and six hundred volumes. They consist, in great part, of letters from Ministers detailing the proceedings of Parliament, and of various political memoranda dealing with home, foreign, and colonial policy; among these are a few drafts of Her Majesty's replies. There are volumes concerned with the affairs of almost every European country; with the history of India, the British Army, the Civil List, the Royal Estates, and all the complicated machinery of the Monarchy and the Constitution. There are letters from monarchs and royal personages, and there is further a whole series of volumes dealing with matters in which the Prince Consort took a special interest. Some of them are arranged chronologically, some by subjects. Among the most interesting volumes are those containing the letters written by Her Majesty to her uncle Leopold, King of the Belgians, and his replies.1 The collection of letters from and to Lord Melbourne forms another hardly less interesting series. In many places Queen Victoria caused extracts, copied from her own private Diaries, dealing with important political events or describing momentous interviews, to be inserted in the volumes, with the evident intention of illustrating and completing the record.

Footnote 1: A set of volumes containing the Queen's letters to Lord John Russell came into our hands too late to be made use of for the present publication.

It became obvious at once that it was impossible to deal with these papers exhaustively. They would provide material for a historical series extending to several hundred volumes. Moreover, on the other hand, there are many gaps, as a great deal of the business of State was transacted by interviews of which no official record is preserved.

His Majesty the King having decided that no attempt should be made to publish these papers in extenso, it was necessary to determine upon some definite principle of selection. It became clear that the only satisfactory plan was to publish specimens of such documents as would serve to bring out the development of the Queen's character and disposition, and to give typical instances of her methods in dealing with political and social matters—to produce, in fact, a book for British citizens and British subjects, rather than a book for students of political history. That the inner working of the unwritten constitution of the country; that some of the unrealised checks and balances; that the delicate equipoise of the component parts of our executive machinery, should stand revealed, was inevitable. We have thought it best, throughout, to abstain from unnecessary comment and illustration. The period is so recent, and has been so often traversed by historians and biographers, that it appeared to us a waste of valuable space to attempt to reconstruct the history of the years from which this correspondence has been selected, especially as Sir Theodore Martin, under the auspices of the Queen herself, has dealt so minutely and exhaustively with the relations of the Queen's innermost circle to the political and social life of the time. It is tempting, of course, to add illustrative anecdotes from the abundant Biographies and Memoirs of the period; but our aim has been to infringe as little as possible upon the space available for the documents themselves, and to provide just sufficient comment to enable an ordinary reader, without special knowledge of the period, to follow the course of events, and to realise the circumstances under which the Queen's childhood was passed, the position of affairs at the time of her accession, and the personalities of those who had influenced her in early years, or by whom she was surrounded.

The development of the Queen's character is clearly indicated in the papers, and it possesses an extraordinary interest. We see one of highly vigorous and active temperament, of strong affections, and with a deep sense of responsibility, placed at an early age, and after a quiet girlhood, in a position the greatness of which it is impossible to exaggerate. We see her character expand and deepen, schooled by mighty experience into patience and sagacity and wisdom, and yet never losing a particle of the strength, the decision, and the devotion with which she had been originally endowed. Up to the year 1861 the Queen's career was one of unexampled prosperity. She was happy in her temperament, in her health, in her education, in her wedded life, in her children. She saw a great Empire grow through troubled times in liberty and power and greatness; yet this prosperity brought with it no shadow of complacency, because the Queen felt with an increasing depth the anxieties and responsibilities inseparable from her great position. Her happiness, instead of making her self-absorbed, only quickened her beneficence and her womanly desire that her subjects should be enabled to enjoy a similar happiness based upon the same simple virtues. Nothing comes out more strongly in these documents than the laborious patience with which the Queen kept herself informed of the minutest details of political and social movements both in her own and other countries.

It is a deeply inspiring spectacle to see one surrounded by every temptation which worldly greatness can present, living from day to day so simple, vivid, and laborious a life; and it is impossible to conceive a more fruitful example of duty and affection and energy, displayed on so august a scale, and in the midst of such magnificent surroundings. We would venture to believe that nothing could so deepen the personal devotion of the Empire to the memory of that great Queen who ruled it so wisely and so long, and its deeply-rooted attachment to the principle of constitutional monarchy, as the gracious act of His Majesty the King in allowing the inner side of that noble life and career to be more clearly revealed to a nation whose devotion to their ancient liberties is inseparably connected with their loyalty to the Throne.

CHAPTER I

Queen Victoria, on her father's side, belonged to the House of Brunswick, which was undoubtedly one of the oldest, and claimed to be actually the oldest, of German princely families. At the time of her birth, it existed in two branches, of which, the one ruled over what was called the Duchy of Brunswick, the other over the Electorate (since 1815 the Kingdom) of Hanover, and had since 1714 occupied the throne of England. There had been frequent intermarriages between the two branches. The Dukes of Brunswick were now, however, represented only by two young princes, who were the sons of the celebrated Duke who fell at Quatre-Bras. Between them and the English Court there was little intercourse. The elder, Charles, had quarrelled with his uncle and guardian, George IV., and had in 1830 been expelled from his dominions. The obvious faults of his character made it impossible for the other German princes to insist on his being restored, and he had been succeeded by his younger brother William, who ruled till his death in 1884. Both died unmarried, and with them the Ducal family came to an end. One Princess of Brunswick had been the wife of George IV., and another, Augusta, was the first wife of Frederick I., King of Würtemberg, who, after her death, married a daughter of George III. The King of Würtemberg was also, by his descent from Frederick Prince of Wales, first cousin once removed of the Queen. We need only notice, in passing, the distant connection with the royal families of Prussia, the Netherlands, and Denmark. The Prince of Orange, who was one of the possible suitors for the young Queen's hand, was her third cousin once removed.

THE HOUSE OF SAXE-COBURG-GOTHA

The House of Saxe-Coburg-Gotha, to which the Queen belonged on her mother's side, and with which she was to be even more intimately connected by her marriage, was one of the numerous branches into which the ancient and celebrated House of Wettin had broken up. Since the 11th century they had ruled over Meissen and the adjoining districts. To these had been added Upper Saxony and Thuringia. In the 15th century the whole possessions of the House had been divided between the two great branches which still exist. The Albertine branch retained Meissen and the Saxon possessions. They held the title of Elector, which in 1806 was exchanged for the title of King. Though the Saxon House had been the chief protectors of the Reformation, Frederick Augustus I. had, on being elected to the throne of Poland, become a Roman Catholic; and thereby the connection between the two branches of the House had to a great extent ceased. The second line, that of the Ernestines, ruled over Thuringia, but, according to the common German custom, had again broken up into numerous branches, among which the Duchies of Thuringia were parcelled out. At the time of the Queen's birth there were five of these, viz., Gotha-Altenburg, Coburg-Saalfeld, Weimar-Eisenach, Meiningen, and Hildburghausen. On the extinction of the Gotha line, in 1825, there was a rearrangement of the family property, by which the Duke of Hildburghausen received Altenburg, Gotha was given to the Duke of Coburg, and Saalfeld with Hildburghausen added to Meiningen. These four lines still exist.

The Ernestine princes had, by this constant division and sub-division, deprived themselves of the opportunity of exercising any predominant influence, or pursuing any independent policy in German affairs; and though they had the good fortune to emerge from the revolution with their possessions unimpaired, their real power was not increased. Like all the other princes, they had, however, at the Congress of Vienna, received the recognition of their full status as sovereign princes of the Germanic Confederation. Together they sent a single representative to the Diet of Frankfort, the total population of the five principalities being only about 300,000 inhabitants.

It was owing to this territorial sub-division and lack of cohesion that these princes could not attach to their independence the same political importance that fell to the share of the larger principalities, such as Hanover and Bavaria, and they were consequently more ready than the other German princes to welcome proposals which would lead to a unification of Germany.

It is notable that the line has produced many of the most enlightened of the German princes; and nowhere in the whole of Germany were the advantages of the division into numerous small States so clearly seen, and the disadvantages so little felt, as at Weimar, Meiningen, Gotha, and Coburg.

THE HOUSE OF COBURG

The House of Coburg had gained a highly conspicuous and influential position, owing, partly, to the high reputation for sagacity and character which the princes of that House had won, and partly to the marriage connections which were entered into about this time by members of the Coburg House with the leading Royal families of Europe. Within ten years, Princes of Coburg were established, one upon the throne of Belgium, and two others next to the throne in Portugal and England, as Consorts of their respective Queens.

By the first marriage of the Duchess of Kent, the Queen was also connected with a third class of German princes—the Mediatised, as those were called who during the revolution had lost their sovereign power. Many of these were of as ancient lineage and had possessed as large estates as some of the regnant princes, who, though not always more deserving, had been fortunate enough to retain their privileges, and had emerged from the revolution ranking among the ruling Houses of Europe. The mediatised princes, though they had ceased to rule, still held important privileges, which were guaranteed at the Congress of Vienna. First, and most important, they were reckoned as "ebenburtig," which means that they could contract equal marriages with the Royal Houses, and these marriages were recognised as valid for the transmission of rights of inheritance. Many of them had vast private estates, and though they were subjected to the sovereignty of the princes in whose dominions these lay, they enjoyed very important privileges, such as exemption from military service, and from many forms of taxation; they also could exercise minor forms of jurisdiction. They formed, therefore, an intermediate class. Since Germany, as a whole, afforded them no proper sphere of political activity, the more ambitious did not disdain to take service with Austria or Prussia, and, to a less extent, even with the smaller States. It was possible, therefore, for the Queen's mother, a Princess of Saxe-Coburg, to marry the Prince of Leiningen without losing caste. Her daughter, the Princess Feodore, the Queen's half-sister, married Ernest, Prince of Hohenlohe-Langenburg, and thus established an interesting connection with perhaps the most widely-spread and most distinguished of all these families. The House of Hohenlohe would probably still have been a reigning family, had not the Prince of Hohenlohe preferred to fight in the Prussian army against Napoleon, rather than receive gifts from him. His lands were consequently confiscated and passed to other princes who were less scrupulous. The family has given two Ministers President to Prussia, a General in chief command of the Prussian army, a Chancellor to the German Empire, and one of the most distinguished of modern military writers. They held, besides their extensive possessions in Würtemberg and Bavaria, the County of Gleichen in Saxe-Coburg.

FAMILY CONNECTIONS

It will be seen therefore that the Queen was intimately connected with all classes that are to be found among the ruling families of Germany, though naturally with the Catholic families, which looked to Austria and Bavaria for guidance, she had no close ties. But it must be borne in mind that her connection with Germany always remained a personal and family matter, and not a political one; this was the fortunate result of the predominance of the Coburg influence. Had that of the House of Hanover been supreme, it could hardly have been possible for the Queen not to have been drawn into the opposition to the unification of Germany by Prussia, in which the House of Hanover was bound to take a leading part, in virtue of its position, wealth, and dignity.

It will be as well here to mention the principal reigning families of Europe to which Queen Victoria was closely allied through her mother.

The Duchess of Kent's eldest brother, Ernest, Duke of Saxe-Coburg, was the father of Albert, Prince Consort. Her sister was the wife of Alexander, Duke of Würtemberg. The Duchess of Kent's nephew, Ferdinand (son of Ferdinand, the Duchess's brother), married Maria da Gloria, Queen of Portugal, and was father of Pedro V. and Luis, both subsequently Kings of Portugal.

The Duchess's third brother, Leopold (afterwards King of the Belgians), married first the Princess Charlotte, daughter of George IV., and afterwards the Princess Louise Marie, eldest daughter of King Louis Philippe. Prince Augustus (son of Ferdinand, the Duchess of Kent's brother) married another daughter of Louis Philippe, the Princess Clémentine, while Prince Augustus's sister, Victoria, married the Duc de Nemours, a son of Louis Philippe. Another nephew, Duke Friedrich Wilhelm Alexander, son of the Duchess of Würtemberg, married the Princess Marie, another daughter of Louis Philippe.

Thus Queen Victoria was closely allied with the royal families of France, Portugal, Belgium, Saxe-Coburg, and Würtemberg.

THE ENGLISH ROYAL FAMILY

On turning to the immediate Royal Family of England, it will be seen that the male line at the time of the Queen's accession was limited to the sons, both named George, of two of the younger brothers of George IV., the Dukes of Cumberland and Cambridge. The sons of George III. played their part in the national life, shared the strong interest in military matters, and showed the great personal courage which was a tradition of the family.

It must be borne in mind that abstention from active political life had been in no sense required, or even thought desirable, in members of the Royal House. George III. himself had waged a lifelong struggle with the Whig party, that powerful oligarchy that since the accession of the House of Hanover had virtually ruled the country; but he did not carry on the conflict so much by encouraging the opponents of the Whigs, as by placing himself at the head of a monarchical faction. He was in fact the leader of a third party in the State. George IV. was at first a strong Whig, and lived on terms of the greatest intimacy with Charles James Fox; but by the time that he was thirty, he had severed the connection with his former political friends, which had indeed originally arisen more out of his personal opposition to his father than from any political convictions. After this date he became, with intervals of vacillation, an advanced Tory of an illiberal type. William IV. had lived so much aloof from politics before his accession, that he had had then no very pronounced opinions, though he was believed to be in favour of the Reform Bill; during his reign his Tory sympathies became more pronounced, and the position of the Whig Ministry was almost an intolerable one. His other THE ROYAL DUKES brothers were men of decided views, and for the most part of high social gifts. They not only attended debates in the House of Peers, but spoke with emotion and vigour; they held political interviews with leading statesmen, and considered themselves entitled, not to over-rule political movements, but to take the part in them to which their strong convictions prompted them. They were particularly prominent in the debates on the Catholic question, and did not hesitate to express their views with an energy that was often embarrassing. The Duke of York and the Duke of Cumberland had used all their influence to encourage the King in his opposition to Catholic Emancipation, while the Duke of Cambridge had supported that policy, and the Duke of Sussex had spoken in the House of Lords in favour of it. The Duke of York, a kindly, generous man, had held important commands in the earlier part of the Revolutionary war; he had not shown tactical nor strategical ability, but he was for many years Commander-in-Chief of the Army, and did good administrative work in initiating and carrying out much-needed military reforms. He had married a Prussian princess, but left no issue, and his death, in 1827, left the succession open to his younger brother, the Duke of Clarence, afterwards King William IV., and after him to the Princess Victoria.

The Duke of Kent was, as we shall have occasion to show, a strong Whig with philanthropic views. But the ablest of the princes, though also the most unpopular, was the Duke of Cumberland, who, until the birth of the Queen's first child, was heir presumptive to the Throne. He had been one of the most active members of the ultra-Tory party, who had opposed to the last the Emancipation of the Catholics and the Reform Bill. He had married a sister-in-law of the King of Prussia, and lived much in Berlin, where he was intimate with the leaders of the military party, who were the centre of reactionary influences in that country, chief among them being his brother-in-law, Prince Charles of Mecklenburg.

In private life the Duke was bluff and soldier-like, of rather a bullying turn, and extraordinarily indifferent to the feelings of others. "Ernest is not a bad fellow," his brother William IV. said of him, "but if anyone has a corn, he will be sure to tread on it." He was very unpopular in England.

On the death of William IV. he succeeded to the throne of Hanover, and from that time seldom visited England. His first act on reaching his kingdom was to declare invalid the Constitution which had been granted in 1833 by William IV. His justification for this was that his consent, as heir presumptive, which was necessary for its validity, had not at the time been asked. The act caused great odium to be attached to his name by all Liberals, both English and Continental, and it was disapproved of even by his old Tory associates. None the less he soon won great popularity in his own dominions by his zeal, good-humour, and energy, and in 1840 he came to terms with the Estates. A new Constitution was drawn up which preserved more of the Royal prerogatives than the instrument of 1833. Few German princes suffered so little in the revolution of 1848. The King died in 1851, at the age of eighty, and left one son, George, who had been blind from his boyhood. He was the last King of Hanover, being expelled by the Prussians in 1866. On the failure of the Ducal line of Brunswick, the grandson of Ernest Augustus became heir to their dominions, he and his sons being now the sole male representatives of all the branches of the House of Brunswick, which a few generations ago was one of the most numerous and widely-spread ruling Houses in Germany.1

Footnote 1: Of the daughters of George III., Princess Amelia had died in 1810, and the Queen of Würtemberg in 1828; two married daughters survived—Elizabeth, wife of the Landgrave of Hesse-Homburg, and Mary, who had married her cousin, the Duke of Gloucester, and lived in England. There were also two unmarried daughters, the Princesses Augusta and Sophia, living in England.

The Duke of Sussex was in sympathy with many Liberal movements, and supported the removal of religious disabilities, the abolition of the Corn Laws, and Parliamentary Reform.

The Duke of Cambridge was a moderate Tory, and the most conciliatory of all the princes. But for more than twenty years he took little part in English politics, as he was occupied with his duties as Regent of Hanover, where he did much by prudent reforms to retain the allegiance of the Hanoverians. On his return to England he resumed the position of a peacemaker, supporting philanthropic movements, and being a generous patron of art and letters. He was recognised as "emphatically the connecting link between the Crown and the people." Another member of the Royal Family was the Duke of Gloucester, nephew and son-in-law of George III.; he was more interested in philanthropic movements than in politics, but was a moderate Conservative, who favoured Catholic Emancipation but was opposed to Parliamentary Reform.

Thus we have the spectacle of seven Royal princes, of whom two succeeded to the Throne, all or nearly all avowed politicians of decided convictions, throwing the weight of their influence and social position for the most part on the side of the Tory party, and believing it to be rather their duty to hold and express strong political opinions than to adopt the moderating and conciliatory attitude in matters of government that is now understood to be the true function of the Royal House.

INDEPENDENCE OF THE QUEEN

The Queen, after her accession, always showed great respect and affection for her uncles, but they were not able to exercise any influence over her character or opinions.

This was partly due to the fact that from an early age she had imbibed a respect for liberal views from her uncle Leopold, King of the Belgians, to whom she was devoted from her earliest childhood, and for whom she entertained feelings of the deepest admiration, affection, and confidence; but still more was it due to the fact that, from the very first, the Queen instinctively formed an independent judgment on any question that concerned her; and though she was undoubtedly influenced in her decisions by her affectionate reliance on her chosen advisers, yet those advisers were always deliberately and shrewdly selected, and their opinions were in no case allowed to do more than modify her own penetrating and clear-sighted judgment.

T.R.H. The Duchess of Kent and the Princess Victoria.

From the miniature by H. Bone, after Sir W. Beechey, at Windsor Castle

To face p. 8, Vol. I

CHAPTER II

Alexandrina Victoria, Queen of Great Britain and Ireland and Empress of India, was born on Monday, 24th May 1819, at Kensington Palace.

THE DUKE AND DUCHESS OF KENT

Her father, Edward, Duke of Kent and Strathearn (1767-1820), the fourth son of George III., was a man of decided character, kindly, pious, punctual, with a strict sense of duty and enlightened ideas. He was a devoted soldier, and, as Queen Victoria once said, "was proud of his profession, and I was always taught to consider myself a soldier's child." He had a wide military experience, having served at Gibraltar, in Canada, and in the West Indies. He had been mentioned in despatches, but was said to be over-strict in matters of unimportant detail. His active career was brought to an end in 1802, when he had been sent to Gibraltar to restore order in a mutinous garrison. Order had been restored, but the Duke was recalled under allegations of having exercised undue severity, and the investigation which he demanded was refused him, though he was afterwards made a Field-Marshal.

He was a man of advanced Liberal ideas. He had spoken in the House of Lords in favour of Catholic Emancipation, and had shown himself interested in the abolition of slavery and in popular education. His tastes were literary, and towards the end of his life he had even manifested a strong sympathy for socialistic theories.

At the time of the death of the Princess Charlotte, 6th November 1817, the married sons of King George III. were without legitimate children, and the surviving daughters were either unmarried or childless. Alliances were accordingly arranged for the three unmarried Royal Dukes, and in the course of the year 1818 the Dukes of Cambridge, Kent, and Clarence led their brides to the altar.

The Duchess of Kent (1786-1861), Victoria Mary Louisa, was a daughter of Francis, Duke of Saxe-Coburg-Saalfeld. She was the widow of Emich Charles, Prince of Leiningen,1 whom she had married in 1803, and who had died in 1814, leaving a son and a daughter by her.

Footnote 1: Leiningen, a mediatised princely House of Germany, dating back to 1096. In 1779 the head of one of the branches into which it had become divided, the Count of Leiningen-Dachsburg-Hardenburg, was raised to the rank of a prince of the Empire, but the Peace of Lunéville (1801) deprived him of his ancient possessions, extending about 232 miles on the left bank of the Rhine. Though no longer an independent Prince, the head of the House retains his rank and wealth, and owns extensive estates in Bavaria and Hesse.

The Duke of Kent died prematurely—though he had always been a conspicuously healthy man—at Sidmouth, on the 23rd of January 1820, only a week before his father.

A paper preserved in the Windsor archives gives a touching account of the Duke's last hours. The Regent, on the 22nd of January, sent to him a message of solicitude and affection, expressing an anxious wish for his recovery. The Duke roused himself to enquire how the Prince was in health, and said, "If I could now shake hands with him, I should die in peace." A few hours before the end, one who stood by the curtain of his bed heard the Duke say with deep emotion, "May the Almighty protect my wife and child, and forgive all the sins I have committed." His last words—addressed to his wife—were, "Do not forget me."

The Duchess of Kent was an affectionate, impulsive woman, with more emotional sympathy than practical wisdom in worldly matters. But her claim on the gratitude of the British nation is that she brought up her illustrious daughter in habits of simplicity, self-sacrifice, and obedience.

As a testimony to the sincere appreciation entertained by the politicians of the time for the way in which the Duchess of Kent had appreciated her responsibilities with regard to the education of a probable heir to the Crown of England, we may quote a few sentences from two speeches made in the House of Commons, in the debate which took place (27th May 1825) on the question of increasing the Parliamentary annuity paid to the Duchess, in order to provide duly for the education of the young Princess.

The Chancellor of the Exchequer, Mr Robinson, afterwards Lord Ripon, said:

"The position in which this Princess stood with respect to the throne of the country could not fail to make her an object of general interest to the nation. He had not himself the honour of being acquainted with the Duchess of Kent, but he believed that she had taken the greatest pains with her daughter's education. She had been brought up in principles of piety and morality, and to feel a proper sense, he meant by that an humble sense, of her own dignity, and the rank which probably awaited her. Perhaps it might have been fit to have brought this matter before Parliament at an earlier period."

Mr Canning said:

"All parties agreed in the propriety of the Grant, and if Government had anything to answer for on this point, it was for having so long delayed bringing it before the House. There could not be a greater compliment to Her Royal Highness than to state the quiet unobtrusive tenor of her life, and that she had never made herself the object of public gaze, but had devoted herself to the education of her child, whom the House was now called upon to adopt."

EARLY REMINISCENCES

In the year 1872 Queen Victoria wrote down with her own hand some reminiscences of her early childhood, the manuscript of which is preserved at Windsor, and which may be quoted here.

"My earliest recollections are connected with Kensington Palace, where I can remember crawling on a yellow carpet spread out for that purpose—and being told that if I cried and was naughty my 'Uncle Sussex' would hear me and punish me, for which reason I always screamed when I saw him! I had a great horror of Bishops on account of their wigs and aprons, but recollect this being partially got over in the case of the then Bishop of Salisbury (Dr Fisher, great-uncle to Mr Fisher, Private Secretary to the Prince of Wales), by his kneeling down and letting me play with his badge of Chancellor of the Order of the Garter. With another Bishop, however, the persuasion of showing him my 'pretty shoes' was of no use. Claremont remains as the brightest epoch of my otherwise rather melancholy childhood—where to be under the roof of that beloved Uncle—to listen to some music in the Hall when there were dinner-parties—and to go and see dear old Louis!—the former faithful and devoted Dresser and friend of Princess

Charlotte—beloved and respected by all who knew her—and who doted on the little Princess who was too much an idol in the House. This dear old lady was visited by every one—and was the only really devoted Attendant of the poor Princess, whose governesses paid little real attention to her—and who never left her, and was with her when she died. I used to ride a donkey given me by my Uncle, the Duke of York, who was very kind to me. I remember him well—tall, rather large, very kind but extremely shy. He always gave me beautiful presents. The last time I saw him was at Mr Greenwood's house, where D. Carlos lived at one time,—when he was already very ill,—and he had Punch and Judy in the garden for me.

"To Ramsgate we used to go frequently in the summer, and I remember living at Townley House (near the town), and going there by steamer. Mamma was very unwell. Dear Uncle Leopold went with us.

"To Tunbridge Wells we also went, living at a house called Mt. Pleasant, now an Hotel. Many pleasant days were spent here, and the return to Kensington in October or November was generally a day of tears.

"I was brought up very simply—never had a room to myself till I was nearly grown up—always slept in my Mother's room till I came to the Throne. At Claremont, and in the small houses at the bathing-places, I sat and took my lessons in my Governess's bedroom. I was not fond of learning as a little child—and baffled every attempt to teach me my letters up to 5 years old—when I consented to learn them by their being written down before me.

GEORGE IV.

"I remember going to Carlton House, when George IV. lived there, as quite a little child before a dinner the King gave. The Duchess of Cambridge and my 2 cousins, George and Augusta, were there. My Aunt, the Queen of Würtemberg (Princess Royal), came over, in the year '26, I think, and I recollect perfectly well seeing her drive through the Park in the King's carriage with red liveries and 4 horses, in a Cap and evening dress,—my Aunt, her sister Princess Augusta, sitting opposite to her, also in evening attire, having dined early with the Duke of Sussex at Kensington. She had adopted all the German fashions and spoke broken English—and had not been in England for many many years. She was very kind and good-humoured but very large and unwieldy. She lived at St James's and had a number of Germans with her. In the year '26 (I think) George IV. asked my Mother, my Sister and me down to Windsor for the first time; he had been on bad terms with my poor father when he died,—and took hardly any notice of the poor widow and little fatherless girl, who were so poor at the time of his (the Duke of Kent's) death, that they could not have travelled back to Kensington Palace had it not been for the kind assistance of my dear Uncle, Prince Leopold. We went to Cumberland Lodge, the King living at the Royal Lodge. Aunt Gloucester was there at the same time. When we arrived at the Royal Lodge the King took me by the hand, saying: 'Give me your little paw.' He was large and gouty but with a wonderful dignity and charm of manner. He wore the wig which was so much worn in those days. Then he said he would give me something for me to wear, and that was his picture set in diamonds, which was worn by the Princesses as an order to a blue ribbon on the left shoulder. I was very proud of this,—and Lady Conyngham pinned it on my shoulder. Her husband, the late Marquis of Conyngham, was the Lord Chamberlain and constantly there, as well as Lord Mt. Charles (as Vice-Chamberlain), the present Lord Conyngham.

"None of the Royal Family or general visitors lived at the Royal Lodge, but only the Conyngham family; all the rest at Cumberland Lodge. Lady Maria Conyngham (now dead, first wife to Lord Athlumney, daughter of Lord Conyngham), then quite young, and Lord Graves (brother-in-law to Lord Anglesey and who afterwards shot himself on account of his wife's conduct, who was a Lady of the Bedchamber), were desired to take me a drive to amuse me. I went with them, and Baroness (then Miss) Lehzen (my governess) in a pony carriage and 4, with 4 grey ponies (like my own), and was driven about the Park and taken to Sandpit Gate where the King had a Menagerie—with wapitis, gazelles, chamois, etc., etc. Then we went (I think the next day) to Virginia Water, and met the King in his phaeton in which he was driving the Duchess of Gloucester,—and he said 'Pop her in,' and I was lifted in and placed between him and Aunt Gloucester, who held me round the waist. (Mamma was much frightened.) I was greatly pleased, and remember that I looked with great respect at the scarlet liveries, etc. (the Royal Family had crimson and green liveries and only the King scarlet and blue in those days). We drove round the nicest part of Virginia Water and stopped at the Fishing Temple. Here there was a large barge and every one went on board and fished, while a band played in another! There were numbers of great people there, amongst whom was the last Duke of Dorset, then Master of the Horse. The King paid great attention to my Sister,2 and some people fancied he might marry her!! She was very lovely then—about 18—and had charming manners, about which the King was extremely particular. I afterwards went with Baroness Lehzen and Lady Maria C. to the Page Whiting's cottage. Whiting had been at one time in my father's service. He lived where Mr Walsh now does (and where he died years ago), in the small cottage close by; and here I had some fruit and amused myself by cramming one of Whiting's children, a little girl, with peaches. I came after dinner to hear the band play in the Conservatory, which is still standing, and which was lit up by coloured lamps—the King, Royal Family, etc., sitting in a corner of the large saloon, which still stands.

Footnote 2: The Princess Feodore of Leiningen, afterwards Princess of Hohenlohe, Queen Victoria's half-sister.

"On the second visit (I think) the following year, also in summer, there was a great encampment of tents (the same which were used at the Camp at Chobham in '53, and some single ones at the Breakfasts at Buckingham Palace in '68-9), and which were quite like a house, made into different compartments. It rained dreadfully on this occasion, I well remember. The King and party dined there, Prince and Princess Lieven, the Russian Ambassador and Ambassadress were there.

"I also remember going to see Aunt Augusta at Frogmore, where she lived always in the summer.

"We lived in a very simple, plain manner; breakfast was at half-past eight, luncheon at half-past one, dinner at seven—to which I came generally (when it was no regular large dinner party)—eating my bread and milk out of a small silver basin. Tea was only allowed as a great treat in later years.

DUCHESS OF SAXE-COBURG-SAALFELD

"In 1826 (I think) my dear Grandmother, the Dowager Duchess of Saxe-Coburg-Saalfeld, came to Claremont, in the summer. Mamma and my sister went on part of the way to meet her, and Uncle Leopold I think had been to fetch her as far as Dover. I recollect the excitement and anxiety I was in, at this event,—going down the great flight of steps to meet her when she got out of the carriage, and hearing her say, when she sat down in her room, and fixed her fine clear blue eyes on her little grand-daughter whom she called in her letters 'the flower of May,' 'Ein schönes Kind'—'a fine child.' She was very clever and adored by her children but especially by her sons. She was a good deal bent and walked with a stick, and frequently with her hands on her back. She took long drives in an open carriage and I was frequently sent out with her, which I am sorry to confess I did not like, as, like most children of that age, I preferred running about. She was excessively kind to children, but could not bear naughty ones—and I shall never forget her coming into the room when I had been crying and naughty at my lessons—from the next room but one, where she had been with Mamma—and scolding me severely, which had a very salutary effect. She dined early in the afternoon and Uncle Leopold asked many of the neighbours and others to dinner to meet her. My brother Prince Leiningen came over with her, and was at that time paying his court to one of her ladies, Countess Klebelsberg, whom he afterwards married—against the wish of his grandmother and mother—but which was afterwards quite made up. In November (I think, or it may have been at the end of October) she left, taking my sister with her back to Coburg. I was very ill at that time, of dysentery, which illness increased to an alarming degree; many children died of it in the village of Esher. The Doctor lost his head, having lost his own child from it, and almost every doctor in London was away. Mr Blagden came down and showed much energy on the occasion. I recovered, and remember well being very cross and screaming dreadfully at having to wear, for a time, flannel next my skin. Up to my 5th year I had been very much indulged by every one, and set pretty well all at defiance. Old Baroness de Späth, the devoted Lady of my Mother, my Nurse Mrs Brock, dear old Mrs Louis—all worshipped the poor little fatherless child whose future then was still very uncertain; my Uncle the Duke of Clarence's poor little child being alive, and the Duchess of Clarence had one or two others later. At 5 years old, Miss Lehzen was placed about me, and though she was most kind, she was very firm and I had a proper respect for her. I was naturally very passionate, but always most contrite afterwards. I was taught from the first to beg my maid's pardon for any naughtiness or rudeness towards her; a feeling I have ever retained, and think every one should own their fault in a kind way to any one, be he or she the lowest—if one has been rude to or injured them by word or deed, especially those below you. People will readily forget an insult or an injury when others own their fault, and express sorrow or regret at what they have done."

THE EDUCATION OF THE PRINCESS

In 1830 the Duchess of Kent wished to be satisfied that the system of education then being pursued with the Princess was based on the right lines, and that due moral and intellectual progress was being made. A memorandum, carefully preserved among the archives, gives an interesting account of the steps which she took to this end.

LETTER TO THE BISHOPS

The Duchess therefore brought the matter under the consideration of those whom, from their eminent piety, great learning, and high station, she considered best calculated to afford her valuable advice upon so important a subject. She stated to the Bishops of London and Lincoln the particular course which had been followed in the Princess's education, and requested their Lordships to test the result by personal examination. The nature and objects of Her Royal Highness's appeal to these eminent prelates will be best shown by the following extracts from her letter to the Bishops:—

"'The Princess will be eleven years of age in May; by the death of her revered father when she was but eight months old, her sole care and charge devolved to me. Stranger as I then was, I became deeply impressed with the absolute necessity of bringing her up entirely in this country, that every feeling should be that of Her native land, and proving thereby my devotion to duty by rejecting all those feelings of home and kindred that divided my heart.

"'When the Princess approached her fifth year I considered it the proper time to begin in a moderate way her education—an education that was to fit Her to be either the Sovereign of these realms, or to fill a junior station in the Royal Family, until the Will of Providence should shew at a later period what Her destiny was to be.

"'A revision of the papers I send you herewith will best shew your Lordships the system pursued, the progress made, etc. I attend almost always myself every lesson, or a part; and as the Lady about the Princess is a competent person, she assists Her in preparing Her lessons for the various masters, as I resolved to act in that manner so as to be Her Governess myself. I naturally hope that I have pursued that course most beneficial to all the great interests at stake. At the present moment no concern can be more momentous, or in which the consequences, the interests of the Country, can be more at stake, than the education of its future Sovereign.

"'I feel the time to be now come that what has been done should be put to some test, that if anything has been done in error of judgment it may be corrected, and that the plan for the future should be open to consideration and revision. I do not presume to have an over-confidence in what I have done; on the contrary, as a female, as a stranger (but only in birth, as I feel that this is my country by the duties I fulfil, and the support I receive), I naturally desire to have a candid opinion from authorities competent to give one. In that view I address your Lordships; I would propose to you that you advert to all I have stated, to the papers I lay before you, and that then you should personally examine the Princess with a view of telling me—

* "'1. If the course hitherto pursued in Her education has been the best; if not, where it was erroneous.

* "'2. If the Princess has made all the Progress she should have made.

* "'3. And if the course I am to follow is that you would recommend, and if not in what respect you would desire a change, and on what grounds.

RELIGIOUS INSTRUCTION

"'Mr Davys will explain to you the nature of the Princess's religious education, which I have confided to him, that she should be brought up in the Church of England as by Law established. When she was at a proper age she commenced attending Divine Service regularly with me, and I have every feeling, that she has religion at Her heart, that she is morally impressed with it to that degree, that she is less liable to error by its application to Her feelings as a Child capable of reflection. The general bent of Her character is strength of intellect, capable of receiving with ease, information, and with a peculiar readiness in coming to a very just and benignant decision on any point Her opinion is asked on. Her adherence to truth is of so marked a character that I feel no apprehension of that Bulwark being broken down by any circumstance.

"'I must conclude by observing that as yet the Princess is not aware of the station that she is likely to fill. She is aware of its duties, and that a Sovereign should live for others; so that when Her innocent mind receives the impression of Her future fate, she receives it with a mind formed to be sensible of what is to be expected from Her, and it is to be hoped, she will be too well grounded in Her principles to be dazzled with the station she is to look to.'"

Charles James Blomfield, Bishop of London, 1828-1853, and John Kaye, Bishop of Lincoln, 1827-1853.

The Rev. George Davys, the Princess's instructor, afterwards successively Dean of Chester and Bishop of Peterborough.

The examination was undertaken by the Bishops, with highly satisfactory results. Their report says:

"The result of the examination has been such as in our opinion amply to justify the plan of instruction which has been adopted. In answering a great variety of questions proposed to her, the Princess displayed an accurate knowledge of the most important features of Scripture History, and of the leading truths and precepts of the Christian Religion as taught by the Church of England, as well as an acquaintance with the Chronology and principal facts of English History remarkable in so young a person. To questions in Geography, the use of the Globes, Arithmetic, and Latin Grammar, the answers which the Princess returned were equally satisfactory.

"Upon the whole, we feel no hesitation in stating our opinion that the Princess should continue, for some time to come, to pursue her studies upon the same plan which has been hitherto followed, and under the same superintendence. Nor do we apprehend that any other alterations in the plan will be required than those which will be gradually made by the judicious director of Her Highness's studies, as the mind expands, and her faculties are strengthened."

RESULT OF EXAMINATION

The Duchess of Kent referred all this correspondence to the Archbishop of Canterbury.5 His memorandum is preserved; it states he has considered the Report, and further, has himself personally examined the Princess. He continues:

"I feel it my duty to say that in my judgment the plan of Her Highness's studies, as detailed in the papers transmitted to me by command of your Royal Highness, is very judicious, and particularly suitable to Her Highness's exalted station; and that from the proficiency exhibited by the Princess in the examination at which I was present, and the general correctness and pertinency of her answers, I am perfectly satisfied that Her Highness's education in regard to cultivation of intellect, improvement of talent, and religious and moral principle, is conducted with so much care and success as to render any alteration of the system undesirable."

Footnote 5: Dr William Howley.

The Princess was gradually and watchfully introduced to public life, and was never allowed to lose sight of the fact that her exalted position carried with it definite and obvious duties. The following speech, delivered at Plymouth in 1832, in answer to a complimentary deputation, may stand as an instance of the view which the Duchess of Kent took of her own and her daughter's responsibilities:—

"It is very agreeable to the Princess and myself to hear the sentiments you convey to us. It is also gratifying to us to be assured that we owe all these kind feelings to the attachment you bear the King, as well as to his Predecessors of the House of Brunswick, from recollections of their paternal sway. The object of my life is to render the Princess worthy of the affectionate solicitude she inspires, and if it be the Will of Providence she should fill a higher station (I trust most fervently at a very distant day), I shall be fully repaid for my anxious care, if she is found competent to discharge the sacred trust; for communicating as the Princess does with all classes of Society, she cannot but perceive that the greater the diffusion of Religion, Knowledge, and the love of freedom in a country, the more orderly, industrious, and wealthy is its population, and that with the desire to preserve the constitutional Prerogatives of the Crown ought to be co-ordinate the protection of the liberties of the people."

CLAREMONT

The strictness of the régime under which the Princess was brought up is remarkable; and it is possible that her later zest for simple social pleasures is partly to be accounted for by the austere routine of her early days. In an interesting letter of 1843 to the Queen, recalling the days of their childhood, Princess Feodore, the Queen's half-sister, wrote—

"Many, many thanks, dearest Victoria, for your kind letter of the 7th from dear Claremont. Oh I understand how you like being there. Claremont is a dear quiet place; to me also the recollection of the few pleasant days I spent during my youth. I always left Claremont with tears for Kensington Palace. When I look back upon those years, which ought to have been the happiest in my life, from fourteen to twenty, I cannot help pitying myself. Not to have enjoyed the pleasures of youth is nothing, but to have been deprived of all intercourse, and not one cheerful thought in that dismal existence of ours, was very hard. My only happy time was going or driving out with you and Lehzen; then I could speak and look as I liked. I escaped some years of imprisonment, which you, my poor darling sister, had to endure after I was married. But God Almighty has changed both our destinies most mercifully, and has made us so happy in our homes—which is the only real happiness in this life; and those years of trial were, I am sure, very useful to us both, though certainly not pleasant. Thank God they are over!... I was much amused in your last letter at your tracing the quickness of our tempers in the female line up to Grandmamma,6 but I must own that you are quite right!"

Footnote 6: Augusta Caroline Sophia, Dowager-Duchess of Saxe-Coburg-Saalfeld, a Princess of Reuss Ebersdorf (1757-1831).

But if there was little amusement, there was, on the other hand, great devotion; the Princess, as a child, had that peculiar combination of self-will and warm-heartedness which is apt to win for a child a special love from its elders. The Princess Feodore wrote to the Queen, in 1843—

"... Späth7 wished me to thank you for the coronation print, as she could not write to you or Albert now, she says! why, I don't see. There certainly never was such devotedness as hers, to all our family, although it sometimes shows itself rather foolishly—with you it always was a sort of idolatry, when she used to go upon her knees before you, when you were a child. She and poor old Louis did all they could to spoil you, if Lehzen had not prevented and scolded them nicely sometimes; it was quite amusing."

Footnote 7: Baroness Späth, Lady-in-Waiting to the Duchess of Kent.

The Princess was brought up with exemplary simplicity at Kensington Palace, where her mother had a set of apartments. She was often at Claremont, which belonged to her uncle Leopold, King of the Belgians; holidays were spent at Ramsgate, Tunbridge Wells, Broadstairs, and elsewhere.

WILLIAM IV.

In June 1830 George IV. died, and William IV. succeeded to the Throne. He had no legitimate offspring living; and it consequently became practically certain that if the Princess outlived her uncle she would succeed him on the Throne. The Duchess of Kent's Parliamentary Grant was increased, and she took advantage of her improved resources to familiarise the Princess with the social life of the nation. They paid visits to historic houses and important towns, and received addresses. This was a wise and prudent course, but the King spoke with ill-humour of his niece's "royal progresses." The chief cause of offence was that the Princess was not allowed by the Duchess of Kent to make her public appearances under his own auspices, as he not unnaturally desired. He also began to suspect that the Princess was deliberately kept away from Court; a painful controversy arose, and the Duchess became gradually estranged from her brother-in-law, in spite of the affectionate attempts of Queen Adelaide to smooth matters over. His resentment culminated in a painful scene, in 1836, when the King, at a State banquet at Windsor, made a speech of a preposterous character; speaking of the Duchess, who sat next him, as "that person," hinting that she was surrounded with evil advisers, and adding that he should insist on the Princess being more at Court. The Princess burst into tears; the Duchess sate in silence: when the banquet was over, the Duchess ordered her carriage, and was with difficulty prevailed upon to remain at Windsor for the night. The King went so far in May 1837 as to offer the Princess an independent income, and the acceptance of this by the Princess caused the Duchess considerable vexation; but the project dropped. The King died in the following month, soon after the Princess had attained her legal majority; he had always hoped that the Duchess would not be Regent, and his wish was thus fulfilled.

It is no exaggeration to say that the accession of the Princess Victoria reinstated the English monarchy in the affections of the people. George IV. had made the Throne unpopular; William IV. had restored its popularity, but not its dignity. Both of these kings were men of decided ability, but of unbalanced temperament. In politics both kings had followed a somewhat similar course. George IV. had begun life as a strong Whig, and had been a close friend of Fox. Later in life his political position resolved itself into a strong dislike of Roman Catholic Relief. William IV. had begun his reign favourably inclined to Parliamentary Reform; but though gratified by the personal popularity which his attitude brought him in the country, he became alarmed at the national temper displayed. It illustrates the tension of the King's mind on the subject that, when he was told that if the Reform Bill did not pass it would bring about a rebellion, he replied that if it did bring about a rebellion he did not care: he should defend London and raise the Royal Standard at Weedon (where there was a military depôt); and that the Duchess of Kent and the Princess Victoria might come in if they could.

The reign of William IV. had witnessed the zenith of Whig efficiency. It had seen the establishment of Parliamentary and Municipal Reform, the Abolition of Slavery, the new Poor Law, and other important measures. But, towards the end of the reign, the Whig party began steadily to lose ground, and the Tories to consolidate themselves. Lord Melbourne had succeeded Lord Grey at the head of the Whigs, and the difference of administration was becoming every month more and more apparent. The King indeed went so far as abruptly to dismiss his Ministers, but Parliament was too strong for him. Lord Melbourne's principles were fully as liberal as Lord Grey's, but he lacked practical initiative, with the result that the Whigs gradually forfeited popular estimation and became discredited. The new reign, however, brought them a decided increase of strength. The Princess had been brought up with strong Whig leanings, and, as is clear from her letters, with an equally strong mistrust of Tory principles and politicians.

CHARACTER AND TEMPERAMENT

A word may here be given to the Princess's own character and temperament. She was high-spirited and wilful, but devotedly affectionate, and almost typically feminine. She had a strong sense of duty and dignity, and strong personal prejudices. Confident, in a sense, as she was, she had the feminine instinct strongly developed of dependence upon some manly adviser. She was full of high spirits, and enjoyed excitement and life to the full. She liked the stir of London, was fond of dancing, of concerts, plays, and operas, and devoted to open-air exercise. Another important trait in her character must be noted. She had strong monarchical views and dynastic sympathies, but she had no aristocratic preferences; at the same time she had no democratic principles, but believed firmly in the due subordination of classes. The result of the parliamentary and municipal reforms of William IV.'s reign had been to give the middle classes a share in the government of the country, and it was supremely fortunate that the Queen, by a providential gift of temperament, thoroughly understood the middle-class point of view. The two qualities that are mostSYMPATHY WITH MIDDLE CLASSES characteristic of British middle-class life are common sense and family affection; and on these particular virtues the Queen's character was based; so that by a happy intuition she was able to interpret and express the spirit and temper of that class which, throughout her reign, was destined to hold the balance of political power in its hands. Behind lay a deep sense of religion, the religion which centres in the belief in the Fatherhood of God, and is impatient of dogmatic distinctions and subtleties.

H.R.H. The Princess Victoria, 1827.
By Plant, after Stewart. From the miniature at Buckingham, Palace
To face p. 16, Vol. I

CHAPTER III

It may be held to have been one of the chief blessings of Queen Victoria's girlhood that she was brought closely under the influence of an enlightened and large-minded Prince, Leopold, her maternal uncle, afterwards King of the Belgians. He was born in 1790, being the youngest son of Francis, Duke of Saxe-Coburg-Saalfeld, and his youth was spent in the Russian military service. He had shown talent and courage in the field, and had commanded a battalion at Lützen and Leipsic. He had married, in 1816, the Princess Charlotte, only child of George IV. For many years his home was at Claremont, where the Princess Charlotte had died; there the Princess Victoria spent many happy holidays, and grew to regard her uncle with the most devoted affection, almost, indeed, in the light of a father. It is said that Prince Leopold had hoped to be named Regent, if a Regency should be necessary.1 He was offered, and accepted, the throne of Greece in 1830, but shrank from the difficulties of the position, and withdrew his acceptance upon the plea that Lord Aberdeen, who was then Foreign Secretary, was not prepared to make such financial arrangements as he considered satisfactory.2

Footnote 1: A practical proof of his interest in his niece may be found in the fact that for years he contributed between three and four thousand a year to the expenses of her education, and for necessary holidays by the sea, at a time when the Duchess of Kent's Parliamentary Grant was unequal to the increasing expenses of her household.

Footnote 2: Greece after having obtained autonomy was in a practically bankrupt condition, and the Powers had guaranteed the financial credit of the country until it was able to develop its own resources.

It is interesting to observe from the correspondence that King Leopold seems for many years to have continued to regret his decision; it was not that he did not devote himself, heart and soul, to the country of his adoption, but there seems to have been a romantic element in his composition, which did not find its full satisfaction in presiding over the destinies of a peaceful commercial nation.

In 1831, when Louis Philippe, under pressure from Lord Palmerston, declined the throne of Belgium for his son the Duc de Nemours, Prince Leopold received and accepted an offer of the Crown. A Dutch invasion followed, and the new King showed great courage and gallantry in an engagement near Louvain, in which his army was hopelessly outnumbered. But, though a sensitive man, the King's high courage and hopefulness never deserted him. He ruled his country with diligence, ability, and wisdom, and devoted himself to encouraging manufactures and commerce. The result of his firm and liberal rule was manifested in 1848, when, on his offering to resign the Crown if it was thought to be for the best interests of the country, he was entreated, with universal acclamation, to retain the sovereignty. Belgium passed through the troubled years of revolution in comparative tranquillity. King Leopold was a model ruler; his deportment was grave and serious; he was conspicuous for honesty and integrity; he was laborious and upright, and at the same time conciliatory and tactful.

He kept up a close correspondence with Queen Victoria, and paid her several visits in England, where he was on intimate terms with many leading Englishmen. It would be difficult to over-estimate the importance of his close relations with the Queen; by example and precept he inspired her with a high sense of duty, and from the first instilled into her mind the necessity of acquainting herself closely with the details of political administration. His wisdom, good sense, and tenderness, as well as the close tie of blood that existed between him and the Queen, placed him in a unique position with regard to her, and it is plain that he was fully aware of the high responsibility thus imposed upon him, which he accepted with a noble generosity. It is true that there were occasions when, as the correspondence reveals, the Queen was disposed to think that King Leopold endeavoured to exercise too minute a control over her in matters of detail, and even to attempt to modify the foreign policy of England rather for the benefit of Belgium than in the best interests of Great Britain; but the Queen was equal to these emergencies; she expressed her dissent from the King's suggestions in considerate and affectionate terms, with her gratitude for his advice, but made no pretence of following it.

QUEEN ADELAIDE

For her aunt, Queen Adelaide, the Princess Victoria had always felt a strong affection; and though it can hardly be said that this gentle and benevolent lady exercised any great influence over her more vigorous and impetuous niece, yet the letters will testify to the closeness of the tie which united them.

Queen Adelaide was the eldest child of George, Duke of Saxe-Meiningen; her mother was a princess of Hohenlohe-Langenburg.

At the age of twenty-six she was married to the Duke of Clarence, then in his fifty-third year, without any preliminary courtship. They lived for a year in Hanover, and then principally at Bushey Park. Two daughters were born to them, the elder of whom lived only a few hours; the younger, Princess Elizabeth, died in the first year of her age. Their married life was a happy one, in spite of the disparity of age. Queen Adelaide was a woman of a deeply affectionate disposition, sensible, sympathetic, and religious. She had a very definite ideal of the duties of a wife and a Queen; she made it her pleasure to meet and anticipate, as far as possible, her husband's wishes; and her husband, hasty and choleric though he was, repaid her with tender affection. To such an extent did the Queen merge her views in those of her husband, that she passed at one time through a period of general unpopularity. It was believed that she was adverse to Reform, and used her influence against it. She was mobbed in the streets at the time when the Reform agitation was at its height; and it is said that when the Melbourne Ministry of 1834 was dismissed, London was (owing to an unjustifiable communication of Lord Brougham to the Times) placarded with posters bearing the words, "The Queen has done it all!"

It is a pathetic instance of the irony of fate that Queen Adelaide should have thus been supposed to desire to take an active part in politics. It is obvious, from her letters, that she had practically no political views at all, except a gentle distrust of all proposed changes, social or political. Her one idea of her position as Queen was to agree with any expression of opinion that fell from the King. She was fond of music, and took a deep interest in her religious duties and in all that concerned the welfare of the Protestant communion. But apart from this, her interests were entirely domestic and personal, and her letters reveal her character in the most amiable light. Her devotion to the King, and the tender and respectful diffidence with which she welcomed her niece to the Throne, show a very sweet nature.

The rest of her life, after King William's death, was passed to a great extent under invalid conditions, though she was only forty-four at the time of her niece's accession. She travelled a good deal in search of health, and lived a quiet life in England, surrounded by a small but devoted circle of friends and relations. Her personal popularity with the nation became very great, not only for the simple kindliness of her life, but for her splendid munificence; it is said that her public subscriptions often exceeded £20,000 a year. She died in December 1849. Queen Victoria was very much attached to her gentle, simple-minded, and tender-hearted aunt, and treated her with the utmost consideration and an almost daughterly affection.

BARONESS LEHZEN

Another person who had a large share in forming the Queen's character was Louise Lehzen, the daughter of a Hanoverian clergyman, who came to England as governess to Princess Feodore of Leiningen, Queen Victoria's half-sister, shortly before the Queen's birth. In 1824 she became governess to the Princess Victoria. In 1827 George IV. conferred upon her the rank of a Hanoverian Baroness. When the Duchess of Northumberland, in 1830, was appointed the Princess's official governess, she remained as lady in attendance. The Princess was devoted to her, but "greatly in awe of her." She remained at Court after the accession till 1842, without holding an official position, and then returned to Germany, where she died in 1870.

BARON STOCKMAR

Baron Stockmar was another of the interesting personalities who came into very close contact with the Queen in her early years. He was forty-nine at the time of the accession, but he had come to England more than twenty years before as private physician to Prince Leopold. He endeared himself to the Princess Charlotte, who died holding his hand. He afterwards became Prince Leopold's private secretary, and took a prominent part as the Prince's representative in the successive negotiations with regard to his candidature for the thrones of Greece and Belgium. Upon the accession of Queen Victoria, Stockmar joined the Court in a private capacity, and for fifteen months he held an unofficial position as her chief adviser. There was a general feeling of dislike in the minds of the English public to the German influences that were supposed to be brought to bear on the Queen; and Lord Melbourne found it necessary to make a public and categorical denial of the statement that Stockmar was acting as the Queen's private secretary. But the statement, if not technically, was virtually true. Stockmar lived at Court, had interviews with the Queen and her Ministers, and though he industriously endeavoured to efface himself, yet there is no doubt that he was consulted on most important questions. In 1838, he had been entrusted by King Leopold, with the Queen's knowledge and consent, with a mission of great delicacy: he was asked to accompany Prince Albert on a tour in Italy, with the idea of completing his education, and in order to satisfy himself that the Prince would be a worthy Consort for the Queen. This task he discharged admirably, and became the most confidential and trusted of all the Prince's friends. There are many letters of Stockmar's to the Prince extant, which prove that Stockmar never shrank from speaking the plainest truth to the Prince on matters of duty and faults of temperament, without any courtier-like attempt to blink criticism that might have been unpalatable. The Prince had the generosity and humility to value this trait of Stockmar's very highly, to such an extent that Stockmar's influence possessed if anything too great a preponderance. Stockmar had jealously nursed two profound political ideals—the unity of Germany under Prussia, and the establishment of close relations between Germany and England. He induced Prince Albert, heavily burdened as he was with work, to devote almost too much time and thought to the former of these aims. Stockmar was a profound student of social and constitutional questions. He had made a close study of English political institutions; but though he grasped the constitutional theory of the English Throne, and saw that the first necessity for the Sovereign was to hold a position independent of party, he never clearly understood that the Monarch should keep as far as possible clear of political details. Stockmar's view of the position was that the Sovereign should be practically Premier as well; and much of the jealousy that was felt, on various occasions, at the position which Prince Albert assumed with regard to political situations, is referable to Stockmar's influence.

He was a very able man, with immense political knowledge, and without personal ambition; Lord Palmerston, who was no friend to Stockmar's theory of government, admitted that he was the most disinterested man he had ever encountered. Stockmar's ambition was to achieve his own political ideals, and to modify the course of events in what he conceived to be beneficial directions; he was entirely indifferent to the trappings of power, and this very disinterestedness made his influence more supreme.

He suffered all his life from feeble health and a hypochondriacal tendency, and was genuinely fond of retirement and quiet life. He certainly deserved the devoted confidence reposed in him by Prince Albert and the Queen; it may perhaps be questioned whether his own doctrinaire bias did not make itself too strongly felt, in the minuteness with which Prince Albert dealt with English politics; but the net result of his influence was that the danger, which lies in wait for strictly constitutional Sovereigns, was averted—the danger, that is, of leaving the administration of State affairs in the hands of specialists, and depriving it of the wise control and independent criticism which only the Crown can adequately supply.

INTRODUCTORY NOTE: TO CHAPTER IV

Queen Victoria, from the very first, took great pleasure in filing the correspondence addressed to her. There are many volumes of letters received from her various relations. We have thought it best to give some of Queen Adelaide's early letters; they indicate in a remarkable manner the growing estrangement between King William IV. and the Duchess of Kent. In the earlier letters the King enquires very affectionately after the Duchess, and constant mention is made of presents sent to her; but the references made to her become less frequent and colder, till at last the King contents himself with sending messages only to the Princess. But the letters of Queen Adelaide are always written in a strain of touching devotion and affection, and reveal her as a woman of large heart and great simplicity of character.

KING LEOPOLD

But the most interesting series of letters are the Queen's own correspondence with King Leopold, of which several hundred are preserved. The letters, too, received by her from the King of the Belgians are preserved in their entirety.

The letters which the Queen wrote to King Leopold are of extraordinary interest; she kept up an unbroken correspondence with him, and spoke freely of all that was in her mind. Two points are worthy of special mention: though she was early convinced of the necessity of holding an independent constitutional position in politics she mentions the Tory party with undisguised mistrust; and further, the name of King William hardly ever occurs until his last illness.

King Leopold's early letters reveal his character in the most amiable light. He familiarised the Queen with all the complicated details of foreign politics; he gave her the most sensible and wise advice; he warned and encouraged her; he answered her enquiries with the minutest care: and the warm affection to which he gave frequent expression is a very sacred and beautiful thing to contemplate.

We have selected several of the Princess Victoria's letters to the King of the Belgians before her accession, because they throw a remarkable light upon her temperament. In the first place, they reveal the deep affectionateness of her character, and, what is still more remarkable at her age, her frankness and outspokenness in expressing her feelings.

In the second place, they show with what interest and eagerness the Princess was following the course of foreign politics. Her view was naturally a personal one, but it may be said that there can have been very few, if any, girls in England, of the Princess's age, who were taking any interest at all in Continental affairs. It is true that King Leopold had early impressed upon the Princess that it was a duty to become acquainted with the course of current events; but the letters show that the interest she felt was congenial and innate, and did not spring from a sense of duty. The allusions to home politics are not so frequent, but still show that here also her attention was alert.

Thirdly, they reveal her abounding vitality, her love of life and amusement, her devotion to music, and the simple unspoilt zest with which she threw herself into all that surrounded her.

There is a special interest which attaches to the correspondence between Queen Victoria and

King Leopold after the Accession. The letters reveal, as no other documents could do, the monarchical point of view. However intimate may be the relations between a Sovereign and a subject, there is bound to appear a certain discretion, and even condescension, on the one hand, and on the other a due degree of deference. But here we have the remarkable spectacle of two monarchs, both of eminent sagacity, and both, so to speak, frankly interested in the task of constitutional government, corresponding freely on all the difficulties and problems inseparable from their momentous task, and with an immense sense of their weighty responsibilities. It is impossible to exaggerate the deep and abiding interest of such a correspondence; and the seriousness, the devotion, the public spirit that are displayed, without affectation or calculated impressiveness, make the whole series of letters singularly memorable.

The King of the Belgians had married Princess Louise of Orleans, daughter of Louis Philippe, in 1832. She was only seven years older than the Princess Victoria, who grew to regard her with the tenderest affection.

The letters from Queen Louise are very numerous. A few are in French, but they are mostly written in brisk, lively English, not always very correct, either in construction or in spelling. They are full of small family details—the movements of various relations, the improvement in her brothers' looks, Court festivities, the childish ailments of her little boys, the journeys and expeditions, recollections of Windsor, their visitors, elaborate descriptions of dresses— interesting to read, but difficult to select from. They are full of heart-felt expressions of the sincerest affection for "your dear Majesty," a quaint phrase that often occurs.

PRINCE ALBERT

After their marriage in 1840, Prince Albert naturally became the Queen's confidential Secretary.

A close study of the Queen's correspondence reveals the character of the Prince in a way which nothing else could effect. Traces of his untiring labour, his conscientious vigilance, his singular devotedness, appear on every page. There are innumerable memoranda in his own hand; the papers are throughout arranged and annotated by him; nothing seems to have escaped him, nothing to have dismayed him. As an instance of the minute laboriousness which characterised the Royal household, it may be mentioned that there are many copies of important letters, forwarded to the Prince for his perusal, the originals of which had to be returned, written not only by the Prince himself, but by the Queen under his direction. But besides keeping a vigilant eye upon politics, the Prince took the lead in all social and educational movements of the time, as well as devoting a close and continuous attention to the affairs of Europe in general, and Germany in particular. It is obvious from the papers that the Prince can hardly ever have taken a holiday; many hours of every day must have been devoted by him to work; yet he was at the same time a tender husband and father, always ready with advice and sympathy, and devoted to quiet domestic life.

After the Queen's marriage the correspondence becomes far more voluminous. It is difficult to exaggerate the amount of conscientious labour bestowed by the Queen and the Prince Consort on all matters which concerned the welfare of the nation. The number of documents which passed through their hands, and which were carefully studied by them, was prodigious.

The drafts of the Queen's replies to letters are in many cases in the handwriting of the Prince Consort, but dated by herself, and often containing interlinear corrections and additions of her own. Whether the Queen indicated the lines of the replies, whether she dictated the substance of them, or whether they contain the result of a discussion on the particular matter, cannot be precisely ascertained. But they contain so many phrases and turns of expression which are characteristic of her outspoken temperament, that it is clear that she not only followed every detail, but that the substance of the communication bore in most cases the impress of her mind. A considerable number of the drafts again are in her own hand, with interlinear corrections and additions by the Prince; and these so strongly resemble in style the drafts in the handwriting of the Prince, that it is clear that the Queen did not merely accept suggestions, but that she had a strong opinion of her own on important matters, and that this opinion was duly expressed.

One fact must, however, be borne in mind. It happens in many cases that a correspondence on some particular point seems to be about to lead up to a definite conclusion, but that the salient and decisive document is absent. In these cases it is clear that the matter was settled at a personal interview; in many cases the Prince prepared a memorandum of an important interview; but there are a considerable number of such correspondences, where no record is preserved of the eventual solution, and this incompleteness is regrettable, but, by the nature of the case, inevitable.

LEADING STATESMEN IN 1837

The young Queen, on coming to the Throne, had little technical knowledge of the details of diplomacy, but she already had a real and intelligent acquaintance with foreign affairs, though it was rather personal than political, and, as we have seen, was more inspired by her interest in the fortunes and position of her numerous maternal relations than by the political views of her paternal relatives. Among the English statesmen of the day there were few who were qualified to help and instruct her. The two men who for over twenty years alternately guided the foreign policy of the country were Lord Aberdeen and Lord Palmerston. They represented two opposed schools. Lord Aberdeen, a Peelite, was naturally and by tradition inclined to desire harmonious relations with all foreign Powers, and to abstain, as far as was consistent with maintaining British interests, from any sort of intervention in European affairs; Palmerston was a disciple of Canning, who had definitely broken with the principles of the Congress of Vienna, and openly avowed his approval of a policy of intervention, to any extent short of actual war, in the interests of liberty and good government. The only other man who had any title to speak with authority on foreign affairs was the Duke of Wellington, who had held the seals as Foreign Secretary for a few months in 1834 and 1835. He had, however, lost much of the reputation for political sagacity which he had held at the time when he was the arbiter of Europe and virtual ruler of France. Moreover, being, as he was, a much occupied man, with varied business to transact, and at the mercy of his almost excessive conscientiousness, he held himself to a considerable extent aloof from current politics, though he never lost his absorbing interest in Continental affairs.

CHAPTER IV

[The first letter ever received by Queen Victoria appears to be the following little note, written by the Duchess of Clarence, afterwards Queen Adelaide, in May 1821, when the Princess entered upon her third year. It is pathetic to recollect that the Duchess's surviving child, Princess Elizabeth, had died, aged three months, in March of the same year.

EARLY LETTERS

My dear little heart,—I hope you are well and don't forget Aunt Adelaide, who loves you so fondly.

Loulou and Wilhelm1 desire their love to you, and Uncle William also.

God bless and preserve you is the constant prayer of your most truly affectionate Aunt, Adelaide.

Footnote 1: Princess Louise and Prince William of Saxe-Weimar, children of Duchess Ida of Saxe-Weimar (sister of the Duchess of Clarence). They were the eldest brother and sister of Prince Edward of Saxe-Weimar.

24th May 1822.

Uncle William and Aunt Adelaide send their love to dear little Victoria with their best wishes on her birthday, and hope that she will now become a very good Girl, being now three years old. Uncle William and Aunt Adelaide also beg little Victoria to give dear Mamma and to dear Sissi2 a kiss in their name, and to Aunt Augusta,3 Aunt Mary4 and Aunt Sophia5 too, and also to the big Doll. Uncle William and Aunt Adelaide are very sorry to be absent on that day and not to see their dear, dear little Victoria, as they are sure she will be very good and obedient to dear Mamma on that day, and on many, many others. They also hope that dear little Victoria will not forget them and know them again when Uncle and Aunt return.

Footnote 2: Princess Feodore, the Queen's half-sister.

Footnote 3: Augusta, daughter of Frederick, Landgrave of Hesse-Cassel, wife of the Duke of Cambridge.

Footnote 4: Princess Mary, a daughter of George III., married to her cousin the Duke of Gloucester.

Footnote 5: Princess Sophia, daughter of George III.

[The following is the earliest letter preserved of the long series written by the Queen to King (then Prince) Leopold. The Princess was then nine years old.

Kensington Palace, 25th November 1823.

My dearest Uncle,—I wish you many happy returns of your birthday; I very often think of you, and I hope to see you soon again, for I am very fond of you. I see my Aunt Sophia6 often, who looks very well, and is very well. I use every day your pretty soup-basin. Is it very warm in Italy? It is so mild here, that I go out every day. Mama is tolerable well and am quite well. Your affectionate Niece,

Victoria.

P.S.—I am very angry with you, Uncle, for you have never written to me once since you went, and that is a long while.

Footnote 6: Princess Sophia, daughter of George III.

Paris, 20th April 1829.

My dearest Love,—Though in a few days I hope to have the happiness of seeing you, still I wish to recall myself even before that time to your recollection, and to tell you how delighted I shall be to embrace my dearest little child. I have travelled far over the world and shall be able to give you some curious information about various matters.

Stockmar, who was very ill, and whom I despaired of seeing here, did arrive before yesterday,8 and you may guess what pleasure it gave me. Now I will conclude; au revoir, and let me find you grown, blooming, and kind to your old and faithful Uncle,

Leopold.

Footnote 7: Afterwards King of the Belgians.

Footnote 8: I.e. avant hier.

BIRTHDAY LETTERS

[May 1829.]

If I had wings and could fly like a bird, I should fly in at your window like the little robin to-day, and wish you many very happy returns of the 24th, and tell you how I love you, dearest sister, and how often I think of you and long to see you. I think if I were once with you again I could not leave you so soon. I should wish to stay with you, and what would poor Ernest9 say if I were to leave him so long? He would perhaps try to fly after me, but I fear he would not get far; he is rather tall and heavy for flying. So you see I have nothing left to do but to write to you, and wish you in this way all possible happiness and joy for this and many, many years to come. I hope you will spend a very merry birthday. How I wish to be with you, dearest Victoire, on that day!

I have not thanked you, I believe, for a very dear letter you have written to me, which gave me the greatest pleasure. Your descriptions of the plays you had seen amused me very much. I wish I had seen your performance too. Your most affectionate Sister,

Feodore.

Footnote 9: The Princess Feodore of Leiningen, the Queen's half-sister, had married, in January 1828, the Prince (Ernest) of Hohenlohe-Langenburg.

Bushey Park, 14th August 1829.

A thousand thanks to you, dear Victoria, for your very nice and well-written letter full of good wishes, which I had the pleasure to receive yesterday; and many thanks more for the pretty gifts your dear Mamma has sent me in your name. I wore them last night for your sake, dearest child, and thought of you very often.

It gives me great satisfaction to hear that you are enjoying the sea air and like the place which you now occupy. I wish I could pay your Mamma a visit there and see you again, my dear little niece, for I long to have that pleasure, and must resign myself at being deprived of it some time longer. Your Uncle desires to be most kindly remembered to you, and hopes to receive soon also a letter from you, of whom he is as fond as I am. We speak of you very often, and trust that you will always consider us to be amongst your best friends....

God bless you, my dear Victoria, is always the prayer of your most truly affectionate Aunt, Adelaide.

Brussels, 22nd May 1832.

My dearest Love,—Let me offer you my sincerest and best wishes on the return of the anniversary of your birthday. May heaven protect and prosper you, and shower all its best blessings on you.

Time flies: it is now thirteen years that you came into the world of trouble; I therefore can hardly venture to call you any longer a little Princess.

This will make you feel, my dear Love, that you must give your attention more and more to graver matters. By the dispensation of Providence you are destined to fill a most eminent station; to fill it well must now become your study. A good heart and a trusty and honourable character are amongst the most indispensable qualifications for that position.

You will always find in your Uncle that faithful friend which he has proved to you from your earliest infancy, and whenever you feel yourself in want of support or advice, call on him with perfect confidence.

If circumstances permitted my leaving Ostend early to-morrow morning, I should be able to place myself my birthday present into your fair hair; as this happiness has not fallen to my lot, your excellent mother has promised to act as my representative.

You will probably have little time to spare. I therefore conclude with the assurance of the sincere attachment and affection with which I shall ever be, my dearest Love, your faithful and devoted Friend and Uncle,

Leopold R.

THE QUEEN OF THE BELGIANS

Laeken,10 31st August 1832.

My dearest Love,—You told me you wished to have a description of your new Aunt.11 I therefore shall both mentally and physically describe her to you.

She is extremely gentle and amiable, her actions are always guided by principles. She is at all times ready and disposed to sacrifice her comfort and inclinations to see others happy. She values goodness, merit, and virtue much more than beauty, riches, and amusements. With all this she is highly informed and very clever; she speaks and writes English, German and Italian; she speaks English very well indeed. In short, my dear Love, you see that I may well recommend her as an example for all young ladies, being Princesses or not.

Now to her appearance. She is about Feodore's height, her hair very fair, light blue eyes, of a very gentle, intelligent and kind expression. A Bourbon nose and small mouth. The figure is much like Feodore's but rather less stout. She rides very well, which she proved to my great alarm the other day, by keeping her seat though a horse of mine ran away with her full speed for at least half a mile. What she does particularly well is dancing. Music unfortunately she is not very fond of, though she plays on the harp; I believe there is some idleness in the case. There exists already great confidence and affection between us; she is desirous of doing everything that can contribute to my happiness, and I study whatever can make her happy and contented.

You will see by these descriptions that though my good little wife is not the tallest Queen, she is a very great prize which I highly value and cherish....

Now it is time I should finish my letter. Say everything that is kind to good Lehzen, and believe me ever, my dearest Love, your faithful Friend and Uncle,

Leopold R.

Footnote 10: The Royal Palace, four miles from Brussels, which Napoleon owned for many years. A monument to King Leopold now stands there.

Footnote 11: Louise Marie, Princess of Orleans, daughter of King Louis Philippe of France, was married to King Leopold on 9th August 1832.

A BIRTHDAY LETTER

Laeken, 21st May 1833.

My dearest Love,—To make quite sure of my birthday congratulations reaching you on that day, I send them by to-day's messenger, and confide them to the care of your illustrious mother.

My sincere good wishes for many happy returns of that day which gave you, dear little soul, to us, will be accompanied by some few reflections, which the serious aspect of our times calls forth. My dearest Love, you are now fourteen years old, a period when the delightful pastimes of childhood must be mixed with thoughts appertaining already to a matured part of your life. I know that you have been very studious, but now comes the time when the judgment must form itself, when the character requires attention; in short when the young tree takes the shape which it retains afterwards through life.

VALUABLE ADVICE

To attain this object it is indispensable to give some little time to reflection. The life in a great town is little calculated for such purposes; however, with some firmness of purpose it can be done.

Self-examination is the most important part of the business, and a very useful mode of proceeding is, for instance, every evening to recapitulate the events of the day, and the motives which made one act oneself, as well as to try to guess what might have been the motives of others. Amiable dispositions like yours will easily perceive if your own motives were good. Persons in high situations must particularly guard themselves against selfishness and vanity. An individual in a high and important situation will easily see a great many persons eager to please the first, and to flatter and encourage the last. Selfishness, however, makes the individual itself miserable, and is the cause of constant disappointment, besides being the surest means of being disliked by everybody.

Vanity, on the other hand, is generally artfully used by ambitious and interested people to make one a tool for purposes of their own, but too often in opposition with one's own happiness and destruction of it.

To learn to know oneself, to judge oneself with truth and impartiality, must be the great objects of one's exertion; they are only attainable by constant and cool self-examination.

The position of what is generally called great people has of late become extremely difficult.

They are more attacked and calumniated, and judged with less indulgence than private individuals. What they have lost in this way, they have not by any means regained in any other. Ever since the revolution of 1790 they are much less secure than they used to be, and the transition from sovereign power to absolute want has been as frequent as sudden.

It becomes, therefore, necessary that the character should be so formed as not to be intoxicated by greatness and success, nor cast down by misfortune. To be able to do so, one must be able to appreciate things according to their real value, and particularly avoid giving to trifles an undue importance.

Nothing is so great and clear a proof of unfitness for greater and nobler actions, than a mind which is seriously occupied with trifles.

Trifling matters may be objects of amusement and relaxation to a clever person, but only a weak mind and a mean spirit consider trifles as important. The good sense must show itself by distinguishing what is and what is not important.

My sermon is now long enough, my dear child. I strongly recommend it, however, to your reflection and consideration.

My gift consists in a set of views of the former Kingdom of the Netherlands, out of which you will be able to discover all those of the present Belgium.

Let me soon hear from you; and may God bless and preserve you. Ever, my dear Love, your affectionate Uncle,

Leopold R.

VISIT TO HEVER CASTLE

Tunbridge Wells, 14th September 1834.

My dearest Uncle,—Allow me to write you a few words, to express how thankful I am for the very kind letter you wrote me. It made me, though, very sad to think that all our hopes of seeing you, which we cherished so long, this year, were over. I had so hoped and wished to have seen you again, my beloved Uncle, and to have made dearest Aunt Louisa's acquaintance. I am delighted to hear that dear Aunt has benefited from the sea air and bathing. We had a very pretty party to Hever Castle yesterday, which perhaps you remember, where Anne Boleyn used to live, before she lost her head. We drove there, and rode home. It was a most beautiful day. We have very good accounts from dear Feodore, who will, by this time, be at Langenburg.

Believe me always, my dearest Uncle, your very affectionate and dutiful Niece,

Victoria.

HISTORICAL READING

Laeken, 18th October 1834.

My dearest Love,—I am happy to learn that Tunbridge Wells has done you good. Health is the first and most important gift of Providence; without it we are poor, miserable creatures, though the whole earth were our property; therefore I trust that you will take great care of your own. I feel convinced that air and exercise are most useful for you. In your leisure moments I hope that you study a little; history is what I think the most important study for you. It will be difficult for you to learn human-kind's ways and manners otherwise than from that important source of knowledge. Your position will more or less render practical knowledge extremely difficult for you, till you get old, and still if you do not prepare yourself for your position, you may become the victim of wicked and designing people, particularly at a period when party spirit runs so high. Our times resemble most those of the Protestant reformation; then people were moved by religious opinions, as they now undoubtedly are by political passions. Unfortunately history is rarely written by those who really were the chief movers of events, nor free from a party colouring; this is particularly the case in the works about English history. In that respect France is much richer, because there we have authenticated memoirs of some of the most important men, and of others who really saw what passed and wrote it down at the time. Political feelings, besides, rarely created permanent parties like those in England, with the exception, perhaps, of the great distinctions of Catholics and Protestants. What I most should recommend is the period before the accession of Henry IV. of France to the throne, then the events after his death till the end of the minority of Louis XIV.; after that period, though interesting, matters have a character which is more personal, and therefore less applicable to the present times. Still even that period may be studied with some profit to get knowledge of mankind. Intrigues and favouritism were the chief features of that period, and Madame de Maintenon's immense influence was very nearly the cause of the destruction of France. What I very particularly recommend to you is to study in the Memoirs of the great and good Sully12 the last years of the reign of Henry IV. of France, and the events which followed his assassination. If you have not got the work, I will forward it to you from hence, or give you the edition which I must have at Claremont.

As my paper draws to a close, I shall finish also by giving you my best blessings, and remain ever, my dearest Love, your faithfully attached Friend and Uncle,

Leopold R.

Footnote 12: Maximilien, Duc de Sully, was Henry's Minister of Finance. A curious feature of the Memoirs is the fact that they are written in the second person: the historian recounts the hero's adventures to him.

THE PRINCESS'S READING

Tunbridge Wells, 22nd October 1834.

My dearest Uncle,—You cannot conceive how happy you have made me, by your very kind letter, which, instead of tiring, delights me beyond everything. I must likewise say how very grateful I feel for the kind and excellent advice you gave me in it.

For the autographs I beg to return my best thanks. They are most valuable and interesting, and will be great additions to my collections. As I have not got Sully's Memoirs, I shall be delighted if you will be so good as to give them to me. Reading history is one of my greatest delights, and perhaps, dear Uncle, you might like to know which books in that line I am now reading. In my lessons with the Dean of Chester,13 I am reading Russell's Modern Europe,14 which is very interesting, and Clarendon's History of the Rebellion. It is drily written, but is full of instruction. I like reading different authors, of different opinions, by which means I learn not to lean on one particular side. Besides my lessons, I read Jones'15 account of the wars in Spain, Portugal and the South of France, from the year 1808 till 1814. It is well done, I think, and amuses me very much. In French, I am now in La Rivalité de la France et de l'Espagne, par Gaillard,16 which is very interesting. I have also begun Rollin.17 I am very fond of making tables of the Kings and Queens, as I go on, and I have lately finished one of the English Sovereigns and their consorts, as, of course, the history of my own country is one of my first duties. I should be fearful of tiring you with so long an account of myself, were I not sure you take so great an interest in my welfare.

Pray give my most affectionate love to dearest Aunt Louisa, and please say to the Queen of the French and the two Princesses how grateful I am for their kind remembrance of me.

Believe me always, my dearest Uncle, your very affectionate, very dutiful, and most attached Niece,

Victoria.

Footnote 13: The Rev. George Davys. See ante, p.

Footnote 14: This History of Modern Europe, in a series of letters from a nobleman to his son, 5 vols. (1779-1784), deals with the rise of modern kingdoms down to the Peace of Westphalia (1648).

Footnote 15: Sir John Thomas Jones, Bart. (1783-1843), a Royal Engineer, who served in the Peninsular War.

Footnote 16: Gabriel Henri Gaillard (1726-1806), Member of the French Academy.

Footnote 17: The Histoire Ancienne, by Charles Rollin (1661-1741), Rector of the University of Paris.

St. Leonards, 19th November 1834.

My dearest Uncle,—It is impossible for me to express how happy you have made me by writing so soon again to me, and how pleased I am to see by your very kind letter that you intend to write to me often. I am much obliged to you, dear Uncle, for the extract about Queen Anne, but must beg you, as you have sent me to show what a Queen ought not to be, that you will send me what a Queen ought to be.18

Might I ask what is the very pretty seal with which the letter I got from you yesterday was closed? It is so peculiar that I am anxious to know.

Believe me always, dear Uncle, your very affectionate, very dutiful, and very attached Niece, Victoria.

Footnote 18: King Leopold had sent the Princess an extract from a French Memoir, containing a severe criticism of the political character of Queen Anne.

Laeken, 2nd December 1834.

My dearest Love,—You have written a very clever, sharp little letter the other day, which gave me great pleasure. Sure enough, when I show you what a Queen ought not to be, I also ought to tell you what she should be, and this task I will very conscientiously take upon myself on the very first occasion which may offer itself for a confidential communication. Now I must conclude, to go to town. I must, however, say that I have given orders to send you Sully's Memoirs. As they have not been written exclusively for young ladies, it will be well to have Lehzen to read it with you, and to judge what ought to be left for some future time. And now

God bless you! Ever, my beloved child, your attached Friend and Uncle,

Leopold R.

A NEW YEAR GREETING

St. Leonards, 28th December 1834.

My dearest Uncle,—I must again, with your permission, write you a few lines, to wish you a very happy new year, not only for this year, but for many to come. I know not how to thank you sufficiently for the invaluable and precious autographs which you were so very kind as to send me. Some of them I received a few days ago, and the others to-day, accompanied by a very kind letter from you, and a beautiful shawl, which will be most useful to me, particularly as a favourite one of mine is growing very old. I wish you could come here, for many reasons, but also to be an eye-witness of my extreme prudence in eating, which would astonish you. The poor sea-gulls are, however, not so happy as you imagine, for they have great enemies in the country-people here, who take pleasure in shooting them.

Believe me always, my dearest Uncle, your very affectionate and most grateful Niece,

Victoria.

Kensington Palace, 2nd February 1835.

My dearest Uncle,—I know not how to thank you sufficiently for the most valuable autographs you were kind enough to send me. I am particularly delighted with that of Louis Quatorze, "le grand Roi," and my great admiration.... You will not, I hope, think me very troublesome if I venture to ask for two more autographs which I should very particularly like to have; they are Mme. de Sévigné's19 and Racine's; as I am reading the letters of the former, and the tragedies of the latter, I should prize them highly. Believe me always, my dearest Uncle, your most affectionate and dutiful Niece,

Victoria.

Footnote 19: Marie de Rabutin Chantal, Marquise de Sévigné, born 1626. At twenty-four she was left a widow, and devoted herself to her children's education. When her daughter married the Count de Grignan, she began that correspondence with her on which her reputation chiefly rests. She died in 1696, and the letters were first published in 1726.

THE PRINCESS'S CONFIRMATION

Camp of Beverloo

(in the North of the Province of Limburg),

3rd August 1835.

My dear Love,—By your Mother's letter of the 31st ulto., I learned of the serious and important action in your young life20 which has passed recently, and I cannot let it pass without saying some words on the subject. I am perhaps rather strangely situated for a preaching— somewhat in the style of those old camp preachers who held forth to many thousand people on some heath in Scotland. I am also on an immense heath, surrounded by 16,000 men, mostly young and gay, cooking, singing, working, and not very like the stern old Covenanters; however, I shall try. First of all, let me congratulate you that it passed happily and well off. Secondly, let me entreat you to look with a serious and reflective mind on the day which is past. Many are the religions, many the shades of those religions, but it must be confessed the principles of the Christian religion are the most perfect and the most beautiful that can be imagined.... There is one virtue which is particularly Christian; this is the knowledge of our own heart in real humility. Hypocrisy is a besetting sin of all times, but particularly of the present, and many are the wolves in sheep's clothes. I am sorry to say, with all my affection for old England, the very state of its Society and politics renders many in that country essentially humbugs and deceivers; the appearance of the thing is generally more considered than the reality; provided matters go off well, and opinion may be gained, the real good is matter of the most perfect indifference. Defend yourself, my dear love, against this system; let your dear character always be true and loyal; this does not exclude prudence—worldly concerns are now unfortunately so organised that you must be cautious or you may injure yourself and others—but it does not prevent the being sterling and true. Nothing in persons gives greater reliance, greater weight, than when they are known to be true. HONESTY AND SINCERITY From your earliest childhood I was anxious to see in you this important virtue saved and developed, and Lehzen will still be able to recollect that. If it is God's pleasure that you should once21 fill the arduous situation to which you seem destined, you will find the importance of what I now say to you. And when others may tremble to have at last their real character found out, and to meet all the contempt which they may deserve, your mind and heart will be still and happy, because it will know that it acts honestly, that truth and goodness are the motives of its actions. I press you now against my heart; may God bless you as I wish and hope it, and may you always feel some affection for your sincerely devoted camp preacher and Uncle,

Leopold R.

Footnote 20: The Princess was confirmed at the Chapel Royal, on 30th July 1835.

Footnote 21: King Leopold not infrequently uses "once" like the Latin olim, as referring to any indefinite date in the future as well as in the past. "Some day" is what is intended here.

INTRODUCTORY NOTE: TO CHAPTER V

The year 1836 was not an eventful one at home; the Whig Ministry were too weak to carry measures of first-rate importance, and could hardly have maintained themselves in power against the formidable opposition of Sir Robert Peel without the support of O'Connell. Parliament was chiefly occupied by the consideration of the Secret Societies in Ireland, Tithes, Municipal Corporations, and such matters; the Marriage Act, and the Act for the Registration of Births have probably been the most important measures of the year to the country. Troubles which were destined to become more acute arose in Lower Canada and Jamaica, both taking the form of disputes between the executive and the legislature.

On the continent of Europe, affairs were more disturbing. Several attempts were made on the life of the King of the French, while an abortive insurrection with a view of establishing a military empire was made by Louis Bonaparte at Strasburg. The Prince was allowed to leave the country and go to the United States, but his accomplices were detained for trial. In Algiers the French Government determined to prosecute operations against the Arab Chief Abd-el-Kader, and they sent an expedition to Constantin.

Holland and Belgium were occupied with a dispute about their boundary line, the cession to Belgium of Luxemburg being the chief point of difference. The difficulties that arose in passing an important Municipal Act for Belgium caused King Leopold temporarily to regret he had not accepted the throne of Greece.

Portugal was still convulsed by revolutionary agitation. Dom Pedro, the eldest son of King John VI., had been proclaimed Emperor of Brazil in his father's lifetime, and had abdicated the throne of Portugal in favour of his daughter Donna Maria, a child seven years old, while Dom Miguel, his younger brother, who had acted in opposition to his father in Portugal, claimed the throne for himself. Dom Pedro had agreed that his daughter should marry Miguel, who was in 1827 appointed Regent. Miguel, had he acted wisely, might have maintained himself on the throne, but Dom Pedro, who had been expelled from Brazil by a revolution, took active steps to recover the Portuguese throne for his daughter, and equipped an expedition for that end with English and French volunteers. In this way, Donna Maria, who had spent part of her exile in England, and formed a friendship with the Princess Victoria, was through British instrumentality placed on her throne, but still could only maintain herself with difficulty against Miguel. She was a few weeks older than the Princess Victoria, and had recently lost her first husband, the Duc de Leuchtenberg. She was married by proxy on the 1st of January 1836, and in person on the 9th of April, to Prince Ferdinand of Saxe-Coburg.

There was also a disputed succession in Spain, where by the ancient law women might succeed to the throne. Ferdinand VII., who had revoked the Pragmatic Sanction of 1711 and restored the former system, died in 1833, leaving no son. His elder daughter Isabella, then three years of age, was proclaimed Queen (her mother Christina being appointed Regent), and Isabella's claims were recognised by England and France. The late King's brother, Don Carlos, taking his stand upon the Salic Law as established by the Pragmatic Sanction, raised the standard of revolt and allied himself with Dom Miguel, the young Queens Maria and Isabella mutually recognising each other, and being supported by France and England against the "Holy Alliance" of Austria, Russia, and Prussia. A seven years' civil war resulted, which did not end till, from sheer exhaustion, the Carlists had to cease fighting the Christinos, as the loyal party was called. The English Government in the previous year had sanctioned the enlistment of 10,000 men; who, commanded by Colonel (afterwards Sir de Lacy) Evans, landed at San Sebastian in August to assist the Christinos. A British auxiliary contingent was already with the Spanish army, while a naval squadron under Lord John Hay was active on the coast. Mendizabal was Prime Minister at the beginning of the year 1836, and was succeeded in May by Isturitz. Riots took place at Madrid, and Isturitz fled to France; Calatrava succeeding him, assisted by Mendizabal. The Christino cause did not much advance during the year.

CHAPTER V

4th March 1836.

My dearly beloved Child,—You wrote me again a long, dear, good letter, like all those which I received from your kind hands. Time approaches now for the arrival of the cousins, and most probably of your Uncle Ferdinand also. He has informed me of his arrival for the 7th or 8th; notwithstanding this, I mean to leave everything settled as it has been arranged. They will set off on the 7th, arrive at Paris on the 8th, and leave it again on the 12th.... Fernando1 has still a very bad cold; change of air is likely to cure that. The stay here has done Fernando a great deal of good, and it cannot be denied that he is quite another person. It has given me some trouble, but I have written down for him everything which he ought to know about the organisation of a government in general, and what will be necessary in specie to carry on successfully the Government in Portugal.... My inclinations, as you are aware, would have led me to the East, but certainly the only thing which reconciles me with my not having done so is that it has made me to remain near you, and will enable me to see you and to be useful to you.

Footnote 1: The Queen's first cousin, Prince Ferdinand (son of Prince Ferdinand of Saxe-Coburg, who was brother of the Duchess of Kent and the King of the Belgians), aged nineteen, who married the Queen of Portugal on 9th April. He was at this time visiting the King of the Belgians on his way to Portugal.

Kensington Palace, 7th March 1836.

... You are very kind, my dearest, best Uncle, to say that "the only thing which reconciles you" for not having gone to Greece is, that you are near me and can see me. Thank Heaven that you did not go there! it would have been dreadful for me and for all your relations to be thus, as it were, cut off from almost all intercourse! It is hard enough, that you are as far as you are, when I recollect the happy time when I could see you, and be with you, every day!...

Kensington Palace, 29th March 1836.

My dearest Uncle,— ... As concerning the "fatigues" we are said to have undergone, they were none to me, and made me very happy; I only wish they could have lasted longer, for all, all is over now, and our beloved Ferdinand2 himself leaves our shores this very morning. We accompanied them all on Sunday, where we took a final leave of our dear Ferdinand, and I cannot tell you how sorry I was, and am, to see him go, for I love him dearly. He is so truly excellent, kind, and good, and endears himself so much by his simplicity and good-heartedness! I may venture to say, that no one has his prosperity and happiness more at heart than I have. I am extremely sanguine about his success. He goes there full of courage, spirits, and goodwill, and being naturally clever and observant, I doubt not that with good counsel, and prudence, he will do very well. Your kind advice will be of the greatest and most important use to him, the more so as he is so exceedingly fond of you.... Ferdinand leaves behind him here a most favourable impression on all parties, for I have even heard from some great Tories themselves that there was a great feeling for him in this country.

Footnote 2: See ante, p. He had latterly been visiting the Duchess of Kent.

THE PRINCES ERNEST AND ALBERT

Stuttgart, 16th April 1836.

... You will like our two Coburg cousins also, I think; they are more manly than I think the two others are, after the description. I am very fond of them both. Ernest is my favourite, although Albert is much handsomer, and cleverer too, but Ernest is so honest and good-natured. I shall be very curious to hear your opinion upon them....

Kensington Palace, 26th April 1836.

My dearest, best Uncle,— ... You will, I am sure, have been delighted with M. de Neumann's3 account of the complete success of our dear Ferdinand. All has gone off better than even our most sanguine hopes could have desired. He is much pleased with the good Queen, and she is delighted with him, and M. de Neumann says that they are already quite happy together. This is really a great blessing, but I fear that all the exterior affairs are not in quite so good a state. I hope, however, that the good people will not make any more difficulties about Fernando's being Commander-in-Chief, as I hear from all accounts it is necessary he should be so....

Uncle Ernest and my cousins will probably come here in the beginning of next month, I hear, and will visit you on their return.

You ask me about Sully's Memoirs, and if I have finished them. I have not finished them, but am reading them with great interest, and find there is a great deal in them which applies to the present times, and a great deal of good advice and reasoning in them. As you say, very truly, it is extremely necessary for me to follow the "events of the day," and to do so impartially. I am always both grateful and happy when you give me any advice, and hope you will continue to do so as long as I live.

I am glad to hear you approve my singing, and I cannot tell you how delightful it would be for me, if you could join with us. À propos, dear Uncle, you did not answer what I said to you in a former letter about your visiting us again. You know, dear Uncle, that this is a subject upon which I am very earnest and very eager, and as the summer approaches I grow more and more anxious about it. You know, also, that pleasure does more good than a hundred walks and rides.

Believe me always, my dearest Uncle, your truly devoted and attached Niece,

Victoria.

Footnote 3: Baron Neumann, who acted as Minister Plenipotentiary during the absences of Prince Esterhazy, succeeded him as Austrian Minister in 1842. He married Lady Augusta Somerset in 1844.

THE PRINCE OF ORANGE

13th May 1836.

My dearest Child,—I got this time a very small letter from your good little Ladyship, and I shall repay it probably in larger coin, as my letter going through a messenger of my own will become longer, as it will be more confidential than through the usual mode of conveyance.

I am really astonished at the conduct of your old Uncle the King; this invitation of the Prince of Orange and his sons, this forcing him upon others, is very extraordinary.4 It is so, because persons in political stations and champions of great political passions cannot put aside their known character as you would lay your hat upon a table.

Not later than yesterday I got a half official communication from England, insinuating that it would be highly desirable that the visit of your relatives should not take place, this year—qu'en dites-vous? The relations of the Queen and the King, therefore, to the God-knows-what degree, are to come in shoals and rule the land, when your relations are to be forbidden the country, and that when, as you know, the whole of your relations have ever been very dutiful and kind to the King. Really and truly I never heard or saw anything like it, and I hope it will a little rouse your spirit; now that slavery is even abolished in the British Colonies, I do not comprehend why your lot alone should be to be kept, a white little slavey in England, for the pleasure of the Court, who never bought you, as I am not aware of their having gone to any expense on that head, or the King's even having spent a sixpence for your existence. I expect that my visits in England will also be prohibited by an Order in Council. Oh consistency and political or other honesty, where must one look for you!

I have not the least doubt that the King, in his passion for the Oranges, will be excessively rude to your relations; this, however, will not signify much; they are your guests and not his, and will therefore not mind it....

Footnote 4: King Leopold had for some time cherished a hope of uniting the Princess Victoria in marriage with her cousin, Prince Albert of Coburg. He therefore arranged that the Prince, with his elder brother, Prince Ernest, should pay a visit to the Duchess of Kent at Kensington Palace. King William naturally opposed a scheme which he knew met with the approval of his sister-in-law. He accordingly invited the Prince of Orange and his two sons at the same time, and favoured the candidature of the younger son, Prince Alexander. The King (it is believed) went so far as to say that no other marriage should ever take place, and that the Duke of Saxe-Coburg and his son should never put foot in the country; they should not be allowed to land, and must go back whence they came.

The Prince of Orange had himself been a candidate for the hand of Princess Charlotte, and had no reason to be friendly to King Leopold, of whom it is recorded that he said, "Voilà un homme qui a pris ma femme et mon royaume."

ARRIVAL OF PRINCE ALBERT

23rd May 1836.

My dearest Uncle,— ... Uncle Ernest and my cousins arrived here on Wednesday, sains et saufs. Uncle is looking remarkably well, and my cousins are most delightful young people. I will give you no detailed description of them, as you will so soon see them yourself. But I must say, that they are both very amiable, very kind and good, and extremely merry, just as young people should be; with all that, they are extremely sensible, and very fond of occupation. Albert is extremely handsome, which Ernest certainly is not, but he has a most good-natured, honest, and intelligent countenance. We took them to the Opera on Friday, to see the Puritani, and as they are excessively fond of music, like me, they were in perfect ecstasies, having never heard any of the singers before....

PRINCE ALBERT

7th June 1836.

My dearest Uncle,—These few lines will be given to you by my dear Uncle Ernest when he sees you.

I must thank you, my beloved Uncle, for the prospect of great happiness you have contributed to give me, in the person of dear Albert. Allow me, then, my dearest Uncle, to tell you how delighted I am with him, and how much I like him in every way. He possesses every quality that could be desired to render me perfectly happy. He is so sensible, so kind, and so good, and so amiable too. He has, besides, the most pleasing and delightful exterior and appearance you can possibly see.

I have only now to beg you, my dearest Uncle, to take care of the health of one, now so dear to me, and to take him under your special protection. I hope and trust that all will go on prosperously and well on this subject of so much importance to me.

Believe me always, my dearest Uncle, your most affectionate, devoted, and grateful Niece, Victoria.

CONVERSATION

17th June 1836.

My dearest and most beloved Child,—I begged your Mother, in the meantime, to offer you my best thanks for your very pretty drawing representing the Provost of Bruges and his daughter5; I admired also that for your Aunt. They do your spirit of invention honour, and it is a very good plan to draw subjects from books or plays which interest you. You will feel the loss of a pleasant society in the old Palace, the more so as your relations are good unsophisticated people, a thing which one does not so often meet with. I suppose that part of your London amusements will soon be over. You were going to Windsor, which you will probably have left by this time. I hope you were very prudent; I cannot disguise from you, that though the inhabitants are good-natured people, still that I think you want all your natural caution with them. Never permit yourself to be induced to tell them any opinion or sentiment of yours which is beyond the sphere of common conversation and its ordinary topics. Bad use would be made of it against yourself, and you cannot in that subject be too much guarded. I know well the people we have to deal with. I am extremely impartial, but I shall also always be equally watchful.... God bless you! Ever, my dear child, your very devoted Uncle and Friend,

Leopold R.

Footnote 5: Leading characters in The Heiress of Bruges, by Grattan.

9th August 1836.

My beloved Uncle,— ... I was sure you would be very much pleased with Ernest and Albert as soon as you knew them more; there cannot be two more good and sensible young men than they are. Pray, dear Uncle, say everything most kind from me to them.

We go to Buxted6 to-morrow morning, and stay there till next Monday.

All the gaieties are now over. We took leave of the Opera on Saturday, and a most brilliant conclusion to the season it was. Yesterday I took my farewell lesson with Lablache,7 which I was very sorry to do. I have had twenty-six lessons with him, and I look forward with pleasure to resume them again next spring.

Footnote 6: Lord Liverpool's house. Charles Cecil Cope Jenkinson, third Earl of Liverpool, was fifty-three years old at the time of the Queen's accession. He was a moderate Tory, and had held office as Under-Secretary for the Home Department in 1807, and in 1809 as Under-Secretary for War and the Colonies. He succeeded to the Earldom in 1828. The title, since revived, became extinct on his death in 1851. He was a friend of the Duchess of Kent, who often stayed with him at Buxted Park in Sussex, and at Pitchford in Shropshire. At three successive visits at the latter house the Princess occupied the same small room without a fireplace.

Footnote 7: Luigi Lablache (1794-1858), a famous opera-singer, was the Princess's singing-master.

2nd September 1836.

My dearest Uncle,— ... The state of Spain is most alarming and unfortunate.8 I do hope something will be done. The news were rather better yesterday and the day before. The Christinos had gained a victory over the Carlists.9 I take a great interest in the whole of this unfortunate affair. I hope and trust Portugal may not suffer by all the affairs of Spain, but much is to be feared. Dieskau will have told you much about the internal affairs, which seem to go on very prosperously. Pray has the Duchess of Braganza10 written to you or Aunt Louise since Ferdinand's marriage?

You did not send me the King of Naples'11 letter, as you said you would; pray do so in your next letter. I hope he will come here next year. You do not mention France, so I hope all is quiet. The Duke of Orleans is quite well again, I am happy to hear from Aunt Louise. Now I must conclude, begging you to believe me, always, your most truly attached and really devoted Niece,

Victoria.

Footnote 8: See Introductory Note for the year, ante,

Footnote 9: The civil war was favourable to the Carlists at this time, General Gomez obtaining a victory on 30th August. By the end of the year he had twice traversed the kingdom, hampered with plunder and prisoners, and surrounded by armies greater than his own, and in no district did he find the inhabitants disposed to act against him.

Footnote 10: Step-mother of the Queen of Portugal.

Footnote 11: Ferdinand II., commonly named "Bomba." He married en secondes noces, the Archduchess Theresa of Austria.

A FAREWELL LETTER

Claremont, 21st September 1836.

My most dearly beloved Uncle,—As I hear that Mamma is going to send a letter to you which will reach you at Dover, and though it is only an hour and a half since we parted, I must write you one line to tell you how very, very sad I am that you have left us, and to repeat, what I think you know pretty well, how much I love you. When I think that but two hours ago we were happily together, and that now you are travelling every instant farther and farther away from us, and that I shall with all probability not see you for a year, it makes me cry. Yes, dearest Uncle, it is dreadful in this life, that one is destined, and particularly unhappy me, to be almost always separated from those one loves most dearly. I live, however, in the hopes of your visit next year with dear Aunt, and I cannot say how thankful and happy I am that we have had you here for six short, and to me most bright happy days! I shall look back with the greatest delight on them.

Believe me, always, your ever devoted and most affectionately attached Niece and Child,

Victoria.

Footnote 12: Written at the conclusion of the King's visit to England.

THE PRINCESS AND THE CHURCH

Laeken, 11th November 1836.

My very dear Child,— ...I know attempts have been made to represent you as indifferent to the established Church. You know that in England the Sovereign is the head of the Church, and that the Church looks upon the Protestant religion as it is established as the State Religion. In times like the present, when the Crown is already a good deal weakened, I believe that it is of importance to maintain as much as possible this state of affairs, and I believe that you will do well, whenever an occasion offers itself to do so without affectation, to express your sincere interest for the Church, and that you comprehend its position and count upon its good-will. The poor Church will be a good deal persecuted, I have no doubt, but it would be desirable that the men belonging to it should be united, sensible, and moderate....

Ramsgate, 14th November 1836.

... What you say to me relative to Church matters I quite comprehend, and always am very thankful for advice from you.

I am reading away famously. I like Mrs. Hutchinson's Life of her husband13 only comme cela; she is so dreadfully violent. She and Clarendon are so totally opposite, that it is quite absurd, and I only believe the juste milieu....

Your speech interested me very much; it is very fine indeed; you wrote it yourself, did you not?

Belgium is indeed the happiest country in the world, and it is all, all owing to your great care and kindness. "Nous étions des enfans perdus," General Goblet14 said to me at Claremont, "quand le Roi est venu nous sauver." And so it is....

Pray, dear Uncle, say everything most kind from me to Ernest and Albert, and believe me, always, your affectionate Niece,

Victoria.

Pray, dear Uncle, is the report of the King of Naples' marriage to the Archduchess Theresa true? I hear the king has behaved uncommonly well at Naples during the cholera panic. I enclose the measure of my finger.

Footnote 13: The regicide, Colonel Hutchinson's, fame rests more on his wife's commemoration of him than on his own exploits. She was the daughter of Sir Allen Apsley, Lieutenant of the Tower of London, and highly educated. Between 1664 and 1671 she wrote the biography of her husband, first published in 1806. "The figure of Colonel Hutchinson," says J. R. Green, "stands out from his wife's canvas with the grace and tenderness of a portrait by Van Dyck."

Footnote 14: The Belgian General, Albert Joseph Goblet. Count d'Alviella.

DEATH OF CHARLES X

Laeken, 18th November 1836.

... Poor Charles X. is dead, it is said of the cholera. I regret him; few people were ever kinder to me than the good old man. He was blinded by certain absolute ideas, but a good man, and deserving to be loved. History will state that Louis XVIII. was a most liberal monarch, reigning with great mildness and justice to his end, but that his brother, from his despotic and harsh disposition, upset all the other had done, and lost the throne. Louis XVIII. was a clever, hard-hearted man, shackled by no principle, very proud and false. Charles X. an honest man, a kind friend, an honourable master, sincere in his opinions, and inclined to do everything that is right. That teaches us what we ought to believe in history as it is compiled according to ostensible events and results known to the generality of people. Memoirs are much more instructive, if written honestly and not purposely fabricated, as it happens too often nowadays, particularly at Paris.... I shall not fail to read the books you so kindly recommend. I join you a small copy of our very liberal Constitution, hitherto conscientiously executed—no easy matter. You may communicate it to your Mother; it is the best answer to an infamous Radical or Tory-Radical paper, the Constitutional, which seems determined to run down the Coburg family. I don't understand the meaning of it; the only happiness poor Charlotte knew was during her short wedded existence, and there was but one voice on that subject, that we offered a bright prospect to the nation. Since that period I have (though been abused, and vilified merely for drawing an income which was the consequence of a Treaty ratified by both Houses of Parliament, and that without one dissenting voice, a thing not very likely to happen again) done everything to see England prosperous and powerful. I have spared her, in 1831, much trouble and expense, as without my coming here very serious complications, war and all the expensive operations connected with it, must have taken place. I give the whole of my income, without the reservation of a farthing, to the country; I preserve unity on the Continent, have frequently prevented mischief at Paris, and to thank me for all that, I get the most scurrilous abuse, in which the good people from constant practice so much excel.... The conclusion of all this—and that by people whose very existence in political life may be but of a few years' standing—is scurrilous abuse of the Coburg family. I should like to know what harm the Coburg family has done to England? But enough of this. Your principle is very good; one must not mind what newspapers say. Their power is a fiction of the worst description, and their efforts marked by the worst faith and the greatest untruths. If all the Editors of the papers in the countries where the liberty of the press exists were to be assembled, we should have a crew to which you would not confide a dog that you would value, still less your honour and reputation....

REVOLUTION AT LISBON

21st November 1836.

My most dearly beloved Uncle,—You cannot imagine how happy you have made me by your very dear, kind, long, and interesting letter of the 18th, which I received yesterday morning, and for which I beg you to accept my very warmest and best thanks. You know, I think, my dearest

Uncle, that no creature on earth loves you more dearly, or has a higher sense of admiration for you, than I have. Independent of all that you have done—which I never, never can be grateful enough for—my love for you exceeds all that words can express; it is innate in me, for from my earliest years the name of Uncle was the dearest I knew, the word Uncle, alone, meant no other but you!

Your letter is so interesting and instructive that I could read it over and over again. I hope, dear Uncle, you will in process of time give me the aperçu you mention, which would be so very interesting for me.

I cannot tell you how distressed I was by the late unfortunate contre-révolution manquée at Lisbon,15 and how sorry I was to see by the letter you wrote me, that you were still unaware of it on the 18th. Mamma received a letter from Lord Palmerston yesterday morning, which she has sent you, and which is consolatory, I think. He speaks in the highest terms of our beloved Ferdinand, which proves that he becomes daily more and more worthy of his arduous situation, and says that the Queen's situation "is better than it was," less bad than it might have been "after such an affair," and not so good as it would have been had poor Donna Maria waited patiently till all was ripe for action. Dietz16 wrote Mamma a most desponding letter, so much so, that had we not got Lord Palmerston's letter we must have thought all, all was over.17 I hope, dear Uncle, you will tell me your feeling about the whole, which will only satisfy me; no one else could, for I take an interest in Ferdinand's welfare as though he were my brother.

THE PRINCESS'S NAME

Allow me, dearest Uncle, to say a few words respecting my name, to which you allude. You are aware, I believe, that about a year after the accession of the present King there was a desire to change my favourite and dear name Victoria to that of Charlotte, also most dear, to which the King willingly consented. On its being told me, I said nothing, though I felt grieved beyond measure at the thought of any change. Not long after this, Lord Grey, and also the Archbishop of Canterbury, acquainted Mamma that the country, having been accustomed to hear me called Victoria, had become used to it, enfin, liked it, and therefore, to my great delight, the idea of a change was given up.18

I was sure the death of old Charles X. would strike you....

I thank you much for the Constitution de la Belgique. Those attacks on you are infamous, but must not be minded; they are the language of a few jealous, envious people. En revanche, I enclose a paragraph from a speech of O'Connell's19 I think worth your reading.

Pray, dearest Uncle, say everything most kind to my beloved and dearest Aunt, and thank her in my name for her kind letter, which I shall answer on Friday. I am happy she and the dear little man are well.

Believe me, always, your most devoted and affectionately attached Niece,
Victoria.

Footnote 15: Prince Ferdinand was appointed Commander-in-Chief of the Portuguese army on the advice of the Duc de Terceira, then Prime Minister. The appointment was highly unpopular; riots broke out, the army mutinied, and rose against the authorities, with the result that the Queen of Portugal was compelled to accept the Radical Constitution of 1820, in the place of Dom Pedro's constitutional Charter of 1826. Later in the year the Queen, assisted by Palmella, Terceira, and Saldanha, made a counter-move, believing that the people of Lisbon would support her, and proposed to dismiss her Ministers; she had, however, been misled as to the popular aid forthcoming, and had to give up the struggle, Sá da Bandeira becoming Prime Minister. The Queen, virtually a captive, had to accede to the revolutionary requirements.

Footnote 16: Dietz was a former Governor of Prince Ferdinand, who accompanied him to Portugal on his marriage with Donna Maria, and took a considerable part in political affairs.

Footnote 17: A former Minister of the Interior was killed by the National Guards, who threatened to march on Belem, where the Queen was; she had to apply to the British Marines for protection.

Footnote 18: In the course of the debate (3rd August 1831) on Lord Althorp's proposition to add £10,000 a year to the Duchess of Kent's income, Sir M. W. Ridley suggested changing the Princess's name to Elizabeth, as being "more accordant to the feelings of the people," saying that he had heard the subject "frequently and seriously argued." Hunt, the Radical, who opposed the grant, saw no objection to the change, and Lord Althorp thought the matter of no particular consequence. The Princess's own feelings, and those of her mother, do not seem to have been considered. See Hansard, 3rd series, vol. v. 591, 654 et seq.

Footnote 19: Probably that on the Irish Church Question at the General (formerly "Catholic") Association, Dublin.

Claremont, 5th December 1836.

My dearest Uncle,—... I have begun since a few days Lord Clive's Life, by Sir John Malcolm,20 which is very interesting, as it gives much insight into the affairs of India, over parts of which, I fear, it would be well to throw a veil. I am reading it by myself, et je vous le recommande....

Footnote 20: The book reviewed by Macaulay, who spoke of Sir John Malcolm as one whose "love passes the love of biographers, and who can see nothing but wisdom and justice in the actions of his idol."

INTRODUCTORY NOTE: TO CHAPTER VI

The closing months of the reign of William IV. were not marked by any stirring events at home. The Conservative opposition to the Melbourne Ministry was strengthened before the meeting of Parliament by a great speech by Sir Robert Peel at Glasgow, and Lord Brougham later on emerged from his retirement to become the able and venomous critic of his former friends. The Government failed to carry important measures on Church Rates and Irish Municipal Corporations, while the Radical group pressed persistently their favourite motions in support of the Ballot, and against the Property qualification of members, Primogeniture, the Septennial Act, the Bishops' seats and Proxy Voting in the House of Lords. The Ministry was saved from shipwreck by the demise of the Crown and by the accession of the Princess Victoria, who, on attaining her legal majority a month earlier, had received marked signs of enthusiastic popular favour.

The General Election in the Autumn did not materially affect the position of parties, the Radicals losing and O'Connell gaining seats; but the prestige of Lord Melbourne was increased by the unique position he now held in reference to the Sovereign. Parliament was opened in person by the Queen on 20th November, and the Civil List dealt with, the amount allocated being £385,000 as against £510,000 in the late reign (of which £75,000, formerly paid in pensions, was now struck off, and other arrangements made).

For some time past the state of Canada had caused grave anxiety. By an Act of 1791, it had been divided into Upper and Lower Canada, each with a Governor, Council, and House of Representatives, Lower Canada being in the main French, while Upper Canada was occupied by British settlers. Friction first arose in the former, between the nominee Council and the popular Assembly, the Assembly declining to pay the salaries of officials whom they had censured, but whom the Executive had retained in their posts. Mr Papineau, who had been Speaker of the Assembly, was leader in the popular movement. Lord Gosford, the Governor of Lower Canada, dismissed some Militia officers who had taken part in political demonstrations, and warrants were issued for the apprehension of certain members of the Assembly, on the charge of high treason: within a short time the discontented party broke out into rebellion. The course which events would take in Upper Canada was for a time doubtful. Sir Francis Head, the Governor, placed his regular troops at the service of Lord Gosford, preferring to rely on the militia. This unusual action was successful, but was not approved by the Colonial Office. The state of affairs became very alarming at the close of the year, when it was announced in Parliament that Lord Gosford had resigned and that Sir John Colborne (afterwards Lord Seaton) had been appointed to succeed him.

In France the confederates of Louis Napoleon in the Strasburg outbreak were tried and acquitted; a treaty was concluded at Tafna with Abd-el-Kader, but negotiations for a similar agreement with Achmet Bey were less successful, and operations were continued against Constantin with successful results, the town being carried by an assault on 13th October, with some loss of officers and men on the French side.

Affairs continued unsettled in the Peninsula. In Spain General Evans was defeated near San Sebastian, but afterwards, in conjunction with Lord John Hay, captured Irun, the frontier town. Don Carlos meanwhile marched on Madrid, but was encountered by Espartero, Commander-in-Chief of the Christinos, who was Prime Minister for a brief period during the year. The British legion was dissolved, and Evans returned to England.

In Portugal the English were becoming unpopular for their supposed intervention: Ferdinand, the Queen's consort, who was naturally believed to be in harmony with the British Cabinet, acted tactlessly in accepting the Commandership-in-Chief, and internal hostilities continued throughout the year.

In Hanover a reactionary step was taken by King Ernest, who had succeeded his brother, William IV. of England, on the throne of Hanover; by letters patent he abrogated the Constitution of 1833, an action which, imperfect and open to criticism though the Constitution was, naturally aroused anxiety among the supporters of representative institutions throughout Europe.

CHAPTER VI

SPAIN AND PORTUGAL

16th January 1837.

My dearest Uncle,— ... We saw Van de Weyer1 on Tuesday, and his conversation was most interesting. He praises our dear Ferdinand most exceedingly, but as for the poor Queen, what he told us does not redound much to her credit; one good quality, however, she has, which is her excessive fondness for and real obedience to Ferdinand. She is unfortunately surrounded by a camarilla2 who poison her ears, and fetter all her actions; poor soul! she is much to be pitied. About Lavradio3 you will also have, I fear, heard but too much. Honesty and single-heartedness seems to have left Portugal. Van de Weyer is so clear in all that he says, so sensible, so quiet, so clever, and, last but not least, so agreeable; I hope we shall soon see him again. You see, dear Uncle, how much interest I take in Portugal; but I must say that I think every one who knows dear Ferdinand, and particularly who loves him as I do, must feel a very deep interest as to the fate of the unhappy country in which he is destined to play so prominent and difficult a part.

I have been reading to-day a very clever speech of Sir Robert Peel's (not a political one) to the University at Glasgow, on the occasion of his being elected Lord Rector of that college. There is another speech of his at the dinner at Glasgow which is political, but which I have not yet read....4

Footnote 1: Sylvain Van de Weyer (b. 1802) was, in 1830, Belgian Plenipotentiary at the Conference of London. He returned to his own country and became Foreign Minister. His exertions contributed greatly to render successful the candidature of Prince Leopold for the throne of Belgium. The King appointed him Belgian Minister in London, to which post he returned in 1851, and held it till 1867. He was treated by the Queen until his death in 1874 as a very intimate friend and adviser.

Footnote 2: I.e. a clique.

Footnote 3: The Portuguese Statesman who had gone to Gotha to arrange the Queen's marriage, and was destined to act in a similar manner for her son in 1857.

Footnote 4: Sir R. Peel was installed as Lord Rector of Glasgow on 11th January, and delivered an address on the principles of Education: strong political feeling was manifested, groans being given for Lord Melbourne and the Ministry. At a civic banquet given in Sir R. Peel's honour, he expounded the principles of Conservative Reform.

23rd January 1837.

My dearest Uncle,— ... The affairs of the Peninsula are indeed very distressing,5 and what you tell me in your letter of the 20th, as also in the former one, is highly interesting and, alas! but too true. I trust, not withstanding what you say, I may yet live to see Spain and Portugal settled. But I greatly fear that the time is far distant.

Do you know Mendizabal?6 I saw him at our house in 1835. Alava7 presented him to us; he is a tall, dark, fine, and clever-looking man. I remember his being so much struck with my likeness to Donna Maria, which I was not aware was the case. Pray, dear Uncle, may I ask you a silly question?—is not the Queen of Spain8 rather clever? You know her, and what do you think of her? And do you know what sort of people are about poor little Queen Isabel?9 Poor, good Donna Maria! I feel much for her; her education was one of the worst that could be. As long as those Ficalhos and Melos remain about her, nothing can be done. Could they not be got rid of in time?

I was sorry to see that the French Chambers were rather stormy.10

I thank you much for the list of the ball of the 18th, which must have been very splendid. The last ball I was at was our own, and I concluded that very ball at half-past three in the morning with a country dance, Albert being my partner.

Pray, dear Uncle, tell both young gentlemen, with my kindest love, that I often think of that night and of many other pleasant evenings we passed together. The singing will come all in time. Who is their singing-master? I wish they had my worthy Lablache. I sing regularly every evening, as I think it better to do so every day to keep the voice manageable. Oh, my beloved Uncle, could you join us, how delightful that would be! How I should delight in singing with you all our favourite things from La Gazza, Otello, Il Barbiere, etc., etc.

The little Cousin11 must be a little love: oh, could I but see him and play with him! Pray, dear Uncle, does he know such a thing as that he has got an Aunt and Cousin on the other side of the water? ...

Pray, dear Uncle, have you read Sir R. Peel's two speeches? I wish you would, and give me your opinion of them.

Footnote 5: Some interesting observations on these events may be read in Borrow's Bible in Spain.

Footnote 6: Don Juan Alvarez y Mendizabal (1790-1853), Spanish politician and financier.

Footnote 7: Miguel Ricardo di Alava (1771-1843), Spanish General; he acted as the representative of Spain at Paris, at the Court of the Bourbons; he was a great friend of the Duke of Wellington, and was with him at his headquarters during the Peninsular War.

Footnote 8: The Queen Regent, Christina.

Footnote 9: Then six years old; she died in 1904.

Footnote 10: This was in reference to the trial at Strasburg of the confederates of Prince Louis Bonaparte (afterwards Napoleon III.) in his abortive attempt to establish a military despotism on 30th October. The Prince was permitted to go to the United States, being conveyed in a French frigate; the other conspirators were acquitted.

Footnote 11: Leopold, born in 1835, afterwards Duke of Brabant, the present King of the Belgians.

PARLIAMENTARY LANGUAGE

Claremont, 30th January 1837.

My dearest Uncle,— ... I am very sorry that the Portuguese news are still so very unfavourable; I trust that, in time, things will come right. The Portuguese are, as you say, a most inconceivable set of selfish politicians.

Our friend, Mr Hume,12 made a most violent speech at a dinner given to him and old George

Byng13 at Drury Lane last week.14 He called Sir R. Peel and some other Tories "the cloven foot," which I think rather strong. I think that great violence and striving such a pity, on both sides, don't you, dear Uncle? They irritate one another so uselessly by calling one another fools, blockheads, liars, and so forth for no purpose. I think violence so bad in everything. They should imitate you, and be calm, for you have had, God knows! enough cause for irritation from your worthy Dutch neighbours and others. You will, I fear, laugh at my politics, but I like telling you my feelings, for you alone can put me right on such subjects.

Footnote 12: Joseph Hume, leader of the Radical party, was now M.P. for Middlesex.

Footnote 13: George Byng, for many years Member for Middlesex, was great-grandson of William Wentworth, Earl of Strafford, of the 1711 creation. His younger brother, Sir John Byng, the well-known General of the Peninsula and Waterloo, was created Earl of Strafford in 1817.

Footnote 14: This was a dinner given by the Middlesex reformers to their representatives. Grote also spoke and said that the Tories well knew that their dominion rested upon everything that was antiquated and corrupt and anti-popular in the nation—upon oligarchical predominance in the State, and sectarian pride and privileges in the Church.

POLITICAL PASSION

3rd February 1837.

My dear Child,— ... I am sorry to see so much violence in England at this moment; I consider it as the most lamentable circumstance, as it renders matters so very difficult to settle. Besides, the poor Crown is more or less the loser in all this, as it generally ends with the abolition of something or other which might have proved useful for the carrying on of Government. A rule which you may thus early impress on your mind is, that people are far from acting generally according to the dictates of their interests, but oftener in consequence of their passions, though it may even prove injurious to their interests. If the Tory part of Parliament could have brought themselves to act without passion, much in the reform of Parliament might have been settled much more in conformity with their best interests. I was authorised, in 1831, to speak in this sense to the Duke of Wellington by Lord Grey;15 the effect would have been highly beneficial to both parties, but passion made it impossible to succeed. This is a dangerous part of the business, and we must see during the present session of Parliament if parties are grown wiser. I fear they are not. The business of the highest in a State is certainly, in my opinion, to act with great impartiality and a spirit of justice for the good of all, and not of this or that party.16

Footnote 15: This refers to the rejection of the Reform Bill by the House of Lords in 1831; as a consequence, mobs broke the windows of Apsley House, and fired Nottingham Castle.

Footnote 16: On 14th April 1837, Sir Robert Peel wrote to J. W. Croker:— ... "We are, in short, in this state of things. All the convictions and inclinations of the Government are with their Conservative opponents. Half their actions and all their speeches are with the Radicals." (Croker Papers, ii. 306.)

Claremont, 6th February 1837.

My beloved Uncle,— ... I do not know quite for certain when we leave this place, but I should think to-day week. You must be pleased, dear Uncle, I think, for we shall have been six months in the country next Thursday, as we left town on the 10th of August last, and I am sure you will stand by me for my having my season fully, as you may understand that my Operatic and Terpsichorean feelings are pretty strong, now that the season is returning, and I have been a very good child, not even wishing to come to town till now. We shall certainly come here for the Easter week.

Dr Clark17 arrived here quite happy last night, bringing the news that Van de Weyer had had the best news from Lisbon he had received since his return, that all had gone off quietly, that Ferdinand was daily gaining popularity, and that both he and the Queen had been very well received at the theatre. The man who threw a stone at Ferdinand was a Frenchman, whom, it seems, Ferdinand had relieved with money over and over again. A fine specimen of gratitude!

I hope and trust with you that there will be less violence in Parliament this year, but much is to be feared.

You will miss my good cousins Ernest and Albert very much, I am sure; I hope you will instil into them to take enough exercise and not to study too much.

There were two questions in my last letter but one, which you have not answered, dear Uncle. They are: 1st, What you think of the Queen Christina of Spain, what opinion you have of her, as one cannot believe reports? 2nd, If you know what sort of people are about poor little Queen Isabel, and if she is being well or ill brought up?...

Footnote 17: Afterwards Sir James Clark, and Physician-in-Ordinary to the Queen.

A DINNER PARTY

14th March 1837.

... We had a dinner on Saturday which amused me, as I am very fond of pleasant society, and we have been for these last three weeks immured within our old palace, and I longed sadly for some gaiety. After being so very long in the country I was preparing to go out in right earnest, whereas I have only been twice to the play since our return, which is marvellous! However, we are to have another dinner to-morrow, and are going to the play and Opera. After Easter I trust I shall make ample amends for all this solitariness. I hope to begin singing with Lablache shortly after Easter. But to return to last Saturday's dinner. We had the Archbishop of Dublin,18 a clever but singular man, and his lady; Lord Palmerston, with whom I had much pleasant and amusing conversation after dinner—you know how agreeable he is; then Lady Cadogan,19 who enquired much after you and Aunt Louise; Lord and Lady Rosebery,20 Mr and Mrs E. Stanley,21 Lord Morpeth,22 Lord Templetown,23 Sir John Cam Hobhouse,24 Dr Lushington,25 and Mr Woulfe,26 the Solicitor-General for Ireland, a Roman Catholic and a very clever man. Lady Cadogan, who is not long come back from Paris, says that the Duke of Orleans has been going out very little and is remarkably well. I saw a report in the papers that he and the Duc de Nemours were coming over here, which I fear is not true; I wish it was....

THE THRONE OF GREECE

There is one thing in your former letter which I must answer, or, rather, more advert to. You said to me, that if it was not for me, you would regret Greece very much. Now, I assure you, dearest Uncle, you ought not to regret it, though there is not a doubt that Greece would be much happier were you there. But I have heard from various people who have been staying in Greece that they very soon got to like the Turks much better than the Greeks, who are very untrue, and are quite banditti-like; then, again, the country, though undoubtedly fine in parts, is a rocky and barren country, and also you are constantly exposed to the effects of the Plague, that most dreadful of all evils; and then, lastly, how very, very far you would be, how cut off from all those who are dear to you, and how exposed to dangers of all kinds!

I much grieve that they are quarrelling so much in the French Chambers.27 I must now conclude.

Footnote 18: Richard Whateley, formerly Principal of St Alban Hall, and Drummond Professor of Political Economy at Oxford.

Footnote 19: Louisa Honoria, wife of the third Earl, and sister of Joseph, first Lord Wallscourt.

Footnote 20: Archibald, fourth Earl of Rosebery, and Anne Margaret, his second wife, daughter of the first Viscount Anson.

Footnote 21: Edward Stanley, afterwards fourteenth Earl of Derby, thrice Prime Minister.

Footnote 22: Chief Secretary for Ireland.

Footnote 23: John Henry, first Viscount, formerly M.P. for Bury St Edmunds.

Footnote 24: Sir John Cam Hobhouse, a Radical, and a friend of Byron, at whose wedding he acted as best man; he was imprisoned in 1819 for breach of privilege. He was elected M.P. for Westminster in 1820 as Burdett's colleague, and afterwards for Nottingham and Harwich. Commissioner of Woods and Forests (the old Houses of Parliament being burned down during his term of office), and later President of Board of Control. Created Lord Broughton, 1851.

Footnote 25: Stephen Lushington, advocate in the old Ecclesiastical Court, M.P. for Ilchester and the Tower Hamlets, and a Judge in the Ecclesiastical and Admiralty Courts from 1828 to 1867.

Footnote 26: Stephen Woulfe, M.P. for Carlisle, Solicitor-General, and subsequently Attorney-General, for Ireland, becoming Chief Baron in 1838.

Footnote 27: On 10th March a heated debate took place in the French Chamber on the question of the Queen of the Belgians' dowry, a Deputy calling for the production of King Louis Philippe's rent-roll, and a complete statement of his income.

Laeken, 31st March 1837.

My beloved Child,—Your dear letter of the 28th gave me the greatest pleasure. I was sure from your constant affection for us that you would feel much interested in the event of the 24th. It was a moment of some anxiety, but all passed over very well. Your Aunt is going on very well, and the little cousin28 also. He is smaller than his brother was, but promises to be like him; the features are much the same, the shape of the forehead and mouth. The elder Prince was much interested about his frère, and anxious to see him; at first, however, he declared after a long contemplation, "pas beau frère!" Now he thinks better of him, but makes a very odd little face when he sees him. The name of the little one will be Philippe Eugène Ferdinand Marie Clément Baudouin (Baldwin)—a name of the old Counts of Flanders—Léopold Georges. My Aunt, who is his godmother, wished he should be called Philippe in honour of his grandfather, and as

Philippe le Bon was one of the most powerful Princes of this country, I gave him the name with pleasure. Eugène is her own name, Ferdinand that of Chartres, Marie of the Queen and also of Princess Marie, Clément of Princess Clémentine; Léopold your Aunt wished, and George in honour of St George of England and of George IV. Probably I shall hereafter give to Léopold the title of Duke of Brabant, and to Philippe that of Count of Flanders, both fine old titles.

Footnote 28: Philippe, second son of King Leopold, afterwards Count of Flanders. He died in 1905.

PRESS COMMENTS

Laeken, 7th April 1837.

My dearest Child,—... You have been the subject of all sorts of newspaper paragraphs; your good and sensible way of looking on these very creditable productions will be of use to you. If the press says useful things, and makes observations which merit attention, there is no doubt that sometimes, though God knows very rarely, something useful may be gleaned from them. But when you see its present state, when the one side says black and the other white, when the opposite political characters are treated by their respective antagonists as rogues, fools, blockheads, wretches, and all the other names in which the English political dictionary is so very rich, one stands like the ass, between two bundles of hay, considerably embarrassed which ought to be chosen....

THE PRINCESS'S ESTABLISHMENT

Laeken, 11th April 1837.

... As I believe the visit at Windsor is fixed for the 15th, I hope this letter will arrive in time. Perhaps the King will speak to you about the necessity of forming you an establishment.29... Your position, having a Mother with whom you very naturally remain, would render a complete independent establishment perhaps matter of real inconvenience; still something like that which Charlotte had will become desirable. My idea, if it meets with your approbation, would be this: The Duchess of Northumberland would remain your first Lady, Baroness Lehzen would fill a position similar to that of Mrs Campbell, who had been Charlotte's governess in her younger days, and the Dean30 would step into the position which good Dr Short31 held. An Equerry, I do not think—as you will not go out without your Mother—you would require. On the other hand, it may become matter of examination if you will perhaps like to have some young ladies attendants in the style of Lady Catherine Jenkinson;32 should this be your wish, it would become necessary to make very good choices, else perhaps you would derive more trouble than comfort from the arrangement; cela va sans dire, that the choice could only be made by yourself, and that nobody should be given you against your wishes. Should the King speak to you on the subject, I would at once express this my wish if you should approve some such arrangement, and beg him to let you choose. Resist mildly but positively any nomination of a Gentleman other than the Dean; it is highly probable that any other would be put about you as a spy, and turn out at all events a great bore, which is better avoided....

I received a messenger from Coburg. I enclose the letters and also a packet with fans. Ever, my beloved child, your faithfully attached Uncle and Friend,

Leopold R.

Footnote 29: The Princess was to attain her legal majority on 24th May.

Footnote 30: George Davys, the Princess Victoria's instructor, Dean of Chester, and afterwards Bishop of Peterborough.

Footnote 31: Thomas Vowler Short, Rector of St George's, Bloomsbury, appointed in 1841 Bishop of Sodor and Man.

Footnote 32: Lady Catherine Jenkinson, daughter of the Earl of Liverpool, soon after the Queen's accession married Colonel Francis Vernon Harcourt.

12th April 1837.

... What you say about the newspapers is very true and very flattering. They are indeed a curious compound of truth and untruth. I am so used to newspaper nonsense and attacks that I do not mind it in the least....

How happy I am that that beloved Aunt is going on so well and does not suffer from the cold, as also the jeune Philippe. Leopold must be great fun with his Aunt Marie;33 does he still say "pas beau frère!" or is he more reconciled to his brother? It is very noble in the Duc de Nemours to have thus given up his apanage;34 I am sorry there were such difficulties about it. There is no Ministry formed yet, I see by the papers.

Footnote 33: Princess Marie of Orleans, born 1813, daughter of King Louis Philippe, and thus sister to the Queen of the Belgians.

Footnote 34: This grant was surrendered in order that due provision might be made by the Legislature for the elder brother, the Duke of Orleans, on the occasion of his marriage with the Princess Hélène of Mecklenburg-Schwerin.

THE IRISH MUNICIPAL BILL

28th April 1837.

My most beloved Uncle,—.... Sir Henry Hardinge's35 motion was quite lost, I am happy to say, and don't you think, dearest Uncle, that it has almost done good, as it proves that the Tories have lost all chance of getting in? It was a trial of strength, and the Ministry have triumphed. I have been reading in the papers, what I suppose you already know, that it is believed that the Lords will pass the Irish Corporation Bill;36 and also that Ministers mean to drop for the present the question about Church Rates,37 as the Radicals, being angry with Ministers relative to the Canada business, would not support them well.

Footnote 35: On a motion for going into supply, Sir H. Hardinge proposed an amendment censuring the Government for the authorisation of the raising of a force of Volunteers to assist the Spanish Government, and for the method in which that force had been organised. The amendment was lost by a majority of 36, on 19th April.

Footnote 36: The Irish Municipal Bill, to convert Corporations of Municipalities into Electoral Councils, was introduced in the House of Commons on the 15th of February. The Bill was opposed by the Conservatives, but passed the House of Commons. In the Lords an amendment of Lyndhurst's struck out the constructive clauses, and the Act became, on the 18th of May, an Act for the Abolition of Municipalities in Ireland. Lord John Russell brought forward a motion to reconstruct the Bill. But the Peers declined to pass it, and it was postponed.

Footnote 37: As Ministers only obtained a majority of 5 in a house of 569, the measure was dropped.

Laeken, 28th April 1837.

... I hope you occupy yourself with the several great questions which agitate parties. I think a good mode will be to talk concerning them sometimes with the Dean. He is a good moderate man, and still well able to give you sufficient information. From conversation with clever people, such as dine sometimes with you, much may be very usefully gathered, and you will do well to attend to this. I am no enemy to this way of instruction, and have seen people who were sharp enough to profit wonderfully by it. You hear in this way the opinions of a variety of persons, and it rests with your own good sense to classify and appreciate them....

MINISTERIAL ANXIETY

2nd May 1837.

... You may depend upon it that I shall profit by your excellent advice respecting Politics. Pray, dear Uncle, have you read Lord Palmerston's speech concerning the Spanish affairs,38 which he delivered the night of the division on Sir Henry Hardinge's motion? It is much admired. The Irish Tithes question came on last night in the House of Commons,39 and I am very anxious for the morning papers, to see what has been done. Lord Melbourne looks remarkably well, Lord Palmerston not very well, and as for poor little Lord John Russell, he is only a shadow of himself. It must be dreadfully fagging work for them; they sit so very late too, for when the Spanish question came on, the division only took place at four o'clock in the morning, and I saw them at the Drawing-Room the same day afterwards....

Footnote 38: Lord Palmerston indignantly asked whether England should continue to fulfil her nengagement with the Queen of Spain, or disgracefully abandon an ally whom she had pledged herself to succour.

Footnote 39: The Irish Tithe Bill, a measure to facilitate the collection of tithes, was abandoned because the Tories would not consent to any secular appropriation of Church revenues, and the Whigs would not consent to the withdrawal of their amendments. A remarkable feature in the Bill was a proposal that a portion of every clergyman's income should be applied to education, as was already prescribed by a former Act.

9th May 1837.

My dearest Uncle,—It was very kind of you to write to me from your new château; I hardly ventured to hope for my usual letter, and yet I should have been much disappointed had I not received it. I am sorry that the house is so bad, but hope you will have found a good position for a new one....

Pray, dearest Uncle, may I ask such an indiscreet question as, if Major Stroekens is a clever man; he was so nervous and embarrassed when he came here, that I could not make him out. He brought me a very nice letter from Donna Maria.

I am anxiously waiting to hear the issue of the battle between the Carlists and Christinos, which is, they say, to decide a great deal.40

Now farewell, dearest Uncle. I beg my affectionate love to my dear Aunt, and my most respectful hommages to the Members of the Family with you. Believe me, always, your affectionate Niece,

Victoria.

Old Pozzo41 dined here last Wednesday, and he gave me a long, I must say clever, dissertation about the state of France, during dinner-time.

Footnote 40: After an obstinate investment by the Carlists, Espartero had relieved Bilbao on Christmas Day, 1836. The Christino commanders then began to concert a combined movement on the Carlist lines, which stretched from Irun to Villafranca.

Footnote 41: Count Pozzo di Borgo (1764-1842), Russian Ambassador. By birth a Corsican and a devoted patriot, he was a life-long opponent of Napoleon and his designs. He entered the Russian diplomatic service in 1803, and after Waterloo became Russian Ambassador in Paris. He was Ambassador in London for two years, when his health gave way.

THE PRINCESS'S ESTABLISHMENT

Laeken, 25th May 1837.

My dearest Child,—You have had some battles and difficulties of which I am completely in the dark. The thing I am most curious to learn is what the King proposed to you concerning your establishment.... I shall reserve my opinion till I am better informed, but by what I heard I did not approve of it, because I thought it ill-timed. Stockmar will be able to do much. Two things seem necessary; not to be fettered by any establishment other than what will be comfortable to you, and then to avoid any breach with your mother. I have fully instructed Stockmar, and I must say he left me in such good disposition that I think he will be able to be of great use to you. The great thing is to act without precipitation and with caution. The King seems better again. I am very curious to know what he proposed; you will have it in your power to modify his proposition, as it is difficult your approbation should be dispensed with; it would be a great fault in your situation to submit to this.... They seemed to think the King dying, which does not appear to be the case. Be steady, my good child, and not put out by anything; as long as I live you will not want a faithful friend and supporter....

Here your somewhat curious little soul has at least the outlines of things....

26th.—I received yesterday the whole of the papers concerning the King's propositions.42 I approve your letter to the King, as it is amiable and generous, and this in your position will always tell favourably. I think that if he is well advised he will chiefly consult your wishes. This is the footing on which you must place matters. It is not worth while to be told that one is in some sort of age when the consequence is that you are not consulted in what concerns you most personally. Avoid in future to say much about your great youth and inexperience. Who made the letter? Was it yourself, or came it from your Mother? You have now the Baron at your elbow, and even your Mother was most anxious for his arrival. Speak sometimes with him; it is necessary to accustom you to the thing.

About the King's health.43 I am doubtful what to think. We have foreseen the case and treated it formerly. The great thing would be to make no change, to keep Ministers and everything as it is, and to gain time; in this way no one is hurt and no amour-propre blessé. For this reason I lean to your keeping, to begin with, Sir Herbert Taylor44 for your official secretary, though I am not quite decided on the subject. He knows the manner in which the daily business is carried on; this is important. I believe him, and have found him to be an honest man, that would do for State matters; it would not be required that he should be your confidential adviser. Now I conclude, and send you this letter through Stockmar. My best regards to Lehzen. Ever your faithful Uncle and Friend,

Leopold R.

Footnote 42: The King had offered the Princess an establishment of £10,000 a year, independent of her mother. This was accepted, to the great vexation of the Duchess of Kent, but the arrangement was not carried into effect.

Footnote 43: King William's health was at this time causing much anxiety.

Footnote 44: Private Secretary to King William IV.

BIRTHDAY REJOICINGS

26th May 1837.

... The demonstrations of affection and kindness from all sides towards me on my birthday, were most gratifying. The parks and streets were crowded all day as though something very extraordinary had happened. Yesterday I received twenty-two Addresses from various places, all very pretty and loyal; one in particular was very well written which was presented by Mr. Attwood45 from the Political Union at Birmingham.

I am delighted to hear Stockmar is at length arrived; he reached London on Wednesday, and we shall see him to-day.

How distressed I am that poor dear Ernest46 has been so ill! Thank God! that he is now better.

The Spanish affairs have turned out better than you had expected; the triumphant capture of Irun47 was a great thing for the Christinos.

The King is much better.

Footnote 45: Thomas Attwood founded in 1829 the Birmingham Political Union, which helped to pass the Reform Act. Previously he had been known for his opposition to the Orders in Council, and the resumption of cash payments. Birmingham elected him without opposition in 1832, and he sat till 1840.

Footnote 46: Prince Ernest of Saxe-Coburg.

Footnote 47: The frontier town of Spain, near St Sebastian, captured, 16th May, by the Christinos, supported by British troops.

ADVICE AND ENCOURAGEMENT

Tuileries, 7th June 1837.

... The entrée48 last Sunday was something remarkably splendid; we saw it from the Tuileries, as we had nothing to do with the business itself, and your Aunt's rank would have clashed with that of the Duchess of Orleans. The effect of all this on the people of this great town has been very great, and evidently much ground has been solidly regained. The King, getting out of that sort of confinement in which it was necessary to keep, has gained much in personal comfort, and also in a political point of view; because to have a King who cannot show himself without being shot at, is a state of society which lowers his authority....

For the present the best plan is to continue to act as you have done hitherto; to avoid quarrels, but also to stick firmly to your resolution when once taken. The violence which is sometimes shown is so well known to you, you know also so well that you have nothing to fear from these people, that you must keep up your usual cool spirit, whatever may be tried in the House to teaze you out of it. I mean to wait some more detailed accounts of what is going on in England before I give my opinion on what ought to be done in the case that the King's disease should take a more fatal turn.

As I told you before, however, when we treated this subject verbally and in writing, I believe it to be your interest to act very mildly, to begin by taking everything as the King leaves it. By this system you avoid disappointing those whose hopes may remain unchanged, as your own choices, as it were, are not yet made. Parties, which at present are so nearly balanced, remain in statu quo, and you gain time.

I must conclude now this letter. My winding up is, keep your mind cool and easy; be not alarmed at the prospect of becoming perhaps sooner than you expected Queen; aid will not be wanting, and the great thing is that you should have some honest people about you who have your welfare really at heart. Stockmar will be in this respect all we can wish, and we must hope that useful occupation will prevent his health from suffering. Now once more God bless you. Ever, my dear child, your faithful Uncle and Friend,

Leopold R.

Footnote 48: The entry into Paris of the Duke and Duchess of Orleans, who had been married at Fontainebleau on May 30th.

THE ACCESSION IMMINENT

Laeken, 15th June 1837.

My beloved Child,—I hope that to-day will not pass over without bringing me a letter from you. In the meantime I will begin this epistle, which will go by a messenger of my own to-morrow. In every letter I shall write to you I mean to repeat to you, as a fundamental rule, to be courageous, firm and honest, as you have been till now. You may count upon my faithful good offices in all difficulties, and you have at your command Stockmar, whose judgment, heart, and character offer all the guarantees we can wish for. I wish nothing but to see you happy and prosperous, and by Sunday I shall probably write you a long letter, which will enter into details about most things.

My object is that you should be no one's tool, and though young, and naturally not yet experienced, your good natural sense and the truth of your character will, with faithful and proper advice, get you very well through the difficulties of your future position, should it be the will of Providence to take the King from this earthly life. Of his real position I am still not quite able to judge, there being so much contradictory in the reports. Be this as it may, the great thing for you is, not to be hurried into important measures, and to gain time. A new reign is always a time of hope; everybody is disposed to see something for his own wishes and prospects. The policy of a new Sovereign must therefore be to act in such a manner as to hurt as little as possible the amour-propre of people, to let circumstances and the force of things bring about the disappointments which no human power could prevent coming sooner or later: that they should come as late as possible is in your interest. Should anything happen to the King before I can enter more fully into the necessary details, limit yourself to taking kindly and in a friendly manner the present Administration into your service. They are naturally friendly to your interests, as you are in fact the only possible Sovereign of the whole family, with the exception of the Duke of Sussex, they can serve with sincerity and attachment. This is of great importance to you, as it is by no means the same thing to have people who aid and assist you with feelings of real attachment, or merely from cold and calculating motives of political expediency and self-interest. This being done, no other step should be taken without consulting seriously. The very time which is necessary to attain this end is favourable to you, as it is your greatest interest for the present moment to act most cautiously and to gain as much time as possible. In high positions it is excessively difficult to retrace a false move to get out of a mistake; and there exists very rarely, except in time of war and civil feuds, a necessity for an immediate decision. Your part must be, to resume once more what I said before, to remain as long as possible agreeable to all parties, and after the formation of the Ministry, to be most careful how you take any measure of importance....

H.M. King William IV.

From a miniature at Windsor Castle

To face p. 72, Vol. I

THE KING'S ILLNESS

16th June 1837.

My beloved Uncle,—... I cannot say how happy I am that the entrée publique into Paris succeeded so well, and that the dear King was so well received; I trust he will now at last be rewarded for all the troubles and anxiety he has had ever since 1830. Lord Palmerston said that the French say that l'assassinat est hors de mode. I hope and trust in Heaven that this may be the case, and for ever!

You know, of course, dear Uncle, how very ill the King is; it may all be over at any moment, and yet may last a few days. Consequently, we have not been out anywhere in public since Tuesday, 6th, and since Wednesday all my lessons are stopped, as the news may arrive very suddenly....

Laeken, 17th June 1837.

My beloved Child,—... I shall to-day enter on the subject of what is to be done when the King ceases to live. The moment you get official communication of it, you will entrust Lord Melbourne with the office of retaining the present Administration as your Ministers. You will do this in that honest and kind way which is quite your own, and say some kind things on the subject. The fact is that the present Ministers are those who will serve you personally with the greatest sincerity and, I trust, attachment. For them, as well as for the Liberals at large, you are the only Sovereign that offers them des chances d'existence et de durée. With the exception of the Duke of Sussex, there is no one in the family that offers them anything like what they can reasonably hope from you, and your immediate successor, with the mustaches,49 is enough to frighten them into the most violent attachment for you.

... The irksome position in which you have lived will have the merit to have given you the habit of discretion and prudence, as in your position you never can have too much of either. Great measures of State I hope you will be able to avoid at first. I have already—if you would read it over, and perhaps let Stockmar see it—written to you some months ago on the subject of the necessity of maintaining the influence of conservative principles, and of protecting the Church. You will do well to keep both objects in view. You will do wisely by showing yourself attached to the English Protestant Church as it exists in the State; you are particularly where you are, because you are a Protestant. I know you are averse to persecution, and you are right; miss, however, no opportunity to show your sincere feeling for the existing Church; it is right and meet that you should do so. I must repeat that you will do well as long as it will be possible to hurt no one's hopes or prospects. That this will not always, or very long, be possible is the consequence of the state of parties; still, one may be frank and honest, and still kind to all. Concerning foreign policy I shall write on some future occasion. In the meantime I trust you will protect the two Queens in the Peninsula, who are miserably ill off. I am sure, with your good sense you will not find it difficult to judge questions yourself. I cannot too much recommend this, as it will then become a habit, and even an amusement to you. Cultivate always a genuine feeling of right and wrong, and be very true and honourable in your dealings; this gives great strength. I have taken into consideration the advantage or disadvantage of my coming over to you immediately. The result of my examen is that I think it better to visit you later. If, however, you wanted me at any time, I should come in a moment. People might fancy I came to enslave you, while I glory in the contrary; and, thirdly, that they might be jealous, or affect it at least, of my coming, as if I thought of ruling the realm for purposes of my own....

I am now at the end, I think, of what I had to say. May Heaven bless you and keep up your spirits. Ever, my beloved child, your faithful Uncle and Friend,

Leopold R.

Pardon the hurry in which this letter was written.

Footnote 49: The Duke of Cumberland.

THE KING'S CONDITION HOPELESS

19th June 1837.

My dearly beloved Uncle,—Your kind and dear letter, containing most wholesome, prudent, sound and excellent advice, was given me by our good and invaluable honest friend, Stockmar, and I beg you to accept my best thanks for it. Before I say anything else, let me tell you how happy and thankful I am to have Stockmar here; he has been, and is, of the greatest possible use, and be assured, dearest Uncle, that he possesses my most entire confidence!

The King's state, I may fairly say, is hopeless; he may perhaps linger a few days, but he cannot recover ultimately. Yesterday the physicians declared he could not live till the morning, but to-day he is a little better; the great fear is his excessive weakness and no pulse at all. Poor old man!

I feel sorry for him; he was always personally kind to me, and I should be ungrateful and devoid of feeling if I did not remember this.

I look forward to the event which it seems is likely to occur soon, with calmness and quietness; I am not alarmed at it, and yet I do not suppose myself quite equal to all; I trust, however, that with good-will, honesty, and courage I shall not, at all events, fail. Your advice is most excellent, and you may depend upon it I shall make use of it, and follow it, as also what Stockmar says. I never showed myself, openly, to belong to any party, and I do not belong to any party. The Administration will undoubtedly be well received by me, the more so as I have real confidence in them, and in particular in Lord Melbourne, who is a straightforward, honest, clever and good man.

I need not add much more, dearest Uncle, but that I trust that the all-powerful Being who has so long watched over my destinies will guide and support me, in whatever situation and station it may please Him to place me!...

THE ACCESSION

South Street, 20th June 1837.

Viscount Melbourne50 presents his humble duty to your Majesty, and being aware that your Majesty has already received the melancholy intelligence of the death of his late Majesty, will do himself the honour of waiting upon your Majesty a little before nine this morning. Viscount Melbourne has requested the Marquis of Lansdowne51 to name eleven as the hour for the meeting of the Council at Kensington Palace.

Footnote 50: Lord Melbourne, so far as can be augured from his handwriting, which is extremely difficult to decipher, appears always to have written his own name Melburne. But it is not the correct spelling, and no one else seems to have employed it.

Footnote 51: Lord President of the Council; formerly for a brief period (1806-7) Chancellor of the Exchequer.

20th June 1837 (half-past eight a.m.).

Dearest, most beloved Uncle,—Two words only, to tell you that my poor Uncle, the King, expired this morning at twelve minutes past two. The melancholy news were brought to me by Lord Conyngham52 and the Archbishop of Canterbury53 at six. I expect Lord Melbourne almost immediately, and hold a Council at eleven. Ever, my beloved Uncle, your devoted and attached Niece,

Victoria R.

Footnote 52: Francis Nathaniel, second Marquis of Conyngham, had been M.P. for Westbury and Donegal, and was now Lord Chamberlain.

Footnote 53: William Howley (1766-1848), Bishop of London 1813-1828, Primate 1828-1848.

Windsor Castle, 20th June 1837.

My dearest Niece ... I feel most grateful for your kind letter full of sympathy with my irreparable loss, and thank you with all my heart for your feeling expressions on this melancholy occasion. I am, as you may suppose, deeply affected by all the sad scenes I have gone through lately; but I have the great comfort to dwell upon the recollection of the perfect resignation, piety, and patience with which the dear King bore his trials and sufferings, and the truly Christian-like manner of his death.

Excuse my writing more at present, my heart is overwhelmed and my head aches very much. Accept the assurance of my most affectionate devotion, and allow me to consider myself always as your Majesty's most affectionate Friend, Aunt, and Subject,

Adelaide.

THE QUEEN'S JOURNAL

I was awoke at 6 o'clock by Mamma, who told me that the Archbishop of Canterbury and Lord Conyngham were here, and wished to see me. I got out of bed and went into my sitting-room (only in my dressing-gown) and alone, and saw them. Lord Conyngham (the Lord Chamberlain) then acquainted me that my poor Uncle, the King, was no more, and had expired at 12 minutes past 2 this morning, and consequently that I am Queen. Lord Conyngham knelt down and kissed my hand, at the same time delivering to me the official announcement of the poor King's demise. The Archbishop then told me that the Queen was desirous that he should come and tell me the details of the last moments of my poor good Uncle; he said that he had directed his mind to religion, and had died in a perfectly happy, quiet state of mind, and was quite prepared for his death. He added that the King's sufferings at the last were not very great but that there was a good deal of uneasiness. Lord Conyngham, whom I charged to express my feelings of condolence and sorrow to the poor Queen, returned directly to Windsor. I then went to my room and dressed.

Since it has pleased Providence to place me in this station, I shall do my utmost to fulfil my duty towards my country; I am very young and perhaps in many, though not in all things, inexperienced, but I am sure that very few have more real goodwill and more real desire to do what is fit and right than I have.

THE QUEEN'S FIRST COUNCIL

Breakfasted, during which time good, faithful Stockmar came and talked to me. Wrote a letter to dear Uncle Leopold and a few words to dear good Feodore. Received a letter from Lord Melbourne in which he said he would wait upon me at a little before 9. At 9 came Lord Melbourne, whom I saw in my room, and of course quite alone, as I shall always do all my Ministers. He kissed my hand, and I then acquainted him that it had long been my intention to retain him and the rest of the present Ministry at the head of affairs, and that it could not be in better hands than his. He again then kissed my hand. He then read to me the Declaration which I was to read to the Council, which he wrote himself, and which is a very fine one. I then talked with him some little time longer, after which he left me. He was in full dress. I like him very much, and feel confidence in him. He is a very straightforward, honest, clever and good man. I then wrote a letter to the Queen. At about 11 Lord Melbourne came again to me, and spoke to me upon various subjects. At about half-past 11 I went downstairs and held a Council in the red saloon.

I went in of course quite alone and remained seated the whole time. My two Uncles, the Dukes of Cumberland and Sussex, and Lord Melbourne conducted me. The Declaration, the various forms, the swearing in of the Privy Councillors, of which there were a great number present, and the reception of some of the Lords of the Council, previous to the Council, in an adjacent room (likewise alone) I subjoin here. I was not at all nervous and had the satisfaction of hearing that people were satisfied with what I had done and how I had done it. Received after this, audiences of Lord Melbourne, Lord John Russell, Lord Albemarle (Master of the Horse), and the Archbishop of Canterbury, all in my room and alone. Saw Stockmar. Saw Clark, whom I named my physician. Saw Mary. Wrote to Uncle Ernest. Saw Ernest Hohenlohe, who brought me a kind and very feeling letter from the poor Queen. I feel very much for her, and really feel that the poor good King was always so kind personally to me, that I should be ungrateful were I not to recollect it and feel grieved at his death. The poor Queen is wonderfully composed now, I hear.

Wrote my journal. Took my dinner upstairs alone. Went downstairs. Saw Stockmar. At about twenty minutes to 9 came Lord Melbourne and remained till near 10. I had a very important and a very comfortable conversation with him. Each time I see him I feel more confidence in him; I find him very kind in his manner too. Saw Stockmar. Went down and said good-night to Mamma, etc. My dear Lehzen will always remain with me as my friend, but will take no situation about me, and I think she is right.

THE HOUSE OF COMMONS

Wilton Crescent, 22nd June 1837.

Lord John Russell54 presents his humble duty to your Majesty, and has the honour to report that he presented to the House of Commons this day your Majesty's gracious Message.

He then moved an Address of Condolence and Congratulation, which was seconded by Sir Robert Peel. Sir Robert Peel very properly took occasion to speak in terms of high admiration of the deportment of your Majesty before the Privy Council on Tuesday. The Address was agreed to without a dissentient voice, and your Majesty may rest assured that the House of Commons is animated by a feeling of loyalty to the Throne, and of devotion to your Majesty.

Footnote 54: Writing as Leader of the House of Commons.

(Undated—22nd or 23rd June 1837.)

My dearest Niece,—I am most grateful for your amiable letter and truly kind offer to come and see me next week. Any day convenient to your Majesty will be agreeable to me, the sooner the better, for I am equally anxious to see you again, and to express to you in person all that I feel for you at this trying moment. If Monday will suit you I shall be ready to receive you and your dear Mother on that day. My prayers are with you and my blessing follows you in all you have to go through. My health is as well as it can be after the great exertions I have suffered, and I try to keep up under my heavy trial and deep affliction.

My best wishes attend you, my dearest Niece, and I am for ever your Majesty's most affectionate and faithful Friend, Aunt and Subject,

Adelaide.

CONGRATULATIONS

Paris, le 23 Juin 1837.

Madame ma Sœur,—J'ai appris avec une vive peine la perte que votre Majesté vient de faire dans la personne de son très cher et bien aimé Oncle le Roi Guillaume IV. d'auguste et vénérable mémoire. La vive et sincère amitié que je porte à votre Majesté, et à ceux qui lui sont chers, les liens de parenté qui rapprochent nos deux familles par l'alliance de ma fille chérie avec le Roi des Belges votre Oncle bien aimé, et enfin le souvenir qui m'est toujours bien cher de la tendre amitié qui m'attachait au feu Prince votre Père, depuis que nous nous étions vus en Amérique, il y a déjà trente-huit ans,55 me déterminent à ne pas attendre les formalités d'usage, pour offrir à votre Majesté mes félicitations sur son avènement au Trône de la Grande-Bretagne. Il m'est doux de penser que l'heureuse direction que la Princesse votre excellente et bien aimée Mère a si sagement donnée à votre jeune âge, vous met à portée de supporter dignement le grand fardeau qui vous est échu. Je fais les vœux les plus sincères pour que la Providence bénisse votre Règne, et qu'il soit une époque de bonheur et de prospérité pour les peuples que vous êtes appelée a gouverner. Puissiez-vous aussi jouir longtemps de tout le bonheur personnel que je vous souhaite du fond de mon cœur. Je serai toujours bien empressé de manifester à votre Majesté tous les sentiments d'attachement et d'affection que je lui porte. Qu'elle me permette d'y ajouter l'expression de la haute estime et de l'inviolable amitié avec lesquelles je ne cesserai d'être, Madame ma Sœur, de votre Majesté Le Bon Frère,

Louis Philippe R.

Footnote 55: In 1799 the Duke of Kent was Commander-in-Chief in British North America.
Laeken, 23rd June 1837.

My beloved Child,—Your new dignities will not change or increase my old affection for you; may Heaven assist you, and may I have the happiness of being able to be of use to you, and to contribute to those successes in your new career for which I am so anxious. Your letter of the 19th, written very shortly before the important event took place, gave me great satisfaction; it showed me a temper of mind well calculated for the occasion. To see the difficulties of the task without shrinking from them or feeling alarm, and to meet them with courage, is the way to succeed. I have often seen that the confidence of success has been the cause of the success itself, and you will do well to preserve that sentiment.

I have been most happy to learn that the swearing in of the Council passed so well. The Declaration in the newspapers I find simple and appropriate. The translation in the papers says, "J'ai été élevés en Angleterre." 1. I should advise to say as often as possible that you are born in England. George III. gloried in this, and as none of your cousins are born in England, it is your interest de faire reporter cela fortement. 2. You never can say too much in praise of your country and its inhabitants. Two nations in Europe are really almost ridiculous in their own exaggerated praises of themselves; these are the English and the French. Your being very national is highly important, and as you happen to be born in England and never to have left it a moment,56 it would be odd enough if people tried to make out the contrary. 3. The Established Church I also recommend strongly; you cannot, without pledging yourself to anything particular, say too much on the subject. 4. Before you decide on anything important I should be glad if you would consult me; this would also have the advantage of giving you time. In politics most measures will come in time within a certain number of days; to retrace or back out of a measure is on the contrary extremely difficult, and almost always injurious to the highest authority.

Footnote 56: The Duke and Duchess of Kent were settled at Amorbach, in Leiningen, till a short time before the birth of their child, when they came to Kensington.

THE MINISTERS

25th June 1837.

My beloved Uncle,—Though I have an immense deal of business to do, I shall write you a few lines to thank you for your kind and useful letter of the 23rd, which I have just received. Your advice is always of the greatest importance to me.

Respecting Claremont, Stockmar will be able to explain to you the total impossibility of my being out of London, as I must see my Ministers every day. I am very well, sleep well, and drive every evening in the country; it is so hot that walking is out of the question. Before I go further let me pause to tell you how fortunate I am to have at the head of the Government a man like Lord Melbourne. I have seen him now every day, with the exception of Friday, and the more I see him, the more confidence I have in him; he is not only a clever statesman and an honest man, but a good and a kind-hearted man, whose aim is to do his duty for his country and not for a party. He is of the greatest use to me both politically and privately.

I have seen almost all my other Ministers, and do regular, hard, but to me delightful, work with them. It is to me the greatest pleasure to do my duty for my country and my people, and no fatigue, however great, will be burdensome to me if it is for the welfare of the nation. Stockmar will tell you all these things. I have reason to be highly pleased with all my Ministers, and hope to God that the Elections57 may be favourable, as I well know that the present Ministry is the best and most moderate we can have.

Do not, my dearly beloved Uncle, fear for my health; I shall take good care of it. I beg your advice on the enclosed paper.

Ever your devoted and grateful Niece and affectionate Child,

Victoria R.

Footnote 57: At that time rendered necessary by the demise of the Crown.

DELIBERATION ADVISED

Laeken, 27th June 1837.

My dear Child,—... Now I must touch on another subject which is of vital importance for you and your comfort, viz. the habits of business which you will contract now. The best plan is to devote certain hours to it; if you do that, you will get through it with great ease. I think you would do well to tell your Ministers that for the present you would be ready to receive those who should wish to see you between the hours of eleven and half-past one. This will not plague you much, and will be sufficient in most cases for the usual business that is to be transacted.

I shall add to this a piece of advice. Whenever a question is of some importance, it should not be decided on the day when it is submitted to you. Whenever it is not an urgent one, I make it a rule not to let any question be forced upon my immediate decision; it is really not doing oneself justice de décider des questions sur le pouce. And even when in my mind I am disposed to accede, still I always keep the papers with me some little time before I return them. The best mode for you will be, that each Minister should bring his box with him, and when he submits to you the papers, explain them to you. Then you will keep the papers, either to think yourself upon it or to consult somebody, and either return them the next time you see the Minister to whom they belong, or send them to him. Good habits formed now may for ever afterwards be kept up, and will become so natural to you that you will not find them at all fatiguing.

Kensington Palace, 29th June 1837.

The Queen has received Lord Melbourne's communication, and thinks, as Prince Ernest of Hesse goes to the funeral, it would be proper the Prince of Leiningen should do just the same. The Queen requests that Lord Melbourne will be so good as to take care that the Prince of Leiningen is informed as to the proper dress he ought to wear on the occasion.

Lord Albemarle mentioned yesterday to the Queen, that all the ladies' saddle-horses, including the Queen-Dowager's own favourite horses, belonged to the Queen; but it strikes her that it would be well if the Queen was to give the Queen-Dowager the choice of two or three of her own horses, and that she might keep them. The Queen would wish Lord Melbourne to give her his opinion on this subject....

STOCKMAR

Laeken, 30th June 1837.

My dearest Child,—... I am glad to see that you are so much pleased with Lord Melbourne. I believe him to be as you think him. His character is a guarantee which is valuable, and remember that cleverness and talent, without an honest heart and character, will never do for your Minister. I shall name nobody, but what I said just now applies to some people you have recently seen.

I am so happy that you enter into the important affairs which Providence has entrusted to you with so much interest and spirit; if you continue you will be sure of success, and your own conscience will give you the most delightful and satisfactory feelings. To be National is the great thing, and I was sure you would agree with what I said repeatedly to you on this vital subject, and you will be certain in this way of the love of the nation you govern.

I recommend to your kind attention what Stockmar will think it his duty to tell you; he will never press anything, never plague you with anything, without the thorough conviction that it is indispensable for your welfare. I can guarantee his independence of mind and disinterestedness; nothing makes an impression upon him but what his experience makes him feel to be of importance for you. I am delighted with your plan. You will recollect that I pressed upon you repeatedly how necessary it was for you to continue your studies on a more extended scale, more appropriate to the station you were destined once to fill. No one is better qualified to direct those studies for the next few years than Stockmar, few people possess more general information, and very, very few have been like him educated, as it were, by fate itself since 1816. There is no branch of information in which he may not prove useful—

SUBJECTS FOR STUDY

(1) History, considered in a practical and philosophical way; (2) International Law and everything connected with it; (3) Political Economy, an important branch nowadays; (4) Classic studies; (5) belles lettres in general; (6) Physical Science in all its branches, etc., etc.—the list

would be very long if I were to enumerate it all. The sooner you do this the better; in all countries and at all times men like Stockmar have filled similar situations, even in the most bigoted and jealous countries, such as Spain, Austria, etc. You will have him in this case constantly near you without anybody having the right of finding fault with it, and to be useful to you he should be near you. Stockmar would have the immense advantage, for so young a Queen, to be a living dictionary of all matters scientific and politic that happened these thirty years, which to you is of the greatest importance, because you must study the political history of at least the last thirty-seven years more particularly. I had begun something of the sort with you, even so far back as George II.; you will do well to go through the reign of George III., and to follow the various circumstances which brought on finally the present state of affairs....

My letter grows too long, and you will not have time to read it; I will therefore come to an end, remaining ever, my beloved Victoria, your faithfully attached Uncle and Friend,

Leopold R.

SPANISH AFFAIRS

3rd July 1837.

My dearest Uncle,—I had the happiness of receiving your kind letter of 30th June yesterday, and hasten to thank you for it. Your dear and kind letters, full of kind and excellent advice, will always be of the greatest use to me, and will always be my delight. You may depend upon it that I shall profit by your advice, as I have already so often done.

I was sure you would be of my opinion relative to Lord Melbourne. Indeed, dearest Uncle, nothing is to be done without a good heart and an honest mind; I have, alas! seen so much of bad hearts and dishonest and double minds, that I know how to value and appreciate real worth.

All is going on well at present, and the elections promise to be favourable. God grant they may be so! I had a very long and highly interesting conversation with Palmerston on Saturday, about Turkey, Russia, etc., etc. I trust something may be done for my sister Queens. They have got a Constitution in Spain at length, and the Cortes have done very well. We hope also to conclude a treaty of commerce with the Spaniards shortly, which would be an immense thing.

If you could get my kind and dear friend Louis Philippe, whom I do so respect, and for whom I have a great affection, to do something for poor Spain, it would be of great use.

I am quite penetrated by the King's kindness in sending good old General Baudrand58 and the Duc d'Elchingen59 over to compliment me; Baudrand did it very well, and with much good feeling. In Portugal, affairs look very black, I grieve to say. They have no money, and the Chartists want to bring about another counter-revolution, which would be fatal to the poor Queen's interests, I fear.

That you approve my plan about Stockmar I am delighted to hear.

I hope to go into Buckingham Palace very shortly after the funeral.

Now, dearest Uncle, I must invite you en forme. I should be most delighted if you, dearest Aunt Louise, and Leopold (j'insiste) could come about the middle or end of August. Then I should beg you would stay a little longer than usual, a fortnight at least. You could bring as many gentlemen, ladies, bonnes, etc., etc., as you pleased, and I should be too happy and proud to have you under my own roof....

Footnote 58: General Comte Baudrand (1774-1848).

Footnote 59: Son of Marshal Ney.

5th July 1837.

Went about half-past ten o'clock to Apsley House, and told the Duke of Wellington the whole of my communication with the Queen, Duchess of Kent, and Sir John Conroy on 15th June, also of my communication subsequently with Lord Melbourne, all of which he very much approved of. He said that he was quite sure that the Queen would find Lord Melbourne an honourable man, and one in whom Her Majesty might put confidence; that he was a man apt to treat matters too lightly, or, as he expressed it, a poco curante, but in the main an honest and an honourable man. Upon my speaking to him of the kind and paternal conduct of King Leopold towards his Niece, he said that he was fully persuaded of this, and should at all and any time be ready to uphold it by his approbation, but that he had no immediate connection with the Press, whose attacks indeed he held very cheap, though they were frequently very offensive. He then asked me whether it was not true that the Queen had thought of some reviews at which she would appear on horseback. I said there had been some talk of it. He desired me to say that he thought this would be very dangerous, that she had much better do this in an open carriage, as no one except such as himself knew how difficult it was to get steady riding horses, and besides that, she could not be attended by any female, and that this would appear indelicate.

QUEEN ADELAIDE

Windsor Castle, 7th July 1837.

My dearest Niece,—I must, before I leave this dear Castle, once more express to you the grateful sense I entertain for the kind treatment I have experienced from you since it has pleased our heavenly Father to put you in possession of it. You have contributed much to my comfort under all the painful and distressing circumstances of this time of woe, and I assure you that I ever shall remember it with sincere gratitude.

I hope that you continue quite well and do not suffer from the exertions and duties of your new position. My best wishes and prayers attend you on all occasions, for I shall be for the rest of my life devoted and attached to you as your most affectionate Aunt and Subject,

Adelaide.

Kensington Palace, 10th July 1837.

The Queen regrets very much to hear of Lord Melbourne's indisposition, and trusts it will be of no duration.

The Queen has just seen the Lord Chamberlain and has given him all her orders. The Lord Chamberlain says that he will do everything in his power to facilitate the Queen's going into Buckingham Palace on Thursday.

The Queen fears that there may have been some mistake with respect to the Chapter of the Garter, for Lord Conyngham,60 as well as several others, imagined it would be held on Wednesday instead of Friday. The Queen requests Lord Melbourne to rectify this mistake, as it is the Queen's intention to hold the Chapter on Friday.

Footnote 60: The Lord Chamberlain.
11th July 1837.

My dearest, best Uncle,—... I have got very little time and very little to say. I really and truly go into Buckingham Palace the day after to-morrow, but I must say, though I am very glad to do so, I feel sorry to leave for ever my poor old birthplace....

25th.—I shall not go out of town, I think, before the 20th or thereabouts of next month. Windsor requires thorough cleaning, and I must say I could not think of going in sooner after the poor King's death. Windsor always appears very melancholy to me, and there are so many sad associations with it. These will vanish, I daresay, if I see you there soon after my arrival there.

I have very pleasant large dinners every day. I invite my Premier generally once a week to dinner as I think it right to show publicly that I esteem him and have confidence in him, as he has behaved so well. Stockmar is of this opinion and is his great admirer....

MADAME DE LIEVEN

Neuilly, 12th July 1837.

... Having still a few moments before a special messenger sets off, I take advantage of it to add a few words. By all I can hear, there are many intrigues on foot in England at this moment. Princess Lieven[61] and another individual recently imported from her country seem to be very active in what concerns them not; beware of them. A rule which I cannot sufficiently recommend is, never to permit people to speak on subjects concerning yourself or your affairs, without your having yourself desired them to do so. The moment a person behaves improperly on this subject, change the conversation, and make the individual feel that he has made a mistake.... People will certainly try to speak to you on your own personal affairs; decline it boldly, and they will leave you alone....

Now I conclude with my warmest wishes for your happiness. Ever, my dear Victoria, your faithfully attached Uncle and Friend,

Leopold R.

Footnote 61: The Princess Dorothea de Benckendorff married the Count de Lieven at fifteen; in 1812, he became Russian Minister (and later Ambassador) in London, whither she accompanied him. She was a woman of extraordinary cleverness, enjoying the confidence of George IV., Liverpool, Canning, Castlereagh, and Wellington. Inspiring the efforts, and even composing the despatches of her husband, she became herself the confidential correspondent of Nesselrode, Esterhazy, Posso di Borgo, Guizot, and Lord Aberdeen. In 1834, the Lievens returned to St Petersburg, where the Emperor Nicholas, though indifferent to the society of women of talent, showed her special marks of regard. Her husband died at Rome, in January 1838, and she established herself in Paris, afterwards seeking a home in England during the troubles of 1848. Returning to Paris, her salon became again the resort of diplomatists, politicians, and men of the world. She died in January 1857.

Madame de Lieven about this time told Greville that she had had an audience of the Queen, "who was very civil and gracious, but timid and embarrassed, and talked of nothing but commonplaces"; and Greville adds that the Queen "had probably been told that the Princess was an intrigante, and was afraid of committing herself."

Madame de Lieven wrote to Lord Aberdeen on the 30th July 1837:—

J'ai vu la Reine deux fois, je l'ai vue seule, et je l'ai vue dans la société du soir, et avec son Premier Ministre. Elle a un aplomb, un air de commandement, de dignité, qui avec son visage enfantin, sa petite taille, et son joli sourire, forment certainement le spectacle le plus extraordinaire qu'il soit possible de se figurer. Elle est d'une extrême réserve dans son discours. On croit que la prudence est une de ses premières qualités. Lord Melbourne a auprès d'elle un air d'amour, de contentement, de vanité même, et tout cela mêlé avec beaucoup de respect, des attitudes très à son aise, une habitude de première place dans son salon, de la rêverie, de la gaieté, vous voyez tout cela. La Reine est pleine d'aimables sourires pour lui.

La société le soir n'était composée que du household de la Reine, de tout le household de la Duchesse de Kent (moins la famille Conroy, qui n'approche pas du Palais), et de quelques étrangers. La Duchesse de Kent est parfaitement mécontente,—elle m'en a même parlé. Je doute que la mère et la fllle habitent longtemps sous le même toit. Quant à Lord Melbourne, il me semble que la Duchesse le déteste. Il est évident qu'il est dans la possession entière et exclusive de la confiance de la Reine, et que ses ressentiments, comme ses peines passées, sont confiés sans réserve à son Premier Ministre....

PARLIAMENT PROROGUED

18th July 1837.

My beloved Uncle,—... I have been so busy, I can say but two words more, which are that I prorogued Parliament yesterday in person, was very well received, and am not at all tired to-day, but quite frisky. There is to be no review this year, as I was determined to have it only if I could ride, and as I have not ridden for two years, it was better not. Believe me, always, your devoted Niece,

Victoria R.

Stanhope Street, 22nd July 1837.

... With regard to Count Orloff,62 your Majesty will probably renew to him, on his taking leave, the assurances which your Majesty has already given, of your desire to cement and maintain the friendly alliance which subsists between the two Crowns; and an expression might be repeated of the pleasure which your Majesty has derived from the selection of a person who possesses the confidence and esteem of the Emperor so fully as Count Orloff is known to do.

It might, perhaps, be as well to avoid any allusion to your Majesty's not being personally acquainted with the Emperor, or anything that might be construed into an invitation to that Sovereign to come to England, because Viscount Palmerston has reason to believe that any such hint would be eagerly caught at, while at the same time such a visit does not, under all circumstances, seem to be a thing particularly to be desired....

Footnote 62: The Russian Ambassador.

DISCRETION ADVISED

Laeken, 24th July 1837.

My dearest Child,—... I hear that the Levée went off very well, and I have no doubt that the

Drawing-Room did the same. Your spirit in all these new and trying proceedings makes me happy beyond expression. Believe me, with courage and honesty, you will get on beautifully and successfully. The firmness you displayed at the beginning of your reign will be for your quiet of the utmost importance. People must come to the opinion it is of no use intriguing, because when her mind is once made up, and she thinks a thing right, no earthly power will make her change. To these qualities must be added one which is of great importance, this is discretion; humble as it seems, it has often brought about successes in which talent failed and genius did not succeed. Discretion in the great affairs of the world does wonders, and safety depends frequently and is chiefly derived from it....

Now I must quickly conclude, with the prayer that you will not permit anybody, be it even your Prime Minister, to speak to you on matters that concern you personally, without your having expressed the wish of its being done. You have no idea of the importance of this for your peace and comfort and safety. I always act on this principle, and I can say with great success.

Believe me ever, my dearest Victoria, your devoted Uncle,

Leopold R.

Laeken, 29th July 1837.

My dearest Child,—Your dear letter of the 24th inst. is, amongst so many kind letters, almost the kindest I yet received from your dear hands. My happiness and my greatest pride will always be, to be a tender and devoted father to you, my beloved child, and to watch over you and stand by you with heart and soul as long as the heart which loves you so sincerely will beat.

I have no doubt that Lord Melbourne will always do everything in his power to be useful to you. His position is become extremely happy; after having been, under the late King at least, in an awkward position, he is now sure of enjoying your confidence and sincere support. If the elections turn out favourably to the Ministry, it will, I hope, give them the means of trying to conciliate the great mass of the moderate Tories, who from their nature and in consequence of their opinions are safe and desirable supporters of the Crown. The two extremes will give them trouble, and the ultra-Tories appear to me to be even the more unreasonable of the two.

I am most happy to see you on your guard against Princess Lieven and such-like people. Your life amongst intriguers and tormented with intrigues has given you an experience on this important subject which you will do well not to lose sight of, as it will unfortunately often reproduce itself, though the names and manner of carrying on the thing may not be the same.

I also think Windsor a little melancholy, but I believe that one likes it more and more, as the Park in particular is uncommonly beautiful. We shall try our best to enliven it by our presence, and probably soon after your arrival. I am most happy to see you so spirited and happy in your new position; it will go a great way to ensure your success, and your spirit and courage will never be de trop.

Now I will conclude for the day, not to bore you, and beg you always to believe me, my dear and beloved Victoria, your devoted Uncle and Friend,

Leopold R.

PRINCESS HOHENLOHE

Langenburg, 31st July 1837.

My dearest Victoria,—On arriving here, I found your dear letter of the 9th of this month; and some days ago I received the one of the 16th. Many, many thanks for them both; it is indeed kind of you to write to me now when you have so much to do. You have no idea what a feeling it is, to hear and read of you, and to think that it is you, my own dear sister, who are the object of general observation, and, I may say, admiration; it is sometimes like a dream. For those who are near you it is quite different than for me, who have not seen you yet in your new position, but must represent to myself all through the report of others. The description in the papers of your proroguing Parliament I read with great interest; it must have been an imposing moment for you, your standing for the first time in your life in the middle of that assembly where the interests and welfare of your country are discussed and decided upon. It is with pride, pleasure, and anxiety I think of you at the description of such scenes and occurrences. I saw too by the papers that your incognito at the Opera was not quite kept as you wished it....

THE ELECTIONS

Buckingham Palace, 1st August 1837.

My dearest Uncle,—... I should be most happy to "peep once" into your country, and wish that it could be.

With respect to Politics, Lord Melbourne told me this morning that he thinks the Lords will be more moderate and reasonable next Session. The Duke of Wellington made a speech shortly before the Dissolution of Parliament, in which he said that he wished as much as the Government did to pass the questions now pending.

You do not think Alexander63 near handsome enough in my opinion; you know, ladies are much better judges. He is somewhat colossal, I own, but very proportionate and good-looking, I think. I am all impatience to hear more about all this, and when you imagine the marriage will take place.

I have resumed my singing lessons with Lablache64 twice a week, which form an agreeable recreation in the midst of all the business I have to do. He is such a good old soul, and greatly pleased that I go on with him. I admire the music of the Huguenots very much, but do not sing it, as I prefer Italian to French for singing greatly. I have been learning in the beginning of the season many of your old favourites, which I hope to sing with you when we meet. I wish I could keep Lablache to sing with us, but he will be gone by that time, I greatly fear.

Now farewell, my beloved Uncle. Give my affectionate love to my dear Aunt, and believe me always, your devoted Niece,

Victoria R.

J'embrasse Léopold et Philippe.

Footnote 63: Prince Alexander of Wurtemberg, betrothed to Princess Marie of Orleans, daughter of Louis Philippe. She died 10th January 1839. See of Queen Victoria to the King of the Belgians, 11th January 1839.

Footnote 64: See ante, p.

THE ELECTIONS

9th August 1837.

My beloved Uncle,—... With respect to the Elections, they are, I'm thankful to say, rather favourable, though not quite so much so as we could wish. But upon the whole we shall have as good a House as we had, and, I hope (as Lord Melbourne does also), a more moderate one than the last one. The Irish Elections are very favourable to us; we have gained six in the English boroughs, and lost, I grieve to say, several in the counties.

The country is very quiet, and I have good reason to believe all will do very well.

The King of Würtemberg is to arrive to-night, under the name of Count Teck, and wishes to be in strict incognito. He comes on purpose to see me; you know he is my second cousin—his mother65 was sister to Queen Caroline and daughter to my grand-aunt.66 I shall give the King a large dinner on Friday and a little concert after it....

Footnote 65: Queen Augusta of Würtemberg.

Footnote 66: Augusta, Duchess of Brunswick, sister of George III.

Endsleigh, 15th August 1837.

Lord John Russell presents his humble duty to your Majesty, and has the honour to lay before your Majesty a general statement of the result of the elections, which, with the exception of one or two doubtful counties in Ireland, may be said to be completed....

It is not to be denied that this near balance of parties makes the task of conducting the government difficult for any Ministry. On the other hand, the circumstances of the country do not present any extraordinary difficulty, and were any such to arise, the general composition of the new House of Commons affords a security that the maintenance of the Constitution and the welfare of the country would be permanent objects to the majority of its Members.67

Lord John Russell had some time ago the honour of stating to your Majesty that the return of Mr Fox Maule for Perthshire, and of Mr Hume for Middlesex, were hardly to be expected. In this as in many other instances the superior organisation of the Tory party have enabled them to gain the appearance of a change of opinion, which has not in fact taken place.

Lord John Russell is sorry to add that bribery, intimidation, and drunkenness have been very prevalent at the late elections, and that in many cases the disposition to riot has only been checked by the appearance of the Military, who have in all cases conducted themselves with great temper and judgment.

Footnote 67: While the extreme Radicals were in several cases defeated, the number of O'Connell's followers was decidedly increased. The general balance of parties was not much affected, though the complaint made by Mr Roebuck, the Radical Member for Bath, in the last days of William IV.'s reign, that there was no Government, and that the machinery of legislation was at a dead stop, was no longer warranted.

THE ELECTIONS

Endsleigh, 21st August 1837.

Lord John Russell presents his humble duty to your Majesty, and has the honour to submit to your Majesty a letter from the Earl of Coventry requesting an Audience.

It is usual for the Sovereign to receive any Peer who may be desirous of an Audience, without any other person being present. But if the Peer who is thus admitted to the honour of an Audience should enter upon political topics, it has been the custom for your Majesty's predecessors merely to hear what is offered, and not to give any opinion, or to enter into any discussion or conversation upon such topics.

Should your Majesty be pleased to grant Lord Coventry's request of an Audience, perhaps the most convenient course will be that the Lord-in-Waiting should signify to him, direct from Windsor, your Majesty's pleasure.

Windsor Castle, 19th September 1837. (20 m(inutes) p(ast) 11.)

My dearest, most beloved Uncle,—One line to express to you, imperfectly, my thanks for all your very great kindness to me, and my great, great grief at your departure! God knows how sad, how forlorn, I feel! How I shall miss you, my dearest, dear Uncle! every, every where! How I shall miss your conversation! How I shall miss your protection out riding! Oh! I feel very, very sad, and cannot speak of you both without crying!

Farewell, my beloved Uncle and father! may Heaven bless and protect you; and do not forget your most affectionate, devoted, and attached Niece and Child,

Victoria R.

Footnote 68: Written on the conclusion of a visit of the King of the Belgians to England.

Windsor Castle, 3rd October 1837.

My beloved Uncle,—... I am quite sad to leave this fine place, where, if it had not been for the meeting of Parliament so early this year, I would have remained till November. I have passed such a pleasant time here, the pleasantest summer I have ever passed in my life; I have had the great happiness of having you and my beloved Aunt here, I have had pleasant people staying with me, and I have had delicious rides which have done me more good than anything. It will be such a break-up of our little circle! Besides my own people, Lord Melbourne and Lord Palmerston are the only people who have been staying here, and this little party was very social and agreeable. The Princess Augusta of Saxony69 has been here for two nights; she is neither young nor handsome, but a very kind good person.

The news from Portugal are bad which I got this morning. The Civil War is ended, and the Chartists have been completely defeated; this is sad enough, but I was fearful of it: a counter-revolution never does well.70

En revanche, the news from Spain are by far better....

Believe me always, in haste, your devoted and affectionate Niece,

Victoria R.

Footnote 69: Daughter of King Frederick Augustus of Saxony.

Footnote 70: On July 1st a new Ministry had come into power in Portugal. The finances of the country were in great confusion, a military insurrection broke out in the North at Braga, the Ministry resigned, and a new Ministry came into office in August. On the 18th August, the Duke of Terceira, followed by many persons of distinction, joined the insurgents, and, establishing himself at Mafra, advanced upon Lisbon with the Chartist troops, issuing a proclamation of provisional regency. A Convention was eventually signed, and the Cortes proceeded to discuss measures of Constitutional Reform.

RECEPTION AT BRIGHTON

6th October 1837.

Lord Melbourne presents his humble duty to your Majesty, and in acknowledging your Majesty's gracious communication, of yesterday returns his thanks for the very lively account which your Majesty has given of the journey and the entrance into Brighton. Lord Melbourne entirely partakes in the wish your Majesty has been graciously pleased to express that he had been there to witness the scene; but your Majesty will at once perceive that it was better that he was not, as in that case Lord Melbourne would have been accused of an attempt to take a political advantage of the general enthusiasm and to mix himself and the Government with your Majesty's personal popularity. Lord Melbourne fears that for some time your Majesty will find yourself somewhat incommoded by the desire, which naturally prevails amongst all ranks and classes, to obtain an opportunity of seeing your Majesty....

Laeken, 9th October 1837.

... I have also told Stockmar to try to settle something for regular safe communication; in quiet times like the present, one a week would be sufficient. You know now that all letters are read, and that should not be always the case with ours. There is, however, one thing about which I think it right to warn you. This way of reading people's letters is often taken advantage of by the writers of them, who are not so ignorant of the thing as is imagined to write the very subject which they wish to convey to the ears of persons without compromising themselves. I will give you an example: we are still plagued by Prussia concerning those fortresses; now, to tell the Prussian Government many things, which we should not like to tell them officially, the Minister is going to write a despatch to our man at Berlin, sending it by post; the Prussians are sure to read it, and to learn in this way what we wish them to hear. The diplomats in England may resort to this same mode of proceeding to injure people, to calumniate, and to convey to your knowledge such things as they may hope to have the effect of injuring some people they may fear, in your eyes. I tell you the trick, that you should be able to guard against it; it is of importance, and I have no doubt will be resorted to by various political people.... Ever, my dearest Victoria, your faithfully devoted Uncle and Friend,

Leopold R.

ENGLAND AND FRANCE LOUIS PHILIPPE'S POLICY

Trianon, 19th October 1837.

My dearest Victoria,—... There is a great disposition here to be on the best possible terms with England. As it has but too often happened that the diplomatic agents of the two countries have drawn, or been believed to draw, different ways,COUNT MOLÉ I recommended strongly to Count Molé71 to give strong and clear instructions to his people, particularly at Madrid, Lisbon, and Athens.... He is going to read them to Lord Granville, and also to communicate as much as possible all the despatches of the French diplomats to the English Government. This will be a proof of confidence, and it will besides have the advantage of giving often useful information, enabling thereby the English Government to hear two opinions instead of one. It cannot be denied that the idea that the Plenipotentiaries of the two countries were following two different lines of policy has been hurtful to the causes of the two Queens in the Peninsula. To put a stop to this double action is the only benefit which the Queens will at present derive from a better understanding between England and France; but as it is, it will be still of some importance to them, and take away from the different political parties the possibility of using the pretended misunderstanding against the Government of the Queens. I trust that you will tell your Ministers to meet this friendly disposition with frankness and kindness. The wish of the King here is, to have matters concerted between the Plenipotentiaries of both countries. In this way it would become difficult for the parties in Spain or Portugal to say that the two Plenipotentiaries support different candidates for Ministerial power, and the division in the parties connected with the Queens might be in this manner prevented or reconciled. Many and many are the ill-natured hints thrown out against the King's policy here, and because he is clever, he is suspected of having ambitious schemes without end; it may not be without some importance to set this, in your mind at least, to rights. Whatever may have been the King's views immediately after the revolution of July72 I will not decide; perhaps he may a moment have wished to be able to do something for France. Supposing this for the sake of argument to have been so, two months of his reign were sufficient to show him that the great question was not to conquer territories or foreign influence, but to save Monarchy. He saw clearly that though he might begin a war, necessarily it would soon degenerate into a war of propaganda, and that he and his family would be the first victims of it. His struggle has constantly been to strengthen his Government, to keep together or create anew the elements indispensable for a Monarchical Government, and this struggle is far from being at its end, and most probably the remainder of his life will be devoted to this important task; and whatever may be the more lively disposition of the Duke of Orleans, great part of his reign if he comes to the throne, and perhaps the whole of it, will, bon gré mal gré, take the same turn. That it should be so is very natural, because of what use would be some foreign provinces if they would only add to the difficulty of governing the old? Therefore, knowing as I do all the proceedings of the King and his Cabinet, even more fully than I do those of your Government; seeing constantly in the most unreserved manner the whole of the despatches; knowing as the nearest neighbour the system that they constantly followed up towards us, I must say that no one is more against acquiring influence in foreign States, or even getting burthened with family aggrandisement in them, than he. He rejected most positively the marriage of Joinville with Donna Maria because he will not have anything to do with Portugal. He rejects a mille times the idea of a future union of the Queen of Spain with Aumale, because he will not have a son where it is not his intention to support him.

His fear of being drawn into a real intervention has been the cause of his having been so anxious not to have a French Legion in Spain. He may be right or wrong on this subject—I do not decide this, as I was of a different opinion last year; but his fear of being drawn too far, like a man whose clothes get caught by a steam-engine, is natural enough. His dislike to the ultra-Liberals in the Peninsula is also very natural, because they uphold principles of Government which render Monarchy impossible, and the application of which to France would be the ruin of the King. England, from the peculiarity of its position, can do many things which in France would upset everything.... I must close my letter, and shall answer yours to-morrow. God bless you! Ever, my dearest Victoria, your devoted Uncle,

Leopold R.

Footnote 71: French Premier and Foreign Secretary.

Footnote 72: 1830.

Pavilion, Brighton, 25th October 1837.

... Now, dearest Uncle, I must speak to you un peu de Politique. I made Lord Melbourne read the political part of your letter. He wished me to communicate to you part of the contents of a letter of Lord Granville's which we received yesterday. Lord Granville complains a good deal of Molé,73 and says, that though he is apparently very cordial and friendly towards us, and talks of his desire that we should be on a better footing as to our foreign Ministers than we have hitherto been, that whenever Lord Granville urges him to do anything decisive (to use Lord G.'s own words) "he shrinks from the discussion," says he must have time to reflect before he can give any answer, and evades giving any reply, whenever anything of importance is required. This, you see, dear Uncle, is not satisfactory. I merely tell you this, as I think you would like to know what Molé tells our Ambassador; this differs from what he told you. What you say about Louis Philippe I am sure is very true; his situation is a very peculiar and a very difficult one....

Footnote 73: See ante, p.

THE FRENCH IN AFRICA

Trianon, 27th October 1837.

... Political matters I shall not touch upon to-day; there is nothing very particular except the taking of Constantin.74 The Duc de Nemours has greatly distinguished himself. I am sorry to see that in England people are sometimes sufficiently absurd to be jealous of these French conquests. Nothing indeed can be more absurd, as nothing is of greater importance to the peace of Europe than that a powerful and military nation like the French should have this outlet for their love of military display. If one had named a council of wise men to fix upon a spot where this might be done with the least mischief to the rest of the world, one should have named the coast of Africa. By their being there they will render to civilisation a country which for about 800 years has been growing worse and worse, and which was in the times of the Romans one of the richest provinces. It settles, besides, upon the French a constant petite guerre with the natives, which is the very thing that will do them good.

Footnote 74: The French losses amounted to 19 officers and 86 men killed, with 38 officers and 468 men wounded. The French Government had failed in its efforts for an amicable arrangement with Achmet Bey, and it appeared probable that the Turkish fleet would also oppose them. The commander, however, merely landed some men at Tripoli, and the French success was complete.

Buckingham Palace, 19th November 1837.

... Now, dearest Uncle, before I say anything more, I will answer the various questions in your letter, which I have communicated to Lord Melbourne and Lord Palmerston. (1) With respect to

Ferdinand's question to you, it is impossible for us to say beforehand what we shall do in such an emergency; it depends so entirely on the peculiar circumstances of the moment that we cannot say what we should do. You know, dear Uncle, that the fleet has orders to protect the King and Queen in case they should be in any personal danger. As to Lord Howard,75 though what you say about him is true enough, it would not do to recall him at present; it would give Bois le Comte76 all the advantage he wishes for, and which would be injurious to our interests and influence.

(2) With regard to Spain, a very decided mention is made of the Queen herself in the speech which is to be delivered by me to-morrow in the House of Lords.

We have great reason to know that, of late, the Queen has positively declared her intention to remain at Madrid to the very last.

Villiers'77 conduct has been, I fear, much misrepresented, for his own opinions are not at all those of the ultra-Liberal kind; and his only aim has been, to be on good terms with the Spanish Ministry for the time being.

(3) Concerning France, I need not repeat to you, dear Uncle, how very anxious we all are to be upon the best and most friendly terms with her, and to co-operate with her.

Footnote 75: Lord Howard de Walden, British Minister at Lisbon.

Footnote 76: French Minister at Madrid.

Footnote 77: British Minister at Madrid, afterwards fourth Earl of Clarendon, and twice Foreign Secretary.

CLOSE OF THE SESSION

Buckingham Palace, 25th December 1837.

My dearest Uncle,—... You will, I am sure, be happy to hear that this Session is happily closed, and that the whole has gone off very satisfactorily, much more so even than any of us could hope. I went on Saturday to the House of Lords to give my Assent to the Civil List Bill. I shall return to town on the 16th of January, when Parliament meets again; it meets sooner than it was at first intended it should, on account of the affairs of Canada.

Laeken, 26th December 1837.

My dearest Child,—You were somewhat irritable when you wrote to me!... Affairs stand now as follows: the studies at Bonn take the whole of April, and may be concluded at the beginning of May. From May till the end of August, if you approved of the visit, the time should be utilisé. A séjour at Coburg would not be of much use; here we are generally absent in the summer. To confide therefore the young gentleman to his Uncle Mensdorff79 for three months, would give him so much time for some manly accomplishments, which do no harm to a young man. To make him enter the Service would not do at all. What you say about his imbibing principles of a political nature, there is no great fear of that. First of all, Prague is not a town where politics are at all agitated; these topics are very rarely touched upon; besides, Albert is clever, and it is not at the eleventh hour that anybody in three months will make him imbibe political principles. Perhaps you will turn in your mind what you think on the subject, and communicate me the result of it....

Footnote 78: This letter refers to the course of study which Prince Albert was about to pursue.

Footnote 79: Count Emmanuel de Mensdorff-Pouilly, who married, in 1804, Sophia, Princess of Saxe-Coburg-Saalfeld.

CANADA

27th December 1837.

Lord Melbourne presents his humble duty to your Majesty, and acquaints your Majesty that he has this morning received a letter from the Speaker80 consenting to remain until Whitsuntide. This is inconvenient enough, but the delay relieves your present embarrassment upon this head, and puts off changes until a period of the Session when public affairs will be more decisively settled.

Lord Melbourne is sorry to have to inform your Majesty that there was a good deal of difference of opinion yesterday in the Cabinet upon the affairs of Canada.81 All are of opinion that strong measures should be taken for the repression of the insurrection, but some, and more particularly Lord Howick, think that these measures of vigour should be accompanied by measures of amendment and conciliation. We are to have a Cabinet again upon the subject on Wednesday next, when Lord Melbourne hopes that some practical result will be come to without serious difference.

Footnote 80: Mr James Abercromby, afterwards Lord Dunfermline. He remained in the Chair till 1839. He had little hold over the House, and many regrettable scenes occurred.

Footnote 81: See Introductory Note, p. .

Windsor Castle, 28th December 1837.

The Queen received Lord Melbourne's communication yesterday evening, and is glad to see that the Speaker consents to remain a little while longer, though, as Lord Melbourne says, it is still very inconvenient.

The Queen regrets that there should have been any difference of opinion with respect to Canada, but hopes with Lord Melbourne that some final arrangement may be come to next Wednesday.

The Queen is very sorry to learn that Lord Melbourne will be detained in London until Saturday. She omitted to ask Lord Melbourne when he thinks it would be convenient for Lord Palmerston to come down to Windsor for a few days, as it is the Queen's wish to ask him in the course of the Recess. The Queen is very thankful to Lord Melbourne for his kind enquiries after her health; she is sorry to say she had one of her bad headaches yesterday, but feels very well this morning and thinks a drive will quite cure her.

ARMY ESTIMATES

Windsor Castle, 29th December 1837.

The Queen received Lord Melbourne's two letters yesterday evening, and another this morning, enclosing one from Lord Duncannon.82 The Queen is very much gratified by the kind expressions in the letter she got last night; she is grieved to see Lord Melbourne is so much oppressed with business.

The Queen thinks Lord Melbourne has acted with the greatest judgment with respect to Sir J.

Conroy,83 and highly approves the course he intends pursuing.

The Queen regrets that there should be so much difficulty with respect to the Report of the Army Estimates, but fervently trusts that no serious difficulties will arise from it; she will be very anxious to talk about this and many other matters when she sees Lord Melbourne, which the Queen hopes (as Lord Melbourne says nothing to the contrary) she will do on the 3rd or 4th.

The Queen thinks that it will be quite right if Lord Melbourne writes to Lord John about the Staffordshire Yeomanry. The Queen will be delighted to see Lady John Russell's little girl, and would be very happy if Lady John was to bring the Baby also. The Queen begs Lord Melbourne to invite them (Lord and Lady John) in her name on the 8th, and to stay till the 11th.

The Duke and Duchess of Cambridge are here, and the Queen is very sorry to say, that from what she sees and hears, she has reason to fear all is not as it should be; her mother is most markedly civil and affectionate towards both the Duke and Duchess, and spoke Politics with the former. The Queen will tell Lord Melbourne more about this when she sees him.

The weather was beautiful yesterday, and the Queen had a long drive and walk, which have done her great good; it is still finer to-day.

Footnote 82: Commissioner of Woods and Forests and Lord Privy Seal.

Footnote 83: Sir J. Conroy, who had been Comptroller to the Duchess of Kent, made certain claims which it was not considered expedient to grant. He received a pension and a baronetcy.

CANADA

30th December 1837.

... Lord Melbourne will do his utmost to compose these differences respecting Canada and the Army,84 but your Majesty must contemplate the possibility, not to say the probability, of his not being able to succeed. It will not do for the sake of temporary accommodation to sacrifice the honour of your Majesty's Crown or the interests of your Majesty's subjects.

Footnote 84: See Introductory Notes for 1837 and 1838, pp. and

STATE DEPARTMENTS

31st December 1837.

... Lord Melbourne has not yet been able to leave London. In order to have a chance of arranging these troublesome affairs it is necessary continually to see those who are principally engaged in them. From a conversation which he has had this evening with Lord Howick, Lord Melbourne has better hopes of producing a general agreement upon Canadian affairs, but the question of the administration of the Army, which is of less immediate importance, is of more difficulty. Your Majesty knows the importance attached by the King of the Belgians to this matter. The opinion of the Duke of Wellington is also strongly against the projected alteration. On the other hand, five Cabinet Ministers have pledged themselves to it by signing the report, and consider themselves as having publicly undertaken to the House of Commons that some such measure shall be proposed. Lord Melbourne has asked for the opinions of Lord Hill85 and Sir Hussey Vivian86 in writing. When Lord Melbourne receives them he must submit them to your Majesty with as short and as clear a statement as he can make of a question which is of a technical and official character, and with which Lord Melbourne does not feel himself to be very familiar. Lord Melbourne transmits a copy of the proposed Order in Council to carry the recommendation of the report into effect, which will acquaint your Majesty precisely what the powers and duties are which it is intended to transfer from the Secretary of State87 to the Secretary-at-War. It is the more necessary to be cautious, because it can be done without taking the opinion or having recourse to the authority of Parliament.

Your Majesty will not suppose that Lord Melbourne by laying before you the whole case has an idea of throwing the weight of such a decision entirely upon your Majesty. Lord Melbourne will deem it his duty to offer your Majesty a decided opinion upon the subject.

Lord Melbourne is much rejoiced to hear that your Majesty enjoys Windsor. The Duchess of Sutherland,88 who appreciates both the grand and the beautiful, could not be otherwise than delighted with it....

Lord Melbourne has the pleasure of wishing your Majesty a happy and prosperous New Year.

Footnote 85: Commander-in-Chief.

Footnote 86: Master-General of the Ordnance.

Footnote 87: The Secretaries of State (then three, now five in number) have co-extensive authority, that is to say, any one of them can legally execute the duties of all, although separate spheres of action are for convenience assigned to them; at that time the administration of Colonial and Military affairs were combined, the Secretary-at-War not being a Secretary of State. After the Crimean War a fourth Secretary was appointed, and after the Indian Mutiny a fifth was added, entrusted severally with the supervision of Military affairs and the administration of India. See letters of Lord Melbourne of , , and November 1841.

Footnote 88: Harriet Elizabeth Georgiana, Duchess of Sutherland (1806-1868), was the daughter of the sixth Earl of Carlisle, and married her cousin, Earl Gower (1786-1861), who became Duke of Sutherland in 1833. On the accession of the Queen, the Duchess of Sutherland became Mistress of the Robes, a post which she held till 1841, and on three subsequent occasions. The Duchess was a cultivated woman with many tastes, and made Stafford House a great social centre. She was deeply interested in philanthropic and social movements, such as the Abolition of Slavery, and had a strong sympathy for national movements, which she showed by entertaining Garibaldi in 1864. She combined a considerable sense of humour with a rare capacity for affection, and became one of the Queen's closest friends; after the Prince Consort's death she was for some weeks the Queen's constant companion.

INTRODUCTORY NOTE: TO CHAPTER VII

The Melbourne Ministry were able to maintain themselves in office during the year (1838), but were too weak to carry important measures. The prevailing distress led to much criticism of the Poor Law Act of 1834, and the disturbances in Canada turned the tide of emigration to Australia. But public interest in politics was eclipsed by the gaieties of the Coronation, in which all ranks partook. The events of Imperial importance elsewhere centred in Jamaica and Canada, the apprenticeship system in the former place leading to a renewal of the anti-slavery agitation at home, and the passing of a Colonial Bill for absolute emancipation. The Canadian troubles brought about the passing of an Imperial Act for the suspension for two years of the Legislative Assembly of Lower Canada, and Lord Durham, an impulsive and generous-hearted man, was sent out as High Commissioner. Having dismissed the Executive Council of his predecessor, he nominated a fresh one, but an ordinance thereafter promulgated in reference to the rebels was severely criticised. Lord Brougham, rejoicing at the opportunity of paying off old scores, castigated the Government, especially Lord Glenelg, the Colonial Secretary, and carried a measure censuring their Canadian policy. The Ministry disallowed the ordinance of Lord Durham, who, finding himself unsupported, resigned his Commission and returned home. On his arrival at Plymouth, he made a speech, in which he described the rebellion as finally at an end; the news, however, subsequently arrived that after his departure from Canada, disturbances had broken out afresh. Sir John Colborne was appointed to succeed Lord Durham with full powers.

The Civil War continued in Spain through the year, and intermittent rioting took place in Portugal, a country which was now verging on bankruptcy. The old Dutch and Belgian controversy as to the possession of Luxemburg was revived, the King of Holland, who had obstinately withheld his concurrence for six years from the Articles on the faith of which King Leopold accepted the throne of Belgium, now showing overt hostility in the disputed territory. As was natural, France was in sympathy with Belgium, and the two countries entered into a treaty of commerce and reciprocity.

CHAPTER VII

1st January 1838.

... Lord Melbourne feels most deeply the extreme kindness of your Majesty's expressions. Whatever may happen in the course of events, it will always be to Lord Melbourne a source of the most lively satisfaction to have assisted your Majesty in the commencement of your reign, which was not without trouble and difficulty, and your Majesty may depend that whether in or out of office Lord Melbourne's conduct will always be directed by the strongest attachment to your Majesty's person, and by the most ardent desire to promote your Majesty's interests, which from his knowledge of your Majesty's character and disposition Lord Melbourne feels certain will be always identified with the interests of your People.

CANADA

14th January 1838.

Lord Melbourne presents his humble duty to your Majesty, and has the honour of acknowledging your Majesty's gracious communication, which he received this evening. Lord Melbourne has this morning seen Lord Durham upon the subject of his assuming the Government of Canada,1 and has had a long conversation with him. Lord Melbourne is to receive his final answer before the Cabinet to-morrow, which meets at ten o'clock. Lord Durham is anxious that your Majesty should express to him your wish, or rather, as he phrased it, lay upon him your commands that he should undertake this duty, and also that, as his absence will be but temporary, that Lady Durham2 should retain her situation in your Majesty's household. Lord Melbourne thinks that your Majesty may properly gratify him in both these points. Lord Durham made some other stipulations, which Lord Melbourne will explain to your Majesty, but, upon the whole, Lord Melbourne feels little doubt that he will accept.

Lord Glenelg3 is on Monday to make a statement to the House of Lords upon the subject of Canada, on which a debate may not improbably arise by which Lord Melbourne may be detained. On Wednesday there is neither House of Lords nor Cabinet dinner. Wednesday, Friday, and Sunday will therefore be festive days, on which Lord Melbourne will have great pleasure in obeying your Majesty's commands and also on Monday, if he should not be kept in the House of Lords.

Lord Melbourne thinks it was prudent in your Majesty not to expose yourself to the cold of the Chapel. He is himself better, but has still much cough, though he has kept himself very quiet and been very careful of his diet since he has been in London.

Footnote 1: In the room of Lord Gosford. See ante, p.

Footnote 2: Daughter of Earl Grey.

Footnote 3: Colonial Secretary.

Windsor Castle, 15th January 1838.

(Half-past nine o'clock.)

The Queen has written approved on Lord Melbourne's letter as he desired; but adds a line to express her satisfaction at Lord Durham's having accepted the office of Governor-General of

Canada.

The Queen will be very happy to see Lord Melbourne at half-past three.

INFLUENCE OF THE CROWN

Brussels, 16th January 1838.

My dearly beloved Child,—... I am very grateful for Lord Melbourne's kind recollection of me. I have a sincere regard for him, and I think that our intercourse has satisfied him of one thing, that I have nothing so much at heart than your welfare, and what is for the good of your Empire. I wish very much that you would speak with him on the subject of what ought to be done to keep for the Crown the little influence it still may possess. His views on this important subject are the more trustworthy as he always has belonged to the moderate Liberals, and therefore has had the means of judging the matter with great impartiality. Monarchy to be carried on requires certain elements, and the occupation of the Sovereign must be constantly to preserve these elements, or should they have been too much weakened by untoward circumstances, to contrive by every means to strengthen them again. You are too clever not to know, that it is not the being called Queen or King, which can be of the least consequence, when to the title there is not also annexed the power indispensable for the exercise of those functions. All trades must be learned, and nowadays the trade of a constitutional Sovereign, to do it well, is a very difficult one.

... I must end, and remain ever, most affectionately, my dear Child, your devoted Uncle,

Leopold R.

24th January 1838.

My dearest Niece,—Having just been informed of your gracious consideration of, and your generosity towards, the dear King's children,4 I must express to you how deeply I feel this kind proof of your attachment to the late King, whose memory you respect by the generous continuance of their former allowances from the Privy Purse. Nothing could have given me more real satisfaction, and I trust and hope that they will prove their gratitude and entire devotion to you by their future conduct. Let me thank you, dearest Victoria, from the bottom of my heart, and be assured that the heavenly blessing of our beloved King will be upon you for your generous kindness to those he loved so much in this world.

I hope that you have not suffered at all from the severity of the weather, and are as well as all your subjects can wish you to be, amongst whom there is none more anxiously praying for your welfare and happiness than, my dear Niece, your most devoted and affectionate Aunt,

Adelaide.

Footnote 4: The eldest of the five illegitimate sons of William IV. and Mrs. Jordan had been created Earl of Munster, and his sisters and brothers had been given the precedence of the daughters and younger sons of a Marquis. The Queen now continued the same allowances as they had received from the late King.

DANIEL O'CONNELL

Buckingham Palace, 22nd February 1838.

My dear Uncle,—... I had a very brilliant Levée again yesterday, at which O'Connell and all his sons, son-in-law, nephew, etc., appeared. I received him, as you may imagine, with a very smiling face; he has been behaving very well this year.5 It was quite a treat for me to see him, as I had for long wished it.

We are going on most prosperously here, which will, I am sure, give you as much pleasure as it does me. We have no fear for any of the questions. Lord John Russell is much pleased with the temper of the House of Commons, which he says is remarkably good, and the Duke of Wellington is behaving uncommonly well, going with Ministers, and behaving like an honest man should do....

Footnote 5: Ever since the Accession, O'Connell's speeches had been full of expressions of loyalty, and he had been acting in concert with the Whigs.

DEPARTMENTS OF STATE

Stanhope Street, 25th February 1838.

Viscount Palmerston presents his humble duty to your Majesty, and with reference to your Majesty's question upon the subjects to which Lord William Russell's recent despatch relates, he has the honour to state: that in the Governments of the Continent, and more especially in those which have no representative Assemblies, the second class of persons in the public offices possess and exercise much more power and influence than the corresponding class of persons do in this country. In England the Ministers who are at the head of the several departments of the State, are liable any day and every day to defend themselves in Parliament; in order to do this, they must be minutely acquainted with all the details of the business of their offices, and the only way of being constantly armed with such information is to conduct and direct those details themselves.

On the Continent, where Ministers of State are not liable so to be called to account for their conduct, the Ministers are tempted to leave the details of their business much more to their Under-Secretaries and to their chief clerks. Thus it happens that all the routine of business is generally managed by these subordinate agents; and to such an extent is this carried, that Viscount Palmerston believes that the Ministers for Foreign Affairs, in France, Austria, Prussia, and Russia, seldom take the trouble of writing their own despatches, except, perhaps, upon some very particular and important occasion.

Your Majesty will easily see how greatly such a system must place in the hands of the subordinate members of the public departments the power of directing the policy and the measures of the Government; because the value and tendency, and the consequences of a measure, frequently depend as much upon the manner in which that measure is worked out, as upon the intention and spirit with which it was planned.

Another circumstance tends also to give great power to these second-class men, and that is their permanence in office.

In England when, in consequence of some great political change, the Heads of Departments go out, the greater part of the Under-Secretaries go out also; thus the Under-Secretary (with two or three exceptions) having come in with his Chief, has probably no more experience than his Chief, and can seldom set up his own knowledge to overrule the opinion, or to guide the judgment, of his superior.

But on the Continent, changes of Ministers are oftener changes of individual men from personal causes, than changes of parties from political convulsions; and therefore when the Chief retires, the Under-Secretary remains. There are consequently in all the public offices abroad a number of men who have spent the greater part of their lives in their respective departments, and who by their long experience are full of knowledge of what has been done in former times, and of the most convenient and easy manner of doing what may be required in the time present. This affords to the Chiefs an additional motive for leaning upon their subordinates, and gives to those subordinates still more real influence.

BUREAUCRACY

This class of subordinate men has, from the fact of its being possessed of so much power, been invested by the jargon of the day with the title of "Bureaucratic"—a name fabricated in imitation of the words "aristocratic" and "democratic," each being compounded of the word "cratic," which is a corruption from the Greek word "kratos," which means power; and the prefix, denoting the particular class of society whose power is meant to be expressed. Thus "aristo-cratic" is the power of the upper, or, as in Greek it is called, the "aristos" class of society; "demo-cratic" is the power of the people, which in Greek is called the "demos"; and "bureau-cratic" is the power of the public offices or "bureaus," for which latter the French name has been taken instead of a Greek word.

It appears, then, to be the opinion of Lord William Russell, that this second class of public men in Prussia are animated by a desire to see the general policy of their country rendered more national and independent than it has hitherto been; that for this purpose they were desirous of urging on the Government to take its stand against foreign influence upon some point or other, not much caring what that point might be; that they thought it would be difficult to choose a political question, because on such a question the King of Prussia might be against them, and that consequently they chose a religious question, on which they knew they should have the King with them; and that accordingly they led the Government on to a quarrel with the Court of Rome, and with the Catholic or Austrian party in Germany, more with a view to place Prussia in an independent national position than from any particular importance which they attached to the question itself upon which the rupture was to be effected.

21st March 1838.

Lord Melbourne presents his humble duty to your Majesty. The House sate until half-past eleven last night. Lord Stanhope6 made a long declamatory speech, very violent, but having in it nothing defined or specific, and was answered by Lord Brougham in a most able and triumphant defence and maintenance of the late Act for Amending the Laws for the Relief of the Poor.7

Lord Melbourne was very sorry to be prevented from waiting upon your Majesty. He is very grateful for your Majesty's enquiries, and feels very well this morning....

Lord Minto8 told Lord Melbourne last night to acquaint your Majesty that Lord Amelius Beauclerck,9 your Majesty's first Naval Aide-de-Camp, intended to ask an Audience to-day of your Majesty, and that the object of it was to request that he and the other Aides-de-Camp might wear sashes. This was always refused by the late King as being absurd and ridiculous—as it is, particularly considering Lord Amelius's figure—and your Majesty had perhaps better say that you can make no change.

Lord Melbourne will be at St James's twenty minutes before ten.

Footnote 6: Philip Henry, fourth Earl.

Footnote 7: Before 1834 a great source of public abuse was the out-door relief given to able-bodied paupers, either in kind or money. The Act of that year was based on the principle that no one must perish through the want of the bare necessities of life. Poor Law Commissioners were established, England was divided into Districts, and the Districts into Unions. Out-door relief was to be given, on the order of two justices, to poor persons wholly unable, from age or infirmity, to work. But there was much opposition to the new law; it was considered a grievance that old couples were refused relief at home, and that the sexes must be separated at the workhouse, to which the name of "Bastille" began to be attached. In Devonshire it was even believed that the bread distributed by the relieving officers was mixed with poisonous ingredients.

Footnote 8: The First Lord of the Admiralty.

Footnote 9: A son of the eighth Duke of St Albans.

PRESSURE OF BUSINESS

Buckingham Palace, 4th April 1838.

My dearest Uncle,—Vous ne m'en voudrez pas, I sincerely hope, for not having written to you sooner to thank you for your kind letter, which I received last week, but I really could not do so. As honesty is the best policy, I will tell you the simple fact. I have been out riding every day for about three hours, which quite renovates me, and when I come home I have consequently a good deal to do, what with seeing people, reading despatches, writing, etc. You will, I trust, now quite forgive your poor niece, whom you so often call "the little Queen," which is, I fear, true; but her feelings of affection are not so small as her body is, I can assure you.

The Prince de Ligne10 will be received with every possible attention, I can promise; it would have been so without his being recommended; his rank, and, above all, his being one of your subjects, would of course entitle him to a good reception from me....

There is another sujet which I wish to mention to you, et que j'ai bien à cœur, which is, if you would consult Stockmar with respect to the finishing of Albert's education; he knows best my feelings and wishes on that subject....

Footnote 10: He was appointed to attend the Coronation as Minister Extraordinary from King Leopold.

5th April 1838.

Lord Melbourne presents his humble duty to your Majesty, and is much distressed that, being in the House of Lords, he was unable to answer your Majesty's letter as soon as he received it. Lord Melbourne went to the Palace about half-past four, but learning from the porter at the gate that your Majesty was not returned, went away thinking that there was not left time to see your Majesty before the House of Lords. Lord Melbourne is very much concerned that your Majesty should have hastened at all, and most earnestly requests your Majesty never will do so upon his account. Lord Melbourne hears with great pleasure that your Majesty has had a pleasant ride, and likes your horse. Lord Melbourne is very well himself, and will wait upon your Majesty to-morrow morning about ten minutes before ten.

FAVOURITE HORSES

Buckingham Palace, 10th April 1838.

My dearest Uncle,—I received your kind letter of the 5th on Sunday, and return you my best thanks for it. I shall, before I say another word, answer your question about the horses which I ride, which I do the more willingly as I have got two darlings, if I may use that word. They are, both of them, quite perfect in every sense of the word; very handsome, full of spirit, delightful easy-goers, very quiet, and never shying at anything. Is not this perfection? The one called Tartar (which belonged to Lord Conyngham), an Irish horse, is a very dark brown, a beautiful creature; the other, which Lord Uxbridge11 got for me, is called Uxbridge; he is smaller than Tartar, and is a dark chestnut, with a beautiful little Arabian head. I am afraid I shall have bored you with this long account of my horses.

I am going to Windsor to-morrow afternoon, and have got a great deal to do in consequence....

Poor dear Louie12 lingers on, but, alas! I can only say lingers; she does not gain strength. I cannot say how it grieves me, I am so sincerely attached to the good old soul, who has known me ever since my birth. But I still entertain a hope that she may get over it.

We shall have a fortnight's respite from our Political Campaign. I trust we shall do as well as we have done when Parliament meets again. Believe me always, your devoted Niece,

Victoria R.

Footnote 11: Henry, Earl of Uxbridge, afterwards second Marquis of Anglesey (1797-1869).

Footnote 12: Louisa Louis was born at Erbach in 1771. The Queen erected a tablet to her memory in St Martin's-in-the-Fields, where she is described as "the faithful and devoted friend of Princess Charlotte of Wales, and from earliest infancy honoured by the affectionate attachment of Her Majesty Queen Victoria." See Reminiscences, ante, p.

PRINCE ALBERT'S EDUCATION

13th April 1838.

... Concerning the education of our friend Albert, it has been the best plan you could have fixed upon, to name Stockmar your commissary-general; it will give unité d'action et de l'ensemble, which otherwise we should not have had. I have communicated to him what your uncle and the young gentleman seem to wish, and what strikes me as the best for the moment. Stockmar will make a regular report to you on this subject. They will return to Bonn at the beginning of May, and remain till the end of August.... I agree with this, as nothing enlarges the mind so much as travelling. But Stockmar will best treat this affair verbally with you. The young gentlemen wished to pay me another visit at the beginning of May, prior to their return to Bonn. Nothing definite is, however, as yet settled about it. On one thing you can rely, that it is my great anxiety to see Albert a very good and distinguished young man, and no pains will be thought too much on my part if this end can be attained....

(Undated.)

Your Majesty will perceive by this box, which I received this morning but had not time to open, that Marshal Soult, Duke of Dalmatia,13 has been appointed Ambassador to the Coronation....

Footnote 13: Soult entered the French army in 1785, and became Marshal of France in 1804. After distinguishing himself at Austerlitz in 1805, he was made Duke of Dalmatia in 1807. Serving in the Peninsular War, he pursued Moore to Corunna, and became Commander-in-Chief in Spain in 1809. Subsequently he conducted the French retreat before Wellington in Southern France, 1813-14; was banished, but recalled and created a peer. He was Minister of War 1830-34.

OLD SERVANTS

Windsor Castle, 17th April 1838.

My dearest Uncle,—... You will by this time have learnt the sad loss we have all sustained in the death of dearest, faithful, excellent Louie, who breathed her last, without a struggle or a suffering, on Sunday night at nine o'clock. I don't think I have ever been so much overcome or distressed by anything, almost, as by the death of this my earliest friend; it is the first link that has been broken of my first and infantine affections. I always loved Louie, and shall cherish her memory as that of the purest and best of mortals as long as I live! I took leave of her before I left London on Wednesday, and never, never shall I forget the blessing she gave me, and the grasp she gave my hand! I was quite upset by it! And I feared and felt I should behold her on earth no more; it was, however, a beautiful lesson of calmness and contentment and resignation to the will of her God! Prepared as she was at every moment of her life to meet her heavenly Father, she was full of hope of recovery, and quite unconscious of her approaching end. You will, I am sure, dearest Uncle, feel the loss of this excellent creature; I cannot restrain my tears while writing this. One great consolation I have, which is, that I have been the means of making her last days as happy as she could wish to be, after having lost what she loved most!

... Poor Mason, our faithful coachman for so many years, is also dead. These old servants cannot be replaced; and to see those whom one has known from one's birth drop off, one by one, is melancholy! You will think this letter a very sad one, but I feel sad....

Marlborough House, 17th April 1838.

... I can well enter into all your feelings of regret at the death of one so truly attached and so faithful as dear old Louie had been to you from your infancy, and I quite understand your grief; yet I feel sure that you will also rejoice for her, that she has been relieved from her earthly sufferings. For her the change of existence was a happy one; good and pious as she was, we may trust that her state at present is one of felicity and bliss through the redeeming grace of our Saviour....

THE CORONATION

17th April 1838.

... The Parliamentary affairs will, please Heaven, continue to go on well; I am more than ever bound to wish it, as I am not anxious to exchange my clever and well-informed friend Palmerston, with Lord Aberdeen, for instance, of whose sweetness the Greek negotiation14 has given me very fair means of judging. Now I will conclude by touching on one subject which concerns your great goodness to us. When we left England you expressed a wish to see us at the time of the Coronation, which was then believed to take place at the end of May. More mature reflection has made me think that a King and Queen at your dear Coronation might perhaps be a hors-d'œuvre, and I think, if it meets with your approbation, that it may be better to pay you our respects at some other period, which you might like to fix upon. I do not deny that having been deprived by circumstances from the happiness of wishing you joy at your birthday, since 1831, in person, I feel strongly tempted to make a short apparition to see you, as seeing and speaking is much pleasanter than ink and paper....

Footnote 14: Referring to the offer of the throne of Greece to King Leopold in 1830.

Buckingham Palace, 25th April 1838.

My beloved Uncle,—... With respect to the happiness of seeing you and my dearest Aunt, I shall now respectfully state my feelings. It would have made me very happy to see you both at the Coronation, but I think upon the whole it is perhaps better you should not do so. Then, with respect to your coming for my old birthday, I must observe that I could not enjoy you or my Aunt at all à mon aise. First of all, I could not lodge you, and if one is not in the same house together, there is no real seeing one another; secondly, the town will be so full of all sorts of foreigners that I should have no peace to see you and Aunt quietly. If therefore, dearest Uncle, it suits you and Aunt Louise, would you come about the end of August, and stay with me as long as you can? I trust, dearest Uncle, que vous me comprendrez bien, and that you are assured of the great happiness it is for me to see you at any time.

Since I have written to you we have received from Lord Granville the news of Marshal Soult's appointment as Ambassador for the Coronation, and of the Duc de Nemours' intention of coming here as a spectator. You may be assured that I shall be delighted to see the Duke, as I always am any of the dear French family. With regard to Soult, I am sure you are aware that whoever the King chose to send would be equally well received by me and the Government.

THE TRAIN-BEARERS

Buckingham Palace, 5th May 1838.

The Queen sends the papers relating to the Coronation as Lord Melbourne wished. The Queen also transmits the names of the young ladies who she proposes should carry her train. If Lord Melbourne sees any objection to any of these she hopes he will say so.

The Queen has put down Lady Mary Talbot, as being the daughter of the oldest Earl in the Kingdom15 and a Roman Catholic; and Lady Anne Fitzwilliam, as she is anxious to show civility to Lord Fitzwilliam, who has been very kind to the Queen.

Perhaps, when the names are agreed to, Lord Melbourne would kindly undertake to speak or write to the parents of the young ladies proposing it to them.

* Lady Caroline Lennox.
* Lady Adelaide Paget.
* Lady Fanny Cowper.
* Lady Wilhelmina Stanhope.

* Lady Mary Talbot.

* Lady Anne Fitzwilliam.

* Lady Mary Grimston.

* Lady Louisa Jenkinson.

Footnote 15: John, sixteenth Earl of Shrewsbury (1791-1852).

17th May 1838.

Lord Melbourne presents his humble duty to your Majesty, and thinks that your Majesty had better direct Lord Conyngham to ask the Archbishop, before the Audience, who has generally been there and how it ought to be conducted.

Your Majesty had better read the Answer and not give it to the Archbishop, as Lord Melbourne apprehends the Archbishop does not give your Majesty the Address.

Your Majesty had better say something kind to each of the Bishops as they are presented. They are presented to your Majesty in this manner as a sort of privilege, instead of being presented at the Drawing-Room with others, and your Majesty should conduct yourself towards them exactly as if they had been presented in the usual circle. The time is about half-past one, and your Majesty had better be punctual so as not to delay the Drawing-Room.

THE SLAVE TRADE

In the same letter is enclosed a draft of a letter which it was suggested by Lord Melbourne that the Queen should write to the King of Portugal, with regard to the suppression of the Slave Trade.

That you hope that the King and Queen of Portugal will not consider the strong representations made by your Government on the subject of the Slave Trade as arising from any desire to embarrass them. That there is every disposition to make allowance for the difficulties of Portugal, but allowance must also be made for the feelings of the people of England; that those feelings on the Slave Trade are as strong as they are just. That England has made great sacrifices for the suppression of that crime, that she has made sacrifices to Portugal, and that she has been extremely indignant at finding that traffic so obstinately continued to be sheltered and protected under the flag of Portugal. That Portugal must not expect that England will much longer refrain from taking effectual measures for preventing these practices. That you have spoken thus openly because you wish them to be aware of the truth, and that you entreat both the Queen and the King to use their power and influence in procuring such a treaty to be concluded without delay, as will satisfy England and exonerate Portugal from the reproach under which she now labours.

This is the substance of what might be written. It is perhaps a little harshly worded, but your Majesty may soften it.

Buckingham Palace, 25th May 1838.

My dearest Uncle,—I am most thankful for your very kind letter, and for the beautiful little sword, which delights me.

I have been dancing till past four o'clock this morning; we have had a charming ball, and I have spent the happiest birthday that I have had for many years; oh, how different to last year! Everybody was so kind and so friendly to me.

We have got a number of Austrians and Milanese here, among whom are a Prince Odescalchi, and a Count Eugène Zichy, renowned for his magnificent turquoises and his famous valzing, a good-natured élégant; we have also Esterhazy's daughter Marie—now Countess Chorinsky—a Count and Countess Grippa, and a Marquis and Marchioness of Trivalzi, etc.

Old Talleyrand16 is at last dead. I hear he showed wonderful composure and firmness to the last. He was one of those people who I thought never would die. Did you know what Pozzo said to somebody here about him? He said he (Talleyrand) would not die yet, "parce que le Diable ne voulait pas l'avoir."

Footnote 16: Died 17th May, aged eighty-four.

INDEPENDENCE OF BELGIUM

Laeken, 2nd June 1838.

... I have not all this time touched on our affairs, from motives of great discretion, but as the battle draws nigh,17 I cannot very well help writing a few words on the subject. I found an Article in the French Constitutionnel which paints our position in pretty true colours. As it is not very long, I beg you to have the goodness to read it. You have given me so many proofs of affection, and your kind speech at Windsor is so fresh in my memory, that it would be very wrong in me to think that in so short a time, and without any cause, those feelings which are so precious to me could have changed. This makes me appeal to those sentiments.

The independent existence of the Provinces which form this Kingdom has always been an object of importance to England; the surest proof of it is, that for centuries England has made the greatest sacrifices of blood and treasure for that object. The last time I saw the late King at Windsor, in 1836, he said to me: "If ever France or any other Power invades your country, it will be a question of immediate war for England; we cannot suffer that." I answered him I was happy to hear him speak so, as I also did not want any foreign Power to invade us....

All I want from your kind Majesty is, that you will occasionally express to your Ministers, and particularly to good Lord Melbourne, that, as far as it is compatible with the interests of your own dominions, you do not wish that your Government should take the lead in such measures as might in a short time bring on the destruction of this country, as well as that of your uncle and his family.

Europe has enjoyed ever since 1833, in our part of it, a state of profound peace and real happiness and prosperity. None can deny that the measures which I adopted to organise this country have greatly contributed to this happy state of affairs; this makes me think that the changes which are to take place should be brought about in a very gentle manner....

I am sorry to have you to listen to so much about politics, but it is not my fault; I wished nothing so much as to be left alone. I shall do all I can to bring about a good conclusion, but it must not be forgotten that these seven years all the dangers, all the trouble, fell constantly to my share....

Now I will make haste to conclude, and remain ever, my dearest Victoria, your truly devoted Uncle,

Leopold R.

Footnote 17: The execution of the treaty of 1831, called the Twenty-four Articles, assigning part of Luxemburg to Holland, had been reluctantly agreed to by Leopold, but the King of Holland withheld his assent for seven years.

ANGLO-BELGIAN RELATIONS

Buckingham Palace, 10th June 1838.

My dearest Uncle,—It is indeed a long while since I have written to you, and I fear you will think me very lazy; but I must in turn say, dearest Uncle, that your silence was longer than mine, and that it grieved me, and m'a beaucoup peinée. I know, however, you have had, and still have, much to do. Many thanks, my dear Uncle, for your very kind letter of the 2nd inst....

It would indeed, dearest Uncle, be very wrong of you, if you thought my feelings of warm and devoted attachment to you, and of great affection for you, could be changed. Nothing can ever change them! Independent of my feelings of affection for you, my beloved Uncle, you must be aware that the ancient and hereditary policy of this country with respect to Belgium must make me most anxious that my Government not only should not be parties to any measure that would be prejudicial to Belgium, but that my Ministers should, as far as may not conflict with the interests or engagements of this country, do everything in their power to promote the prosperity and welfare of your Kingdom.

My Ministers, I can assure you, share all my feelings on this subject, and are most anxious to see everything settled in a satisfactory manner between Belgium and Holland.

PROGRESS OF BELGIUM

We all feel that we cannot sufficiently or adequately express how much Belgium owes to your wise system of government, which has rendered that country so flourishing in every way, and how much all Europe is indebted to you for the preservation of general peace; because it is certain that when you ascended the throne of Belgium that country was the one from which the occasion of a general war was much to be feared; whereas now it is become a link to secure the continuance of peace; and by the happy circumstances of your double near relationship to me and to the King of the French, Belgium—which was in former times the cause of discord between England and France—becomes now a mutual tie to keep them together.

This, my beloved Uncle, we owe to you, and it must be a source of pride and gratification to you.

I perfectly understand and feel that your position with respect to all these affairs is very difficult and trying, and the feelings of your subjects are far from unnatural; yet I sincerely hope that you will use the great influence you possess over the minds of the leading men in Belgium, to mitigate discontent and calm irritation, and procure acquiescence in whatever arrangements may ultimately be found inevitable.

You are right in saying that I, though but a child of twelve years old when you went to Belgium, remember much of what took place, and I have since then had the whole matter fully explained to me. The Treaty of November 1831 was perhaps not so advantageous to the Belgians as could have been wished, yet it cannot have been thought very advantageous to the Dutch, else they would have most probably urged their Government before this time to accept it; besides, when these conditions were framed, England was only one out of five Powers whose concurrence was required, and consequently they were made under very difficult circumstances. This treaty having been ratified, it is become binding, and therefore it is almost impossible to consider it as otherwise, and to set aside those parts of it which have been ratified by all the parties.

I feel I must in turn, dearest Uncle, entreat your indulgence for so long a letter, and for such full explanations, but I felt it my duty to do so, as you had spoken to me on the subject.

You may be assured, my beloved Uncle, that both Lord Melbourne and Lord Palmerston are most anxious at all times for the prosperity and welfare of Belgium, and are consequently most desirous of seeing this difficult question brought to a conclusion which may be satisfactory to you. Allow me once more therefore, dearest Uncle, to beseech you to use your powerful influence over your subjects, and to strive to moderate their excited feelings on these matters. Your situation is a very difficult one, and nobody feels more for you than I do.

I trust, dearest Uncle, that you will, at all times, believe me your devoted and most affectionate Niece,

Victoria R.

FOREIGN POLICY

Laeken, June 18 1838.

My dearest and most beloved Victoria,—You have written me a very dear and long letter, which has given me great pleasure and satisfaction. I was much moved with the expressions of truly felt affection, which it contains, and I shall never again doubt your affection for me, but rely on your dear heart and the constancy of your character.

I will now tell you honestly that I had some misgivings; I did not exactly think that you had quite forgotten me, but I thought I had been put aside as one does with a piece of furniture which is no longer wanted. I did not complain, because I fear if affection is once on the decline, reproaches only diminish it the faster. I therefore said nothing, but in a life full of grief and disappointments like mine, the loss of your affection would have been one of the most severe. It was in this point of view that the declaration made by Lord Palmerston at the beginning of May to the Prussian Government chagrined me much.19 It was premature, because the negotiation was not yet renewed. It looked as if the English Government had been anxious to say to the Northern Powers, who always steadfastly protected Holland, "You imagine, perhaps, that we mean to have égards for the uncle of the Queen; there you see we shall make even shorter work with him now than we did under our late master."

This impression had been general on the Continent; they considered the declaration to Prussia in this way: "La Reine et ses Ministres sont donc entièrement indifférents sur le compte du Roi L.; cela change entièrement la position, et nous allons faire mains basses sur lui." From that moment their language became extremely imperious; they spoke of nothing but acts of coercion, bombardment, etc., etc. I firmly believe, because I have been these many years on terms of great and sincere friendship with Palmerston, that he did not himself quite foresee the importance which would be attached to his declaration. I must say it hurt me more in my English capacity than in my Belgian, as I came to this country from England, and was chosen for that very reason. Besides, I am happy to say, I was never as yet in the position to ask for any act of kindness from you, so that whatever little service I may have rendered you, remained on a basis of perfect disinterestedness. That the first diplomatic step in our affairs should seem by your Government to be directed against me, created therefore all over the Continent a considerable sensation. I shall never ask any favours of you, or anything that could in the least be considered as incompatible with the interests of England; but you will comprehend that there is a great difference in claiming favours and in being treated as an enemy....

I will conclude my overgrown letter with the assurance that you never were in greater favour, and that I love you dearly. Believe me, therefore, ever, my best beloved Victoria, your devoted Uncle,

Leopold R.

Footnote 18: The day of the month is not given.

Footnote 19: Prussia was giving unmistakable evidence of a disposition to support Holland against Belgium.

THE CORONATION

Marlboro' House, 28th June 1838.

(At a quarter before 12 o'clock on the Coronation Day.)

My dearest Niece,—The guns are just announcing your approach to the Abbey, and as I am not near you, and cannot take part in the sacred ceremony of your Coronation, I must address you in writing to assure you that my thoughts and my whole heart are with you, and my prayers are offered up to Heaven for your happiness, and the prosperity and glory of your reign. May our Heavenly Father bless and preserve you, and His Holy Ghost dwell within you to give you that peace which the world cannot give! Accept of these my best wishes, and the blessing of your most devoted and attached Aunt,

Adelaide.

I was awoke at four o'clock by the guns in the Park, and could not get much sleep afterwards on account of the noise of the people, bands, etc., etc. Got up at seven, feeling strong and well; the Park presented a curious spectacle, crowds of people up to Constitution Hill, soldiers, bands, etc. I dressed, having taken a little breakfast before I dressed, and a little after. At half-past 9 I went into the next room, dressed exactly in my House of Lords costume; and met Uncle Ernest, Charles,20 and Feodore (who had come a few minutes before into my dressing-room), Lady Lansdowne, Lady Normanby, the Duchess of Sutherland, and Lady Barham, all in their robes.

Footnote 20: Prince Charles of Leiningen, the Queen's half-brother.

THE ABBEY

At 10 I got into the State Coach with the Duchess of Sutherland and Lord Albemarle and we began our Progress. I subjoin a minute account of the whole Procession and of the whole Proceeding,—the route, etc. It was a fine day, and the crowds of people exceeded what I have ever seen; many as there were the day I went to the City, it was nothing, nothing to the multitudes, the millions of my loyal subjects, who were assembled in every spot to witness the

Procession. Their good humour and excessive loyalty was beyond everything, and I really cannot say how proud I feel to be the Queen of such a Nation. I was alarmed at times for fear that the people would be crushed and squeezed on account of the tremendous rush and pressure.

I reached the Abbey amid deafening cheers at a little after half-past eleven; I first went into a robing-room quite close to the entrance where I found my eight train-bearers: Lady Caroline Lennox, Lady Adelaide Paget, Lady Mary Talbot, Lady Fanny Cowper, Lady Wilhelmina Stanhope, Lady Anne Fitzwilliam, Lady Mary Grimston, and Lady Louisa Jenkinson—all dressed alike and beautifully in white satin and silver tissue with wreaths of silver corn-ears in front, and a small one of pink roses round the plait behind, and pink roses in the trimming of the dresses.

After putting on my mantle, and the young ladies having properly got hold of it and Lord Conyngham holding the end of it, I left the robing-room and the Procession began as is described in the annexed account, and all that followed and took place. The sight was splendid; the bank of Peeresses quite beautiful all in their robes, and the Peers on the other side. My young train-bearers were always near me, and helped me whenever I wanted anything. The Bishop of Durham21 stood on the side near me, but he was, as Lord Melbourne told me, remarkably maladroit, and never could tell me what was to take place. At the beginning of the Anthem, where I've made a mark, I retired to St Edward's Chapel, a dark small place immediately behind the Altar, with my ladies and train-bearers—took off my crimson robe and kirtle, and put on the supertunica of cloth of gold, also in the shape of a kirtle, which was put over a singular sort of little gown of linen trimmed with lace; I also took off my circlet of diamonds and then proceeded bareheaded into the Abbey; I was then seated upon St Edward's chair, where the Dalmatic robe was clasped round me by the Lord Great Chamberlain. Then followed all the various things; and last (of those things) the Crown being placed on my head—which was, I must own, a most beautiful impressive moment; all the Peers and Peeresses put on their coronets at the same instant.

Footnote 21: Edward Maltby, 1770-1859.

My excellent Lord Melbourne, who stood very close to me throughout the whole ceremony, was completely overcome at this moment, and very much affected; he gave me such a kind, and I may say fatherly look. The shouts, which were very great, the drums, the trumpets, the firing of the guns, all at the same instant, rendered the spectacle most imposing.

HOMAGE

The Enthronisation and the Homage of, first, all the Bishops, and then my Uncles, and lastly of all the Peers, in their respective order was very fine. The Duke of Norfolk (holding for me the Sceptre with a Cross) with Lord Melbourne stood close to me on my right, and the Duke of Richmond with the other Sceptre on my left, etc., etc. All my train-bearers, etc., standing behind the Throne. Poor old Lord Rolle, who is 82, and dreadfully infirm, in attempting to ascend the steps fell and rolled quite down, but was not the least hurt; when he attempted to re-ascend them I got up and advanced to the end of the steps, in order to prevent another fall. When Lord Melbourne's turn to do Homage came, there was loud cheering; they also cheered Lord Grey and the Duke of Wellington; it's a pretty ceremony; they first all touch the Crown, and then kiss my hand. When my good Lord Melbourne knelt down and kissed my hand, he pressed my hand and I grasped his with all my heart, at which he looked up with his eyes filled with tears and seemed much touched, as he was, I observed, throughout the whole ceremony. After the Homage was concluded I left the Throne, took off my Crown and received the Sacrament; I then put on my Crown again, and re-ascended the Throne, leaning on Lord Melbourne's arm. At the commencement of the Anthem I descended from the Throne, and went into St Edward's Chapel with my Ladies, Train-bearers, and Lord Willoughby, where I took off the Dalmatic robe, supertunica, etc., and put on the Purple Velvet Kirtle and Mantle, and proceeded again to the Throne, which I ascended leaning on Lord Melbourne's hand.

There was another most dear Being present at this ceremony, in the box immediately above the royal box, and who witnessed all; it was my dearly beloved angelic Lehzen, whose eyes I caught when on the Throne, and we exchanged smiles. She and Späth, Lady John Russell, and Mr. Murray saw me leave the Palace, arrive at the Abbey, leave the Abbey and again return to the Palace!!

POPULAR ENTHUSIASM

I then again descended from the Throne, and repaired with all the Peers bearing the Regalia, my Ladies and Trainbearers, to St Edward's Chapel, as it is called; but which, as Lord Melbourne said, was more unlike a Chapel than anything he had ever seen; for what was called an Altar was covered with sandwiches, bottles of wine, etc., etc. The Archbishop came in and ought to have delivered the Orb to me, but I had already got it, and he (as usual) was so confused and puzzled and knew nothing, and—went away. Here we waited some minutes. Lord Melbourne took a glass of wine, for he seemed completely tired. The Procession being formed, I replaced my Crown (which I had taken off for a few minutes), took the Orb in my left hand and the Sceptre in my right, and thus loaded, proceeded through the Abbey—which resounded with cheers, to the first robing-room; where I found the Duchess of Gloucester, Mamma, and the Duchess of Cambridge with their Ladies. And here we waited for at least an hour, with all my ladies and train-bearers; the Princesses went away about half an hour before I did. The Archbishop had (most awkwardly) put the ring on the wrong finger, and the consequence was that I had the greatest difficulty to take it off again, which I at last did with great pain. Lady Fanny, Lady Wilhelmina, and Lady Mary Grimston looked quite beautiful. At about half-past four I re-entered my carriage, the Crown on my head, and the Sceptre and Orb in my hands, and we proceeded the same way as we came—the crowds if possible having increased. The enthusiasm, affection, and loyalty were really touching, and I shall ever remember this day as the Proudest of my life! I came home at a little after six, really not feeling tired.

INCIDENTS OF THE CORONATION

At eight we dined. Besides we thirteen—my Uncles, sister, brother, Späth, and the Duke's gentlemen—my excellent Lord Melbourne and Lord Surrey dined here. Lord Melbourne came up to me and said: "I must congratulate you on this most brilliant day," and that all had gone off so well. He said he was not tired, and was in high spirits. I sat between Uncle Ernest22 and Lord

Melbourne; and Lord Melbourne between me and Feodore, whom he had led in. My kind Lord Melbourne was much affected in speaking of the whole ceremony. He asked kindly if I was tired; said the Sword he carried (the first, the Sword of State) was excessively heavy. I said that the Crown hurt me a good deal. He was so much amused at Uncle Ernest's being astonished at our still having the Litany. We agreed that the whole thing was a very fine sight. He thought the robes, and particularly the Dalmatic, "looked remarkably well." "And you did it all so well—excellent!" said he, with tears in his eyes. He said he thought I looked rather pale and "moved by all the people" when I arrived; "and that's natural; and that's better." The Archbishop's and Dean's copes, which were remarkably handsome, were from James the Second's time; the very same that were worn at his Coronation, Lord Melbourne told me. Spoke of the Bishop of Durham's awkwardness, Lord Rolle's fall, etc. Of the Duc de Nemours being like his father in face; of the young ladies' (train-bearers') dresses; which he thought beautiful; and he said he thought the Duchess of Richmond (who had ordered the make of the dresses, etc., and had been much condemned by some of the young ladies for it) quite right. She said to him: "One thing I was determined about; that I would have no discussion with their Mammas about it." Spoke of Talleyrand and Soult having been very much struck by the ceremony of the Coronation; of the English being far too generous not to be kind to Soult. Lord Melbourne went home the night before, and slept very deeply till he was woke at six in the morning. I said I did not sleep well. Spoke of the Illuminations and Uncle Ernest's wish to see them.

Footnote 22: The King of Hanover.

After dinner, before we sat down, we (that is Charles, Lord Melbourne, and I) spoke of the numbers of Peers at the Coronation, which, Lord Melbourne said, with the tears in his eyes, was unprecedented. I observed that there were very few Viscounts; he said: "There are very few Viscounts," that they were an odd sort of title and not really English; that they came from Vice-Comités; that Dukes and Barons were the only real English titles; that Marquises were likewise not English; and that they made people Marquises when they did not wish to make them Dukes. Spoke of Lord Audley who came as the First Baron, and who Lord Melbourne said was a very odd young man, but of a very old family; his ancestor was a Sir Something Audley in the time of the Black Prince, who, with Chandos, gained the Battle of Poictiers.

I then sat on the sofa for a little while with Lady Barham and then with Charles; Lord Melbourne sitting near me the whole evening. Mamma and Feodore remained to see the illuminations and only came in later, and Mamma went away before I did. Uncle Ernest drove out to see the Illuminations.

PAGES OF HONOUR

I said to Lord Melbourne when I first sat down that I felt a little tired on my feet; "You must be very tired," he said. Spoke of the weight of the Robes, etc., etc., the Coronets; and he turned round to me with the tears in his eyes, and said so kindly: "And you did it beautifully—every part of it, with so much taste; it's a thing that you can't give a person advice upon; it must be left to a person." To hear this, from this kind impartial friend, gave me great and real pleasure. Mamma and Feodore came back just after he said this. Spoke of the Bishops' Copes, about which he was very funny; of the Pages who were such a nice set of boys, and who were so handy, Lord Melbourne said, that they kept them the whole time. Little Lord Stafford and Slane (Lord Mountcharles) were pages to their fathers and looked lovely; Lord Paget (not a fine boy) was Lord Melbourne's page and remarkably handy, he said. Spoke again of the young ladies' dresses, about which he was very amusing; he waited for his carriage with Lady Mary Talbot and Lady Wilhelmina; he thinks Lady Fanny does not make as much show as other girls, which I would not allow. He set off for the Abbey from his house at half-past eight, and was there long before anybody else; he only got home at half-past six and had to go round by Kensington. He said there was a large breakfast in the Jerusalem Chamber where they met before all began; he said, laughing, that whenever the Clergy, or a Dean and Chapter, had anything to do with anything, there's sure to be plen'y to eat.

Spoke of my intending to go to bed, etc.; he said, "You may depend upon it, you are more tired than you think you are." I said I had slept badly the night before; he said that was my mind, that nothing kept people more awake than any consciousness of a great event going to take place, and being agitated. He was not sure if he was not going to the Duke of Wellington's.

Stayed in the dining room till twenty minutes past eleven, but remained on Mamma's balcony looking at the fireworks in Green Park, which were quite beautiful.

Uncle Ernest, Charles, Feodore, and the Ladies and Gentlemen (like Lehzen, etc.) saw me leave the Palace, arrive at the Abbey, leave the Abbey, and return to the Palace. Got a long letter from Aunt Louise.

EXTRA HOLIDAYS FOR SCHOOLS

Buckingham Palace, 29th June 1838.

The Queen is very anxious to hear if Lord Melbourne got home safe, and if he is not tired, and quite well this morning.

Lord Melbourne will be glad to hear that the Queen had an excellent night, is not the least tired, and is perfectly well this morning; indeed she feels much better than she has done for some days.

The Queen hears that it is usual to ask for an additional week's holiday for the boys at the various Public Schools, on the occasion of the Coronation. Perhaps Lord Melbourne will enquire about this, in order that there may be no neglect on my part.

Buckingham Palace, 2nd July 1838.

My dearest Uncle,—Many thanks for two kind letters, one which I got last Monday and one this morning. The kind interest you take in me and my country (of which, and of the nation, I'm more proud than I ever was, since I've witnessed their excessive affection and loyalty to me) makes me certain that you will be glad to hear how beautifully everything went off. It was a memorable and glorious day for me. The millions assembled to witness the progress to and from the Abbey was beyond belief, and all in the highest good-humour. It is a fine ceremony, and a scene I shall ever remember, and with pleasure. I likewise venture to add that people thought I did my part very well.

The amiable Duc de Nemours dined with me on Friday, comes to my ball to-night, and dines again with me on Wednesday. Pray tell dearest Aunt Louise that I thank her much for her very kind letter, and will avail myself of her kindness and not write to her this mail.

Feodore is writing in my room, well and happy. Uncle Ernest still very lame, and Charles well. There's an account of the family. Ever and ever your most devoted Niece,

Victoria R.

8th July 1838.

Lord Melbourne presents his humble duty to your Majesty. As your Majesty does not ride, the question is between driving down the line or not going down it at all,23 and it appears to Lord Melbourne that the first is the best, namely, to drive down; but if your Majesty feels a strong repugnance, there is no more to be said.

Lord Melbourne thinks it safer and more prudent that your Majesty should not ride; but still it might have been done, and if Lord Melbourne had thought that your Majesty wished it much, he would not have dissuaded it.

Footnote 23: Referring to the Hyde Park review on the next day.

LOYAL DEMONSTRATIONS

Neuilly, 12th July 1838.

My dearest Victoria,—I am very grateful for your kind letter; it is extremely meritorious, amidst such fatigues and festivities and occupations of every kind, to find a moment to write. I expressed already the great satisfaction with which I read and heard all the accounts of the Coronation, and I believe that there never was anything like it. The only one which in point of loyal demonstration may approach it is that of George III., but I think it fell short of yours.

I am happy to see that it has increased, if possible, your affection and attachment to your country, and this is in every respect a great blessing. You will remember that I have never varied on that subject, the great thing is to be the National Sovereign of your own country, and to love its very faults. This strengthens the mutual attachment, and that can never be too strong....

Believe me, ever, my dearest Victoria, your very devoted Uncle,

Leopold R.

The whole of the family here offer their best hommages.

Neuilly, 20th July 1838.

I feel most grateful for your dear kind letter of the 10th inst., which I received a few days ago. I hear that the review was something most splendid, and I feel always some regret at having been deprived of the happiness of seeing you en fonction, which you do in a degree of rare perfection. May the remembrance of all this long remain in your mind, to cheer and strengthen you when occasionally there will be a darker sky....

LORD DURHAM

10th August 1838.

Lord Melbourne presents his humble duty to your Majesty. The very difficult and embarrassing situation in which Lord Durham and the Canadas and the Ministry are left by the vote of the House of Lords of last night, requires that a Cabinet should be held to-day, and Lord Melbourne has directed one to be summoned at two. Lord Melbourne will wait upon your Majesty either before that hour or after, about four o'clock. The vote of last night and the Bill of Lord Brougham24 is a direct censure upon Lord Durham. Lord Durham's conduct has been most rash and indiscreet, and, as far as we can see, unaccountable. But to censure him now would either be to cause his resignation, which would produce great embarrassment, and might produce great evil, or to weaken his authority, which is evidently most undesirable....

Footnote 24: This Bill (which emphasised the illegality of Lord Durham's ordinance) was read a second time by 54 to 36. On the following day Lord Melbourne announced to the Peers that Ministers had resolved to advise that the ordinance should be disallowed.

10th August 1838.

Lord Melbourne presents his humble duty to your Majesty, and begs to inform you that the Cabinet have determined to advise your Majesty to disallow Lord Durham's ordinance, and to announce the same to the House of Lords.25

This is absolutely necessary, but very disagreeable, and will be very much so to Lord Durham.

Footnote 25: See Introductory Note for the year, ante, p.

25th September 1838.

My most beloved Victoria,—I can never thank you enough for the dear letter which I found on my table on arriving here, Sunday evening. It was most kind of you to have written so soon after our departure, and such an affectionate, good, kind letter. The tears came to my eyes as I read it, and I felt quite moved. Short as has been our stay, and great, as always, the pain of leaving you, it has been a great happiness for me to see you again, a happiness for which I shall always thank God, you, and your dear Uncle. I need not add how very precious is your affection to me, and how very grateful I am for every new proof of it. You know my feelings on this point, and you know they are better felt than expressed. Your calling me Louise, and in such a kind way, gave me great pleasure. Almost all those dear to me call me so, and I think it looks more affectionate; I would fain say now sister-like, although I am rather an old sister for you now....

Leopold is half crazy with the steam-engine, and particularly with the tools which you sent him. I enclose here the expression of his gratitude. I wrote exactly what he told me to write, and I did not add a word. He has found again his kie (key), and he wears it suspended to his neck by a blue riband, with the Duchess's little seal. He felt deeply the attention you had to have an L engraved on each tool, and after his letter was closed he charged me to thank you for it, and to tell you that it gave him great pleasure. An iron spade was the greatest object of his ambition, and he worked so hard yesterday with it, that I feared he would hurt himself with the exertion. He will go to-day to the races with us, in the Scotch dress which the Duchess had the kindness to send him. It fits very well, and he is very proud of having a coat shaped like that of a man....

IRELAND AND O'CONNELL

25th October 1838.

Lord Melbourne presents his humble duty to your Majesty....

Mr Stanley of the Treasury26 arrived in London yesterday, and acquaints me that Lord Normanby makes no secret of his willingness, and indeed his desire, to undertake the government of Canada. It would have been better if Lord Normanby had acquainted Lord

Melbourne quietly of this, and not made it at once public to all the world. It is not necessary to do anything at present. If Lord Durham remains, which Lord Melbourne does not, however, think likely, there will be no successor to be appointed, and if he returns, the authority of Governor of Lower Canada will devolve upon Sir John Colborne,27 in whose hands it may be very safely left for the present.

If Ireland should be vacant, there is a strong feeling amongst many that it would be nice to name the Duke of Sussex. It is said that it would be popular in Ireland, that the name of one of the Royal Family would do good there, and that it would afford to O'Connell a pretext and opportunity for giving up his new scheme of agitation. It is also added that the Duke would suffer himself to be guided on all essential matters by the advice of his Chief Secretary, and that he would content himself with discharging the ceremonial duties. Here are the reasons for it— your Majesty is so well acquainted with the reasons on the other side, that it is unnecessary for me to detail them.

I am afraid that times of some trouble are approaching, for which your Majesty must hold yourself prepared; but your Majesty is too well acquainted with the nature of human affairs not to be well aware that they cannot very well go on even as quietly as they have gone on during the last sixteen months.

Footnote 26: "Ben" Stanley, afterwards Lord Stanley of Alderley, Secretary to the Treasury.

Footnote 27: Field-Marshal Sir John Colborne, afterwards Lord Seaton, had been Military Secretary to Sir John Moore, had commanded a brigade with much distinction in the Peninsula, and had contributed greatly to the success of the British arms at Waterloo.

4th November 1838.

Lord Melbourne is very well, but Sir James Clark,28 a Scotchman and a physician, and therefore neither by country nor by profession very religious, detained him from Church in order to go through the report upon the state of Buckingham Palace. This is not a very good excuse, but it is the true one. Lord Melbourne is very grateful to your Majesty for your enquiries, and having some letters to submit, will be happy to attend upon your Majesty.

Footnote 28: Physician-in-Ordinary to the Queen.

DEATH OF LADY JOHN RUSSELL

Windsor Castle, 6th November 1838.

My dear Uncle,—.... We have all been much distressed by the melancholy and untimely death of poor Lady John Russell,29 which took place on the 1st. She was safely confined on the 20th of October with a little girl, who bears my name, and seemed to be going on very well; but on Wednesday she began to sink from weakness, not disease, and died at three o'clock on Thursday. It is a dreadful blow to him, for he was so attached to her, and I don't believe two people ever were happier together. I send you his pretty letter to me, which I think you may be interested to see; he is dreadfully beat down by it, but struggles manfully against his grief, which makes one pity him more. She has left four children by her first husband, now orphans, the eldest a sweet girl twelve years old, and two little girls by Lord John; the eldest of these two is two and a half, and the youngest a fortnight. I had known her very well and liked her, and I assure you I was dreadfully shocked at it. You may also imagine what a loss she is to poor Miss Lister, who has no mother, and whose only sister she was. I fear, dear Uncle, I have made a sad and melancholy letter of this, but I have been so much engrossed by all this misery, and knowing you take an interest in poor Lord John, that I let my pen run on almost involuntarily.

We have very good accounts of the Queen-Dowager from Gibraltar.

Please return me Lord John's letter when you have done with it.

Lord and Lady Howard30 have been here, and I urged him to bear Dietz as an inevitable evil, and I think he seems very anxious to do what is right. I have likewise written to Ferdinand, urging him and Dietz to be reasonable.

Will you tell Aunt Louise that she will receive a box containing the Limerick lace dress (just like mine), which I lay at her feet. I fear, dear Uncle, you will think I'm making you my commissioner de toilette, as in these two letters I have plagued you with commissions on that subject....

Footnote 29: Daughter of Mr Thomas Lister. She had been widow of the second Lord Ribblesdale, and married Lord John Russell in April 1835.

Footnote 30: Charles Augustus, sixth Lord Howard de Walden, was the British Minister at Lisbon, and afterwards (1846-1868) at Brussels.

Laeken, 9th November 1838.

My dearest Victoria,—Your kind and interesting letter of the 6th reached me yesterday morning. I hail in you those simple and unaffected feelings which it contains. May you always preserve that great warmth and truth of character which you now possess, and rest assured that it will be an ornament to you, and the means of finding the same truth and warmth of feeling in others. Those who serve, from whatever motive it may be, have always their eyes wide open on their superiors, and no qualities impose so much on them the necessity of respect, which they gladly avoid, than a warm and noble character that knows how to feel for others, and how to sympathise with their sorrows. I pity Lord John from all my heart, having always had for him sentiments of the sincerest regard. I fear that as a political man it may prove also a severe blow. All depends on how he takes it, if he will wish to forget his grief by occupying himself with political strife or if his greater sensibility will make him wish to indulge it in solitude....

LORD JOHN RUSSELL

Windsor Castle, 12th November 1838.

My dearest Uncle,—I was certain you would take interest in and feel for poor Lord John; he is, I hear, still dreadfully shaken, and quite unequal to do any business at present. His chief consolation is in attending to the children.

I felt much for you, and still more for poor dear Aunt Louise, when the sad separation from poor Marie31 took place; it is so melancholy to see a dear relation depart who is so ill.

I have this morning heard from Ferdinand that the good Queen is at last confined, after keeping us for two months and more dans l'attente of the event. It took place on the 3rd, and Ferdinand writes such a funny letter, saying, "nous sommes tous bien heureux surtout moi qui craignais que ce ne fût une petite fille ce qui m'eût été un peu désagréable, car en fait d'enfants j'aime mieux les

petits garçons, parce qu'ils sont plus gais et plus tapageurs."32 Isn't this very good?
I believe the King of the French is to be godfather....

Footnote 31: See post, p. .

Footnote 32: The Prince received the title of Duke of Oporto.

20th November 1838.

Lord Melbourne presents his humble duty to your Majesty, and transmits a copy of Mr. Macaulay's letter.33...

Lord Melbourne fears, from what he hears of the language of Lord Howick and Mr. Monson, that much difficulty will be found in making arrangements and deciding upon questions. But Lord Melbourne will use every effort in his power in order to keep the Administration together and to carry on the public service. Lord Melbourne hears with concern from Mr Fox Maule that Lord John Russell does not return to business as readily as Mr Maule had hoped that he would, and Lord Melbourne fears that he will not do whilst he remains at Cassiobury with the children. Solitude and retirement cherish and encourage grief. Employment and exertion are the only means of dissipating it.

Footnote 33: Declining to join the Government. The original is not preserved among the Queen's papers.

CANADA AND LORD DURHAM

22nd November 1838.

Lord Melbourne presents his humble duty to your Majesty, and begs to acknowledge your Majesty's gracious communication received yesterday. Lord Melbourne had nothing particular to lay before your Majesty, but still regrets that he did not write, as your Majesty might have wished to hear from him.

Lord Melbourne returns the King of Portugal's34 letter, which, as your Majesty observes, is very rough and ill-tempered with reference to Lord Howard.35 Lord Melbourne read it with much concern, as it shows so much dislike and alienation, as renders it very improbable that they should ever go on together well and in a friendly spirit. Lord Melbourne fears that the epithets applied to Lord Howard, though very severe and full of resentment, are not entirely ill-chosen and inappropriate.

All the Ministers, except Lord Duncannon36 and Lord John Russell, dined here yesterday, and they all appeared to be in very good-humour and disposed to co-operate in order to meet the difficulties by which we are surrounded....

With respect to Canada, Lord Melbourne feels that it may be considered somewhat presumptuous in him to undervalue danger, which is considered by those upon the spot to be so great and so imminent, but still he cannot feel the alarm which seems to be felt there. Lord Durham, Lord Melbourne is convinced, exaggerates the peril in order to give greater éclat to his own departure. The worst symptom which Lord Melbourne perceives is the general fear which seems to prevail there, and which makes every danger ten times as great as it really is.

Footnote 34: The birth of an heir on 16th September 1837 conferred on Prince Ferdinand the right to the title of King.

Footnote 35: See ante, p.

Footnote 36: Lord Duncannon (1781-1847), at this time Lord Privy Seal and First Commissioner of Woods and Forests, was afterwards (as Earl of Bessborough) Lord-Lieutenant of Ireland. He must not be confused with the Lord Dungannon who sat in the House of Commons as Mr Hill-Trevor from 1830-1841, and, as Viscount Dungannon, was elected in 1843, but immediately unseated on petition.

BELGIUM AND ENGLAND

Laeken, 24th November 1838.

My dear Victoria,—Van Praet37 is bearer of this letter. The present moment being one of some importance—which may, if imprudently managed, cause great disturbances in the West of Europe, and exercise a reaction on your own Government—I think it my duty to inform you of what is going on.

I join a copy of a letter to Lord Palmerston. I should feel obliged to you if you would read it in the presence of good Lord Melbourne, in whose fairness and sense of justice I must say I feel great confidence....

I will not complain, only one subject I must touch upon as really very unfair. That your Ministers should take a line unfavourable to this country may be explained by their political position, but why should they press so much on the French Government? I really see no cause for it. England is in an excellent position for a mediator, and for all parties it is highly desirable that that position should be maintained.38

I will not plague with a longer letter. You know from experience that I never ask anything of you. I prefer remaining in the position of having rendered services without wanting any return for it but your affection; but, as I said before, if we are not careful we may see serious consequences which may affect more or less everybody, and this ought to be the object of our most anxious attention. I remain, my dear Victoria, your affectionate Uncle,

Leopold R.

Footnote 37: Jules van Praet, author of a History of Flanders, was Secretary of the Belgian Legation in London in 1831, and took a leading part in the negotiations which placed King Leopold on the throne.

Footnote 38: King Leopold considered that the interests of Belgium were being neglected by the four Powers, and in his speech at the opening of his Parliament, on 13th November, stated amid loud acclamations that those interests would be defended with perseverance and courage. The Deputies, in reply, said that Belgium had consented to painful sacrifices only under a formal guarantee by the Powers, which they now shrank from carrying out.

BELGIUM AND HOLLAND

2nd December 1838.

Lord Melbourne presents his humble duty to your Majesty, and returns this letter with the enclosures. He has read it and them with great attention. Your Majesty will probably think it right to acquaint the King that your Majesty had already seen his letter to Lord Palmerston.

Lord Melbourne cannot perceive the justice of the King's complaint. For the sake of the King himself and of the Belgian nation, we are most anxious to settle speedily and definitely the questions so long pending between Belgium and Holland, and which arose from the separation of the two countries in 1830. We can only settle it by the agreement of the four Great Powers who constitute the Conference to which the question was referred, viz., Austria, Prussia, England, France. Of course it is of vital importance for us to carry them all along with us, and for that reason we press France. If she differs from us, there is a ground immediately laid for difference and war.

Lord Melbourne would suggest that your Majesty should say "that your great affection for the King, as well as your anxiety for the interests of your own country, and your desire for the promotion of peace, render you most solicitous to have the Belgian question speedily and definitively settled; that it appears to you that it can only be settled by the agreement of the four Powers who constitute the Conference, and that therefore you cannot but wish most strongly to carry France as well as the two others along with you."39

Footnote 39: See the Queen's letter of 5th December to the King of the Belgians.

3rd December 1838.

Lord Melbourne presents his humble duty to your Majesty, and begs to acquaint that as soon as he arrived at half-past two, Sir George Grey40 ran in to acquaint him that the whole insurrection in Canada was put down and suppressed.41 Despatches have been received from Sir John Colborne to say that the British turned out with the utmost alacrity, the volunteers beat the French wherever they met them, the whole are dispersed, and Sir John says that he feels no doubt of the tranquillity of the Colony during the rest of the winter. Unless, therefore, the Americans make an attempt upon Upper Canada, all is well. Lord Melbourne will have the pleasure of returning to Windsor to-morrow, unless there should be any impediment, of which Lord Melbourne will inform your Majesty.

Footnote 40: Sir George Grey (1799-1882), at this time Under-Secretary for the Colonies, afterwards Secretary of State successively for Home and Colonial Affairs.

Footnote 41: On the 3rd of November, however, the insurrection had broken out anew in Lower Canada, while in Upper Canada many American "sympathyzers" joined the insurgents there; these were decisively defeated at Prescott. This fight cost the British 45 in killed and wounded; 159 of their opponents (including 131 natives of the United States) were taken, and conveyed to Kingston, to be tried by court-martial.

BELGIAN AFFAIRS

Windsor Castle, 5th December 1838.

My dear Uncle,—I have to thank you for two letters, one brought by Van Praet, and the other received on Tuesday. Before I proceed further I must tell you that both Lord Melbourne and I had already seen your letter to Lord Palmerston, which he sent to us immediately on receiving it. I have read these letters with the greatest attention, and can quite understand that your difficulties are great in trying to restrain the eagerness and violence of some of your people.

My great affection for you, of course, makes me most anxious to see these troublesome and long pending affairs settled, for the sake of a continuance of peace and tranquillity; but, dear

Uncle, as it appears to me that these affairs can only be settled by the agreement of the four Powers, it is absolutely necessary that France should go with us as well as the others, and I think, dear Uncle, you wrong us in thinking that we urged France too much and unfairly. You must not, dear Uncle, think that it is from want of interest that I, in general, abstain from touching upon these matters in my letters to you; but I am fearful, if I were to do so, to change our present delightful and familiar correspondence into a formal and stiff discussion upon political matters which would not be agreeable to either of us, and which I should deeply regret. These are my reasons, and I trust you will understand them, and be convinced of my unalterable and very great affection for you, my dearest Uncle, and of the great interest I take in all that concerns your welfare and happiness and the prosperity of your country....

Pray give my affectionate love to Aunt Louise and the children, and believe me, always, your most affectionate Niece,

Victoria R.

LORD DURHAM'S RESIGNATION

8th December 1838.

Lord Melbourne presents his humble duty to your Majesty, and has just received your Majesty's letters. Lord Durham arrived yesterday evening, and Lord Melbourne has just seen Mr. Stanley, who has seen him. He represents him as calm, but much hurt and vexed at the last despatch which expresses your Majesty's disapprobation of his conduct in issuing the proclamation.42 Lord Durham said that he should immediately write an answer to it, in which he should state that he would communicate to the Government all the information which he had collected upon the state of the Canadas. That he should not ask an audience of your Majesty. This is his present decision. He may alter it; if he should, and through any channel request an audience, Lord Melbourne is now clearly of opinion that your Majesty should merely say that an answer will be sent and the propriety of granting an audience may then be fully considered by your Majesty's confidential servants. Mr Stanley represents Lord Durham as not speaking with much violence or asperity, but seeming to feel much the censure conveyed in the last despatch.

Your Majesty will receive from the Colonial Office a précis of Sir John Colborne's despatches. Nothing can be more honourable. The American force which made an incursion into Upper Canada have all been taken prisoners....

Lord Melbourne thinks that as long as Lord Durham is here and some communication has been received from him, he had better remain to-night in London. He will return to Windsor to-morrow....

Footnote 42: Lord Durham stated at Devonport: "I shall, when Parliament meets, be prepared to make a representation of facts wholly unknown here, and disclosures which the Parliament and people have no conception of."

8th December 1838.

Lord Melbourne presents his humble duty to your Majesty, and begs to acquaint your Majesty that Lord Glenelg has this evening received a letter from Lord Durham, tendering formally his resignation, and stating that his general report upon the affairs of Canada must be delayed until the gentlemen connected with his Mission return from that country, which they were to leave on or about the 20th of last month, and therefore may be shortly expected here. It will be necessary to ask Lord Durham whether he has no intelligence of immediate importance to give.

AN ENGLISH CHURCH FOR MALTA

Palace, Valetta,43 13th December 1838.

My dearest Niece,—The English mail going to-day gives me another opportunity to address you, and to name a subject to you which I think deserves your consideration, and about which I feel most anxious. It is the want of a Protestant church in this place which I mean. There are so many English residents here, it is the seat of an English Government, and there is not one church belonging to the Church of England.... The consequence of this want of church accommodation has been that the Dissenters have established themselves in considerable numbers, and one cannot blame persons for attending their meetings when they have no church of their own.

I address myself to you, as the head of the Church of England, and entreat you to consider well this important subject, and to talk it over with your Ministers and the Archbishop, in order to devise the best means of remedying a want so discreditable to our country. Should there be no funds at your disposal to effect this object, most happy shall I feel to contribute to any subscription which may be set on foot, and I believe that a considerable sum may be raised amongst the Protestants of this island, where all parties are most anxious to see a proper place of divine worship erected; without assistance from England, however, it cannot be effected. I therefore most humbly and confidently submit this subject to you, dearest Victoria, who will bestow upon your Protestant subjects of this island an everlasting benefit by granting them what they want most.44...

I hope this will find you quite well and happy, and that I shall soon again have the pleasure of hearing from you. Give my affectionate love to your dear Mother, and all my dear sisters, and believe me ever, my dearest Niece, your most devoted and faithfully attached Aunt,

Adelaide.

Footnote 43: The Queen-Dowager was at this time cruising in the Mediterranean, and made some stay at Malta.

Footnote 44: Queen Adelaide herself erected the church at a cost of £10,000.

LORD MELBOURNE'S ANXIETIES

21st December 1838.

... Lord Melbourne saw Mr. Stephenson this morning and learns from him that the Duke of Sussex45 is in the highest degree discontented at being informed decisively that there is no intention of sending him to Ireland. He is very loud against the Government, and is also very angry with Mr Stephenson, and the latter expects that he shall receive his dismissal.... Mr Stephenson assures Lord Melbourne that he has mentioned this matter to no one but Lord Melbourne and Lady Mary, and it is of importance that it should be kept secret. Lord Melbourne thinks it his duty to apprise your Majesty of the feelings of the Duke, and of the possible origin of them.

Lord and Lady Holland return to London to-day and Lord Melbourne is going to dine with them.

Footnote 45: The Duke of Sussex was anxious to be appointed Viceroy of Ireland. Mr Stephenson was his Private Secretary. See ante, p.

22nd December 1838.

Lord Melbourne presents his humble duty to your Majesty, and cannot express how deeply concerned he is to find himself restrained from obeying your Majesty's commands, and repairing without delay to Brighton. Both his duty and his inclination would prompt him to do this without a moment's delay, if he did not find it incumbent upon him to represent to your Majesty the very important circumstances which require his presence for two or three days longer in London. The session of Parliament approaches; the questions which are to be considered and prepared are of the most appalling magnitude, and of the greatest difficulty. Many of your Majesty's servants, who fill the most important offices, are compelled by domestic calamity to be absent, and it is absolutely necessary that there should be some general superintendence of the measures to be proposed, and some consideration of the arrangements to be made. Lord Melbourne assures your Majesty that he would not delay in London if he did not feel it to be absolutely necessary for your Majesty's service....

BRIGHTON

Laeken, 28th December 1838.

My dearest Victoria,—I have to thank you for two extremely kind and dear letters, which made me very happy, and your kind heart would be pleased to know how happy. Sir H. Seymour[46] gave me a very favourable account of your dearest Majesty, and was deeply gratified by your gracious reception.

I am glad to find that you like Brighton better than last year. I think Brighton very agreeable at this time of the year, till the east winds set in. It also gives the possibility of seeing people without having them on one's hands the whole day, as is the case in the country. The Pavilion, besides, is comfortable; that cannot be denied. Before my marriage it was there that I met the Regent. Charlotte afterwards came with old Queen Charlotte. How distant all this already, but still how present to one's memory.

The portrait of your Aunt and Leopold is nicely done. Don Leopoldo is like, and has at times even a more intelligent look; he would amuse you—he is very original and very sly. I often call him the little tyrant, because nobody knows so well de faire aller le monde.... My most beloved Victoria, your devoted Uncle,

Leopold R.

Footnote 46: Sir Hamilton Seymour, Minister at Brussels.

INTRODUCTORY NOTE: TO CHAPTER VIII

The chief political event of the year (1839) at home arose out of the troubles in Jamaica. In addition to the apprenticeship question, the state of the prisons, much overcrowded owing to the planters' severity, had excited attention, and an Imperial Act was passed for their regulation. To this action the Colonial Assembly showed marked hostility, and, after the dissolution by Sir Lionel Smith, the Governor, the new House was no more placable. Accordingly, the home Government brought in a Bill, in April, to suspend temporarily the Jamaica Constitution, but on a division had a majority of five only in a house of five hundred and eighty-three. The Ministers therefore resigned, and Sir Robert Peel was sent for; a difficulty as to the Ladies of the Household, commonly called the Bedchamber Plot, compelled him to resign the task, and the Whigs, much injured in reputation, resumed office. Some changes took place, Macaulay joining the Ministry, and Lord Normanby, who had succeeded Lord Glenelg at the Colonial Office, exchanging places with Lord John Russell, the Home Secretary. The trial of strength over the Speakership ended in a victory for the Ministerial candidate, Mr Shaw Lefevre, by a majority of eighteen in a house of six hundred and sixteen.

Penny Postage was introduced by an Act of this session.

The Princes Ernest and Albert of Saxe-Coburg arrived on a visit to the Queen in October, and on the 14th the Queen's engagement to the latter was announced by herself to Lord Melbourne. A few weeks later the Queen announced her betrothal at a meeting of the Privy Council.

During the year risings in favour of the "people's charter" took place in various parts of the country, especially Birmingham and Newport, the six points demanded being the ballot, universal suffrage, annual Parliaments, payment of members, the abolition of a property qualification for members, and equal electoral districts. At Newport one Frost, a linen-draper whom Lord John Russell had made a magistrate, headed a riot. He was tried with his confederates by a special commission at Monmouth, and, with two others, sentenced to death; a sentence afterwards commuted.

In the East, war broke out between the Sultan Mahmoud and the Pasha of Egypt, Mehemet Ali, who had originally helped Turkey against Greece, but had since revolted and driven the Turks from Syria. On that occasion (1833) Turkey had been saved by Russian intervention, a defensive alliance, known as the treaty of Unkiar Skelessi, made between Russia and Turkey, and Mehemet granted Syria as well as Egypt. On the revival of hostilities, Ibrahim, son of Mehemet, defeated the Turkish army on June 24; a week later the Sultan Mahmoud died, and the Turkish admiral treacherously delivered over the Turkish fleet to Mehemet at Alexandria. Once more the four Powers (Great Britain, Austria, Prussia, and Russia) interfered to save the Sultan. The Czar accepted the principle of a joint mediation, the advance of the Egyptians was stopped, and the Sultan was informed that no terms of peace would be accepted which had not received the approval of the Powers. The terms were settled at a congress held in London. Mehemet refused to accept the terms, and was encouraged by France to persevere in his refusal.

The dispute between Belgium and Holland as to the Luxemburg territory was settled by a treaty in the course of the year. Lord Durham presented his report on Canada, a document drafted by Charles Buller but inspired by Lord Durham himself; though legislation did not take place this year, this document laid the foundation of the federal union of the Canadas, and of the Constitution of other autonomous colonies, but for the present the ex-Commissioner met with much criticism of his actions.

Our troops were engaged during the year against Dost Mahommed, the Ameer of Afghanistan, a usurper who many years earlier had driven Shah Sooja into exile. Lord Auckland, the Viceroy of India, had sent Captain (afterwards Sir Alexander) Burnes on a Mission to Cabul, and the Ameer had received him hospitably at first, but subsequently dismissed him from his Court. Lord Auckland thereupon resolved to restore Shah Sooja, and in the autumn of 1838 issued a manifesto dethroning Dost Mahommed. Operations were accordingly directed against him under Sir John (afterwards Lord) Keane, who, on August 6, 1839, entered Cabul and placed Shah Sooja on the throne. However open to criticism, the news of this result was enthusiastically received in England, and Lord Auckland was promoted to an Earldom.

In China a dispute of long standing became acute. With the renewal of the East India Company's charter, in 1834, the Chinese ports had been thrown open, and the opium trade became a source of great profit to private traders. In spite of the prohibition which the Chinese Government laid on importation of opium, the traffic was actively carried on, and, as a result of the strained relations which ensued, Captain Elliot, the British Chief Superintendent, requested that warships should proceed to China for the protection of British life and property.

CHAPTER VIII

Pavilion [Brighton], 1st January 1839.

My dear Uncle,—... I don't like your croaking so about damp climates; if a niece may venture to say such a thing, I might almost say it is ungrateful to your faithful and attached Belgians.

The Queen-Dowager's letters do tantalize one a good deal, I must own.1 You will see that old Lord Clarendon2 is dead, which makes our friend Villiers Earl of Clarendon, but I am afraid not with a large income.

Lord Palmerston has been unwell and obliged to go to Broadlands, where he still is. He had gone through so much grief and labour, that it was absolutely necessary for him to recruit his strength. The Normanbys spent two nights here.3 Lord Melbourne is the only person staying in the house besides several of my Court and my suite, and, I am sorry to say, is not very well; he has also had, I fear, too much business to do.

Lady Breadalbane4 is my new Lady of the Bedchamber, and a very nice person. Ever your devoted Niece,

Victoria R.

Forgive this short scrawl.

Footnote 1: Queen Adelaide had described the orange-trees and tropical fruits in the gardens of the Palace of St Antonio, Valetta.

Footnote 2: John Charles, third Earl, Chief Justice-in-eyre, North of Trent. His successor, who had been Minister to Spain since 1833, was afterwards the celebrated Foreign Secretary.

Footnote 3: Lord Normanby, at this time Lord-Lieutenant of Ireland, became successively during the year, Colonial and Home Secretary. Lady Normanby, who had been a Lady-in-Waiting since the accession, was a daughter of the first Lord Ravensworth.

Footnote 4: Eliza, daughter of George Baillie of Jerviswood. Her brother afterwards became tenth Earl of Haddington.

MURDER OF LORD NORBURY

6th January 1839.

Lord Melbourne presents his humble duty to your Majesty, and returns his best and warmest thanks for the very kind and gracious communication which he had the honour and pleasure of receiving from your Majesty yesterday evening. Your Majesty will have seen in the newspapers that Lord Norbury was shot at in his own grounds and dangerously wounded.5 Lord Melbourne learns to-day by a letter from Lord Morpeth that Lord Norbury is since dead. This is a shocking event, and will, of course, create a strong sensation, much stronger than the death in the same manner of several persons of inferior degree. It is almost the first time that an attempt of this kind has been directed against an individual of that rank or station....

Lord Melbourne has seen Sir Henry Halford,6 who says that his pulse is low and his system languid. He has prescribed some draughts, which Lord Melbourne trusts will be of service, but he feels much depressed to-day. He dined yesterday at Lady Holland's, where he met Mr Ellice,7 civil and friendly enough in appearance, but Lord Melbourne fears hostile at heart, and a determined partisan of Lord Durham. Lord Durham has not yet made to Lord Glenelg the promised communication of his report and plan, but it is said that he will do so soon....

Footnote 5: At Kilbeggan Abbey, County Meath. The murderer escaped.

Footnote 6: The celebrated physician: he attended George IV. and William IV., as well as Queen Victoria.

Footnote 7: Son-in-law of Lord Grey, as was also Lord Durham.

Buckingham Palace, 11th January 1839.

My dear Uncle,—The dreadful moment has arrived, and dear Marie[8] is no more to bless her loving relations with her presence on this earth of grief and troubles! It is a heavy dispensation, and one that it is difficult to comprehend, but we must submit.

I thought it best to write to my poor dear Aunt, for whom this will be a sad blow; but I abstained from doing so to the dear Queen of the French just as yet. I have no letters, and only learnt the melancholy event by the papers. Poor wretched Alexander! What a loss, what a change for him, poor fellow!

You will, I am sure, regret that sweet amiable creature, as poor Marie was, very much, having known her so well, and her attachment to you was great.

I will not prolong this letter, but merely repeat how much I feel for you all, and beg you to believe me, your most affectionate Niece,

Victoria R.

Footnote 8: Princess Marie of Orleans, born 1813, sister to the Queen of the Belgians, had married Prince Alexander of Wurtemberg, in 1837.

HOLLAND AND BELGIUM

Laeken, 18th January 1839.

... Your Aunt as well as myself are very anxious to be of use to poor Alexander. The dispositions of the whole family are extremely kind towards him, but he is shy and a little helpless; his present melancholy situation is of course calculated to increase this. His position puts me in mind of mine in 1817.... He, besides, is surrounded by people who are kind to him. Of George IV., then Regent, it was observed that for years he had not been in such good spirits than by the loss of his daughter. She was more popular than himself—that was, since her mariage, her only crime....

I feel very grateful for Lord Melbourne's kindness on the subject of our sad loss. He is so feeling and kindhearted that he, much more than most men who have lived so much in the grand monde, has preserved a certain warmth and freshness of feeling....

Your cousins kiss your hands, and I remain, my dearest Victoria, your devoted Uncle,

Leopold R.

Stanhope Street, 27th January 1839.

Viscount Palmerston presents his humble duty to your Majesty, and returns to your Majesty the accompanying papers which he received from Viscount Melbourne. Your Majesty will have seen by Sir Edward Disbrowe's[9] despatches that the concentration of Dutch troops mentioned in these reports was purely defensive, and was the consequence of the military demonstrations previously made by the Belgians; and it appears, moreover, that the Dutch force is inferior in number to the Belgian force opposite to it; and that affords an additional security against the chance of an invasion of Belgium by the Dutch. It is, however, undeniable that when two armies are drawn up in face of each other, separated by a small distance, and animated by mutual hatred, the chances of collision become great and imminent. But it is to be hoped in the present case that the communication made by the Conference to the two parties on Thursday last may avert danger of hostilities between the Dutch and Belgians.10

Footnote 9: Minister at the Hague.

Footnote 10: See next letter.

BELGIUM AND ENGLAND

Buckingham Palace, 7th February 1839.

My dear Uncle,—I am much grieved to learn that poor Philippe11 has given you such anxiety. My poor Aunt! it really is too much upon her to have these cares added to her recent severe affliction. I hope to God that I shall get news of Philippe's complete recovery to-morrow.

I regret to hear that your Government gives you so much trouble, but trust that you will exert all your influence, as you have so frequently done, to persuade your Ministers to be reasonable, and not to resist the favourable offers made to the Government. Everybody here is exceedingly anxious for the conclusion of these long pending affairs, and hope that the answer from Belgium will soon arrive.12 You will forgive me, dear Uncle, if I express to you my earnest hope that these expectations may not be disappointed, for I feel that since the Dutch have so instantly accepted the proposition of the Conference, Belgium would suffer in the eyes of this country were she to delay, and, what I am still more fearful of, my beloved Uncle, you might be blamed, and suffer for what your Government may do. You will, I know, forgive this freedom, which is prompted by my great anxiety for your welfare and happiness (which I know you are well aware of), and for the preservation of the inestimable blessings of peace. No one feels more for you than I do at this difficult moment, nor than I have done throughout these trying and embarrassing affairs. That all may be peaceably and amicably settled is my earnest prayer.

Everything went off well yesterday,13 and we are again launched into a political campaign, which it is impossible not to contemplate with a certain degree of anxiety.

Adieu! my dear Uncle. Give my love to my dear Aunt, and believe me, always, your most devoted Niece,

Victoria R.

Footnote 11: See ante, p.

Footnote 12: The twenty-four Articles, to which Belgium had acceded in 1831, had then been rejected by Holland. Now, however, Holland wished to adopt them. The Belgian Government vainly proposed different schemes, but at last the Bill for ratifying the proposal of the Powers (made 23rd January 1839, and accepted by Holland on 11th February) passed the Belgian Chambers.

Footnote 13: The Queen opened Parliament in person on 6th February.

CABINET DISSENSION

10th February 1839.

Lord Melbourne presents his humble duty to your Majesty, and thinks it right and necessary to acquaint your Majesty that the Cabinet yesterday was very stormy and unpleasant. Lord John Russell brought on the question of the Civil Government of the Army, in a temperate and judicious manner, but Lord Howick made a most violent speech, strongly condemning the whole of the present system and arraigning the conduct of the Treasury and other Departments, saying that he should not throw up his office because no measure was brought forward, but that, when questioned upon the subject by Mr Hume in the House of Commons, as it was certain that he would be, he should say that Government would do nothing upon the subject, until he (Mr Hume) compelled them, and that he should express his entire disapprobation of the present system, and his reasons in detail for that disapprobation. Your Majesty will perceive that nothing could be more violent than this course. It was borne with great patience by the rest of the Cabinet, although Mr. Rice,14 against whom the greater part of Lord Howick's speech was directed, felt himself most deeply hurt, and so expressed himself in private afterwards to Lord Melbourne. Upon the whole, Lord Melbourne cannot but consider that affairs are in a most precarious state, and that whilst there is so much discontent fermenting within the Cabinet itself, there must be great doubt of Lord Melbourne's being much longer able to hold the Administration together.

Footnote 14: The Chancellor of the Exchequer.

10th February 1839.

Lord Melbourne presents his humble duty to your Majesty, and is very sorry that his communication has occasioned your Majesty so much alarm and uneasiness. Lord Melbourne hopes that there is nothing imminent and immediate, but this sort of outbreak and contention may so soon become serious, that Lord Melbourne thought it his duty to take an early opportunity of informing your Majesty of what had taken place. Lord Melbourne would wait upon your Majesty without delay, but trusts that this letter will be sufficient to dispel any disquietude which his former communication may have excited.

Wilton Crescent, 20th February 1839.

Lord John Russell presents his humble duty to your Majesty, and has the honour to report that Mr Charles Villiers15 moved yesterday, after a very able speech, that the petitioners against the Corn Laws should be heard at the Bar of the House.

Sir Robert Peel opposed the Motion on the ground that he meant to resist any change in the Corn Laws. He made a very skilful use of the returns of cotton, etc., exported.

Footnote 15: M.P. for Wolverhampton 1835-1898, becoming "Father of the House."

THE DUKE OF LUCCA

Stanhope Street, 5th March 1839.

Viscount Palmerston presents his humble duty to your Majesty, and requests to be honoured with your Majesty's commands upon the accompanying letter from Count Pollon.16 Viscount Palmerston at the same time begs to state that he has reason to believe, from what Count Pollon said to him in conversation two days ago, that the Duke of Lucca17 has a notion that Sovereign

Princes who have had the honour of dining with your Majesty, have been invited by note and not by card. If that should be so, and if your Majesty should invite the Duke of Lucca to dine at the Palace before his departure, perhaps the invitation might be made by note, instead of by card, as it was when the Duke last dined at the Palace. Your Majesty may think this a small matter, but the Duke is a small Sovereign.

Footnote 16: For many years Sardinian Minister in England.

Footnote 17: Lucca was an independent Italian State.

PORTUGAL

9th March 1839.

Lord Melbourne presents his humble duty to your Majesty, and feels very deeply the very kind and gracious concern which your Majesty expresses for his health, as well as your Majesty's solicitude and interest upon all occasions. Lord Melbourne will take your Majesty's advice, but his experience teaches him that illness is not so easily put off, and that it will have its course in spite of precaution....

Lord Melbourne thinks, upon the whole, that your Majesty had perhaps better write by messenger a few lines of kindness and recollection. It can be no descent on your Majesty's part to do so, and as we may be obliged to take very strong measures with respect to Portugal, it is as well that there should be no appearance of any deficiency of affection or attention. Lord Melbourne [thinks] that, for the reason given by your Majesty, your Majesty may perhaps as well not go to the play this evening, but is very sorry to hear that your Majesty is low and out of spirits.

Buckingham Palace, 14th March 1839.

My dear Uncle,—Many thanks for two letters, one which I received last Sunday, and the other enclosing a letter from Stockmar this morning. I am glad you agree with me about Victoire.18 Since I wrote to you, I got these two letters from the Portuguese children—as I disrespectfully but very deservedly call them—which I send you, in order that you may see how they wish Victoire to come to them, which I fear and think is totally impracticable, for it would never do for Victoire to go so far without her mother. Nevertheless, I thought it but right by them to send you these letters, and I have written to them giving them little hope.

The French Ministry are gone, and I am sure the poor King will be much vexed by it. They talk of Broglie as Minister for Foreign Affairs,19 but I am afraid Thiers is inevitable. We are rather in fear of Thiers here, but it is a pity that Louis Philippe should show so much dislike to a man he must take, for it will have the effect of a defeat.

I have no time to add more, but to beg you to believe me, always, your most affectionate Niece,

Victoria R.

Footnote 18: Daughter of Prince Ferdinand of Saxe-Coburg, and married in April 1840 to the Duc de Nemours.

Footnote 19: After a provisional Cabinet, in which the Duc de Montebello was Foreign Minister, the King appointed a Ministry with Soult as Premier and Foreign Minister.

DIFFICULTIES OF THE MINISTRY

22nd March 1839.

Lord Melbourne presents his humble duty to your Majesty, and begs to acquaint your Majesty that the Cabinet have decided—

If we lose that question, or carry it by a small majority, we must resign. If we carry it, we may go on.

This is a plain statement of the case, and this course will at least give your Majesty time to consider what is to be done.

Footnote 20: By 63 to 58 Lord Roden carried a motion for a Select Committee to enquire into the state of Ireland; the Ministry replied by obtaining a vote of the House of Commons in their favour by 318 to 296.

Brocket Hall,21 1st April 1839.

Lord Melbourne presents his humble duty to your Majesty, and has just received your Majesty's letters, for which he returns many and warm thanks. Nothing could be more prosperous than his journey down, although it rained hard the greater part of the way. Lord Melbourne slept well, and has walked out this morning, although it was still showery. Nothing is so fatiguing as the first exposure to the air of the country, and Lord Melbourne feels the influence of it.

Lord Melbourne returns the letters of the King of the Belgians. He accounts very naturally for the conduct of the poor Duchess,22 but she should have recollected the extreme disadvantage and discredit which attaches to a change of religion. Un gentilhomme ne change jamais la religion, was the saying of Napoleon, and is very just. It is difficult to understand the movements and motives of parties in a foreign country, and therefore Lord Melbourne does not feel able to pronounce any opinion upon the transactions in France. Lord Melbourne had seen G——'s letters, a pert jackanapes, who always takes the worst view of every subject, and does as much mischief as he can....

Lord Melbourne is just starting for Panshanger.23 The evening is better than the morning was, but cold.

Footnote 21: Lord Melbourne's house on the Lea, about three miles north of Hatfield. Its construction was begun by Sir Matthew Lamb, and completed by his son, Sir Peniston, the first Lord Melbourne.

Footnote 22: Princess Alexander of Würtemberg. On her death-bed, she had expressed a wish to her husband that he should join the Roman Catholic Church.

Footnote 23: Panshanger, not far distant from Brocket, the house of Lord Melbourne's brother-in-law, Lord Cowper, and celebrated for its pictures, was bought by Lord Chancellor Cowper, temp. Queen Anne.

ENGLAND AND BELGIUM

Buckingham Palace, 9th April 1839.

My dear Uncle,—... I regret to learn you are still not easy about your own affairs, but trust all will now be speedily adjusted. You always allow me, dear Uncle, to speak frankly to you; you will, therefore, I hope, not be displeased if I venture to make a few observations on one or two parts of your letter.

You say that the anger of the Belgians is principally directed against England.24 Now, I must say you are very unjust towards us, and (if I could) I might be even a little angry with you, dear Uncle. We only pressed Belgium for her own good, and not for ours. It may seem hard at first, but the time will come when you will see that we were right in urging you not to delay any longer the signature of the treaty.

I think that you will see in this frank expression of my sentiments no wish to annoy or hurt you, but only an anxious desire to prove to you that England is Belgium's sincere friend, and that my Government are ever desirous of doing what is in their power for the welfare, security, and prosperity of yourself and your kingdom.

I regret much the state of affairs in France,25 which cannot but make us all somewhat anxious; you will, I hope tell me what news you hear from Paris.

Pray, dearest Uncle, receive my best, my very warmest, wishes for many happy returns of dear Leopold's birthday, and also, though somewhat late, for Philippe's birthday.

Give my love to my dear Aunt, and believe me, always, your most devoted Niece,

Victoria R.

Footnote 24: He had written on 5th April:—"The feeling is strongest against England, in which the people expected to see a support, and only found a strong determination to decide everything against them and at their expense. If there was a great explosion in France, it would not be astonishing to see the people here join it; it would rather be astonishing to see it otherwise, after the kind treatment they received from the Powers."

Footnote 25: The King was for a time without any Ministry, and the meeting of the Chambers had to be postponed.

PRINCE ALBERT IN ITALY

Naples, 16th April 1839.

Madam,—As it is some time that I had the honour to address your Majesty, I hope that a further account of our crusades will meet with a favourable reception.

It is now somewhat better than a month that we left Florence, I may say with regret, for we were there very comfortably in every respect. On our route to Rome we enjoyed the beautiful sight of the cataract at Terni, the place where Queen Caroline sojourned for some time. We were particularly fortunate that day, as the brightest sunshine heightened its picturesque effects beyond description. We found old Rome very full, and to see it and its ecclesiastic governors to advantage, the Holy Week is certainly the properest time. From morning to noon the Prince was at seeing sights, and he made so good a use of his time, that I don't think that something really remarkable was left unseen. Upon this very principle, we paid our respects to the Holy Father,26 of which interview the Prince made so admirable a sketch, so very worthy of H.B.,27 that I am very much tempted to send it for the inspection of your Majesty. We assisted at the Church ceremonies of the Holy Week from the beginning to the end. The music of the Sistine Chapel, which is only vocal, may be well considered as unique, and has not failed to make a lasting impression upon a mind so musical as the Prince's....

I never think of your Majesty—and I take the liberty of thinking very frequently of you—without praying for health, serenity of mind, comfort and success for you, and I can well say that I am from my heart, your Majesty's sincerely attached and devoted Servant,

Stockmar.

Footnote 26: Gregory XVI.

Footnote 27: Initials adopted by Mr Doyle, father of Richard Doyle, in his Reform Caricatures.

BELGIUM

19th April 1839.

... I am glad I extracted some spark of politics from your dear Majesty, very kindly and nicely expressed. I know that your generous little heart would not have wished at any time but what was good for a country in which you were much beloved. But the fact is, that certainly your Government have taken the lead in maintaining a condition which time had rendered difficult to comply with. Physicians will tell you that often an operation, which might have been performed at one time, could not, without great danger for the patient, be undertaken some years later. We have not been listened to, and arrangements are forced on us, in themselves full of seeds of danger, when by consulting the real interests of Holland and Belgium, both countries might have been placed on a footing of sincere peace and good neighbourhood. This country feels now humbled and désenchanté with its soi-disant political independence as it pleased the Conference to settle it. They will take a dislike to a political state which wounds their vanity, and will, in consequence of this, not wish it to continue. Two things will happen, therefore, on the very first opportunity, either that this country will be involved in war to better a position which it thinks too humiliating, or that it will voluntarily throw up a nominal independence in which it is now hemmed in between France and Holland, which begins on the North Sea, and ends, of all the things in this world, on the Moselle!

I think old Pirson, who said in the Chamber that if the treaty was carried into execution I was likely to be the first and last King of the country, was not wrong. Whenever this will happen, it will be very awkward for England, and deservedly so. To see, after eight years of hard work, blooming and thriving political plantations cut and maimed, and that by those who have a real interest to protect them, is very melancholy. I do not say these things with the most distant idea of bringing about any change, but only because in the high and very responsible position in which Providence has placed you, it is good to tell you the truth, as you ought to have weight and influence on the affairs of Europe; and England, not being in the possibility of making territorial acquisition, has a real and permanent interest in the proper maintenance of a balance of political power in Europe. Now I will leave you to enjoy the beginning of Spring, which a mild rain seems to push on prodigiously. Believe me ever, my dear Victoria, your very attached Uncle,

Leopold R.

JAMAICA

26th April 1839.

Lord Melbourne presents his humble duty to your Majesty, and begs to inform your Majesty that the result of the Cabinet has been a decision to stand by the Bill as we have introduced it, and not to accede to Sir Robert Peel's proposal. The Bill is for suspending the functions of the Legislative Assembly of Jamaica, and governing that island for five years by a Governor and Council.28 If Sir Robert Peel should persist in his proposal, and a majority of the House of Commons should concur with him, it will be such a mark of want of confidence as it will be impossible for your Majesty's Government to submit to.

Footnote 28: See Introductory Note, ante, p.

Buckingham Palace, 30th April 1839.

My dear Uncle,—I have to thank you for your last letter, which I received on Sunday. Though you seem not to dislike my political sparks, I think it is better not to increase them, as they might finally take fire, particularly as I see with regret that upon this one subject we cannot agree. I shall therefore limit myself to my expressions of very sincere wishes for the welfare and prosperity of Belgium.

The Grand Duke,29 after a long delay, is at length to arrive on Friday night; I shall put myself out of my way in order to be very civil to such a great personage. I am already thinking how I shall lodge all my relations; you must prepare Uncle Ferdinand for its not being very ample, but this Palace, though large, is not calculated to hold many visitors....

Believe me, always, your very affectionate Niece,

Victoria R.

Footnote 29: The Hereditary Grand Duke of Russia, afterwards the Emperor Alexander II.

MINISTERIAL CRISIS

7th May 1839.

Lord Melbourne presents his humble duty to your Majesty, and has to acquaint your Majesty that the division upon the Jamaica Bill, which took place about two this morning, was two hundred and ninety-nine against the measure, and three hundred and four in favour of it.30 Lord Melbourne has not heard from Lord John Russell since this event, but a Cabinet will of course be summoned early this morning, and Lord Melbourne cannot conceal from your Majesty that in his opinion the determination of the Cabinet must be that the relative numbers upon this vote, joined to the consideration of no less than nine members of those who have hitherto invariably supported the Government having gone against it now, leave your Majesty's confidential servants no alternative but to resign their offices into your Majesty's hands. They cannot give up the Bill either with honour or satisfaction to their own consciences, and in the face of such an opposition they cannot persevere in it with any hope of success. Lord Melbourne is certain that your Majesty will not deem him too presuming if he expresses his fear that this decision will be both painful and embarrassing to your Majesty, but your Majesty will meet this crisis with that firmness which belongs to your character, and with that rectitude and sincerity which will carry your Majesty through all difficulties. It will also be greatly painful to Lord Melbourne to quit the service of a Mistress who has treated him with such unvarying kindness and unlimited confidence; but in whatever station he may be placed, he will always feel the deepest anxiety for your Majesty's interests and happiness, and will do the utmost in his power to promote and secure them.

Footnote 30: The numbers are apparently incorrectly stated. The division was 294 to 289.

RESIGNATION IMMINENT

7th May 1839.

The present circumstances have been for some time so probable, or rather so certain, that Lord Melbourne has naturally been led to weigh and consider maturely the advice which, if called upon, he should tender to your Majesty when they did arrive. That advice is, at once to send for the Duke of Wellington. Your Majesty appears to Lord Melbourne to have no other alternative. The Radicals have neither ability, honesty, nor numbers. They have no leaders of any character. Lord Durham was raised, one hardly knows how, into something of a factitious importance by his own extreme opinions, by the panegyrics of those who thought he would serve them as an instrument, and by the management of the Press, but any little public reputation which he might once have acquired has been entirely dissipated and destroyed by the continued folly of his conduct in his Canadian Government. There is no party in the State to which your Majesty can now resort, except that great party which calls itself Conservative, and of that party, his rank, station, reputation, and experience point out the Duke of Wellington as the person to whom your Majesty should apply.

Lord Melbourne therefore advises that your Majesty should send for the Duke of Wellington, and should acquaint him, provided your Majesty so feels, that you were entirely satisfied with your late Government, and that you part from them with reluctance; but that as he and the party of which he is the head have been the means of removing them from office, you naturally look to him to advise you as to the means of supplying their places and carrying on the business of the country.

If the Duke should be unwilling to form the Government himself, and should desire to devolve the task upon Sir Robert Peel, Lord Melbourne would advise your Majesty to accede to that suggestion; but Lord Melbourne would counsel your Majesty to be very unwilling to suffer the Government to be formed by Sir Robert Peel, without the active assistance in office of the Duke of Wellington.

With respect both to measures and appointments, your Majesty should place the fullest confidence in those to whom you entrust the management of affairs, exercising at the same time, and fully expressing, your own judgment upon both.

Your Majesty will do well to be from the beginning very vigilant that all measures and all appointments are stated to your Majesty in the first instance, and your Majesty's pleasure taken thereon previously to any instruments being drawn out for carrying them into effect, and submitted to your Majesty's signature. It is the more necessary to be watchful and active in this respect, as the extreme confidence which your Majesty has reposed in me may have led to some omission at times of these most necessary preliminaries.

The patronage of the Lord Chamberlain's Department is of the greatest importance, and may be made to conduce at once to the beneficial influence of the Crown, and to the elevation and encouragement of the professions of the Church and of Medicine. This patronage, by being left to the uncontrolled exercise of successive Lord Chamberlains, has been administered not only wastefully but perniciously. The physicians to the late King were many of them men of little eminence; the chaplains are still a sorry set. Your Majesty should insist with the new Ministers that this patronage should be disposed of, not by the Lord Chamberlain, but, as it has hitherto been during your Majesty's reign, by your Majesty upon consultation with your Prime Minister.

DISTRESS OF THE QUEEN

Buckingham Palace, 9th May 1839.

The Queen thinks Lord Melbourne may possibly wish to know how she is this morning; the Queen is somewhat calmer; she was in a wretched state till nine o'clock last night, when she tried to occupy herself and try to think less gloomily of this dreadful change, and she succeeded in calming herself till she went to bed at twelve, and she slept well; but on waking this morning, all—all that had happened in one short eventful day came most forcibly to her mind, and brought back her grief; the Queen, however, feels better now; but she couldn't touch a morsel of food last night, nor can she this morning. The Queen trusts Lord Melbourne slept well, and is well this morning; and that he will come precisely at eleven o'clock. The Queen has received no answer from the Duke, which is very odd, for she knows he got her letter. The Queen hopes Lord Melbourne received her letter last night.

8th May 1839.

Lord Melbourne presents his humble duty to your Majesty, and is much grieved that he did not answer your Majesty's letter yesterday evening, as your Majesty desired, but he did not get it till late, and he felt much tired and harassed by all that had passed during the day. The situation is very painful, but it is necessary for your Majesty to be prudent and firm. It is of all things necessary not to be suspected of any unfair dealing. Whilst Lord Melbourne holds his office, everything of course may be written to him as usual; but still the resolutions for the formation of the new Government will now commence, and it will never do, whilst they are going on, either for appearance or in reality, that Lord Melbourne should dine with your Majesty, as he did before this disturbance. It would create feeling, possibly lead to remonstrance, and throw a doubt upon the fairness and integrity of your Majesty's conduct. All this is very painful both to do and to say, but it is unavoidable; it must be said, and it must be done. Lord Melbourne will wait upon your Majesty at eleven.31

Footnote 31: Lord Melbourne had made the not unnatural mistake of recommending to the Queen, as members of her first Household, ladies who were nearly related to himself and his Whig colleagues. No doubt these were the ladies whom he knew best, and in whom he had entire confidence; but he ought to have had sufficient prescience to see that the Queen would probably form strong attachments to the ladies who first served her: and that if the appointments had not in the first instance a political complexion, yet that the Whig tendencies which these Ladies represented were likely to affect the Queen, in the direction of allying her closely with a particular party in the State.

THE DUKE OF WELLINGTON

8th May 1839.

The Queen told Lord Melbourne she would give him an account of what passed, which she is very anxious to do. She saw the Duke for about twenty minutes; the Queen said she supposed he knew why she sent for him, upon which the Duke said, No, he had no idea. The Queen then said that she had had the greatest confidence in her late Ministry, and had parted with them with the greatest reluctance; upon which the Duke observed that he could assure me no one felt more pain in hearing the announcement of their resignation than he did, and that he was deeply grieved at it. The Queen then continued, that as his party had been instrumental in removing them, that she must look to him to form a new Government. The Duke answered that he had no power whatever in the House of Commons, "that if he was to say black was white,32 they would say it was not," and that he advised me to send for Sir Robert Peel, in whom I could place confidence, and who was a gentleman and a man of honour and integrity. The Queen then said she hoped he would at all events have a place in the new Cabinet. The Duke at first rather refused, and said he was so deaf, and so old and unfit for any discussion, that if he were to consult his own feelings he would rather not do it, and remain quite aloof; but that as he was very anxious to do anything that would tend to the Queen's comfort, and would do everything and at all times that could be of use to the Queen, and therefore if she and her Prime Minister urged his accepting office, he would. The Queen said she had more confidence in him than in any of the others of his party. The Queen then mentioned the subject of the Household, and of those who were not in Parliament. The Duke did not give any decisive answer about it, but advised the Queen not to begin with conditions of this sort, and wait till the matter was proposed. The Queen then said that she felt certain he would understand the great friendship she had for Lord Melbourne, who had been to her quite a parent, and the Duke said no one felt and knew that better than he did, and that no one could still be of greater use to the Queen than Lord Melbourne. The Duke spoke of his personal friendship for Lord Melbourne, and that he hoped I knew that he had often done all he could to help your (Lord Melbourne's) Government. The Queen then mentioned her intention to prove her great fairness to her new Government in telling them, that they might know there was no unfair dealing, that I meant to see you often as a friend, as I owed so much to you. The Duke said he quite understood it, and knew I would not exercise this to weaken the Government, and that he would take my part about it, and felt for me. He was very kind, and said he called it "a misfortune" that you had all left me.

SIR ROBERT PEEL

The Queen wrote to Peel, who came after two, embarrassed and put out. The Queen repeated what she had said to the Duke about her former Government, and asked Sir Robert to form a new Ministry. He does not seem sanguine; says entering the Government in a minority is very difficult; he felt unequal to the task, and far from exulting in what had happened, as he knew what pain it must give me; he quite approved that the Duke should take office, and saw the importance of it; meant to offer him the post of Secretary for Foreign Affairs, and if he refused, Lord Aberdeen; Lord Lyndhurst, Chancellor; hoped to secure Stanley and Graham; Goulburn to be the candidate for the Speaker's Chair; he expects a severe conflict then, and if he should be beat must either resign or dissolve Parliament. Before this the Queen said she was against a dissolution, in which he quite agreed, but of course wished no conditions should be made; he felt the task arduous, and that he would require me to demonstrate (a certain degree, if any I can only feel) confidence in the Government, and that my Household would be one of the marks of that. The Queen mentioned the same thing about her Household, to which he at present would give no answer, and said nothing should be done without my knowledge or approbation. He repeated his surprise at the course you had all taken in resigning, which he did not expect. The Queen talked of her great friendship for, and gratitude to Lord Melbourne, and repeated what she had said to the Duke, in which Peel agreed; but he is such a cold, odd man she can't make out what he means. He said he couldn't expect me to have the confidence in him I had in you (and which he never can have) as he has not deserved it. My impression is, he is not happy and sanguine. He comes to me to-morrow at one to report progress in his formation of the new Government. The Queen don't like his manner after—oh! how different, how dreadfully different, to that frank, open, natural and most kind, warm manner of Lord Melbourne.33 The Duke I like by far better to Peel. The Queen trusts Lord Melbourne will excuse this long letter, but she was so very anxious he should know all. The Queen was very much collected, and betrayed no agitation during these two trying Audiences. But afterwards again all gave way. She feels Lord Melbourne will understand it, amongst enemies to those she most relied on and esteemed, and people who seem to have no heart; but what is worst of all is the being deprived of seeing Lord Melbourne as she used to do.

Footnote 32: Sic: an obvious mistake for "black was black."

Footnote 33: Lady de Grey had written to Peel on 7th May:—"The Queen has always expressed herself much impressed with Lord Melbourne's open manner, and his truth. The latter quality you possess, the former not.

"Now, dear Peel, the first impression on so young a girl's mind is of immense consequence, accustomed as she has been to the open and affectionate manner of Lord Melbourne, who, entre nous, treats her as a father, and, with all his faults, feels for her as such."—Sir Robert Peel, Parker, vol. ii. p. 389.

LORD MELBOURNE'S ADVICE

9th May 1839.

Lord Melbourne presents his humble duty to your Majesty. He has read with the greatest attention the very clear and distinct account which your Majesty has written of that which passed at the Audiences which your Majesty has given to the Duke of Wellington and Sir Robert Peel. Nothing could have been more proper and judicious than your Majesty's conduct, and they appear to have acted upon their part with propriety and sincerity. Lord Melbourne has no doubt that both with respect to him (Lord Melbourne) and to themselves and their own feelings and position, they expressed what they really think. The Duke was right in saying that in general, in affairs of this nature, it is best not to begin with conditions; but this matter of the Household is so personal to yourself, that it was best to give an intimation of your feelings upon it in the first instance. Lord Melbourne has little doubt that if they could have acted from themselves, they would have acceded to your Majesty's wish at once; but your Majesty must recollect that they have others to satisfy, and must not attribute entirely to them anything that is harsh and unreasonable. Lord Melbourne advises your Majesty to urge this question of the Household strongly as a matter due to yourself and your own wishes; but if Sir Robert is unable to concede it, it will not do to refuse and to put off the negotiation upon it. Lord Melbourne would strongly advise your Majesty to do everything to facilitate the formation of the Government. Everything is to be done and to be endured rather than run the risk of getting into the situation in which they are in France, of no party being able to form a Government and conduct the affairs of the country.34

The Dissolution of Parliament is a matter of still more importance, and if this should be again pressed upon your Majesty, Lord Melbourne would advise your Majesty to reserve your opinion, not to give a promise that you will dissolve, nor to say positively that you will not. You may say that you do not think it right to fetter the Prerogative of the Crown by previous engagements, that a dissolution of Parliament is to be decided according to the circumstances at the time, that you mean to give full confidence to the Government that shall be formed, and to do everything in your power to support them, and that you will consider whether Parliament shall be dissolved, when you are advised to dissolve it, and have before you the reasons for such a measure.

Lord Melbourne earnestly entreats your Majesty not to suffer yourself to be affected by any faultiness of manner which you may observe. Depend upon it, there is no personal hostility to Lord Melbourne nor any bitter feelings against him. Sir Robert is the most cautious and reserved of mankind. Nobody seems to Lord Melbourne to know him, but he is not therefore deceitful or dishonest. Many a very false man has a very open sincere manner, and vice versâ....

Lord Melbourne earnestly hopes that your Majesty is better this morning.

Footnote 34: Alluding to the successive failures of Soult, Thiers, and Broglie.

Buckingham Palace, 9th May 1839.

The Queen cannot sufficiently thank Lord Melbourne for his most kind letter, and for his excellent advice, which is at once the greatest comfort and of the greatest use to her; the Queen will follow it in every respect, and nothing of importance shall be done without due reflection; and she trusts Lord Melbourne will help her and be to her what she told him he was, and begged him still ever to be—a father to one who never wanted support more than she does now.

Lord Melbourne shall hear again after she sees Peel this morning....

The Queen has just now heard Lord Liverpool is not in town.

The Queen hopes Lord Melbourne is able to read her letters; if ever there is anything he cannot read, he must send them back, and mark what he can't read.

LORD PALMERSTON'S GRATITUDE

Stanhope Street, 9th May 1839.

Viscount Palmerston presents his humble duty to your Majesty, and begs to return your Majesty his grateful thanks for your Majesty's gracious communication of this morning. It affords Viscount Palmerston the most heartfelt satisfaction to know that his humble but zealous endeavours to promote the interests of his country and to uphold the honour of your Majesty's Crown, have had the good fortune to meet with your Majesty's approbation; and he begs most respectfully to assure your Majesty that the deep impression produced by the condescending kindness which he has upon all occasions experienced from your Majesty can never be effaced from his mind.

THE HOUSEHOLD

9th May 1839.

Lord Melbourne presents his humble duty to your Majesty, and begs to suggest that if Sir Robert Peel presses for the dismissal of those of your Household who are not in Parliament, you may observe that in so doing he is pressing your Majesty more hardly than any Minister ever pressed a Sovereign before.

When the Government was changed in 1830, the principal posts of the Household were placed at the disposal of Lord Grey, but the Grooms and Equerries were not removed.

When Sir Robert Peel himself became Minister in 1834, no part of the Household were removed except those who were in Parliament.

When I became Prime Minister again in 1835, none of the Grooms or Equerries were removed because none of them were in Parliament.

They press upon your Majesty, whose personal feelings ought from your circumstances to be more consulted, a measure which no Minister before ever pressed upon a Sovereign.

If this is put to him by your Majesty, Lord Melbourne does not see how he can resist it.

Buckingham Palace, 9th May 1839.

The Queen writes one line to prepare Lord Melbourne for what may happen in a very few hours. Sir Robert Peel has behaved very ill, and has insisted on my giving up my Ladies, to which I replied that I never would consent, and I never saw a man so frightened. He said he must go to the Duke of Wellington and consult with him, when both would return, and he said this must suspend all further proceedings, and he asked whether I should be ready to receive a decision, which I said I should; he was quite perturbed—but this is infamous. I said, besides many other things, that if he or the Duke of Wellington had been at the head of the Government when I came to the Throne, perhaps there might have been a few more Tory Ladies, but that then if you had come into Office you would never have dreamt of changing them. I was calm but very decided, and I think you would have been pleased to see my composure and great firmness; the Queen of England will not submit to such trickery. Keep yourself in readiness, for you may soon be wanted.

PROPOSED NEW CABINET

At half-past two I saw the Duke of Wellington. I remained firm, and he told Sir Robert that I remained firm. I then saw Sir Robert Peel, who stopped a few minutes with me; he must consult those (of whom I annex the List) whom he had named:

and he said he would return in two or three hours with the result, which I said I should await.35

Footnote 35: It was a curious circumstance, much commented on at the time, that in the Globe of 9th May, a Ministerial evening paper, which would probably have gone to press at two o'clock in the afternoon, the following paragraph appeared: "The determination which it is well known Her Majesty has taken, not to allow the change in the Government to interfere with the ladies of her Court, has given great offence to the Tories."

Buckingham Palace, 9th May 1839.

The Queen has received Lord Melbourne's letter. Lord Melbourne will since have heard what has taken place. Lord Melbourne must not think the Queen rash in her conduct; she saw both the Duke and Sir Robert again, and declared to them she could not change her opinion. The Ladies are not (as the Duke imagined was stated in the Civil List Bill) in the place of the Lords; and the Queen felt this was an attempt to see whether she could be led and managed like a child; if it should lead to Sir Robert Peel's refusing to undertake the formation of the Government, which would be absurd, the Queen will feel satisfied that she has only been defending her own rights, on a point which so nearly concerned her person, and which, if they had succeeded in, would have led to every sort of unfair attempt at power; the Queen maintains all her ladies,—and thinks her Prime Minister will cut a sorry figure indeed if he resigns on this. Sir Robert is gone to consult with his friends, and will return in two or three hours with his decision. The Queen also maintained the Mistress of the Robes, for as he said only those who are in Parliament shall be removed, I should like to know if they mean to give the Ladies seats in Parliament?

We shall see what will be done. The Queen would not have stood so firmly on the Grooms and Equerries, but her Ladies are entirely her own affair, and not the Ministers'.

THE CRISIS

9th May 1839.

Lord Melbourne presents his humble duty to your Majesty. Lord Melbourne had certainly never expected that this demand would be urged, and therefore had never advised your Majesty as to what was to be done in such a case. Lord Melbourne strongly advises your Majesty to hear what the Duke of Wellington and Sir Robert Peel urge, but to take time before you come to a peremptory and final decision.

9th May 1839.

Lord Melbourne presents his humble duty to your Majesty. This is a matter of so much importance, and may have such grave results, that any advice which Lord Melbourne could give would be of little importance unless it coincided with the opinions of others, and particularly of all those who were and intend still [to] continue to be his colleagues.

It will depend upon their determination whether your Majesty is to be supported or not. The best course will perhaps be that you should hear Sir Robert Peel's determination, say nothing, but send for Lord Melbourne, and lay the matter before him. Lord Melbourne will then summon a Cabinet to consider of it.

THE LADIES OF THE BEDCHAMBER

At half-past six came Lord Melbourne and stayed with me till ten minutes past seven.

I then began by giving him a detailed account of the whole proceeding, which I shall state here as briefly as possible. I first again related what took place in the two first interviews, and when I said that the Duke said he had assisted my Government often very much, Lord Melbourne said: "Well, that is true enough, but the Duke did all he could about this vote." "Well, then," I said, "when Sir Robert Peel came this morning, he began first about the Ministry. I consented, though

I said I might have my personal feelings about Lord Lyndhurst and Lord Aberdeen, but that I would suppress every personal feeling and be quite fair. I then repeated that I wished to retain about me those who were not in Parliament, and Sir Robert pretended that I had the preceding day expressed a wish to keep about me those who were in Parliament. I mentioned my wish to have Lord Liverpool, to which Sir Robert readily acceded, saying he would offer him the place of Lord Steward, or of Lord in Waiting. He then suggested my having Lord Ashley,36 which I said I should like, as Treasurer or Comptroller.THE LADIES Soon after this Sir Robert said: 'Now, about the Ladies,' upon which I said I could not give up any of my Ladies, and never had imagined such a thing. He asked if I meant to retain all. 'All,' I said. 'The Mistress of the Robes and the Ladies of the Bedchamber?' I replied, 'All,'—for he said they were the wives of the opponents of the Government, mentioning Lady Normanby37 in particular as one of the late Ministers' wives. I said that would not interfere; that I never talked politics with them, and that they were related, many of them, to Tories, and I enumerated those of my Bedchamber women and Maids of Honour; upon which he said he did not mean all the Bedchamber women and all the Maids of Honour, he meant the Mistress of the Robes and the Ladies of the Bedchamber; to which I replied they were of more consequence than the others, and that I could not consent, and that it had never been done before. He said I was a Queen Regnant, and that made the difference. 'Not here,' I said—and I maintained my right. Sir Robert then urged it upon public grounds only, but I said here I could not consent. He then begged to be allowed to consult with the Duke upon such an important matter. I expressed a wish also to see the Duke, if Sir Robert approved, which he said he did, and that he would return with the Duke, if I would then be prepared for the decision, which I said I would. Well," I continued, "the Duke and Sir Robert returned soon, and I first saw the Duke, who talked first of his being ready to take the post of Secretary for Foreign Affairs, which I had pressed Peel to urge on him (the Duke having first wished to be in the Cabinet, without accepting office), and the Duke said, 'I am able to do anything,' for I asked him if it would not be too much for him. Then I told him that I had been very well satisfied with Sir Robert yesterday, and asked the Duke if Sir Robert had told him what had passed about the Ladies. He said he had, and then I repeated all my arguments, and the Duke his; but the Duke and Sir Robert differed considerably on two points. The Duke said the opinions of the Ladies were nothing, but it was the principle, whether the Minister could remove the Ladies or not, and that he (the Duke) had understood it was stated in the Civil List Bill, 'that the Ladies were instead of the Lords,' which is quite false, and I told the Duke that there were not twelve Lords, as the expense with the Ladies would have been too great." Lord Melbourne said: "There you had the better of him, and what did he say?" "Not much," I replied. I repeated many of my arguments, all which pleased Lord Melbourne, and which he agreed to, amongst others, that I said to the Duke, Was Sir Robert so weak that even the Ladies must be of his opinion? The Duke denied that. The Duke then took my decision to Sir Robert, who was waiting in the next room; after a few minutes Sir Robert returned. After stopping a few minutes, as I have already stated, Sir Robert went to see his colleagues, and returned at five: said he had consulted with those who were to have been his colleagues, and that they agreed that, with the probability of being beat the first night about the Speaker, and beginning with a Minority in the House of Commons, that unless there was some (all the Officers of State and Lords I gave up) demonstration of my confidence, and if I retained all my Ladies this would not be, "they agreed unanimously they could not go on." I replied I would reflect, that I felt certain I should not change my mind, but that I should do nothing in a hurry, and would write him my decision either that evening or the next morning. He said, meanwhile, he would suspend all further proceedings.

Footnote 36: Afterwards Earl of Shaftesbury, the well-known Philanthropist.

Footnote 37: J. W. Croker wrote to the King of Hanover:—

"11th May 1839.

"... This is the sum of the whole affair. Sir R. Peel could not admit that broad principle that all were to remain. Lady Normanby (whom the Queen particularly wishes for), for instance, the wife of the very Minister whose measures have been the cause of the change, two sisters of Lord Morpeth, the sisters-in-law of Lord John Russell, the daughter of the Privy Seal and the Chancellor of the Exchequer....

"Her Majesty's ball last night was, I am told, rather dull, though she herself seemed in high spirits, as if she were pleased at retaining her Ministers. She has a great concert on the 13th, but to both, as I hear, the invitations have been on a very exclusive principle, no Tories being invited who could on any pretence be left out. These are small matters, but everything tends to create a public impression that Her Majesty takes a personal and strong interest in the Whigs—a new ingredient of difficulty."—Croker Papers, II. 347.

I also told Lord Melbourne that I feared I had embarrassed the Government; that I acted quite alone. Lord Melbourne saw, and said I could not do otherwise. "I must summon the Cabinet," said Lord Melbourne, at half-past nine. "It may have very serious consequences. If we can't go on with this House of Commons, we may have to dissolve Parliament, and we don't know if we may get as good a House of Commons." I begged him to come, and he said: "I'll come if it is in any time—if it's twelve; but if it's one or two, I'll write."

After dinner (as usual with the Household) I went to my room, and sat up till a quarter past two. At a quarter to two I received the following letter from Lord Melbourne, written at one o'clock:—

THE QUEEN'S ULTIMATUM

10th May 1839 (1 a.m.).

Lord Melbourne presents his humble duty to your Majesty. The Cabinet has sate until now, and, after much discussion, advises your Majesty to return the following answer to Sir Robert Peel:—

"The Queen having considered the proposal made to her yesterday by Sir Robert Peel to remove the Ladies of her Bedchamber, cannot consent to adopt a course which she conceives to be contrary to usage, and which is repugnant to her feelings."38

Footnote 38: Greville asserts that the plan adopted by the outgoing Cabinet, of meeting and suggesting that this letter should be despatched, was "utterly anomalous and unprecedented, and a course as dangerous as unconstitutional.... They ought to have explained to her that until Sir

Robert Peel had formally and finally resigned his commission into her hands, they could tender no advice.... The Cabinet of Lord Melbourne discussed the proposals of that of Sir Robert Peel, and they dictated to the Queen the reply in which she refused to consent to the advice tendered to her by the man who was at that moment her Minister."—Greville's Journal, 12th May 1839.

10th May 1839.

The Queen having considered the proposal made to her yesterday by Sir Robert Peel, to remove the Ladies of her Bedchamber, cannot consent to adopt a course which she conceives to be contrary to usage, and which is repugnant to her feelings.39

Footnote 39: Sixty years later the Queen, during a conversation at Osborne with Sir Arthur Bigge, her Private Secretary, after eulogising Sir Robert Peel, said: "I was very young then, and perhaps I should act differently if it was all to be done again."

Buckingham Palace, 10th May 1839.

The Queen wrote the letter before she went to bed, and sent it at nine this morning; she has received no answer, and concludes she will receive none, as Sir Robert told the Queen if the Ladies were not removed, his party would fall directly, and could not go on, and that he only awaited the Queen's decision. The Queen therefore wishes to see Lord Melbourne about half-past twelve or one, if that would do.

The Queen fears Lord Melbourne has much trouble in consequence of all this; but the Queen was fully prepared, and fully intended to give these people a fair trial, though she always told Lord Melbourne she knew they couldn't stand; and she must rejoice at having got out of the hands of people who would have sacrificed every personal feeling and instinct of the Queen's to their bad party purposes.

How is Lord Melbourne this morning?

AN ANXIOUS WEEK

Buckingham Palace, 10th May 1839.

Half-past one will do as well as one; any hour will do that Lord Melbourne likes, for the Queen will not go out.

There is no answer from Peel.

The Queen is wonderfully well, considering all the fatigue of yesterday, and not getting to bed till near half-past two, which is somewhat of a fatigue for to-night when the Queen must be very late. Really all these Fêtes in the midst of such very serious and anxious business are quite overwhelming.

Buckingham Palace, 10th May 1839.

The Queen forgot to ask Lord Melbourne if he thought there would be any harm in her writing to the Duke of Cambridge that she really was fearful of fatiguing herself, if she went out to a party at Gloucester House on Tuesday, an Ancient Concert on Wednesday, and a ball at Northumberland House on Thursday, considering how much she had to do these last four days. If she went to the Ancient Concert on Wednesday, having besides a concert of her own here on Monday, it would be four nights of fatigue, really exhausted as the Queen is.

But if Lord Melbourne thinks that as there are only to be English singers at the Ancient

Concert, she ought to go, she could go there for one act; but she would much rather, if possible, get out of it, for it is a fatiguing time....

As the negotiations with the Tories are quite at an end, and Lord Melbourne has been here, the Queen hopes Lord Melbourne will not object to dining with her on Sunday?

RESIGNATION OF PEEL

10th May 1839.

Sir Robert Peel presents his humble duty to your Majesty, and has had the honour of receiving your Majesty's note of this morning.

In respectfully submitting to your Majesty's pleasure, and humbly returning into your Majesty's hands the important trust which your Majesty had been graciously pleased to commit to him, Sir Robert Peel trusts that your Majesty will permit him to state to your Majesty his impression with respect to the circumstances which have led to the termination of his attempt to form an Administration for the conduct of your Majesty's Service.

In the interview with which your Majesty honoured Sir Robert Peel yesterday morning, after he had submitted to your Majesty the names of those whom he proposed to recommend to your Majesty for the principal executive appointments, he mentioned to your Majesty his earnest wish to be enabled, with your Majesty's sanction, so to constitute your Majesty's Household that your Majesty's confidential servants might have the advantage of a public demonstration of your Majesty's full support and confidence, and that at the same time, as far as possible consistently with that demonstration, each individual appointment in the Household should be entirely acceptable to your Majesty's personal feelings.

On your Majesty's expressing a desire that the Earl of Liverpool40 should hold an office in the Household, Sir Robert Peel requested your Majesty's permission at once to offer to Lord Liverpool the office of Lord Steward, or any other which he might prefer.

Sir Robert Peel then observed that he should have every wish to apply a similar principle to the chief appointments which are filled by the Ladies of your Majesty's Household, upon which your Majesty was pleased to remark that you must reserve the whole of those appointments, and that it was your Majesty's pleasure that the whole should continue as at present, without any change.

The Duke of Wellington, in the interview to which your Majesty subsequently admitted him, understood also that this was your Majesty's determination, and concurred with Sir Robert Peel in opinion that, considering the great difficulties of the present crisis, and the expediency of making every effort in the first instance to conduct the public business of the country with the aid of the present Parliament, it was essential to the success of the Commission with which your Majesty had honoured Sir Robert Peel, that he should have that public proof of your Majesty's entire support and confidence which would be afforded by the permission to make some changes in that part of your Majesty's Household which your Majesty resolved on maintaining entirely without change.

Having had the opportunity through your Majesty's gracious consideration, of reflecting upon this point, he humbly submits to your Majesty that he is reluctantly compelled, by a sense of public duty and of the interests of your Majesty's service, to adhere to his opinion which he ventured to express to your Majesty.

He trusts he may be permitted at the same time to express to your Majesty his grateful acknowledgments for the distinction which your Majesty conferred upon him by requiring his advice and assistance in the attempt to form an Administration, and his earnest prayers that whatever arrangements your Majesty may be enabled to make for that purpose may be most conducive to your Majesty's personal comfort and happiness, and to the promotion of the public welfare.

Footnote 40: Charles Cecil Cope Jenkinson, third Earl, 1784-1851, became Lord Steward in 1841.

THE QUEEN'S JOURNAL

Lord Melbourne came to me at two and stayed with me till ten minutes to three. I placed in his hands Sir Robert Peel's answer, which he read. He started at one part where he (Sir Robert) says, "some changes"—but some or all, I said, was the same; and Lord Melbourne said, "I must submit this to the Cabinet." Lord Melbourne showed me a letter from Lord Grey about it—a good deal alarmed, thinking I was right, and yet half doubtful; one from Spring Rice, dreadfully frightened, and wishing the Whig ladies should resign; and one from Lord Lansdowne wishing to state that the ladies would have resigned. Lord Melbourne had also seen the Duke of Richmond, and Lord Melbourne said we might be beat; I said I never would yield, and would never apply to Peel again. Lord Melbourne said, "You are for standing out, then?" I said, "Certainly." I asked how the Cabinet felt. "John Russell, strongly for standing out," he said; "Duncannon, very much so; Holland, Lord Minto, Hobhouse, and the Chancellor, all for standing out; Poulett Thomson too, and Normanby also; S. Rice and Howick alarmed."

CABINET MINUTE

Present.

* The Lord Chancellor.
* The Lord President.
* The Lord Privy Seal.
* Viscount Melbourne.
* The Marquis of Normanby.
* The Earl of Minto.
* The Chancellor of the Duchy of Lancaster.
* The Lord John Russell.
* The Viscount Palmerston.
* The Viscount Howick.
* The Viscount Morpeth.
* Sir John Hobhouse, Bart.
* The Chancellor of the Exchequer.
* Mr. Poulett Thomson.

Her Majesty's Confidential Servants having taken into consideration the letter addressed by Her Majesty to Sir Robert Peel on the 10th of May, and the reply of Sir Robert Peel of the same day, are of opinion that for the purpose of giving to an Administration that character of efficiency and stability and those marks of the constitutional support of the Crown, which are required to enable it to act usefully for the public service, it is reasonable that the great offices of the Court and the situations in the Household held by members of either House of Parliament should be included in the political arrangements made on a change of Administration; but they are not of opinion that a similar principle should be applied or extended to the offices held by Ladies in Her Majesty's Household.41

Footnote 41: This paragraph was read by Lord John Russell to the House of Commons during the course of the Ministerial explanations on 13th May.

Her Majesty's Confidential Servants are therefore prepared to support Her Majesty in refusing to assent to the removal of the Ladies of her Household, which Her Majesty conceived to be contrary to usage, and which is repugnant to her feelings, and are prepared to continue in their offices on these grounds.

Viscount Howick concurs in the opinion expressed in the foregoing Minute that the removal of the Ladies of Her Majesty's Household ought not to form part of the arrangements consequent upon a change of Administration, and shares in the readiness his colleagues have declared to support Her Majesty in acting upon this opinion; but he thinks it his duty to state his conviction that the immediate resumption of their offices by Her Majesty's Confidential Servants is not the mode in which their support can be most effectively afforded and is not calculated to promote the good of Her Majesty's service.

He conceives that before it is determined that the present Administration should be continued, further explanation should be sought with Sir Robert Peel, by which it is not impossible that his concession to Her Majesty's just objection to the removal of the Ladies of her Household might have been obtained, while the endeavour to arrive at this result, even though unsuccessful, would at all events tend to secure additional support to Her Majesty's present Servants, and thus to enable them to surmount those difficulties, which have recently compelled them humbly to tender their resignations to Her Majesty, and which he fears will be found not to have been diminished by the course it has now been determined to pursue.

In humbly submitting this opinion to Her Majesty, Viscount Howick begs permission to add that he nevertheless acquiesces in the determination of his colleagues, and will render them the best assistance in his power in their endeavour to carry on Her Majesty's service.

MELBOURNE RESUMES OFFICE

Buckingham Palace, 11th May 1839.

The Queen is very anxious to hear that Lord Melbourne has not suffered from the ball last night, as it was very hot at first. The beginning was rather dull and heavy, but after supper it got very animated, and we kept it up till a quarter past three; the Queen enjoyed herself very much and isn't at all tired; she felt much the kindness of many of her kind friends, who are her only real friends. Lady Cowper and Lord and Lady Minto, the Duchess of Somerset, and Lord Anglesey were particularly kind. On the other hand, there were some gloomy faces to be seen, and the Duchess of Gloucester was very cross.

The Queen is ashamed to say it, but she has forgotten when she appointed the Judge Advocate; when will the Cabinet be over?

The Queen danced the first and the last dance with the Grand Duke,42 made him sit near her, and tried to be very civil to him, and I think we are great friends already and get on very well; I like him exceedingly.

Footnote 42: The Hereditary Grand Duke of Russia, afterwards the Emperor Alexander II.

Buckingham Palace, 12th May 1839.

The Queen anxiously hopes Lord Melbourne is quite well this morning, and has not suffered from the dinner at Pozzo's.

The Queen wishes to know if she ought to say anything to the Duchess, of the noble manner in which her Government mean to stand by her? The account in the Observer of the whole proceeding is the most correct both as to details and facts, that the Queen has yet seen; were they told what to put in? There was considerable applause when the Queen entered the Theatre, which she, however, thought best and most delicate not to encourage, and she was cheered when she drove up to the Theatre and got out, which she never is in general.

The Grand Duke came and sat with the Queen in her box, for at least half an hour last night—and the Queen asked him if he knew exactly what had happened, which he said he did not—and the Queen accordingly gave him an account of what passed, and he was shocked at Sir Robert Peel's proposal, thought his resignation on that account absurd, and was delighted at the continuance in office of my present Government.

The Queen supposes and fears that Lord Melbourne dines with the Lansdownes to-morrow, but she wishes to know if Wednesday, Saturday, and Sunday would suit him?

Lord Melbourne must not forget the List of our supporters in the House of Commons, which the Queen is very anxious to have as soon as possible. If Lord Melbourne can dine here to-morrow the Queen would be glad, of course.

LORD JOHN RUSSELL'S OPINION

13th May 1839.

Lord John Russell presents his humble duty to your Majesty, and has the honour to report that he this day made his statement to the House, in answer to Sir Robert Peel.

Sir Robert Peel made a skilful, and not unfair statement. He, however, spoke only of his intention of changing some of the Ladies of the Bedchamber. But he did not say that he had made this intention clear to your Majesty; only that he had so arranged the matter with his political friends. The popular impression is greatly in favour of the course pursued by your Majesty.

14th May 1839.

Lord Melbourne presents his humble duty to your Majesty, and is most sorry to hear that your Majesty does not feel well. It is very natural that your Majesty does not. Lord Melbourne does not believe that there was anything wanting in your Majesty's manner yesterday evening,43 but depend upon it, if there was, every allowance would be made for the fatigue and anxiety which your Majesty has gone through, and for the painful and embarrassing situation in which your

Majesty is still placed.

Lord Melbourne will wait upon your Majesty at two, and will have the honour of conversing with your Majesty upon Peel's speech.

Footnote 43: At the State Concert.

THE QUEEN'S VIEW

Buckingham Palace, 14th May 1839.

My dear Uncle,—I begin to think you have forgotten me, and you will think I have forgotten you, but I am certain you will have guessed the cause of my silence. How much has taken place since Monday the 7th to yesterday the 13th. You will have easily imagined how dreadful the resignation of my Government—and particularly of that truly inestimable and excellent man, Lord Melbourne—was for me, and you will have felt for me! What I suffered I cannot describe! To have to take people whom I should have no confidence in, ... was most painful and disagreeable; but I felt I must do it, and made up my mind to it—nobly advised and supported by Lord Melbourne, whose character seems to me still more perfect and noble since I have gone through all this.

I sent for the Duke of Wellington, who referred me to Peel, whom I accordingly saw.

Everything fair and just I assented to, even to having Lord Lyndhurst as Chancellor, and Sir H. Hardinge and Lord Ellenborough in the Cabinet; I insisted upon the Duke in the Foreign Office, instead of Lord Aberdeen.... All this I granted, as also to give up all the Officers of State and all those of my Household who are in Parliament.

When to my utter astonishment he asked me to change my Ladies—my principal Ladies!—this I of course refused; and he upon this resigned, saying, as he felt he should be beat the very first night upon the Speaker, and having to begin with a minority, that unless he had this demonstration of my confidence he could not go on!

You will easily imagine that I firmly resisted this attack upon my power, from these people who pride themselves upon upholding the prerogative! I acted quite alone, but I have been, and shall be, supported by my country, who are very enthusiastic about it, and loudly cheered me on going to church on Sunday. My Government have nobly stood by me, and have resumed their posts, strengthened by the feelings of the country....

Pray tell my dearest Aunt that I really cannot write to her to-day, for you have no conception of what I have to do, for there are balls, concerts, and dinners all going on besides. Adieu! my beloved Uncle. Ever your devoted Niece,

Victoria R.

APPROVAL OF KING LEOPOLD

Laeken, 17th May 1839.

My dearest Victoria,—I feel deeply grateful for your very kind and interesting letter, which reached me yesterday, inclusive of the papers.

You have passed a time of great agitation and difficulty, which will, however, contribute to enlarge the circle of your experience. I approve very highly of the whole mode in which you proceeded; you acted with great good faith and fairness, and when finally propositions were made which you considered you could not submit to, you were very right to resist them. The march of the whole affair is very clear and fair, and does you great credit.... Peel in making his demand misjudged you; he remembered George IV., and even the late King, and dreamt of Court influence of people near the Sovereign. You have the great merit, for which you cannot be too much praised, of being extremely honest and honourable in your dealings. If you had kept Peel, you would have acted honestly by him, without any Lady's having a chance of doing him a bad turn. When he asked the measure as an expression of your great confidence in him, it was not fair, because you had not wished to take him; he was forced upon you, and therefore, even if you had granted his request, nobody would have seen in it a proof of your confidence in him, but rather a sacrifice to a far-stretched pretence.

Besides, that he was to have encountered difficulties as a Minister was partly the consequence of the policy of his party, and you were not bound to give him any assistance beyond what he had a right to ask as a Minister. I was sure that Lord Melbourne would give you both the fairest and the most honourable advice in this painful crisis. He was kind enough last year to speak to me on the subject, and I could but approve what he said on the subject. Altogether, keeping now your old Ministers, you will have reason to congratulate yourself on the result; it is likely to strengthen them, by showing the Radicals what may be the consequences.

Rumour spoke of their wishing to add some Radicals to the Cabinet; I don't see that they could improve the Ministry by it, which is perfectly well composed as it is at present, and new elements often have a dissolving effect. It was very kind of you to have explained everything so clearly to me, but I deserve it for the great interest I take in all that concerns you....

H.R.H. The Prince Consort, 1840.

From the portrait by John Partridge at Buckingham Palace

To face p. 176, Vol. I

6th June 1839.

Lord John Russell presents his humble duty to your Majesty, and has the honour to report that Sir Robert Peel's Bill44 was discussed yesterday in the House of Commons, with great fairness and an entire absence of party spirit.

Viscount Melbourne will have acquainted your Majesty with the result of the Cabinet of yesterday. It appears to Lord John Russell that the Liberal party, with some explanation, will be satisfied with the state of things for the present, and that the great difficulties which attend the complete union of the majority will be deferred till the commencement of next Session. It is always well to have some breathing-time.

Footnote 44: The Jamaica Bill for the temporary suspension of the Constitution.

Wilton Crescent, 11th June 1839.

Lord John Russell presents his humble duty to your Majesty, and has the honour to state that the division of last night was extremely encouraging to the future prospects of the Government.

Combined with the division on the Speakership,45 it shows that the Liberal party have still a clear though small majority in the House of Commons, and that it may probably not be necessary to resort to a dissolution. Indeed, such a measure in present circumstances would be of very doubtful issue.

Lord John Russell stated last night that he would not divide on the Canada resolutions, but move for leave to bring in a Bill.

Footnote 45: Mr Shaw Lefevre was elected by 317 against 299 for Mr Goulburn.

6th July 1839.

Lord John Russell presents his humble duty to your Majesty, and has the honour to report that Mr. Rice yesterday brought forward his financial statement with great ability.

He moved a resolution in favour of a penny postage, which Sir Robert Peel declared it to be his intention to oppose on the report. This will be on Friday next. This seems a mistake on the part of the Opposition.46

Footnote 46: The penny postage scheme came into operation on 10th January 1840.

THE QUEEN AND PRINCE ALBERT

Buckingham Palace, 12th July 1839.

(20 minutes to 12.)

The Queen is really quite shocked to see that her box was taken to Lord Melbourne to Park Lane, and she fears (by the manner in which Lord Melbourne's note is written) that he was at dinner at Lady Elizabeth H. Vere's when he got it. The Queen had imagined that the House of Lords was still sitting, and therefore desired them to take the box there, but never had intended it should follow him to dinner; she begs Lord Melbourne to excuse this mistake which must have appeared so strange.

Did the dinner go off well at Lady Elizabeth H. Vere's, and were there many people there? Did Lord Melbourne go to Lady R. Grosvenor's party or did he go home?

The Queen hopes Lord Melbourne is quite well and not tired.

Monday at two o'clock for the Judge Advocate.

The Queen hears Lady Sandwich is very much delighted at her appointment.

My dear Uncle,—I have no letter from you, but hope to get one soon....

I shall send this letter by a courier, as I am anxious to put several questions to you, and to mention some feelings of mine upon the subject of my cousins' visit, which I am desirous should not transpire. First of all, I wish to know if Albert is aware of the wish of his Father and you relative to me? Secondly, if he knows that there is no engagement between us? I am anxious that you should acquaint Uncle Ernest, that if I should like Albert, that I can make no final promise this year, for, at the very earliest, any such event could not take place till two or three years hence. For, independent of my youth, and my great repugnance to change my present position, there is no anxiety evinced in this country for such an event, and it would be more prudent, in my opinion, to wait till some such demonstration is shown,—else if it were hurried it might produce discontent.

Though all the reports of Albert are most favourable, and though I have little doubt I shall like him, still one can never answer beforehand for feelings, and I may not have the feeling for him which is requisite to ensure happiness. I may like him as a friend, and as a cousin, and as a brother, but not more; and should this be the case (which is not likely), I am very anxious that it should be understood that I am not guilty of any breach of promise, for I never gave any. I am sure you will understand my anxiety, for I should otherwise, were this not completely understood, be in a very painful position. As it is, I am rather nervous about the visit, for the subject I allude to is not an agreeable one to me. I have little else to say, dear Uncle, as I have now spoken openly to you, which I was very, very anxious to do.

You will be at Paris, I suppose, when you get this letter, and I therefore beg you to lay me at the feet of the whole family, and to believe me ever your very devoted Niece,

Victoria R.

Buckingham Palace, 20th July 1839.

The Queen anxiously hopes Lord Melbourne has slept well, and has not suffered from last night. It was very wrong of him not to wish the Queen good-night, as she expected he would in so small a party, for she saw that he did not go away immediately after supper. When did he get home? It was great pleasure to the Queen that he came last night. We kept up the dancing till past three, and the Queen was much amused, and slept soundly from four till half-past ten, which she is ashamed of. She is quite well, but has got a good deal of cold in her head; she hopes to see Lord Melbourne at two.

THE DUCHESS OF BRAGANZA

Buckingham Palace, 25th July 1839.

The Queen has seen the Duchess of Braganza,47 who, though a good deal changed, is still handsome, and very amiable; she seemed so glad, too, to see the Queen again. The child48 is grown a dear fine girl. Lord Palmerston thought it right that I should ask her to dinner also on Saturday and take her to the Opera; and on Sunday, as she came on purpose to see the Queen, and goes on Monday.

On Sunday (besides Lord Melbourne) the Queen proposes asking Palmerston, Normanby, Uxbridge, and Surrey, and no one else except the Duchess's suite. The Queen hopes Lord Melbourne will approve of this. He will not forget to let the Queen know how the debate is going on, at about nine or ten, as she will be curious to know. She trusts he will not suffer from the fatigue of to-night.

Footnote 47: The step-mother of Donna Maria. Pedro I. assumed the title of Duke of Braganza after his abdication.

Footnote 48: Probably the princess known as "Chica," afterwards Princesse de Joinville.

SYRIAN AFFAIRS

St Cloud, 26th July 1839.

... Everything is pretty quiet, and the grâce accordée à Barbès49 has put down the rage against the King personally, at least for some little time. The affairs of the Orient interest a good deal. I think that it is better the Porte should be on a favourable footing with Mehemet Ali than if that gentleman had pushed on in arms, as it will put the casus foederis out of the question, and the Turks will not call in the assistance of the Russians. Whoever pushed the late Sultan into this war has done an act of great folly, as it could only bring the Porte into jeopardy.

Footnote 49: Armand Barbès, the leader of a fatal riot in Paris, was sentenced to death, a sentence afterwards remitted.

3rd August 1839.

Lord Melbourne will wait upon your Majesty at a quarter before five, if possible, but there is much to discuss at the Cabinet. The Caspian Pasha has taken the Turkish fleet to Alexandria,50 and Mehemet Ali says that he will not give it up to the Sultan until he dismisses the Grand Vizier, and acknowledges the hereditary right of the Pasha to the countries which he at present governs. This is to make the Sultan his subject and his vassal.

The accounts from Birmingham are by no means good.51 There has been no disturbance of the peace, but the general disposition is both violent and determined.

Footnote 50: The Viceroy of Egypt had revolted against the Porte, and on 8th June the Sultan purported to deprive him and Ibrahim, his son, of their dignities. War was declared, and the Turkish fleet despatched to Syria. But the Admiral treacherously sailed to Alexandria, and the Ottoman troops, under Hafiz, who had succeeded Mehemet Ali in the Government of Egypt, were utterly routed. With the traitorous conduct of the Turkish admiral, Disraeli, a few years later, compared Peel's conversion to Free Trade.

Footnote 51: Chartist riots were very frequent at the time. See Introductory Note, ante, p.

THE OPERA

Buckingham Palace, 4th August 1839.

The Queen hopes Lord Melbourne is quite well this morning, and did not sit up working very late last night; the Queen met him twice yesterday in the Park, and really wondered how anybody could ride, for she came home much hotter than she went out, and thought the air quite like as if it came out of an oven; to-day we can breathe again. It was intensely hot at the Opera; the Queen-Dowager visited the Queen in her box, as did also the young Grand Duke of Weimar, who is just returned from Scotland, and whom the Queen has asked to come after dinner to-morrow. The Queen has not asked the Duke of Sussex to come after dinner to-morrow, as she thought he would be bored by such a sort of party; does not Lord Melbourne think so? and she means to ask him to dinner soon.

The Queen has not asked Lord Melbourne about any days this week besides to-morrow (when she trusts he may be able to come, but she does not know what there is in the House) and Wednesday; but perhaps Lord Melbourne will consent to leave Thursday and Friday open in case he should be able to come one or both of those days.

Buckingham Palace, 4th August 1839.

The Queen has just received Lord Melbourne's letter; and wishes to know if Lord Melbourne means by "to-day" that he is also coming to see her this afternoon, (which she does not expect) as well as this evening? for she did not ask him in her note of this morning if he would come to-night (for she felt sure of that), but if he could come to-morrow, about which he has not answered her, as to whether he expects there will be anything of great length in the House of Lords. Lord Melbourne will forgive the Queen's troubling him again, but she felt a little puzzled by his letter; she sent him a card for Wednesday without previously asking him, as she thought that would suit him, and hopes it does?

The Queen will follow Lord Melbourne's advice respecting the Duke of Sussex.

We have just returned from hearing not only a very long, and very bad, but also, a very ludicrous, sermon.

The heat is somewhat less, but the Queen is undecided as to driving out or not.

KING LOUIS PHILIPPE

Laeken, 9th August 1839.

... I am sorry that you are less pleased with the old Duke, but party spirit is in England an incurable disease. These last two years he had rendered essential service to the present Administration; perhaps he has been soured by last summer's events. It was my intention to have answered your questions sooner, but from Paris I had not the means. Now the time draws so near when I hope to have the happiness of seeing you, that I think it will be better to treat the matter verbally, the more so as my most beloved Majesty is easily displeased with what may be written with the best intention, instead that in conversation the immediate reply renders any misunderstanding, however small, very difficult; and as I do not wish to have any great or small with you, and see no occasion for it, I will give my answer de vive voix.

Now comes a subject which will astonish you. I am charged de sonder your will and pleasure on the following subject. The King my father-in-law goes to Eu, where he hopes to remain till the 5th or 6th of September. Having at his disposition some very fine steamers, his great wish would be to go over to Brighton, just for one afternoon and night, to offer you his respects in person. He would in such a case bring with him the Queen, my Aunt, Clémentine,52 Aumale and Montpensier. The first step in this business is to know what your pleasure is, and to learn that very frankly, as he perfectly understands that, however short such a visit, it must be submitted to the advice even of some of your Ministers. What renders the thing very difficult, in my opinion, is that in a country like France, and with so many Ministerial difficulties, the King to the last hour will hardly know if he can undertake the thing. As, however, the first object is to know your will, he begged me to ascertain that, and to tell you that if you had the smallest objection you would not be carried away by the apprehension of hurting him by telling me honestly that you did not see how the affair could be arranged, but to speak out, that he knew enough how often objections may arise, and that even with himself he could only be sure of the thing at the last moment.

Footnote 52: Who afterwards married Queen Victoria's cousin, Prince Augustus (Gusti) of Coburg.

THE NEW SULTAN

Foreign Office, 19th August 1839.

Viscount Palmerston presents his humble duty to your Majesty, and in submitting the accompanying private letter from the Earl Granville53 begs to state that neither Viscount Melbourne nor Viscount Palmerston are of opinion that it would be expedient that your Majesty should send an Ambassador Extraordinary to compliment the young Sultan54 on his accession. The circumstances connected with his accession are indeed fitter matter for condolence than for congratulation, and he would probably be better pleased by the restoration of his fleet than by the arrival of Ambassadors Extraordinary. Moreover, it has not been customary for the Sovereign of England to send such missions upon the accession of Sultans.

Footnote 53: The first Earl Granville (1773-1846), formerly Ambassador Extraordinary to the Russian Court, at this time Ambassador at Paris.

Footnote 54: Abdul Medjid, a lad of sixteen, succeeded the Sultan Mahmoud. The majority of the Powers agreed to place him under the protection of Europe, and to warn Mehemet Ali that the matter was for Europe, not him, to decide. France, however, wished to support Mehemet, and direct the Alliance against Russia. But Nicholas I. of Russia was prepared to support England as far as regarded the affairs of Turkey and Egypt, and to close the Dardanelles and Bosphorus to war-ships of all nations, it being stipulated that Russian ships of war only were to pass the Bosphorus, as acting under the mandate of Europe in defence of the Turks. See further, Introductory Notes for and

LOUIS PHILIPPE'S VISIT

Ostende, 24th August 1839.

... The King's intention would be to leave Eu in the evening, let us say at eight or nine o'clock, and to land, perhaps at ten or eleven, at Brighton on the following morning. He would have the honour of dining with you, and would re-embark in the evening of the same day, so as to be back on the following morning at Eu. He will therefore, as you see, not sleep in England.

If you cannot give any pied-à-terre in the Palace for these few hours, they will remain in an hotel. But I must say that as the King and Queen put themselves to some inconvenience in coming to see you, it would be rather desirable to offer them rooms in the Palace, which I think might be easily managed. As far as we are concerned, it does not matter if we are housed in an hotel or where we bivouac. I will charge Van de Weyer to take rooms for us somewhere....

Do not imagine that I have done the least to bring this about for my own satisfaction, which is very limited in this business, but the King wished much to see you once, and so did the Queen, who abhors sailing more than anybody, and this is perhaps the only opportunity which may ever offer of doing it, even with some political benefit, as it certainly is desirable that it should appear that the two maritime Powers are on good terms.... And now, God bless you! Ever, my dearest Victoria, your devoted Uncle,

Leopold R.

Ostende, 25th August 1839.

(La St Louis.)

My dear Victoria,—To keep up the fire of letters, I write again, having received this morning interesting news. As I must forward this letter by Calais, and know not who may read it in these times of curiosity, I am forced to be guarded; but the news are as follows, of the 23rd—curious coincidence, as your letter was also of that date—that, the moment approaching, many and serious difficulties arise, and that the expedition was considered imprudent by some people, that, besides, the presence would perhaps be required, before the possible departure, at the usual home of the person interested, that therefore for the present it would perhaps be best to give it up. I must say that I am most happy that matters have come to this pass, because it would have been next to impossible to arrange affairs properly in proper time. You may now consider everything as over, and settle your plans without reference to it....

THE VISIT POSTPONED

Buckingham Palace, 26th August 1839.

My dearest Uncle,—I had already written you a letter when I received your two very kind ones, and I shall therefore not send my first. My friendship for the dear King and Queen makes me, as you may easily understand, wish most exceedingly to see them and to make the acquaintance of the Queen and all the family. And I feel the immense kindness of them all in wishing to see me, and in coming over for only a few hours. Politically it would be wished by us all, and the only difficulty I see is the following, which is, that I do not feel quite equal to going to Brighton and receiving them all, so soon after the Prorogation.55 I do not feel well; I feel thoroughly exhausted from all that I have gone through this Session, and am quite knocked up by the two little trips I made to Windsor. This makes me fear, uncertain as it all is, with such a pressure of business, so many affairs, and with so much going on, that I should be unequal to the journey and the whole thing. This, and this alone, could make me express a wish that this most kind visit should take place next year instead of this year. I feel such regret really in saying this—I should so wish to see them, and yet I feel I am not quite up to it. You will understand me, dear Uncle, I am certain, as I know the anxiety you always express for my health. For once I long to leave London, and shall do so on Friday. If you could be at Windsor by the 4th, I should be delighted.

The dear Ferdinands, whom I all dearly love, will await you here. I have had so much to do and so many people to see, that I feel quite confused, and have written shockingly, which you must forgive. Ever your devoted Niece,

Victoria R.

Footnote 55: On 27th August.

THE QUEEN'S SPEECH

Buckingham Palace, 26 August 1839. (10 minutes to 12.)

The Queen has received both Lord Melbourne's notes; she was a good deal vexed at his not coming, as she had begged him herself to do so, and as he wrote to say he would, and also as she thinks it right and of importance that Lord Melbourne should be here at large dinners; the Queen insists upon his coming to dinner to-morrow, and also begs him to do so on Wednesday, her two last nights in town, and as she will probably not see him at all for two days when she goes on Friday; the Queen would wish to see Lord Melbourne after the Prorogation to-morrow at any hour before five he likes best.

The Queen has been a good deal annoyed this evening at Normanby's telling her that John Russell was coming to town next Monday in order to change with him.56 Lord Melbourne never told the Queen that this was definitely settled; on the contrary, he said it would "remain in our hands," to use Lord Melbourne's own words, and only be settled during the Vacation; considering all that the Queen has said on the subject to Lord Melbourne, and considering the great confidence the Queen has in Lord Melbourne, she thinks and feels he ought to have told her that this was settled, and not let the Queen be the last person to hear what is settled and done in her own name; Lord Melbourne will excuse the Queen's being a little eager about this, but it has happened once before that she learnt from other people what had been decided on.

The Queen has such unlimited confidence in Lord Melbourne that she knows all that he does is right, but she cannot help being a little vexed at not being told things, when she is accustomed to great confidence on Lord Melbourne's part.

Lord Melbourne may rely on the Queen's secrecy respecting Howick; he knows the Queen always keeps things to herself; Normanby hinted at his wish to get rid of Howick.

The Speech is safely arrived, has been read over twice, and shall not be forgotten to-morrow; the Queen wishes they would not use such thin and slippery paper—for it is difficult to hold with nervous, and, as Lord Melbourne knows, shaking hands. The Queen trusts Lord Melbourne will be less tired in the morning.

Footnote 56: See Introductory Note, ante, p.

Ostende, 21st September 1839.

My dearest Victoria,—Your delightful little letter has just arrived and went like an arrow to my heart. Yes, my beloved Victoria! I do love you tenderly, and with all the power of affection which is often found in characters who do not make much outward show of it. I love you for yourself, and I love in you the dear child whose welfare I carefully watched. My great wish is always that you should know that I am desirous of being useful to you, without hoping for any other return than some little affection from your warm and kind heart. I am even so far pleased that my eternal political affairs are settled, as it takes away the last possibility of imagining that I may want something or other. I have all the honours that can be given, and I am, politically speaking, very solidly established, more so than most Sovereigns in Europe. The only political longing I still have is for the Orient, where I perhaps shall once end my life, unlike the sun, rising in the West and setting in the East. I never press my services on you, nor my councils, though I may say with some truth that from the extraordinary fate which the higher Powers had ordained for me, my experience, both political and of private life, is great. I am always ready to be useful to you when and where it may be, and I repeat it, all I want in return is some little sincere affection from you....

And now I conclude for to-day, not without expressing again my satisfaction and pleasure at having seen you yesterday morning with your dear honest face, looking so dear in your morning attire. Our time was spent very satisfactorily, and only the weather crossed our wishes, and to that one can submit when everything else is delightful. Once more, God bless you! Ever, my dearest Victoria, your devoted Uncle,

Leopold R.

VISIT OF PRINCE ALBERT

Windsor Castle, 25th September 1839.

My dear Uncle,—You will, I think, laugh when you get this letter, and will think I only mean to employ you in stopping my relations at Brussels, but I think you will approve of my wish. In the first place I don't think one can reckon on the Cousins arriving here on the 30th. Well, all I want is that you should detain them one or two days longer, in order that they may arrive here on Thursday, the 3rd, if possible early. My reason for this is as follows: a number of the Ministers are coming down here on Monday to stay till Thursday, on affairs of great importance, and as you know that people are always on the alert to make remarks, I think if all the Ministers were to be down here when they arrive, people would say—it was to settle matters. At all events it is better to avoid this. I think indeed a day or two at Brussels will do these young gentlemen good, and they can be properly fitted out there for their visit. Ever yours devotedly,

Victoria R.

Windsor Castle, 1st October 1839.

My dear Uncle,—I received your kind letter on Sunday, for which many thanks. The retard of these young people puts me rather out, but of course cannot be helped. I had a letter from Albert yesterday saying they could not set off, he thought, before the 6th. I think they don't exhibit much empressement to come here, which rather shocks me.

I got a very nice letter from dear Alexander yesterday from Reinhardtsbrun;57 he says Albert is very much improved, but not taller than Augustus. His description of him is as follows:— "Albert, I found, had become stronger and more handsome; still he has not grown much taller; he is of about the same size as Augustus; he is a most pleasant, intelligent young man. I find, too, that he has become more lively than he was, and that sits well on him, too." (Translation.) I think you may like to hear this, as I know Alexander is a very correct observer of persons, and his opinion may be relied upon. He adds that Albert plagues Leopold beyond measure.

I shall take care and send a gentleman and carriages to meet my cousins, either at Woolwich or the Tower, at whichever place you inform me they land at. The sooner they come the better. I have got the house full of Ministers. On Monday the Queen Dowager is coming to sleep here for two nights; it is the first time, and will be a severe trial. Ever your devoted Niece,

Victoria R.

Footnote 57: A picturesque castle, about eight miles from Gotha.

A CHARM AGAINST EVIL

Windsor Castle, 7th October 1839.

The Queen sends the little charm which she hopes may keep Lord Melbourne from all evil, and which it will make her very happy if he will put [? it with] his keys. If the ring is too small Lord Melbourne must send it back to her, and she will have it altered.

The Queen has made up her mind at length to ask Lady Clanricarde, as Lord Melbourne wishes it so much. Shall Surrey invite her, or Lord Palmerston? and from Thursday to Friday?

Windsor Castle, 8th October 1839.

My dear Uncle,—I have to thank you for three kind letters of the 1st, 4th, and 5th, the last which I received yesterday. I received another letter from Alex. M. yesterday, since Ernest's arrival, and he says that they have determined on setting off, so as to embark at Antwerp on the 9th and be here after all on the 10th! I suppose you will have also heard. I shall therefore (unless I hear from you to the contrary) send one of my equerries and two carriages to the Tower on Thursday.

I am sorry to hear of the serious disturbances at Ghent; I trust it is all got under now. If you should hear anything more of Roi Guillaume's58 marriage, pray let me hear it, as it is such an odd story. Old Alava, who was here for two nights last week, told me he knew Pauline d'Oultremont many years ago, when she was young and very gay and pretty, but that he wonders much at this marriage, as the King hates Catholics. Alava is rayonnant de bonheur.

I told Lord Melbourne of your alarms respecting the financial crisis, which we did not bring on—those wild American speculations are the cause of it—and he desires me to assure you that we will pursue as moderate and cautious a course as possible.

The Queen Dowager came here yesterday and stays till to-morrow; she is very cheerful and in good spirits....

I must conclude in haste. Ever your devoted Niece,

Victoria R.

Many thanks for the two supplies of ortolans, which were delicious.

Footnote 58: William I., King of the Netherlands, was greatly attached to the Roman Catholic Countess d'Oultremont, and in October 1840, being sixty-seven, abdicated his Crown to marry her. He was father of the Prince of Orange, who succeeded him.

ARRIVAL OF PRINCE ALBERT

Windsor Castle, 12th October 1839.

My dear Uncle,—... The dear cousins arrived at half-past seven on Thursday, after a very bad and almost dangerous passage, but looking both very well, and much improved. Having no clothes, they could not appear at dinner, but nevertheless débutéd after dinner in their négligé. Ernest is grown quite handsome; Albert's beauty is most striking, and he so amiable and unaffected—in short, very fascinating; he is excessively admired here. The Granvilles and Lord Clanricarde59 happened just to be here, but are gone again to-day. We rode out yesterday and danced after dinner. The young men are very amiable, delightful companions, and I am very happy to have them here; they are playing some Symphonies of Haydn under me at this very moment; they are passionately fond of music.

In the way of news I have got nothing to tell you to-day. Everything is quiet here, and we have no particular news from abroad. In Spain the Fueros60 seem to give sad difficulty to the Cortes.

Ever, my dearest Uncle, your devoted Niece,

Victoria R.

Footnote 59: Ulick John, first Marquis of Clanricarde (1802-1874), Ambassador at St Petersburg, afterwards Lord Privy Seal.

Footnote 60: Certain rights and privileges of the Basques.

A MOMENTOUS DECISION

Windsor Castle, 15th October 1839.

My dearest Uncle,—This letter will, I am sure, give you pleasure, for you have always shown and taken so warm an interest in all that concerns me. My mind is quite made up—and I told Albert this morning of it; the warm affection he showed me on learning this gave me great pleasure. He seems perfection, and I think that I have the prospect of very great happiness before me. I love him more than I can say, and I shall do everything in my power to render the sacrifice he has made (for a sacrifice in my opinion it is) as small as I can. He seems to have a very great tact—a very necessary thing in his position. These last few days have passed like a dream to me, and I am so much bewildered by it all that I know hardly how to write; but I do feel very, very happy.

It is absolutely necessary that this determination of mine should be known to no one but yourself, and Uncle Ernest—till the meeting of Parliament—as it would be considered otherwise neglectful on my part not to have assembled Parliament at once to have informed them of it.... Lord Melbourne, whom I of course have consulted about the whole affair, quite approves my choice, and expresses great satisfaction at the event, which he thinks in every way highly desirable. Lord Melbourne has acted in this business, as he has always done towards me, with the greatest kindness and affection.

We also think it better, and Albert quite approves of it, that we should be married very soon after Parliament meets, about the beginning of February; and indeed, loving Albert as I do, I cannot wish it should be delayed. My feelings are a little changed, I must say, since last Spring, when I said I couldn't think of marrying for three or four years; but seeing Albert has changed all this.

Pray, dearest Uncle, forward these two letters to Uncle Ernest (to whom I beg you will enjoin strict secrecy, and explain these details, which I have not time to do) and to faithful Stockmar.

I think you might tell Louise of it, but none of her family. I should wish to keep the dear young gentlemen here till the end of next month. Ernest's sincere pleasure gave me great delight. He does so adore dearest Albert. Ever, dearest Uncle, your devoted Niece,

Victoria R.

Windsor Castle, 16th October 1839.

Lord Melbourne will be ready to wait upon your Majesty at a little before one.

Lord Melbourne reads with great satisfaction your Majesty's expression of feeling, as your Majesty's happiness must ever be one of Lord Melbourne's first objects and strongest interests.

KING LEOPOLD'S SATISFACTION

Wiesbaden, 24th October 1839.

My dearest Victoria,—Nothing could have given me greater pleasure than your dear letter. I had, when I saw your decision, almost the feeling of old Zacharias61—"Now lettest Thou Thy servant depart in peace"! Your choice had been for these last years my conviction of what might and would be best for your happiness; and just because I was convinced of it, and knowing how strangely fate often deranges what one tries to bring about as being the best plan one could fix upon, the maximum of a good arrangement, I feared that it would not happen. In your position, which may and will, perhaps, become in future even more difficult in a political point of view, you could not exist without having a happy and an agreeable intérieur.

And I am much deceived—which I think I am not—or you will find in Albert just the very qualities and dispositions which are indispensable for your happiness, and which will suit your own character, temper, and mode of life. You say most amiably that you consider it a sacrifice on the part of Albert. This is true in many points, because his position will be a difficult one; but much, I may say all, will depend on your affection for him. If you love him, and are kind to him, he will easily bear the burthen of the position; and there is a steadiness and at the same time cheerfulness in his character which will facilitate this. I think your plans excellent. If Parliament had been called at an unusual time it would make them uncomfortable, and if, therefore, they receive the communication at the opening of the Session, it will be best. The marriage, as you say, might then follow as closely as possible.

Lord Melbourne has shown himself the amiable and excellent man I always took him for. Another man in his position, instead of your happiness, might have merely looked to his own personal views and imaginary interests. Not so our good friend; he saw what was best for you, and I feel it deeply to his praise.

Your keeping the cousins next month with you strikes me as a very good plan. It will even show that you had sufficient opportunity of judging of Albert's character....

AUSTRIA AND THE PORTE

On the 22nd, Prince Metternich came to see me. He was very kind, and talked most confidentially about political affairs, particularly the Oriental concerns.62 M. de Brunnow had been with him. The short of his views is this: he wishes that the Powers could be unanimous, as he sees in this the best chance of avoiding measures of violence against the Pasha of Egypt, which he considers dangerous, either as not sufficiently effective, or of a nature to bring on complications most earnestly to be avoided, such as making use of Russian troops. Austria naturally would like to bring about the best possible arrangement for the Porte, but it will adhere to any arrangement or proposition which can be agreed upon by England and France. He is, however, positive that Candia must be given back to the Porte, its position being too threatening, and therefore constantly alarming the Porte. He made me write the import of our conversation to King Louis Philippe, which I did send after him to Frankfort, where he was to forward it to Paris. Perhaps you will have the goodness to communicate this political scrap to good Lord Melbourne with my best regards. He spoke in praise of Lord Beauvale.63 The Prince is better, but grown very old and looking tired. It gave me great pleasure to see him again.

I drink the waters now four days, and can therefore not yet judge of their good or bad effects. My palpitations are rather increased here; if my stupid heart will get diseased I shall soon be departing for some other world. I would it could be soon then.

Till further orders I shall say nothing to your Mother, Charles, or Feodore.

Now I will conclude with my best blessings, and remain, my dearest and most beloved Victoria, your devoted Uncle,

Leopold R.

Footnote 61: An obvious slip for Simeon.

Footnote 62: See Introductory Notes for and

Footnote 63: Frederick Lamb, younger brother of Lord Melbourne, Ambassador Extraordinary at Vienna, who had recently been made a Peer.

THE QUEEN'S HAPPINESS

Windsor Castle, 29th October 1839.

My dearest Uncle,—Your most kind and most welcome letter of the 24th arrived yesterday, and gave me very, very great pleasure. I was sure you would be satisfied and pleased with our proceedings.

Before I proceed further, I wish just to mention one or two alterations in the plan of announcing the event.

As Parliament has nothing whatever to say respecting the marriage, can neither approve nor disapprove it (I mean in a manner which might affect it), it is now proposed that, as soon as the cousins are gone (which they now intend to do on the 12th or 14th of November, as time presses), I should assemble all the Privy Councillors and announce to them my intention....

Oh! dear Uncle, I do feel so happy! I do so adore Albert! he is quite an angel, and so very, very kind to me, and seems so fond of me, which touches me much. I trust and hope I shall be able to make him as happy as he ought to be! I cannot bear to part from him, for we spend such happy, delightful hours together.

Poor Ernest has been suffering since Wednesday last with the jaundice, which is very distressing and troublesome, though not alarming.... I love him dearly too, and look upon him quite as a brother.

What you say about Lord Melbourne has given me great pleasure; it is very just and very true. There are not many such honest kind friends to be found in this world. He desires me to say that he is deeply sensible of your good opinion, and that he can have no other object than that which he considers best to secure my happiness, which is closely connected with the well-being of the country.

I am glad you saw Prince Metternich, and that you were satisfied with the interview.

I hope and trust you may derive much benefit from your stay at Wiesbaden. Pray name me to good Stockmar, and believe me, always, your most devoted Niece and Child,

Victoria R.

CONGRATULATIONS

Laeken, 9th November 1839.

My most beloved Victoria,—Your Uncle has already told you, I trust, with what feelings of deep affection and gratitude I received the so interesting and important communication which you permitted him to make to me; but I was longing for an opportunity to speak to you myself of the great subject which fills now our hearts, and to tell you how very grateful I have been, I am, and will ever be, for the confidence and trust which you so kindly placed in me. All I can say is that you did full justice to my feelings, for nothing could interest more my heart than your marriage, my most dearly loved Victoria, and I could not have heard even of that of Clémentine with more anxious affection and sisterly love. I cannot really tell you with words how deeply and strongly I was moved and affected by the great news itself, and by your dear, unaffected, confiding, happy letter. When I received it I could do nothing but cry, and say internally, "May God bless her now and ever!" Ah! may God bless you, my most beloved Victoria! may He shower on you His best blessings, fulfil all your heart's wishes and hopes, and let you enjoy for many, many years the happiness which the dearest ties of affection alone can give, and which is the only real one, the only worthy of the name in this uncertain and transitory world!

I have seen much of dear Albert two years ago, I have watched him, as you may well think, with particular care, attention, and interest, and although he was very young then, I am well convinced that he is not only fit for the situation which he is now called to fulfil, but, what is still more important in my eyes, that he has all those qualities of the heart and the mind which can give and ensure happiness. I think even that his disposition is particularly well calculated to suit yours, and I am fully confident that you will be both happy together. What you tell me of your fear of not being worthy of him, and able to make him sufficiently happy, is for me but a proof more of it. Deep affection makes us always diffident and very humble. Those that we love stand so high in our own esteem, and are in our opinion so much above us and all others that we naturally feel unworthy of them and unequal to the task of making them happy: but there is, I think, a mingled charm in this feeling, for although we regret not to be what we should wish to be for them, feeling and acknowledging the superiority of those we love and must always love and respect, is a great satisfaction, and an increasing and everlasting one. You will feel it, I am sure, as well as I do....

You will excuse my blots and hurried scribbling when I will tell you that in order to profit of the private messenger which goes to-morrow morning I write to you at ten in the evening, a thing quite unusual for me, and even rather forbidden: but after having been deprived of expending my heart for so many days, I could not not avail myself of the present opportunity. When I write to you by the ordinary messenger I will continue to be silent; but I trust you will permit me to say some time a word, when a safe opportunity presents itself, for my heart is with you more than I can tell. I would that I could see you, when it could be, for an hour. I remain, my most beloved Victoria, ever and ever your most affectionate

Louise.

THE ANNOUNCEMENT

Windsor Castle, 11th November 1839.

My dear Uncle,—The affection which you have shown me makes me feel certain that you will take interest in an event which so nearly concerns the future happiness of my life; I cannot, therefore, delay any longer to inform you of my intended marriage with my Cousin Albert, the merits of whose character are so well known by all who are acquainted with him, that I need say no more than that I feel as assured of my own happiness as I can be of anything in this world.

As it is not to be publicly known, I beg you not to mention it except to our own Family.

I hope you are well and enjoying yourself. Believe me, always, your affectionate Niece,

Victoria R.64

Footnote 64: Similar letters with slight variations were written to the Duke of Cambridge, the Princess Augusta, the Princess Sophia, the Duchess of Gloucester, the Princess Sophia Matilda, the King of Hanover, and the Princess Elizabeth (Landgravine of Hesse-Homburg).

Windsor Castle, 14th November 1839.

My dear Aunt,—Your constant kindness and the affection you have ever shown me make me certain that you will take much interest in an event which so nearly concerns the future happiness of my life; I cannot, therefore, any longer delay to inform you of my intended marriage with my Cousin Albert. The merits of his character are so well known to all who are acquainted with him, that I need say no more than that I feel as assured of my own happiness as I can be of anything here below, and only hope that I may be able to make him as happy as he deserves to be. It was both my duty and my inclination to tell you of this as soon as it was determined upon; but, as it is not to be yet publicly announced I beg you not to mention it except to our own Family. I thank you much for your kind letter, and rejoice to hear you have enjoyed yourself so much. Believe me, always, your very affectionate Niece,

Victoria R.

Windsor Castle, 18th November 1839.

The Queen just writes two lines to send Lord Melbourne the accompanying civil letter from the Queen Dowager, and to give him an account of the visit of the Cambridges. They were all very kind and civil, George grown but not embellished, and much less reserved with the Queen, and evidently happy to be clear of me. He gave a very indifferent account of the King of Greece, but a favourable one of the Queen.

The Duchess said she had expected the Queen would marry Albert, and was not surprised at the event. They were very discreet and asked no questions, but described the Duchess of Gloucester to be suffering much from the necessity of keeping the secret.

The weather cleared up, and the Queen has just returned from a walk. She hopes Lord Melbourne got safe to London in spite of the wet and the water on the road; and she hopes he will take great care of himself. She would be thankful if he would let her know to-morrow if he will dine with her also on Thursday or not.

Windsor Castle, 19th November 1839.

My dear Uncle,—Many thanks for your kind letter of the 5th, received last week. I am in a great hurry, and therefore have only time to write to you a line to tell you, first, that on the 15th I wrote to all the Royal Family announcing the event to them, and that they answered all very kindly and civilly; the Duchess of Cambridge and Augusta, with the Duke and George, came over on purpose to congratulate me yesterday; secondly, that the marriage is to be publicly announced in an Open Council on the 23rd, at Buckingham Palace, where I am going to-morrow. I return here after the Council on the 23rd. I am so happy to think I need not then conceal my feelings any longer. I have also written to the King of Hanover and the Landgravine,65 and to all our relations abroad. I hope, dear Uncle, you will not have ill-treated my dearest Albert! I am very anxious to hear from him from Wiesbaden. Ever your devoted Niece,

Victoria R.

Footnote 65: Princess Elizabeth (1770-1840), daughter of George III. and widow of the Landgrave Frederick Joseph Louis of Hesse-Homburg.

LETTERS TO PRINCE ALBERT

[The following extracts of letters from the Queen to Prince Albert were written partly in English and partly in German. The English portions are printed in italics, the German, translated, in ordinary type. These letters are all written in terms of profound affection, which deepened very shortly into complete and absolute devotion to the Prince.]

Buckingham Palace, 21st November 1839.

... It is desired here that the matter should be declared at Coburg as soon as possible, and immediately after that I shall send you the Order.66

Your rank will be settled just before you come over, as also your rank in the Army. Everything will be very easily arranged. Lord Melbourne showed me yesterday the Declaration, which is very simple and nice. I will send it you as soon as possible....

Lord Melbourne told me yesterday, that the whole Cabinet are strongly of opinion that you should not be made a Peer. I will write that to Uncle....

Footnote 66: The Garter.

THE RELIGIOUS QUESTION

22nd November 1839.

... Lord Melbourne has just been with me, and greatly wishes the Declaration to be made at Coburg as soon as possible. He also desired me to ask you to see if you can ... a short History of the House of Saxe-Coburg, who our direct ancestors were, and what part they took in the Protestant, or rather Lutheran, religion; he wishes to hear this in order to make people here know exactly who your ancestors are, for a few stupid people here try to say you are a Catholic, but nobody will believe it. Send (it) as soon as possible; perhaps good Mr. Schenk would write it out in English....

As there is nothing to be settled for me, we require no treaty of marriage; but if you should require anything to be settled, the best will be to send it here. Respecting the succession, in case Ernest should die without children, it would not do to stipulate now, but your second son, if you had one, should reside at Coburg. That can easily be arranged if the thing should happen hereafter, and the English would not like it to be arranged now....

THE DECLARATION

Windsor Castle, 23rd November 1839.

... Just arrived here, 5.30. Everything has gone off very well. The Council67 was held at two o'clock; more than a hundred persons were present, and there I had to read the Declaration. It was rather an awful moment, to be obliged to announce this to so many people, many of whom were quite strangers, but they told me I did it very well, and I felt so happy to do it.

Good Lord Melbourne was deeply moved about it, and Uxbridge likewise; it lasted only two or three minutes. Everybody, they tell me, is very much pleased, and I wish you could have seen the crowds of people who cheered me loudly as I left the Palace for Windsor. I am so happy to-day! oh, if only you could be here! I wish that you were able to participate in all the kindness which is shown to me. To-day I can only send you the Declaration.68 The description of the whole I will send after this....

Send me as soon as possible the report of the announcement at Coburg. I wear your dear picture mornings and evenings, and wore it also at the meeting of the Conseil.

Footnote 67: A Special Meeting of the Privy Council was held on the 23rd November, to receive the Queen's intimation of her engagement. The Queen wrote in her Journal:—

"I went in; the room was full, but I hardly knew who was there. Lord M. I saw, looking at me with tears in his eyes, but he was not near me. I then read my short Declaration. I felt my hands shook, but I did not make one mistake. I felt more happy and thankful when it was over."

Footnote 68: J. W. Croker wrote to Lady Hardwicke:—

"24th November 1839.

"... She then unfolded a paper and read her Declaration, which you will, before this can reach you, have seen in the newspapers. I cannot describe to you with what a mixture of self-possession and feminine delicacy she read the paper. Her voice, which is naturally beautiful, was clear and untroubled; and her eye was bright and calm, neither bold nor downcast, but firm and soft. There was a blush on her cheek which made her look both handsomer and more interesting; and certainly she did look as interesting and as handsome as any young lady I ever saw.

"I happened to stand behind the Duke of Wellington's chair, and caught her eye twice as she directed it towards him, which I fancy she did with a good-natured interest.... The crowd, which was not great but very decent, I might almost say respectable, expressed their approbation of the Duke of Wellington and Sir R. Peel, and their disapprobation of the Ministers very loudly. Lord John and Lord Normanby, they tell me, were positively hooted.... Lord Melbourne ... seemed to me to look careworn, and on the whole the meeting had a sombre air."—Croker Papers, ii. 359.

THE PEERAGE QUESTION

Wiesbaden, 22nd November 1839.

My dearest Victoria,—I was delighted with your dear little letter. You write these kind of letters with a very great facility, and they are generally so natural and clever, that it makes one very happy to receive them. I had written less of late, because I thought you occupied more agreeably than to read my letters. I have on purpose kept back a courier, to be able to send you the latest news from here of M. Albert. The young people arrived here only on the 20th, in the morning, having very kindly stopped at Bonn. I find them looking well, particularly Albert; it proves that happiness is an excellent remedy, and keeps people in better health than any other. He is much attached to you, and moved when he speaks of you. He is, besides, in great spirits and gaiety, and full of fun; he is a very amiable companion.

Concerning the peerage, that is a matter to be considered at any time; the only reason why I do wish it is, that Albert's foreignership should disappear as much as possible. I have, in different circumstances to be sure, suffered greatly from my having declined conditionally the peerage when it was offered me in 1816.69 Your Uncle70 writes to you in German: as far as I understood him, he speaks of the necessity of a marriage treaty; that is a matter of course. There is, however, something additional to be regulated concerning the possible succession in the Coburg-Gotha dominions, there being betwixt it and Albert but good Ernest. Some regulation becomes therefore necessary, at least reasonable. The Duke wishes also to know if the treaty is to be made in England or in Germany. Should the last of the two be fixed upon, he thinks that one of your Ministers abroad would be the proper person for it. Ever, my dear Victoria, your devoted Uncle,

Leopold R.

Footnote 69: The Dukedom of Kendal was offered to, and, after consideration, declined by, Prince Leopold.

Footnote 70: The Duke of Saxe-Coburg (Ernest I.).

Windsor Castle, 26th November 1839.

My dear Uncle,—I thank you for your kind letter which I received the day before yesterday; but I fear you must have been very dull at Wiesbaden....

Everything went off uncommonly well on the 23rd, but it was rather formidable;[71] eighty-two Privy Councillors present; everybody very much pleased—and I was loudly greeted on leaving the Palace after the Council.

The whole Cabinet agree with me in being strongly of opinion that Albert should not be a Peer; indeed, I see everything against it and nothing for it; the English are very jealous at the idea of Albert's having any political power, or meddling with affairs here—which I know from himself he will not do.

As Wiesbaden is half-way (or thereabouts) to Coburg, I take the liberty of enclosing a large letter to Albert, which I beg you to send on to him.

We are quite flooded here, and the road to Datchet is quite impassable. Ever your devoted Niece,

Victoria R.

Footnote 71: Greville mentions that the Queen's hands trembled so, that she could hardly read the Declaration which she was holding.

BRITISH SUSCEPTIBILITIES

27th November 1839.

Lord Melbourne presents his humble duty to your Majesty....

A little civility would be well bestowed upon Lord and Lady Tankerville, and might not be without its effect, but if your Majesty does not like it, it cannot be helped.

The others also shall, if possible, be kept in good humour.

The misrepresentation, respecting Prince Alexander[72] your Majesty will see corrected in the Morning Chronicle of that morning, but of course your Majesty will not expect that this contradiction will put an end to bitter and offensive remarks. It will now be said that, knowing the true religion, he has given over his children to the false, and that he has sacrificed their eternal welfare to his own worldly objects.[73] There is nothing which cannot be turned in an hostile and malignant manner by malignant and perverted ingenuity.

Can your Majesty inform Lord Melbourne what is the arrangement respecting King Leopold's children? They are, Lord Melbourne presumes, to be brought up Roman Catholics.

Lord Melbourne earnestly hopes to hear that your Majesty is better and more free from pain. He is himself very well.

Footnote 72: Prince Alexander of Würtemberg.

Footnote 73: See ante, p.

Windsor Castle, 27th November 1839.

The English are very jealous of any foreigner interfering in the government of this country, and have already in some of the papers (which are friendly to me and you) expressed a hope that you would not interfere. Now, though I know you never would, still, if you were a Peer, they would all say, the Prince meant to play a political part. I am certain you will understand this, but it is much better not to say anything more about it now, and to let the whole matter rest. The Tories make a great disturbance (saying) that you are a Papist, because the words "a Protestant Prince" have not been put into the Declaration—a thing which would be quite unnecessary, seeing that I cannot marry a Papist....

29th November 1839.

I had a talk with Lord Melbourne last night. He thinks your view about the Peerage question quite correct. Uncle seems to me, after all, much more reasonable about it. We had a good talk this morning about your arrangements for our marriage, and also about your official attendants, and he[74] has told me that young Mr. Anson (his Private Secretary), who is with him, greatly wishes to be with you. I am very much in favour of it, because he is an excellent young man, and very modest, very honest, very steady, very well-informed, and will be of much use to you. He is not a member of the House of Commons, which is also convenient; so long as Lord Melbourne is in office he remains his Secretary—but William Cowper[75] was also for some time Secretary to his Uncle, and at the same time my Groom-in-Waiting. Lord Melbourne feared it was not advisable for you to have Mr. Anson, and also his uncle, but I told him that did not matter if the people are fit for the posts....

Footnote 74: Lord Melbourne.

Footnote 75: Afterwards William Cowper-Temple and Lord Mount Temple, author of the well-known amendment to the Education Act of 1870.

THE QUEEN OF PORTUGAL

Lisbonne, 1 Décembre 1839.

Ma bien chère Victoire,—Hier ayant reçu la communication de votre mariage avec Albert, je ne veux pas tarder un seul instant à vous en féliciter sur votre heureux choix, et en même temps vous prier de croire aux vœux sincères que je forme pour votre bonheur avec votre excellent cœur il n'est pas possible le contraire. Permettez que je vous dise que votre choix ne m'a pas dû étonner, car sachant combien Albert est bon, vous ne pouviez pas choisir un autre dont vous fussiez aussi sûre qu'il puisse vous rendre aussi heureuse comme vous le méritez, chère Victoire. Pour que tous mes souhaits soient exaucés je vous désire un bonheur aussi complet que l'est le mien. Qu'Albert soit comme Ferdinand et vous serez parfaitement heureuse. Adieu! ma chère Victoire. Je vous prie de me croire, votre dévouée Cousine,

Marie.

Ferdinand vous fait dire mille choses.

THE PRINCE'S HOUSEHOLD

Windsor Castle, 8th December 1839.

As to your wish about your gentlemen, my dear Albert, I must tell you quite honestly that it will not do. You may entirely rely upon me that the people who will be about you will be absolutely pleasant people, of high standing and good character. These gentlemen will not be in continual attendance on you; only on great occasions, and to accompany you when you go anywhere, and to dinners, etc. Seymour is your confidential attendant, and also Schenk and Anson,76 whom Lehzen has written to you about.

Old Sir George Anson has been told of your gracious wish to have him as Groom of the Bedchamber and is delighted.

I can only have Lords, and they will not be Peers, but Lords, the eldest sons of Dukes or Marquesses, or Earls (Counts), and who as far as possible are not in Parliament, for then they need not change, but your people are appointed by you and not by me (nominally), and therefore, unless they were to vote against my Government (which would be awkward), they need not change. You may rely upon my care that you shall have proper people, and not idle and not too young, and Lord Melbourne has already mentioned several to me who would be very suitable....

I have received to-day an ungracious letter from Uncle Leopold. He appears to me to be nettled because I no longer ask for his advice, but dear Uncle is given to believe that he must rule the roast everywhere. However, that is not a necessity. As he has written to Melbourne, Melbourne will reply to him on every point, and will also tell him that Stockmar ought to come here as soon as possible to arrange everything about the treaty. That will be a very good thing, because Stockmar understands all English things so well.

The Second, as you always called Palmerston, is to be married within the next few days to Lady Cowper, the sister of my Premier (Primus); I have known this for a long time, but Melbourne asked me not to tell it to any one. They are, both of them, above fifty, and I think that they are quite right so to act, because Palmerston, since the death of his sisters, is quite alone in the world, and Lady C. is a very clever woman, and much attached to him; still, I feel sure it will make you smile.

Footnote 76: Mr George Anson had been Private Secretary to Lord Melbourne; it was on Lord Melbourne's recommendation that the Queen appointed him Private Secretary to Prince Albert. The Prince was inclined to resent the selection, and to think that in the case of so confidential an official he should have been allowed to make his own nomination. But they became firm friends, and the Prince found Mr Anson's capacity, common sense, and entire disinterestedness of the greatest value to him. Later he became keeper of the Prince's Privy Purse, and died in 1849.

(Continued on the 9th).—To-day I have had a Conseil, and then I knighted the Mayor of Newport77 (who distinguished himself so much in that riot of the Chartists78); he is a very timid, modest man, and was very happy when I told him orally how exceedingly satisfied I am with his conduct.... The officers have been rewarded too.... I am plaguing you already with tiresome politics, but you will in that find a proof of my [confidence] love,79 because I must share with you everything that rejoices me, everything that vexes or grieves me, and I am certain you will take your part in it....

To-day I saw Lord William Russell—you know him, don't you? I forgot to tell you that you will have a great Officer of State at the head of your Household, who is called the Groom of the Stole; it is a position in the Court for prestige only, without any business; he will be a Peer....

Footnote 77: Mr T. Phillips, the Mayor of Newport, Monmouthshire, had behaved with great coolness and courage during the riot on 4th November. He read the Riot Act among showers of bullets before ordering the troops to fire.

Footnote 78: Frost, Williams, and others, afterwards convicted at Monmouth.

Footnote 79: The Queen had begun the word "confidence" but struck it out and substituted "love."

(Continued 10th December).—I am very impatient at your bust not having yet arrived; the Duchess of Sutherland wrote to me she had seen it in Rome, and it was so beautiful!...

Who has made the little copy which you sent me, and who the original? Feodore writes to me so much about you....

We expect Queen Adelaide to-day, who will stay here until the day after to-morrow. Melbourne has asked me to enquire of you whether you know Lord Grosvenor? He is the eldest son of the Marquis of Westminster, and does not belong to any party; he is not in Parliament. He is very pleasant, speaks German very well, and has been a good deal on the Continent. If he accepts, he might be one of your gentlemen. Lord Melbourne is particularly desirous of doing everything that is most agreeable to you. I have a request to make, too, viz., that you will appoint poor Clark your physician; you need not consult him unless you wish it. It is only an honorary title, and would make him very happy....

THE PROTESTANT QUESTION

Windsor Castle, 9th December 1839.

My dear Uncle,—... I was quite miserable at not hearing from Albert for ten days; such a long silence is quite insupportable for any one in my position towards Albert, and I was overjoyed on receiving yesterday the most dear, most affectionate, delightful long letter from him. He writes so beautifully, and so simply and unaffectedly. I hope, dear Uncle, you received my last letter (quite a packet) for Albert, on the 5th or 6th? I send you another now. I fear I am very indiscreet about these letters, but I have so much to tell him, and it will only last two months, so that I trust you will forgive it, and forward them.

I mentioned the topics you spoke of to me in your letter to our good friend Lord Melbourne, and as he is writing, I leave it to him to explain to you, as he writes so much better than I do. He will explain to you why the word Protestant was left out in the Declaration, which I think was quite right; for do what one will, nothing will please these Tories.... I shall be delighted to see Stockmar here, for so many reasons, and the quicker he comes the better....

I have a favour to ask you, dear Uncle, which I hope you will grant, unless it should be indiscreet in me. It is, if you have still got Aunt Charlotte's bust at Claremont, if you would give it to me to put in the Gallery here, where you would see it oftener than you do at Claremont, and I am so anxious there should be one of her here.

We have vile weather, cold and foggy; such fogs we have here! I move to London for good on the 9th or 10th of January. Ever your devoted Niece,

Victoria R.

Windsor Castle, 11th December 1839.

... I like Lady A—— very much too, only she is a little strict and particular, and too severe towards others, which is not right; for I think one ought always to be indulgent towards other people, as I always think, if we had not been well brought up and well taken care of, we might also have gone astray. That is always my feeling. Yet it is always right to show that one does not like to see what is obviously wrong; but it is very dangerous to be too severe, and I am certain that as a rule such people always greatly regret that in their youth they have not been as careful as they ought to have been. I have explained this so badly, and written it so badly, that I fear you will hardly be able to make it out.

Windsor Castle, 15th December 1839.

... Again no letter from you!... Lord Melbourne left here this morning, but comes back to-morrow evening, after the wedding of his sister. I hope he will remain here, because I am fond of him, and because he has a share in all my happiness, and is the only man with whom I can speak without gêne on everything, which I cannot do with my Court.

"Islay"80 is still plagued by him every evening—a thing which he much enjoys—and constantly begs for the spectacles. I forgot to tell you that Karl has given me a pretty little Rowley, who likewise lives in the house. The multitude of dogs is really terrible!

The ceremony of Declaration must have been very fine and touching, and I am most happy that the good people of Coburg are so pleased with our marriage....

Dec. 17th.—I have spoken to Lord M. about your wish, and he says—what is my own opinion too—that your people ought to be as much as possible out of Parliament when they have hardly any politics, which is the best thing—as your Household must not form a contrast to mine—and therefore you could not have violent Tories amongst your people; but you may be quite certain that both I and Lord Melbourne will take the greatest care to select respectable and distinguished people, and people of good character. Perhaps Lord Grosvenor may be your Groom of the Stole, though he is no Peer; but his rank and family are so high, that he would do very well; and, besides, not belonging to any party, and being out of Parliament, is such a great advantage.

The design of our Arms without supporters is unfortunately not finished, but I send you a little drawing which I have made of it myself. The report of Sir William Woods I beg you will send back, but the Arms you can keep.

I add a little pin as a small Christmas present. I hope you will sometimes wear it.

Footnote 80: A pet dog of the Queen's.

THE PROTESTANT QUESTION

Laeken, 14th December 1839.

My dearest Victoria,—I lived in the hope of receiving some letters for you from Albert, but nothing is arrived to-day. Your dear long letter gave me great pleasure. Before I answer some parts of it, I will say a few words on Lord Melbourne's letter. Perhaps you will be so good to tell him that it gratified me much. It is the letter of an honest and an amiable statesman, practical and straightforward. In the omission of the word "Protestant" he was probably right, and it is equally probable that they would have abused him—maybe even more if he had put it in. There is only this to say, however: the Ernestine branch of the Saxon family has been, there is no doubt, the real cause of the establishment of Protestantism in Germany, and consequently in great parts of Northern Europe. This same line became a martyr to that cause, and was deprived of almost all its possessions in consequence of it.

Recently there have been two cases of Catholic marriages, but the main branch has remained, and is, in fact, very sincerely Protestant. Both Ernest and Albert are much attached to it, and when deviations took place they were connected more with new branches transplanted out of the parent soil than with what more properly must be considered as the reigning family.

The Peerage question may remain as it is, but it will not be denied that the great object must be to make Albert as English as possible, and that nothing will render this more difficult than a foreign name....

I shall be most happy to see poor Charlotte's bust in the Gallery at Windsor, and it is kind of you to have had the thought. She was a high and noble-minded creature, and her affection and kindness for me very great. She had placed the most unbounded confidence in me; our principle had been never to let a single day pass over any little subject of irritation. The only subjects of that sort we had were about the family, particularly the Regent, and then the old Queen Charlotte. Now I must conclude with my best love. Ever, my dearest Victoria, your devoted Uncle,

Leopold R.

A MISSING LETTER

Windsor Castle, 17th December 1839.

My dear Uncle,—Many thanks for your two most kind letters. I suppose I may send for Aunt Charlotte's bust, for which I am most grateful—and say I have your authority to do so? You are very kind to think about my stupid health; I don't think I ever, at least not for very long, have walked so regularly as I have done this last month—out in fog, and mist, and wind, and cold. But I cannot be otherwise than agitated; getting no letter makes me ill, and getting them excites me....

I have much to write, and therefore cannot make this a long letter, but one thing more I must mention. The very day of the Declaration in Council, on the 23rd ult., I sent off a letter to Albert, by Van de Weyer, saying it was to be forwarded sans délai to Coburg; now, Albert never has received that letter, which was a long one, and thanks me for two, of the 26th and 29th. This vexes me much, and I can't help thinking the letter is lying either at Wiesbaden or Brussels. Would you graciously enquire, for I should not like it to be lost.

Forgive my writing such a letter so full of myself. Ever, dearest Uncle, your devoted Niece, Victoria R.

THE PRINCE'S SECRETARY

Windsor Castle.

The 22nd.—I have but little time to write. The Duchess of Sutherland is here, who admires you much, and is very sympathetic....

The 23rd.—Your letter of the 15th just received. I will now answer at once. It is, as you rightly suppose, my greatest, my most anxious wish to do everything most agreeable to you, but I must differ with you respecting Mr Anson.... What I said about Anson giving you advice, means, that if you like to ask him, he can and will be of the greatest use to you, as he is a very well-informed person. He will leave Lord Melbourne as soon as he is appointed about you. With regard to your last objection, that it would make you a party man if you took the Secretary of the Prime Minister as your Treasurer, I do not agree in it; for, though I am very anxious you should not appear to belong to a Party, still it is necessary that your Household should not form a too strong contrast to mine, else they will say, "Oh, we know the Prince says he belongs to no party, but we are sure he is a Tory!" Therefore it is also necessary that it should appear that you went with me in having some of your people who are staunch Whigs; but Anson is not in Parliament, and never was, and therefore he is not a violent politician. Do not think because I urge this, Lord M. prefers it; on the contrary, he never urged it, and I only do it as I know it is for your own good. You will pardon this long story. It will also not do to wait till you come to appoint all your people. I am distressed to tell you what I fear you do not like, but it is necessary, my dearest, most excellent Albert. Once more I tell you that you can perfectly rely on me in these matters....

THE TORIES

Windsor Castle, 26th December 1839.

... The Historical Sketch has interested us greatly; Lord Melbourne read it through immediately. I greatly thank you also for the genealogical tree you sent me.

Now, my dearest, to be about what is not so pleasant or amusing. I mean, now for business. I always think it safer to write that in English, as I can explain myself better, and I hope you can read my English, as I try to be very legible. I am much grieved that you feel disappointed about my wish respecting your gentlemen, but very glad that you consent to it, and that you feel confidence in my choice. Respecting the Treasurer, my dearest Albert, I have already written at great length in my last letter, so I will not say much more about it to-day, but I will just observe that, tho' I fully understand (indeed no one could feel more for you in the very trying position you will be placed in than I do) your feelings, it is absolutely necessary that an Englishman should be at the head of your affairs; therefore (tho' I will not force Mr. Anson on you) I ask you if it is not better to take a man in whom I have confidence, and whom I know well enough to trust perfectly, than a man who is quite a stranger, and whom I know nothing of?

I am very glad that your father knows Lord Grosvenor. As to the Tories, I am still in a rage;[81] they abuse and grumble incessantly in the most incredible manner.

I will tell good Lord Melbourne that you are very grateful. That you will write to him is very nice of you, and makes me glad. I shall always feel very happy if you, my dearest Albert, will be very friendly to this good and just man; and I am convinced that, when you will know him more intimately, you will be as fond of him as I am. No one is more abused by bad people than Lord M.—and nobody is so forgiving....

I have just learned that my two uncles, the Dukes of Sussex and Cambridge (to whom Lord M. had written) very willingly consent to let you take precedence of them; it was, of course, necessary to ask them about it....

Footnote 81: Lit. raging (wuthend). The phrase was a favourite one of King Leopold's, from whom the Queen had adopted it.

Windsor Castle, 27th December 1839.

My dear Uncle,—Just two words (though you don't deserve half a one, as your silence is unpardonable) to say I have just heard from Albert, who, I am glad to say, consents to my choosing his people; so one essential point is gained, and we have only the Treasurer to carry now. I am sure, as you are so anxious Albert should be thoroughly English, you will see how necessary it is that an Englishman should be at the head of his financial affairs.

I see that you wrote to Lord Melbourne that you were glad to hear I took more walking exercise, but I must tell you that ever since I have done so I sleep badly, and feel unwell! If the weather would only allow me to ride I should be quite well. Ever your devoted Niece,

Victoria R.

THE PRINCE AND LORD MELBOURNE

Windsor Castle, 30th December 1839.

... I here enclose Lord Melbourne's letter. I have read it, and I think that nothing could be better; it is just what I told you, and it is the honest and impartial advice of a very clever, very honest, and very impartial man, whose greatest wish is to secure your and my happiness. Follow this advice and you may be sure of success. Lord Melbourne told me that he had it written on purpose in a clear hand, by one of his secretaries, as he thought and feared you would not be able to read his own hand, which I daresay would have been the case, as he writes a very peculiar hand; he has therefore only signed it.

I saw to-day the Duke of Cambridge, who has shown me your letter, with which he is quite delighted—and, indeed, it is a very nice one. The Duke told Lord Melbourne he had always greatly desired our marriage, and never thought of George; but that I do not believe.

I must conclude, my dearest, beloved Albert. Be careful as to your valuable health, and be assured that no one loves you as much as your faithful Victoria.

INTRODUCTORY NOTE: TO CHAPTER IX

The marriage of the Queen and Prince Albert took place amid great splendour and general rejoicings on the 10th of February; the general satisfaction being unaffected by the tactless conduct of Ministers who, by not acting in conjunction with the Opposition, had been defeated on the question of the amount of the Prince's annuity, the House of Commons reducing it from £50,000 to £30,000.

At home, the Privilege Question aroused great interest, a point which for months convulsed the Courts and Parliament being whether a report, ordered by the House to be printed, of a Committee appointed by the House, was protected by privilege against being the subject of an action for libel. The Courts having decided that it was not, an Act was passed to alter the rule for the future, but meanwhile the sheriffs had been imprisoned by the House for executing the judgment in the usual course.

The Ministry tottered on, getting a majority of nine only on their China policy, and twenty-one on a direct vote of confidence. The Bill for the union of the two Canadas was, however, passed without difficulty.

An attempt by a barman named Oxford to assassinate the Queen on Constitution Hill fortunately failed, and Oxford was committed, after trial, to a lunatic asylum. In July, the prospect of an heir being born to the throne led to the passing of a Regency Bill, naming Prince Albert Regent, should the Queen die leaving issue; the Duke of Sussex alone entered a formal protest against it.

Afghanistan continued unsettled, and Lord Auckland's policy seemed hardly justified by the unpopularity at Cabul of Shah Sooja; Dost Mahommed still made efforts to regain his position, but he ultimately surrendered to Sir William Macnaghten, the British Envoy at Cabul. The disputes with China continued, and hostilities broke out; British ships proceeded to China, and Chusan was captured.

In France an attempt against the Government was made by Louis Napoleon, who landed at Boulogne in a British steamer, was captured, and sentenced to life imprisonment. More serious difficulties between this country and France arose out of Eastern affairs. The Four Powers, England, Russia, Austria, and Prussia, had addressed an ultimatum to Mehemet, requiring him to evacuate North Syria, France declining to take part in the conference on the subject. An Anglo-Austrian army undertook to eject him, St Jean d'Acre was stormed, and France thrust into a position of unwilling isolation. Thiers, who had been made Minister, expected that Mehemet would be able to retain his conquests, and for a time it looked as though France would interfere to protect him. Ultimately, in spite of some ostentatious preparations in France, peaceful counsels prevailed, and Thiers found it advisable to retire in favour of Guizot.

In Holland, William I. (then sixty-seven) abdicated in favour of his son, the Prince of Orange (William II.). The need of a younger and firmer ruler was the reason officially stated in the Royal Proclamation. The real reasons were probably the King's attachment to the Roman Catholic Countess d'Oultremont, whom he now privately married, and the humiliation he felt at the unfavourable termination of the Belgian dispute.

CHAPTER IX

Buckingham Palace, 11th January 1840.

Stockmar is here; I saw him yesterday and to-day, and have begged him to explain to you all the Court affairs, and the affairs concerning the Treaty, in my name. He will explain to you the Treasury affair, and will do it much better than I should. I am very happy to see him again, and to have him here; he can give such good advice to both of us, and he understands England so fully.... Stocky (as I always used to call him) is so sensible about everything, and is so much attached to you.

I shall have no great dinners, because the large rooms in the upper story here are not yet ready. My good old Primus1 usually dines with me three or four times a week, almost always on Sundays, when I cannot invite other people to dinner, as it is not reckoned right here for me to give dinners on Sunday, or to invite many people. Your song (the bust has been mentioned before) is very fine; there is something touching in it which I like so much....

Footnote 1: I.e. Premier.

OPENING OF PARLIAMENT

Buckingham Palace, 12th January 1840.

This letter will be handed you by Torrington personally. I recommend you not to leave late, so as to make the journey without hurry. I did not go to church to-day; the weather is very cold, and I have to be careful not to catch cold before the 16th, because I open Parliament in person. This is always a nervous proceeding, and the announcement of my marriage at the beginning of my speech is really a very nervous and awful affair for me. I have never failed yet, and this is the sixth time that I have done it, and yet I am just as frightened as if I had never done it before. They say that feeling of nervousness is never got over, and that Wm. Pitt himself never got up to make a speech without thinking he should fail. But then I only read my speech.

I had to-day a visit from George2 whom I received alone, and he was very courteous. His Papa I have also seen.

Footnote 2: Prince George of Cambridge.

Buckingham Palace, 17th January 1840.

... Yesterday just as I came home from the House of Lords,3 I received your dear letter of the 10th. I cannot understand at all why you have received no letters from me, seeing that I always wrote twice a week, regularly....

I observe with horror that I have not formally invited your father; though that is a matter of course. My last letter will have set that right. I ought not to have written to you on picture notepaper, seeing that we are in deep mourning for my poor Aunt, the Landgravine,4 but it was quite impossible for me to write to you on mourning paper....

But this will not interfere with our marriage in the least; the mourning will be taken off for that day, and for two or three days after, and then put on again.

Everything went off exceedingly well yesterday. There was an immense multitude of people, and perhaps never, certainly not for a long time, have I been received so well; and what is remarkable, I was not nervous, and read the speech really well. The Tories began immediately afterwards to conduct themselves very badly and to plague us. But everyone praised you very much. Melbourne made a very fine speech about you and your ancestors. To-day I receive the Address of the House of Lords, and, perhaps, also that of the House of Commons.

Footnote 3: The Queen had opened Parliament in person, and announced her intended marriage.

Footnote 4: The Princess Elizabeth (born 1770), third daughter of George III. and widow of the Landgrave Frederick Joseph Louis of Hesse-Homburg. See p.

TORIES, WHIGS, AND RADICALS

Buckingham Palace, 21st January 1840.

I am awaiting with immense impatience a letter from you. Here hardly anything to relate to-day, because we are living in great retirement, until informed that my poor Aunt has been buried. With the exception of Melbourne and my own people, no one has dined for the last week.

We are all of us very much preoccupied with politics. The Tories really are very astonishing; as they cannot and dare not attack us in Parliament, they do everything that they can to be personally rude to me.... The Whigs are the only safe and loyal people, and the Radicals will also rally round their Queen to protect her from the Tories; but it is a curious sight to see those, who as Tories, used to pique themselves upon their excessive loyalty, doing everything to degrade their young Sovereign in the eyes of the people. Of course there are exceptions.

Buckingham Palace, 31st January 1840.

... You have written to me in one of your letters about our stay at Windsor, but, dear Albert, you have not at all understood the matter. You forget, my dearest Love, that I am the Sovereign, and that business can stop and wait for nothing. Parliament is sitting, and something occurs almost every day, for which I may be required, and it is quite impossible for me to be absent from London; therefore two or three days is already a long time to be absent. I am never easy a moment, if I am not on the spot, and see and hear what is going on, and everybody, including all my Aunts (who are very knowing in all these things), says I must come out after the second day, for, as I must be surrounded by my Court, I cannot keep alone. This is also my own wish in every way.

Now as to the Arms: as an English Prince you have no right, and Uncle Leopold had no right to quarter the English Arms, but the Sovereign has the power to allow it by Royal Command: this was done for Uncle Leopold by the Prince Regent, and I will do it again for you. But it can only be done by Royal Command.

I will, therefore, without delay, have a seal engraved for you.

You will certainly feel very happy too, at the news of the coming union of my much-beloved Vecto5 with Nemours. It gives me quite infinite pleasure, because then I can see the dear child more frequently.

I read in the newspaper that you, dear Albert, have received many Orders; also that the Queen of Spain will send you the Golden Fleece....

Farewell, dearest Albert, and think often of thy faithful

Victoria R.

THE PRINCE'S GRANT

Brussels, 31st January 1840.

My dearest Victoria,—I am most grateful for your long letter of the 27th and 28th inst. I send a messenger to be able to answer quite confidentially. I must confess that I never saw anything so disgraceful than the discussion and vote in the Commons.6 The whole mode and way in which those who opposed the grant treated the question was so extremely vulgar and disrespectful, that I cannot comprehend the Tories. The men who uphold the dignity of the Crown to treat their Sovereign in such a manner, on such an occasion! Even in private life the most sour and saturnine people relax and grow gay and mildly disposed on occasions like this. Clearly, as you are Queen Regnant, Albert's position is to all intents and purposes that of a male Queen Consort, and the same privileges and charges ought to be attached to it which were attached to Queen Adelaide's position. The giving up the income which the Queen-Dowager came into, and which I hope and trust Albert would never have, or have had, any chance of having had himself, was in reality giving up a thing which custom had sanctioned. That Prince George of Denmark7 was considered to be in the same position as a Queen Consort there can be, I think, no doubt about, and when one considers the immense difference in the value of money then and now, it renders matters still more striking. I must say such conduct in Parliament I did not expect, and the less when I consider that your Civil List was rather curtailed than otherwise, perhaps not quite fairly. I rejoice to think that I induced Lord Melbourne to propose to you not to accede to the giving up of the Duchy of Lancaster. Parliament did not deserve it, and by good management I think something may be made of it.

Another thing which made me think that Parliament would have acted with more decency, is that I return to the country now near £40,000 a year, not because I thought my income too large, as worthy Sir Robert Peel said, but from motives of political delicacy, which at least might be acknowledged on such occasions. I was placed by my marriage treaty in the position of a Princess of Wales, which in reality it was, though not yet by law, there existing a possibility of a Prince of Wales as long as George IV. lived. I can only conclude by crying shame, shame!...

I hope and trust you will not be too much worried with all these unpleasant things, and that Albert will prove a comforter and support to you. And so good-bye for to-day. Ever, my dearest Victoria, your devoted Uncle,

Leopold R.

THE PRINCE AT BRUSSELS

Brussels, 1st February 1840.

My dearest Victoria,—I hope you will be pleased with me, as I send a messenger on purpose to inform you of Albert's arrival. He will write himself this night, though rather inclined to surrender himself to Morpheus.

He looks well and handsome, but a little interesting, being very much irritated by what happened in the House of Commons. He does not care about the money, but he is much shocked and exasperated by the disrespect of the thing, as he well may.

I do not yet know the exact day of their departure, but I suppose it will be on the 5th, to be able to cross on the 6th. I have already had some conversation with him, and mean to talk à fond to him to-morrow. My wish is to see you both happy and thoroughly united and of one mind, and I trust that both of you will ever find in me a faithful, honest, and attached friend.

As it is eleven o'clock at night, I offer you my respects, and remain, ever, my dearest Victoria, your devoted Uncle,

Leopold R.

Your poor Aunt fainted this morning; she is much given to this, but it was rather too long to-day.

AMIABILITY OF THE PRINCE

Brussels, 4th February 1840.

My dearest Victoria,—I have now treated all the questions you wished me to touch upon with Albert, and I was much pleased with his amiable disposition. At a certain distance explanations by letter are next to impossible, and each party in the end thinks the other unreasonable. When he arrived he was rather exasperated about various things, and pretty full of grievances. But our conversations have dissipated these clouds, and now there will only remain the new parliamentary events and consequences, which change a good deal of what one could reasonably have foreseen or arranged. You will best treat these questions now verbally. Albert is quick, not obstinate, in conversation, and open to conviction if good arguments are brought forward. When he thinks himself right he only wishes to have it proved that he misunderstands the case, to give it up without ill-humour. He is not inclined to be sulky, but I think that he may be rendered a little melancholy if he thinks himself unfairly or unjustly treated, but being together and remaining together, there never can arise, I hope, any occasion for any disagreement even on trifling subjects.... Ever, my dearest Victoria, your devoted Uncle,

Leopold R.

Brussels, 8th February 1840.

My dearest Victoria,—This letter will arrive when I trust you will be most happily occupied; I don't mean therefore to trespass on your time.

May Heaven render you as happy as I always wished you to be, and as I always tried hard to see you. There is every prospect of it, and I am sure you will be mistress in that respect of your own avenir. Perfect confidence will best ensure and consolidate this happiness. Our rule in poor Charlotte's time was never to permit one single day to pass over ein Missverständniss, however trifling it might be.8 I must do Charlotte the justice to say that she kept this compact most religiously, and at times even more so than myself, as in my younger days I was sometimes inclined to be sulky and silently displeased. With this rule no misunderstandings can take root and be increased or complicated by new ones being added to the old. Albert is gentle and open to reason; all will therefore always be easily explained, and he is determined never to be occupied but by what is important or useful to you....

Now I conclude, with my renewed warmest and sincerest good wishes for you, ever, my dearest Victoria, your devoted Uncle,

Leopold.

Footnote 8: (From an unpublished Contemporary Memoir by Admiral Sir William Hotham, G.C.B.)

"Her Royal Highness was now and then apt to give way to a high flow of animal spirits, natural at her time of life, and from carelessness more than unkindness to ridicule others. In one of these sallies of inconsiderate mirth, she perceived the Prince, sombre and cold, taking no apparent notice of what was going on, or if he did, evidently displeased. She at length spoke to him about it, and he at once manifested reluctance to join in the conversation, saying that though he had been a tolerably apt scholar in many things, he had yet to learn in England what pleasure was derived from the exercise of that faculty understood to be called "quizzing"; that he could by no means reconcile it to himself according to any rule either of good breeding or benevolence. The tears instantly started in her eye, and feeling at once the severity and justice of the reproof, assured him most affectionately that, as it was the first time she had ever merited His Royal Highness's reproof on this subject, she assured him most solemnly it should be the last."

THE WEDDING-DAY

10th February 1840.

Dearest,—... How are you to-day, and have you slept well? I have rested very well, and feel very comfortable to-day. What weather! I believe, however, the rain will cease.

Send one word when you, my most dearly loved bridegroom, will be ready. Thy ever-faithful, Victoria R.

Footnote 9: A note folded in billet form, to be taken by hand. Addressed:

"His Royal Highness the Prince.

"The Queen."

This was the day of their marriage at the Chapel Royal. After the wedding breakfast at Buckingham Palace they drove to Windsor, and on the 14th they returned to London.

Windsor Castle, 11th February 1840.

My dearest Uncle,—I write to you from here, the happiest, happiest Being that ever existed. Really, I do not think it possible for any one in the world to be happier, or as happy as I am. He is an Angel, and his kindness and affection for me is really touching. To look in those dear eyes, and that dear sunny face, is enough to make me adore him. What I can do to make him happy will be my greatest delight. Independent of my great personal happiness, the reception we both met with yesterday was the most gratifying and enthusiastic I ever experienced; there was no end of the crowds in London, and all along the road. I was a good deal tired last night, but am quite well again to-day, and happy....

My love to dear Louise. Ever your affectionate,

Victoria R.

Brussels, 21st February 1840.

My dearest Victoria,—I am more grateful than I can express that, notwithstanding your many empêchements and occupations, you still found a little moment to write to me. News from you are always most precious to me, and now almost more than ever. This is such an important moment in your life, it will so much decide how the remainder is to be, that I am deeply interested in all I can hear on the subject. Hitherto, with the exception of your own dear and Royal self, I have not been spoiled, et j'ai puisé beaucoup de mes nouvelles in the Times and such like sources.

God be praised that the dear ménage is so happy! I can only say may it be so for ever and ever. I always thought that with your warm and feeling heart and susceptibility for strong and lasting affection, you would prefer this genre of happiness, if you once possessed it, to every other. It must be confessed that it is less frequent than could be wished for the good of mankind, but when it does exist, there is something delightful to a generous heart like yours in this sacred tie, in this attachment for better for worse, and I think the English Church service expresses it in a simple and touching manner.

I was happy to see that the Addresses of both Houses of Parliament were voted in a decent and becoming way. How mean people are! If they had not seen the public at large take a great interest in your marriage and show you great affection, perhaps some would again have tried to bring on unpleasant subjects....

My letter is grown long; I will therefore conclude it with the expression of my great affection for your dear self. Ever, my most beloved Victoria, your devoted Uncle,

Leopold R.

POPULAR ENTHUSIASM

6th March 1840.

... As your Majesty has by your Lord Chamberlain permitted plays to be acted on Wednesdays and Fridays in Lent, it would be condemning yourself if you did not go to see them if you like to do so....

... Lord Melbourne is much pleased to hear that your Majesty and the Prince liked The School for Scandal. It is upon the whole the cleverest comedy in the English language, the fullest of wit and at the same time the most free from grossness.

THE CORN LAWS

4th April 1840.

Lord John Russell presents his humble duty to your Majesty, and has the honour to state that the House of Commons having resumed the consideration of the Corn Laws, the debate was closed by Sir Robert Peel, in a speech much inferior to those which he usually makes. Mr Warburton moved an adjournment, which caused many members to leave the House. The motion being opposed, there were on a division 240 against adjournment, and only 125 in favour of it.

Mr Warburton then by some blunder moved that the House adjourn, which puts an end to the debate. This was eagerly caught at by the opposite party, and agreed to. So that the question is lost by this ridiculous termination, and it is to be feared that it will produce much discontent in the manufacturing class.10

Footnote 10: The opposition to the Corn Laws was now increasing in the North.

5th April 1840.

Lord Melbourne presents his humble duty to your Majesty. He is quite well but much tired. He has so much to do this morning that he will not be able to speak to Albemarle,11 but if Albemarle dines at the Palace, he certainly will then.

Lord Melbourne always feared anything like a mixture of the Stable establishments. It would have been much better that what horses the Prince had should have been kept quite separate, and that the horses of your Majesty's which he should have to use should have been settled, and some plan arranged by which they could have been obtained when wanted. Horses to be used by one set of people and kept and fed by another will never do. Servants and subordinate agents in England are quite unmanageable in these respects. If they get [matters] into their hands neither the Deity nor the Devil, nor both together, can make them agree. Lord Melbourne writes this in ignorance of the actual facts of the case, and therefore it may be inapplicable.

Footnote 11: Master of the Horse.

8th April 1840.

Lord John Russell presents his humble duty to your Majesty, and has the honour to state that Sir James Graham yesterday brought forward his motion on China in a speech of nearly three hours.12 He was answered by Mr Macaulay in a manner most satisfactory to his audience, and with great eloquence. Sir William Follett spoke with much ingenuity, but in the confined spirit of a lawyer.

Footnote 12: The motion was to censure Ministers for their want of foresight in their dealings with China in connection with the extension of commerce, and with the opium trade. The motion was rejected by 271 to 262.

ENGLAND AND CHINA

9th April 1840.

Lord John Russell presents his humble duty to your Majesty, and has the honour to report that the debate went on yesterday, when Mr Hawes spoke against the motion. In the course of the debate Mr Gladstone13 said the Chinese had a right to poison the wells, to keep away the English! The debate was adjourned.

Footnote 13: Mr Gladstone had been member for Newark since 1832.

2nd May 1840.

Mr Cowper has just come in and tells me that they have determined to begin the disturbance to-night at the Opera, at the very commencement of the performance.14 This may be awkward, as your Majesty will arrive in the middle of the tumult. It is the intention not to permit the opera to proceed until Laporte gives way.

Lord Melbourne is afraid that if the row has already begun, your Majesty's presence will not put an end to it; and it might be as well not to go until your Majesty hears that it is over and that the performance is proceeding quietly. Some one might be sent to attend and send word.

Footnote 14: A fracas took place at the Opera on 29th April. The Manager, Laporte, not having engaged Tamburini to sing, the audience made a hostile demonstration at the conclusion of the performance of I Puritani. An explanation made by Laporte only made matters worse, and eventually the Tamburinists took possession of the stage.

6th May 1840.

Lord Melbourne presents his humble duty to your Majesty. He has just received this from Lord John Russell—a most shocking event,15 which your Majesty has probably by this time heard of. The persons who did it came for the purpose of robbing the house; they entered by the back of the house and went out at the front door.16 The servants in the house, only a man and a maid, never heard anything, and the maid, when she came down to her master's door in the morning, found the horrid deed perpetrated....

Footnote 15: The murder of Lord William Russell by his valet, Courvoisier, in Norfolk Street, Park Lane.

Footnote 16: This was the original theory.

MURDER OF LORD WILLIAM RUSSELL

6th May 1840.

Lord Melbourne presents his humble duty to your Majesty. Since he wrote to your Majesty, he has seen Mr Fox Maule,17 who had been at the house in Norfolk Street. He says that it is a most mysterious affair. Lord William Russell was found in his bed, quite dead, cold and stiff, showing that the act had been perpetrated some time. The bed was of course deluged with blood, but there were no marks of blood in any other part of the room; so that he had been killed in his bed and by one blow, upon the throat, which had nearly divided his head from his body. The back door of the house was broken open, but there were no traces of persons having approached the door from without. His writing-desk was also broken open and the money taken out, but otherwise little or nothing had been taken away. The police upon duty in the streets had neither heard nor seen anything during the night. In these circumstances strong suspicion lights upon the persons in the house, two maids and a man, the latter a foreigner18 and who had only been with Lord William about five weeks. These persons are now separately confined, and the Commissioners of Police are actively employed in enquiring into the affair. An inquest will of course be held upon the body without delay.

Lord Melbourne has just received your Majesty's letter, and will immediately convey to Lord John your Majesty's kind expressions of sympathy.

Footnote 17: Under-Secretary for Home Affairs; afterwards, as Lord Panmure, Secretary for War.

Footnote 18: Courvoisier.

MRS NORTON

Laeken, 22nd May 1840.

My dearest Victoria,—I received yesterday a most kind and dear letter from your august hands. Charles,19 who wanted to cross yesterday, will have had very bad weather. He is prepared not to make too long a stay in England. He dined here on the 19th. Louise was prepared to come to dinner, but was not quite equal to it; she therefore came after it. He came also to see me on the 20th, before his departure for Ostende. It is very gracious of you to have given him subsidies, but in fact poor Feo stands more in need of it. She really is too poor; when one thinks that they have but £600 a year, and that large castles, etc., are to be kept up with it, one cannot conceive how they manage it. It was a very generous feeling which prompted you to see Mrs Norton, and I have been too much her friend to find fault with it. True it is that Norton was freely accepted by her, but she was very poor, and could therefore hardly venture to refuse him. Many people will flirt with a clever, handsome, but poor girl, though not marry her—besides, the idea of having old Shery20 for a grandfather had nothing very captivating. A very unpleasant husband Norton certainly was, and one who had little tact. I can well believe that she was much frightened, having so many eyes on her, some of which, perhaps, not with the most amiable expression.

PRINCESS CHARLOTTE

I was delighted to learn that you meant to visit poor Claremont, and to pass there part of your precious birthday. Claremont is the place where in younger days you were least plagued, and generally I saw you there in good spirits. You will also nolens volens be compelled to think of me, and maybe of poor Charlotte.

This gives me an opening for saying a few words on this subject. I found several times that some people had given you the impression that poor Charlotte had been hasty and violent even to imperiousness and rudeness. I can you assure that it was not so; she was quick, and even violent, but I never have seen anybody so open to conviction, and so fair and candid when wrong. The proverb says, and not without some truth, that ladies come always back to the first words, to avoid any symptom of having been convinced. Generous minds, however, do not do this; they fight courageously their battles, but when they clearly see that they are wrong, and that the reasons and arguments submitted to them are true, they frankly admit the truth. Charlotte had eminently this disposition; besides, she was so anxious to please me, that often she would say: "Let it be as it may; provided you wish it, I will do it." I always answered: "I never want anything for myself; when I press something on you, it is from a conviction that it is for your interest and for your good." I know that you have been told that she ordered everything in the house and liked to show that she was the mistress. It was not so. On the contrary, her pride was to make me appear to my best advantage, and even to display respect and obedience, when I least wanted it from her. She would almost exaggerate the feeling, to show very clearly that she considered me as her lord and master.

And on the day of the marriage, as most people suspected her of a very different disposition, everybody was struck with the manner in which she pronounced the promise of obedience. I must say that I was much more the master of the house than is generally the case in private life. Besides, there was something generous and royal in her mind which alone would have prevented her doing anything vulgar or ill-bred. What rendered her sometimes a little violent was a slight disposition to jealousy. Poor Lady Maryborough,21 at all times some twelve or fifteen years older than myself, but whom I had much known in 1814, was once much the cause of a fit of that description. I told her it was quite childish, but she said, "it is not, because she is a very coquettish, dissipated woman." The most difficult task I had was to change her manners; she had something brusque and too rash in her movements, which made the Regent quite unhappy, and which sometimes was occasioned by a struggle between shyness and the necessity of exerting herself. I had—I may say so without seeming to boast—the manners of the best society of Europe, having early moved in it, and been rather what is called in French de la fleur des pois. A good judge I therefore was, but Charlotte found it rather hard to be so scrutinised, and grumbled occasionally how I could so often find fault with her.

Nothing perhaps speaks such volumes as the positive fact of her manners getting quite changed within a year's time, and that to the openly pronounced satisfaction of the very fastidious and not over-partial Regent. To explain how it came that manners were a little odd in England, it is necessary to remember that England had been for more than ten years completely cut off from the rest of the world....

We have bitter cold weather which has given colds to both the children. Uncle Ferdinand 22 is now only arriving si dice on Sunday next. He has been robbed of 15,000 francs in his own room au Palais-Royal, which is very unpleasant for all parties.

My letter is so long that I must haste to conclude it, remaining ever, my beloved Victoria, your devoted Uncle,

Leopold R.

My love to Alberto.

Footnote 19: Prince Charles of Leiningen.

Footnote 20: The three sisters, Mrs Norton, Lady Dufferin, and Lady Seymour (afterwards Duchess of Somerset), the latter of whom was "Queen of Beauty" at the Eglinton Tournament, were grand-daughters of R. B. Sheridan. Lord Melbourne was much in Mrs Norton's company, and Norton, for whom the Premier had found a legal appointment, sued him in the Court of Common Pleas for crim. con.; the jury found for the defendant.

Footnote 21: Lord Maryborough (1763-1845) was William Wellesley Pole, brother of the Marquess Wellesley and the Duke of Wellington. He married Katherine Elizabeth Forbes, granddaughter of the third Earl of Granard.

Footnote 22: Prince Ferdinand of Saxe-Coburg, King Leopold's brother.

THE QUEEN AND THE PRINCE

Lord Melbourne.—"I have spoken to the Queen, who says the Prince complains of a want of confidence on trivial matters, and on all matters connected with the politics of this country. She said it proceeded entirely from indolence; she knew it was wrong, but when she was with the Prince she preferred talking upon other subjects. I told Her Majesty that she should try and alter this, and that there was no objection to her conversing with the Prince upon any subject she pleased. My impression is that the chief obstacle in Her Majesty's mind is the fear of difference of opinion, and she thinks that domestic harmony is more likely to follow from avoiding subjects likely to create difference. My own experience leads me to think that subjects between man and wife, even where difference is sure to ensue, are much better discussed than avoided, for the latter course is sure to beget distrust. I do not think that the Baroness23 is the cause of this want of openness, though her name to me is never mentioned by the Queen."

Baron Stockmar.—"I wish to have a talk with you. The Prince leans more on you than any one else, and gives you his entire confidence; you are honest, moral, and religious, and will not belie that trust. The Queen has not started upon a right principle. She should by degrees impart everything to him, but there is danger in his wishing it all at once. A case may be laid before him; he may give some crude and unformed opinion; the opinion may be taken and the result disastrous, and a forcible argument is thus raised against advice being asked for the future.

"The Queen is influenced more than she is aware of by the Baroness. In consequence of that influence, she is not so ingenuous as she was two years ago. I do not think that the withholding of her confidence does proceed wholly from indolence, though it may partly arise, as the Prince suggests, from the entire confidence which she reposes in her present Ministers, making her inattentive to the plans and measures proposed, and thinking it unnecessary entirely to comprehend them; she is of necessity unable to impart their views and projects to him who ought to be her friend and counsellor."

Footnote 23: Baroness Lehzen.

OXFORD'S ATTEMPT

Carlton Terrace, 10th June 1840.

Viscount Palmerston presents his humble duty to your Majesty, and though your Majesty must be overwhelmed with congratulations at your Majesty's escape from the aim of the assassin,24 yet Viscount Palmerston trusts that he may be allowed to express the horror with which he heard of the diabolical attempt, and the deep thankfulness which he feels at your Majesty's providential preservation.

Viscount Palmerston humbly trusts that the failure of this atrocious attempt may be considered as an indication that your Majesty is reserved for a long and prosperous reign, and is destined to assure, for many years to come, the welfare and happiness of this nation.

Footnote 24: Edward Oxford, a pot-boy, aged eighteen, fired twice at the Queen on Constitution Hill. The Queen, who was untouched either shot, immediately drove to the Duchess of Kent's house to announce her safety. On his trial, Oxford was found to be insane.

11 Juin 1840.

Madame ma Sœur,—C'est avec une profonde indignation que je viens d'apprendre l'horrible attentat qui a menacé les précieux jours de votre Majesté. Je rends grâce du fond de mon cœur à la Divine Providence qui les a miraculeusement conservés, et qui semble n'avoir permis qu'ils fussent exposés à un si grand danger, que pour faire briller aux yeux de tous, votre courage, votre sang-froid, et toutes les qualités qui vous distinguent.

J'ose espérer que votre Majesté me permettra de recourir à son entremise pour offrir à S.A.R. le Prince Albert, l'expression de tous les sentiments dont je suis pénétré, et qu'elle voudra bien recevoir l'assurance de tous ceux que je lui porte, ainsi que celle de ma haute estime, de mon inaltérable attachement et de mon inviolable amitié. Je suis, Madame ma Sœur, de votre Majesté, le bon Frère,

Louis Philippe R.

A PROVIDENTIAL ESCAPE

11th June 1840.

Lord Melbourne presents his humble duty to your Majesty, and returns your Majesty many, many thanks for your letter. Lord Melbourne was indeed most anxious to learn that your Majesty was well this morning. It was indeed a most awful and providential escape. It is impossible not to shudder at the thought of it.

Lord Melbourne thinks that it will be necessary to have an examination of this man before such of your Majesty's confidential servants as are of the Privy Council;25 it should take place this morning.

Addresses will be moved in both Houses immediately upon their meeting.

Footnote 25: I.e., the Cabinet.

Laeken, 13th June 1840.

My dearest and most beloved Victoria,—I cannot find words strong enough to express to you my horror at what happened on the 10th, and my happiness and delight to see your escape from a danger which was really very great. In your good little heart I hope that it made you feel grateful to God for a protection which was very signal. It does good and is a consolation to think that matters are not quite left to take care of themselves, but that an all-powerful Hand guides them.

Louise I told the affair mildly, as it might have made too great an impression on her otherwise. She always feels so much for you and loves you so much, that she was rejoiced beyond measure that you escaped so well and took the thing with so much courage. That you have shown great fortitude is not to be doubted, and will make a very great and good impression. I see that the general feeling is excellent, but what a melancholy thing to see a young man, without provocation, capable of such a diabolical act! That attempts of that sort took place against George III., and even George IV., one can comprehend; but you have not only been extremely liberal, but in no instance have you hitherto come into contact with any popular feeling or prejudice; besides, one should think that your being a lady would alone prevent such unmanly conduct. It shows what an effect bad example and the bad press have. I am sure that this act is une singerie of what passes in France, that it is a fancy of some of those societies de Mort aux Rois et Souverains, without knowing wherefore, merely as a sort of fashion....

EGYPT AND THE POWERS

St Cloud, 26th July 1840.

My dearest Victoria,—Your dear letter of the 19th greatly delighted me....

Let me now add a few words on politics. The secret way in which the arrangement about the arbitration of the Turco-Egyptian affairs has been signed, the keeping out of France in an affair so near it and touching its interests in various ways, has had here a very disastrous effect.26 I cannot disguise from you that the consequences may be very serious, and the more so as the Thiers Ministry is supported by the movement party, and as reckless of consequences as your own Minister for Foreign Affairs, even much more so, as Thiers himself would not be sorry to see everything existing upset. He is strongly impregnated with all the notions of fame and glory which belonged to part of the Republican and the Imperial times; he would not even be much alarmed at the idea of a Convention ruling again France, as he thinks that he would be the man to rule the Assembly, and has told me last year that he thinks it for France perhaps the most powerful form of Government.27

The mode in this affair ought to have been, as soon as the Four Powers had agreed on a proposition, to communicate it officially to France, to join it. France had but two ways, either to join or to refuse its adhesion. If it had chosen the last, it would have been a free decision on her part, and a secession which had nothing offensive in the eyes of the nation.

But there is a material difference between leaving a company from motives of one's own, or being kicked out of it. I must beg you to speak seriously to Lord Melbourne, who is the head of your Government, on these important affairs; they may upset everything in Europe if the mistake is not corrected and moderated.

I shall write again to you next Friday from hence, and on Saturday, 1st August, we set off. Ever, my dearest Victoria, your devoted Uncle,

Leopold R.

Footnote 26: On the 15th of July a convention was signed in London by representatives of England, Russia, Austria, and Prussia, offering an ultimatum to the Viceroy of Egypt. The exclusion of France was hotly resented in Paris. Guizot, then Ambassador in London, had been kept in ignorance of the project, but the Foreign Secretary, Lord Palmerston, denied that there had been any discourtesy intended, or want of consideration shown.

Footnote 27: Louis Adolphe Thiers (1797-1877), who through the Press had contributed to the downfall of the Bourbons, had held various Cabinet offices under Louis Philippe, and, from March to October 1840, was for the second time Premier.

PRINCE LOUIS NAPOLEON

7th August 1840. (10 p.m.)

Lord Melbourne presents his humble duty to your Majesty. The House of Lords lasted until eight, and Lord Melbourne might by an exertion have got to the Palace to dinner, but as he had the Speech, by no means an easy one, to prepare for the consideration of the Cabinet to-morrow, he thought it better to take this evening for that purpose, and he hopes therefore that your Majesty will excuse his not coming, which is to him a great sacrifice to have made.

Your Majesty will have probably seen by this time the report from your Majesty's Consul at Boulogne of the mad attempt of Louis Bonaparte.28 It is rather unfortunate that it should have taken place at this moment, as the violent and excited temper of the French nation will certainly lead them to attribute it to England. It will also be highly embarrassing to the King of the French to have in his possession a member of the family of Bonaparte and so many Bonapartists who have certainly deserved death but whom it may not be prudent or politic to execute.

Footnote 28: The Prince, afterwards the Emperor Napoleon III., descended on Boulogne with fifty-three persons, and a tame eagle which had been intended, with stage effect, to alight on the Colonne de Napoléon. He was captured, tried for high treason, and sentenced to perpetual imprisonment. He effected his escape, which was undoubtedly connived at by the authorities, in 1846.

THE CONVENTION OF 1828

Wiesbaden, 22nd September 1840.

My dearest Victoria,—I was most happy in receiving this morning per messenger your dear little letter of the 15th, though it is grown a little elderly. The life one leads here is not favourable to writing, which, besides, is prohibited, and easily gives me palpitation enough to sing "di tanti palpiti!" I get up at half after six and begin to drink this hot water; what with drinking and walking one comes to ten o'clock or half after ten for breakfast. Then I read papers and such like things. At one o'clock I have been generally bored with some visit or other till two o'clock. I try to finish some writing, and then I walk and ride out till dinner-time, generally at seven. In the evening I have written sometimes, but it certainly does one harm. You see that there remains but little time for writing.

I am most happy to find that you are well; the papers, which don't know what to invent to lower the Funds, said that you had been unwell on the 10th, which, God be praised! is not at all true.

I pity poor Princess Augusta29 from all my heart. I am sure that if she had in proper time taken care of herself she might have lived to a great age. I have not time to-day to write at any length on the politics of the day, but I am far from thinking that the French acted wisely in the Oriental affair. I must say that I think the King meant well, but I should not have abstained from the Conference as he did, though, in France, interference with Mehemet Ali was certainly not popular. In England much of the fond is logical, but the form towards France was, and is still, harsh and insulting. I don't think France, which these ten years behaved well, and the poor King, who was nearly murdered I don't remember how often, deserved to be treated so unkindly, and all that seemingly to please the great Autocrat. We must not forget what were the fruits of the first Convention of July 1828—I think the 16th or 26th of that month; I ought to remember it, as I took its name in vain often enough in the Greek affair.

This first Convention brought about the battle of Navarino and the second campaign of the Russians, which ended with, in fact, the demise of the poor old Porte, the Treaty of Adrianople.30 Your Majesty was then afflicted with the age of ten, in itself a good age, and may not remember much about it except that in 1829 the affair about my going to Greece began, and that your affectionate heart took some interest in that. Lord Melbourne, however, you must encourage to speak about this matter. Canning's intention was this: he said we must remain with Russia, and by this means prevent mischief. The Duke of Wellington, who came to me shooting at Claremont in 1828, really did cry, though he is not of a crying disposition, and said "by this Convention the Russians will have the power of doing all they never would have dared to do single-handed, and shielded by this infernal Convention, it will not be in our power to stop them." Russia is again in this very snug and comfortable position, that the special protection of the Porte is confided to its tender mercies—la chèvre gardant le chou, the wolf the sheep, as I suppose I must not compare the Turcs to lambs. The Power which ruined the Ottoman Empire, which since a hundred and forty years nearly pared it all round nearly in every direction, is to be the protector and guardian of that same empire; and we are told that it is the most scandalous calumny to suspect the Russians to have any other than the most humane and disinterested views! "ainsi soit-il," as the French say at the end of their sermons. This part of the Convention of the 15th of July 1840 strikes impartial people as strange, the more so as nothing lowers the Porte so much in the eyes of the few patriotic Turks who remain than the protection of the arch-enemy of the concern, Russia. I beg you to read this part of my letter to my good and dear friend, Lord Melbourne, to whom I beg to be kindly remembered.

Footnote 29: Princess Augusta, second daughter of George III. See below [second letter, 26th September, 1840.].

Footnote 30: Under this treaty (14th September 1829) the Danubian principalities were made virtually independent States, the treaty rights of Russia in the navigation of the Bosphorus and Dardanelles were confirmed, and Greek affairs were arranged, by incorporating in the treaty the terms of the Protocol of 22nd March 1829.

A THREATENED CRISIS

Windsor Castle, 26th September 1840.

This is certainly awkward; but the latter part about Peel is most absurd; to him I can never apply, we must do everything but that. But for God's sake do not bring on a crisis;32 the Queen really could not go through that now, and it might make her seriously ill if she were to be kept in a state of agitation and excitement if a crisis were to come on; she has had already so much lately in the distressing illness of her poor Aunt to harass her. I beseech you, think of all this, and the consequences it might cause, not only to me, but to all Europe, as it would show our weakness in a way that would be seriously injurious to this country.

Footnote 31: The letter, to which this is a reply, seems not to have been preserved. The Queen's letter, having been shown to Lord John Russell and copied by him, has hitherto been supposed to be a letter from Lord Melbourne to Lord John Russell. See Walpole's Russell, vol. i., chap. xiii.

Footnote 32: The Cabinet met on the 28th to consider the Oriental Question. The Government was on the verge of dissolution, as Lord Palmerston and Lord John Russell were in conflict. The meeting was adjourned till 1st October.

FRANCE AND THE EAST

Windsor Castle, 26th September 1840.

My dearest Uncle,—I have unfortunately very little time to-day, but I will try and answer your kind letters of the 13th and 19th briefly. You know now that the sufferings of good excellent Aunt Augusta were terminated on the 22nd of this month. I regret her very, very sincerely, though for herself we are all most thankful for the release of such unexampled sufferings, borne with such unexampled patience. Almost the last thing she said when she was still conscious, the day before she died, was to Mr More (the apothecary), who wrote me every morning a Report: "Have you written to my darling?" Is this not touching? The Queen-Dowager had her hand in hers when she died, and closed her eyes when all was over; all the Family were present.

I have seen your letters to Palmerston, and his answer to you, and I also send you a paper from Lord Melbourne. I assure you that I do give these affairs my most serious attention: it would be indeed most desirable if France could come back to us, and I think what Metternich suggests very sagacious and well-judged.33 You must allow me to state that France has put herself into this unfortunate state. I know (as I saw all the papers) how she was engaged to join us—and I know how strangely she refused; I know also, that France agrees in the principle, but only doubts the efficacy of the measures. Where then is "La France outragée"? wherefore arm when there is no enemy? wherefore raise the war-cry? But this has been done, and has taken more effect than I think the French Government now like; and now she has to undo all this and to calm the general agitation and excitement, which is not so easy. Still, though France is in the wrong, and quite in the wrong, still I am most anxious, as I am sure my Government also are, that France should be pacified and should again take her place amongst the five Powers. I am sure she might easily do this....

Albert, who sends his love, is much occupied with the Eastern affairs, and is quite of my opinion....

Footnote 33: Metternich's suggestion was that if other means of coercion failed, the allies should renew their deliberations in conjunction with France.

Windsor Castle, 30th September 1840.

Lord Melbourne presents his humble duty to your Majesty. He is quite well, and will be ready at half-past one.

The Prince's34 observations are just, but still the making an advance to France now, coupled with our constant inability to carry into effect the terms of our Convention, will be an humiliating step.

Lord Melbourne sends a letter which he has received this morning from Lord Normanby, whom he had desired to see Lord Palmerston and Lord John Russell, and try what he could do.

Lord Melbourne also sends a letter which he has received from Lord Lansdowne.

Lord Melbourne would beg your Majesty to return them both.

Footnote 34: Prince Metternich.

Downing Street, 1st October 1840.

Lord Melbourne presents his humble duty to your Majesty. We have had the Cabinet and it has passed over quietly. We have agreed to make a proposition to France founded upon the communication of Prince Metternich to the King of the Belgians.35 Palmerston will propose to-morrow to Neumann,36 the Prussian Minister, and Brunnow,37 that he should write to Granville, authorising him to acquaint Thiers that if France will concur in respecting the principle of the treaty, we, without expecting her to adopt coercive measures, will concert with her the further course to be adopted for the purpose of carrying the principle into effect. This is so far so good. Lord Melbourne trusts that it will get over the present entanglement, but of course we must expect that in a matter so complicated and which we have not the power of immediately terminating, further difficulties will arise.

Footnote 35: See p.

Footnote 36: Austrian Minister.

Footnote 37: Russian Minister.

MEHEMET ALI

Downing Street, 2nd October 1840.

Lord Melbourne presents his humble duty to your Majesty. We have just had another Cabinet,38 which was rendered necessary by Brunnow and the Prussian Minister refusing to concur in what we determined yesterday without reference to their Courts and authority from them. This makes it impossible for us to take the step in the way we proposed, but we have now settled that Palmerston should direct Granville to submit the proposition to Thiers, and ask him how he would be disposed to receive it if it were formally made to him. This, so far as we are concerned, will have all the effect which could have been attained in the other way.

Very important despatches of the 14th inst. have come from Constantinople. The Ministers of the Porte held the last proposition of Mehemet Ali as a positive refusal of the terms of the Convention, and proceeded by the advice of Lord Ponsonby39 at once to divest Mehemet Ali of the Pashalik of Egypt; to direct a blockade of the coasts both of Syria and Egypt, and to recall the four Consuls from Alexandria. These are serious measures, and there are despatches from Lord Beauvale40 stating that Prince Metternich is much alarmed at them, and thinks that measures should be immediately taken to diminish and guard against the effect which they may have in France. Lord Melbourne humbly begs your Majesty's pardon for this hurried scrawl upon matters of such importance, but Lord Melbourne will have the opportunity of speaking to your Majesty more fully upon them to-morrow.

Footnote 38: The peace party in the Cabinet were defeated and Palmerston triumphant.

Footnote 39: British Ambassador at Constantinople.

Footnote 40: Frederick James Lamb, younger brother of Lord Melbourne, and his successor in the title (1782-1853). He was at this time Ambassador at Vienna, having previously been Ambassador at Lisbon.

PALMERSTON AND FRANCE

Wiesbaden, 2nd October 1840.

... There is an idea that Mehemet Ali suffers from what one calls un charbon, a sort of dangerous ulcer which, with old people, is never without some danger. If this is true, it only shows how little one can say that the Pashalik of Aleppo is to decide who is to be the master of the Ottoman Empire in Europe and Asia, the Sultan or Mehemet? It is highly probable that if the old gentleman dies, his concern will go to pieces; a division will be attempted by the children, but that in the East hardly ever succeeds. There everything is personal, except the sort of Caliphate which the Sultan possesses, and when the man is gone, his empire also goes. Runjeet Singh41 is a proof of this; his formidable power will certainly go to the dogs, though the Sikhs have a social link which does not exist in the Egyptian concern. If we now were to set everything in Europe on a blaze, have a war which may change totally all that now exists, and in the midst of it we should hear that Mehemet is no more, and his whole boutique broken up, would it not be really laughable, if it was not melancholy? And still the war once raging, it would no longer put a stop to it, but go on for other reasons.

I cannot understand what has rendered Palmerston so extremely hostile to the King and Government of France. A little civility would have gone a great way with the French; if in your

Speech on the 11th of August some regret had been expressed, it would have greatly modified the feelings of the French. But Palmerston likes to put his foot on their necks! Now, no statesman must triumph over an enemy that is not quite dead, because people forget a real loss, a real misfortune, but they won't forget an insult. Napoleon made great mistakes that way; he hated Prussia, insulted it on all occasions, but still left it alive. The consequence was that in 1813 they rose to a man in Prussia, even children and women took arms, not only because they had been injured, but because they had been treated with contempt and insulted. I will here copy what the King wrote to me lately from Paris:

VIEWS OF LOUIS PHILIPPE

"Vous ne vous faites pas d'idée à quel point l'approbation publique soutient les armements, c'est universel. Je regrette que cela aille bien au-delà, car la fureur contre l'Angleterre s'accroît et un des points que je regrette le plus, c'est que tout notre peuple est persuadé que l'Angleterre veut réduire la France au rang de Puissance secondaire, et vous savez ce que c'est que l'orgueil national et la vanité dc tous les peuples. Je crois donc bien urgent que la crise actuelle se termine bientôt pacifiquement. Plus je crois que l'union de l'Angleterre et de la France est la base du repos du monde, plue je regrette de voir susciter tant d'irritation entre nos deux Nations. La question est de savoir ce que veut véritablement le Gouvernement Anglais. J'avoue que je ne suis pas sans crainte et sans inquiétude à cet égard quand je récapitule dans ma tête tout ce que Lord Ponsonby a fait pour l'allumer et tout ce qu'il fait encore. Je n'aurais aucune inquiétude si je croyais que le Gouvernement suivrait la voix de sa Nation, et les véritables intérêts de son pays qui repoussent l'alliance Russe et indiquent celle de la France, ce qui est tout-à-fait conforme à mes vœux personnels. Mais ma vieille expérience me rappelle ce que font les passions personnelles, qui prédominent bien plus de nos jours que les véritables intérêts, et ce que peut le Gouvernement Anglais pour entraîner son pays, et je crains beaucoup l'art de la Russie ou plutôt de l'Empereur Nicolas de captiver, par les plus immenses flatteries, les Ministres Anglais, preuve Lord Durham. Or si ces deux Gouvernements veulent ou osent entreprendre l'abaissement de la France, la guerre s'allumera, et pour mon compte alors je m'y jetterai à outrance, mais si comme je l'espère encore, malgré mes soupçons, ils ne veulent pas la guerre, alors l'affaire de l'Orient, s'arrangera à l'amiable, et le cri de toutes les Nations fera de nouveau justice de ces humeurs belliqueuses et consolidera la paix générale, comme cela est arrivé dans les premières années de mon règne."

I think it right to give you this extract, as it is written from the very bottom of the King's heart, and shows the way in which he considers the present position of affairs. Perhaps you will be so kind to read it or to let it be read by Lord Melbourne. It is this abaissement de la France which now sticks in their throats. Chartres42 has quite the same feeling, and then the refrain is, plutôt périr que de souffrir cette ignominie!

Really my paper is abominable, but it is a great shame that in the residence of such a rich Prince nothing can be had. My letter being long, I conclude it with my best blessings. Ever, my dearest Victoria, your devoted Uncle,

Leopold R.

Footnote 41: Runjeet Singh, known as the Lion of the Punjab, had died in 1839, having consolidated the Sikh power. As an outcome of the Sikh wars in 1846 and 1848, the Punjab was annexed by Great Britain in 1849.

Footnote 42: Ferdinand, Duke of Orléans, who died 13th July 1842, was generally called Chartres in the family circle; this title, which he had previously borne, was conferred on his younger son, born 9th November 1840.

NEGOTIATIONS WITH FRANCE

Claremont, 6th October 1840.

Lord Melbourne presents his humble duty to your Majesty. The King's letter to Lord Melbourne is in many respects just and true.43 The practical measure which it recommends, namely, that Lord Granville should make to Thiers a general proposition for settling the whole matter, is very much the same as that which we agreed upon at the Cabinet should be adopted. Lord Melbourne expects that this has been carried into effect, and if it has not, Lord Melbourne has urged that it should be done without delay.

These affairs are very troublesome and vexatious, but they are, unfortunately, more than troublesome, they are pregnant with danger.

Footnote 43: The King of the Belgians had written a letter to Lord Melbourne on 1st October, which he had sent to Queen Victoria, asking her to read it and forward it to Lord Melbourne.

Wiesbaden, 6th October 1840.

... It is to-day the poor King of the French's birthday; he is sixty-seven years old, and these last ten years he has had a pleasant time of it. And now he has this serious and difficult complication to deal with, and still I find him always fair and amiable in his way of looking at all these things, and bearing the almost unbearable annoyance and plagues of his arduous position with a degree of firmness and courage worthy of kinder treatment from the European Powers than he has received....

South Street, 9th October 1840.

Lord Melbourne presents his humble duty to your Majesty. Lord John Russell has directed a Cabinet to be summoned for to-morrow at three o'clock, at which he intends to propose that "Instructions should be sent to Lord Granville to ascertain from the French Government what terms France would consider satisfactory for the immediate arrangement of the affairs of the East."

That if such terms shall appear satisfactory, Mr Henry Bulwer44 or some person of similar rank should be sent to Constantinople to urge their acceptance on the Sultan, and that our Allies should be invited to co-operate in that negotiation.

That the French Government should be informed that the only mode in which the pacification can be carried into effect is by Mehemet Ali's accepting the terms of the treaty and then receiving from the Sultan the terms which shall have been previously agreed upon by his Allies.

Lord Melbourne feels certain that Lord Palmerston will not accede to these proposals, and indeed Lord Melbourne himself much doubts whether, after all that has passed, it would be right to submit the whole matter, as it were, to the decision and arbitration of France. Lord John

Russell seems very much determined to press this question to a decision to-morrow, and Lord Melbourne much fears that such a decision may lead to serious consequences.

Lord Melbourne is much grieved to have to send your Majesty intelligence which he knows will greatly disquiet your Majesty, but there is no remedy for it.

Lord Melbourne's lumbago is somewhat better to-day but not much. His being compelled to attend at the House of Lords yesterday prevented him from recovering. He has remained in bed to-day, and hopes to be better to-morrow.

Footnote 44: Henry Bulwer (1801-1872), afterwards Lord Dalling, then First Secretary of the Embassy in Paris, became Minister to Spain, 1843-1848; to the United States, 1849-1852; to Tuscany, 1852-1855; and Ambassador to Turkey, 1858-1865.

PACIFIC INSTRUCTIONS

South Street, 9th October 1840.

Lord Melbourne presents his humble duty to your Majesty. He has just received your Majesty's box. He will do all he can to put everything together, and it does not appear to him that there is any necessity on any side for a decisive step at present. A letter is arrived to-day from Bulwer, which states that the instructions given to Guizot are, through the interposition of the King, of a very pacific character. It would surely be well to see what they are, and whether they will not afford the means of arranging the whole affair.

Lord Melbourne thought with your Majesty that the letter to Lord Granville upon Prince Metternich's proposition was a great deal too short and dry and slight, but the importance of this step is now a good deal superseded by what has taken place, and the position of affairs has already become different from that in which it was resolved upon.

Lord Melbourne very much thanks the Prince for his letter, which may do much service and have an effect upon the antagonists.

Lord Melbourne has just seen Dr Holland.45 Lord Melbourne is very much crippled and disabled. Lord Melbourne does not think that the shooting has had anything to do with it. His stomach has lately been out of order, which is always the cause of these sort of attacks. Lord Melbourne will come down on Sunday if he possibly can, and unless he should be still disabled from moving.

Footnote 45: Dr (afterwards Sir) Henry Holland, Physician-in-Ordinary to the Queen, 1850-1873, father of Lord Knutsford.

South Street, 10th October 1840.

Lord Melbourne presents his humble duty to your Majesty.... All the question at the Cabinet to-day as to whether we should write a communication to France was fortunately put an end to by Guizot desiring to see Palmerston in the morning and making a communication to him. This communication is very much in substance what Mr. Bulwer's note had led us to expect. It is a strong condemnation of the act of the Porte depriving Mehemet Ali of the Government of Egypt, an expression of satisfaction at having already learned from Lord Palmerston and Count Apponyi46 that Austria and England are not prepared to consider this act as irrevocable, and a threat on the part of France that he considers the power of Mehemet Ali in Egypt a constituent part of the balance of Europe, and that he cannot permit him to be deprived of that province without interfering. It was determined that this intimation should be met in an amicable spirit, and that Lord Palmerston should see the Ministers of the other Powers and agree with them to acquaint the French that they with England would use their good offices to induce the Porte not to insist upon the deprivation of Mehemet Ali as far as Egypt is concerned. Lord Melbourne hopes that this transaction may lead to a general settlement of the whole question.

Lord Melbourne feels himself much fatigued to-night. Though better, he is yet far from well, and he knows by experience that this malady when once it lays hold of him does not easily let go. It was so when he was younger. He fears, therefore, that it will not be prudent for him to leave town so early as Monday, but will do so as soon as he can with safety.

Footnote 46: Born 1782; at this time the Austrian Ambassador in France.

MEHEMET ALI

Panshanger, 11th October 1840.

Viscount Palmerston presents his humble duty to your Majesty.

Viscount Palmerston submits to your Majesty some interesting letters, which he received some days ago from Paris, showing that there never has been any real foundation for the alarm of war with France which was felt by some persons in this country.

Viscount Palmerston also submits a despatch from Mons. Thiers to Mons. Guizot which was communicated to him yesterday by Mons. Guizot, and which seems to open a prospect of an amicable and satisfactory understanding between France and the Four Powers.

Viscount Palmerston also submits a note from Mr Bulwer intimating that the French Government would be contented with an arrangement which should leave Mehemet Ali in possession of Egypt alone, without any part of Syria, and Viscount Palmerston submits that such is the arrangement which it would on all accounts be desirable to accomplish. There seems reason to think that the bombardment of Beyrout47 and the deposal of Mehemet Ali by the Sultan have greatly contributed to render the French more reasonable on this question, by exciting in their minds an apprehension that unless some arrangement be speedily effected, the operations now going on in the Levant will end in the entire overthrow of Mehemet Ali.

Footnote 47: On 10th October Ibrahim was defeated by the Allies, and next day Beyrout was occupied by British, Austrian, and Turkish troops.

GUIZOT AND THIERS

South Street, 11th October 1840.

Lord Melbourne presents his humble duty to your Majesty. He has not written before to-day, because he had nothing new to lay before your Majesty. Lord Melbourne anxiously hopes she feels some confidence that the present state of the Eastern affairs is such as may lead to a speedy, amicable termination—at the same time, with a nation so irritable as the French, and with the Constitution which they have and which they are unused to exercise, it is impossible to feel secure for a moment. Guizot, when he gave the despatch of Thiers to Lord Palmerston, said that he had nothing to do with the reasonings of that despatch, and would not enter into any argument upon them.

He delivered them only in his official capacity as the Ambassador of the King of France. All he would say was that they were the result of a great effort of that party in France which was for peace. This was a sufficient intimation that he himself did not approve of them, but it was not possible to collect from what he said upon what grounds his dissent was founded. Lord Melbourne has since heard that he says, that he considers that France has taken too low a tone and has made too much concession, and that he could not have been a party to this step if he had been one of the King's Ministers. The step is also probably contrary to the declared opinion of M. Thiers; whether it be contrary to his real opinion is another question. But if it was written principally by the influence of the King, it is a measure at once bold and friendly upon his part, and the success of which will much depend upon its being met in an amicable spirit here.

Lord Melbourne returns the letter of the King of the Belgians. Lord Melbourne kept it because he wished to show it to Lord John Russell, and some others, as containing an authentic statement of the feelings of the King of the French, which it is well that they should know....

Windsor Castle, 12th October 1840.

The Queen in returning these letters must express to Lord Palmerston her very great satisfaction at the favourable turn affairs have taken, and the Queen earnestly trusts that this demonstration of returning amity on the part of France will be met in a very friendly spirit by Lord Palmerston and the rest of her Government. The Queen feels certain that this change on the part of France is also greatly owing to the peaceable disposition of the King of the French, and she thinks that in consideration of the difficulties the King has had to contend with, and which he seems finally to have overcome, we should make some return; and indeed, as Lord Palmerston states, the arrangement proposed is the best which can be desired.

FEELING IN FRANCE

South Street, 12th October 1840.

Lord Melbourne presents his humble duty to your Majesty. He is much better to-day, free from pain and difficulty of moving, but he thinks that it would not be prudent, and that he should run the risk of bringing back the complaint, if he should leave town to-morrow.

He thinks it might also be imprudent in another point of view, as affairs are still in a very unsettled state, and the rest of the Cabinet watch with great impatience, and, to say the truth, not without suspicion, the manner in which Palmerston will carry into effect the decision of Saturday. They are particularly anxious for speed, and I have written both last night and this morning to Palmerston, to urge him not to delay. He will go down to Windsor to-morrow, and your Majesty will then have an opportunity of speaking to him, upon which Lord Melbourne will write again to your Majesty.

Guizot has been with Lord Melbourne this morning for the purpose of repeating what he had before said to Palmerston, that the Note which he delivered on Saturday was the result of a great effort made by the party who are for peace, that it had been conquered against a strong opposition, that if it were not taken advantage of here now, it would not be renewed, that the conduct of affairs in France would probably fall into the hands of the violent party, and that it would be no longer possible to control the excited feelings of the people of France.

The worst is that Palmerston, and John Russell, with now the greater part of the Cabinet, proceed upon principles, opinions, and expectations which are entirely different from one another, and which therefore necessarily lead to a different course of action. We are anxious to finish the business speedily, because we fear that there is danger of the Government of France being forced into violent measures by popular outcry. Palmerston, on the contrary, thinks that there is no danger of war, that the French do not mean war, and that there is no feeling in France but what has been produced by the Ministry and their instruments the Press.

We are anxious that the opportunity should be seized now whilst we have the appearance of success in Syria, not being at all confident of the ultimate result. Palmerston, on the contrary, is so confident of complete success, that he wishes to delay concluding the affair until he can have the benefit of the full advantages, which he anticipates, in the negotiation.

We should be too glad to see the matter settled, leaving Mehemet Ali in possession of Egypt. Palmerston has both the wish and the hope of getting him out of Egypt, as well as Syria.

These great differences of view, object, and expectation render it difficult for those who hold them to pursue the same line of conduct.

There is also, as your Majesty knows, much suspicion, distrust and irritation, and all these circumstances throw great obstacles in the way of the progress of affairs, but Lord Melbourne hopes that they will all be overcome, and that we shall arrive at a safe conclusion.

RELATIONS WITH FRANCE

South Street, 13th October 1840.

Lord Melbourne presents his humble duty to your Majesty. It is absolutely necessary that we should have a Cabinet on Thursday. There is so much natural impatience, and so deep an interest taken in what is now going on, that it cannot be avoided....

Your Majesty will naturally seize this opportunity of stating strongly to Palmerston your wishes that this opportunity should be taken advantage of, with a view to the speedy accommodation of the whole difference. Your Majesty will see the necessity of at the same time not appearing to take too much the part of France, which might irritate and indispose.

Your Majesty will find John Russell perfectly right and reasonable. He was before somewhat embarrassed by the position in which he was placed. Having agreed to the Convention, it was difficult for him to take steps which might appear to be in departure from its policy, and to be occasioned by the gravity of its consequences. But this step upon the part of France will enable all the friends of peace to act cordially together. John Russell thinks that you have not been put fully in possession of his sentiments. Lord Melbourne thinks this is not the case; but it would be well if your Majesty would try to efface this impression from his mind as much as possible.

13th October 1840.

My dearest Uncle,— ... I have three kind letters of yours unanswered before me, of the 1st, 2nd, and 6th, for which many thanks. My time is very short indeed to-day, but Albert has, I know, written to you about the favourable turn which the Oriental affairs have taken, and of the proposition of France, which is very amicably received here; Austria and Prussia are quite ready to agree, but Brunnow has been making already difficulties (this is in confidence to you). I hope and trust that this will at length settle the affair, and that peace, the blessings of which are innumerable, will be preserved. I feel we owe much of the change of the conduct of France to the peaceable disposition of the dear King, for which I feel grateful.48 Pray, dear Uncle, when an opportunity offers, do offer the King my best, sincerest wishes for his health and happiness in every way, on the occasion of his birthday; may he live many years, for the benefit of all Europe!...

Footnote 48: The King of the French was alarmed at the warlike language of his Ministers. He checked the preparations for war which Thiers was making; he went further, and on the 24th of October he dismissed the Thiers Ministry, and entrusted the management of affairs to Soult and Guizot, who were pacifically inclined and anxious to preserve the Anglo-French entente.

THE QUEEN'S INFLUENCE

Windsor Castle, 16th October 1840.

My dearest Uncle,—I received your kind but anxious letter of the 10th, the day before yesterday, and hasten to reply to it by the courier who goes to-day. Indeed, dearest Uncle, I have worked hard this last week to bring about something conciliatory, and I hope and trust I have succeeded. Lord Melbourne, who left Claremont on the same day as we did, was confined to the house till yesterday, when he arrived here, by a lumbago and bilious attack; but I had a constant correspondence with him on this unfortunate and alarming question, and he is, I can assure you, fully aware of the danger, and as anxious as we are to set matters right; and so is Lord John, and Palmerston, I hope, is getting more reasonable. They have settled in consequence of Thiers' two despatches that Palmerston should write to Lord Ponsonby to urge the Porte not to dispossess Mehemet Ali finally of Egypt, and I believe the other foreign Ministers at Constantinople will receive similar instructions; this despatch Palmerston will send to Granville (to-night, I believe) to be communicated to Thiers, and I have made Palmerston promise to put into the despatch to Granville "that it would be a source of great satisfaction to England, if this would be the cause of bringing back France to that alliance (with the other Four Powers) from which we had seen her depart with so much regret." I hope this will have a good effect. Now, in my humble opinion (but this I say of myself and without anybody's knowledge), if France, upon this, were to make some sort of advance, and were to cease arming, I think all would do; for you see, if France goes on arming, we shall hardly be justified in not doing the same, and that would be very bad. Couldn't you suggest this to the King and Thiers, as of yourself? My anxiety is great for the return of amity and concord, I can assure you. I think our child ought to have besides its other names those of Turco Egypto, as we think of nothing else! I had a long talk with Palmerston on Wednesday, and also with J. Russell.

I hope I have done good. The Dutch don't like the abdication. I'm so sorry for poor little Paris!49

Pray excuse this dreadful scrawl, but I am so hurried. Ever your devoted Niece,

Victoria R.

Footnote 49: The Comte de Paris, born 24th August 1838, eldest son of Ferdinand, Duke of Orleans, who was Louis Philippe's eldest son.

ATTEMPT ON LOUIS PHILIPPE

LAEKEN, 17th October 1840.

My dearest Victoria,—You will, I am sure, have been very much shocked on hearing that on the 15th there was a new attempt made to kill the poor good King at Paris.50 The place was cleverly chosen, as the King generally puts his head out of the carriage window to bow to the guard. I join the letter which he had the goodness to forward us through an estafette.51 May this melancholy attentat impress on your Ministers the necessity of aiding the King in his arduous task.... You will have the goodness to show this letter to Albert.

Louise was much alarmed when it arrived at such an unusual hour; it was ten o'clock. At first we thought it might be something about poor little Paris, who is not yet so well as one could wish.

We have gloomy miserable weather, and I feel much disgusted with this part of the world. Ever, my beloved Victoria, your devoted Uncle,

Leopold R.

Footnote 50: The King was fired at as he was leaving the Tuileries, by Darmes, a Marseillais. As Croker wrote to Lord Brougham on the 31st of October 1840:—"Poor Louis Philippe lives the life of a mad dog, and will soon, I fear, suffer the death of that general object of every man's shot."

Footnote 51: Express messenger.

FRANCE AND EGYPT

Laeken, 20th October 1840.

My most beloved Victoria,—I must write to you a few lines by M. Drouet, who returns to-morrow morning to England. God bless you for the great zeal you have mis en action for our great work, the maintenance of peace; it is one of the greatest importance for everything worth caring for in Europe. You know well that no personal interest guides me in my exertions; I am in fact bored with being here, and shall ever regret to have remained in these regions, when I might so easily have gone myself to the Orient, the great object of my predilection.

I never shall advise anything which would be against the interests and honour of yourself, your Government, or your country, in which I have so great a stake myself. The great thing now is not to refuse to negotiate with France, even if it should end in nothing. Still for the King Louis Philippe there is an immense strength and facility in that word "nous négocions"; with this he may get over the opening of the session, and this once done, one may hope to come to a conclusion. Since I wrote to Lord Melbourne to-day, I have received a letter from the King, of the 19th, i.e. yesterday, in which he tells me, "Pourvu qu'il y ait, pour commencer, des négociations, cela me donne une grande force."

I have written yesterday to him most fully a letter he may show Thiers also concerning the armaments. I think that my arguments will make some impression on Thiers. The King writes me word that by dint of great exertion he had brought Thiers to be more moderate. If it was possible to bring France and Mehemet Ali to agree to the greatest part of the Treaty, it will be worth while for everybody to consent. The way to bring France to join in some arrangement, and to take the engagement to compel Mehemet to accept it, would be the best practical way to come to a conclusion. It is probable, though I know nothing about it in any positive way, that the efforts of getting possession of Syria will fail, if the country itself does not take up arms on a large scale, which seems not to be believed.

To conclude then my somewhat hurried argumentation, the greatest thing is to negotiate. The negotiation cannot now have the effect of weakening the execution as that goes on, and it may have the advantage of covering the non-success if that should take place, which is at all events possible if not probable. May I beg you to read these few confused words to Lord Melbourne as a supplement of my letter to him. Darmes says that if Chartres had been with the King, he would not have fired, but that his reason for wishing to kill the King was his conviction that one could not hope for war till he was dead.

It is really melancholy to see the poor King taking this acharnement very much to heart, and upon my word, the other Powers of Europe owe it to themselves and to him to do everything to ease and strengthen his awful task.

What do you say to poor Christina's departure?52 I am sorry for it, and for the poor children. She is believed to be very rich.

Now I must conclude, but not without thanking you once more for your great and most laudable exertions, and wishing you every happiness, which you so much deserve. Ever, my most beloved Victoria, your devoted Uncle,

Leopold R.

Footnote 52: Queen Christina abdicated the Regency of Spain, and went to Paris. In the following May General Espartero, Duke of Vittoria, was appointed sole Regent.

DEATH OF LORD HOLLAND

Windsor Castle, 23rd October 1840.

My dearest Uncle,—Many thanks for your two kind letters of the 17th and 20th. I have very little time to-day, and it being besides not my regular day, I must beg you to excuse this letter being very short. I return you the King's letters with bien des remercîments. It is a horrid business. We have had accounts of successes on the Syrian coast. Guizot is here since Wednesday, and goes this morning. Albert (who desires me to thank you for your kind letter) has been talking to him, and so have I, and he promised in return for my expressions of sincere anxiety to see matters raccommodées, to do all in his power to do so. "Je ne vais que pour cela," he said.

We were much shocked yesterday at the sudden death of poor good, old Lord Holland.53 I send you Dr Holland's letter to Lord Melbourne about it. He is a great loss, and to Society an irreparable one. I'm sure you will be sorry for it.

Mamma comes back sooner than the 31st. She is in great distress at poor Polly's death. You will regret him. Ever your devoted Niece,

Victoria R.

Pray do try and get the King's Speech to be pacific, else Parliament must meet here in November, which would be dreadful for me.

Footnote 53: Chancellor of the Duchy of Lancaster, who, by reason of his social influence, great wealth, and high intellectual endowments, was one of the most efficient supporters of the Whig party.

Laeken, 26th October 1840.

... The Duke of Cambridge arrived, as you know, before yesterday evening, at Brussels. Your Uncle visited him yesterday, and at six he came to Laeken to dine with us. I found him looking well, and he was as usual very good-natured and kind. I need not tell you that conversation did not flag between us, and that I thought of you almost the whole time. In the course of the evening he took leave. He left Brussels this morning early, on his way to Calais, and I suppose you will hear of him before this letter reaches you. He took charge of all my love and hommages for you, dear Albert, and all the Royal Family. Before dinner the children were presented to him (that is Leopold and Philippe), but I am sorry to say that poor Lippchen was so much frightened with his appearance, loud voice, and black gloves, that he burst out crying, and that we were obliged to send him away. The Duke took his shyness very kindly; but I am still ashamed with his behaviour.

NEWS FROM SYRIA

Carlton Terrace, 8th November 1840.

Viscount Palmerston presents his humble duty to your Majesty, and in addition to the good news from Syria, which confirms the defeat and dispersion of the forces, both of Ibrahim and of Solyman Pasha, with the loss of 8,000 prisoners, 24 pieces of cannon, the whole of their camp, baggage, and stores, followed by the flight of those two Generals with a small escort, he has the satisfaction of informing your Majesty that the new French Ministers had a majority of 68, upon the vote for the election of the President of the Chamber.54

This majority, so far exceeding any previous calculation, seems to place the stability of the Government beyond a doubt, though it must, of course, be expected that upon other questions their majority will not be so overwhelming.

Footnote 54: M. Sauzet was elected in preference to M. Odillon Barrot. Thiers resigned the Premiership on 14th October; in the new Ministry Soult was President of the Council, Guizot Minister of Foreign Affairs, and Duchatel Minister of the Interior.

DISAFFECTION IN FRANCE

Windsor Castle, 11th November 1840.

Viscount Palmerston presents his humble duty to your Majesty, and with reference to your Majesty's memorandum of the 9th inst., he entreats your Majesty not to believe that there exists at present in France that danger of internal revolution and of external war which the French Government, to serve its own diplomatic purposes, endeavours to represent.

There is no doubt a large Party among the leading politicians in France, who have long contemplated the establishment of a virtually, if not actually, independent State in Egypt and Syria, under the direct protection and influence of France, and that Party feel great disappointment and resentment at finding their schemes in this respect baffled. But that Party will not revenge themselves on the Four Powers by making a revolution in France, and they are enlightened enough to see that France cannot revenge herself by making war against the Four Powers, who are much stronger than she is.

... But your Majesty may be assured that there is in France an immense mass of persons, possessed of property, and engaged in pursuits of industry, who are decidedly adverse to unnecessary war, and determined to oppose revolution. And although those persons have not hitherto come prominently forward, yet their voice would have made itself heard, when the question of peace or unprovoked war came practically to be discussed.

With regard to internal revolution, there is undoubtedly in France a large floating mass of Republicans and Anarchists, ready at any moment to make a disturbance if there was no strong power to resist them; but the persons who would lose by convulsion are infinitely more numerous, and the National Guard of Paris, consisting of nearly 60,000 men, are chiefly persons of this description, and are understood to be decidedly for internal order, and for external peace.

It is very natural that the French Government, after having failed to extort concessions upon the Turkish Question, by menaces of foreign war, should now endeavour to obtain those concessions, by appealing to fears of another kind, and should say that such concessions are necessary in order to prevent revolution in France; but Viscount Palmerston would submit to your Majesty his deep conviction that this appeal is not better founded than the other, and that a firm and resolute perseverance on the part of the Four Powers, in the measures which they have taken in hand, will effect a settlement of the affairs of Turkey, which will afford great additional security for the future peace of Europe, without producing in the meantime either war with France, or revolution in France.

France and the rest of Europe are entirely different now from what they were in 1792. The French nation is as much interested now to avoid further revolution, as it was interested then in ridding itself, by any means, of the enormous and intolerable abuses which then existed. France then imagined she had much to gain by foreign war; France now knows she has everything to lose by foreign war.

Europe then (at least the Continental States) had also a strong desire to get rid of innumerable abuses which pressed heavily upon the people of all countries. Those abuses have now in general been removed; the people in many parts of Germany have been admitted, more or less, to a share in the management of their own affairs. A German feeling and a spirit of nationality has sprung up among all the German people, and the Germans, instead of receiving the French as Liberators, as many of them did in 1792-1793, would now rise as one man to repel a hateful invasion. Upon all these grounds Viscount Palmerston deems it his duty to your Majesty to express his strong conviction that the appeals made to your Majesty's good feelings by the King of the French, upon the score of the danger of revolution in France, unless concessions are made to the French Government, have no foundation in truth, and are only exertions of skilful diplomacy.

Viscount Palmerston has to apologise to your Majesty for having inadvertently written a part of this memorandum upon a half-sheet of paper. And he would be glad if, without inconvenience to your Majesty, he could be enabled to read to the Cabinet to-morrow the accompanying despatches from Lord Granville.

THE STATE OF FRANCE

Windsor Castle, 11th November 1840.

The Queen has to acknowledge the receipt of Lord Palmerston's letter of this morning, which she has read with great attention. The Queen will just make a few observations upon various points in it, to which she would wish to draw Lord Palmerston's attention. The Queen does so with strict impartiality, having had ample opportunities of hearing both sides of this intricate and highly-important question.

First of all, it strikes the Queen that, even if M. Thiers did raise the cry, which was so loud, for war in France (but which the Queen cannot believe he did to the extent Lord Palmerston does), that such an excitement once raised in a country like France, where the people are more excitable than almost any other nation, it cannot be so easily controuled and stopped again, and the Queen thinks this will be seen in time.

Secondly, the Queen cannot either quite agree in Lord Palmerston's observation, that the French Government state the danger of internal revolution, if not supported, merely to extract further concessions for Mehemet Ali. The Queen does not pretend to say that this danger is not exaggerated, but depend upon it, a certain degree of danger does exist, and that the situation of the King of the French and the present French Government is not an easy one. The majority, too, cannot be depended upon, as many would vote against Odillon Barrot,56 who would not vote on other occasions with the Soult-Guizot Ministry.

Thirdly, the danger of war is also doubtless greatly exaggerated, as also the numbers of the French troops. But Lord Palmerston must recollect how very warlike the French are, and that if once roused, they will not listen to the calm reasoning of those who wish for peace, or think of the great risk they run of losing by war, but only of the glory and of revenging insult, as they call it.

Fourthly, the Queen sees the difficulty there exists at the present moment of making any specific offer to France, but she must at the same time repeat how highly and exceedingly important she considers it that some sort of conciliatory agreement should be come to with France, for she cannot believe that the appeals made to her by the King of the French are only exertions of skilful diplomacy. The Queen's earnest and only wish is peace, and a maintenance of friendly relations with her allies, consistent with the honour and dignity of her country. She does not think, however, that the last would be compromised by attempts to soften the irritation still existing in France, or by attempts to bring France back to her former position in the Oriental Question.

She earnestly hopes that Lord Palmerston will consider this, will reflect upon the importance of not driving France to extremities, and of conciliatory measures, without showing fear (for our successes on the coast of Syria show our power), or without yielding to threats. France has been humbled, and France is in the wrong, but, therefore, it is easier than if we had failed, to do something to bring matters right again. The Queen has thus frankly stated her own opinion, which she thought it right Lord Palmerston should know, and she is sure he will see it is only dictated by an earnest desire to see all as much united as possible on this important subject.

Footnote 55: A copy of this letter was sent at the same time to Lord Melbourne.
Footnote 56: The unsuccessful candidate for the Presidency of the Chamber.
21st November 1840.

My dear Lord,—I have just received Her Majesty's order to express to you her great desire to have from this day the Prince's name introduced into the Church Prayer. Her own words were: "that I should press it with Lord Melbourne as the wish she had most at heart at this moment." Ever yours most sincerely,

Stockmar.

KING LEOPOLD ON FRENCH AFFAIRS

Laeken, 26th November 1840.

... As to politics, I do not wish to say much to-day. Palmerston, rex and autocrat, is, for a Minister finding himself in such fortunate circumstances, far too irritable and violent. One does not understand the use of showing so much hatred and anger. What he says about the appeal to the personal feeling of the Queen, on the part of the King of the French, is childlike and malicious, for it has never existed.

The King was for many years the great friend of the Duke of Kent, after whose death he remained a friend of Victoria. His relations with the latter have, up to 1837, passed through very varied phases; she was for a long time an object of hatred in the family, who had not treated the Duke of Kent over-amicably, and a proof of this is the fact that the Regent, from the year 1819, forbade the Duke his house and presence—which was probably another nail in the Duke's coffin. Many of these things are quite unknown to Victoria, or forgotten by her. Still it is only fair not to forget the people who were her friends before 1837; after that date there was a violent outbreak of affection among people who in the year 1836 would still not go near Victoria. October 1836, when he sat next her at dinner, was the first time that Palmerston himself had ever seen Victoria except at a distance. As you have the best means of knowing, the King has not even dreamt of applying to Victoria.

As to danger, it was very great in September, on the occasion of the ouvrier riot—for a Paris mob fires at once, a thing which—Heaven be thanked!—English mobs rarely do. Towards the end of October, when Thiers withdrew, there was a possibility of a revolution, and it was only the fear of people of wealth that kept them together, and drew them towards Guizot.

A revolution, at once democratic and bellicose, could not but become most dangerous. That was on the cards, and only a fairly fortunate combination of circumstances saved matters. The King and my poor mother-in-law were terribly low, on both occasions, and I confess that I looked everyday with the greatest anxiety for the news. If the poor King had been murdered, or even if he were now to be murdered, what danger, what confusion would follow! All these things were met by Palmerston with the excessively nonchalante declaration, it was not so, and it is not so! Those are absolutely baseless assertions, and totally valueless. At least I could estimate the danger as well as he and Bulwer—and, indeed, it was an anxious crisis. I should think the Revolution of 1790 et ce qui s'en est suivi had done a brisk enough business in Europe, and to risk a new one of the same kind would really be somewhat scandalous.

What, however, may be the future fruit of the seed of Palmerston's sowing, we do not in the least know as yet; it may, however, prove sufficiently full of misfortune for the future of innocent people. The Eastern affairs will be put on an intelligible footing only when, after these differences with Mehemet Ali, something is done for the poor Porte, which is now so much out of repair. Otherwise there remains a little place which is called Sebastopol, and from which, as the wind is almost constantly favourable, one can get very quickly to Constantinople—and Constantinople is always the one place which exercises the greatest influence, and all the more because the ducats come from that quarter, with results which the marked economy of England is hardly likely to effect....

Victoria has borne herself bravely and properly in the matter, and deserves to be greatly praised....

BIRTH OF THE PRINCESS ROYAL

Laeken, 30th November 1840.

My most beloved Victoria,—I have been longing to write to you ever since we got the joyful tidings,57 but I would not do so before the nine days were at an end. Now that they are over, I hope as you are, thank God, so well, I may venture a few lines to express a part of my feelings, and to wish you joy on the happy birth of your dear little girl. I need not tell you the deep, deep share I took in this most happy event, and all I felt for you, for dear Albert, when I heard of it, and since we last met. You know my affection for you, and I will not trouble you with the repetition of what you know. All I will say is that I thanked God with all my heart, and as I have scarcely thanked Him for any other favour....

Footnote 57: The Princess Royal, afterwards the Empress Frederick of Germany, was born 21st November 1840.

SETTLEMENT OF EASTERN QUESTION

15th December 1840.

My dearest Uncle,—Many thanks for your kind little letter of the 10th from Ardenne. I am very prosperous, walking about the house like myself again, and we go to Windsor on the 22nd or 23rd, which will quite set me up. I am very prudent and careful, you may rely upon it. Your little grand-niece is most flourishing; she gains daily in health, strength and, I may add, beauty; I think she will be very like her dearest father; she grows amazingly; I shall be proud to present her to you.

The dénouement of the Oriental affair is most fortunate, is it not?58

I see Stockmar often, who is very kind about me and the Princess Royal....

Albert sends his affectionate love, and pray believe me always, your devoted Niece,

Victoria R.

Footnote 58: On the 3rd of November St Jean d'Acre was captured by the allied fleet, Admiral Sir Robert Stopford commanding the British contingent; the battle is said to have been the first to test the advantages of steam. Admiral Napier proceeded to Alexandria, and threatened bombardment, unless the Pasha came to terms. On 25th November a Convention was signed, by which Mehemet Ali resigned his claims to Syria, and bound himself to restore the Ottoman Fleet, while the Powers undertook to procure for him undisturbed possession of the Pashalik of Egypt.

Laeken, 26th December 1840.

... I can well understand that you feel quite astonished at finding yourself within a year of your marriage a very respectable mother of a nice little girl, but let us thank Heaven that it is so. Any illness to which, unfortunately, we poor human creatures are very subject, would almost have kept you longer in bed, and make you longer weak and uncomfortable, than an event which in your position as Sovereign is of a very great importance.

Because there is no doubt that a Sovereign without heirs direct, or brothers and sisters, which by their attachment may stand in lieu of them, is much to be pitied, viz., Queen Anne's later years. Moreover, children of our own, besides the affection which one feels for them, have also for their parents sentiments which one rarely obtains from strangers. I flatter myself therefore that you will be a delighted and delightful Maman au milieu d'une belle et nombreuse famille....

INTRODUCTORY NOTE: TO CHAPTER X

At the beginning of the year the Ministry were confronted with monetary difficulties and bad trade; their special weakness in finance, contrasted with Sir Robert Peel's great ability, in addition to their many reverses, indicated that a change was at hand; and confidential communications were, with Lord Melbourne's full approval, opened up by the Prince with Sir Robert Peel, to avert the recurrence of a Bedchamber dispute. The Ministry were defeated on their Budget, but did not resign. A vote of want of confidence was then carried against them by a majority of one, and Parliament was dissolved; the Ministers appealing to the country on the cry of a fixed duty on corn. The Conservative and Protectionist victory was a decisive one, the most significant successes being in the city of London, Northumberland, and the West Riding. Somewhat improving their position in Scotland and Ireland, and just holding their own in the English boroughs, the Whigs were absolutely overwhelmed in the counties, and in the result three hundred and sixty-eight Conservatives and only two hundred and ninety-two Liberals were returned. The modern practice of resigning before meeting Parliament had not then been introduced, and the Ministry was defeated in both Houses on Amendments to the Address, the Duke of Wellington taking the opportunity of eulogising Lord Melbourne's great services to the Queen. A powerful Protectionist Ministry was formed by Sir Robert Peel, including the Duke of Wellington, Lord Aberdeen, Sir James Graham, and Lord Lyndhurst.

Great national rejoicings took place when, on the 9th of November, a male heir to the throne, now His Majesty King Edward VII., was born.

In France the bitter feeling against England, arising out of the Syrian expedition, still continued, but Thiers' supersession by the more pacific Guizot, and the satisfaction with which both the latter and his Sovereign regarded the displacement of Palmerston by Aberdeen, began to lead to a better entente. The scheme of fortifying Paris continued, however, to be debated, while the Orleanist family were still the subjects of futile attentats.

Spain was disturbed, the question of the guardianship of the young Queen giving rise to dissension: insurrections in the interests of the Queen-mother took place at Pampeluna and Vittoria, and her pension was suspended by Espartero, the Regent.

In the east, Mehemet Ali surrendered the whole of the Turkish fleet, and he was subsequently guaranteed the hereditary Pashalik of Egypt by the four European Powers who had intervened in the affairs of the Levant.

In Afghanistan, an insurrection broke out, and Sir Alexander Burnes was murdered; our envoy at Cabul, Sir William Macnaghten, in an unfortunate moment entered into negotiations with Akbar Khan, a son of Dost Mahommed, who treacherously assassinated him. Somewhat humiliating terms were arranged, and the English force of 4,000 soldiers, with 12,000 camp-followers, proceeded to withdraw from Cabul, harassed by the enemy; after endless casualties, General Elphinstone, who was in command, with the women and children, became captives, and one man alone, of the 16,000—Dr Brydon—reached Jellalabad to tell the tale.

In China, operations were continued, Sir Henry Pottinger superseding Captain Elliot, and

Canton soon lying at the mercy of the British arms; the new Superintendent co-operated with Sir Hugh Gough and Admiral Sir William Parker, in the capture of Amoy, Chusan, Chintu, and Ningpo.

In America, the union of the two Canadas was carried into effect, but a sharp dispute with the United States arose out of the Upper Canada disturbances of 1837. Some Canadian loyalists had then resented the interference of a few individual Americans in favour of the rebels, and an American named Durfee had been killed. One M'Leod, a British subject, was now arrested in the State of New York, on a charge of having been concerned in the affray. He was acquitted, reprisals were made by Canadians, and international feeling was for a time highly acute.

Much interest naturally attaches to Lord Melbourne's continued correspondence with the Queen, after the change of Government. Baron Stockmar's remonstrance on the subject shows that he misunderstood the character of the correspondence, and over-estimated its momentousness.

These letters dealt chiefly with social and personal matters, and although full of interest from the light which they throw on Lord Melbourne's relations with the Queen, they show him to have behaved with scrupulous honour and delicacy, and to have tried to augment, rather than undermine, Peel's growing influence with the Queen and Prince. There are comparatively few of Peel's letters in the collection. He wrote rarely at first, and only on strictly official matters. But before long his great natural reserve was broken through, and his intercourse with the Prince, to whom his character was particularly sympathetic, became very close and intimate.

Of all the English Ministers with whom the Prince was brought in contact, it is known that he preferred the stately and upright Commoner, who certainly, of all English Ministers, estimated and appreciated the Prince's character most truly and clearly.

CHAPTER X

5th January 1841.

My dearest Uncle,—I have to thank you for two very kind letters, of the 26th December and 1st January, and for all your very kind and good wishes. I am sorry to hear you have all been plagued with colds; we have as yet escaped them, and I trust will continue to do so. I think, dearest Uncle, you cannot really wish me to be the "Mamma d'une nombreuse famille," for I think you will see with me the great inconvenience a large family would be to us all, and particularly to the country, independent of the hardship and inconvenience to myself; men never think, at least seldom think, what a hard task it is for us women to go through this very often. God's will be done, and if He decrees that we are to have a great number of children, why we must try to bring them up as useful and exemplary members of society. Our young lady flourishes exceedingly, and I hope the Van de Weyers (who have been here for three days), who have seen her twice, will give you a favourable description of her. I think you would be amused to see Albert dancing her in his arms; he makes a capital nurse (which I do not, and she is much too heavy for me to carry), and she already seems so happy to go to him.

The christening will be at Buckingham Palace on the 10th of February, our dear marriage-day. Affairs are certainly still precarious, but I feel confident all will come right....

Ever your devoted Niece,

Victoria R.

Laeken, 8th January 1841.

... I trust also that affairs will come right; what is to be feared is the chapter of accidents. Your name bears glorious fruits in all climes; this globe will soon be too small for you, and something must be done to get at the other planets....

THE QUEEN'S EDUCATION

Lord Melbourne said, "The Prince is bored with the sameness of his chess every evening. He would like to bring literary and scientific people about the Court, vary the society, and infuse a more useful tendency into it. The Queen however has no fancy to encourage such people. This arises from a feeling on her part that her education has not fitted her to take part in such conversation; she would not like conversation to be going on in which she could not take her fair share, and she is far too open and candid in her nature to pretend to one atom more knowledge than she really possesses on such subjects; and yet, as the world goes, she would, as any girl, have been considered accomplished, for she speaks German well and writes it; understands Italian, speaks French fluently, and writes it with great elegance. In addition to this old Davys instilled some Latin into her during his tutorship. The rest of her education she owes to her own natural shrewdness and quickness, and this perhaps has not been the proper education for one who was to wear the Crown of England.

"The Queen is very proud of the Prince's utter indifference to the attractions of all ladies. I told Her Majesty that these were early days to boast, which made her rather indignant. I think she is a little jealous of his talking much even to men."

THE QUEEN'S SPEECH

19th January 1841.

Lord Melbourne presents his humble duty to your Majesty. He has just received your Majesty's letter. Lord Melbourne is very sorry not to come down to Windsor, but he really thinks that his absence from London at this moment might be prejudicial.

Lord Melbourne will do his utmost to have the Speech worded in the most calm manner, and so as in no respect to offend or irritate any feelings. Some mention of the good conduct and gallantry of the Navy there must be—to omit it would be injurious and disheartening—but as to any expressions complimentary to France or expressive of regret at our separation from it, it will be hardly possible to introduce anything of that nature.1 It is quite unusual in our Speeches from the Throne to express either approbation or disapprobation of the conduct of foreign nations and foreign Governments. It is surprising how very seldom it has been done, and the wisdom and prudence of abstaining from it is very manifest. It would be giving an opinion upon that which does not belong to us. Anything which would have the effect of producing satisfaction in France must be of an apologetic character, which there is no ground for, and for which neither the Government nor the country is prepared.

The best course will be a total reserve upon this head, certainly abstaining from anything that can be in the slightest degree offensive.

Footnote 1: France was not mentioned, though the Convention with the other Powers, and the naval operations in conjunction with Austria, were referred to.

22nd January 1841.

Lord Melbourne presents his humble duty to your Majesty.

Lord Melbourne will be most happy to wait upon your Majesty on Saturday and Sunday.

Lord Melbourne is very sorry that your Majesty is compelled to come to London contrary to your inclinations; but Lord Melbourne much rejoices that your Majesty expresses that reluctance, as there is no surer sign of complete happiness and contentment in the married life than a desire to remain quietly in the country, and there is nothing on the earth Lord Melbourne desires more anxiously than the assurance of your Majesty's happiness.

THE QUEEN'S INFANCY

Brussels, 22nd January 1841.

My dearest Victoria,—I thank you very sincerely for your kind letter of the 19th, which I hasten to answer. I should not have bored you by my presence, but the act of the christening is, in my eyes, a sort of closing of the first cyclus of your dear life. I was shooting at the late Lord Craven's in Berkshire, when I received the messenger who brought me the horrifying news of your poor father's deadly illness. I hastened in bitter cold weather to Sidmouth, about two days before his death. His affairs were so much deranged that your Mother would have had no means even of leaving Sidmouth if I had not taken all this under my care and management. That dreary journey, undertaken, I think, on the 26th of January, in bitter cold and damp weather, I shall not easily forget. I looked very sharp after the poor little baby, then about eight months old. Arrived in London we were very unkindly treated by George IV., whose great wish was to get you and your Mamma out of the country, and I must say without my assistance you could not have remained.... I state these facts, because it is useful to remember through what difficulties and hardships one had to struggle. You will also remember that though there existed the possibility of your eventually succeeding to the Crown, that possibility was very doubtful, the then Duchess of Clarence having been confined after your Mother, and there being every reason to think that, though poor little Princess Elizabeth did not live more than some months, other children might appear.2

It was a long time from 1820 to 1837! We got over it, however, and, as far as you are concerned, God be praised! safely and happily. You are married, with every prospect of many happy years to come, and your happiness is crowned, and consolidated, as it were, by the birth of the dear little lady. Having from motives of discretion, perhaps carried even too far, not assisted at your coming to the throne, nor at your Coronation, nor afterwards at your marriage, I wished to assist at the christening of the little Princess, an event which is of great importance....

Footnote 2: Two children were born to the Duke and Duchess of Clarence—Charlotte Augusta Louisa, born and died 29th March 1819, and Elizabeth Georgina Adelaide, born 10th December 1820, and died 4th March 1821.

Carlton Terrace, 1st February 1841.

Viscount Palmerston presents his humble duty to your Majesty, and in submitting this letter from Earl Granville, which coupled with the despatches from Sir Robert Stopford virtually show that the Turkish Question is brought to a close, begs most humbly to congratulate your Majesty upon this rapid and peaceful settlement of a matter which at different periods has assumed appearances so threatening to the peace of Europe.3

Footnote 3: See ante, pp. , .

2nd February 1841.

Lord Melbourne presents his humble duty to your Majesty. Lord Melbourne will be happy to wait upon your Majesty on Thursday, Saturday and Sunday, but he finds that there is to be a Cabinet dinner to-morrow.

Lord Melbourne will speak to Lord Palmerston about Lord John Russell.

Lord Melbourne does not see the name of the Archbishop of Canterbury as a subscriber to this "Parker" Society, and if your Majesty will give him leave, he will ask him about it before he gives your Majesty an answer. It is in some degree a party measure, and levelled against these new Oxford doctrines. The proposal is to republish the works of the older divines up to the time of the death of Queen Elizabeth. Up to that period the doctrines of the Church of England were decidedly Calvinistic. During the reign of James II.,4 and particularly after the Synod of Dort (1618-1619), the English clergy very generally adopted Arminian opinions.

It is proposed to republish the works of the divines who wrote during the first period, and to stop short when they come to the second. There is meaning in this. But, after all, the object is not a bad one, and it may not be worth while to consider it so closely.

Footnote 4: Lord Melbourne must have meant James I.

ILLNESS OF DUKE OF WELLINGTON

5th February 1841 (6 o'clock).

Lord Melbourne presents his humble duty to your Majesty, and is very sorry to have to acquaint your Majesty that the Duke of Wellington was taken ill in the House of Lords this evening with a seizure, probably paralytic, and of the same nature with those which he has had before. Lord Brougham, who was standing opposite to the Duke and addressing the House, observed the Duke's face to be drawn and distorted, and soon afterwards the Duke rose from his seat and walked staggeringly towards the door. He walked down the gallery, supported on each side, but never spoke. A medical man was procured to attend him; he was placed in his carriage and driven home....

THE UNITED STATES

6th March 1841.

Lord John Russell presents his humble duty to your Majesty, and has the honour to state that the remainder of the Navy Estimates, and nearly the whole of the Army Estimates, were voted last night without any serious opposition. Indeed the chief fault found with the Army Estimates was that they are not large enough.

Sir Robert Peel made a remarkable speech. Adverting to the present state of our affairs with the United States,5 he said that much as he disliked war, yet if the honour or interests of the country required it, he should sink all internal differences, and give his best support to the Government of his country.

This declaration was received with loud cheers. It must be considered as very creditable to Sir Robert Peel.

Footnote 5: See Introductory Note, ante, p.

CHINA

Foreign Office, 10th April 1841.

Viscount Palmerston presents his humble duty to your Majesty, and has the honour to submit the accompanying letters, which he received yesterday, about the operations in China, and which have just been returned to him by Viscount Melbourne, whose letter he also transmits.6

Viscount Palmerston has felt greatly mortified and disappointed at this result of the expedition to China, and he much fears that the sequel of the negotiation, which was to follow the conclusion of these preliminary conditions, will not tend to render the arrangement less objectionable. Captain Elliot seems to have wholly disregarded the instructions which had been sent to him, and even when, by the entire success of the operations of the Fleet, he was in a condition to dictate his own terms, he seems to have agreed to very inadequate conditions.7 The amount of compensation for the opium surrendered falls short of the value of that opium, and nothing has been obtained for the expenses of the expedition, nor for the debts of the bankrupt Hong8 merchants. The securities which the plenipotentiaries were expressly ordered to obtain for British residents in China have been abandoned; and the Island of Chusan which they were specifically informed was to be retained till the whole of the pecuniary compensation should have been paid, has been hastily and discreditably evacuated. Even the cession of Hong Kong has been coupled with a condition about the payment of duties, which would render that island not a possession of the British Crown, but, like Macao, a settlement held by sufferance in the territory of the Crown of China.

Viscount Palmerston deems it his duty in laying these papers before your Majesty, to state some few of the objections which he feels to the arrangement, but the Cabinet will have to consider, as soon as they meet after the Recess, what advice they may wish humbly to tender to your Majesty upon these important matters. There is no doubt, however, that much has been accomplished, but it is very mortifying to find that other things which the plenipotentiaries were ordered to obtain, and which the force placed at their command was amply sufficient to enable them to accomplish, have not been attained.

Viscount Palmerston has sent a small map of the Canton River, which your Majesty may like to keep for future reference.

Footnote 6: Captain Elliot, after capturing the Chinese position at the mouth of Canton River, concluded a preliminary treaty with the Chinese Government, which did not satisfy the Chinese, and which was strongly disapproved of by the English Ministry, as containing no mention of the opium traffic, which had been the cause of all the difficulties; Elliot was accordingly recalled, and succeeded by Sir Henry Pottinger.

Footnote 7: They were the cession of Hong-Kong, and payment of an indemnity of 6,000,000 dollars to Great Britain, with provision for commercial facilities and collection of customs.

Footnote 8: The native Canton merchants,—Hong here probably meaning a "row of houses," a "street." Hong Kong (Hiang Kiang) means the "fragrant lagoon."

13th April 1841.

My dearest Uncle,—I thank you much for your kind letter of the 9th, received yesterday. I have just heard from Stockmar (who, I hope, reported favourably of us all) that your Ministry is at last settled, of which I wish you joy. I think, dear Uncle, that you would find the East not only as "absurd" as the West, but very barbarous, cruel, and dangerous into the bargain.

The Chinese business vexes us much, and Palmerston is deeply mortified at it. All we wanted might have been got, if it had not been for the unaccountably strange conduct of Charles Elliot (not Admiral Elliot,9 for he was obliged to come away from ill-health), who completely disobeyed his instructions and tried to get the lowest terms he could.... The attack and storming of the Chorempee Forts on the 7th of January was very gallantly done by the Marines, and immense destruction of the Chinese took place.10 The accounts of the cruelty of the Chinese to one another are horrible. Albert is so much amused at my having got the Island of Hong Kong, and we think Victoria ought to be called Princess of Hong Kong in addition to Princess Royal.

She drives out every day in a close carriage with the window open, since she has been here, which does her worlds of good, and she is to have a walk to-day.

Stockmar writes me word that Charlotte11 is quite beautiful. I am very jealous.

I think Vecto quite right not to travel without Nemours; for it would look just as if she was unhappy, and ran to her parents for help. I am sure if Albert ever should be away (which, however, will and shall never happen, for I would go with him even if he was to go to the North Pole), I should never think of travelling; but I can't make mamma understand this. Now farewell.

Ever your devoted Niece,

Victoria R.

Footnote 9: They were both cousins of Lord Minto, the First Lord of the Admiralty.

Footnote 10: Commodore Bremer very speedily reduced some of the forts, but his further operations were stopped.

Footnote 11: Daughter of King Leopold, who married in 1857 the Archduke Ferdinand of Austria (afterwards Emperor Maximilian of Mexico).

LORD CARDIGAN

24th April 1841.

Lord Melbourne presents his humble duty to your Majesty. Mr Labouchere[12] has desired that the five-pound piece which is about to be issued from the Mint should be submitted for your Majesty's inspection and approbation.

ARMY DISCIPLINE

We have had under our consideration at the Cabinet the unfortunate subject of the conduct of Lord Cardigan.[13] The public feeling upon it is very strong, and it is almost certain that a Motion will be made in the House of Commons for an Address praying your Majesty to remove him from the command of his regiment. Such a Motion, if made, there is very little chance of resisting with success, and nothing is more to be apprehended and deprecated than such an interference of the House of Commons with the interior discipline and government of the Army. It was also felt that the general order issued by the Horse Guards was not sufficient to meet the case, and in these circumstances it was thought proper that Lord Melbourne should see Lord Hill, and should express to him the opinion of the Cabinet, that it was necessary that he should advise your Majesty to take such measures as should have the effect of removing Lord Cardigan from the command of the 11th Hussars. The repeated acts of imprudence of which Lord Cardigan has been guilty, and the repeated censures which he has drawn down upon himself, form a ground amply sufficient for such a proceeding, and indeed seem imperiously to demand it.[14]

Lord Melbourne has seen Lord Hill and made to him this communication, and has left it for his consideration. Lord Hill is deeply chagrined and annoyed, but will consider the matter and confer again with Lord Melbourne upon it to-morrow.

Footnote 12: President of the Board of Trade, afterwards created Lord Taunton.

Footnote 13: "Within the space of a single twelvemonth, one of his [Lord Cardigan's] captains was cashiered for writing him a challenge; he sent a coarse and insulting verbal message to another, and then punished him with prolonged arrest, because he respectfully refused to shake hands with the officer who had been employed to convey the affront; he fought a duel with a lieutenant who had left the corps, and shot him through the body; and he flogged a soldier on Sunday, between the Services, on the very spot where, half an hour before, the man's comrades had been mustered for public worship."—Sir G. Trevelyan, Life and Letters of Lord Macaulay, chap. viii.

Footnote 14: In February he had been acquitted on technical grounds by the House of Lords of shooting a Captain Harvey Garnett Phipps Tuckett. He had accused Tuckett of being the author of letters which had appeared in the papers reflecting on his character; a duel on Wimbledon Common followed, and Tuckett was wounded. The evidence, consisting in part of a visiting card, showed that a Captain Harvey Tuckett had been wounded, which was held to be insufficient evidence of identity.

25th April 1841.

Lord Melbourne presents his humble duty to your Majesty. He is most anxious upon all subjects to be put in possession of Your Majesty's full and entire opinions. It is true that this question may materially affect the discipline of the Army, by subjecting the interior management of regiments to be brought continually under the inspection and control of the House of Commons upon complaints of officers against their superiors, or even of private men against the officers.

The danger of the whole of Lord Cardigan's proceedings has been lest a precedent of this nature should arise out of them. The question is whether it is not more prudent to prevent a question being brought forward in the House of Commons, than to wait for it with the certainty of being obliged to yield to it or of being overpowered by it. But of course this cannot be done unless it is consistent with justice and with the usage and prestige of the Service.

Lord Melbourne has desired the Cabinet Ministers to assemble here to-day at four o'clock, in order to consider the subject. Lord Melbourne has seen Lord Hill again this morning, and Lord Hill has seen and consulted the Duke of Wellington, who has stated his opinion very fully.

The opinion of the Duke is that the Punishment on Sunday was a great impropriety and indiscretion upon the part of Lord Cardigan, but not a Military offence, nor a breach of the Mutiny Act or of the Articles of War; that it called for the censure of the Commander-in-Chief, which censure was pronounced by the General Order upon which the Duke was consulted before it was issued, and that according to the usage of the Service no further step can be taken by the Military Authorities. This opinion Lord Melbourne will submit to-day to the Cabinet Ministers.

Lord Melbourne perceives that he has unintentionally written upon two sheets of paper, which he hopes will cause your Majesty no inconvenience.

THE NOTTINGHAM ELECTION

South Street, 28th April 1841.

Lord Melbourne presents his humble duty to your Majesty. He has himself seen the result of the election at Nottingham15 without the least surprise, from his knowledge of the place and his observation of the circumstances of the contest. What John Russell reported to your Majesty was the opinion of those who act for us in that place, but as soon as Lord Melbourne saw that there was a disposition upon the part of the violent party, Radicals, Chartists, and what not, to support the Tory candidate, he knew that the contest was formidable and dubious. The Tory party is very strong, naturally, at Nottingham, and if it received any accession of strength, was almost certain to prevail. This combination, or rather this accession of one party to the Tories, which has taken place at Nottingham, is very likely, and in Lord Melbourne's opinion almost certain, to take place in many other parts of the country in the case of a general election, and forms very serious matter for consideration as to the prudence of taking such a step as a dissolution of the Parliament.

Lord Melbourne will wait upon your Majesty after the Levée. It signifies not how late, as there is no House of Lords.

Footnote 15: Where Mr Walter, a Tory, was elected with a majority of 238.

THE BUDGET

Wilton Crescent, 1st May 1841.

Lord John Russell presents his humble duty to your Majesty, and has the honour to report that Mr Baring yesterday brought forward the Budget in a remarkably clear and forcible speech.

The changes in the duties on Sugar and Timber,16 and the announcement made by Lord John Russell of a proposal for a fixed duty on Corn, seemed to surprise and irritate the Opposition.

Sir Robert Peel refused to give any opinion on these propositions, and satisfied himself with attacking the Government on the state of the finances.

The supporters of the Government were greatly pleased with Mr Baring's plan, and loud in their cheers.

It is the general opinion that Lord Stanley will not proceed with his Bill,17 and there seems little doubt of this fact.

But the two parties are now evenly balanced, and the absence or defection of some two or three of the Ministerial party may at any time leave the Government in a minority.

Footnote 16: The proposals were to increase the duty on colonial timber from 10s. to 20s. a load, reducing it on foreign timber from 55s. to 50s., to leave the duty on colonial sugar unloaded at 24s. a cwt., reducing that on foreign sugar from 63s. to 36s. a cwt.

Footnote 17: On Irish Registration.

3rd May 1841.

Lord Melbourne presents his humble duty to your Majesty. We decided at the Cabinet on Friday that we could not sanction the agreement which Captain Elliot has probably by this time concluded with the Government of China, but that it would be necessary to demand a larger amount of indemnity for the past injury, and also a more complete security for our trade in future. For this purpose it was determined to send out instructions, in case the armament should not have left the Chinese coasts and have been dispersed, to reoccupy the Island of Chusan,18 a measure which appears to have had a great effect upon the minds of the Chinese Government. It was also determined to recall Captain Elliot, and to send out as soon as possible another officer with full instructions from hence as to the views and intentions of your Majesty's Government. Sir Henry Pottinger,19 an officer in the East India Company's Service, much distinguished in the recent operations in Afghanistan, is designated with your Majesty's approbation for this service, which he has signified his willingness to undertake. It was also thought that it would be proper to entrust Lord Auckland20 with general discretionary powers as to the further conduct of the expedition. These determinations Lord Melbourne hopes that your Majesty will approve.

Lord John Russell informed Lord Melbourne yesterday that he knew that it was not the intention of the Opposition to press Lord Stanley's Bill; but it is not to be expected in the present position of affairs that they will not determine upon taking some decisive and united measure in advance.

In the present state of public measures and of public feeling, when debate may arise at any moment, it would not be fitting for Lord Melbourne to absent himself on any sitting day from the House of Lords. But unless there should be anything so urgent as to prevent him, he will come down after the House on Tuesday evening and stay until Thursday morning.

Fanny is highly delighted and immeasurably grateful for your Majesty's offer of the Lodge in Richmond Park, and most desirous to avail herself of your Majesty's kindness, and so is Jocelyn. Lord Melbourne has little doubt that they will thankfully accept it.21

Footnote 18: The Island of Chusan, off the coast of China, had been occupied in July 1840 as a base of operations, but evacuated by Elliot in 1841. It was retaken in September 1841, after Elliot's recall, by Sir Henry Pottinger.

Footnote 19: He had served in the Mahratta War, and been political agent in Scinde.

Footnote 20: Governor-General of India.

Footnote 21: Lady Fanny Cowper, Lord Melbourne's niece, was married to Lord Jocelyn on 27th April.

CHRISTENING OF COMTE DE PARIS

Paris, 3rd May 1841.

My beloved Victoria,—As you know surely already, the day of yesterday went off very well. The christening22 was very splendid, the weather beautiful, and everything extremely well managed.... The arrival at Notre-Dame, and the coup d'œil of the old church, all hung interiorly with crimson velvet draperies and trophies of flags, was very splendid. There was in the church three rows de tribunes all full of well-dressed people. Les grands corps de l'État étaient rangés de chaque côté et dans le chœur; l'Autel était placé au centre de l'église. Les cardinaux et tout le clergé étaient alentour. When my father arrived, the Archbishop of Paris received him at the door of the church, and we all walked in state. My father ouvrait la marche with the Queen. Prie-dieu and chairs were disposed for us en demi-cercle before the altar, or rather before the baptismal font, which was placed in front of it, in the very middle of the Church. My father and mother stood in the centre of the row near each other. Your uncle, Chartres, and all the Princes followed on the side of my father, and the princesses on the side of my mother. Paris remained with Hélène till the moment of the christening. When the ceremony began he advanced near the font with my father and mother (sponsors), and was taken up in the arms of his nurse. After the christening a Mass and Te Deum were read, and when we came back to the Tuileries the corps municipal brought the sword which the City of Paris has given to the Comte de Paris....

Footnote 22: Of the Comte de Paris, at this time nearly three years old, son of the Duc d'Orléans.

THE SUGAR DUTIES

Wilton Crescent, 4th May 1841.

Lord John Russell presents his humble duty to your Majesty, and has the honour to report that Lord Stanley yesterday postponed his Bill for a fortnight, which at this period of the year is equivalent to its abandonment.

On the other hand, Lord Sandon gave a notice for Friday for a Resolution on Sugar Duties.

If, as is probable, this Motion is made as a party movement, it is probable that, with the addition of those on the Ministerial side who have an interest in the West Indies, the Motion will be successful.

The whole scheme of finance for the year will thus be overturned.

The Tory party seem to expect a dissolution of Parliament, but your Majesty's advisers will hardly be able to recommend to your Majesty such a step.

The cry against the Poor Law is sure to be taken up by the worst politicians of the Tory party, and, as at Nottingham, may be successful against that most useful law.

The friends of Government who represent counties will be taunted with the proposal to alter the Corn Law.

Bribery is sure to be resorted to beyond anything yet seen.

A defeat of the Ministry on a dissolution would be final and irreparable.

On the other hand, their successors in the Government would have to provide for the excess in the expenditure pledged against the best measures that could be resorted to for the purpose. It would be a difficulty of their own seeking, and their want of candour and justice to their opponents would be the cause of their own embarrassments.

The moment is a very important one, and the consequences of the vote of Friday, or probably Monday, cannot fail to be serious.

A MINISTERIAL CRISIS

Lord Melbourne came down from town after the House of Lords. I went with him to his room for an hour after the Queen had retired. He said the main struggle would take place on the Sugar Duties on Friday. His impression was that the Government would be beat, and he must then decide whether to go out or dissolve. He leaned to the former. I said, "I trusted he would not dissolve unless he thought there was some prospect of increasing his strength, and begged him to remember what was done would not be considered the act of the Government but that of himself and the Queen, and that he individually would be held as the responsible person."

He said he had not written to the Queen to prepare H.M. for coming events and the course that it would be incumbent upon her to take, for he felt it extremely difficult and delicate, especially as to the use she should make of the Prince, and of her mode of communication when she required it with Lord Melbourne. He thought she ought never to ask his advice direct, but if she required his opinion there would be no objection to her obtaining it through the Prince.

He said H.M. had relied so implicitly upon him upon all affairs, that he felt that she required in this emergency advice upon almost every subject. That he would tell H.M. that she must carefully abstain from playing the same part she did, again, on Sir R. Peel's attempt to form a Ministry, for that nothing but the forbearance of the Tories had enabled himself and his colleagues to support H.M. at that time. He feared Peel's doggedness and pertinacity might make him insist, as a point of honour, on having all discretion granted to him in regard to the removal of Ladies. I told him of the Prince's suggestion that before the Queen saw Sir R. Peel some negotiation might be entered into with Sir Robert, so that the subject might be avoided by mutual consent, the terms of which might be that Sir Robert should give up his demand to extort the principle. The Queen, on the other hand, should require the resignation of those Ladies objected to by Sir Robert. Lord Melbourne said, however, that the Prince must not have personal communication with Sir Robert on this subject, but he thought that I might through the medium of a common friend.

LORD MELBOURNE'S ADVICE

Saw Lord Melbourne after his interview this morning with the Queen. He says Her Majesty was perfectly calm and reasonable, and seemed quite prepared for the resignation of the Government. He said she was prepared to give way upon the Ladies if required, but much wished that that point might be previously settled by negotiation with Sir R. Peel, to avoid any discussion or difference. Lord Melbourne thinks I might do this. He would also like Peel to be cautioned not to press Her Majesty to decide hastily, but to give Her Majesty time, and that he should feel that if he acted fairly he would be met in the same spirit by the Queen.

With regard to future communication with Lord Melbourne, the Queen said she did not mean that a change should exclude her from Lord Melbourne's society, and when Lord Melbourne said that in society Her Majesty could not procure Lord Melbourne's opinion upon any subject, and suggested that that should be obtained through the Prince, Her Majesty said that that could pass in writing under cover to me, but that she must communicate direct.

The Queen, he says, leans to sending for the Duke of Wellington. Lord Melbourne advised that Her Majesty should make up her mind at once to send for Sir Robert. He told me that it would not be without precedent to send for both at once; this it appears to me would obviate every objection. The Queen, he thinks, has a perfect right to exercise her judgment upon the selection of all persons recommended to Her Majesty for Household appointments, both as to liking, but chiefly as to their character and as to the character of the husband or wife of the person selected. He would advise the Queen to adopt the course which King William did with Lord Melbourne in 1835, viz. desiring Lord Melbourne, before His Majesty approved of any appointments, to send a list of those proposed even to the members of every Board, and the King having them all before him expressed his objections to certain persons, which Lord Melbourne yielded to.

Told Lord Melbourne that the Prince wished him to impress upon the Queen's mind not to act upon the approaching crisis without the Prince, because she would not be able to go through difficulties by herself, and the Prince would not be able to help her when he was ignorant of the considerations which had influenced her actions. He would wish Lord Melbourne when with the Queen to call in the Prince, in order that they might both be set right upon Lord Melbourne's opinions, that he might express in the presence of each other his views, in order that he should not convey different impressions by speaking to them separately, so that they might act in concert.

The Prince says the Queen always sees what is right at a glance, but if her feelings run contrary she avoids the Prince's arguments, which she feels sure agree with her own, and seeks arguments to support her wishes against her convictions from other people.

DISSOLUTION OR RESIGNATION

South Street, 7th May 1841.

Lord Melbourne presents his humble duty to your Majesty, and laments much the prospect that lies before us, more especially as it is so repugnant to your Majesty's feelings. Your Majesty has often observed that these events must come in the course of affairs at some moment or another, but Lord Melbourne knows not whether it is much consolation to reflect that what is very disagreeable is also natural and unavoidable. Lord Melbourne feels certain that your Majesty will consider the situation calmly and impartially, will do that which shall appear the best for your own interests and those of the country, which are identical.

Everything shall be done that can be; the questions which may arise shall be considered well, and upon as full information as can be obtained. But Lord Melbourne has little to add to what he wrote to your Majesty yesterday. So many interests are affected by this Sugar question, the West Indian, the East Indian, the opponents of Slavery and others, that no small number of our supporters will be induced either to stay away or to vote against us, and this must place us in a minority upon the main points of our Budget. In this we can hardly acquiesce, nor can we adopt a different policy and propose other taxes, when in our opinion the necessary revenue can be raised without imposing them. This state of things imposes upon us the alternative of dissolution or of resignation, and to try the former without succeeding in it would be to place both your Majesty and ourselves in a worse situation than that in which we are at present.

South Street, 8th May 1841.

Lord Melbourne presents his humble duty to your Majesty. We have been considering this question of dissolution at the Cabinet, and we have had before us a general statement of the public returns for England and Wales. It is not very favourable, but Lord Melbourne fears that it is more favourable than the reality would prove. The Chancellor,23 Palmerston, and Hobhouse are strongly for dissolution, but the opinion of the majority is the other way, and in that opinion Lord Melbourne is strongly inclined to agree.

Lord Melbourne will have the honour of waiting upon your Majesty to-morrow at three.

Footnote 23: The Earl of Cottenham.

H.M. Queen Victoria, 1841.

From the drawing by E. F. T., after H. E. Dawe, at Buckingham Palace

To face p. 272, Vol. I

SIR ROBERT PEEL

Told Sir Robert that I had wished to have sought him through the medium of a common friend, which would have given him a greater confidence than I had now a right to expect at his hands, but I felt upon so delicate a mission it was safer, and would be more in accordance with his wishes, to come direct.

That the Prince had sent me to him, with the object of removing difficulties upon his coming into office.

That Her Majesty was anxious that the question of the removal of the Ladies of the Bedchamber should not be revived, and would wish that in any personal communication with Sir Robert this question might be avoided.

That it might be arranged that if Sir Robert would not insist upon carrying out his principle,

Her Majesty might procure the resignation of any Ladies whom Sir Robert might object to; that I thought there might be a disposition to yield to the removal of the Mistress of the Robes, Lady Normanby, and the Duchess of Bedford, as being connected with leading political persons in Government.

Endeavoured to impress upon Sir Robert that if he acts fairly and kindly towards the Queen, he will be met in the same spirit.

Sir Robert said he had considered the probable object of my interview, and thought, from my former position with Lord Melbourne, that Lord Melbourne would be aware of my coming. He must be assured of this before he could speak confidentially to me.

Upon this I admitted that Lord Melbourne had knowledge of my intention, but that I was not authorised to say that he had.

Sir Robert said, "I shall put aside all form, and treat you frankly and confidentially. You may depend upon every word you say being held as sacred. No part, without further permission, shall be mentioned even to the Duke, much less to any of my other colleagues.

"I would waive every pretension to office, I declare to God! sooner than that my acceptance of it should be attended with any personal humiliation to the Queen."

He thought that giving in the names of those Ladies whom he considered obnoxious was an offensive course towards the Queen.

For the sake of office, which he did not covet, he could not concede any constitutional principle, but it was not necessary that that principle should be mooted.

"It would be repulsive to my feelings that Her Majesty should part with any of her Ladies, as the result of a forced stipulation on my part; in a party sense it would doubtless be advantageous to me to say that I had demanded from the Queen, and the Queen had conceded to me the appointments of these three Ladies."

The mode he would like, and which he considered as least objectionable for Her Majesty, was for Her Majesty to say to him, "There is no occasion to revive this constitutional question, as those ladies immediately connected with prominent members of the Administration have sent in their resignation."

The vacancies existing before Sir Robert Peel sees Her Majesty, there is no necessity for discussion.

On the one hand, by this means, there was less appearance of insult to the Queen, and on the other, there was no appearance of concession of principle upon his.

Sir Robert was ready to make any personal sacrifice for Her Majesty's comfort, except that of his honour. "Can the Queen for an instant suppose that I would permit my party to urge me on to insist upon anything incompatible with Her Majesty's dignity, which it would be my great aim and honour to defend?"

[This was his indignant reply to my remark upon the rumours that his party would press him to coerce and subdue Her Majesty.]

Sir Robert thinks it better for the Queen to avoid anything in the shape of a stipulation. He would like what he would have done upon a former occasion (and upon which, on the honour of a gentleman, his views had undergone no change) to be taken as a test of what he would be ready to concede to.

Nothing but misconception, he said, could in his opinion have led to failure before. "Had the Queen told me" (after the question was mooted, which it never need have been) "that those three ladies immediately connected with the Government had tendered their resignation, I should have been perfectly satisfied, and should have consulted the Queen's feelings in replacing them."

Sir Robert said this conversation shall remain sacred, and to all effect, as if it had never happened, until he saw me again to-morrow morning.

There is nothing said, he added, which in any way pledges or compromises the Queen, the Prince, or Lord Melbourne.

Footnote 24: See Parker's Sir Robert Peel, vol. ii. p. 455, et seq., where Peel's memorandum of the interview is set out.

SIR ROBERT PEEL

Peel said: "It is essential to my position with the Queen that Her Majesty should understand that I have the feelings of a gentleman, and where my duty does not interfere, I cannot act against her wishes. Her Majesty doubtless knows how pressed I am as the head of a powerful party, but the impression I wish to create in Her Majesty's mind is, that I am bound to defend her against their encroachments."

HOUSEHOLD APPOINTMENTS

In regard to Household appointments the holders of which are not in Parliament, he had not considered the question, but in the meantime he would in no way commit himself to anyone, or to any understanding upon the subject, without previous communication. He had no personal objects to serve, and the Queen's wishes would always be consulted.

He again repeated, that if the Queen's personal feelings would suffer less by forming an Administration to his exclusion, he should not be offended. Private life satisfied him, and he had no ambition beyond it.

Lord Melbourne might rest assured that he fully appreciated his aim, that his only object was to do that which was most for Her Majesty's advantage, and no human being should know that he was privy to this overture. Lord Melbourne might depend upon his honour. If Lord Melbourne was pressed to a dissolution he should still feel the same impression of Lord Melbourne's conduct, that it was honourable and straightforward.

He wished the Prince to send him a list of those Ladies whom it would be agreeable to Her Majesty to have in her Household. Sir Robert must propose it to the Ladies, but will be entirely guided by Her Majesty's wishes. There should be no appearance that Her Majesty has any understanding, as he was bound to his party to make it appear that the appointments emanated from himself.25

Footnote 25: There was a further interview on the following day at which various detailed points were arranged.

The Queen considers it her right (and is aware that her predecessors were peculiarly tenacious of this right) to appoint her Household. She, however, gives up the great officers of State and those of her Lords-in-Waiting, Equerries, and Grooms-in-Waiting, who are in Parliament, to the appointment of the Prime Minister, subject to her approval.

The Queen has always appointed her Ladies of the Bedchamber herself, but has generally mentioned their names to the Prime Minister before appointing them, in order to leave him room for objection in case he should deem their appointment injurious to his Government, when the Queen would probably not appoint the Lady.

The Maids of Honour and Women of the Bedchamber are of course not included amongst those who are mentioned to the Prime Minister before their appointment, but are at once appointed by the Queen.

PRESSURE OF BUSINESS

"At seven minutes to five Lord Melbourne came to me and stayed till half-past five. He gave me the copies of Anson's conversations with Peel. Lord Melbourne then gave me a letter from the Chancellor to read, strongly advocating a dissolution, and wishing that there should be a division also on Lord John Russell's amendment.26

"Lord Melbourne left the letter with me. The first part of the letter, relative to Lord John's amendment, we think good, but the other part we can't quite agree in. 'There is to be a Cabinet to-morrow to consider what is to be done,' said Lord Melbourne, 'for the Chancellor's opinion must be considered. There is a preferment amongst our people for dissolution,' Lord M. added. The feeling in the country good. I asked Lord M., 'Must they resign directly, the next day, after the division (if they intended resigning)?' 'Why,' he said, 'it was awkward not to do so if Parliament was sitting; if the division were only to take place on Friday, then they needn't announce it till Monday,' which we hope will be the case, as we agreed it wouldn't do for me to have a ball the day Lord M. had resigned, and before I had sent for anybody else, and therefore I hoped that it could be managed that the division did not take place till Friday. Lord M. said that in case they resigned, he wished Vernon Smith27 to be made a Privy Councillor; the only addition to the Peers he mentioned the other day he wished to make is Surrey;28 we agreed that too many Peers was always a bad thing."

Footnote 26: To Lord Sandon's resolution on the Sugar Duties.

Footnote 27: Robert Vernon Smith (1800-1873), Under-Secretary for War and the Colonies, afterwards Lord Lyveden.

Footnote 28: The Earl of Surrey (1791-1856) was now M.P. for West Sussex, and Treasurer of the Household, and was afterwards thirteenth Duke of Norfolk.

11th May 1841.

... I am sure you will forgive my writing a very short letter to-day, but I am so harassed and occupied with business that I cannot find time to write letters. You will, I am sure, feel for me; the probability of parting from so kind and excellent a being as Lord Melbourne as a Minister (for a friend he will always remain) is very, very painful, even if one feels it will not probably be for long; to take it philosophically is my great wish, and quietly I certainly shall, but one cannot help feelings of affection and gratitude. Albert is the greatest possible comfort to me in every way, and my position is much more independent than it was before.

I am glad you see the French feeling in the right light. I rejoice that the christening, etc., went off so well. Believe me, ever, your devoted Niece,

Victoria R.

QUESTION OF DISSOLUTION

"Saw Lord Melbourne at a little past four.

"... 'We have had a Cabinet,' Lord Melbourne said, 'and we have been considering the question of dissolution and what is the best course to be pursued; if we were to dissolve, John Russell,' he said, 'would pursue quite a different course; he would then announce the Sugar Duties at once. I (Lord Melbourne) said, that I had been considering well the whole question, and the Chancellor's letter, but that altogether I did not think it advisable to have recourse to a dissolution—and I think the greater part lean towards that opinion; but there are a few who are very much for a dissolution—the Chancellor and Hobhouse very much so, and Palmerston. They have, however, not quite finally decided the matter. I understand the debate will certainly go over to-night,' he said, 'and that they would have time on Saturday and Sunday to consider about Lord John's amendment.'"

"Lord Melbourne came to me at twenty minutes past one, and we talked about this question of dissolution. 'We shall have a long debate upon it this morning at the Cabinet,' Lord Melbourne said. 'The worst thing is, that if we carry the Sugar Duties, we must dissolve. If we were to dissolve,' he continued, 'and were to have the parties equal as they are now, it would be very bad; if we were to have a majority, it would be a great thing; but if we were to have a minority it would be still worse.... We know that Charles I. and Charles II., and even Cromwell, appealed to the country, and had a Parliament returned into their very teeth' (so strong an Opposition), 'and that produced deposition, and convulsion, and bloodshed and death; but since then the Crown has always had a majority returned in favour of it. Even Queen Anne,' he continued, 'who removed Marlborough in the midst of his most glorious victories and dissolved Parliament, had an immense majority, though her measures were miserable; William IV.,' he said, 'even though he had a majority against him which prevented him from keeping his Ministers, had a much stronger feeling for him in that Parliament, than he ever had before. But I am afraid,' he added, 'that for the first time the Crown would have an Opposition returned smack against it; and that would be an affront to which I am very unwilling to expose the Crown.' This is very true."

KING LEOPOLD'S SYMPATHY

Tuileries, 14th May 1841.

My dearest Victoria,—I am deeply grateful for your kind letter, which reached me this morning. Letters from hence ought not to be longer on their way than, at the longest, forty hours; forty-eight is the maximum. I fear that they are delayed at the Foreign Office; here it cannot be, as for instance these lines go this evening.

I can easily understand that the present crisis must have something very painful for you, and you will do well for your health and comfort to try to take it as philosophically as possible; it is a part of the Constitutional system which is for the Sovereign very hard to get over.

Nous savons tous des paroles sur cet air, as the French say. I was convinced that Lord

Melbourne's right and good feeling would make him pause before he proposed to you a dissolution. A general election in England, when great passions must be roused or created to render it efficacious for one party or another, is a dangerous experiment, always calculated to shake the foundations on which have hitherto reposed the great elements of the political power of the country. Albert will be a great comfort to you, and to hear it from yourself has given me the sincerest delight. His judgment is good, and he is mild and safe in his opinions; they deserve your serious attention; young as he is, I have really often been quite surprised how quick and correct his judgment is....

TORY DISSENSIONS

Wilton Crescent, 16th May 1841.

Lord John Russell presents his humble duty to your Majesty, and has the honour to state that the general effect of last week's debate29 has been greatly in favour of the measures of your Majesty's Ministers.

The speeches of Mr Labouchere, Sir George Grey, and Lord Howick, with the powerful argument of the Chancellor of the Exchequer on Friday night, have not been met by any corresponding ability on the other side.

In fact the Opposition seem to have concealed their own views of policy, and to have imagined that the Anti-Slavery feeling would carry them through successfully. But this expectation has been entirely disappointed; debate has unmasked the hollow pretence of humanity, and the meetings at Exeter Hall and in the country have completely counteracted the impressions which Dr Lushington's speech30 had produced.

Lancashire, Cheshire, and the West Riding of Yorkshire have been roused to strong excitement by the prospect of a reduction of the duty on corn. Several of the large towns have expressed their opinions without distinction of party.

These symptoms are said to have created some dissensions among the opponents of your Majesty's present Government.

Sir Robert Peel, Lord Stanley, and nearly all the eminent leaders of the party, profess their adherence to the principles of Mr Huskisson.31 On the other hand, the Duke of Buckingham,32 with many Lords and Commoners, is opposed to any relaxation of the present Corn Laws. This difference must ultimately produce serious consequences, and it is possible they may break out before the present debate is ended.

One consequence of the propositions of the Ministry is the weakening of the power of the Chartists, who have relied on the misrepresentation that neither Whigs nor Tories would ever do anything for the improvement of the condition of the working classes.

All these circumstances have a bearing on the question of a dissolution of Parliament, and are to be weighed against the risks and inconveniences of so bold a measure.

Footnote 29: On Lord Sandon's resolution.

Footnote 30: Against the Budget, on the ground that it tended to encourage slavery.

Footnote 31: Which were opposed to Protection and the Navigation Laws.

Footnote 32: Richard Plantagenet (1797-1861), second Duke of the 1822 creation, M.P. for

Bucks 1818-1839, and author of the "Chandos clause," became Lord Privy Seal this year, but resigned shortly after. He dissipated his property, and had to sell the contents of Stowe.

THE QUEEN'S JOURNAL

"Lord Melbourne came to me at twenty minutes to three. There were no new news. He gave me a letter from the Duke of Roxburgh,33 saying he could not support Government on the Corn Laws, and writing an unnecessarily cold letter. Lord Melbourne fears this would lose Roxburgh in case of an election. A great many of the friends of the Government, however, are against any alteration in the Corn Laws. Talked of the excellent accounts from the country with which the papers are full, and I said I couldn't help thinking the Government would gain by a dissolution, and the feeling in the country so strong, and daily increasing. They would lose the counties, Lord Melbourne thinks, and the question is whether their successes in the manufacturing towns would be sufficient to counterbalance that. The debate may last longer, Lord Melbourne says, as J. Russell says he will continue it as long as their friends wish it. Many of their friends would be very angry if we did not dissolve, Lord Melbourne says. 'I say always,' said Lord Melbourne, 'that your Majesty will be in such a much worse position' (if a majority should be returned against us), 'but they say not, for that the others would dissolve.' I said that if that was so we must dissolve, for then that it would come to just the same thing, and that that changed my opinion very much. 'You would like us then to make the attempt?' Lord Melbourne asked. I said 'Almost.' I asked if he really thought they would dissolve. 'I've great reason to believe they would,' he replied. 'Hardinge34 told Vivian35 "we shall prevent your dissolving, but we shall dissolve."' ... I asked did Lord Melbourne think they (the Conservatives) would remain in long, and Melbourne said: 'One can't tell beforehand what may happen, but you would find their divisions and dissensions amongst themselves sufficient to prevent their staying in long.' ...

"Saw Lord John Russell, who didn't feel certain if the debate would end to-night. Talked of the very good feeling in the country. He said he understood Sir Edward Knatchbull36 was exceedingly displeased at what Peel had said concerning Free Trade, and said in that case Peel would be as bad as the present Government. He thinks the Tories, if in power, might try and collect the Sugar duties without Law, which would do them a great deal of harm and be exceedingly unpopular. He does not think the Tories intend certainly to dissolve. He thinks they would not dissolve now, and that they would hereafter get so entangled by their own dissensions, as to render it unfavourable to them."

Footnote 33: James, sixth Duke. The Duchess was afterwards a Lady of the Bedchamber.

Footnote 34: Sir Henry Hardinge (1785-1856) had been Secretary at War, and Chief Secretary for Ireland, under former Tory Governments.

Footnote 35: Master-General of the Ordnance.

Footnote 36: M.P. for East Kent. He became Paymaster-General in Peel's Cabinet.

18th May 1841.

... I was sure you would feel for me. Since last Monday, the 10th, we have lived in the daily expectation of a final event taking place, and the debate still continues, and it is not certain whether it will even finish to-night, this being the eighth night, it having begun on Friday the 7th, two Saturdays and two Sundays having intervened! Our plans are so unsettled that I can tell you nothing, only that you may depend upon it nothing will be done without having been duly, properly, and maturely weighed. Lord Melbourne's conduct is as usual perfect; fair, calm, and totally disinterested, and I am certain that in whatever position he is you will treat him just as you have always done.

My dearest Angel is indeed a great comfort to me. He takes the greatest interest in what goes on, feeling with and for me, and yet abstaining as he ought from biassing me either way, though we talk much on the subject, and his judgment is, as you say, good and mild....

P.S.—Pray let me hear soon when you come. You, I know, like me to tell you what I hear, and for me to be frank with you. I therefore tell you that it is believed by some people here, and even by some in the Government, that you wish my Government to be out. Now, I never for an instant can believe such an assertion, as I know your liberal feelings, and your interest in my welfare and in that of the country too well to think you could wish for such a thing, and I immediately said I was sure this was not so; but I think you would do well to say to Seymour something which might imply interest in my present Government.

I know you will understand my anxiety on your account, lest such a mischievous report should be believed. It comes, you see, from the idea that your feelings are very French.

THE CORN LAWS

"Saw Lord Melbourne.37 He said Lord John Russell had been to see him, and, 'He now wishes us not to resign, but to give notice immediately of a Motion on the Corn Laws. This, he thinks, will make the others propose a vote of confidence, or make them oppose the Sugar Duties, which, he thinks, will be better for us to resign upon, and when it would be clear to our people that we couldn't dissolve. Everybody says it would be a very bad thing for us to resign now, upon such a question as this, and we must consider the party a little.' I said, of course, this would be agreeable to me as it gave us another chance. I said it would be awkward if they resigned Thursday, on account of the Birthday. Lord Melbourne said I could wait a day and only send for Peel on Saturday, that that wouldn't signify to Peel, as he could come down to Claremont.... I asked, in case they meant to bring on this Corn Law question, when would they do so. 'Perhaps about the 30th,' Lord Melbourne said. It would be a more dangerous question, but it would make them (the Tories) show their colours, which is a great advantage. He said they prevented Sir Edward Knatchbull from speaking last night."

Footnote 37: After eight days' discussions of Lord Sandon's Motion, the Ministers were defeated by 317 to 281.

RESIGNATION POSTPONED

"At twenty minutes to one came Lord Melbourne.... I returned him Lord John Russell's letter, and talked of it, and of John Russell's saying the division and Peel's speech made it absolutely necessary to decide to-day whether to resign or dissolve. I asked what Peel had said in his speech about the Corn Laws. 'I'll tell you, Ma'am, what he said,' Lord Melbourne replied, 'that he was for a sliding duty and not for a fixed duty; but he did not pledge himself as to what rate of duty it should be. I must say,' Lord Melbourne continued, 'I am still against dissolution. I don't think our chances of success are sufficient.' I replied that I couldn't quite believe that, but that I might be wrong. Lord John is for dissolving. 'You wish it?' I said I always did. Talked of the feeling in the City and in the country being so good. Lord Melbourne don't think so much of the feeling in the country. Talked of the majority of thirty-six having not been more than they expected.... Lord Melbourne said people thought the debate was lengthened to please me. I said not at all, but that it was more convenient for me. Anyhow I need do nothing till Saturday. The House of Commons was adjourned to the next day, and the House of Lords to Monday. 'Mr Baring says,' he said, 'if there was only a majority one way or another, it would be better than this state of complete equality.'

"At twenty minutes past four Lord Melbourne returned. 'Well, Ma'am,' he said, 'we've considered this question, and both the sides of it well, and at last we voted upon it; and there were—the Lord Chancellor for dissolution, Lord Minto38 for it, Lord Normanby against it, but greatly modified; Lord John for, Lord Palmerston for, Lord Clarendon for, Lord Morpeth for, Lord Lansdowne for, Labouchere for, Hobhouse for, Duncannon39 for, Baring for, Macaulay for; and under those circumstances of course I felt I could not but go with them.40 Lord Melbourne was much affected in saying all this. 'So we shall go on, bring on the Sugar Duties, and then, if things are in a pretty good state, dissolve. I hope you approve?' I said I did highly ... and that I felt so happy to keep him longer. 'You are aware we may have a majority against us?' he said; he means in our election. The Sugar Duties would probably take a fortnight or three weeks to pass, and they would dissolve in June and meet again in October. He thought they must."

Footnote 38: Lord Minto was First Lord of the Admiralty.

Footnote 39: Then First Commissioner of Land Revenue.

Footnote 40: See Sir John Hobhouse's account of this Cabinet meeting, Edinburgh Review, vol. 133, p. 336.

THE QUEEN AND THE CHURCH
21st May 1841.

Lord Melbourne thinks that what your Majesty proposes to say will do very well, but it is thought best to say "Church as Reformed" at the Reformation.

If your Majesty could say this, it would be well:

"I am very grateful for your congratulations on the return of this day. I am happy to take this opportunity of again expressing to you my firm determination to maintain the Church of England as settled at the Reformation, and my firm belief in her Articles and Creeds, as hitherto understood and interpreted by her soundest divines."

Nothing could go off better than the dinner. Everybody was much pleased with the Prince.

Lord Melbourne is not conscious of having slept.41

Footnote 41: It seems that some one had told the Queen that Lord Melbourne had fallen asleep at dinner.

FEELING IN FRANCE
Brussels, 20th May 1841.

My dearest Victoria,—I receive this very moment your dear letter of the 18th, and without loss of time I begin my answer here, though the messenger can only go to-morrow. I cannot sufficiently express to you my gratitude for the frankness with which you have written to me—and let me entreat you, whenever you have anything sur le cœur, to do the same. I shall begin with your postscript concerning the idea that I wished your present Ministers to retire, because they had become disagreeable to France. The people who avancent quelque chose de la sorte probably have some ill-natured motive which it is not always easy to guess; perhaps in the present instance does it mean, let us say, that? whatever opinion he may then express we can easily counteract it, representing it as the result of strong partiality to France. Let us therefore examine what France has to gain in a change of Administration. Certainly your present Ministers are not much loved now in France, not so much in consequence of the political events of last year themselves, than for the manner in which they came to pass. Nevertheless, when I was at Paris, King and Council were decided to sign the treaty with the four other Powers, which would put an end to the isolement, though many people are stoutly for the isolement. There end the relations which will exist for some time between the two countries—they will be on decent terms; that is all I wish for the present, and it is matter of moonshine who your Ministers are. No doubt, formerly there existed such a predilection in favour of Lord Grey's[42] Administration and those who continued it, that the coming in of the Tories would have been considered as a great public calamity; but even now, though this affection is gone, the Tories will also be looked on with some suspicion. Lord Melbourne's Administration has had the great merit of being liberal, and at the same time prudent, conservative in the good sense of the word, preserving what was good. Monarchy, by an adherence to this system, was very safe, and the popular liberal cry needless.

Footnote 42: 1830-1834.

KING LEOPOLD'S ADVICE

(Continued at) Laeken, 21st May.

I regret that the Corn question was brought forward somewhat abruptly;[43] it is a dangerous one, as it roused the most numerous and poorest classes of society, and may easily degenerate into bloodshed. The dissolution under such circumstances would become still more a source of agitation, as it generally always is in England. Lord Melbourne, I am sure, will think so too.

I am delighted by what you say of Albert; it is just the proper line for him to take, without biassing you either way, to show you honestly the consequences which in his opinion the one or the other may have. As he has really a very clear and logical judgment, his opinion will be valuable for you. I feel very much for you, and these Ministerial complications are of a most painful and perplexing nature, though less in England than on the Continent, as the thing is at least better understood. To amuse you a little, and to prove to you how impartial I must be to be in this way accused by both parties, I must tell you that it is said in France that, conjointly with Lord Melbourne, we artfully ruined the Thiers Administration,[44] to the great detriment of the honour and welfare of France. But what is still stranger is, that the younger branches of the family, seeing that my arrival at Paris was delayed from time to time, became convinced that I would not come at all, and that my intention was to cut them completely, not to compromettre myself with England! Truly people are strange, and the unnecessary suspicions and stories which they love to have, and to tell, a great bore....

Pray have the goodness of giving my kindest regards to Lord Melbourne. I will love him very tenderly in and out of office, as I am really attached to him. Now last, though first, I offer my sincerest wishes on the happy return of your birthday; may every blessing be always bestowed on your beloved head. You possess much, let your warm and honest heart appreciate that. Let me also express the hope that you always will maintain your dear character true and good as it is, and let us also humbly express the hope that our warmth of feeling, a valuable gift, will not be permitted to grow occasionally a little violent, and particularly not against your uncle. You may pull Albertus by the ear, when so inclined, but be never irritated against your uncle. But I have not to complain when other people do not instigate such things; you have always been kind and affectionate, and when you look at my deeds for you, and on behalf of you, these twenty-two years, I think you will not have many hardships to recollect. I am happy to hear of my god-daughter's teeth, and that she is so well. May God keep the whole dear little family well and happy for ever. My dearest Victoria, your devoted Uncle,

Leopold R.

Footnote 43: The Ministerial proposal of a fixed duty instead of a sliding scale.

Footnote 44: The Thiers Government had resigned in the preceding October, owing to the King objecting to the warlike speech which they wished him to pronounce to the Chambers. The Soult-Guizot Cabinet was accordingly formed.

SIR ROBERT PEEL

Called upon Sir Robert Peel this morning. I said I could not feel satisfied without seeing him after the very unexpected course which political affairs had taken. I wished to know that he felt assured, though I trusted there could be no doubt upon his mind, that there had been perfect honesty of purpose on my part towards him, and more especially upon the part of those with whose knowledge I had been acting. I assured Sir Robert that H.M. had acted in the most perfect fairness towards him, and I was most anxious that there should be no erroneous impression upon his mind as to the conduct of either H.M. or the Prince.

I said (quoting the Prince's expression), "that the Queen has a natural modesty upon her constitutional views, and when she receives an advice from men like the Lord Chancellor, Lord John Russell, Mr Baring, Mr Labouchere, and Lord Clarendon, and knows that they have been weighing the question through so many days, she concludes that her judgment cannot be better than theirs, and that she would do wrong to reject their advice."

The Prince, I said, however strongly impressed for or against a question, thinks it wrong and impolitic, considering his age and inexperience and his novelty to the country, to press upon the Queen views of his own in opposition to those of experienced statesmen. Sir Robert said he could relieve my mind entirely; that he was convinced that all that had taken place had been with the most perfect honesty; that he had no feeling whatever of annoyance, or of having been ill-used; that, on the contrary, he had the feeling, and should always retain it, of the deepest gratitude to the Queen for the condescension which Her Majesty had been pleased to show him, and that it had only increased his devotion to Her Majesty's person. He said that much of the reserve which he had shown in treating with me was not on his own account, but that he felt from his own experience that events were by no means certain, and he most cautiously abstained from permitting her Majesty in any way to commit herself, or to bind herself by any engagement which unforeseen circumstances might render inconvenient. Sir Robert said it was very natural to try and remove obstacles which had before created so much confusion, and he was convinced that they would have been practically removed by what had passed. He said that neither Lord Stanley nor Sir James Graham knew a word of what had passed. That Mr Greville had asked his friend Mr Arbuthnot whether some understanding had not been entered into between Lord Melbourne and him. That Mr Arbuthnot had replied that he was certain that nothing of the sort could have passed,45 as, if it had, Sir Robert Peel would have informed him (Mr Arbuthnot) of the fact. Again, Lady de Grey, the night of the ball at the Palace, came up to him and said the Duke of Bedford had been speaking to her about the resignation of the Duchess of Bedford, and asking her whether she thought it necessary. She volunteered to find out from Sir Robert whether he thought it requisite. She asked the question, which Sir Robert tried to evade, but not being able, he said it struck him that if it was a question of doubt the best means of solving it, was for the Duke of Bedford to ask Lord Melbourne for his opinion.

I added that if the dissolution was a failure, which it was generally apprehended would be the case, I felt convinced that Sir Robert would be dealt with in the most perfect fairness by Her Majesty.

Footnote 45: "After I had been told by the Duke of Bedford that Peel was going to insist on certain terms, which was repeated to me by Clarendon, I went to Arbuthnot, told him Melbourne's impression, and asked him what it all meant. He said it was all false, that he was certain Peel had no such intentions, but, on the contrary, as he had before assured me, was disposed to do everything that would be conciliatory and agreeable to the Queen."—Greville's Journal, 19th May 1841.

VOTE OF WANT OF CONFIDENCE

South Street, 24th May 1841.

Lord Melbourne presents his humble duty to your Majesty, and has to acquaint your Majesty that in the House of Commons this evening Sir Robert Peel gave notice that on Thursday next he would move a resolution to the following effect: "That Her Majesty's Ministers not possessing power sufficient to carry into effect the measures which they considered necessary, their retention of office was unconstitutional and contrary to usage."46 These are not the exact words, but they convey the substance. This is a direct vote of want of confidence, and Lord Melbourne would be inclined to doubt whether it will be carried, and if it is, it certainly will not be by so large a majority as the former vote. When the Chancellor of the Exchequer moved the resolution upon the Sugar Duties, Sir Robert Peel seconded the motion, thereby intending to intimate that he did not mean to interfere with the Supplies. This course was determined upon at a meeting held at Sir R. Peel's this morning.

Footnote 46: The closing words of the resolution were as follows: "... That Her Majesty's Ministers do not sufficiently possess the confidence of the House of Commons to enable them to carry through the House measures which they deem of essential importance to the public welfare, and that their continuance in office under such circumstances is at variance with the spirit of the Constitution."

PROSPECT OF DISSOLUTION

Wilton Crescent, 28th May 1841.

Lord John Russell presents his humble duty to your Majesty, and has the honour to state that Sir Robert Peel yesterday brought forward his motion in a remarkably calm and temperate speech.

Sir John Hobhouse and Mr Macaulay completely exposed the fallacy of his resolution, and successfully vindicated the government. Lord Worsley47 declared he would oppose the resolution, which declaration excited great anger, and produced much disappointment in the Tory party.

If the debate is carried on till next week, it is probable the Ministers may have a majority of one or two.

The accounts from the country are encouraging.

It does not appear that Sir Robert Peel, even if he carries this motion, intends to obstruct the measures necessary for a dissolution of Parliament.

Footnote 47: M.P. for Lincolnshire, who had voted for Lord Sandon's motion.

31st May 1841.

... I beg you not to be alarmed about what is to be done; it is not for a Party triumph that Parliament (the longest that has sat for many years) is to be dissolved; it is the fairest and most constitutional mode of proceeding; and you may trust to the moderation and prudence of my whole Government that nothing will be done without due consideration; if the present Government get a majority by the elections they will go on prosperously; if not, the Tories will come in for a short time. The country is quiet and the people very well disposed. I am happy, dearest Uncle, to give you these quieting news, which I assure you are not partial....

KING LEOPOLD'S VIEWS

Laeken 31st May 1841.

My dearest Victoria,—Your Mother48 is safely arrived, though she was received close to Ostende by a formidable thunderstorm. I had given directions that everywhere great civilities should be shown her. She stood the fatigues better than I had expected, and is less sleepy than in England. She seems to be pleased with her séjour here, and inclined in fact to remain rather than to go on; but I am sure, when once in Germany she will be both pleased and interested by it. It will amuse you to hear from herself her own impressions.

I cannot help to add a few political lines. I regret much, I must confess, that the idea of a dissolution has gained ground, and I will try to show in a very few words why I am against it.

In politics, a great rule ought to be to rule with the things which one knows already, and not to jump into something entirely new of which no one can do more than guess the consequences.

The present Parliament has been elected at a moment most favourable to the present Administration after a most popular accession to the throne, everything new and fresh, and with the natural fondness of the great mass of people, a change is always popular; it was known that you were kindly disposed towards your Ministers, everything was therefore à souhait for the election of a new Parliament. In this respect Ministers have nothing like the favourable circumstances which smiled upon them at the last general election. Feeling this, they raise a cry, which may become popular and embarrass their antagonists about cheap bread! I do not think this is quite befitting their dignity; such things do for revolutionaries like Thiers, or my late Ministers.... If the thing rouses the people it may do serious mischief; if not, it will look awkward for the Ministers themselves. If you do not grant a dissolution to your present Ministers you would have, at the coming in of a new Administration, the right to tell them that they must go on with the present Parliament; and I have no doubt that they could do so. The statistics of the present House of Commons are well known to all the men who sit in it, and to keep it a few years longer would be a real advantage.

You know that I have been rather maltreated by the Tories, formerly to please George IV., and since I left the country, because I served, in their opinion, on the revolutionary side of the question. I must say, however, that for your service as well as for the quiet of the country, it would be good to give them a trial. If they could not remain in office it will make them quieter for some time. If by a dissolution the Conservative interest in the House is too much weakened the permanent interests of the country can but suffer from that. If, on the contrary, the Conservatives come in stronger, your position will not be very agreeable, and it may induce them to be perhaps less moderate than they ought to be. I should be very happy if you would discuss these, my hasty views, with Lord Melbourne. I do not give them for more than what they are, mere practical considerations; but, as far as I can judge of the question, if I was myself concerned I should have no dissolution; if even there was but the very banale consideration, qu'on sait ce qu'on a, mais qu'on ne sait nullement ce qu'on aura. The moment is not without importance, and well worthy your earnest consideration, and I feel convinced that Lord Melbourne will agree with me, that, notwithstanding the great political good sense of the people in England, the machine is so complicated that it should be handled with great care and tenderness.

To conclude, I must add that perhaps a permanent duty on corn may be a desirable thing, but that it ought to be sufficiently high to serve as a real protection. It may besides produce this effect, that as it will be necessary, at least at first, to buy a good deal of the to be imported corn with money, the currency will be seriously affected by it. The countries which would have a chance of selling would be chiefly Poland in all its parts, Prussia, Austria, and Russia, the South of Russia on the Black Sea, and maybe Sicily. Germany does not grow a sufficient quantity of wheat to profit by such an arrangement; it will besides not buy more from England for the present than it does now, owing to the Zollverein,49 which must first be altered. But I will not bore you too long, and conclude with my best love to little Victoria, of whom her Grandmama speaks with raptures. Ever, my dearest Victoria, your devoted Uncle,

Leopold R.

Footnote 48: The Duchess of Kent had left England for a tour on the Continent.

Footnote 49: After the fall of Napoleon, the hopes of many Germans for a united national Germany were frustrated by the Congress of Vienna, which perpetuated the practical independence of a number of German States, as well as the predominance within the Germanic confederation of Austria, a Power largely non-German. One of the chief factors in the subsequent unification of Germany was the Zollverein, or Customs Union, by which North Germany was gradually bound together by commercial interest, and thus opposed to Austria. The success of this method of imperial integration has not been without influence on the policies of other lands.

THE OPPOSITION ELATED

Wilton Crescent, 5th June 1841.

Lord John Russell presents his humble duty to your Majesty, and has the honour to state that the House divided about three this morning.

The Opposition were greatly elated by this triumph. Lord Stanley, and Sir Robert Peel who spoke last in the debate, did not deny that the Crown might exercise the prerogative of dissolution in the present case. But they insisted that no time should be lost in previous debates, especially on such a subject as the Corn Laws.

Lord John Russell spoke after Lord Stanley, and defended the whole policy of the Administration.

After the division he stated that he would on Monday propose the remaining estimates, and announce the course which he meant to pursue respecting the Corn Laws.

MARRIAGE OF LORD JOHN RUSSELL

6th June 1841.

... Now, many thanks for two letters of the 31st ult. and 4th June. The former I shall not answer at length, as Albert has done so, and I think has given a very fair view of the state of affairs. Let me only repeat to you again that you need not be alarmed, and that I think you will be pleased and beruhigt when you talk to our friend Lord Melbourne on the subject...

I fear you will again see nothing of the Season, as Parliament will probably be dissolved by the 21st....

As to my letters, dear Uncle, I beg to assure you (for Lord Palmerston was most indignant at the doubt when I once asked) that none of our letters nor any of those coming to us, are ever opened at the Foreign Office. My letters to Brussels and Paris are quite safe, and all those to Germany, which are of any real consequence, I always send through Rothschild, which is perfectly safe and very quick.

We are, and so is everybody here, so charmed with Mme. Rachel;50 she is perfect, et puis, such a nice modest girl; she is going to declaim at Windsor Castle on Monday evening.

Now adieu in haste. Believe me, always, your very devoted Niece,

Victoria R.

Really Leopold must come, or I shall never forgive you.

Footnote 50: The young French actress, who made her début in England on 4th May as

Hermione in Racine's Andromaque. She was received with great enthusiasm.

Windsor Castle, 8th June 1841.

Lord Melbourne presents his humble duty to your Majesty. He is quite well, and has nothing particular to relate to your Majesty, at least nothing that presses; except that he is commissioned by Lord John Russell respectfully to acquaint your Majesty that his marriage is settled, and will take place shortly.

Does Lord Melbourne really mean J. Russell's marriage? and to whom?

VISIT TO NUNEHAM

The Lady Fanny Eliot.51 Lord Melbourne did not name her before, nor does not now, because he did not remember her Christian name.

Footnote 51: Daughter of Lord Minto. Lord Melbourne originally wrote The Lady —— Eliot at the head of his letter (spelling the surname wrong, which should be Elliot). The word "Fanny" is written in subsequently to the completion of the letter.

Nuneham,52 15th June 1841.

Affairs go on, and all will take some shape or other, but it keeps one in hot water all the time. In the meantime, however, the people are in the best possible humour, and I never was better received at Ascot, which is a great test, and also along the roads yesterday. This is a most lovely place; pleasure grounds in the style of Claremont, only much larger, and with the river Thames winding along beneath them, and Oxford in the distance; a beautiful flower and kitchen garden, and all kept up in perfect order. I followed Albert here, faithful to my word, and he is gone to Oxford53 for the whole day, to my great grief. And here I am all alone in a strange house, with not even Lehzen as a companion, in Albert's absence, but I thought she and also Lord Gardner,54 and some gentlemen should remain with little Victoria for the first time. But it is rather a trial for me.

I must take leave, and beg you to believe me always, your most devoted Niece,

Victoria R.

Footnote 52: The house of Edward Vernon Harcourt, Archbishop of York.

Footnote 53: To receive an address at Commemoration.

Footnote 54: Alan Legge, third and last Lord Gardner (1810-1883) was one of the Queen's first Lords-in-Waiting.

THE PRINCE VISITS OXFORD

South Street, 16th June 1841.

Lord Melbourne presents his humble duty to your Majesty. He has just received your Majesty's letter, and will wait upon your Majesty at half-past five. Lord Melbourne is sorry to hear that your Majesty has been at all indisposed. It will suit him much better to wait upon your Majesty at dinner to-morrow than to-day, as his hand shows some disposition to gather, and it may be well to take care of it.

Lord Melbourne is very glad to learn that everything went off well at Oxford. Lord Melbourne expected that the Duke of Sutherland55 would not entirely escape a little public animadversion. Nothing can be more violent or outrageous than the conduct of the students of both Universities upon such occasions; the worst and lowest mobs of Westminster and London are very superior to them in decency and forbearance.

The Archbishop56 is a very agreeable man; but he is not without cunning, and Lord Melbourne can easily understand his eagerness that the Queen should not prorogue Parliament in person. He knows that it will greatly assist the Tories. It is not true that it is universal for the Sovereign to go down upon such occasions. George III. went himself in 1784; he did not go in 1807, because he had been prevented from doing so by his infirmities for three years before. William IV. went down himself in 1830.57

Lord Melbourne sends a note which he has received from Lord Normanby upon this and another subject.

Footnote 55: Who was, of course, associated with the Whig Ministry.

Footnote 56: Archbishop Vernon Harcourt, of York, the Queen's host.

Footnote 57: The Queen prorogued Parliament in person on 22nd June.

Buckingham Palace, 17th June 1841.

My dearest Uncle,—A few lines I must write to you to express to you my very great delight at the certainty, God willing, of seeing you all three next week, and to express a hope, and a great hope, that you will try and arrive a little earlier on Wednesday.... I must again repeat I am so sorry you should come when Society is dispersed and at sixes and sevens, and in such a state that naturally I cannot at the moment of the elections invite many Tories, as that tells so at the elections. But we shall try and do our best to make it as little dull as we can, and you will kindly take the will for the deed.

We came back from Nuneham yesterday afternoon. Albert came back at half-past five on Tuesday from Oxford, where he had been enthusiastically received, but the students ... had the bad taste to show their party feeling in groans and hisses when the name of a Whig was mentioned, which they ought not to have done in my husband's presence.

I must now conclude, begging you ever to believe me, your devoted Niece,

Victoria R.

My Coiffeur will be quite at Louise's disposal, and he can coiffer in any way she likes, if her dresser tells him how she wishes it.

LORD BROUGHAM

Grafton Street, 19th June 1841.

LETTER FROM LORD BROUGHAM

Most gracious Sovereign,—I crave leave humbly to approach your Majesty and to state in writing what I should have submitted to your Royal consideration at an Audience, because I conceive that this course will be attended with less inconvenience to your Majesty.

In the counsel which I ventured with great humility, but with an entire conviction of its soundness, to tender, I cannot be biassed by any personal interest, for I am not a candidate for office; nor by any Parliamentary interest, for I have no concern with elections; nor by any factious interest, for I am unconnected with party. My only motive is to discharge the duty which I owe to both the Crown and the country. Nor am I under the influence of any prejudice against your Majesty's servants or their measures; for I charge your Majesty's servants with nothing beyond an error, a great error, in judgment, and I entirely approve of the measures which they have lately propounded (with a single exception partially applicable to one of them), while I lament and disapprove of the time and manner of propounding them, both on account of the Government and of the measures themselves.

I feel myself, Madam, under the necessity of stating that the dissolution of the Parliament appears to me wholly without justification, either from principle or from policy. They who advise it must needs proceed upon the supposition that a majority will be returned favourable to the continuance of the present Administration and favourable to their lately announced policy. On no other ground is it possible that any such advice should be tendered to your Majesty. For no one could ever think of such a proceeding as advising the Crown to dissolve the Parliament in order to increase the force of the Opposition to its own future Ministers, thus perverting to the mere purposes of party the exercise of by far the most eminent of the Royal prerogatives; and I pass over as wholly unworthy of notice the only other supposition which can with any decency be made, when there is no conflict between the two Houses, namely, that of a dissolution in entire ignorance of the national opinion and for the purpose of ascertaining to which side it inclines. Your Majesty's advisers must, therefore, have believed, and they must still believe, that a majority will be returned favourable both to themselves and their late policy. I, on the other hand, have the most entire conviction that there will be a considerable majority against them, and against their policy a majority larger still, many of their supporters having already joined to swell that majority. Whoever examines the details of the case must be satisfied that the very best result which the Government can possibly hope for is a narrow majority against them—an event which must occasion a second dissolution by whatever Ministry may succeed to the confidence of your Majesty. But those best acquainted with the subject have no doubt at all that the majority will be much more considerable.

I beg leave, Madam, humbly to represent to your Majesty, in my own vindication for not having laid my opinion before your Majesty as soon as I returned from the Continent, that when I first heard of the course taken by the Government early in May, I formed the opinion which I now entertain, but conceived that I must have mistaken the facts upon which they were acting; and when I arrived twelve days ago I was confirmed in the belief (seeing the fixed resolution taken to dissolve) that I must have been under an erroneous impression as to the probable results of the elections. But I have since found ample reason for believing that my original conviction was perfectly well founded, and that no grounds whatever exist sufficient to make any one who considers the subject calmly, and without the bias of either interest or prejudice, really believe that this ill-fated proceeding can have any other result than lasting injury to your Majesty's service, to the progress of sound and just views of policy, and to the influence of those in whom the Crown and the country alike should repose confidence.

That a number of short-sighted persons whose judgments are warped by exclusive attention to a single subject, or by personal feelings, or by party views (and these narrow and erroneous), may have been loudly clamorous for the course apparently about to be pursued, is extremely possible, and affords no kind of excuse for it. Many of these will be the slowest to defend what they have so unfortunately called for; some will be among the first to condemn it when a manifest failure shall have taken place, and general discomfiture shall throw a few local successes into the shade.

My advice is humbly offered to your Majesty, as removed far above such confined and factious views; as the parent of all your people; as both bound and willing to watch over their true interests; and as charged by virtue of your exalted office with the preservation of the public peace, the furtherance of the prosperity, and the maintenance of the liberties of your subjects.

I am, with profound respect, Madam, your Majesty's faithful and dutiful Subject, Brougham.59

Footnote 58: Mention has been made earlier of the resentment which Brougham cherished against his late colleagues, after his exclusion from the Whig Cabinet, and this letter, on the proposal to dissolve Parliament, was, no doubt, prompted by that feeling.

Footnote 59: Parliament, however, notwithstanding this rescript of Lord Brougham, was dissolved, and the Ministry went to the country with the cry of a fixed duty on corn, as against a sliding scale, and they attacked, as monopolists, at once the landowner, who enjoyed protection for his wheat, and the West Indian proprietor, who profited by the duty on foreign sugar. The Conservatives impugned the general policy of the Whig Administration. The result, a majority of seventy-six, was an even greater Conservative triumph than the most sanguine of the party anticipated.—See Introductory Note, ante, p.

VISIT TO WOBURN

Arrived here last night with the Prince and the Queen; this is now the second expedition (Nuneham being the first) which Her Majesty has taken, and on neither occasion has the Baroness accompanied us.

The Prince went yesterday through a review of the many steps he had made to his present position—all within eighteen months from the marriage. Those who intended to keep him from being useful to the Queen, from the fear that he might ambitiously touch upon her prerogatives, have been completely foiled; they thought they had prevented Her Majesty from yielding anything of importance to him by creating distrust through imaginary alarm. The Queen's good sense, however, has seen that the Prince has no other object in all he seeks but a means to Her Majesty's good. The Court from highest to lowest is brought to a proper sense of the position of the Queen's husband. The country has marked its confidence in his character by passing the Regency Bill nem. con. The Queen finds the value of an active right hand and able head to support her and to resort to for advice in time of need. Cabinet Ministers treat him with deference and respect. Arts and science look up to him as their especial patron, and they find this encouragement supported by a full knowledge of the details of every subject. The good and the wise look up to him with pride and gratitude as giving an example, so rarely shown in such a station, of leading a virtuous and religious life.

Windsor Castle, 3rd August 1841.

... Our little tour was most successful, and we enjoyed it of all things; nothing could be more enthusiastic or affectionate than our reception everywhere, and I am happy to hear that our presence has left a favourable impression, which I think will be of great use. The loyalty in this country is certainly very striking. We enjoyed Panshanger60 still more than Woburn; the country is quite beautiful, and the house so pretty and wohnlich; the picture-gallery and pictures very splendid. The Cowpers are such good people too. The visit to Brocket naturally interested us very much for our excellent Lord Melbourne's sake. The park and grounds are beautiful.

I can't admit the Duke of Bedford61 ever was radical; God knows! I wish everybody now was a little so! What is to come hangs over me like a baneful dream, as you will easily understand, and when I am often happy and merry, comes and damps it all!62

But God's will be done! and it is for our best, we must feel, though we can't feel it. I can't say how much we think of our little visit to you, God willing, next year. You will kindly let our good old Grandmother63 come there to see her dear Albert once again before she dies, wouldn't you? And you would get the Nemours to come? And you would persuade the dear Queen64 to come for a little while with Clémentine?

Now farewell! Believe me, always, your most devoted Niece,

Victoria R.

Footnote 60: The house of Earl Cowper.

Footnote 61: The Duke, who had formerly been M.P. for Bedfordshire, was inclined to go further in the direction of Reform than Lord John, yet he applauded the latter's attitude on the occasion of the speech which earned him the nickname of "Finality Jack."

Footnote 62: Alluding to the Ministerial defeat at the polls.

Footnote 63: The Dowager Duchess of Saxe-Gotha-Altenburg.

Footnote 64: Marie Amélie, Queen of the French.

LORD MELBOURNE AND THE GARTER

I went to Lord Melbourne this morning in his room as he had desired me. He said: "The Prince has been urging me to accept the Blue Riband before I quit office, and I wished to tell you that I am very anxious that this should not be pressed upon me by the Queen; it may be a foolish weakness on my part, but I wish to quit office without having any honour conferred upon me; the Queen's confidence towards me is sufficiently known without any public mark of this nature. I have always disregarded these honours, and there would be an inconsistency in my accepting this. I feel it to be much better for my reputation that I should not have it forced upon me. Mr Pitt never accepted an order, and only the Cinque Ports on being pressed to do so. Lord Grenville accepted a peerage, but never any other honour or advantage, and I wish to be permitted to retire in like manner. If I was a poor man, I should have no hesitation in receiving money in the shape of place or pension; I only don't wish for place, because I do not want it."

In the course of conversation Lord Melbourne said that he considered it very improbable that he should ever again form a part of any Administration.

He did not think that a violent course was at all to be apprehended from Lord John Russell; he said Lord John had been far more of a "finality" man than he had, and in the Cabinet had always been averse to violent change. He added, "I think you are in error in forming the opinion which you have of him."

Lord Melbourne thought the Queen very much disliked being talked at upon religion; she particularly disliked what Her Majesty termed a Sunday face, but yet that it was a subject far more thought of and reflected upon than was [thought to be?] the case.

A DREADED MOMENT

South Street, 15th August 1841.

... Lord Melbourne well knows the feeling which your Majesty describes. The expectation of an event which is dreaded and deprecated, and yet felt to be certain and imminent, presents itself continually to the mind and recurs at every moment, and particularly in moments of satisfaction and enjoyment. It is perhaps no consolation to be told that events of this nature are necessary and incidental to your Majesty's high situation, but Lord Melbourne anxiously hopes that the change, when it does take place, will not be found so grievous as your Majesty anticipates, and your Majesty may rely that Lord Melbourne will do everything in his power to reconcile it to your Majesty's feelings.

Windsor Castle, 17th August 1841.

Lord Melbourne is very glad to hear of the Princess's tooth.

Lord Melbourne is much obliged to your Majesty for informing him about the mourning.

He is quite well and will be ready when your Majesty sends.

A CARRIAGE ACCIDENT

Lord John Russell was staying at the Castle, and asked to-day for an audience of Her Majesty, and was closeted for a long time. The Prince asked Her Majesty what Lord John came for. The Queen said he came about several things, but particularly he wished to impress upon the Queen that Her Majesty should not allow Sir Robert Peel to propose any new Grants in Parliament, as they (the Whigs) could not well oppose it, and this being felt, the whole unpopularity would fall upon the Queen's person. An idea existed that the Tories were always jobbing with money, and the grant for the building the new stables at Windsor had shown how suspicious people were.

Lord John did not speak clearly out, but on consultation with Lord Melbourne the Queen thought Lord John must have alluded to Peel having spoken equivocally at the end of his speech relative to the Prince's annuity, and would now probably propose a further grant, and would say the time was now come in order to stand well with the Queen. The Queen replied that she would never allow such a thing to be proposed and that it would be a disgrace to owe any favour to that Party.

The only answer the Prince gave was that these views were very agreeable for him.

Windsor Castle, 24th August 1841.

... Our accident65 was not so very bad, and considering that it is the very first that had happened in the course of five summers, with so many carriages and horses, one cannot be surprised. I beg leave also to say that I can get out very quick. I am very thankful that you agree to the couriers. I am a little sorry that you have put poor Mamma off so late, as she is very much hurt at it, I fear, by what I hear, and accuses me of it. But that will, I trust, be forgiven. You don't say that you sympathise with me in my present heavy trial,66 the heaviest I have ever had to endure, and which will be a sad heartbreaking to me—but I know you do feel for me. I am quiet and prepared, but still I fell very sad, and God knows! very wretched at times, for myself and my country, that such a change must take place. But God in His mercy will support and guide me through all. Yet I feel that my constant headaches are caused by annoyance and vexation!

Adieu, dearest Uncle! God bless you! Ever your devoted Niece,

Victoria R.

Footnote 65: The Queen had driven to Virginia Water to see Prince Albert's beagles hunting, when owing to the hounds running between the horses' legs and frightening them, a pony phaeton and four containing Lord Erroll, Lady Ida Hay, and Miss Cavendish was upset. One of the postillions was (not dangerously) hurt.

Footnote 66: I.e, Lord Melbourne being succeeded by Sir Robert Peel as Prime Minister.

DEBATE ON THE ADDRESS

South Street, 24th August 1841.

Lord Melbourne presents his humble duty to your Majesty. We have just delivered the Speech in the House of Lords, and the debate will commence at five o'clock. We understand that the amendment is to be a repetition of the motion of want of confidence, which Sir Robert Peel made in the House of Commons before the dissolution, and nearly in the same terms. It is to be moved by Lord Ripon67 in the House of Lords, and by Mr. Stuart Wortley68 in the House of Commons. It is understood to be their intention to avoid, as much as possible, debate upon the Corn Laws, and upon the other topics in the Speech, and to place the question entirely upon the result of the General Election and the proof which that affords that the Ministry does not possess the confidence of the country. Lord Melbourne thinks that it will not be found easy to repress debate in the House of Commons, but would not be surprised if the course which it is intended to pursue should much shorten it in the House of Lords. Lord Melbourne will write again to your Majesty after the debate, and will certainly come down to-morrow, unless anything unexpected should occur to prevent him.

It will be necessary to receive the address of the Convocation in some manner or another. Lord Melbourne will write confidentially to the Archbishop69 to learn how it may be received in the quietest manner and with the least trouble. Lord Melbourne has little doubt that the Lords and Commons will send their addresses by the officers of the Household.

Lord Melbourne entreats your Majesty to pick up your spirits.

Footnote 67: The first Earl (1782-1859) who had, as Lord Goderich, been Premier in 1827-1828.

Footnote 68: J. Stuart Wortley (1801-1855), M.P. for the West Riding, afterwards the second Lord Wharncliffe.

Footnote 69: Dr Howley.

COBDEN'S SPEECH

Wilton Crescent, 26th August 1841.

Lord John Russell presents his humble duty to your Majesty, and has the honour to report that nothing remarkable occurred in the debate of yesterday, except a powerful speech from Mr

Cobden, a manufacturer.70

The debate will probably close this evening. No one of the Tory leaders, except Sir Robert Peel, appears disposed to speak.

Should the Address be voted to-night, and reported tomorrow, it may be presented to your Majesty by Lord Marcus Hill71 on Saturday.

But should the debate be continued over this night, the report of the Address can hardly take place till Monday. This, however, is not very likely.

Footnote 70: Cobden had just been elected for the first time for Stockport.

Footnote 71: Son of Lord Downshire, and M.P. for Evesham; afterwards (under a special remainder) the third Lord Sandys.

South Street, 27th August 1841.

Lord Melbourne presents his humble duty to your Majesty. Upon his arrival he found that there was no precedent of the House meeting again after an Address, without receiving an answer from the Crown. Lord Erroll therefore delivered the answer in the terms which had been submitted by Lord Melbourne to your Majesty, and it appeared to give satisfaction. The debate will probably terminate in the House of Commons to-night; at the same time it may not. If it does we must place our resignation in your Majesty's hands on Saturday, and it must be announced to the Houses of Parliament on Monday. Your Majesty will then do well not to delay sending for some other person beyond Tuesday. Lord Melbourne will write to your Majesty more fully upon all these subjects tomorrow, when he will know the result of the night's debate, and be able more surely to point out the course of events.

Lord Melbourne received the Eau-de-Cologne, and returns your Majesty many thanks for it.

Lord Melbourne understands that the Duke of Wellington is, in fact, very desirous of having the Foreign Seals,72 and that if your Majesty feels any preference for him in that department the slightest intimation of your Majesty's wish in that respect will fix him in his desire to have it.

Footnote 72: The Duke had been Foreign Secretary in 1835.

AN OVERWHELMING MAJORITY

Wilton Crescent, 28th August 1841.

Lord John Russell presents his humble duty to your Majesty, and has the honour to report that the Amendment to the Address was carried by 91, the numbers being—

The Tory party proposed that the House should meet this day, and the Speaker signified that he should take the Chair at twelve o'clock. The Address will be carried to Windsor by Lord Marcus Hill this evening if then ready.

Lord John Russell takes this opportunity of closing his Reports again, to express to your Majesty his deep sense of your Majesty's goodness towards him. It is his fervent prayer that your Majesty may enjoy a long and happy reign.

South Street, 28th August 1841.

... Your Majesty must, of course, consider us as having tendered our resignations immediately after the vote of last night, and your Majesty will probably think it right to request us to continue to hold our offices and transact the current business until our successors are appointed.

Lord Melbourne will have the honour of writing again to your Majesty in the course of the day.

THE RESIGNATION

Windsor Castle, 28th August 1841.

... Albert will not stay for the dinner, and I expect him back at about eleven to-night. He went at half-past eleven this morning. It is the first time that we have ever been separated for so long since our marriage, and I am quite melancholy about it.

You will forgive me if I mention it to you, but I understand that the Queen Dowager has been somewhat offended at your not taking leave of her when she came here, and at your not answering her, when she wrote to you. Perhaps you would write to her and soften and smoothen matters. She did not the least expect you to come to her. Believe me always, your most devoted Niece,

Victoria R.

South Street, 28th August 1841.

Lord Melbourne presents his humble duty to your Majesty, and begs to acknowledge gratefully the communication which he has just received from your Majesty. Lord Melbourne feels certain that your Majesty's sense and firmness will enable your Majesty to bear up under this which your Majesty names a severe trial. The kindness of your Majesty's expressions emboldens Lord Melbourne to say that he also feels deeply the pain of separation from a service, which has now for four years and more been no less his pleasure than his pride.

Lord Melbourne would have been anxious to have waited upon your Majesty to-day, but he feels that his presence is in some degree material at a meeting, at which not only the present situation of your Majesty's servants, but also their future conduct and prospects, will be considered.

Lord Melbourne is sure that your Majesty will at once perceive that it would not have a good appearance if he were to return to Windsor immediately after having announced his resignation to the House of Lords on Monday next.

It is right that there should be no appearance of delay or of unwillingness to carry into effect the wishes of both Houses of Parliament, and, therefore, your Majesty will forgive Lord Melbourne if he suggests that it would be well if your Majesty could make up your mind to appoint Sir R. Peel on Monday next, so that there might be as little delay as possible in the formation of a new Government. On all accounts, and particularly on account of the lateness of the Season, it is desirable that this should be done as speedily as possible.

29th August 1841.

Lord Melbourne presents his humble duty to your Majesty. He knows well what that feeling of working under the impression of trouble and annoyance is, but if the first gloom is brushed away, confidence and hope and spirits return, and things begin to appear more cheerful. Lord Melbourne is much obliged by your Majesty's enquiries. He slept well, but waked early, which he always does now, and which is a sure sign of anxiety of mind.

Lord Melbourne will be ready to attend your Majesty at any time.

Lord Melbourne is to take his farewell audience of the Queen to-morrow, and Her Majesty has appointed Sir Robert Peel to come down here at three o'clock to-morrow.

DELAY UNDESIRABLE

I went with Lord Melbourne from luncheon to his room. He seemed in tolerable spirits, though somewhat sad when he alluded to taking leave of the Queen. He said he was anxious that Her Majesty should lose no time in writing to appoint Sir Robert Peel to be here to-morrow, for though he was not afraid of Sir Robert taking affront, his Party would be too ready to construe any delay on the Queen's part into a slight. He said the Prince had been with him just before, and amongst other things had urged him to continue to him and to the Queen his advice and assistance, especially on measures affecting their private concerns and family concerns; he told Lord Melbourne it was on these points that he felt Lord Melbourne's advice had been peculiarly sound, and there was no reason why this should not be continued, and any communication might be made through me. Lord Melbourne said that the Prince had also entered upon the subject of the Baroness, and expressed the constant state of annoyance he was kept in by her interference. Lord Melbourne said to me: "It will be far more difficult to remove her after the change of Government than now, because if pressed to do it by a Tory Minister, the Queen's prejudice would be immediately aroused." I admitted this, but said that though the Prince felt that if he pressed the point against the Baroness remaining, he should be able to carry it, still his good feeling and affection for the Queen prevented him from pressing what he knew would be painful, and what could not be carried without an exciting scene; he must remain on his guard, and patiently abide the result. People were beginning much better to understand that lady's character, and time must surely work its own ends.

On my being sent for by the Prince, Lord Melbourne said, "I shall see you again before I take my leave." I was much affected by the earnestness with which this was said, and said I would certainly be with him before he saw the Queen tomorrow.

PARTING WITH LORD MELBOURNE

The Prince said that Her Majesty was cheerful and in good spirits, and the only part of the approaching scene which he dreaded was the farewell with Lord Melbourne. The Queen had, however, been much relieved by the Prince arranging for her hearing from Lord Melbourne whenever she wished it.

30th August 1841.

Lord Melbourne presents his humble duty to your Majesty, and thanks your Majesty much for the very clever and interesting etchings which your Majesty most kindly sent him yesterday evening. Lord Melbourne will ever treasure them as remembrances of your Majesty's kindness and regard, which he prizes beyond measure.

They will, as your Majesty says, certainly recall to recollection a melancholy day, but still Lord Melbourne hopes and trusts that with the divine blessing it will hereafter be looked back upon with less grief and bitterness of feeling, than it must be regarded at present.

THE PRINCE'S POSITION

Directly I got here this morning the Prince sent for me, and said he had been made somewhat uneasy by a conversation he had just had with the Queen. Her Majesty said that after the manner in which the Tories had treated the Prince (relative to annuity) he ought now to keep them at a distance. She said they would try to flatter him, and would all come to see him; this he should resist, and should refuse to see them, at all events for some time.

The Prince wished me to mention this to Lord Melbourne when I went to take leave of him, and to urge Lord Melbourne to set this right with the Queen by his advice before he parted with the Queen, reminding him that his view had always been that from this moment the Prince would take up a new position, and that the Queen, no longer having Lord Melbourne to resort to in case of need, must from this moment consult and advise with the Prince. That Lord Melbourne should urge the Queen to have no scruple in employing the Prince, and showing that unless a proper understanding existed from the first, he in attempting to do good would be easily misrepresented.

I found Lord Melbourne alone in his dressing-room and put this case before him. He said he had always thought that when he left the service of the Queen the Prince would of necessity be brought forward, and must render great assistance to the Queen; and the Queen's confidence in his judgment having so much increased, this consequence was the more natural. The Prince must, however, be very cautious at first, and in a little time he would fall into it. He must be very careful not to alarm the Queen, by Her Majesty for an instant supposing that the Prince was carrying on business with Peel without her cognisance.

If it were possible for any one to advise Peel, he would recommend that he should write fully to Her Majesty, and elementarily, as Her Majesty always liked to have full knowledge upon everything which was going on. He would advise the Queen to be cautious in giving a verbal decision, that she should not allow herself to be driven into a corner, and forced to decide where she felt her mind was not made up and required reflection.

Peel should be very careful that intelligence came first from him direct. King William was very particular upon this point, so was the Queen.

I asked Lord Melbourne if he had considered the future position of himself with the Queen, and also of Peel with the Queen. He said he owned he had not and would avoid entering into any discussion—he felt sure that he should be regarded with extreme jealousy, not so much by Peel as by the party. He would be looked upon as Lord Bute had been in his relation to George III.,—always suspected of secret intercourse and intrigue. He would make me the medium of any written communication.

With regard to Peel's position with the Queen, he thought that circumstances must make it. He thought the Queen must see him oftener than King William did him, as he thought the present state of things would require more frequent intercourse. The late King used to see him once a week after the Levée, seldom oftener; all the rest of the business was transacted by correspondence, but this mode, though it had its merits in some respect, very much impeded the public business.

The less personal objections the Queen took to any one the better, as any such expression is sure to come out and a personal enemy is made. It was also to be recollected that Peel was in a very different position now, backed by a large majority, to when the other overture was made.

He had the power now to extort what he pleased, and he fancied he saw the blank faces of the heads of the Party when Peel told them that he had agreed to the dismissal or resignation of only three of the Queen's ladies.

Lord Melbourne said the Queen was afraid she never could be at ease with Peel, because his manner was so embarrassed, and that conveyed embarrassment also to her, which it would be very difficult to get over.

The Queen took leave of Lord Melbourne to-day. Her Majesty was much affected, but soon recovered her calmness.

Peel had his first audience at half-past three o'clock.

MELBOURNE'S OPINION OF THE PRINCE

30th August 1841 (6 P.M.).

Lord Melbourne presents his humble duty to your Majesty. The announcement has been made in both Houses of Parliament. A few words were said by Lord Stanley73 in the House of Commons, and nothing in the House of Lords.

Lord Melbourne cannot satisfy himself without again stating to your Majesty in writing what he had the honour of saying to your Majesty respecting his Royal Highness the Prince. Lord Melbourne has formed the highest opinion of His Royal Highness's judgment, temper, and discretion, and he cannot but feel a great consolation and security in the reflection that he leaves your Majesty in a situation in which your Majesty has the inestimable advantage of such advice and assistance. Lord Melbourne feels certain that your Majesty cannot do better than have recourse to it, whenever it is needed, and rely upon it with confidence.

Lord Melbourne will be anxious to hear from your Majesty as to what has passed with Sir R. Peel. Your Majesty will, Lord Melbourne is sure, feel that the same general secrecy which your Majesty has always observed respecting public affairs is more particularly necessary at the present moment.

Lord Melbourne earnestly hopes that your Majesty is well and composed, and with the most anxious wishes for your Majesty's welfare and happiness, remains ever your Majesty's most devoted and attached Servant, and he trusts that he may add, without presumption, your Majesty's faithful and affectionate Friend.

Footnote 73: Who now became Colonial Secretary.

THE HOUSEHOLD

Your Majesty might say, if to your Majesty it seems good, that in consequence of the Addresses voted by both Houses of Parliament, your Majesty's servants had tendered their resignations, and that for the same reason your Majesty had accepted those resignations. That your Majesty's present servants possessed your Majesty's confidence, and that you only parted with them in deference to the opinion of Parliament.

That your Majesty naturally had recourse to Sir Robert Peel as possessing the confidence of the great Party which constitutes the majority of both Houses, and that you were prepared to empower him to form an Administration.

That your Majesty did not conceive that the giving him this commission of itself empowered him to advise the removal of the officers of your Majesty's Household; that you conceive that all that the Constitution required was that the Sovereign's Household should support the Sovereign's Ministers; but that you were prepared to place at his disposal, and to take his advice upon all the offices of the Household at present filled by members of either House of Parliament, with the exception of those whom your Majesty might think proper to name, i.e., Lord Byron74—and it should be understood that this exception was not to extend further than to him.

If Sir Robert Peel should wish that in case of Lord Byron's remaining it should be considered as a fresh appointment made by his advice, this wish might properly be acceded to.

The Ladies.—If any difficulty should arise it may be asked to be stated in writing, and reserved for consideration. But it is of great importance that Sir Robert Peel should return to London with full power to form an Administration. Such must be the final result, and the more readily and graciously it is acquiesced in the better.

Your Majesty must take care not to be driven to the wall, and to be put into a situation in which it is necessary to Aye or No. No positive objection should be taken either to men or measures.

It must be recollected that at the time of the negotiation in 1839 Lord Melbourne and Lord John Russell were still at the head of a majority in the House of Commons. This is not the case now.

Footnote 74: George Anson, seventh Lord Byron (1789-1868), cousin and successor of the poet.

THE NEW CABINET

Footnote 75: The Peel Ministry of 1841 was unique in containing three ex-Premiers: Sir Robert Peel himself, the Earl of Ripon, and the Duke of Wellington, who succeeded Lord Goderich as Premier in 1828. Ripon's career was a curious one; he was a singularly ineffective Prime Minister, and indeed did not, during the course of his Ministry (August 1827-January 1828), ever have to meet Parliament. He was disappointed at not being invited to join the Wellington Ministry, subsequently joined the Reform Ministry of Lord Grey, but followed Lord Stanley, Sir James Graham, and the Duke of Richmond out of it. In August 1841 he moved the vote of want of confidence in the Melbourne Ministry, and became President of the Board of Trade in Peel's Government. In 1846 it fell to him, when President of the Board of Control, to move the Corn Law Repeal Bill in the Lords.

The only later instance of an ex-Premier accepting a subordinate office was in the case of Lord John Russell, who, in 1852, took the Foreign Office under Aberdeen, subsequently vacating the office and sitting in the Cabinet without office. In June 1854, he became Lord President of the Council, and left the Ministry when it was menaced by Roebuck's motion. When Lord Palmerston formed a Ministry in 1855, Lord John, after an interval, became Colonial Secretary, again resigning in five months. Finally, in 1859, he went back to the Foreign Office, where he remained until he succeeded Palmerston as Premier in 1865.

The Government also contained three future Premiers, Aberdeen, Stanley, and Gladstone.

INTERVIEW WITH PEEL

Windsor Castle 30th August 1841.

... The first interview with Sir Robert Peel has gone off well, and only lasted twenty minutes; and he sends the Queen to-morrow, in writing, the proposed arrangements, and will only come down on Wednesday morning. He first wished to come to-morrow, but on the Queen's saying that he need not to do that, but might send it and only come down Wednesday, he thought the Queen might prefer having it to consider a little, which she said she certainly should, though she meant no want of confidence. The Queen, in the first instance, stated that she concluded he was prepared for her sending for him, and then stated exactly what Lord Melbourne wrote, viz., the resignation having taken place in consequence of the Addresses—the Queen's great regret at parting with her present Ministers—the confidence she had in them, and her only acceding in consequence of the Addresses in Parliament, and then that consequently she looked to him (Sir Robert Peel) as possessing the confidence of both Houses of Parliament to form an Administration. He made many protestations of his sorrow, at what must give pain to the Queen (as she said to him it did), but of course said he accepted the task. The Duke of Wellington's health too uncertain, and himself too prone to sleep coming over him—as Peel expressed it—to admit of his taking an office in which he would have much to do, but to be in the Cabinet, which the Queen expressed her wish he should. He named Lord De Grey76 as Lord Lieutenant of Ireland, and Lord Eliot77 as Secretary for Ireland, who, he said, were both moderate people. The Queen said she gaveHOUSEHOLD APPOINTMENTS up to him the officers of State and those of her Household who were in Parliament, and he then asked if Lord Liverpool would be agreeable as Lord Steward (the Queen said he would), and if she would object to Lord Jersey as Master of the Horse (she said she would not), as she believed he understood it perfectly. He said he was so anxious to do everything which could be agreeable to the Queen, that he wished her to name whom she should like as Lord Chamberlain; she said he might suggest some one, but as he would not, and pressed the Queen to name whoever she pleased, she said she should like the Duke of Rutland, and he said he would certainly name it to him. The Queen said that Lord Melbourne had always been very particular to name no one who might be disagreeable to her in the Household, and Sir R. Peel said he felt this, and should be most anxious to do what could be agreeable to me and for my comfort, and that he would even sacrifice any advantage to this. The Queen mentioned the three Ladies' resignation, and her wish not to fill up the three Ladies' places immediately. She mentioned Lady Byron,78 to which he agreed immediately, and then said, as I had alluded to those communications, he hoped that he had been understood respecting the other appointments (meaning the Ladies), that provided I chose some who had a leaning towards the politics of the Administration, I might take any I liked, and that he quite understood that I should notify it to them. The Queen said this was her rule, and that she wished to choose moderate people who should not have scruples to resign in case another Administration should come in, as changing was disagreeable to her. Here it ended, and so far well. He was very anxious the Queen should understand how anxious he was to do everything which was agreeable to the Queen. The Queen wishes to know if Lord Melbourne thinks she should name the Duchess of Buccleuch Mistress of the Robes, on Wednesday, and if she shall ask Sir Robert to sound the Duchess, or some one else, and then write to appoint her? She thinks of proposing Lady de la Warr and Lady

Abercorn by and by as the two Ladies, but these she will sound herself through other people, or Lady Canning, or Lady Rosslyn, in case these others should not take it. She should say she meant to sound those, and no more. What the Queen felt when she parted from her dear, THE QUEEN'S DISTRESS kind friend, Lord Melbourne, is better imagined than described; she was dreadfully affected for some time after, but is calm now. It is very, very sad; and she cannot quite believe it yet. The Prince felt it very, very much too, and really the Queen cannot say how kind and affectionate he is to her, and how anxious to do everything to lighten this heavy trial; he was quite affected at this sad parting. We do, and shall, miss you so dreadfully; Lord Melbourne will easily understand what a change it is, after these four years when she had the happiness of having Lord Melbourne always about her. But it will not be so long till we meet again. Happier and brighter times will come again. We anxiously hope Lord Melbourne is well, and got up well and safe. The Queen trusts he will take care of his valuable health, now more than ever.

Footnote 76: Thomas, Earl de Grey (1781-1859); he was the elder brother of Lord Ripon, who had been previously known as Mr Robinson and Viscount Goderich, and whose son, besides inheriting his father's and uncle's honours, was created Marquis of Ripon.

Footnote 77: Afterwards third Earl of St Germans.

Footnote 78: Lady Byron had been Miss Elizabeth Chandos-Pole.

I was sent up to Town to-day to see Lord Melbourne and Sir Robert Peel. I found Lord Melbourne as usual up in his bedroom. He had received the account of Her Majesty's first interview with Peel, which he thought very satisfactory. Sir Robert very much regretted that he should have been the instrument of obliging Her Majesty to change her Government. The Queen had said to Sir Robert that though she did not conceive the Minister could demand any of the Household appointments, still it was Her Majesty's intention to give up to him the great offices of State, and all other places in the Household filled by people in Parliament. He was to send his proposed list for offices the next day and be at Windsor the morning after that. Lord Melbourne had written to the Queen the night before, stating his opinion of the Prince—that he had great discretion, temper, and judgment, and that he considered him to be well worthy of Her Majesty's confidence, and that now was the time for Her Majesty to feel comfort and assistance from giving him her fullest confidence. He had just received the Queen's answer to this, saying what "pleasure it had given the Queen to receive his letter with this expression of his opinion of her beloved husband, and that what he said could not fail to increase the confidence which she already felt in him. He was indeed a great comfort to her in this trying moment; at times she was very low indeed though she strove to bear up. It would always be a satisfaction to her to feel secure of Lord Melbourne's faithful and affectionate friendship to her and the Prince. She hoped after a time to see him here again, and it would always be a pleasure to her to hear from him frequently."

From South Street I went to Sir Robert Peel's. I told him I came to speak to him about Lord Exeter, whom the Prince proposed to make the head of his Household, should it not interfere with any of Sir Robert's arrangements for the Queen. Sir Robert said he was so good a man and one that he felt sure the Prince would like, and he therefore thought he had better propose the situation to him at once.

MELBOURNE'S OFFICIAL FAREWELL

South Street, 31st August 1841.

Lord Melbourne had the pleasure of receiving last night both your Majesty's letters, the one dated four o'clock, and written immediately after your Majesty's interview with Sir R. Peel, the other dated half-past nine. Lord Melbourne thanks your Majesty much for them both, and for the expressions of kindness contained in them. Lord Melbourne will ever consider the time during which your Majesty is good enough to think that he has been of service to your Majesty the proudest as well as the happiest part of his life.

Lord Melbourne has read with great care your Majesty's very clear and full account of what passed. It appears to Lord Melbourne that nothing could be better. Sir Robert Peel seems to have been anxious to act with the utmost respect and consideration for your Majesty, and your Majesty most properly and wisely met him half-way. In the spirit in which the negotiation has been commenced I see the prospect of a termination of it, which will be not so unsatisfactory to your Majesty as your Majesty anticipated, and not, Lord Melbourne trusts, disadvantageous to the country....

Lord Melbourne concludes with the most anxious wishes for your Majesty's happiness and with expressing a great admiration of the firmness, prudence, and good sense with which your Majesty has conducted yourself.

Lord Melbourne begs to be remembered to His Royal Highness most respectfully, most affectionately.

31st August 1841.

Lord Melbourne presents his humble duty to your Majesty, and has just received your Majesty's letter. Lord Melbourne rejoices much to learn that your Majesty feels more composed and that you are well. Recollect how precious is your Majesty's health, and how much health depends upon tranquillity of mind....

Lord Melbourne will either write to Sir Francis Chantrey79 to-morrow morning, or call upon him and settle without further delay about the Bust. There is no end of subscriptions to Monuments, but perhaps your Majesty will do well to subscribe to Sir David Wilkie's.80

Your Majesty is very good about the blue Ribband, but Lord Melbourne is certain that upon the whole, it is better for his own position and character that he should not have it.

Footnote 79: Sir Francis Chantrey, the sculptor, born in 1781, died on 25th November 1841.

Footnote 80: Sir David Wilkie, Painter-in-Ordinary to the Queen, had died on 1st June, aged fifty-six.

PEEL'S RECEPTION

Grosvenor Crescent, 31st August 1841.

My dear Melbourne,—You may like to know that Peel was perfectly satisfied with his reception yesterday, and does full justice to the Queen's declaration of her regret at parting with her Ministers, which he said it was quite natural she should feel, and quite right she should express. This I know from undoubted authority, and from a person who came to enquire of me whether I could tell what impression Peel had produced upon the Queen, which of course I could not.

He assured the Queen that he had had no communication with his friends, and was not prepared to submit an Administration for her approval, but he is to see her again to-morrow morning.

The only appointment yet settled is De Grey to Ireland; he was very unwilling, but Peel insisted. Yours sincerely,

Clarendon.

Footnote 81: The retiring Lord Privy Seal.

Footnote 82: Letter forwarded by Lord Melbourne to the Queen.

FAREWELL AUDIENCES

Carlton Terrace, 31st August 1841.

... Viscount Palmerston begs to be allowed to tender to your Majesty the grateful thanks of himself and of Viscountess Palmerston for your Majesty's gracious expressions towards them. Viscount Palmerston sees with deep regret the termination of those duties in your Majesty's service, in the course of which he has had the honour of experiencing from your Majesty so much condescending personal kindness, and such flattering official confidence; and it affords him the highest gratification to have obtained your Majesty's approbation.

South Street, 2nd September 1841.

Lord Melbourne presents his humble duty to your Majesty. He received your Majesty's letter yesterday evening, and was very glad to learn from it that your Majesty was not ill satisfied with Sir Robert Peel, and that the arrangements were going on smoothly, which it is highly desirable that they should. Your Majesty should desire Sir Robert Peel to give notice to all those who have insignia of office, such as Seals, Wands, to give up, to attend at Claremont on Friday; but of course he will do this of himself. Your Majesty will have much to go through upon that day and much that is painful. Your Majesty should spare yourself and be spared as much as possible. It will not be necessary for Lord Melbourne to go down. He may be considered as having resigned at the Audience which he had of your Majesty at Windsor, and Lord Melbourne has ventured to tell Lord Lansdowne that he thinks he need not do so either, and that your Majesty will excuse his attendance. Lord Melbourne need say nothing about the Secretaries of State, with all of whom your Majesty is so well acquainted; but perhaps your Majesty will not omit to thank Mr Baring83 cordially for his services. He is a thoroughly honest man and an able public servant. If your Majesty could say to the Lord Chancellor,84 "that you part with him with much sorrow; that you are sensible that much of the strength of the late Administration was derived from the manner in which he discharged the duties of his office, and that you consider his retirement a great and serious loss to the country," it would certainly be no more than he deserves.

It is thought by some who know him here that the Duke of Rutland will be so extremely pleased with the offer being made, and that by your Majesty yourself, that he will accept it; but he is a year older than Lord Melbourne, and therefore hardly fit for any very active duty....

The appointment of Colonel Arbuthnot will of course be very agreeable to the Duke of

Wellington. The Arbuthnots are quiet, demure people before others; but they are not without depth of purpose, and they are very bitter at bottom.

Your Majesty will not forget the two Knights for Mr de la Beche85 and Major Monro.

Lord Melbourne begins to hope that this affair will be got through more satisfactorily and with less annoyance than your Majesty anticipated. As long as your Majesty is desirous of receiving his communications, he will be always most careful to give your Majesty his impartial opinion and the best advice which he has to offer. His most fervent prayer will always be for your Majesty's welfare and happiness.

Footnote 83: The retiring Chancellor of the Exchequer.

Footnote 84: Lord Cottenham.

Footnote 85: Sir Henry T. de la Beche, an eminent geologist.

MELBOURNE'S LAST OFFICIAL LETTER

South Street, 2nd September 1841.

....Lord Melbourne hopes and trusts that when to-morrow is over your Majesty will recover from that depression of spirits under which your Majesty now labours. Lord Melbourne never doubted that it would be so, but is glad to learn from your Majesty the support and consolation which your Majesty finds in the advice and affection of the Prince.

This is the last letter which Lord Melbourne will send in a box. He will to-morrow morning return his keys to the Foreign Office, and after that your Majesty will be good enough to send the letters, with which you may honour Lord Melbourne, through Mr Anson.

Lord Melbourne most anxiously wishes your Majesty every blessing.

COUNCIL AT CLAREMONT

South Street, 3rd September 1841.

Lord Melbourne earnestly hopes that your Majesty is well after this trying day.86 Lord Melbourne has thought and felt for your Majesty all this morning. But now that the matter is settled it will be necessary that your Majesty should take a calm and composed view of the whole situation, which Lord Melbourne trusts that your Majesty will find by no means unsatisfactory.

And first with respect to public affairs. In the concerns of a great nation like this there will always be some difficulties and entanglements, but upon the whole the present state is good and the prospect is good for the future. There is no reason to expect that Sir Robert Peel will either be desirous or be able to take a very different course from that which has been taken by your Majesty's late servants, and some difficulties will certainly be removed, and some obstacles smoothed, by the change which has lately taken place.

With respect to the effect which will be produced upon the comfort of your Majesty's private life, it would be idle in Lord Melbourne, after what your Majesty has said, to doubt of the manner in which your Majesty will feel the change, which must take place in your Majesty, to long accustomed habits and relations. But your Majesty may rest assured of Lord Melbourne's devoted and disinterested attachment to your Majesty, and that he will devote himself to giving to your Majesty such information and advice as may be serviceable to your Majesty with the sole view of promoting your Majesty's public interests and private happiness.

Lord Melbourne hopes, and indeed ventures to expect, that your Majesty, upon reflection and consideration of the real state of circumstances, will recover your spirits, and Lord Melbourne has himself great satisfaction in thinking upon the consideration of the advice which he has given, that it has not tended to impair your Majesty's influence and authority, but, on the contrary, to secure to your Majesty the affection, attachment, approbation, and support of all parties.

In the course of this correspondence Lord Melbourne has thought it his duty to your Majesty to express himself with great freedom upon the characters of many individuals, whose names have come under consideration, but Lord Melbourne thinks it right to say that he may have spoken upon insufficient grounds, that he may have been mistaken, and that the persons in question may turn out to be far better than he has been induced to represent them.

Footnote 86: A Council had been held at Claremont for the outgoing Ministers to give up their Seals of Office, which were bestowed upon Sir Robert Peel and the incoming Cabinet.

MELBOURNE ON THE NEW MINISTRY

South Street, 4th September 1841.

Lord Melbourne presents his humble duty to your Majesty. He was most happy to hear yesterday the best account of everything that had taken place at Claremont. Everybody praised, in the highest manner, the dignity, propriety, and kindness of your Majesty's deportment, and if it can be done without anything of deceit or dissimulation, it is well to take advantage of the powers and qualities which have been given, and which are so well calculated to gain a fair and powerful influence over the minds and feelings of others. Your Majesty may depend upon it, that the impression made upon the minds of all who were present yesterday, is most favourable. Of course, with persons in new and rather awkward situations, some of whom had never been in high office before, all of whom had not been so now for some years, there was a good deal of embarrassment and mistakes. Forms which are only gone through at long intervals of time, and not every day, are necessarily forgotten, and when they are required nobody knows them. But Lord Melbourne cannot really think that they looked cross; most probably they did look shy and embarrassed. Strange faces are apt to give the idea of ill humour....

Lord Melbourne anxiously hopes that your Majesty is well and happy to-day.

South Street, 5th September 1841.

Lord Melbourne presents his humble duty to your Majesty. Your Majesty may depend upon it, that if Lord Melbourne hears anything respecting your Majesty, which it appears to him to be important or advantageous, that your Majesty should know, Lord Melbourne will not fail to convey it to your Majesty.

Lord Melbourne encloses the exact names of the two gentlemen to whom Knighthood has been promised by your Majesty....

Your Majesty is very good, very good indeed, to think of doing what your Majesty mentions for Fanny; but Lord Melbourne fears that it would hardly suit with their present situation, or with the comfort of their domestic life. But Lord Melbourne mentioned the matter yesterday to his sister, and he encloses the letter which she has written to him this morning, after reflecting upon the subject. By that letter your Majesty will perceive that Jocelyn is not so much in debt, as Lord Melbourne's letter had led your Majesty to suppose....

Lord B—— is a very old friend of Lord Melbourne's. They were at Eton together, and intimate there. He is a gentlemanly man and a good man, but not very agreeable. Few of the P——s are, and very bitter in politics; but still Lord Melbourne is glad, for old acquaintance' sake, that your Majesty has taken him. Lord Melbourne must again repeat that when he writes with so much freedom about individual characters, it is only to put your Majesty in possession of what he knows respecting them, and not with a view of inducing your Majesty to object to their being appointed....

Might not Fanny have the Bedchamber Woman's place? It would be a help to her, and would not take her away from home. This only strikes Lord Melbourne as he is writing.

MELBOURNE ON PEEL

6th September 1841.

Lord Melbourne wrote the above yesterday, but had no opportunity of sending it, as there was no post. Lord Melbourne has since seen Lady Palmerston, and finds that his last suggestion about Fanny will not do.

Lord Melbourne encloses Lady Palmerston's two notes upon the subject, which will explain to your Majesty what she wishes. But if Jocelyn is himself to get a place, this will be a better arrangement, and puts an end to all the others.

What Lady Palmerston says about Sir R. Peel is very unjust. There is no shabbiness whatever in his not coming to a decision upon the factory question.87

Footnote 87: Lady Palmerston (no doubt in sympathy with Lord Ashley) expected some factory legislation to be announced.

Claremont, 6th September 1841.

My dearest Lady Gainsborough,—I had the pleasure of receiving your two kind letters of the 24th and 25th ult. yesterday, and thank you much for them. I am so happy that you are really better....

I hoped that you would be pleased at what you thank me for; you see I did not forget what you told me once at Windsor when we were out driving, and I assure you that Lord Melbourne was very anxious to do it. Last week was a most painful, trying one to me, and this separation from my truly excellent and kind friend Lord Melbourne, most distressing. You will understand what a change it must be to me. I am, however, so happy in my home, and have such a perfect angel in the Prince, who has been such a comfort to me, that one must be thankful and grateful for these blessings, and take these hard trials as lessons sent from above, for our best.

Our little girl makes great progress, and suffers comparatively but very little from her teething. We came here to be quiet for a few days, as this place is so very private.

The Baroness will write to Lord Gainsborough to say that I wish much you would take Lady Lyttelton's waiting, which begins on 23rd of November.

The Prince begs to be kindly named to you, and I to Fanny and your brother, and pray believe me always, dearest Lady Gainsborough, ever yours most affectionately,

Victoria R.

Pray thank Fanny for her kind letter.

Footnote 88: Formerly, as Lady Barham, a Lady of the Bedchamber. Lord Barham had been created Earl of Gainsborough in the course of the year (1841).

LORD CHAMBERLAIN'S DEPARTMENT

7th September 1841.

The Queen wishes that Sir Robert Peel would mention to Lord De la Warr89 that he should be very particular in always naming to the Queen any appointment he wishes to make in his department, and always to take her pleasure upon an appointment before he settles on them; this is a point upon which the Queen has always laid great stress. This applies in great measure to the appointment of Physicians and Chaplains, which used to be very badly managed formerly, and who were appointed in a very careless manner; but since the Queen's accession the Physicians and Chaplains have been appointed only for merit and abilities, by the Queen herself, which the Queen is certain Sir Robert Peel will at once see is a far better way, and one which must be of use in every way. Sir Robert Peel may also tell Lord De la Warr that it is unnecessary for him to appear in uniform, as the Queen always dispenses with this in the country. This applies also to the Ministers, who the Queen does not expect or wish should appear in uniform at Councils which are held in the country. The Queen concludes that it will be necessary to hold a Council some time next week to swear in some of the new Officers who are not Privy Councillors; but Sir Robert Peel will be able to tell the Queen when he thinks this will be necessary.

Footnote 89: See ante, p. .

DIPLOMATIC APPOINTMENTS

8th September 1841.

There is a subject which the Queen wishes to mention to Sir Robert Peel, as she is at present so little acquainted with Lord Aberdeen; the Queen is very desirous that, if it were possible, Sir Hamilton Seymour should not be removed from Brussels. The Queen believes that his political views are not violent either way, and she knows that he is peculiarly agreeable to her Uncle, which has, therefore, prompted her to write this to Sir Robert Peel. The Queen seizes the same opportunity to say that she is also very anxious that a moderate and conciliatory person should be sent to Lisbon, as it is of great importance there.

THE FRENCH AMBASSADOR

Claremont, 8th September 1841.

My dearest Uncle,—I begin my letter to-day, for fear I should have no time to write to-morrow. Your kind letter gave me great pleasure, and I must own your silence on all that was going on distressed me very much! It has been indeed a sad time for me, and I am still bewildered, and can't believe that my excellent Lord Melbourne is no longer my Minister, but he will be, as you say, and has already proved himself, very useful and valuable as my friend out of office. He writes to me often, and I write to him, and he gives really the fairest and most impartial advice possible. But after seeing him for four years, with very few exceptions—daily—

you may imagine that I must feel the change; and the longer the time gets since we parted, the more I feel it. Eleven days was the longest I ever was without seeing him, and this time will be elapsed on Saturday, so you may imagine what the change must be. I cannot say what a comfort and support my beloved Angel is to me, and how well and how kindly and properly he behaves. I cannot resist copying for you what Lord Melbourne wrote to me about Albert, the evening after we parted; he has already praised him greatly to me, before he took leave of me. It is as follows:

"Lord Melbourne cannot satisfy himself without again stating to your Majesty in writing what he had the honour of saying to your Majesty respecting H.R.H. the Prince. Lord Melbourne has formed the highest opinion of H.R.H.'s judgment, temper, and discretion, and he cannot but feel a great consolation and security in the reflection that he leaves your Majesty in a situation in which your Majesty has the inestimable advantage of such advice and assistance. Lord Melbourne feels certain that your Majesty cannot do better than have recourse to it, whenever it is needed, and rely upon it with confidence."

This naturally gave me great pleasure, and made me very proud, as it comes from a person who is no flatterer, and would not have said it if he did not think so, or feel so. The new Cabinet you have by this time seen in the papers.

The Household (of which I send you a list) is well constituted—for Tories.

Lord Aberdeen has written to me to say Bourqueney has announced Ste Aulaire90 as Ambassador. This is very well, but let me beg you, for decency's sake, to stop his coming immediately; if even not meant to, it would have the effect of their sending an ambassador the moment the Government changed, which would be too marked, and most offensive personally to me. Indeed Guizot behaved very badly about refusing to sign the Slave Trade Treaty91 which they had so long ago settled to do; it is unwise and foolish to irritate the late Government who may so easily come in again; for Palmerston will not forgive nor forget offences, and then France would be worse off than before, with England. I therefore beg you to stop Ste Aulaire for a little while, else I shall feel it a great personal offence.

9th.—I have had a letter from Lord Melbourne to-day, who is much gratified by yours to him.... Now adieu! Believe me, always, your devoted Niece,

Victoria R.

Footnote 90: See post, p. .

Footnote 91: A treaty on the subject was signed in London, on 20th December, between Great Britain, France, Austria, Prussia, and Russia.

QUEEN ADELAIDE

Sudbury Hall, 8th September 1841.

My dearest Niece,—I have not ventured to disturb you with a letter since we parted, knowing how fully your time was employed with business of importance. I cannot any longer now refrain to enquire after you, after all you have gone through lately, and I must congratulate you with all my heart on having so well completed your difficult task.

There is but one voice of praise, I hear, of your perfect composure and beautiful conduct during the trying scenes of last week. It has gratified me more than I can express, for I had fully expected it of you, and it has made me very happy to find that it has been generally remarked and has given so much satisfaction. Everybody feels deeply for you, and the devotion and zeal in your service is redoubled by the interest your trying position has evoked. May our Heavenly Father support and guide you always as hitherto, is my constant prayer!

I hope that the selection of your Government is to your own satisfaction, and though the change must have been trying to you, I trust that you will have perfect confidence in the able men who form your Council. Our beloved late King's anxious wishes to see Wellington and Peel again at the head of the Administration is now fulfilled. His blessing rests upon you.

Excuse my having touched upon this subject, but I could not keep silent whilst the heart is so full of earnest good wishes for your and the country's prosperity.

I hope that an article of the newspapers, of the indisposition of your darling child, is not true, and that she is quite well. God bless and protect her!...

I am much amused with reading your Life by Miss Strickland,92 which, though full of errors, is earnest on the whole, and very interesting to me. However, I wish she would correct the gross errors which otherwise will go down to posterity. She ought to have taken first better information before she published her work....

With my affectionate love to dear Prince Albert, believe me ever, my dearest Niece, your most devoted and affectionate Aunt,

Adelaide.

Footnote 92: Miss Agnes Strickland (1808-1874), who also edited Letters of Mary Queen of Scots, etc.

The Ministerial arrangements are now nearly completed. Writs for new elections moved last night.

Wrote to Sir Robert, telling him the Queen ought to have heard from him respecting the adjournment of the House of Commons, instead of seeing it first in the public papers. Told him also of its being the Queen's wish that a short report of the debates in each House should always be sent to Her Majesty, from him in the Commons and from the Duke of Wellington in the Lords.

The Queen had a letter to-day from the Queen Dowager, which was kindly meant, but which made Her Majesty rather angry, complimenting Her Majesty on the good grace with which she had changed her Government, and saying that the late King's blessing rested upon her for calling the Duke of Wellington and Peel to her Councils, etc....

THE QUEEN CRITICISES APPOINTMENTS

9th September 1841.

The Queen takes this opportunity of writing to Sir Robert Peel confidentially about another person: this is about Lord ——. The Queen is strongly of opinion that Lord —— should not be employed in any post of importance, as his being so would, in her opinion, be detrimental to the interests of the country. The Queen wishes Sir Robert to state this to Lord Aberdeen as her opinion. The Queen is certain that Sir Robert will take care that it should not be known generally that this is her opinion, for she is always most anxious to avoid anything that might appear personal towards anybody. The Queen cannot refrain from saying that she cannot quite approve of Sir Charles Bagot's appointment,93 as from what she has heard of his qualities she does not think that they are of a character quite to suit in the arduous and difficult position in which he will be placed. At the same time the Queen does not mean to object to his appointment (for she has already formally approved of it), but she feels it her duty to state frankly and at all times her opinion, as she begs Sir Robert also to do unreservedly to her. For the future, it appears to the Queen that it would be best in all appointments of such importance that before a direct communication was entered into with the individual intended to be proposed, that the Queen should be informed of it, so that she might talk to her Ministers fully about it; not because it is likely that she would object to the appointment, but merely that she might have time to be acquainted with the qualities and abilities of the person. The Queen has stated this thus freely to Sir Robert as she feels certain that he will understand and appreciate the motives which prompt her to do so. The Queen would wish the Council to be at two on Tuesday, and she begs Sir Robert would inform her which of the Ministers besides him will attend.

Footnote 93: As Governor-General of Canada.

9th September 1841.

... Sir Robert Peel will have the honour of writing to your Majesty to-morrow on the subjects adverted to in the note which he has just received from your Majesty.

He begs for the present to assure your Majesty that he shall consider every communication which your Majesty may be pleased to address to him in reference to the personal merits or disqualifications of individuals as of a most confidential character.

PEEL APOLOGISES

Whitehall, 10th September 1841.

My dear Sir,—I am sorry if I have failed to make any communication to Her Majesty respecting public matters, which Her Majesty has been in the habit of receiving, or which she would have wished to receive.

Having been occupied in the execution of the important trust committed to me not less than sixteen or eighteen hours of the twenty-four for several days past, it may be that I have made some omissions in this respect, which under other circumstances I might have avoided. I did not think Her Majesty would wish to be informed of the issue of writs, necessarily following the appointments to certain offices, of all which Her Majesty had approved. I certainly ought to have written to Her Majesty previously to the adjournment of the House of Commons until Thursday the 16th of September. It was an inadvertent omission on my part, amid the mass of business which I have had to transact, and I have little doubt that if I had been in Parliament I should have avoided it.

The circumstances of my having vacated my seat, and of having thus been compelled to leave to others the duty of proposing the adjournment of the House, was one cause of my inadvertence.

Both the Duke of Wellington and I fully intended to make a report to Her Majesty after the close of the Parliamentary business of each day, and will do so without fail on the reassembling of Parliament.

I am, my dear Sir, very faithfully yours,

Robert Peel.

DIPLOMATIC APPOINTMENTS

South Street, 10th September 1841.

... Lord Melbourne has no doubt that Sir Robert Peel has the most anxious wish to do everything that can be agreeable to your Majesty.

Your Majesty should not omit to speak fully and seriously to him upon the disposal of great appointments. Their Diplomatic Corps, from which Ambassadors and Governors are generally taken, is the weakest part of their establishment. They have amongst them men of moderate abilities and of doubtful integrity, who yet have held high offices and have strong claims upon them. The public service may suffer most essentially by the employment of such men. Lord Melbourne would say to Peel that "affairs depend more upon the hands to which they are entrusted than upon any other cause, and that you hope he will well consider those whose appointment to high and important situations he sanctions, and that he will not suffer claims of connection or of support to overbalance a due regard for your Majesty's service and the welfare of the country." Such an expression of your Majesty's opinion may possibly be a support to Sir Robert Peel against pretensions which he would be otherwise unable to resist; but this is entirely submitted to your Majesty's judgment, seeing that your Majesty, from an exact knowledge of all that is passing, must be able to form a much more correct opinion of the propriety and discretion of any step than Lord Melbourne can do....

Lord Melbourne has a letter from Lord John Russell, rather eager for active opposition; but Lord Melbourne will write to your Majesty more fully upon these subjects from Woburn.

CANADA

Woburn Abbey, 12th September 1841.

Lord Melbourne has this morning received your Majesty's letter of yesterday. Lord Melbourne entirely agrees with your Majesty about appointments. He knows, as your Majesty does from experience, that with all the claims which there are to satisfy, with all the prejudices which are to be encountered, and with all the interests which require to be reconciled, it is impossible to select the best men, or even always those properly qualified. He is the last man who would wish that a Minister who has the whole machine of the Government before him should be necessarily thwarted or interfered with in the selection of those whom he may be desirous to employ. Lord Melbourne would therefore by no means advise your Majesty to throw difficulty in the way of the diplomatic arrangements which may be proposed, unless there should be in them anything manifestly and glaringly bad. The nomination of Lord —— would have been so, but otherwise it cannot very greatly signify who is the Ambassador at Vienna, or even at Petersburg or Paris. Stuart de Rothesay94 and Strangford95 are not good men, either of them, but it will be difficult for Lord Aberdeen to neglect their claims altogether. Heytesbury96 is an able man, the best they have. Sir Robert Gordon97 is an honest man, slow but not illiberal. It would be well if your Majesty showed Lord Aberdeen that you know these men, and have an opinion upon the subject of them.

Canada is another matter. It is a most difficult and most hazardous task. There has been recent rebellion in the country. A new Constitution has lately been imposed upon it by Parliament. The two Provinces have been united, and the united Province is bordered by a most hostile and uncontrollable community, the United States of North America. To govern such a country at such a moment requires a man of great abilities, a man experienced and practical in the management of popular assemblies.... It is possible that matters may go smoothly there, and that if difficulties do arise Sir C. Bagot may prove more equal to them than from his general knowledge of his character Lord Melbourne would judge him to be....

Upon the subject of diplomatic appointments Lord Melbourne has forgotten to make one general observation which he thinks of importance. Upon a change of Government a very great and sudden change of all or many of the Ministers at Foreign Courts is an evil and to be avoided, inasmuch as it induces an idea of a general change of policy, and disturbs everything that has been settled. George III. always set his face against and discouraged such numerous removals as tending to shake confidence abroad in the Government of England generally and to give it a character of uncertainty and instability. It would be well if your Majesty could make this remark to Lord Aberdeen.

Footnote 94: The new Ambassador to St Petersburg.

Footnote 95: Percy, sixth Viscount Strangford (1780-1855), formerly Ambassador to Constantinople, whom Byron described as

"Hibernian Strangford, with thine eyes of blue, And boasted locks of red or auburn hue."

Footnote 96: See post, p. .

Footnote 97: The new Ambassador to Vienna.

LORD ELLENBOROUGH'S REPORT INDIA AND AFGHANISTAN

Lord Ellenborough presents his most humble duty to your Majesty, and humbly acquaints your Majesty that having, on the morning after the Council held at Claremont on the third of this month, requested the clerks of the India Board to put him in possession of the latest information with respect to the Political, Military, and Financial affairs of India, he ascertained that on the 4th of June instructions had been addressed to the Governor-General of India in Council in the following terms:—"We direct that unless circumstances now unknown to us should induce you to adopt a different course, an adequate force be advanced upon Herat, and that that city and its dependencies may be occupied by our troops, and dispositions made for annexing them to the kingdom of Cabul."99

The last letters from Calcutta, dated the 9th of July, did not intimate any intention on the part of the Governor-General in Council of directing any hostile movement against Herat, and the Governor-General himself having always evinced much reluctance to extend the operations of the army to that city, it seemed almost probable that the execution of the orders of the 4th of June would have been suspended until further communication could be had with the Home Authorities.

Nevertheless, in a matter of so much moment it did not appear to be prudent to leave anything to probability, and at Lord Ellenborough's instance your Majesty's confidential servants came to the conclusion that no time should be lost in addressing to the Governor-General in Council a letter in the following terms—such letter being sent, as your Majesty must be aware, not directly by the Commissioners for the Affairs of India, but, as the Act of Parliament prescribes in affairs requiring secrecy, by their direction through and in the name of the Secret Committee of the Court of Directors:—

"From the Secret Committee of the Court of Directors of the East India Company to the Governor-General of India in Council.

"Her Majesty having been pleased to form a new Administration, we think it expedient that no step should be taken with respect to Herat which would have the effect of compelling the prosecution of a specific line of Policy in the countries beyond the Indus, until the new Ministers shall have had time to take the subject into their deliberate consideration, and to communicate to us their opinions thereupon.

"We therefore direct that, unless you should have already taken measures in pursuance of our Instructions of the 4th of June 1841—which commit the honour of your Government to the prosecution of the line of Policy which we thereby ordered you to adopt, or which could not be arrested without prejudice to the Public interests, or danger to the troops employed—you will consider those Instructions to be suspended.

"We shall not fail to communicate to you at an early period our fixed decision upon this subject."

It was not possible to bring this subject before your Majesty's confidential servants before the afternoon of Saturday the 4th. The mail for India, which should have been despatched on the 1st, had been detained till Monday the 6th by the direction of your Majesty's late Ministers, in order to enable your Majesty's present servants to transmit to India and China any orders which it might seem to them to be expedient to issue forthwith. Further delay would have been productive of much mercantile inconvenience, and in India probably of much alarm. In this emergency your Majesty's Ministers thought that your Majesty would be graciously pleased to approve of their exercising at once the power of directing the immediate transmission to India of these Instructions.

Your Majesty must have had frequently before you strong proofs of the deep interest taken by Russia in the affairs of Herat, and your Majesty cannot but be sensible of the difficulty of maintaining in Europe that good understanding with Russia which has such an important bearing upon the general peace, if serious differences should exist between your Majesty and that Power with respect to the States of Central Asia.

But even if the annexation of Herat to the kingdom of Cabul were not to have the effect of endangering the continuance of the good understanding between your Majesty and Russia, still your Majesty will not have failed to observe that the further advance of your Majesty's forces 360 miles into the interior of Central Asia for the purpose of effecting that annexation, could not but render more difficult of accomplishment the original intention of your Majesty, publicly announced to the world, of withdrawing your Majesty's troops from Afghanistan as soon as Shah Sooja should be firmly established upon the throne he owes to your Majesty's aid.

These considerations alone would have led Lord Ellenborough to desire that the execution of the orders given on the 4th of June should at least be delayed until your Majesty's confidential servants had had time to consider maturely the Policy which it might be their duty to advise your Majesty to sanction with respect to the countries on the right bank of the Indus; but financial considerations strengthened this desire, and seemed to render it an imperative duty to endeavour to obtain time for mature reflection before any step should be taken which might seriously affect the tranquillity of Europe, and must necessarily have disastrous effects upon the Administration of India.

INDIAN FINANCES

It appeared that the political and military charges now incurred beyond the Indus amounted to £1,250,000 a year—that the estimate of the expense of the additions made to the Army in India, since April 1838, was £1,138,750 a year, and that the deficit of Indian Revenue in 1839-40 having been £2,425,625, a further deficit of £1,987,000 was expected in 1840-41.

Your Majesty must be too well informed of the many evils consequent upon financial embarrassment, and entertains too deep a natural affection for all your Majesty's subjects, not to desire that in whatever advice your Majesty's confidential servants may tender to your Majesty with respect to the Policy to be observed in Afghanistan, they should have especial regard to the effect which the protracted continuance of military operations in that country, still more any extension of them to a new and distant field, would have upon the Finances of India, and thereby upon the welfare of eighty millions of people who there acknowledge your Majesty's rule.

Footnote 98: President of the Board of Control.

Footnote 99: For the progress of affairs in Afghanistan, see Introductory Notes for 1839-1842.

[; ; ; .]

Windsor Castle, 19th September 1841.

The Queen thanks Lord Ellenborough for this clear and interesting Memorandum he has sent. It seems to the Queen that the course intended to be pursued—namely to take time to consider the affairs of India without making any precipitate change in the Policy hitherto pursued, and without involving the country hastily in expenses, is far the best and safest.

DIPLOMATIC APPOINTMENTS

Windsor Castle, 19th September 1841.

In the conversation that the Queen had with Lord Aberdeen last week, she omitted mentioning two persons to him. The one is Lord Heytesbury; the Queen believes him to be a very able man, and would it not therefore be a good thing to employ him in some important mission? The other person is Mr Aston, who is at Madrid; the Queen hopes it may be possible to leave him there, for she thinks that he acted with great discretion, prudence, and moderation since he has been there, and the post is one of considerable importance. He was, the Queen believes, long Secretary to the Legation at Paris.

Foreign Office, 21st September 1841.

Lord Aberdeen presents his most humble duty to your Majesty....

Lord Aberdeen has seen the favourable opinion which your Majesty has been graciously pleased to express of Lord Heytesbury, and he humbly presumes to think that this honour is not unmerited. The situation of Governor-General of India has recently been proposed by Sir Robert Peel for Lord Heytesbury's acceptance, which has been declined by him, and it is understood that Lord Heytesbury is not at present desirous of public employment.100

Your Majesty's servants have not yet fully considered the propriety of submitting to your Majesty any proposal of a change in the Spanish Mission; but the opinion which your Majesty has been pleased to signify respecting the conduct of Mr Aston at Madrid appears, in the humble judgment of Lord Aberdeen, to be fully confirmed by the correspondence in this Office.

Lord Aberdeen would, however, venture humbly to mention that the person filling this Mission has usually been replaced on a change of the Administration at home. Should this be the case in the present instance, Lord Aberdeen begs to assure your Majesty that the greatest care will be taken to select an individual for your Majesty's approbation who may be qualified to carry into effect the wise, just, and moderate policy which your Majesty has been graciously pleased to recognise in the conduct of Mr Aston.

Footnote 100: He was made Governor and Captain of the Isle of Wight, and Governor of Carisbrooke Castle.

MELBOURNE AND PEEL

Saw Baron Stockmar this morning at the Castle, and had a good deal of conversation with him on various matters. He is very apprehensive that evil will spring out of the correspondence now carried on between the Queen and Lord Melbourne. He thinks it is productive of the greatest possible danger, and especially to Lord Melbourne; he thought no Government could stand such undermining influence. I might tell this to Lord Melbourne, and say that if he was totally disconnected from his Party, instead of being the acknowledged head, there would not be the same objection. He said, Remind Lord Melbourne of the time immediately after the Queen's accession, when he had promised the King of the Belgians to write to him from time to time an account of all that was going on in this country; and upon Lord Melbourne telling him of this promise, he replied, This will not do. It cannot be kept a secret that you keep up this correspondence, and jealousy and distrust will be the fruit of a knowledge of it. "Leave it to me," he said, "to arrange with the King; you cease to write, and I will put it straight with the King."

The Baron seemed to expect Lord Melbourne to draw the inference from this that a correspondence between Lord Melbourne and the Queen was fraught with the same danger, and would, when known, be followed by distrust and jealousy on the part of Sir Robert Peel. I said I reconciled it to myself because I felt that it had been productive of much good and no harm—and that, feeling that it was conducted on such honourable terms, I should not, if it were necessary, scruple to acquaint Sir Robert Peel of its existence. The Baron said, "Ask Lord Melbourne whether he would object to it." He said Peel, when he heard it, would not, on the first impression, at all approve of it; but prudence and caution would be immediately summoned to his aid, and he would see that it was his policy to play the generous part—and would say he felt all was honourably intended, and he had no objection to offer—"but," said the Baron, "look to the result. Distrust, being implanted from the first, whenever the first misunderstanding arose, or things took a wrong turn, all would, in Peel's mind, be immediately attributed to this cause."

Windsor Castle, 24th September 1841.

My dearest Uncle,—I have already thanked you for your two kind letters, but I did not wish to answer them but by a Messenger. I feel thankful for your praise of my conduct; all is going on well, but it would be needless to attempt to deny that I feel the change, and I own I am much happier when I need not see the Ministers; luckily they do not want to see me often. I feel much the King's kindness about Ste Aulaire;101 I shall see him here on Tuesday next.

I return you our excellent friend Melbourne's letter, which I had already seen, as he sent it me to read, and then seal and send. I miss him much, but I often hear from him, which is a great pleasure to me. It is a great satisfaction to us to have Stockmar here; he is a great resource, and is now in excellent spirits.

Mamma is, I suppose, with you now, and we may expect her here either next Thursday or Friday. How much she will have to tell us! I am very grateful for what you say of Claremont, which could so easily be made perfect; and I must say we enjoy ourselves there always particulièrement.... Albert begs me to make you his excuses for not writing, but I can bear testimony that he really has not time to-day. And now addio! dearest Uncle, and pray believe me, always, your devoted Niece,

Victoria R.

Footnote 101: See post, p. .

FINE ARTS COMMISSION

26th September 1841.

Sir Robert Peel presents his humble duty to your Majesty, and begs to be permitted to submit for your Majesty's consideration a suggestion which has occurred to Sir Robert Peel, and which has reference to the communication which he recently addressed to your Majesty on the subject of the promotion of the Fine Arts in connection with the building of the new Houses of Parliament.

Sir Robert Peel would humbly enquire from your Majesty whether (in the event of your Majesty's being graciously pleased to approve of the appointment of a Royal Commission for the further investigation and consideration of a subject of such deep importance and interest to the encouragement of art in this country) your Majesty would deem it desirable that the Prince should be invited in the name of your Majesty to place himself at the head of this Commission, and to give to it the authority and influence of his high name, and the advantage of his taste and knowledge.

Sir Robert Peel will not of course mention this subject to any one, until he has had the honour of receiving from your Majesty an intimation of your Majesty's opinions and wishes on this subject.

DIPLOMATIC APPOINTMENTS

South Street, 28th September 1841.

... The diplomatic appointments are as well as they could be made. At least Lord Melbourne thinks so—at least as much in consequence of those whom they exclude, as of those whom they admit. The Duke of Beaufort will do better for Petersburg than for Vienna. He is hardly equal to the place, which requires a clever man, it being more difficult to get information there, and to find out what is going on, than in any other country in Europe.... But Lord Melbourne does not much regard this, and the Duke of Beaufort possesses one advantage, which is of the greatest importance in that country. He is a soldier, was the Duke of Wellington's Aide-de-Camp, and served during much of the Peninsular War. He will therefore be able to accompany the Emperor to reviews, and to talk with him about troops and manœuvres. Sir Robert Gordon and Sir S. Canning will do very well.102

Lord Melbourne is very glad to hear that your Majesty was pleased and impressed with Archdeacon Wilberforce's103 sermon and his manner of delivering it. Lord Melbourne has never seen nor heard him. His father had as beautiful and touching a voice as ever was heard. It was very fine in itself. He spoiled it a little by giving it a methodistical and precatory intonation.

Hayter has been to Lord Melbourne to-day to press him to sit to him, which he will do as soon as he has done with Chantrey. Chantrey says that all Lord Melbourne's face is very easy except the mouth. The mouth, he says, is always the most difficult feature, and he can rarely satisfy himself with the delineation of any mouth, but Lord Melbourne's is so flexible and changeable that it is almost impossible to catch it.

Footnote 102: For Vienna and Constantinople.

Footnote 103: Samuel, son of William Wilberforce, at this date Archdeacon of Surrey, and chaplain to Prince Albert; afterwards, in 1844, appointed Bishop of Oxford, and eventually translated to the See of Winchester.

MELBOURNE'S ADVICE

South Street, 1st October 1841.

Lord Melbourne presents his humble duty to your Majesty. He received your Majesty's letter yesterday evening, and cannot express to your Majesty how much obliged he feels by your Majesty's taking the trouble to give him so much information upon so many points. Ste Aulaire's hair-powder seems to make a very deep and general impression.104 Everybody talks about it. "He appears to be very amiable and agreeable," everybody says, but then adds, "I never saw a man wear so much powder." A head so whitened with flour is quite a novelty and a prodigy in these times. Lord Melbourne has not yet seen him, but means to call upon him immediately. Lord Melbourne is upon the whole glad that the Duke of Beaufort has declined St Petersburg. It is an appointment that might have been acquiesced in, but would not have been approved. Bulwer105 will not be a bad choice to accompany Sir Charles106 to Canada. Your Majesty knows Bulwer well. He is clever, keen, active; somewhat bitter and caustic, and rather suspicious. A man of a more straight-forward character would have done better, but it would be easy to have found many who would have done worse. Lord Melbourne is very glad that it has been offered to the Prince to be at the head of this Commission, and that His Royal Highness has accepted it. It is an easy, unexceptionable manner of seeing and becoming acquainted with a great many people, and of observing the mode of transacting business in this country. The Commission itself will be a scene of very considerable difference of opinion. Lord Melbourne is for decorating the interior of the Houses of Parliament, if it be right to do so, but he is not for doing it, whether right or wrong, for the purpose of spending the public money in the encouragement of the Fine Arts. Whether it is to be painting or sculpture, or both; if painting, what sort of painting, what are to be the subjects chosen, and who are to be the artists employed? All these questions furnish ample food for discussion, difference, and dispute. Chantrey says fresco will never do; it stands ill in every climate, will never stand long in this, even in the interior of a building, and in a public work such as this is, durability is the first object to be aimed at. He says that there is in the Vatican a compartment of which the middle portion has been painted by Giulio Romano107 in fresco, and at each of the ends there is a figure painted by Raphael in oil. The fresco painting has been so often repaired in consequence of decay, that not a vestige of the original work remains; while the two figures painted by Raphael in oil still stand out in all their original freshness, and even improved from what they were when first executed....

Lord Melbourne dined and slept on Wednesday at Wimbledon.108 He met there Lord and Lady Cottenham, Lord109 and Lady Langdale, Lord Glenelg and his brother, Mr Wm. Grant, who was his private secretary, and is an amusing man. Lord Melbourne is going there again to-morrow to stay until Monday. The place is beautiful; it is not like Claremont, but it is quite of the same character, and always puts Lord Melbourne in mind of it. The Duchess has many merits, but amongst them is the not small one of having one of the best cooks in England.

Footnote 104: Madame de Lieven wrote to Aberdeen, 12th September 1841: "Ne jugez pas cet Ambassadeur par son exterieur; il personnifie un peu les Marquis de Molière.... Passez-lui ses cheveux poudrés, son air galant et papillon auprès des femmes. He cannot help it."

Footnote 105: Sir Henry Bulwer, afterwards Lord Dalling.

Footnote 106: Sir Charles Bagot.

Footnote 107: He was a pupil of Raphael, celebrated for (among other works) his "Fall of the Titans."

Footnote 108: The word is almost illegible. Wimbledon was at that time in the occupation of the Duke of Somerset.

Footnote 109: Master of the Rolls.

PEERS AND AUDIENCES

Whitehall, 2nd October 1841.

Sir James Graham with humble duty begs to lay before your Majesty two letters, which he has received from the Earl of Radnor,110 together with the copy of the answer which Sir James Graham returned to the first of the two letters.

If the presentation of Petitions were the sole subject of the Audience, it might be needless to impose on your Majesty the trouble incident to this mode of receiving them, since they might be transmitted through the accustomed channel of one of the Secretaries of State; but Sir James Graham infers from a conversation which, since the receipt of the letters he has had with Lord Radnor, that the Audience is asked in exercise of a right claimed by Peers of the Realm.

The existence of this right is not recognised by Statute; but it rests in ancient usage, and is noticed by Judge Blackstone in his Commentaries on the Laws of England in the following terms:—

"It is usually looked upon to be the right of each particular Peer of the Realm to demand an Audience of the King, and to lay before him, with decency and respect, such matters as he shall judge of importance to the public weal."

The general practice on the part of the Sovereign has been not to refuse these Audiences when Peers have asked them....

The above is humbly submitted by your Majesty's dutiful Subject and Servant,

J. R. G. Graham.

Footnote 110: William, third Earl, formerly M.P. for Salisbury.

Windsor Castle, 3rd October 1841.

The Queen has received Sir James Graham's communication with the enclosures. She thinks that it would be extremely inconvenient if Audiences were to be granted to Peers for the purpose of presenting Petitions or Addresses. The Queen knows that it has always been considered a sort of right of theirs to ask for and receive an Audience of the King or Queen. But the Queen knows that upon several occasions Lord Melbourne and Lord John Russell wrote to the Peers who requested Audiences, stating that it would be very inconvenient for the Queen, particularly in the country, and that they had better either put off asking for it, till the Queen came to town, or send what they had to say; communicate in writing—which was complied with. If, therefore, Sir James Graham would state this to Lord Radnor, he may probably give up pressing for an Audience. Should he, however, urge his wish very strongly, the Queen will see him in the manner proposed by Sir James. The Queen would wish to hear from Sir James again before she gives a final answer.

THE CHINESE CAMPAIGN

India Board, 2nd October 1841.

Lord Ellenborough, with his most humble duty to your Majesty, humbly acquaints your Majesty that your Majesty's Ministers, taking into consideration the smallness of the force with which the campaign in China was commenced this year, and the advanced period of the season at which the reinforcements would arrive (which reinforcements would not so raise the strength of the Army as to afford any reasonable expectation that its operations will produce during the present year any decisive results), have deemed it expedient that instructions would be at once issued to the Indian Government with a view to the making of timely preparations for the campaign of 1842.111

Your Majesty's Ministers are of opinion that the War with China should be conducted on an enlarged scale, and the Indian Government will be directed to have all their disposable military and naval force at Singapore in April, so that the operations may commence at the earliest period which the season allows.

Lord Ellenborough cannot but entertain a sanguine expectation that that force so commencing its operations, and directed upon a point where it will intercept the principal internal communication of the Chinese Empire, will finally compel the Chinese Government to accede to terms of Peace honourable to your Majesty, and affording future security to the trade of your

Majesty's subjects.

Footnote 111: Ningpo was taken by Sir Hugh Gough on 13th October 1841, and no further operations took place till the spring of the following year. See Introductory Note, ante, p.

Sat by the Queen last night at dinner. Her Majesty alluded to Sir Robert Peel's awkward manner, which she felt she could not get over. I asked if Her Majesty had yet made any effort, which I was good-humouredly assured Her Majesty "thought she really had done."

Sir Robert's ignorance of character was most striking and unaccountable; feeling this, made it difficult for Her Majesty to place reliance upon his judgment in recommendations.

ENGLISH AND FOREIGN ARTISTS

South Street, 4th October 1811.

Lord Melbourne presents his humble duty to your Majesty. He had the honour of receiving your Majesty's letter of the 2nd inst. yesterday, at Wimbledon. If Lord Melbourne should hear of anything of what your Majesty asks respecting the impression made upon Sir Robert and Lady Peel, he will take care and inform your Majesty, but, of course, they will speak very favourably, and if they feel otherwise will not breathe it except in the most secret and confidential manner.

Lord Melbourne is very much rejoiced to hear that the Duchess of Kent arrived safe and well and in good spirits.

SIR FRANCIS CHANTREY

Lord Melbourne sat to Sir F. Chantrey on Saturday last. He will, Lord Melbourne believes, require only one more sitting, which he wishes to be at the distance of a week from the last, in order that he may take a fresh view of the bust, and not become reconciled to its imperfections by continually looking at it. It may give the Prince some idea of the national feeling which prevails here, when he is told that Lord Melbourne upon asking Sir F. Chantrey what ought to be done if foreign artists were employed to paint the Houses of Parliament, received from him the following answer: "Why, their heads ought to be broke and they driven out of the country, and, old as I am, I should like to lend a hand for that purpose."

South Street, 5th October 1841.

... Lord Melbourne, by telling your Majesty what Sir Francis Chantrey said respecting foreign artists, and by requesting your Majesty to repeat it to the Prince, by no means intended to imply that there was any disposition on the part of His Royal Highness to recommend the employment of foreigners. He only meant to convey the idea of the strength of the prejudice which is felt by enlightened and able men upon the subject. Lord Melbourne has been sitting this morning to Hayter for the picture of the marriage, and he (Hayter) held an entirely contrary language. His tone is: "If foreign artists are more capable than English, let them be employed. All I require is that the work should be done as well as it can be." The English are certainly very jealous of foreigners, and so, Lord Melbourne apprehends, are the rest of mankind, but not knowing himself any nation except the English, he cannot venture to make positively that assertion. Lord Melbourne has been reading the evidence given before the committee of the House of Commons upon this subject. It is well worth attention, particularly Mr Eastlake's,112 which appears to Lord Melbourne to be very enlightened, dispassionate, and just....

Footnote 112: Afterwards Sir Charles Eastlake, Keeper of the National Gallery, 1843-1847, President of the Royal Academy, 1850-1865.

THE PRINCE'S GRANT

Sat by Her Majesty last night at dinner.

The Queen had written to Lord Melbourne about coming to the Castle, but in his answer he had made no allusion to it; she did not know whether this was accidental or intentional, for he very often gave no answer to questions which were put.

I told Her Majesty that I feared he had raised an obstacle to his visit by making a strong speech against the Government just at the time he was thinking of coming. That this attack had identified him as the leader of his Party, at a moment when I had been most anxious that he should abstain from taking an active part, and by withdrawing himself from politics he would enable himself to become the more useful friend to Her Majesty. The Queen had not seen the speech, was sorry he had felt himself obliged to make it, but it would be difficult for him to avoid it after having been so long Prime Minister.

Her Majesty told me that previous to the exit of the late Government, Lord John had earnestly cautioned Her Majesty not to propose any new grant of money, as it would in the case of £70,000 for the new stables, however unfairly, bring great unpopularity upon the Queen. I said in regard to any increase to the Prince's annuity, I thought it would be very imprudent in him to think of it, except under very peculiar circumstances which might arise, but which could not yet be foreseen. The Queen said that nothing should induce Her Majesty to accept such a favour from these Ministers. Peel probably now regretted his opposition to the grant, but it was, and was intended to be, a personal insult to herself, and it was followed up [by] opposition to her private wishes in the precedency question, where the Duke of Wellington took the lead against her wishes, as Peel had done in the Commons against the Prince's grant. She never could forget it, and no favour to her should come from such a quarter. I told Her Majesty I could not rest the Prince's case on Her Majesty's objections if they were the only ones which could be brought forward. If the case again rose I feared Her Majesty would find many who before, from Party views, voted according to Her Majesty's wishes, would now rank on the opposite side.

Her Majesty asked Dr Hawtrey the evening before who was the cleverest boy at Eton.

Dr Hawtrey made a profound bow to the Queen and said, "I trust your Majesty will excuse my answering, for if I did I make 600 enemies at once."

The Queen had asked Lord Melbourne whether he would soon visit her at Windsor. He had not replied on that point, but had written to Prince Albert in order to learn first the Prince's opinion on the feasibility of the matter.

The Prince sent for me and consulted with me. I was of opinion that the Prince had better refrain from giving an answer, and that I should give my opinion in the written form of a Memorandum, with which Anson should betake himself to town. He was to read it aloud to Melbourne, and orally to add what amplifications might be necessary.

And so it was done.

RELATIONS WITH PEEL

My Memorandum was as follows:—

Sir Robert Peel has yet to make his position opposite113 the Queen, which for him to obtain is important and desirable for obvious reasons. I have good cause to doubt that Sir Robert is sure within himself of the good-will and confidence of the Queen. As long as the secret communication exists between Her Majesty and Lord Melbourne, this ground, upon which alone Sir Robert could obtain the position necessary to him as Premier, must remain cut away from under his feet. I hold, therefore, this secret interchange an essential injustice to Sir Robert's present situation. I think it equally wrong to call upon the Prince to give an opinion on the subject, as he has not the means to cause his opinion to be either regarded or complied with. In this particular matter nobody has paramount power to do right or wrong but the Queen, and more especially Lord Melbourne himself. To any danger which may come out of this to Her Majesty's character, the caution and objection must come from him, and from him alone; and if I was standing in his shoes I would show the Queen, of my own accord, and upon constitutional grounds too, that a continued correspondence of that sort must be fraught with imminent danger to the Queen, especially to Lord Melbourne, and to the State.

Footnote 113: I.e. with.

I then gave Anson the further arguments with which he was to accompany the reading out of this Memo.

DISCRETION URGED ON MELBOURNE

On the next day Anson went to Melbourne and told him that his note to him had raised a great consultation, that the Prince felt much averse to giving any opinion in a case upon which he could exercise no control, and in which, if it was known that he had given his sanction, he would be held responsible for any mischief which might arise. He had consulted Baron Stockmar, who had written the enclosed opinion, which the Prince had desired Anson to read to Lord Melbourne. Melbourne read it attentively twice through, with an occasional change of countenance and compression of lips. He said on concluding it: "This is a most decided opinion indeed, quite an 'apple114 opinion.'" Anson told him that the Prince felt that if the Queen's confidence in Peel was in a way to be established, it would be extremely shaken by his (Lord Melbourne's) visit at such a moment. He felt that it would be better that Lord Melbourne's appearance should be in London, where he would meet the Queen only on the terms of general society, but at the same time he (the Prince) was extremely reluctant to give an opinion upon a case which Lord Melbourne's own sense of right ought to decide. Anson added how he feared his speech of yesterday in the House of Lords115 had added another impediment to his coming at this moment, as it had identified him with and established as the head of the Opposition party, which he (Anson) had hoped Melbourne would have been able to avoid. Melbourne, who was then sitting on the sofa, rushed up upon this, and went up and down the room in a violent frenzy, exclaiming—"God eternally d—n it!" etc., etc. "Flesh and blood cannot stand this. I only spoke upon the defensive, which Ripon's speech at the beginning of the session rendered quite necessary. I cannot be expected to give up my position in the country, neither do I think that it is to the Queen's interest that I should."

MELBOURNE'S INFLUENCE

Anson continued that the Baron thought that no Ministry could stand the force of such an undercurrent influence, that all the good that was to be derived from pacifying the Queen's mind at the change had been gained, and that the danger which we were liable to, and which threatened him in particular, could only be averted by his own straightforward decision with the Queen. Anson asked him if he saw any danger likely to arise from this correspondence. After a long pause he said, "I certainly cannot think it right," though he felt sure that some medium of communication of this sort was no new precedent. He took care never to say anything which could bring his opinion in opposition to Sir Robert's, and he should distinctly advise the Queen to adhere to her Ministers in everything,116 unless he saw the time had arrived at which it might be resisted.117 The principal evil, replied Anson, to be dreaded from the continuance of Lord Melbourne's influence was, according to the Baron's opinion, that so long as the Queen felt she could resort to Lord Melbourne for his advice, she never would be disposed (from not feeling the necessity) to place any real confidence in the advice she received from Peel.

Footnote 114: No doubt Lord Melbourne said an "apple-pie" opinion.

Footnote 115: At the opening of the Session Lord Ripon had reprobated the late Government for resorting to temporary expedients, and Lord Melbourne, on the second reading of the Exchequer-bills Funding Bill, caustically but good-humouredly replied to the attack.

Footnote 116: Note by Baron Stockmar.—If he wishes to carry this out consistently and quite honestly, what then is the value of his advice, if it be only the copy of that of Sir R. Peel?

Footnote 117: Note by Baron Stockmar.—This means, in my way of reading it: "The Queen, by her correspondence with me, puts Peel into my hands, and there I mean to let him stay unhurt, until time and extraneous circumstances—but more especially the advantage that will accrue to me by my secret correspondence with the Queen—shall enable me to plunge, in all security, the dagger into his back."

Fife House, 7th October 1841.

My dear Baron,—Peel sent for me this morning to speak to me about the contents of his letter to me. After some general conversation on matters respecting the Royal Household, he said that he had had much satisfaction in his intercourse lately with Her Majesty, and specifically yesterday, and he asked me whether I had seen Her Majesty or the Prince yesterday, and whether they were satisfied with him. I told him that except in public I had not seen Her Majesty, and except for a moment in your room I had not seen the Prince; but that as he spoke to me on this matter, I must take the opportunity of saying a word to him about you, from whom I had learnt yesterday that both the Queen and Prince are extremely well pleased with him. That I had known you very long, but that our great intimacy began when King Leopold sent you over just previous to the Queen's accession; that we had acted together on that occasion, and that our mutual esteem and intimacy had increased; that your position was a very peculiar one, and that you might be truly said to be a species of second parent to the Queen and the Prince; that your only object was their welfare, and your only ambition to be of service to them; that in this sense you had communicated with Melbourne, and that I wished that in this sense you should communicate with him (Peel). He said that he saw the matter exactly as I did, that he wished to communicate with you, and felt the greatest anxiety to do everything to meet the wishes of the Queen and Prince in all matters within his power, and as far as consistent with his known and avowed political principles; that in all matters respecting the Household and their private feelings that the smallest hint sufficed to guide him, as he would not give way to any party feeling or job which should in any way militate against Her Majesty or His Royal Highness's comfort; that he wished particularly that it should be known that he never had a thought of riding roughshod over Her Majesty's wishes; that if you would come to him at any time, and be candid and explicit with him, you might depend upon his frankness and discretion; that above all, if you had said anything to him, and expressed a wish that it might not be communicated even to the Duke of Wellington, (that was his expression), that he wished me to assure you that your wishes should be strictly attended to. Pray give me a line to say that you do not disapprove of what I have done. We had a great deal more conversation, but with this I will not now load my letter, being ever sincerely yours,

Liverpool.

Direct your answer to this house.

Footnote 118: This letter was submitted to the Queen.

AUDIENCES OF PEERS

South Street, 8th October 1841.

Lord Melbourne presents his humble duty to your Majesty. He has this morning received your Majesty's letter of yesterday. There can be no doubt that your Majesty is right about the Audiences which have been requested....

Sir Robert Peel is probably right in supposing that the claim of a Peer to an Audience of the Sovereign originated in early times, and before the present course of government by responsible advisers was fully and decidedly established, which it hardly can be said to have been until after the accession of the House of Hanover, but the custom of asking for such Audiences, and of their being in general granted, was well known, and has for the most part been observed and adhered to. Lord Melbourne remembers that during the part of the French War, when considerable alarm began to prevail respecting its duration, and the serious aspect which it was assuming, George III. gave Audiences to the Duke of Norfolk and others which he certainly would not have been inclined to do if he had not thought himself bound by his duty and by Constitutional precedent. At the time of the passing of the Roman Catholic Relief Act, George IV. received very many Peers, much no doubt against his will, who came to remonstrate with him upon the course which his Ministers were pursuing. William IV. did the same at the time of the Reform Bill, and certainly spoke upon the subject in a manner which Lord Melbourne always thought indiscreet and imprudent. Upon the whole, the practice has been so much acted upon and established, that Lord Melbourne will certainly not think it wise to make any alteration now, especially as it has in itself beneficial effects, especially as in a time of strong political feeling it is a satisfaction to the people to think that their wishes and opinions are laid before the Sovereign fairly and impartially. It is not likely to be a very heavy burthen, inasmuch as such Audiences are only asked at particular moments, and they are not in themselves very burthensome nor difficult to deal with. It is only for the Sovereign to say that he is convinced of the good motives which have actuated the step, and that consideration will be given to the matter and arguments which have been stated.

Lord Melbourne has one vague recollection of a correspondence upon this subject between Lord Holland and some King, but does not remember the circumstances with any accuracy.

Duncannon119 persuaded Brougham to give up asking an Audience upon condition of Lord Melbourne's promising to place his letters in your Majesty's hands, which he did.120 Lord Charlemont121 also was prevented in some manner or another, which Lord Melbourne forgets.

Upon the whole, Lord Melbourne thinks that it is best to concede this privilege of the Peerage, whether it actually exists or not, but to restrain it within due and reasonable bounds, which in ordinary times it is not difficult to do. Extraordinary times must be dealt with as they can be....

Lady A—— is, as your Majesty says, good-natured. She talks three or four times as much as she ought, and like many such women often says exactly the things she ought not to say. Lady B—— has ten times the sense of her mother, and a little residue of her folly.

Footnote 119: Ex-First Commissioner of Land Revenue.

Footnote 120: See ante, pp. and .

Footnote 121: Francis William, fifth Viscount Charlemont (1775-1863), created a Peer of the United Kingdom in 1837.

GOVERNOR-GENERALSHIP OF INDIA

9th October 1841.

Sir Robert Peel, with his humble duty to your Majesty, begs leave to inform your Majesty that in consequence of the opinion which your Majesty was graciously pleased to express when Sir Robert Peel last had the honour of waiting upon your Majesty, with respect to the superior qualifications of Lord Ellenborough for the important trust of Governor-General of India, Sir Robert Peel saw his Lordship yesterday, and enquired whether he would permit Sir Robert Peel to propose his appointment to your Majesty.

LORD ELLENBOROUGH

Lord Ellenborough was very much gratified by the proposal, admitted at once that it was very difficult to find an unexceptionable candidate for an office of such pre-eminent importance, but made some difficulty on two points.

First—Considerations of health, which though disregarded personally, might, he feared, interfere with the execution of such unremitting and laborious duties as would devolve upon the Governor-General of India.

Secondly—The consideration that on his acceptance of the office he would be required by law to give up during his tenure of it no less than £7,500 per annum, the amount of compensation now paid to him in consequence of the abolition of a very valuable office122 which he held in the Courts of Law.

During Lord Ellenborough's conversation with Sir Robert Peel, and while the mind of Lord Ellenborough was very much in doubt as to the policy of his acceptance of the office, the box which contained your Majesty's note of yesterday was brought to Sir Robert Peel.

Sir Robert Peel humbly acquaints your Majesty that he ventured to read to Lord Ellenborough on the instant the concluding paragraph of your Majesty's note, namely—

"The more the Queen thinks of it, the more she thinks that Lord Ellenborough would be far the most fit person to send to India."

Sir Robert Peel is perfectly convinced that this opinion of your Majesty, so graciously expressed, removed every doubt and difficulty from Lord Ellenborough's mind, and decided him to forgo every personal consideration rather than appear unmindful of such a favourable impression of his qualifications for public service on the part of his Sovereign.

Sir Robert Peel humbly hopes that your Majesty will not disapprove of the use which he made of a confidential note from your Majesty.

As your Majesty kindly permitted Sir Robert Peel to send occasionally letters to your Majesty of a private rather than a public character, he ventures to enclose one from the Duke of Wellington on the subject of the appointment of Governor-General.

Sir Robert Peel had observed to the Duke of Wellington that he had great confidence in Lord Ellenborough's integrity, unremitting industry, and intimate knowledge of Indian affairs; that his only fear was that Lord Ellenborough might err from over-activity and eagerness—but that he hoped his tendency to hasty decisions would be checked by the experience and mature judgment of Indian advisers on the spot.

The Duke of Wellington's comments have reference to these observations of Sir Robert Peel. Your Majesty will nevertheless perceive that the Duke considers, upon the whole, "that Lord Ellenborough is better qualified than any man in England for the office of Governor-General."

Footnote 122: He was Joint Chief Clerk of the Pleas in the Queen's Bench, a sinecure conferred on him by his father, who was Lord Chief Justice of the King's Bench, 1802-1818.

AFFAIRS IN SPAIN

Windsor Castle, 12th October 1841.

My dearest Uncle,—— ... Respecting the Spanish affairs,123 I can give you perfectly satisfactory intelligence concerning the Infants' return. Espartero sees them return with the greatest regret, but said he felt he could not prevent them from doing so. If, however, they should be found to intrigue at all, they will not be allowed to remain. Respecting a marriage with the eldest son of Dona Carlotta, I know positively that Espartero never would hear of it; but, on the other hand, he is equally strongly opposed to poor little Isabel marrying any French Prince, and I must add that we could never allow that. You will see that I have given you a frank and fair account....

Footnote 123: The Queen-mother, who was living in Paris, had been deprived by a vote of the Cortes of the guardianship of the young Queen, Isabella II., and risings in her interest now took place at Pampeluna and Vittoria. On the 7th October, a bold attempt was made at Madrid to storm the Palace and get possession of the person of the young Queen. Queen Christina denied complicity, but the Regent, Espartero, suspended her pension on the ground that she had encouraged the conspirators.

South Street, 12th October 1841.

Lord Melbourne presents his humble duty to your Majesty, and returns many thanks for the letter received yesterday informing Lord Melbourne of the time of your Majesty's coming to London. Lord Melbourne earnestly hopes that your Majesty continues well.

Lord Melbourne is very glad to hear of the appointment of Lord Ellenborough. The reasons which your Majesty gives are sound and just, and it is of great importance that a man not only of great ability but of high station, and perfectly in the confidence of the Government at home, should be named to this important post. Lord Ellenborough is a man of great abilities, of much knowledge of India, of great industry and of very accurate habits of business, and Lord Melbourne knows of no objection to his appointment, except the loss of him here, where, whether in or out of office, he has always been of great service. He has hitherto been an unpopular man and his manners have been considered contemptuous and overbearing, but he is evidently much softened and amended in this respect, as most men are by time, experience, and observation. Lord Fitzgerald124 is a very able public man, Lord Melbourne would say one of the most able, if not the most able they have; but Lord Melbourne is told by others, who know Lord Fitzgerald better, that Lord Melbourne overrates him. He is a very good speaker, he has not naturally much industry, and his health is bad, which will probably disable him from a very close and assiduous attention to business. It is, however, upon the whole an adequate appointment, and he is perhaps more likely to go on smoothly with the Court of Directors, which is a great matter, than Lord Ellenborough.

Footnote 124: On Lord Ellenborough becoming Governor-General, Lord Fitzgerald and Vesci, an ex-M.P., and former Chancellor of the Irish Exchequer, succeeded him at the Board of Control.

FRANCE AND SPAIN

Foreign Office, 16th October 1841.

Lord Aberdeen, with his most humble duty, begs to lay before your Majesty a private letter from M. Guizot, which has just been communicated to him by M. de Ste-Aulaire, on the recent attempt in favour of Queen Christina in Spain. Your Majesty will see that although M. Guizot denies, with every appearance of sincerity, all participation of the French Government in this attempt, he does not conceal that it has their cordial good wishes for its success. These feelings, on the part of such a Government as that of France, will probably be connected with practical assistance of some kind, although M. Guizot's declarations may perhaps be literally true.

The Queen must say that she fears the French are at the bottom of it, for their jealousy of our influence in Spain is such, that the Queen fears they would not be indisposed to see civil war to a certain degree restored rather than that Spain should go on quietly supported by us.125 The Queen, however, hopes that, as far as it is possible, the English Government will support the present Regent, who is thoroughly attached to England, and who, from all that the Queen hears of him, is the fittest man they have in Spain for the post he occupies; and indeed matters till now had gone on much more quietly than they had for some time previous, since Espartero is at the head of the Government. The French intrigues should really be frustrated. The Queen certainly thinks that M. Guizot's veracity is generally not to be doubted, but the conduct of France regarding Spain has always been very equivocal.

Footnote 125: See post, p. .

MASTERSHIP OF TRINITY

16th October 1841.

Sir Robert Peel, with his humble duty to your Majesty, begs leave to acquaint your Majesty that the Master of Trinity College, Cambridge, has formally signified his wish to retire from the duties of that important trust.

Sir Robert Peel has reason to believe that it would be advantageous that the selection of a successor to Dr. Wordsworth should be made from members of Trinity College who are or have been fellows of the College. Of these, the most eminent in respect to the qualifications required in the office of Master, and to academical distinction, are:—

The latter is a highly distinguished scholar, but his success as Head Master of Harrow has not been such as to overcome the objection which applies on general grounds to the succession of a father by a son in an office of this description.

Professor Whewell is a member of Trinity College of the highest scientific attainments. His name is probably familiar to your Majesty as the author of one of the Bridgewater Treatises,129 and of other works which have attracted considerable notice.

He is a general favourite among all who have had intercourse with him from his good temper and easy and conciliatory manners. Though not peculiarly eminent as a divine (less so at least than a writer on scientific and philosophical subjects), his works manifest a deep sense of the importance of religion and sound religious views. The Archbishop of Canterbury130 and the Bishop of London131 (himself of Trinity College) incline to think that the most satisfactory appointment upon the whole would be that of Professor Whewell.

Sir Robert Peel, after making every enquiry into the subject, and with a deep conviction of the importance of the appointment, has arrived at the same conclusion, and humbly therefore recommends to your Majesty that Professor Whewell should succeed Dr Wordsworth as Master of Trinity College, Cambridge.

Footnote 126: Then Knightsbridge Professor of Moral Philosophy.

Footnote 127: Francis Martin, afterwards Vice-Master, died 1868.

Footnote 128: Christopher Wordsworth, afterwards Bishop of Lincoln.

Footnote 129: By the will (dated 1825) of the eighth Earl of Bridgewater—who must not be confounded with the third and last Duke, projector of inland navigation—£8,000 was left for the best work on the "Goodness of God as manifested in the Creation." The money was divided amongst eight persons, including Whewell, who wrote on Astronomy considered in reference to Natural Theology.

Footnote 130: William Howley.

Footnote 131: O. J. Blomfield.

QUEEN ISABELLA

17th October 1841.

The Queen received Lord Aberdeen's letter yesterday evening, and quite approves of the draft to Mr Aston, and of Lord Aberdeen's having sent it off at once. Her earnest wish is that the English Government should be firm, and uphold the Regent as far as it is in our power. The Queen has perused M. Guizot's letter with great attention, but she cannot help fearing that assistance and encouragement has been given in some shape or other to the revolts which have taken place. The Queen Christina's residence at Paris is very suspicious, and much to be regretted; every one who saw the Queen and knew her when Regent, knew her to be clever and capable of governing, had she but attended to her duties. This she did not, but wasted her time in frivolous amusements and neglected her children sadly, and finally left them. It was her own doing, and therefore it is not the kindest conduct towards her children, but the very worst, to try and disturb the tranquillity of a country which was just beginning to recover from the baneful effects of one of the most bloody civil wars imaginable.

THE SPANISH MARRIAGE

The Queen is certain that Lord Aberdeen will feel with her of what importance it is to England that Spain should not become subject to French interests, as it is evident France wishes to make it. The marriage of Queen Isabel is a most important question, and the Queen is likewise certain that Lord Aberdeen sees at once that we could never let her marry a French Prince. Ere long the Queen must speak to Lord Aberdeen on this subject. In the meantime the Queen thought it might be of use to Lord Aberdeen to put him in possession of her feelings on the state of Spain, in which the Queen has always taken a very warm interest.

Panshanger, 21st October 1841.

Lord Melbourne presents his humble duty to your Majesty. He received here yesterday your Majesty's letter of the 19th inst., and he earnestly hopes that your Majesty has arrived quite safe and well in London. Besides the family, we have had hardly anybody here except Lady Clanricarde.132 Yesterday Sir Edward L. Bulwer133 came, beating his brother hollow in ridiculousness of attire, ridiculous as the other is. He has, however, much in him, and is agreeable when you come to converse with him....

Lord Melbourne is rather in doubt about his own movements. Lord Leicester134 presses him much to go to Holkham, where Lord Fortescue,135 Mr Ellice136 and others are to be, and considering Lord Leicester's age, Lord Melbourne thinks that it will gratify him to see Lord Melbourne again there. But at Holkham they shoot from morning until night, and if you do not shoot you are like a fish upon dry land. Lord Melbourne hardly feels equal to the exertion, and therefore thinks that he shall establish himself for the present at Melbourne, where he will be within reach of Trentham, Beau Desert,137 Wentworth,138 and Castle Howard,138 if he likes to go to them. The only annoyance is that it is close to Lord and Lady G——, whom he will be perpetually meeting.

Footnote 132: A daughter of George Canning, the Prime Minister.
Footnote 133: Afterwards Lord Lytton, the novelist.
Footnote 134: The famous country gentleman, "Mr Coke of Norfolk."
Footnote 135: Hugh, second Earl, K.G.
Footnote 136: The Right Hon. Edward Ellice, M.P. ("Bear" Ellice).

Footnote 137: Near Lichfield, a seat of Lord Anglesey.
Footnote 138: Lord Fitzwilliam's house, near Rotherham.
Footnote 139: Lord Carlisle's house, near York, built by Vanbrugh.
HOLLAND AND BELGIUM

Laeken, 22 October 1841.

... In France there is a great outcry that a Bourbon must be the future husband of the Queen of Spain, etc. I must say that as the Spaniards and the late King changed themselves the Salic custom which Philip V. had brought from France,140 it is natural for the rest of Europe to wish that no Bourbon should go there. Besides, it must be confessed that the thing is not even easy, as there is great hatred amongst the various branches of that family. The King of the French himself has always been opposed to the idea of one of his sons going there; in France, however, that opinion still exists, and Thiers had it, strongly.

I confess that I regret that Queen Christina was encouraged to settle at Paris, as it gave the thing the appearance of something preconcerted. I believe that a wish existed that Christina would retire peaceably and par la force des circonstances, but now this took a turn which I am sure the King does not like; it places him, besides, into une position ingrate; the Radicals hate him, the Moderates will cry out that he has left them in the lurch, and the Carlists are kept under key, and of course also not much pleased. I meant to have remained in my wilds till yesterday, but my Ministers were so anxious for my return, there being a good many things on the tapis, that I came back on Tuesday, the 19th....

Here one is exactly shut up as if one was in a menagerie, walking round and round like a tame bear. One breathes here also a mixture of all sorts of moist compounds, which one is told is fresh air, but which is not the least like it. I suppose, however, that my neighbour in Holland, where they have not even got a hill as high as yours in Buckingham Gardens, would consider Laeken as an Alpine country. The tender meeting of the old King and the new King,141 as one can hardly call him a young King, must be most amusing. I am told that if the old King had not made that love-match, he would be perfectly able to dethrone his son; I heard that yesterday from a person rather attached to the son and hating the father. In the meantime, though one can hardly say that he is well at home, some strange mixture of cut-throats and ruined soldiers of fortune had a mind to play us some tricks here; we have got more and more insight into this. Is it by instigation from him personally, or does he only know of it without being a party to it? That is difficult to tell, the more so as he makes immense demonstration of friendly dispositions towards us, and me in particular. I would I could make a chassez croisez with Otho;142 he would be the gainer in solids, and I should have sun and an interesting country; I will try to make him understand this, the more so as you do not any longer want me in the West.

Footnote 140: The Pragmatic Sanction of Philip V. was repealed in 1792 by the Cortes, but the repeal was not promulgated by the King. Under the Salic Law, Don Carlos would have been on the throne. See ante, p. .

Footnote 141: William I., who had abdicated in order to marry again, and William II., his son, who was nearly fifty.

Footnote 142: The King of Greece, elected in 1833.

AMBASSADORS' AUDIENCES

25th October 1841.

With respect to the appointment of Chief Justice of the Queen's Bench, the Queen approves of Mr Pennefather143 for that office. The Queen may be mistaken, for she is not very well acquainted with the judicial officers in Ireland, but it strikes her that Serjeant Jackson belonged to the very violent Orange party in Ireland, and if this should be the case she suggests to Sir Robert Peel whether it would not be better not to appoint him. If, on the other hand, the Queen should be mistaken as to his political opinions, she would not disapprove of his succeeding Mr Pennefather.

The Queen saw in the papers that Lord Stuart de Rothesay is already gone. The Queen can hardly believe this, as no Ambassador or Minister ever left England without previously asking for an Audience and receiving one, as the Queen wishes always to see them before they repair to their posts. Would Sir Robert be so very good as to ask Lord Aberdeen whether Lord Stuart de Rothesay is gone or not, and if he should be, to tell Lord Aberdeen that in future she would wish him always to inform her when they intend to go, and to ask for an Audience, which, if the Queen is well, she would always grant. It is possible that as the Queen said the other day that she did not wish to give many Audiences after the Council, that Lord Aberdeen may have misunderstood this and thought the Queen would give none, which was not her intention. The Queen would be thankful to Sir Robert if he would undertake to clear up this mistake, which she is certain (should Lord Stuart be gone) arose entirely from misapprehension.

The Queen also wishes Sir Robert to desire Lord Haddington to send her some details of the intended reductions in the Fleet which she sees by a draft of Lord Aberdeen's to Mr Bulwer have taken place.144

Footnote 143: Recently appointed Solicitor-General; Sergeant J. D. Jackson now succeeded him.

Footnote 144: The statement of the Royal Navy in Commission at the beginning of 1841 sets out 160 vessels carrying 4,277 guns.

STOCKMAR AND MELBOURNE

... I told [Lord Melbourne] that, as I read the English Constitution, it meant to assign to the Sovereign in his functions a deliberative part—that I was not sure the Queen had the means within herself to execute this deliberative part properly, but I was sure that the only way for her to execute her functions at all was to be strictly honest to those men who at the time being were her Ministers. That it was chiefly on this account that I had been so very sorry to have found now, on my return from the Continent, that on the change of the Ministry a capital opportunity to read a great Constitutional maxim to the Queen had not only been lost by Lord Melbourne, but that he had himself turned an instrument for working great good into an instrument which must produce mischief and danger. That I was afraid that, from what Lord Melbourne had been so weak as to have allowed himself to be driven into, against his own and better conviction, the Queen must have received a most pernicious bias, which on any future occasion would make her inclined to act in a similar position similarly to that what she does now, being convinced that what she does now must be right on all future occasions, or else Lord Melbourne would not have sanctioned it. Upon this, Lord Melbourne endeavoured to palliate, to represent the danger, which would arise from his secret correspondence with the Queen as very little, to adduce precedents from history, and to screen his present conduct behind what he imagined Lord Bute's conduct had been under George III.145 I listened patiently, and replied in the end: All this might be mighty fine and quite calculated to lay a flattering unction on his own soul, or it might suffice to tranquillize the minds of the Prince and Anson, but that I was too old to find the slightest argument in what I had just now heard, nor could it in any way allay my apprehension. I began then to dissect all that he had produced for his excusation, and showed him—as I thought clearly, and as he admitted convincingly—that it would be impossible to carry on this secret commerce with the Sovereign for any length of time without exposing the Queen's character and creating mighty embarrassments in the quiet and regular working of a Constitutional machine.

STOCKMAR'S ADVICE

My representations seemed to make a very deep impression, and Lord Melbourne became visibly nervous, perplexed, and distressed. After he had recovered a little I said, "I never was inclined to obtrude advice; but if you don't dislike to hear my opinion, I am prepared to give it to you." He said, "What is it?" I said, "You allow the Queen's confinement to pass over quietly, and you wait till her perfect recovery of it. As soon as this period has arrived, you state of your own accord to Her Majesty that this secret and confidential correspondence with her must cease; that you gave in to it, much against your feelings, and with a decided notion of its impropriety and danger, and merely out of a sincere solicitude to calm Her Majesty's mind in a critical time, and to prevent the ill effects which great and mental agitation might have produced on her health. That this part of your purpose now being most happily achieved, you thought yourself in duty bound to advise Her Majesty to cease all her communications to you on political subjects, as you felt it wrong within yourself to receive them, and to return your political advice and opinions on such matters; that painful as such a step must be to your feelings, which to the last moment of your life will remain those of the most loyal attachment and devotion to the Queen's person, it is dictated to you by a deep sense of what you owe to the country, to your Sovereign, and to yourself."

Footnote 145: For some time after the accession of George III., Bute, though neither in the Cabinet nor in Parliament, was virtually Prime Minister, but he became Secretary of State on 25th March 1761. George II. had disliked him, but he was generally believed to have exercised an undue influence over the consort of Prince Frederic of Wales, mother of George III.

26th October 1841.

With respect to Serjeant Jackson, the Queen will not oppose his appointment, in consequence of the high character Sir Robert Peel gives him; but she cannot refrain from saying that she very much fears that the favourable effect which has hitherto been produced by the formation of so mild and conciliatory a Government in Ireland, may be endangered by this appointment, which the Queen would sincerely regret.

South Street, 26th October 1841.

Lord Melbourne presents his humble duty to your Majesty, and returns your Majesty the letters of the King of the Belgians, with many thanks. It certainly is a very unfortunate thing that the Queen Christina was encouraged to fix her residence at Paris, and the suspicion arising, therefore, cannot but be very injurious both to the King of the French and to the French nation.

Lord Melbourne returns his warmest thanks for your Majesty's kind expressions. He felt the greatest pleasure at seeing your Majesty again and looking so well, and he hopes that his high spirits did not betray him into talking too much or too heedlessly, which he is conscious that they sometimes do.

The King Leopold, Lord Melbourne perceives, still hankers after Greece; but Crowns will not bear to be chopped and changed about in this manner. These new Kingdoms are not too firmly fixed as it is, and it will not do to add to the uncertainty by alteration....

DISPUTE WITH UNITED STATES

Whitehall, 28th October 1841.

... Sir Robert Peel humbly assures your Majesty that he fully participates in the surprise which your Majesty so naturally expresses at the extraordinary intimation conveyed to Mr Fox146 by the President of the United States.147

Immediately after reading Mr Fox's despatch upon that subject, Sir Robert Peel sought an interview with Lord Aberdeen. The measure contemplated by the President is a perfectly novel one, a measure of a hostile and unjustifiable character adopted with pacific intentions.

Sir Robert Peel does not comprehend the object of the President, and giving him credit for the desire to prevent the interruption of amicable relations with this country, Sir Robert Peel fears that the forcible detention of the British Minister, after the demand of passports, will produce a different impression on the public mind, both here and in the United States, from that which the President must (if he be sincere) have anticipated. It appears to Sir Robert Peel that the object which the President professes to have in view would be better answered by the immediate compliance with Mr Fox's demand for passports, and the simultaneous despatch of a special mission to this country conveying whatever explanations or offers of reparation the President may have in contemplation.

Sir Robert Peel humbly assures your Majesty that he has advised such measures of preparation to be taken in respect to the amount of disposable naval force, and the position of it, as without bearing the character of menace or causing needless disquietude and alarm, may provide for an unfavourable issue of our present differences with the United States.

Sir Robert Peel fears that when the President ventured to make to Mr Fox the communication which he did make, he must have laboured under apprehension that M'Leod might be executed in spite of the efforts of the general Government of the United States to save his life.

Footnote 146: British Minister at Washington.

Footnote 147: One Alexander M'Leod was tried at Utica on the charge of being implicated in the destruction of the Caroline (an American vessel engaged in carrying arms to the Canadian rebels), in 1837, and in the death of Mr Durfee, an American. The vessel had been boarded by

Canadian loyalists when lying in American waters, set on fire and sent over Niagara Falls, and in the affray Durfee was killed. M'Leod was apprehended on American territory, and hence arose the friction between the two countries. M'Leod was acquitted 12th October 1841.

PORTUGAL

Buckingham Palace, 31st October 1841.

The Queen received yesterday evening Lord Aberdeen's letter with the accompanying despatches and draft. She certainly is surprised at the strange and improper tone in which Lord Howard's148 despatches are written, and can only attribute them to an over-eager and, she fully believes, mistaken feeling of the danger to which he believes the throne of the Queen to be exposed.

The Queen has carefully perused Lord Aberdeen's draft, which she highly approves, but wishes to suggest to Lord Aberdeen whether upon further consideration it might not perhaps be as well to soften the words under which she has drawn a pencil line, as she fears they might irritate Lord Howard very much.

The Queen is induced to copy the following sentences from a letter she received from her cousin, the King of Portugal, a few days ago, and which it may be satisfactory to Lord Aberdeen to see:—

"Je dois encore vous dire que nous avons toutes les raisons de nous louer de la manière dont le Portugal est traité par votre Ministre des Affaires Étrangères, et nous ferons de notre côté notre possible pour prouver notre bonne volonté."

Footnote 148: Lord Howard de Walden, Minister Plenipotentiary at Lisbon.

SECRETARIES OF STATE

South Street, 1st November 1841.

... Now for His Royal Highness's questions....

How the power of Prime Ministry grew up into its present form it is difficult to trace precisely, as well as how it became attached, as it were, to the office of First Commissioner of the Treasury. But Lord Melbourne apprehends that Sir Robert Walpole was the first man in whose person this union of powers was decidedly established, and that its being so arose from the very great confidence which both George I. and George II. reposed in him, and from the difficulty which they had in transacting business, particularly George I., from their imperfect knowledge of the language of the country.

With respect to the Secretary of State, Lord Melbourne is not prepared from memory to state the dates at which the different arrangements of that office have taken place. There was originally but one officer, and at the present the three are but the heads of the different departments of one office. The first division was into two, and they were called the Secretary for the Northern and the Secretary for the Southern department. They drew a line across the world, and each transacted the business connected with the countries within his own portion of the globe. Another division then took place, and the Foreign affairs were confided to one Secretary of State, and the Home and Colonial affairs to the other; but the present arrangement was finally settled in the year 1793, when the junction was formed between Mr Pitt on the one hand, and those friends of Mr Fox who left him because they differed with him upon the French Revolution. The Home affairs were placed in the hands of one Secretary of State, the Foreign of another, and the Colonial and Military affairs of a third, and this arrangement has continued ever since.149 The persons then appointed were the Duke of Portland,150 Lord Grenville,151 and Mr Dundas,152 Home, Foreign, and Colonial Secretaries.

Writing from recollection, it is very possible that Lord Melbourne may be wrong in some of the dates which he has ventured to specify.153

Footnote 149: A fourth Secretary of State was added at the time of the Crimean War, so as to separate Colonial and Military affairs, and a fifth after the Indian Mutiny to supersede the President of the Board of Control. See Lord Melbourne's letter of 31st December 1837, ante, p.

Footnote 150: Third Duke (1738-1809).

Footnote 151: William Wyndham, Lord Grenville (1759-1834).

Footnote 152: Henry Dundas (1742-1811), afterwards Lord Melville.

Footnote 153: See post, pp. , .

THE ENGLISH CONSTITUTION

South Street, 4th November 1841.

Lord Melbourne presents his humble duty to your Majesty. He has this morning had the honour and pleasure of receiving your Majesty's letter of yesterday....

Lord Melbourne sends a letter which he has received from his sister, which may not be unentertaining. Lady Palmerston is struck, as everybody is who goes to Ireland, with the candid warmth and vehement demonstration of feeling. England always appears cold, heartless, and sulky in comparison....

With respect to the questions put to me by your Majesty at the desire of His Royal Highness, Lord Melbourne begs leave to assure your Majesty that he will be at all times most ready and anxious to give any information in his power upon points of this sort, which are very curious, very important, very worthy to be enquired into, and upon which accurate information is not easily to be found. All the political part of the English Constitution is fully understood, and distinctly stated in Blackstone and many other books, but the Ministerial part, the work of conducting the executive government, has rested so much on practice, on usage, on understanding, that there is no publication to which reference can be made for the explanation and description of it. It is to be sought in debates, in protests, in letters, in memoirs, and wherever it can be picked up. It seems to be stupid not to be able to say at once when two Secretaries of State were established; but Lord Melbourne is not able. He apprehends that there was but one until the end of Queen Anne's reign, and that two were instituted by George I., probably because upon his frequent journeys to Hanover he wanted the Secretary of State with him, and at the same time it was necessary that there should be an officer of the same authority left at home to transact the domestic affairs.

Prime Minister is a term belonging to the last century. Lord Melbourne doubts its being to be found in English Parliamentary language previously. Sir Robert Walpole was always accused of having introduced and arrogated to himself an office previously unknown to the Law and

Constitution, that of Prime or Sole Minister, and we learn from Lady Charlotte Lindsay's154 accounts of her father, that in his own family Lord North would never suffer himself to be called prime Minister, because it was an office unknown to the Constitution. This was a notion derived from the combined Whig and Tory opposition to Sir Robert Walpole, to which Lord North and his family had belonged.

Lord Melbourne is very sorry to hear that the Princess Royal continues to suffer from some degree of indisposition. From what your Majesty had said more than once before, Lord Melbourne had felt anxiety upon this subject, and he saw the Baron yesterday, who conversed with him much upon it, and informed him of what had taken place. Lord Melbourne hopes that your Majesty will attribute it only to Lord Melbourne's anxious desire for the security and increase of your Majesty's happiness, if he ventures to say that the Baron appears to him to have much reason in what he urges, and in the view which he takes. It is absolutely required that confidence should be reposed in those who are to have the management and bear the responsibility, and that they should not be too much interrupted or interfered with.

Footnote 154: Daughter of Lord North (afterwards Earl of Guilford) and wife of Lieut.-Colonel the Hon. John Lindsay. She lived till 1849—a link with the past.

SECRETARIES OF STATE

South Street, 5th November 1841.

Lord Melbourne presents his humble duty to your Majesty. Not feeling satisfied of the correctness of the information which he had given to your Majesty respecting the office of Secretary of State, he yesterday evening requested Mr Allen155 to look into the matter, and he has just received from him the enclosed short memorandum, which he has the honour of transmitting to your Majesty. This shows that Lord Melbourne was quite wrong with respect to the period at which two Secretaries of State were first employed, and that it was much earlier than he had imagined.

The year 1782, when the third Secretary of State was abolished, was the period of the adoption of the great measure of Economical Reform which had been introduced by Mr. Burke in 1780.

The present arrangement was settled in 1794, which is about the time which Lord Melbourne stated.

Footnote 155: Secretary and Librarian at Holland House.

LORD MELBOURNE'S POSITION

South Street, 7th November 1841.

... Your Majesty asks whether Lord Melbourne thinks that Prince Metternich holds the opinion of Sir Robert Gordon, which he expresses to Lord Beauvale. It is difficult to say what Prince Metternich's real sentiments are. Lord Melbourne takes him not to have a very high opinion of the abilities of others in general, and he is not unlikely to depreciate Sir Robert Gordon to Lord Beauvale. Sir Robert Gordon is a man of integrity, but he is tiresome, long and pompous, which cannot be agreeable to the Prince, who has about him much of the French vivacity, and also much of their settled and regular style of argument....

With respect to the latter part of your Majesty's letter, Lord Melbourne returns for the expressions of your Majesty's kindness his warm and grateful thanks. Your Majesty may rest assured that he will always speak to your Majesty without scruple or reserve, and that he will never ask anything of your Majesty, or ever make a suggestion, which he does not consider to be for your Majesty's service and advantage. Lord Melbourne is of opinion that his visits to the Palace should not only avoid exciting suspicion and uneasiness in your Majesty's present advisers, a result of which he has very little apprehension, but they should not be so frequent as to attract public notice, comment, and observation, of which he would be more fearful. A public rumour, however unfounded and absurd, has more force in this country than objections which have in them more of truth and reality. Upon these grounds, and as your Majesty will probably not see much company at present, and the parties therefore will be a good deal confined to the actual Household, Lord Melbourne thinks it would perhaps be as well if he were not again to dine at the Palace at present.

The course which it may be prudent to take hereafter will depend very much upon that which cannot now be foreseen, namely, upon the general course which will be taken by politics and political parties. In this Lord Melbourne does not at present discern his way, and he will not therefore hazard opinions which would not be founded upon any certainty, and might be liable to immediate change and alteration.

STOCKMAR'S ADVICE

The apprehension which haunts me since my return to England is well known to you. It was my intention to have written to you upon it some time hereafter, but the contents of a certain letter, sent by you just before your departure, accelerates the execution of my design. From your own expressions used some time back, I was led to expect that you would be glad to take advantage of any fair opportunity which might contribute towards that devoutly to be wished for object, viz., to let a certain correspondence die a natural death. You may easily conceive how much I felt disappointed when I heard that you had written again, without a challenge, and that, without apparent cause, you had volunteered the promise to write from time to time. This happens at a moment when your harassing apprehension received new life and strength from two incidents which I think it my duty to make known to you, and of which the one came to pass before, the other after, your departure from here. Some weeks back I was walking in the streets with Dr Prætorius,156 when, finding myself opposite the house of one of my friends, it came across my mind to give him a call. Prætorius wanted to leave me, on a conception that, as a stranger, he might obstruct the freedom of our conversation. I insisted, however, on his remaining with me, and we were shown into the drawing-room, where in all there were five of us. For some minutes the conversation had turned on insignificant things, when the person talking to me said quite abruptly: "So I find the Queen is in daily correspondence with Lord Melbourne." I replied, "Who told you this?" The answer was, "Mrs Norton; she told me the other evening. Don't you believe that Lord Melbourne has lost his influence over the Queen's mind; he daily writes to her, and receives as many answers, in which she communicates everything to him." Without betraying much emotion I said, "I don't believe a word of it; the Queen may have written once or twice on private matters, but the daily correspondence on all matters is certainly the amplification of a thoughtless and imprudent person, who is not aware of such exaggerated assertions." My speech was followed by a general silence, after which we talked of other things, and soon took our leave. When we were fairly in the open air, Prætorius expressed to me his amazement at what he had heard, and he remained for some time at a loss to comprehend the character of the person who, from mere giddiness, let out so momentous a secret.

The other fact took place the day after you had left. From the late events at Brussels, it had become desirable that I should see Sir Robert Peel. From Belgium we travelled over to Home politics. I expressed my delight at seeing the Queen so happy, and added a hope that more and more she would seek and find her real happiness in her domestic relations only. He evidently caught at this, and assured me that he should at all times be too happy to have a share in anything which might be thought conducive to the welfare of Her Majesty. That no consideration of personal inconvenience would ever prevent him from indulging the Queen in all her wishes relating to matters of a private nature, and that the only return for his sincere endeavours to please Her Majesty he looked to, was honesty in public affairs. Becoming then suddenly emphatic, he continued, "But on this I must insist, and I do assure you, that that moment I was to learn that the Queen takes advice upon public matters in another place, I shall throw up; for such a thing I conceive the country could not stand, and I would not remain an hour, whatever the consequences of my resignation may be."

Fully sensible that he was talking at me, I received the charge with the calmness of a good conscience, and our time being exhausted I prepared for retreat. But he did not allow me to do so, before he had found means to come a second time to the topic uppermost in his own mind, and he repeated, it appeared to me with increased force of tone, his determination to throw up, fearless of all consequences, that moment he found himself and the country dishonestly dealt by.

STOCKMAR'S EXPOSTULATIONS

I think I have now reported to you correctly the two occurrences which of late have added so much to my antecedent suspicions and fears. Permit me to join to this a few general considerations which, from the nature of the recited incidents alone, and without the slightest intervention of any other cause, must have presented themselves to my mind. The first is, that I derive from the events related quite ground enough for concluding that the danger I dread is great and imminent, and that, if ill luck is to have its will, no human power can prevent an explosion for a day, or even for an hour. The second is the contemplation—what state will the Queen be placed in by such a catastrophe? That in my position, portraying to myself all the consequences of such a possibility, I look chiefly to the Queen, needs hardly, I trust, an excuse.... Can you hope that the Queen's character will ever recover from a shock received by a collision with Peel, upon such a cause? Pray illustrate to yourself this particular question by taking a purely political and general survey of the time and period we live in at this moment. In doing so must you not admit that all England is agreed that the Tories must have another trial, and that there is a decided desire in the nation that it should be a fair one? Would you have it said that Sir Robert Peel failed in his trial, merely because the Queen alone was not fair to him, and that principally you had aided her in the game of dishonesty? And can you hope that this game can be played with security, even for a short time only, when a person has means of looking into your cards whom you yourself have described to me some years ago as a most passionate, giddy, imprudent and dangerous woman? I am sure beforehand that your loyalty and devotion has nothing to oppose to the force of my exposition. There are, however, some other and minor reasons which ought likewise to be considered before you come to the determination of trusting entirely to possibilities and chance. For the results of your deliberation you will have to come to will in their working and effects go beyond yourself, and must affect two other persons. These will have a right to expect that your decision will not be taken regardless of that position, which accidental circumstances have assigned to them, in an affair the fate of which is placed entirely within your discretion. This is an additional argument why you should deliberate very conscientiously. A mistake of yours in this respect might by itself produce fresh difficulties and have a complicating and perplexing retro effect upon the existing ones; because both, seeing that they must be sufferers in the end, may begin to look only to their own safety, and become inclined to refuse that passive obedience which till now constitutes the vehicle of your hazardous enterprize.

Approaching the conclusion of this letter, I beg to remind you of a conversation I had with you on the same subject in South Street, the 25th of last month.157Though you did not avow it then in direct words, I could read from your countenance and manner that you assented in your head and heart to all I had said, and in particular to the advice I volunteered at the end of my speech. At that time I pointed out to you a period when I thought a decisive step ought to be taken on your part. This period seems to me to have arrived. Placing unreserved confidence into your candour and manliness, I remain, for ever, very faithfully yours,

Stockmar.

Footnote 156: Librarian and German Secretary to Prince Albert.

Footnote 157: Ante, pp. .

MELBOURNE'S REPLY

24th November 1841.

My dear Baron,—I have just received your letter; I think it unnecessary to detain your messenger. I will write to you upon the subject and send it through Anson. Yours faithfully,

Melbourne.

THE HEIR APPARENT

Buckingham Palace, 29th November 1841.

My dearest Uncle,—I have to thank you for four most kind letters, of the 4th, 6th, 19th and 26th; the last I received yesterday. I would have written sooner, had I not been a little bilious, which made me very low, and not in spirits to write. The weather has been so exceedingly relaxing, that it made me at the end of the fortnight quite bilious, and this, you know, affects the spirits. I am much better, but they think that I shall not get my appetite and spirits back till I can get out of town; we are therefore going in a week at latest. I am going for a drive this morning, and am certain it will do me good. In all essentials, I am better, if possible, than last year. Our little boy158 is a wonderfully strong and large child, with very large dark blue eyes, a finely formed but somewhat large nose, and a pretty little mouth; I hope and pray he may be like his dearest Papa. He is to be called Albert, and Edward is to be his second name. Pussy, dear child, is still the great pet amongst us all, and is getting so fat and strong again.

I beg my most affectionate love to dearest Louise and the dear children. The Queen-Dowager is recovering wonderfully.

I beg you to forgive this letter being so badly written, but my feet are being rubbed, and as I have got the box on which I am writing on my knee, it is not easy to write quite straight—but you must not think my hand trembles. Ever your devoted Niece,

Victoria R.

Pussy is not at all pleased with her brother.

Footnote 158: His Majesty King Edward VII., born 9th November.

THE INFANT PRINCE

Trentham, 1st December 1841.

Lord Melbourne presents his humble duty to your Majesty, and has had the honour of receiving here your Majesty's letters of yesterday, by which he learns with sincere pleasure and satisfaction that your Majesty is so much recovered as to go to Windsor on so early a day as your Majesty names. Lord Melbourne hears with great concern that your Majesty has been suffering under depression and lowness of spirits.... Lord Melbourne well knows how to feel for those who suffer under it, especially as he has lately had much of it himself.

Lord Melbourne is much rejoiced to hear so good an account of the Heir Apparent and of the Princess Royal, and feels himself greatly obliged by the information respecting the intended names and the sponsors. Lord Melbourne supposes that your Majesty has determined yourself upon the relative position of the two names, but Edward is a good English appellation, and has a certain degree of popularity attached to it from ancient recollections. Albert is also an old Anglo-Saxon name—the same, Lord Melbourne believes, as Ethelred—but it has not been so common nor so much in use since the Conquest. However, your Majesty's feelings, which Lord Melbourne perfectly understands, must determine this point. The notion of the King of Prussia159 gives great satisfaction here, and will do so with all but Puseyites and Newmanites and those who lean to the Roman Catholic faith. His strong Protestant feelings, and his acting with us in the matter of the Syrian Bishop, have made the King of Prussia highly popular in this country, and particularly with the more religious part of the community.

Your Majesty cannot offer up for the young Prince a more safe and judicious prayer than that he may resemble his father. The character, in Lord Melbourne's opinion, depends much upon the race, and on both sides he has a good chance. Be not over solicitous about education. It may be able to do much, but it does not do so much as is expected from it. It may mould and direct the character, but it rarely alters it. George IV. and the Duke of York were educated quite like English boys, by English schoolmasters, and in the manner and upon the system of English schools. The consequence was that, whatever were their faults, they were quite Englishmen. The others, who were sent earlier abroad, and more to foreign universities, were not quite so much so. The late king was educated as a sailor, and was a complete sailor....

Lord Melbourne will tell your Majesty exactly what he thinks of John Russell's reply to the

Plymouth address. It is very angry and very bitter, and anger and bitterness are never very dignified. Lord Melbourne certainly would not have put in those sarcasms upon the Duke of Wellington and Sir Robert Peel, for their change of opinion and conduct upon the Roman Catholic question. But the tone of the rest of the answer is, in Lord Melbourne's opinion, just and right. We certainly delivered the affairs of the country into their hands in a good state, both at home and abroad, and we should be acting unfairly by ourselves if we did not maintain and assert this upon every occasion. Lord Melbourne's notion of the conduct which he has to pursue is, that it should not be aggressive, but that it must be defensive. He would oppose no right measures, but he cannot suffer the course of policy which has been condemned in him to be adopted by others without observation upon the inconsistency and injustice....

Lord Melbourne concludes with again wishing your Majesty health and happiness, and much enjoyment of the country.

Footnote 159: King Frederick William IV., who was to be a sponsor.

PRINCE OF WALES

Whitehall, 6th December 1841.

Sir James Graham, with humble duty, begs to enclose for the Signature of your Majesty the Letters Patent creating His Royal Highness, the Prince of the United Kingdom, Prince of Wales and Earl of Chester.160

Understanding that it is your Majesty's pleasure to have this Creation inserted in the Gazette of to-morrow night, Sir James Graham has given directions, which will ensure the publication, though the Letters Patent themselves may not be completed. The Warrant already signed by your Majesty is a sufficient authority.

The above is humbly submitted by your Majesty's dutiful Subject and Servant,

J. R. G. Graham.

Footnote 160: His present Majesty had been referred to in letters of the previous month as the Duke of Cornwall. "Know ye," ran the present Letters Patent, "that we have made ... our most dear son, the Prince of the United Kingdom of Great Britain and Ireland (Duke of Saxony, Duke of Cornwall ...) Prince of Wales and Earl of Chester ... and him our said most dear son, ... as has been accustomed, we do ennoble and invest with the said Principality and Earldom, by girding him with a sword, by putting a coronet on his head, and a gold ring on his finger, and also by delivering a gold rod into his hand, that he may preside there, and may direct and defend those parts...."

Windsor Castle, 7th December 1841.

My dearest Uncle,—We arrived here sains et saufs with our awfully large Nursery Establishment yesterday morning. It was a nasty warm and very rainy day, but to-day is very bright, clear and dry, and we walked out early and felt like prisoners freed from some dungeon. Many thanks for your kind letter of the 2nd, by which I grieve to see that you are not quite well. But let me repeat again, you must not despond so; you must not be so out of spirits. I have likewise been suffering so from lowness that it made me quite miserable, and I know how difficult it is to fight against it. I am delighted to hear that all the children are so well. I wonder very much who our little boy will be like. You will understand how fervent my prayers and I am [sure] everybody's must be, to see him resemble his angelic dearest Father in every, every respect, both in body and mind. Oh! my dearest Uncle, I am sure if you knew how happy, how blessed I feel, and how proud I feel in possessing such a perfect being as my husband, as he is, and if you think that you have been instrumental in bringing about this union, it must gladden your heart! How happy should I be to see our child grow up just like him! Dear Pussy travelled with us and behaved like a grown-up person, so quiet and looking about and coquetting with the Hussars on either side of the carriage. Now adieu! Ever your devoted Niece,

Victoria R.

THE APPROACHING CHRISTENING
Castle Howard, 22nd December 1841.

... Lord Melbourne will consider himself most highly honoured by being invited to the christening, and will hold himself in readiness to attend, whenever it may take place. He has written to Mr Anson in answer to the letter which he received from him this morning. Lord Melbourne has been obliged to consent to receive an address from Derby, and has fixed Monday the 27th inst. for that purpose. He could have wished to have avoided this, but it was impossible, and he must make the best of it that he can, which he conceives will be effected by conceiving his reply in very guarded terms, and in a tone defensive of his own administration, but not offensive to those who have succeeded him....

Lord Melbourne is very glad to hear of the feelings of the King of Prussia. For religious matters he is at present very popular with many in this country, and popularity, though transient and uncertain, is a good thing while it lasts. The King of the Belgians should not be surprised or mortified at the conduct of the King of Holland. We must expect that people will act according to their nature and feelings. The Union of Belgium and Holland has been for a long time the first wish and the daily dream of the House of Orange. It has been the great object of their lives, and by the separation, which took place in 1830, they saw their fondest hopes disappointed and destroyed at once. It must be expected that under such a state of things, they will be unquiet, and will try to obtain what they so eagerly desire and have once possessed.

Lord Melbourne is much rejoiced to hear that your Majesty is in the enjoyment of such good health. Your Majesty's observations upon your own situation are in the highest degree just and prudent, and it is a sign of a right mind and of good feelings to prize the blessings we enjoy, and not to suffer them to be too much altered by circumstances, which may not turn out exactly according to our wishes.

THE UNITED STATES
Foreign Office, 24th December 1841.

Lord Aberdeen presents his most humble duty to your Majesty. He ventures to request your Majesty's attention for a moment to the character of your Majesty's present relations with the Government of the United States. Your Majesty is aware that several questions of great difficulty and importance have been long pending between the two Governments.161 Some of these have become more complicated than they were ten years ago; and any of them might, at any moment, lead to consequences of the most disastrous nature.

Instead of continuing negotiations, necessarily tedious and which promise to be interminable, your Majesty's servants are humbly of opinion that an effort ought to be made, by a Special Mission at Washington, to bring all these differences promptly to an adjustment. The public feeling in the United States at this time does not appear to be unfavourable for such an attempt. Should it be undertaken by a person whose rank, character, and abilities would ensure respect, and whose knowledge of the subjects under discussion, and of the people of the country, together with his conciliatory manners, would render him generally acceptable, your Majesty might perhaps indulge the hope of a successful result.

Lord Aberdeen humbly ventures to think that such a person may be found in Lord Ashburton,162 whom he submits for your Majesty's gracious approbation.

Footnote 161: The question of the North-West Boundary had long been one source of dispute; another was the right the British Government claimed of searching vessels suspected of being engaged in the slave trade.

Footnote 162: Alexander, first Lord Ashburton, who had held office in Peel's short Ministry, and married Miss Bingham of Philadelphia. See post, p. .

CHRISTMAS

Christmas has brought its usual routine of festivity and its agreeable accompaniment of Christmas presents. The Queen was not at all well again yesterday, being again troubled with lowness. The Melbourne correspondence still is carried on, but I think not in its pristine vigour by any means. He has taken no notice of the Baron's remonstrance to him, and we are in the dark in what manner, if at all, he means to deal with it.

I have sat by Her Majesty at dinner several times lately. I should say that Her Majesty interests herself less and less about politics, and that her dislike is less than it was to her present Ministers, though she would not be prepared to acknowledge it. Her Majesty is a good deal occupied with the little Princess Royal, who begins to assume companionable qualities. In the evening, instead of her usual conversation with her old Prime Minister, some round game at cards is substituted, which always terminates at eleven. The Prince, to amuse the Queen at this, has nearly left off his chess; his amusements—shooting or hunting—always commence and terminate between eleven and two, not to interfere with Her Majesty's arrangements, in which he is included as her companion.

Melbourne, 29th December 1841.

Lord Melbourne presents his humble duty to your Majesty. He received here yesterday your Majesty's letter of the 25th inst., upon a paper adorned with many quaint and humorous Christmas devices, and Lord Melbourne begs to offer to your Majesty, most sincerely and most fervently, the good wishes of the Season. Lord Melbourne will be in town on Friday evening next, and after that day will wait upon your Majesty, whenever your Majesty is pleased to command....

Lord Melbourne is very glad to hear that the King of the Belgians is reassured by his journey to Mons and his reception upon it. He need not mind the King of Holland, if he can keep all right at

Paris.

The railway smash163 is awful and tremendous, as all railway mishaps are, and Lord Melbourne fears must always be. These slips and falls of earth from the banks are the greatest danger that now impends over them, and if they take place suddenly and in the dark, Lord Melbourne does not see how the fatal consequences of them are to be effectually guarded against. They are peculiarly likely to happen now, as the cuttings have been recently and hastily made, the banks are very steep, and the season has been peculiarly wet, interrupted by severe frosts.

Lord Melbourne received the deputation from Derby, a large and respectable one, here on Monday last. The address was very guarded, temperate, and judicious, and Lord Melbourne strove to construct his answer in the same manner.

Footnote 163: This accident took place on 24th December in the Sonning Hill cutting, two and a half miles from Reading. Eight persons were killed on the spot.

INTRODUCTORY NOTE: TO CHAPTER XI

The session was mainly occupied by the great Ministerial measure of finance, direct taxation by means of income tax being imposed, and the import duties on a large number of articles being removed or relaxed, Mr Gladstone, now at the Board of Trade, taking charge of the bills. Two more attempts on the Queen's life were made, the former again on Constitution Hill by one Francis, whose capital sentence was commuted; the latter by a hunchback, Bean, who was sentenced to eighteen months' imprisonment. An Act was promptly passed to deal with such outrages in future as misdemeanours, without giving them the importance of high treason. Lord Ashley's Bill was passed, prohibiting woman and child labour in mines and collieries. But the Anti-Corn Law League of Manchester was not satisfied with the policy of the Government and objected to the income tax; while riots broke out in the manufacturing districts of the North.

In Afghanistan, the disasters of the previous year were retrieved; Sir Robert Sale, who was gallantly defending Jellalabad, made a sortie and defeated Akbar Khan; General Nott arrived at Ghuznee, but found it evacuated; he destroyed the citadel and removed the Gates of Somnauth. General Pollock swept the Khyber Pass and entered Cabul. The captives taken on the retreat from Cabul were recovered—Lady Macnaghten and Lady Sale among them. In retribution for the murder of Macnaghten, the great bazaar of Cabul, where his remains had been dishonoured, was destroyed by Pollock; the British force was then withdrawn. Dost Mahommed made himself again ruler of Cabul, and a proclamation of Lord Ellenborough announced that the British Government accepted any Sovereign and Constitution approved by the Afghans themselves.

In China, also, operations were successfully terminated, Chapoo being taken in May, and an attack by Admiral Parker upon Nanking being only averted by the conclusion of a favourable treaty, involving an indemnity, the cession by China of Hong Kong, and the opening of important ports to commerce.

A dispute had arisen between this country and the United States as to the boundary line between the latter country and the British Possessions in North America. Lord Ashburton was accordingly sent out on a special mission to effect the adjustment of this and other disputes, and a treaty was concluded for the purpose of defining each country's territorial rights, and imposing mutual obligations for the suppression of the Slave Trade.

CHAPTER XI

Sudbury Hall, 4th January 1842.

My dear Niece,—Most grateful for your very amiable kind letter full of good wishes for me, I hasten to answer it and to assure you that I deeply feel all your affectionate kindness to me in wishing my life to be prolonged. From ill-health I have become such a useless member of your family, that I must wonder you have not long been tired of me. I wish I was more able to be of any use to you which you might like to make of me. My services would be most faithful, I can assure you. Should my life be spared, there may perhaps yet be a time when I can prove to you, that what I say is not merely a façon de parler, but my sincere wish.

Your domestic happiness, dearest Victoria, gives me great satisfaction whenever I think of it, and that is very often. God continue it so, uninterrupted, is my daily prayer.

Your approbation of my little offering to my dear godchild gives me much pleasure. It occupied me several days during my illness to make the drawing, weak as I then was, and it was a pleasant occupation.

We have frost again, with a clear blue sky, which is much better for me than the damp close weather of last week, which oppressed me so much. I breathe again, and my spirits get their usual tone, which they had lost, but I still cough a great deal, which is very fatiguing.

Will you kiss your darlings in my name and bless them, and pray believe me ever, my dear Niece, your most affectionately devoted Aunt,

Adelaide.

WINDSOR

Broadlands,1 5th January 1842.

Lord Melbourne presents his humble duty to your Majesty, and begs to return to your Majesty and to His Royal Highness his thanks for all the kindness shown him at Windsor. He was very happy to find himself there again and in your Majesty's society. He has seen many fine places and much fine country, but after all there is nothing like Windsor and the Park. Twenty very fine places might easily be made out of the latter. Lord Melbourne as he drove to Bagshot was very glad to see the plantations at and about Cumberland Lodge and onwards so well and judiciously thinned. He had a very prosperous journey here. It is a lovely place, with the greatest beauty that a place can have, a very swift, clear, natural stream, running and winding in front of the house. The whole place is much improved since Lord Melbourne saw it last; a great deal of new pleasure-ground has been made. The trees, cypresses, elders, planes, elms, white poplars and acacias are very fine indeed....

Lord Melbourne thinks of staying here six or seven days, and then returning to London and going to Brocket Hall and Panshanger, but he has not fixed his plans decidedly, which he is never very fond of doing.

Lord Melbourne was delighted at thinking that he left your Majesty in good health, which he earnestly hopes and fervently prays may, together with every other blessing, long continue.

Footnote 1: The house of Lord Palmerston in Hants.

Foreign Office, 6th January 1842.

... Sir Robert Peel has informed Lord Aberdeen that he had mentioned to your Majesty the suggestion of the King of Prussia to confer the Order of the Black Eagle2 upon the Prince of Wales, immediately after the christening of his Royal Highness. Lord Aberdeen therefore abstains from troubling your Majesty with any observations on this subject.

Footnote 2: Founded by Frederick I. in 1701.

DISASTERS IN AFGHANISTAN

8th January 1842.

Lord Fitzgerald, with his most humble duty to your Majesty, begs leave humbly to inform your Majesty that despatches have been this day received at the India House from the Earl of Auckland, Governor-General of India, which most officially confirm to too great an extent the disastrous intelligence contained in the public journals of yesterday, the particulars of which the editors of these journals had received by express messengers from Marseilles.3

This intelligence is of a most painful character, and though the details which have arrived do high honour to the courage and the gallantry of your Majesty's forces, as well as of the East India Company's Army, yet the loss sustained has been very great, and many valuable officers have fallen the victims of a widespread conspiracy which seems to have embraced within its confederation the most warlike tribes of the Afghan nation.

Lord Fitzgerald begs leave most humbly to lay before your Majesty an interesting despatch from Lord Auckland, comprising the most important details of the late events in Afghanistan.

It is very satisfactory to Lord Fitzgerald to be enabled humbly to acquaint your Majesty that Lord Auckland has decided on waiting the arrival of his successor, Lord Ellenborough, and states to Lord Fitzgerald that he will feel it to be his duty to remain in his [Government], in the present critical state of affairs, until he is relieved by the new Governor-General.

All of which is most humbly submitted to your Majesty, by your Majesty's most dutiful Subject and Servant,

Fitzgerald and Vesci.

Footnote 3: See Introductory Note, 1841, ante, p. The rebellion broke out at Cabul on 2nd November, and Sir Alexander Burnes was murdered.

THE OXFORD MOVEMENT

Broadlands, 12th January 1842.

Lord Melbourne presents his humble duty to your Majesty. He has this morning received your Majesty's letter of the 10th inst., and is glad to infer from it that your Majesty and the Prince are both well and in good spirits.

With respect to the Oxford affair, your Majesty is aware that for a long time a serious difference has been fermenting and showing itself in the Church of England, one party leaning back towards Popery, and the other either wishing to keep doctrines as they are, or, perhaps, to approach somewhat nearer to the dissenting Churches. This difference has particularly manifested itself in a publication, now discontinued, but which has been long going on at Oxford, entitled Tracts for the Times, and generally called the Oxford Tracts. The Professorship of Poetry is now vacant at Oxford, and two candidates have been put forward, the one Mr Williams, who is the author of one or two of the most questionable of the Oxford Tracts, and the other Mr Garbett, who is a representative of the opposite party. Of course the result of this election, which is made by the Masters of Arts of the University, is looked to with much interest and anxiety, as likely to afford no unequivocal sign of which is the strongest party in the University and amongst the clergy generally. It is expected that Mr Garbett will be chosen by a large majority....

THE MORNING CHRONICLE
South Street, 17th January 1842.

Lord Melbourne presents his humble duty to your Majesty, and begs to acknowledge your Majesty's letter of the 15th, which he has received here this morning.

Lord Melbourne does not think this Puseyite difference in the Church so serious or dangerous as others do. If it is discreetly managed, it will calm down or blow over or sink into disputes of little significance. All Lord Melbourne fears is lest the Bishops should be induced to act hastily and should get into the wrong. The Puseyites have the most learning, or rather, have considered the points more recently and more accurately than their opponents.

Lord Melbourne hopes that the Spanish affair will be settled. Lord Melbourne cannot doubt that the French are wrong. Even if the precedents are in their favour, the Spanish Court has a right to settle its own etiquette and its own mode of transacting business, and to change them if it thinks proper.4

Lord Melbourne was at Broadlands when the Article to which your Majesty alludes appeared in the Morning Chronicle, and he talked it over with Palmerston. He does not think that Palmerston wrote it, because there were in it errors, and those errors to Palmerston's disadvantage; but it was written by Easthope under the impression that it conveyed Palmerston's notions and opinions. Your Majesty knows very well that Palmerston has long had much communication with the Morning Chronicle and much influence over it, and has made great use of it for the purpose of maintaining and defending his own policy. In this sort of matter there is much to be said upon both sides. A Minister has a great advantage in stating his own views to the public, and if Palmerston in the Syrian affair had not had as devoted an assistant as the Morning Chronicle, he would hardly have been able to maintain his course or carry through his measures. It has always been Lord Melbourne's policy to keep himself aloof from the public press and to hold it at arm's-length, and he considers it the best course, but it is subject to disadvantages. You are never in that case strongly supported by them, nor are the motives and reasons of your conduct given to the public with that force and distinctness which they might be.

Lord Melbourne has no doubt that your Majesty's assurance is well founded, and that the present Government are anxious for the welfare and prosperity and tranquillity of Spain. It cannot be otherwise.

Palmerston dislikes Aberdeen and has a low opinion of him. He thinks him weak and timid, and likely to let down the character and influence of the country. Your Majesty knows that Lord Melbourne does not partake these opinions, certainly not at least to anything like the extent to which Palmerston carries them.

Lord Melbourne is going down to Panshanger to-morrow, where he understands that he is to meet Lord and Lady Lansdowne and Lord and Lady Leveson.5 Lord Melbourne will take care and say nothing about Brighton, but is glad to hear that your Majesty is going thither.

Footnote 4: An Ambassador, M. de Salvandy, had been sent from France to Madrid. Espartero, the Regent, required the credentials to be presented to him and not to the young Queen. The French Ambassador having refused to comply, an unseemly dispute arose, and M. de Salvandy left Madrid.

Footnote 5: The late Lord Granville and his first wife, only child of the Duc de Dalberg, and widow of Sir Ferdinand Acton.

Windsor Castle, 18th January 1842.

My dear Uncle,—Not to miss my day, I write a line to thank you for your kind letters of the 10th and 13th, but shall write fully by the messenger. Our Claremont trip was very enjoyable, only we missed Pussy so much; another time we shall take her with us; the dear child was so pleased to see us again, particularly dear Albert, whom she is so fond of.... We think of going to Brighton early in February, as the physicians think it will do the children great good, and perhaps it may me; for I am very strong as to fatigue and exertion, but not quite right otherwise; I am growing thinner, and there is a want of tone, which the sea may correct.

Albert's great fonction6 yesterday went off beautifully, and he was so much admired in all ways; he always fascinates the people wherever he goes, by his very modest and unostentatious yet dignified ways. He only came back at twelve last night; it was very kind of him to come. The King of Prussia means, I believe, to cross on the 20th. Now addio. Ever your most affectionate Niece,

Victoria R.

Footnote 6: The Prince laid the foundation stone of the new Royal Exchange.

THE DUKE OF WELLINGTON

London, 21st January 1842.

Field-Marshal the Duke of Wellington presents his humble duty to your Majesty. He is much flattered by your Majesty's most gracious desire that he should bear the Sword of State at the ceremony of the christening of His Royal Highness the Prince of Wales.

He had already received from Sir Robert Peel an intimation of your Majesty's gracious pleasure on this subject. He is in such good health, as to be able to perform any duty upon which your Majesty may think proper to employ him; and he will attend your Majesty's gracious ceremony at Windsor Castle on Tuesday morning, the 25th Jan. inst.

All of which is humbly submitted to your Majesty by your Majesty's most dutiful and devoted Subject and Servant,

Wellington.

Windsor Castle, 22nd January 1842.

The Queen cannot say how grieved she is, and the Prince also, at hearing of Lord Melbourne's serious indisposition, by his letter this morning. How very provoking if he cannot come on

Tuesday. It will be the only important ceremony during the Queen's reign which Lord Melbourne has not been present at, and it grieves her deeply. It was already a deep mortification not to see him in his old place, but not to see him at all is too provoking. If Lord Melbourne should soon get well we shall hope to see him later during the King's7 stay. The Prince is gone to Greenwich to meet the King, and I expect them about five o'clock.

The Queen hopes to hear soon of Lord Melbourne's being better, and expresses again her very sincere regret at his being prevented from coming.

Footnote 7: Frederick Wilham IV., King of Prussia.

THE SLAVE TRADE

28th January 1842.

Lord Aberdeen presents his most humble duty to your Majesty. Some time ago, your Majesty was graciously pleased to express a desire to have a copy of the Treaty concluded by your Majesty with the Four Great Powers of Europe, for the more effectual suppression of the Slave Trade.8 Lord Aberdeen has had one prepared for your Majesty's use, which he humbly begs to lay before your Majesty.

In obeying your Majesty's commands Lord Aberdeen thinks it his duty, at the same time, to state to your Majesty that, with the exception of some alterations and additions of little importance, the Treaty in its present form had existed for a considerable time in the Foreign Office. He found, also, that there had been a reluctance to sign it on the part of the French Government; but as the objection was chiefly of a personal nature, it was speedily removed. The only share, therefore, which Lord Aberdeen can properly be said to have had in this transaction is that of having been enabled to afford your Majesty the great satisfaction of completing this blessed work at an earlier period than would otherwise have been the case.

Footnote 8: The treaty conferred a mutual right of search.

South Street, 1st February 1842.

Lord Melbourne presents his humble duty to your Majesty, and has to thank your Majesty for the letters of the 28th and the 31st ult., the last of which he received this morning.

Lord Melbourne is very glad that your Majesty opens the Parliament in person. Your Majesty knows Lord Melbourne's opinion, that it ought always to be done, when it can be, without reference to Ministers, politics, or political questions. Lord Melbourne hopes to be able to go to the House in the evening, but he fears that it would be too much for him if he were to attempt to attend also in the morning.

Lord Melbourne was in despair at hearing of poor Eos.9 Favourites often get shot; Lord Melbourne has known it happen often in his time. That is the worst of dogs; they add another strong interest to a life which has already of itself interest enough, and those, God knows! sufficiently subject both to accident and decay.

Lord Melbourne is sorry to do anything that could trouble your Majesty in the slightest degree, but he doubts not that your Majesty is already aware of the matter, and therefore he has less scruple in sending to your Majesty a letter10 which he has received from the Duke of Sussex. Upon the plea of not being well, Lord Melbourne has put off seeing the Duke upon this subject until after Monday next, and when he does see him, he will try to keep him quiet, which your Majesty knows when he has got a thing of this sort into his head, is no easy matter.

Footnote 9: A favourite greyhound of the Prince, accidentally shot by Prince Ferdinand. See King Leopold's letter, 4th February.

Footnote 10: This letter is not preserved among the Queen's papers.

THE KING OF PRUSSIA

Windsor Castle, 1st February 1842.

My dear Uncle,—I have to thank you for a kind, short note of the 27th inst., which I received on Sunday. I gave your kind message to the King of Prussia, who was much touché by it. He is a most amiable man, so kind and well-meaning, and seems so much beloved. He is so amusing too. He is very anxious that Belgium should become liée with Germany, and I think, dearest Uncle, that it would be for the real good of Belgium if it could be so. You will have heard how perfectly and splendidly everything went off on the 25th. Nothing could have done better, and little Albert (what a pleasure that he has that dearest name!) behaved so well. The King left us yesterday morning to go to town, where we follow him to-morrow; he was quite sad to leave Windsor, which he admired so much. He dined with the Sutherlands yesterday, and dines with the Duke of Wellington to-day, and the Cambridges to-morrow. On Thursday he dines with us (he lodges in Buckingham Palace), and on Friday takes his departure. He is really a most agreeable visitor, though I must own that I am somewhat knocked up by our great exertions.

Uncle Ferdinand is very well, and we are delighted with dear Leopold;11 he is so much improved, and is such a modest, sensible boy.

I can't say much for poor Gusti,12 though I love him, but he is really too odd and inanimate. I hope Louise will see the King of Prussia. You have heard our great misfortune about dear Eos; she is going on well, but slowly, and still makes us rather anxious. It made me quite ill the first day, and keeps me fidgety still, till we know that she is quite safe. Ever your devoted Niece,

Victoria R.

We were grieved to hear Papa had been so ill.

Footnote 11: Son of Prince Ferdinand of Saxe-Coburg, and brother of the King of Portugal, afterwards a candidate for the hand of Queen Isabella of Spain. See post, p. .

Footnote 12: Prince Augustus, afterwards married to the Princess Clémentine, daughter of King Louis Philippe.

THE KING OF PRUSSIA

Laeken, 4th February 1842.

My dear Victoria,—Thousand thanks for your kind letter of the 1st, which I received yesterday.

The King of Prussia is a very delightful person;13 he is so clever and amiable, and, owing to his good-nature, not by any means fatiguing. I fear you had cold weather yesterday for the opening of Parliament. To-day we have here a tremendous fog; Heaven grant that it may not be so heavy on the Thames! else the King's journey will be rendered difficult.

We expect him to-morrow about eleven o'clock; he wishes to be at Antwerp at five, which would indicate his departure from hence at three o'clock. There can be no doubt that nothing could be better than to link this country as much as possible to Germany. The public feeling was and is still favourable to this, but in Germany some years ago they were childishly ultra, and kicked us off most unnecessarily, which renders everything of the sort now much less easy. In a political point of view the King's journey will prove useful, as it takes him still more out of the clutches of Russia and gives him more correct views of what is going on in the West of Europe.

I wish the King may also talk to his helter-skelter cousin in Holland; if the man goes on in his wild intrigues, though he will get most probably nothing by it himself, he may do a great deal of harm, and may force us to incline more towards France for fear of his intrigues with France.

I was extremely sorry to hear the accident which befell dear Eos, a great friend of mine. I do not understand how your uncle managed it; he ought rather to have shot somebody else of the family. Ernest has then been going on fast enough; all I hear of the lady is very satisfactory.14 I don't yet know when he means to come here.

Now I must conclude. In haste, ever, my dear Victoria, your affectionate Uncle,
Leopold R.

Footnote 13: Lord Aberdeen wrote to Madame de Lieven: "I passed a great deal of time with the King of Prussia when he was in this country, and perfectly subscribe to the truth of the description you gave me of him before his arrival—intelligent, high-minded, and sincere. Like all Germans, he is sometimes a little in the clouds, but his projects are generous, and he wishes to do what is right."

Footnote 14: He married the Princess Alexandrina of Baden on 3rd May 1842.

Windsor Castle, 8th February 1842.

My dearest Uncle,—I thank you de tout mon cœur for your kind letter of the 4th, which I received the day before yesterday. You have now seen our good, kind, amiable King of Prussia, for whom I have really the greatest affection and respect. We were quite sorry to lose him, and he was much affected at going. He is so open and natural, and seems really so anxious to do good whenever he can. His liberality and generosity here has been immense. He is very much displeased with his "helter-skelter cousin,"15 and quite unhappy at the state of things in that country....

BETROTHAL OF PRINCE ERNEST

Ernest's marriage is a great, great delight to us; thank God! I say, as I so ardently wished it, and Alexandrina is said to be really so perfect. I have begged Ernest beforehand to pass his honeymoon with us, and I beg you to urge him to do it; for he witnessed our first happiness, and we must therefore witness his.

Leopold is a dear, sweet boy, really, so full of feeling, and so very good-tempered and modest; the King was charmed with him and he with the King. I am happy to say faithful Eos is quite convalescent; she walks about wrapped up in flannel.

We are off for Brighton the day after to-morrow; I can't say I like it at all. We were, and the boy too, all three, vaccinated from the same child yesterday! Now adieu! Ever your devoted Niece,
Victoria R.

Fanny Jocelyn is taking her first waiting, and makes a most excellent and sedate Dame d'Honneur. I am sorry she is so very thin still.

Footnote 15: The King of Holland. See King Leopold's letter of 4th February.

CHRISTENING OF PRINCE OF WALES

Marlborough House, 5th February 1842.

My dear Niece,—I thank you a thousand times for your kind letter, just received, and am delighted with the hope of seeing you, if you have time to spare, when you come to town next week. I hardly dare to expect it, but it will make me very happy should you be able to fulfil your kind intention.

I was happy to hear how well the holy ceremony went off on Tuesday, and how splendid the whole was. The earnest attention of the King of Prussia to the ceremony, and the manner with which he read the responses, was universally remarked and admired. May your dear child, our beloved Prince of Wales, follow his pious example in future, and become as truly estimable and amiable and good as his Godfather really is. He is indeed most charming, and so very agreeable and affable to every one, that he must be loved and respected by all who have the good fortune to approach him. I hope he does not over-fatigue himself, for he does a great deal in the short time of his stay in England. He expresses himself delighted with his reception.

I regret to find that your dear little girl is still suffering so much from her teeth. God bless and guard her and her brother!—who by all descriptions must be a very fine babe. The King of Prussia admires little Victoria very much; he described her to me as the most lovely child he ever saw.

I enclose the impression of my seal, according to your wish....

With my best love to dear Albert, I beg you to believe me ever, dearest Victoria, your most attached and devoted Aunt,

Adelaide.

May I ask you to give my affectionate respects to the King of Prussia, and my love to your Mamma?

Whitehall, 14th February, Monday Night.

(Half-past 1 a.m.)

Sir Robert Peel, with his humble duty to your Majesty, begs leave to acquaint your Majesty that Lord John Russell proposed this evening in the House of Commons a resolution condemnatory of the principle of the plan for the adjustment of the Corn Laws, brought forward by your Majesty's servants.

Lord John Russell was followed in the debate by Mr Gladstone, the Vice-President of the Board of Trade, who vindicated the plan....

Sir Robert Peel had a meeting yesterday of the friends of the Government in the House of Commons, and he is convinced that although many may have wished that the plan of the Government had given an increased degree of protection to agriculture, the great body will support the measure, and that we shall have no difficulty in resisting any detached efforts that may be made to add to the duties on foreign corn.

PEEL AND PRINCE ALBERT

Whitehall, 15th February(?) 1842.

Sir,—When I had the honour of last seeing your Royal Highness at Windsor Castle, I stated to your Royal Highness that it would give me great satisfaction to have the opportunity from time to time of apprising your Royal Highness of the legislative measures in contemplation of Her Majesty's servants, and of explaining in detail any matters in respect to which your Royal Highness might wish for information.

In conformity with this feeling on my part, I take the liberty of sending to your Royal Highness two confidential Memoranda prepared for the information of Her Majesty's servants on the important subjects respectively of the state of Slavery in the East Indies, and of the Poor Laws in this country.

They may probably be interesting to your Royal Highness, and if your Royal Highness should encourage me to do so, I will, as occasion may arise, make similar communications to your Royal Highness. I have the honour to be, Sir, with sincere respect, your Royal Highness's most faithful and humble servant,

Robert Peel.

P.S.—I do not think that the measure which I have brought forward for the diminution of the duties on the import of foreign corn, will deprive us of any portion of the support or goodwill of our friends. Many wish that the reduction had not been carried so far, but almost all are aware of the consequences of rejecting or obstructing the measure.

AFGHANISTAN

India Board, 1st March 1842.

Lord Fitzgerald, with his most humble duty to your Majesty, requests permission humbly to submit to your Majesty, that the communications received yesterday at the India House present a dark and alarming picture of the position and danger of the British troops in Afghanistan.16

Although the Governor-General's despatch announcing these melancholy tidings also states that no strictly official intelligence had reached him from Cabul, yet the opinion of Lord Auckland evidently is, that the reports on which his despatch is founded are but too likely to be true.

From them it would appear that a numerous and excited native population had succeeded in intercepting all supplies, that the army at Cabul laboured under severe privations, and that in consequence of the strict investment of the cantonments by the enemy, there remained, according to a letter from the late Sir William Macnaghten to an officer with Sir Robert Sale's force, only three days' provision in the camp.

Under such circumstances it can perhaps be but faintly hoped that any degree of gallantry and devotion on the part of your Majesty's forces can have extricated them from the difficulties by which they were encompassed on every side.

Capitulation had been spoken of, and it may, unhappily, have become inevitable, as the relieving column, expected from Candahar, had been compelled by the severity of an unusual season to retrace its march.

The despatches from Calcutta being voluminous, and embracing minute unofficial reports, Lord Fitzgerald has extracted and copied those parts which relate to the military operations in Afghanistan, and most humbly submits them to your Majesty.

He at the same time solicits permission to annex a précis of some of the most important of the private letters which have been forwarded from India; and, as your Majesty was graciously pleased to peruse with interest some passages from the first journal of Lady Sale, Lord Fitzgerald ventures to add the further extracts, transmitted by Lord Auckland, in which Lady Sale describes successive actions with the enemy, and paints the state of the sufferings of the army, as late as the 9th of December.

Nothing contained in any of these communications encourages the hope of Sir Alexander Burnes's safety. In one letter the death of an individual is mentioned, who is described as the assassin of that lamented officer.

All of which is most humbly submitted to your Majesty by your Majesty's most dutiful Subject and Servant,

Fitzgerald and Vesci.

Footnote 16: See Introductory Note, ante, pp. ,

A MARINE EXCURSION

Pavilion, 4th March 1842.

The Queen thanks Lord Melbourne for his kind letter, received the day before yesterday, by which she is glad to see he is well, and Fanny got safe to Dublin.

Our excursion was most successful and gratifying. It rained very much all Monday evening at Portsmouth, but, nevertheless, we visited the St Vincent and the Royal George yacht, and the Prince went all over the Dockyards.

It stormed and rained all night, and rained when we set off on bord the Black Eagle (the Firebrand that was) for Spithead on Tuesday morning; it, however, got quite fine when we got there, and we went on board the Queen, and a glorious sight it was; she is a magnificent ship, so wide and roomy, and though only just commissioned, in the best order. With marines, etc., her crew is near upon a thousand men! We saw the men at dinner, and tasted the grog and soup, which pleased them very much. Old Sir Edward Owen is very proud of her.

It was a great pleasure for the Queen to be at sea again, and not a creature thought even of being sick. The saluting of all those great ships in the harbour at once, as we came out and returned, has a splendid effect.

The Queen was also much pleased at seeing four of the crew of the Emerald again whom she knew so well nine years ago! The Prince was delighted with all he saw, as were also our Uncle and Cousins; these last, we are sorry to say, leave us on Monday,—and we go up to Town on Tuesday, where the Queen hopes to see Lord Melbourne soon.

The Queen sends Lord Melbourne a letter from the Queen of Portugal, all which tends to show how wrong it is to think that they connive at the restoration of the Charter....

Lady Dunmore is in waiting, and makes an excellent Lady-in-Waiting. Lord Hardwicke the Queen likes very much, he seems so straightforward. He took the greatest care of the Queen when on board ship.

Was not his father drowned at Spithead or Portsmouth?17

The Queen hopes to hear that Lord Melbourne is very well.

Footnote 17: "His father, Sir Joseph Yorke," Lord Melbourne replied, "was drowned in the Southampton River, off Netley Abbey, when sailing for pleasure. The boat was supposed to have been struck by lightning. His cousin, Lord Royston, was drowned in the year 1807 in the Baltic, at Cronstadt" [according to Burke in 1808, off Lubeck, æt. twenty-three], "which event, together with the death of two younger sons of Lord Hardwicke, gave the earldom ultimately to the present Lord."

Pavilion, 7th March 1842.

My dear Uncle,—As I wrote you so long a letter yesterday, I shall only write you a few lines to-day, to thank you for your kind letter of the 4th, received yesterday. Our dear Uncle and dear Cousins have just left us, and we are very sorry to see them go; for the longer one is together the more intimate one gets, and they were quite become as belonging to us, and were so quiet and unassuming, that we shall miss them much, particularly dear Leopold, whom poor Uncle Ferdinand recommended to my especial care, and therefore am really very anxious that we should settle something for his future. Uncle Ferdinand likes the idea of his passing some time at Brussels, and some time here, very much, and I hope we may be able to settle that. Uncle and Cousins were sorry to go.

You will have heard how well our Portsmouth expedition went off; the sea was quite smooth on Tuesday, and we had a delightful visit to the Queen, which is a splendid ship. I think it is in these immense wooden walls that our real greatness exists, and I am proud to think that no other nation can equal us in this....

Now addio! Ever your most affectionate Niece,

Victoria R.

THE FALL OF CABUL

10th March 1842.

Lord Fitzgerald, with his most humble duty to your Majesty, begs leave most humbly and with deep sorrow to lay before your Majesty reports which he has only within this hour received.

They are to be found in a despatch from the Governor and Council of Bombay, and unhappily confirm, to an appalling degree, the disastrous intelligence from Afghanistan. The commercial expresses, which reached London yesterday, gave to the public some of the details of the fall of Cabul; and Lord Fitzgerald laments that it is his painful duty most humbly to inform your Majesty that the despatches just arrived confirm to their full extent the particulars of Sir William Macnaghten's fate, and of the fate of that remnant of gallant men who, on the faith of a capitulation, had evacuated that cantonment which they had defended with unavailing courage.

In addition to the despatch from the Council of Bombay, Lord Fitzgerald humbly ventures to submit to your Majesty a letter addressed to him by Mr Anderson, the Acting-Governor of that Presidency, with further details of these melancholy events.

The despatches from the Governor-General of India come down to the date of the 22nd of

January (three days previous to the tragical death of Sir William Macnaghten). Lord Auckland was then uninformed of the actual state of the force in Cabul, though not unprepared for severe reverses.

THE GARTER

Whitehall, 20th March 1842.

Sir Robert Peel presents his humble duty to your Majesty, and will take an opportunity to-morrow of ascertaining your Majesty's pleasure with respect to the remaining Garter which still remains undisposed of, as your Majesty may probably think it advisable that the Investiture of all the Knights selected for the vacant Garters should take place at the same time.

Sir Robert Peel humbly represents to your Majesty that those Peers who may severally be considered from their rank and station candidates for this high distinction, have behaved very well in respect to it, as since Sir Robert Peel has had the honour of serving your Majesty he has never received, excepting in the cases of the Duke of Buckingham and recently of Lord Cardigan, a direct application on the subject of the Garter.

Of those who from their position and rank in the Peerage, and from the Garter having been heretofore conferred on their ancestors or relations, may be regarded as competitors, the principal appear to Sir Robert Peel to be the following:—

* The Duke of Cleveland
* The Duke of Montrose
* The Marquis of Hertford
* The Marquis of Bute
* The Marquis of Abercorn
* The Marquis Camden
* The Marquis of Londonderry.

Sir Robert Peel names all, without meaning to imply that the pretensions of all are very valid ones. He would humbly represent for your Majesty's consideration, whether on account of rank, fortune and general character and station in the country, the claims of the Duke of Cleveland do not upon the whole predominate.18

His Grace is very much mortified and disappointed at Sir Robert Peel's having humbly advised your Majesty to apply the general rule against the son's succeeding the father immediately in the Lieutenancy of a county to his case in reference to his county of Durham.

Sir Robert Peel thinks it better to write to your Majesty upon this subject, as your Majesty may wish to have an opportunity of considering it.

Footnote 18: The Garter was conferred on the Duke of Cleveland.

THE EARL OF MUNSTER

South Street, 21st March 1842.

Lord Melbourne presents his humble duty to your Majesty. A letter from Charles Fox to Lady Holland, and which she has sent to me, informs me of the shocking end of Munster,19 which your Majesty will have heard long before you receive this. Charles Fox attributes it entirely to the vexatious and uneasy life which he led with Lady Munster, but he was always, as your

Majesty knows, an unhappy and discontented man, and there is something in that unfortunate condition of illegitimacy which seems to distort the mind and feelings and render them incapable of justice or contentment.

It is not impossible that upon this event application may be made to your Majesty for the continuance of the pension upon the Privy Purse to his son. As Lord Melbourne advised your Majesty to continue these pensions upon the late King's death, perhaps it may not be improper that he should now say that it is his strong opinion that they should not be continued further. There is no reason for it. They are not very rich, but neither are they poor, and they have very opulent connections and relations. It appears to me that the first opportunity should be taken to show that it is not your Majesty's intention to charge the Crown with the maintenance and support of all these families, which will otherwise be the case. Lord Melbourne thinks it not improper to mention this matter thus early, as otherwise the [compassionate] feelings naturally raised by such an event might lead to a different determination.

THE QUEEN AND THE INCOME TAX

There is another matter mentioned in your Majesty's letter, relating to money, which is of considerable importance, and that is the determination taken by your Majesty to subject your own provision to the proposed duty on income. When it was put to your Majesty Lord Melbourne is disposed to think that your Majesty's determination20 was right, and it certainly will be very popular, which in the present circumstances of the country and state of public feelings is a great advantage.

At the same time it is giving up a principle of the Constitution, which has hitherto exempted the Sovereign from all direct taxation, and there are very great doubts entertained whether the announcement to Parliament of the intention was not in a constitutional point of view objectionable, inasmuch as it pronounced the opinion of the Crown upon a tax which was still under discussion. It is also a great pecuniary sacrifice, and, as your Majesty says, together with the loss of the Duchy of Cornwall and other revenues, will make a great change in your Majesty's pecuniary circumstances. These defalcations can only be repaired by care and economy. Your Majesty has all the most right feelings and the best judgment about money, and Lord Melbourne has no doubt that your Majesty will so act as to avoid pecuniary embarrassment—the only difficulty which Lord Melbourne fears for your Majesty, and the only contingency which could involve your Majesty in serious personal inconvenience.

Lord Melbourne thanks your Majesty much for the kindness of your letter....

Everybody says that the marriage between Miss Stuart and Lord Waterford21 is likely to take place. It is said that he would do almost anything rather than go to St. Petersburg. Lord Melbourne has not seen Lord Waterford, but he is said to be very good-looking; we know him to be rich and of high rank, and, after all, that sort of character is not disliked by all ladies. Perhaps also she counts upon the effect of her influence to soften, to tranquillise, and to restrain.

Lord Melbourne hears a very bad account of Lord Anglesey's affairs. His case is a hard one, for these pecuniary difficulties are owing to the extravagance of others, and by no means to his own. Lord Melbourne saw Uxbridge and Ellen at Lady Palmerston's on Saturday evening. The latter seemed in good spirits, and said that she did not mean to shut herself up too closely in Hertfordshire.

Lord Melbourne thought that your Majesty would be pleased with Lambeth. The view from the great window in the drawing-room over the river, and to the Houses of Parliament and the Abbey, is very fine indeed, but like all London views can rarely be seen in consequence of the foggy atmosphere....

No doubt your Majesty and His Royal Highness must be anxious for a little quiet and repose, which Lord Melbourne hopes that your Majesty will enjoy. Lord Melbourne had feared that your Majesty's health was not quite so good as it appeared.... Lord Melbourne concludes this very long letter with the most fervent expression of his most sincere wishes for your Majesty's health and happiness.

Lord Melbourne in speaking of poor Lord Munster forgot to mention that at the Levée on Wednesday last he followed Lord Melbourne down the long gallery as he was going away, came up to him with great emotion of manner, pressed his hand warmly, and said that he wished to take the earliest opportunity of thanking Lord Melbourne for all the kindness he had shown him whilst he had been in office.

Footnote 19: The Earl of Munster, son of William IV. and Mrs. Jordan, shot himself, 20th March. His wife was a daughter of the Earl of Egremont.

Footnote 20: The Queen had decided that she would herself pay Income Tax.

Footnote 21: Henry, third Marquis, and Louisa, second daughter of Lord Stuart de Rothesay, were married on 8th June.

STRAWBERRY HILL

Panshanger, 31st March 1842.

Lord Melbourne presents his humble duty to your Majesty. He is much rejoiced to learn that your Majesty has had fine weather and has enjoyed it. It rained here hard yesterday in the morning, but cleared up about half-past twelve and was very fine indeed. Lord Melbourne went over to Brocket Hall and enjoyed it much. He does not intend to return to London until Monday next, when the House of Lords reassembles. It is to be hoped that we shall then soon have the Corn Bill up from the Commons and pass it. The Income Tax will give some trouble, but that done, and the Poor Law Bill, the end of the Session may begin to be looked forward to.

The sale of Strawberry Hill22 naturally excites interest, and things are not unlikely to be sold high. The collection has after all been kept together, and the place has remained in the family of his niece,23 the Duchess of Gloucester, to whom he bequeathed it, longer than he himself expected. He says in one of his letters that he would send a statue down to Linton, Sir Horace Mann's place in Kent, because there it had a better chance of remaining permanently, "for as to this poor bauble of a place," he adds, "it will be knocked to pieces in a very few years after my decease." It has stood, however, and remained five-and-forty years, a longer period than he had anticipated. Some of the works, such as the bell by Benvenuto Cellini, and the antique Eagle, are very fine; others are only curious. Lord Melbourne would not give much money for a mere curiosity, unless there were also some intrinsic merits or beauty.

What is the value of Cardinal Wolsey's cap, for instance? It was not different from that of any other Cardinal, and a Cardinal's cap is no great wonder.

Lord Melbourne returns Lord Munster's letter. It is without date, but was evidently written in contemplation of the dreadful act which he afterwards perpetrated. It is very melancholy. Lord Melbourne was certain that your Majesty would send to Lord Adolphus[24] the assurance which you have done, and that you would be anxious to assist his children, and promote their interests by every means in your power. But both their brothers and they must be made sensible that they must make some effort for themselves.

Lord Melbourne is very glad to learn that your Majesty intends to offer the Round Tower[25] to the Duke of Sussex. It is in every respect kind. It will be of essential service to him, and it will gratify him most exceedingly.

THE ROYAL GOVERNESS

Lord Melbourne thinks that your Majesty's decision respecting the Governess[26] is right. It should be a lady of rank; but that she should be a woman of sense and discretion, and capable of fulfilling the duties of the office, is of more importance than whether she is a Duchess, a Marchioness, or a Countess. The selection is difficult, but if your Majesty can find a person, it would not be well to consider either high or low rank as a disqualification.

Lord Melbourne intends to take advantage of his freedom from the restraints of office in order to see a little of the bloom of spring and summer, which he has missed for so many years. He has got one or two horses, which he likes well enough, and has begun to ride again a little. Lord Melbourne wishes your Majesty much of the same enjoyment, together with all health, happiness, and prosperity.

Footnote 22: Near Twickenham, formerly the residence of Horace Walpole, and filled with his collection of pictures and objets de vertu.

Footnote 23: The Duke of Gloucester, brother of George III., married in 1766 Maria, Countess-Dowager Waldegrave, illegitimate daughter of Sir Edward Walpole, and niece of Horace Walpole. This, and the Duke of Cumberland's marriage in 1771 to Lady Anne Horton, occasioned the passing of the Royal Marriages Act.

Footnote 24: Lord Adolphus FitzClarence (1802-1856), a Rear-Admiral, brother of the Earl of Munster.

Footnote 25: The Earl of Munster had held the office of Governor and Constable of Windsor Castle, with a salary of £1,000 a year.

Footnote 26: To the Royal children. Lady Lyttelton was ultimately appointed.

PARTY POLITICS

Brocket Hall, 6th April 1842.

Lord Melbourne presents his humble duty to your Majesty, and has this morning received your Majesty's very kind and confidential letter, for which he greatly thanks your Majesty. Your Majesty may depend upon it that Lord Melbourne will do everything in his power to discourage and restrain factious and vexatious opposition, not only on account of your Majesty's wish, but because he disapproves it as much as your Majesty can possibly do. But everything in his power he fears is but little. The leaders of a party, or those who are so called, have but little sway over their followers, particularly when not in Government, and when they have it not in their power to threaten them with any very serious consequences, such as the dissolution of the Administration. Mr Pulteney, afterwards Earl of Bath, is reported to have said that political parties were like snakes, guided not by their heads, but by their tails. Lord Melbourne does not know whether this is true of the snake, but it is certainly so of the party. The conduct of the Opposition upon the resolution respecting the Income Tax is rendered peculiarly ridiculous by the result. They forcibly put it off until after the holidays, and then upon the first day of the meeting they vote it without a division. What is this but admitting that they looked to a movement in the country which they have not been able to create? Moreover, all Oppositions that Lord Melbourne has ever seen are more or less factious. The Opposition of Mr Fox to Mr Pitt was the least so, but these were great men, greater than any that exist at the present day, although Lord Melbourne is by no means inclined to depreciate his own times. The factiousness of one Opposition naturally produces the same in the next. They say, "They did so to us; why should we not do so to them?" Your Majesty may rest assured that Lord Melbourne will do everything he can to prevent delay, and to accelerate the transaction of the public business.

Lord Melbourne sends a letter which he has received this morning from the Duke of Sussex, and which expresses very right and proper feeling. Lord Melbourne has written in reply that, "Your Majesty was no doubt influenced principally by your natural affection for him, and by your sense of the generosity of his conduct towards Lord Munster, but that if any thought of Lord Melbourne intervened, your Majesty could not have given a higher or a more acceptable proof of your approbation and regard."

THE GARTER

The Garters27 seem to Lord Melbourne to be given well enough. Your Majesty's feelings upon the subject are most kind and amiable. But these things cannot be helped, and it is upon the whole advantageous that each party should have their portion of patronage and honours. If there is very distinguished service, the Garter should be bestowed upon it. Otherwise, in Lord Melbourne's opinion, it is better given to noblemen of high rank and great property. The chapter in Ecclesiasticus, read in St George's Chapel on Obiit Sunday, well describes those who ought to have it, with the exception of those "who find out musical tunes." Lord Melbourne does not think it well given to Ministers. It is always then subject to the imputation of their giving it to themselves, and pronouncing an approbation of their own conduct.

Lord Melbourne hopes that the Pope's standing sponsor for the young Prince of Portugal is a sign of complete reconciliation with the See of Rome. It is a very awkward thing for a Roman Catholic Government to be at variance with the Pope. He is still a very ugly customer.

Lord Melbourne is very much concerned to hear of the Baron's28 illness—very much indeed; he is an excellent and most valuable man, with one of the soundest and coolest judgments that Lord Melbourne has ever met with. Your Majesty knows that Lord Melbourne has never had a favourable opinion of his health. There seems to be about him a settled weakness of the stomach, which is in fact the seat of health, strength, thought and life. Lord Melbourne sees that a great physician says that Napoleon lost the battle of Leipsic in consequence of some very greasy soup which he ate the day before, and which clouded his judgment and obscured his perceptions.

Lord Melbourne is very glad to hear that your Majesty has amused yourself so well in the country, and is not surprised that you are unwilling to quit it. He means himself to see a little of the coming in of the spring, which he has not done for many years.

Footnote 27: The recipients had been the King of Saxony, the Duke of Beaufort, the Duke of Buckingham, the Marquess of Salisbury, the Duke of Cleveland.

Footnote 28: Baron Stockmar.

A BRILLIANT BALL

Buckingham Palace, 19th April 1842.

Dearest Uncle,—I am so sorry to see by your kind letter of the 15th that you are all so enrhumés, but hear to-day from Vecto that Charlotte is quite well again. I am quite bewildered with all the arrangements for our bal costumé, which I wish you could see; we are to be Edward III. and Queen Philippa, and a great number of our Court to be dressed like the people in those times, and very correctly, so as to make a grand Aufzug; but there is such asking, and so many silks and drawings and crowns, and God knows what, to look at, that I, who hate being troubled about dress, am quite confuse.

To get a little rest we mean to run down to Claremont with the children from Friday to Monday. My last ball was very splendid, and I have a concert on Monday next....

I hope Ernest and dear Alexandrine will come in June, and stay some time quietly with us in the country. I saw another beautiful letter of hers, so well and sensibly and religiously written, it would have pleased you. Now adieu! Ever your devoted Niece,

Victoria R.

South Street, 20th April 1842.

Lord Melbourne presents his humble duty to your Majesty, and thanks your Majesty much for your letter of the 17th inst. Lord Melbourne has been so much occupied with the debates in the House of Lords during the last two days, that he has ventured to put off replying to your Majesty's letters, which he trusts that your Majesty will excuse.

Lord Melbourne did not leave the ball until ten minutes after one, and as there were so many persons there, which Lord Melbourne thinks quite right and was very glad to see, Lord Melbourne had little hope of seeing your Majesty again, and therefore ventured to take advantage of having ordered his carriage at half-past twelve and of its having come at the time that it was ordered. It was a very brilliant and very beautiful and a very gay ball.

Lord Melbourne is very sorry to be obliged to express his fear that your Majesty will prove more in the right than he was about the duration of Parliament. There will be much debate in the Committee upon the details of the Income Tax, and the discussions upon the Tariff of duties, which affects so many interests, are likely to be very long indeed. There is one good thing in the House of Lords, and that is that it never much delays or obstructs public business....

As Lord Melbourne drove down the Park on Saturday evening last to dine with his sister, he could see clearly into your Majesty's room, so as to be able to distinguish the pictures, tables, etc., the candles being lighted and the curtains not drawn. Your Majesty was just setting off for the Opera.

PRINCE ALBERT AND THE ARMY

Buckingham Palace, 20th April 1842.

The Queen encloses the Prince's letter to Sir Robert Peel, containing his acceptance of the Guards. At the same time, both the Prince and Queen feel much regret at the Prince's leaving the 11th, which is, if possible, enhanced by seeing the Regiment out to-day, which is in beautiful order. It was, besides, the Regiment which escorted the Prince from Dover to Canterbury on his arrival in England in February '40. The Queen fears, indeed knows, that Lord Cardigan will be deeply mortified at the Prince's leaving the Regiment, and that it will have the effect of appearing like another slight to him; therefore, the Queen much wishes that at some fit opportunity29 a mark of favour should be bestowed upon him....

The Queen hopes Sir Robert will think of this.

Footnote 29: Lord Cardigan was promoted Major-General in 1847. He became Inspector-General of Cavalry, and received the K.C.B. in 1855.

South Street, 26th April 1842.

Lord Melbourne presents his humble duty to your Majesty, and acknowledges with many thanks your Majesty's letter of the 24th inst., which he received yesterday morning. Lord Melbourne learns with the greatest satisfaction that Lady Lyttelton has undertaken the important and interesting charge, for which she is so well fitted. Lord Melbourne is most sincerely of opinion that no other person so well qualified could have been selected. Lord Melbourne will keep the matter strictly secret; he has not yet mentioned it to any one, nor has he heard it mentioned by any other person, which, as it must be known to some, rather surprises him. Unreserved approbation cannot be expected for anything, but when it is known, Lord Melbourne anticipates that it will meet with as general an assent as could be anticipated for a choice in which all the community will take, and indeed have, so deep an interest.

GOETHE AND SCHILLER

Brocket Hall, 15th May 1842.

Lord Melbourne presents his humble duty to your Majesty. He is very sorry indeed, and entreats your Majesty's pardon for his great omission on Monday evening. He was never told that he was to pass before your Majesty at the beginning; at the same time he admits that it was a blundering piece of stupidity not to find this out of himself. After this he never saw the glimmer of a chance of being able to get near to your Majesty.

Lord Melbourne wonders much who could have whispered to your Majesty that he felt or expressed anything but the most unqualified admiration of the ball, which was the most magnificent and beautiful spectacle that he ever beheld. Lord Melbourne also believes it to be very popular, for the reasons which your Majesty mentions.

Your Majesty having generally chosen handsome and attractive girls for the Maids of Honour, which is very right, must expect to lose them in this way. Lord Melbourne is very glad of the marriage. Lord Emlyn30 always seemed to him a very pleasing young man, and well calculated to make a woman happy.

Lord Melbourne felt quite sure that there had been a mistake about Ben Stanley, which was the reason that he mentioned his name. He is sorry that he has made a fool of himself by writing. Having had so much to do with invitations during the two last years, he was not altogether unnaturally mortified to find himself not invited there.31 Stanley is not a man to whom Lord Melbourne is very partial, but we must give every one his due. Lord Melbourne always discourages to the utmost of his power the notion of any one's having a right or claim to be asked, which notion, however, has a strong possession of the minds of people in general.

Lord Melbourne is come down here again, being determined to see this spring thoroughly and completely. His feelings are like those, so beautifully described by Schiller, of Max Piccolomini,32 when, after a youth passed entirely in war, he for the first time sees a country which has enjoyed the blessings of peace. The Germans seem to Lord Melbourne generally to prefer Goethe to Schiller, a decision which surprises him, although he feels that he has no right to dictate to a people, of whose language he does not understand a word, their judgment upon their own authors. But the one, Schiller, seems to him to be all truth, clearness, nature and beauty; the other, principally mysticism, obscurity, and unintelligibility.

Lord Melbourne intends to return on Wednesday, and will have the honour and pleasure of waiting upon your Majesty on Thursday.

Footnote 30: The second Earl Cawdor, who married Miss Sarah Mary Cavendish.

Footnote 31: Edward John, afterwards second Lord Stanley of Alderley, was nicknamed Ben, after "Sir Benjamin Backbite." He had mentioned to Lord Melbourne that he was disappointed at not receiving an invitation to the Royal Ball.

Footnote 32: In the Wallenstein Trilogy.

Laeken, 20th May 1842.

My dearest Victoria,—I found here yesterday a very long and dear letter from your august hand, which made me very happy. Your fête I believe to have been most probably one of the most splendid ever given. There is hardly a country where so much magnificence exists; Austria has some of the means, but the Court is not elegant from its nature. We regret sincerely not to have been able to witness it, and will admire the exhibition of your splendid costume.

MR EDWIN LANDSEER

Whitehall, 27th May 1842.

... Sir Robert Peel humbly submits his opinion to your Majesty that Mr Landseer's eminence as an artist would fully justify his having the honour of Knighthood, and would not give any legitimate ground of complaint to any other artist on account of a similar distinction not being conferred on him.

Sir Robert Peel proposes therefore to write to Mr Landseer on the subject, as your Majesty's opinion appears to be in favour of his name appearing with the others, should he wish for the distinction....

Buckingham Palace, 28th May 1842.

The Queen is quite vexed at having been quite unable to write to Lord Melbourne sooner, but we have been so occupied that she could not. She was so vexed too to have not had her head turned the other way when she met him yesterday, but she was looking at the Prince, her Uncle, and Cousins riding, and only turned to see Lord Melbourne's groom whom she instantly recognised, but too late, alas! The Queen spent a very merry, happy birthday at dear old Claremont, and we finished by dancing in the gallery. She was grieved Lord Melbourne could not be there.

We have got our dear Uncle Mensdorff33 and his four sons here, which is a great happiness to us. Dear Uncle (who Lord Melbourne is aware is a most distinguished officer) is a delightful and amiable old man, and the sons are all so nice and amiable and kind and good; Lord Melbourne remembers seeing Alexander here in 1839, and that the Queen was very partial to him. The two eldest and the youngest—Hugo, Alphonse, and Arthur—are all amiable, though none near so good-looking, but so very well brought up and so unassuming. The second is very clever. And it is quite beautiful to see the love the father has for his sons, and vice versâ—and the affection the four brothers have for one another; this is so rarely seen that it does one's heart good to witness it. The Queen has appointed the Duchess of Norfolk in Lady Lyttelton's place, and intends appointing Lady Canning in Lady Dalhousie's, who has resigned from ill-health.

Lady Lyttelton is established here in her new office, and does everything admirably.

The Queen must conclude here as she has got so much to do—hoping Lord Melbourne is well.

Footnote 33: See p.

LANDSEER DECLINES KNIGHTHOOD

Whitehall, 31st May 1842.

Sir Robert Peel, with his humble duty to your Majesty, begs leave to acquaint your Majesty, that he has just seen Mr Landseer.

Mr Landseer repeated his expressions of deep and sincere gratitude for the favour and kindness with which your Majesty had contemplated his claims for professional distinction, but appeared to retain the impression that he had yet scarcely done enough to entitle him to the honour which it was contemplated to bestow upon him.

In the course of conversation he observed that he was now occupied upon works of a more important character than any that he had yet completed, and mentioned particularly an equestrian portrait of your Majesty. He said that when these works were finished, and should they prove successful and meet with your Majesty's approbation, he might feel himself better entitled to receive a mark of your Majesty's favour.

As these were evidently his sincere impressions and wishes, Sir Robert Peel forbore from pressing upon him the immediate acceptance of the honour of Knighthood.

ATTEMPT ON THE QUEEN

Buckingham Palace, 31st May 1842.

My dearest Uncle.—I wish to be the first to inform you of what happened yesterday evening, and to tell you that we are saines et sauves. On returning from the chapel on Sunday, Albert was observing how civil the people were, and then suddenly turned to me and said it appeared to him as though a man had held out a pistol to the carriage, and that it had hung fire; accordingly, when we came home he mentioned it to Colonel Arbuthnot, who was only to tell it to Sir J. Graham and Sir Robert Peel, and have the police instructed, and nobody else. No one, however, who was with us, such as footmen, etc., had seen anything at all. Albert began to doubt what he believed he had seen. Well, yesterday morning (Monday) a lad came to Murray34 (who of course knew nothing) and said that he saw a man in the crowd as we came home from church, present a pistol to the carriage, which, however, did not go off, and heard the man say, "Fool that I was not to fire!" The man then vanished, and this boy followed another man (an old man) up St James's Street who repeated twice, "How very extraordinary!" but instead of saying anything to the police, asked the boy for his direction and disappeared. The boy accordingly was sent to Sir Robert Peel, and (doubtful as it all still was) every precaution was taken, still keeping the thing completely secret, not a soul in the house knowing a word, and accordingly after some consultation, as nothing could be done, we drove out—many police then in plain clothes being distributed in and about the parks, and the two Equerries riding so close on each side that they must have been hit, if anybody had; still the feeling of looking out for such a man was not des plus agréables; however, we drove through the parks, up to Hampstead, and back again. All was so quiet that we almost thought of nothing,—when, as we drove down Constitution Hill, very fast, we heard the report of a pistol, but not at all loud, so that had we not been on the alert we should hardly have taken notice of it. We saw the man seized by a policeman next to whom he was standing when he fired, but we did not stop. Colonel Arbuthnot and two others saw him take aim, but we only heard the report (looking both the other way). We felt both very glad that our drive had had the effect of having the man seized. Whether it was loaded or not we cannot yet tell, but we are again full of gratitude to Providence for invariably protecting us! The feeling of horror is very great in the public, and great affection is shown us. The man was yesterday examinedJOHN FRANCIS at the Home Office, is called John Francis, is a cabinet-maker, and son of a machine-maker of Covent Garden Theatre, is good-looking (they say). I have never seen him at all close, but Arbuthnot gave the description of him from what he saw on Sunday, which exactly answered. Only twenty or twenty-one years old, and not the least mad—but very cunning. The boy identified him this morning, amongst many others. Everything is to be kept secret this time, which is very right, and altogether I think it is being well done. Every further particular you shall hear. I was really not at all frightened, and feel very proud at dear Uncle Mensdorff calling me "sehr muthig," which I shall ever remember with peculiar pride, coming from so distinguished an officer as he is! Thank God, my Angel is also well! but he says that had the man fired on Sunday, he must have been hit in the head! God is merciful; that indeed we must feel daily more! Uncle and cousins were quite horrified.... Ever your devoted Niece,

Victoria R.

You will tell Louise all, of course.

Footnote 34: The Hon. Charles Augustus Murray, Master of the Household, afterwards Consul-General of Egypt, and Minister in Persia and at Dresden.

Bushey House (Monday night), May 1842.

My dear Niece,—I must write a line to express to you what I felt when I took up the newspapers which informed me of what had happened yesterday. Is it possible?—can it be true? was my first question. However, the detailed accounts leave no doubt that a pistol was pointed at you again, though not fired. It is really shocking that such wretches exist who dare tempt (sic) to alarm you—though in this instance there was nothing alarming except the evil spirit which inspired the boy.

How grateful must we not feel to our merciful God, who protects you so visibly, and gives you courage and confidence in Him, who is and ever will be your safest guard and support. Trust in Him and you will not fail to be well guided.

I hope it is true that you were not aware of what had happened when you went to church, not to be disturbed in your devotions, and that the account did not agitate you.

Edward35 came yesterday from town, but he knew nothing but that a pistol had been taken from a man in the Park. We hardly believed the story till the papers informed us of the truth. Pray say to dear Albert what I feel for and with you both, and how I thank God and pray that His merciful protection may never fail you.

We are going to Frogmore to-morrow, and from there shall drive in the Park and to St George's Chapel. I hope the weather will be as fine as it was to-day. God bless and guard you ever and ever! dearest Victoria, prays your most devotedly attached Aunt,

Adelaide.

Footnote 35: Prince Edward of Saxe-Weimar.

South Street, 1st June 1842.

Lord Melbourne presents his humble duty to your Majesty. He was much shocked at learning, which he did not do until six o'clock yesterday evening, the event which took place on Monday. After what took place on Sunday, it must have been a trial to your Majesty's nerves, and still more to those of the Prince, to go out on Monday; but it appears to Lord Melbourne that your Majesty judged quite correctly in doing so. Lord Melbourne hardly knows what to say of this repeated attempt. It is a depravity and a malice as unintelligible as it is atrocious. Lord Melbourne is at least as grateful as any one of your Majesty's subjects, and the gratitude is universal and fervent for your Majesty's safety.

Lord Melbourne had ridden over in the morning to visit Lord and Lady Uxbridge in their rural retirement, and upon his return to Brocket Hall, about six o'clock, found the morning newspaper with the accounts of what had happened. If they had sent him down a messenger on Monday night, which it would have been better to have done, he would have been yesterday in his place in the House of Lords.

Lord Melbourne found Uxbridge enveloped in parcels and boxes, which he was busy unpacking, Lady Uxbridge reclining by the stream under the shade of a plane-tree, and the two young ladies somewhat pensive. The place looked beautiful, but Lord Melbourne fears that all its beauty will not be a compensation to them for London at this time of the year.

THE ADDRESS

Whitehall, 1st June 1842.

Sir James Graham, with humble duty to your Majesty, submits a copy of the Answer to the

Address; and an alteration has been made in the Answer which Sir James Graham hopes may render it conformable to the tender and generous feelings which your Majesty has deigned to express with reference to the Prince.

The two Houses of Parliament followed the exact precedent which has been established in Oxford's case; and although the life of the Prince, so dear to your Majesty, is highly valued by all your loving subjects, yet the crime of treason attaches only to an attack on the sacred person of your Majesty; and the expressions used by Parliament with reference to these atrocious crimes, when directed against the Sovereign, are necessarily inapplicable to any other person, and could not be used with propriety. Hence the omission in the former case of all allusion to the Prince; and the silence of Parliament on the present occasion is to be ascribed to the same cause—not to any cold indifference, which the general feeling of attachment to the Prince entirely forbids.

The above is humbly submitted by your Majesty's dutiful Subject and Servant,

J. R. G. Graham.

Windsor Castle, 6th June 1842.

My dearest Uncle,—I was sure of the kind interest you would take in the event of the 29th and 30th. I am most thankful for your very kind, long letter of the 3rd, which I received the day before yesterday. I have so little time—as we are just setting off for Ascot—that I can hardly write anything to you. There seems no doubt whatever that Francis is totally without accomplices, and a mauvais sujet. We shall be able probably to tell you more when we see you. I am grieved that you have deferred your visit again. We are then to expect your arrival either on the Tuesday or Wednesday? Very thankful we should be soon to hear whom you bring with you.

Dear Uncle and the Cousins are delighted with Windsor, and the weather is beautiful, only unfortunately too hot to be pleasant. I rode on my little Barb at a review of Cavalry at Wormwood Scrubbs on Saturday, dont je suis bien fière. Now adieu! dearest Uncle. In haste, your devoted Niece,

Victoria R.

NEWS FROM AFGHANISTAN

India Board, 7th June 1842.

Lord Fitzgerald, with his most humble duty to your Majesty, humbly acquaints your Majesty that despatches have been this day received from the Governor-General and the several Presidencies of India.

SALE AND POLLOCK

They announce a signal victory, achieved by Sir Robert Sale and his admirable garrison.36

The circumstances attending his glorious success, and the consequences likely to result from it, are amongst the most important of this hurtful war.

They are described in Sir Robert Sale's Report, as published in the Bombay Gazette, a copy of which is most humbly submitted to your Majesty.

The despatches further bring the gratifying intelligence that General Pollock had forced the Khyber Pass, and, defeating the enemy on every point, had surmounted the chief obstacles of that dangerous defile.37

The relief of the brave men under Sir Robert Sale, to which their own gallantry and their late victory have so mainly contributed, may now be regarded as certain from the success of General Pollock's advance.

It is with regret that Lord Fitzgerald has to add that the citadel of Ghuznee has surrendered on the faith of a capitulation, perhaps already violated, and that General England, who had marched with a convoy of treasure, and other supplies for the Army at Candahar, had been forced to retrace his steps and had arrived at Quetta.

At the same time, however, General Nott had dispersed considerable assemblages of rebel tribes, whom he had defeated with loss, while an attack made during his absence on the city of Candahar had been effectually repulsed by that portion of his force which had been left for its defence.

The Governor-General having proceeded in person to the North-Western Provinces of Bengal, had issued at Benares General Orders congratulating the Army on the return of victory to its ranks, and on the fresh lustre thus added to your Majesty's Arms.

Fitzgerald and Vesci.

Footnote 36: Sir R. Sale, who with his column had thrown himself into Jellalabad on 13th November 1841, and had heard Brydon's narrative, made a sortie on 7th April, and secured a great victory over Akbar Khan, whose force outnumbered Sale's by five to one.

Footnote 37: General Pollock, whom Auckland had selected for the command, and who found everything in confusion on the frontier, swept the Khyber Pass of the enemy, and joined Sale. The insurrection had spread to Candahar, where General (afterwards Sir William) Nott was in command with a force of 10,000 men. He heard of Macnaghten's murder on 31st January, and, like Sale, refused to follow the order received (under coercion, as he believed) from Elphinstone to return to India. On the contrary, he ordered all Afghans to leave Candahar, marched out himself and attacked and dispersed the enemy, 12,000 strong; while a flank movement made by the enemy on the city was repulsed with great loss. General (afterwards Sir Richard) England started from Quetta with reinforcements, but met with a reverse at Haikalzai; meanwhile also Colonel Palmer had had to make terms at Ghuznee, and had to encounter treachery. Nott, who was badly in want of money and ammunition for the troops, sent imperative orders to General England to reinforce him, which he did early in May.

DEBATE ON THE INCOME TAX

South Street, 10th June 1842.

Lord Melbourne presents his humble duty to your Majesty. He has thought it better not to interrupt your Majesty with letters during the bustle of the last week, but he cannot omit to express to your Majesty how much he was struck with the letter of the 2nd inst. which he received, and how entirely he concurs in the justice and propriety of your Majesty's feelings and observations. Let us hope that we shall have no more of these horrid attempts, which are generated by the wild notions of the time, and by the expectation, extravagant and unfounded, so industriously inculcated into the public mind, of advantages to be derived from change and confusion; Lord Melbourne anxiously hopes that the painful impressions which such events are calculated to produce upon your Majesty's mind, and which they necessarily must produce, will pass away and that nothing will happen to renew and revive them.

Lord Melbourne is happy to hear from Normanby that everything passed off well and successfully at Windsor and at Ascot. The last is always rather a doubtful and disagreeable ordeal to pass through.

We should have got through the debate upon the Income Tax this evening in the House of Lords, if Lansdowne had not unfortunately this morning had an access of gout in the hand, which prevented him from attending, and obliged the debate to be deferred. Lord Melbourne hopes that the resolution which Lansdowne is to move38 is put in such a shape as to vindicate our course, and at the same time not to condemn that which has been adopted overmuch, nor to pledge us for the future....

Lord Melbourne earnestly hopes that your Majesty is well and not too much affected by the heat of this weather, which does not suit Lord Melbourne very well. In conjunction with a large dinner which we had at the Reform Club in honour of the Duke of Sussex, it has given Lord Melbourne a good deal of headache and indisposition. The Duke was in very good humour, and much pleased with the dinner, but he was by no means well or strong.

Footnote 38: This Resolution was in favour of altering the Corn, Sugar, and Timber Duties, in preference to imposing an Income Tax. It was negatived by 112 to 52.

QUEEN'S FIRST RAILWAY JOURNEY

Buckingham Palace, 14th June 1842.

My dearest Uncle,—Though I shall have the inexpressible happiness of seeing you and dearest Louise so soon, I write these few lines to thank you for your very kind letter of the 9th. We arrived here yesterday morning, having come by the railroad, from Windsor, in half an hour, free from dust and crowd and heat, and I am quite charmed with it.39 We spent a delightful time at Windsor, which would have been still pleasanter had not the heat been such, ever since Saturday week, that one is quite overcome; the grass is quite brown, and the earth full of wide cracks; there has not been a drop of rain since the 24th, my birthday! We rode and walked and danced, and I think I never was better than in all this fatigue and exercise....

I get every day fonder of dearest, excellent Uncle Mensdorff and the dear cousins, who are so amiable and good and unassuming; really, in society they keep quite in the background. They are out and out the nicest cousins we have. I am sure what I can do for them I shall be too happy to do. Alexander is the most distinguished and solid, but Alphonse and Arthur the most unassuming. There is something so peculiarly good in dear Arthur! and they are all five so fond of Pussy, and she so fond of them.... Ever your devoted Niece,

Victoria R.

Footnote 39: This was the Queen's first journey on the Great Western Railway. The Prince had often used it, and had been known to say, on descending from the train, "Not quite so fast next time, Mr Conductor, if you please."—Acworth, The Railways of England, p. 17.

THE INCOME TAX BILL

South Street, 19th June 1842.

Lord Melbourne presents his humble duty to your Majesty, and offers many thanks for the letter, which he received yesterday evening. Lord Melbourne is very glad to hear that your Majesty has enjoyed in the society of your near and dear relations so much happiness, which, like all other things, must have its portion of alloy in their departure. Lord Melbourne was much pleased with the short conversation which he had with Count Mensdorff at Stafford House, and it is highly interesting to see at this distance of time a man who has been engaged in affairs so important and of so awful and melancholy a character. Your Majesty is surely right in terming your cousins young men; if the health and constitution be good, thirty-six is a young man, twenty-nine and thirty-two very young men, and twenty-five quite a boy. The weather has been very hot but very fine. The rain was so much required that Lord Melbourne cannot lament its coming, but he also regrets the hot suns which it has banished.

The course which had been taken upon the Income Tax in the House of Commons,40 contrary to Lord Melbourne's wish and opinion, rendered it impossible for Lord Melbourne directly to support the Bill in the House of Lords without offending and separating himself from the whole body of those who supported the last Government.

He therefore acquiesced in the resolution, which was moved by Lord Lansdowne, and which did not oppose the measure, but declared that it might have been avoided if the course which we had proposed had been taken. In the debate Lord Melbourne argued as strongly as he could in favour of the tax, and ended by declaring that if it was imposed, he could not pledge himself for the future against maintaining and even extending it. Lord Melbourne is anxious to make this explanation of his conduct to your Majesty, and hopes therefore that your Majesty will forgive his writing thus much upon this subject. Lord Melbourne very much lamented that the business did not terminate as amiably as it began, and that a contest should have been got into respecting the third reading of the Bill; but considering that the measure had passed by accident through its first stages without any debate, and that there were Lords who were still desirous of speaking upon it, it was imprudent of the Ministers not at once to give another day for that purpose, especially as they were sure to be compelled to do so by repeated motions of adjournment.

The feelings which your Majesty expresses upon the conviction of this man41 are natural, and such as must arise in your Majesty's bosom; but Lord Melbourne knows very well that your Majesty will at once see the necessity of not yielding to your own feelings, and of leaving the issue entirely in the hands of your advisers.

Without any reference to personal or particular circumstances, without adverting to your Majesty's age, sex, qualities mental or personal, without attending to any sentiments of attachment or affection which may be felt for your Majesty's person, it must be remembered that your Majesty's life is, from the position which you occupy and the office which you fill, the most important life in these realms; it is also too clear that it is the most exposed life in the country, the life the most obnoxious42 to danger; and therefore it is a duty to throw around it every protection which the law and the execution of the law can afford.

Lord Melbourne was sure that your Majesty, being fond of speed, would be delighted with the railway. Lord Melbourne hopes that your Majesty was not much affected by the heat, which he feared that you would be.

Has your Majesty read the last volume of Madame D'Arblay's (Miss Burney) Diary, which contains the account of her service in the family of George III.?43 It is a curious [work], gives a curious account of the intérieur, and shows the King and Queen and the Princesses in a very amiable light.

Footnote 40: Lord John Russell had strenuously opposed the Income Tax Bill, but had been defeated by large majorities.

Footnote 41: Frances was tried on 17th June, and convicted. The death sentence was commuted to one of transportation for life.

Footnote 42: Used in the classical sense of "exposed to"; cf. "obnoxia fato."

Footnote 43: The first five volumes were published this year, Madame D'Arblay having died in 1840, at the age of eighty-seven. Croker somewhat rancorously attacked them in the Quarterly, to which Macaulay replied in the Edinburgh.

A PRESENT FROM MUSCAT

Foreign Office, 28th June 1842.

Lord Aberdeen, with his humble duty, begs to enclose for your Majesty's information a list of the presents brought by the Envoy of the Imam of Muscat for your Majesty.

Lord Aberdeen will attend to-morrow with the Envoy, at the hour your Majesty has been pleased to command; and he will suggest that the presents should be sent previously to the Palace, in order to be laid before your Majesty.

[List of Articles sent for Her Most Gracious Majesty, The Mighty Queen, a trifling Gift scarce worth being mentioned.]

Footnote 44: I.e. accept.

India Board, 4th July 1842.

... From the seat of war, the intelligence is most satisfactory. The conduct of the army, its perseverance and its courage, have not been surpassed in the military history of British India.

Recent events have not, however, changed the views of Lord Ellenborough as to the general policy which he recommends to be pursued.

He regards as the best result of that success which has attended the Arms of your Majesty, that it admits of withdrawing, without dishonour, the British force to positions of safety, having certain and uninterrupted communications with the British territory.

From other quarters the reports are equally favourable. The successful advance of a division commanded by Brigadier-General England may be regarded as ensuring the safety of the force at Candahar.

In the Indian Dominions and in the native Army the best spirit prevails.

All of which is most humbly submitted to your Majesty, by your Majesty's most dutiful Subject and Servant,

Fitzgerald and Vesci.

BEAN'S ATTEMPT ON THE QUEEN

South Street, 4th July 1842.

Lord Melbourne presents his humble duty to your Majesty, and is anxious to express his earnest hope that your Majesty is well and not disturbed by the event[45] which took place yesterday, and which, although it appears not to have been dangerous in itself, is formidable as affording additional evidence of the ease with which persons of the lower orders can incite themselves, or be incited by others, to the contemplation and commission of such acts. The only observation that can be made upon these attempts is, that hitherto they appear to have been made by those who have not the means of executing their own wicked designs, and that they are not marked by the same determination and the same long and ferocious preparation which characterised in France the conduct of Fieschi and Alibaud.[46] Lord Melbourne is not of opinion that the extension of mercy to Francis—which from what Lord Melbourne hears of the opinion of the judges he apprehends to have been unavoidable—could have had any effect in encouraging this man to a similar act; at the same time it is impossible to say what may have had an effect upon the mind, and we can only collect the intentions of men from the deeds which they perform.

Lord Melbourne thanks your Majesty much for your letter of the 26th ult. Lord Melbourne again expresses his fervent wishes for your Majesty's health, safety, and tranquillity of mind.

Footnote 45: Bean, a deformed lad, presented a pistol at the Queen in the Mall.

Footnote 46: The perpetrators of attempts on King Louis Philippe.

DEATH OF THE DUKE OF ORLEANS

Claremont, 14th July 1842.

My dearest Uncle,—These two horrible news of poor dear Chartres'[47] fatal accident have quite overcome us. It is the most dreadful misfortune I ever remember, and will be felt everywhere. I can't say how I feel it; I liked and admired him, and know how he was adored by all of you, and by poor wretched Hélène, whom this will kill. Those poor helpless little children! it is too melancholy. After escaping from so many dangers, to be cut off in this way is too dreadful! God knows what is for our best, but this does seem difficult to understand. I pray and hope that you will all be mercifully supported under this heavy bereavement. I think it is so dreadful that poor Hélène could not be with him in his last moments! God be with you all, and believe me, ever your devoted Niece,

Victoria R.

I had begun a letter to poor Chartres this morning.

Footnote 47: On 13th July the Duke of Orleans (formerly Duc de Chartres), eldest son of Louis Philippe, was thrown from his phaeton near the Porte Maillot, Paris, and died shortly afterwards. He was the father of the Comte de Paris and the Duc de Chartres.

ACCOUNT OF THE ACCIDENT

Laeken, 15th July 1842.

My beloved Victoria,—You have surely already heard of the heavy visitation God has sent us. My beloved brother was unexpectedly taken away from us before yesterday evening. Before yesterday morning he went to Neuilly to take leave of my parents, previous to his departure for

St Omer. The horses ran away: he had the unfortunate idea to jump out from his barouche—a thing I cannot understand, as he had on all occasions an uncommon presence of mind—fell upon his head, and expired a few hours afterwards, in presence of my too unfortunate parents, without having recovered his consciousness. It is the greatest misfortune that could happen to us.

We are quite stunned by the sudden and horrid blow, and I cannot believe it yet, although I have before me the letter of my poor parents. They are full of courage and resignation to the will of Providence; but I do not understand what will become of them, particularly of my mother, who loved so fondly, and with so much reason, my brother, and of the too unfortunate Hélène. May God help them and have mercy on them! Clémentine and Victoire are gone to Plombières to give to Hélène the fatal news, and bring her back: it will most probably be her death. My parents wished to see us immediately, and we go to-morrow to Paris.

I am sure, my beloved Victoria, of the share you will take in the misfortune, the greatest which could befall us, and I thank you beforehand for it. God's will be done! May He at least always bless you, and preserve those you love from all evil and danger! In affliction as in joy, I am, ever, my beloved Victoria, yours most devotedly,

Louise.

Claremont, 16th July 1842.

The Queen is anxious to draw Sir Robert Peel's attention to a circumstance which she has already some months ago mentioned to him: this is relative to Sir Edward Disbrowe.48 The Queen knows that Sir Robert Peel shares her opinion as to Sir Edward Disbrowe's abilities not being of the first order, but this is not the only thing; what she chiefly complains of is his decided unfairness towards Belgium, which she thinks has always shown itself, and again most strongly in his last despatches. The King of the Belgians has never dropped a word on the subject, but the Queen really feels it her duty by her Uncle to state this frankly to Sir Robert Peel, and to say that she thinks it highly important that Sir Edward Disbrowe should be removed to some other Mission. Of course she wishes that this should be done quietly, but she thinks that with a man like the present King of the Netherlands, who is continually intriguing in Belgium and making her Uncle's position very painful, it is of the utmost importance that our Minister there should be totally unbiassed—which Sir Edward Disbrowe most decidedly is not. Could not Sir T. Cartwright be sent there, and Sir Edward Disbrowe go to Stockholm? The Queen merely suggests this; but, of course, as long as the man sent to the Hague is sensible and fair, it is indifferent to her who goes there....

Footnote 48: Then British Minister at the Hague.

GRIEF OF THE QUEEN

Claremont, 17th July 1842.

The Queen had intended to have written to Lord Melbourne some time ago to have thanked him for his kind letter of the 5th, but she was so occupied, first of all with the arrival of our brother and sister, with our removal here, and lastly by the dreadful misfortune at Paris, which has completely overpowered her, and made her quite ill—that it prevented her from doing so. The Queen is sure that Lord Melbourne will have warmly shared the universal horror and regret at the untimely and fearfully sudden end of so amiable and distinguished a Prince as poor Chartres (as we all called the Duke of Orleans) was! The loss to France, and indeed Europe, is very great; but to the Royal Family, dearest Louise (who all doted on him), and above all to poor unfortunate Hélène, who adored him (and he was a most devoted husband to her), and to his two poor little boys of four and one years old—he is an irreparable loss. The Queen has heard from none yet, but has seen a letter from Guizot, who was a witness of the last scene, which is quite truly reported in the papers; he says it was fearful—the poor Duke lying and dying on a mattress on the floor surrounded by his parents and sisters, kneeling and praying around their dearly beloved Child! Alas! poor Hélène had not even that comfort!

The Queen is very glad that the Bill for the better security of her person has passed so quickly and in so gratifying a manner through both Houses.

We are here since yesterday week, enjoying the fine weather, and great quiet and peace; but the news from Paris have damped our spirits.

The Queen is charmed with her new sister,49 who is a most amiable, sensible, and gentle creature, and without being really handsome, very pretty and pleasing.

We return to town to-morrow and the Queen hopes soon to see Lord Melbourne. We intend going to Windsor to settle, on Saturday.

The Queen trusts Lord Melbourne is quite well.

Footnote 49: The Duchess Ernest of Saxe-Coburg.

LETTER FROM KING LOUIS PHILIPPE

Neuilly, 17 Juillet 1842.

Madame ma bien chère et bien bonne Sœur,—J'ai bien reconnu le cœur de votre Majesté dans l'empressement qu'elle a mis à m'exprimer la part qu'elle prend à mon malheur. Ma malheureuse Reine en est également bien touchée, et si elle ne le témoigne pas elle-même dès aujourd'hui à votre Majesté, c'est qu'elle est encore dans l'impossibilité d'écrire. Nous osons lui demander tous les deux, d'être notre interprète auprès du Prince Albert, et de lui dire combien nous sommes sensibles à son intérêt. S'il pouvait y avoir une consolation au coup affreux qui a frappé nos vieux jours, ce serait ces témoignages d'intérêt, et les regrets dont on entoure le tombeau de mon enfant chéri, et la perte immense que tous ont faite en lui! C'est à présent qu'on sent ce qu'il était, et ce qu'il devenait chaque jour de plus en plus.

Je remercie de nouveau votre Majesté, du fond de mon cœur brisé, de tous les sentiments dont elle veut bien me donner tant de preuves, et je la prie d'agréer l'expression de la haute estime et de l'inviolable amitié avec lesquelles, je suis, Madame, ma très chère Sœur, de votre Majesté, le bien affectionné Frère,

Louis Philippe R.

Neuilly, 19 Juillet 1842.

Madame ma très chère Sœur,—Je comptais que votre Majesté et le Prince Albert s'associeraient à notre immense douleur; que Dieu vous bénisse pour les tendres expressions de votre lettre. Nous sommes anéantis par le coup dont Dieu nous a frappés, que sa Sainte Volonté soit faite! J'ai perdu l'objet de ma plus vive tendresse, celui qui depuis 32 ans avait été mon amour, mon bonheur, et ma gloire, plein de vie, d'avenir, ma tête n'y est plus, mon cœur est flétri, je tâche de me résigner, je pleure et je prie pour cette Ame qui m'était si chère et pour que Dieu nous conserve l'infortuné et précieux Roi dont la douleur est incommensurable; nous tâchons de nous réunir tous pour faire un faisceau autour de lui. Notre ange de Louise et votre excellent oncle sont arrivés avant-hier; leur présence nous a fait du bien. Hélène, anéantie par la douleur, a un courage admirable, sa santé se soutient. Nemours, dont l'affliction est inexprimable, tâche de prendre des forces pour nous consoler tous, et les bonnes Victoire et Clémentine après l'horrible et douleureuse scène à laquelle elles avaient assisté, ont passé trois nuits pour aller chercher leur infortunée Belle-Sœur. Enfin, Dieu veut que nous vivions pour nous soutenir les uns les autres, que ce Dieu Tout Puissant vous bénisse, Madame, et vous préserve à jamais de pareilles douleurs, c'est le vœu bien sincère de celle qui se dit de tout son cœur, Madame, De votre Majesté la toute dévouée Sœur,

Marie Amélie.

LEIGH HUNT

South Street, 22nd July 1842.

Lord Melbourne presents his humble duty, and ventures to transmit the copy of Mr Leigh Hunt's poem, which he mentioned to your Majesty in his last letter. Lord Melbourne also sends the letter which Mr Leigh Hunt has taken the liberty of addressing to your Majesty, as well as that which he has addressed to Lord Melbourne. Lord Melbourne will inform Mr Hunt that he has done this, and it is not at all required that any further notice should be taken.50

It is a very gay and lively work, and has in it some wit and fun.

Lord Melbourne had great pleasure yesterday in seeing your Majesty well and in good spirits.

Footnote 50: The poem was no doubt The Palfrey; a Love-Story of Old Times.

32 Edwardes Square, Kensington, 15th July 1842.

My Lord,—I was once speaking to Mr Fonblanque51 of my unwillingness to trouble your Lordship, when Prime Minister, with a request to lay my tragedy of the Legend of Florence52 before Her Majesty; and he said that he was sure your good-nature would not have been displeased with it. This is the reason why I now venture to ask whether a similar kindness might be shown the accompanying little poem, supposing no etiquette to stand in the way of it. I have no Tory channels of communication with the Palace, nor wish to seek any; neither can I trespass upon any friendships of Her Majesty's, unless they can find my excuse in some previous knowledge of me. On the other hand, I have no fear of being supposed by your Lordship to approach one who is no longer Premier with less respect than when he was in power. I would even venture to say, if the mode of testifying it were not so poor a one, that it is in a double spirit of respectfulness the application is made. Should it be of a nature calculated to give your Lordship any perplexity, I can only blush for having been the occasion of it, and beg it may be laid to the account of an ignorance which lives very much out of the world. The same reason will plead my excuse for not knowing whether a letter to Her Majesty ought, or ought not, to accompany the book; and for begging your Lordship, after its perusal, to suppress it or otherwise accordingly, in case you can oblige me in the other part of my request. Your Lordship will perceive that the Address prefixed to the poem, not having ventured to ask Her Majesty's permission, does not presume to call itself a dedication; neither does it leave the public under any erroneous impression whatsoever as to the nature of its intentions: and on this account I not only expect, of course, no acknowledgment of its receipt on the part of any one about Her Majesty's person, but shall be more than content to understand by your Lordship's own silence that my book has reached its destination, and therefore not been considered altogether unworthy of it.

The bookseller tells me that it is no longer "the mode" for authors to present their volumes bound; but in regard to books intended to go to Court, he is not quite so certain; and I find it so difficult to disassociate the idea of dress from any such proceeding, that I trust my inexperience in this respect also will procure me whatever pardon it may require.

I have the honour to be, my Lord, your Lordship's ever grateful and faithful Servant,

Leigh Hunt.

Footnote 51: Hunt had founded The Examiner in 1808, and Albany Fonblanque (1793-1872) had succeeded him on it as leader writer.

Footnote 52: Leigh Hunt's play, A Legend of Florence, had had a great success at Covent Garden in 1840; in 1852 it was performed at Windsor by the Queen's command.

THE AFFLICTED FAMILY

Neuilly, 21st July 1842.

My beloved Victoria,—I was unable to thank you the other day for your kind and feeling letter of the 14th, although I was greatly touched by it, and I trust you will have excused me. I thank you to-day very sincerely for both your letters, and for the share and sympathy you and dear Albert take in our great misfortune. I know it is very heartfelt, and we are all very grateful for it. Victoire and my poor mother have already given you news from the unfortunate Hélène. She has sustained and outlived the first shock and shows wonderful courage. She is even well in health, and much better and stronger in all ways than I had expected. She takes very much upon herself on account of the poor children, to prevent that any melancholy or painful feeling should be connected for them with the remembrance of their beloved and unfortunate father. My parents show great fortitude and resignation, but their hearts are for ever broke. They are only sustained by their feeling of duty. My poor mother bears up for my father, and my father bears up to fulfil his duties of father and of king. Their health is, thank God! good, and my father retains all his strength of mind and quickness of judgment; but they are both grown old in looks, and their hairs are turned quite white.

The first days, my poor father could do nothing but sob, and it was really heartbreaking to see him. He begins now to have more command upon his grief, and the presence of your uncle, whom he dearly loves, seems to do him good. The poor children are well and merry and seem unconscious of their dreadful loss. From time to time only they jump round us as if looking for protection. The contrast of their gaiety with their horrid misfortune is very painful. Paris is looking remarkably well and strong. Robert53 is much grown, extremely quick and lively, and begins to speak. The remainder of the family is, as you may easily imagine, in the deepest affliction. Nemours especially is quite broken down with grief. Chartres was more than a brother to him, as he was more than a second father to us all. He was the head and the heart and soul of the whole family. We all looked up to him, and we found him on all occasions. A better, or even such a brother was never seen; our loss is as great as irreparable; but God's will be done! He had surely His motives in sending on my unfortunate parents the horrid affliction in their old days, and in removing from us the being who seemed the most necessary to the hope and happiness of all; we must submit to His decrees, hard as they are; but it is impossible not to regret that my poor brother has not at least found the death of a soldier, which he had always wished for, instead of such a useless, horrid, and miserable one! It seems, for no one saw him fall, that he did not jump, as we had thought at first, but that he was thrown from the barouche, while standing; and I like it in some measure better so, as God's will is still more manifest in this way. It is equally manifest in all the circumstances attending the catastrophe. My poor brother was not even to have come to Neuilly. He had taken leave of my parents the day before, and would not have gone again if my unfortunate mother had not asked him, and if my parents, who were to go to Paris, had not delayed their departure....

I thank you again and again, my beloved Victoria, for all your interest and sympathy. I was sure you would think of us and of me: you know how much I loved my brother. I little expected to outlive him, as I had done my beloved Mary;54 but once more, God's will be done. I remain now and ever, yours most devotedly,

Louise.

I perceive I forgot mentioning Ernest. Pray thank him for his sympathy also. He knows what a brother is, and may feel for us! We expect on Saturday poor Joinville. My father will have thus his four remaining sons round him for the opening of the Session, which takes place on the 26th, and at which he must preside in person. It is a hard duty for him.

Footnote 53: The young Duc de Chartres, born in 1840.

Footnote 54: See ante, p. .

THE CORN LAWS

Whitehall, 23rd July 1842.

Sir Robert Peel, with his humble duty to your Majesty, begs leave to acquaint your Majesty that last night was occupied in the House of Commons with another debate on the Corn Laws, again impeding any progress with the Government business. The debate was entirely confined to those members who act in concert with the Anti-Corn Law League.55 It continued until twelve, when Mr Cobden, the Member for Stockport, moved an adjournment of the House, on the ground that none of your Majesty's servants had taken a part in the debate....

Several members of the Opposition voted with the Government, and declared that they would not be parties to such vexatious proceedings.

A division on the main question—a Committee to enquire into the state of the country with a view to the Repeal of the Corn Laws—then took place.

The motion was negatived by a majority of 156 to 64—92. The House did not adjourn until three this morning.

Footnote 55: The Anti-Corn Law League was rapidly gaining importance, and fiscal policy occupied a great part of the session of 1842. Peel was already reducing import duties on articles other than corn. Cobden had been elected at Stockport, for the first time, in 1841.

FURTHER PARTICULARS OF ACCIDENT

Neuilly, 22nd July 1842.

My dearest Victoria,—I was anxious to write to you on the 18th, but I was so overpowered with all that surrounded me that I could really not. Yesterday I received your dear letter of the 19th, and I will answer it, so as to give you a clear view of the sad case. On the 12th, Tuesday, Chartres had taken leave, as he meant to go to St Omer, the 13th; however, in the family the Queen and others said he ought to come once more to see them. The King had ordered his carriage to go to town on the 13th, to a Council; Chartres meant to have called shortly after ten.

It is necessary to tell you all this, as it shows how strangely circumstances turned fatally. Chartres did not want to return once more to Neuilly, and the King, if exact, might see him once more in town. Chartres, however, instead of coming early, set off after eleven; his Off. d'Ordonnance, M. Bertin de Veaux, his valet de chambre, a German, Holder, begged him not to go quite alone in that small phaeton through Paris, as he was in uniform, but all this did not avail; he insisted to go in the phaeton and to go alone. He set out later than he expected, and if the King had set out exactly as he had named, the parents and the son would probably have met on the rising avenue of the Champs Elysees, towards the Barrière de l'Étoile and Arc de Triomphe. However, the King delayed his departure and the son set off. At the place where from the great avenue one turns off towards Neuilly, the horses, which were not even young horses, as I am told that he has had them some years, moved by that stupid longing to get to Neuilly, where they knew their stables, got rather above the postillion, and ran quasi away. Chartres got up and asked the postillion if he could hold his horses no longer; the boy called out "Non, Monseigneur"; he had looked back when he said this, and saw his master for the last time standing in the phaeton. People at some distance saw him come out of his carriage and describe a sort of semicircle falling down. Nobody knows exactly if he jumped out of the carriage, or if he lost his position and fell out. I am inclined to think that, trusting to his lightness and agility, he wanted to jump out, forgetting the impulse which a quick-going carriage gives, as there were marks on his knees as if he had first fallen that way. The principal blow was, however, on the head, the skull being entirely fractured. He was taken up senseless, that is to say confused, but not fainting, and carried into a small inn. At first his appearance, sitting in a chair, was so little altered that people thought it was nothing of any consequence.

He knew no one, and only spoke a few incoherent words in German. The accident happened about a quarter before twelve, and at four he was no more.

I refer for some other details to Albert. Poor Louise looks like a shadow, and only her great devotion for me supports her. It may serve as a lesson how fragile all human affairs are. Poor Chartres, it seems, with the prospect of these camps and altogether, was never in better spirits. But I must end. Ever, my dearest Victoria, your devoted Uncle,

Leopold R.

SIR EDWARD DISBROWE

Windsor Castle, 27th July 1842.

The Queen thanks Lord Aberdeen for the letter she has this morning received.

The Queen thinks that a reprimand would hardly do, as it is not so much from any particular despatch that she has formed this opinion of Sir Edward Disbrowe, but more from the general tenor of his conduct and despatches; therefore she thinks it would be difficult to censure him, which would probably not have the desired effect.[56] For this reason the Queen would prefer his being removed without his being told that it was for his conduct, and without his being able to find this out, which, the Queen concludes from Lord Aberdeen's letter, could easily be done.

Footnote 56: See p. Lord Aberdeen had suggested sending Sir Edward Disbrowe a private admonition.

Windsor Castle, 2nd August 1842.

Dearest Uncle,—I had the pleasure of receiving your kind letter of the 29th, late on Sunday evening. You know all we have felt, and do feel, for the dear and exemplary French family. Really it is too dreadful, but God's will be done! Perhaps poor Chartres is saved great sorrow and grief. Him we must not pity!

God grant all may go off well on these dreadful days, and may He support the dear afflicted parents, widow, and brothers and sisters! My dearest Louise! I hope and trust that her dear children will occupy her and divert her attention; only don't let her swallow and suppress her grief and keep it to herself; that is dreadful, and very hurtful. Let her give way to her sorrow, and talk of it to her.

Pray, dearest Uncle, will not and ought not Paris to be Duke of Orleans now? Hélène is sole guardian, is she not?...

Dear Louise will, I trust, excuse my not answering her kind letter to-day; pray give her my best love, and believe me, always, your most devoted Niece,

Victoria R.

THE FATHERLESS CHILDREN

Laeken, 5th August 1842.

My dearest Victoria,—... Little Paris,[57] who has gained much of late, will keep the name of Paris, at least for the present. Hélène will be, after the poor King's demise, sole guardian of her children; till then the King as head of the family will be supreme in all matters relating to the children.... Your devoted Uncle,

Leopold R.

Footnote 57: The late Comte de Paris, who bore this title to the end of his life, father of the present Duc d'Orléans.

Laeken, 5th August 1842.

My beloved Victoria,—... Poor little Paris is aware of his misfortune in the way he can be. Hélène told him that he saw everybody weep because he would see no more his beloved father. The poor child wept then very much, and he has done several times since, when the same thing was repeated to him. He wonders why he does not go any more in his unfortunate father's room, and why there is no more "de cher Papa," as he says: else he makes no question or observation and is very quiet and cheerful. He cannot yet feel what he has lost and his melancholy fate: but Hélène does what she can to keep alive in him the remembrance of his father.... Yours most affectionately,

Louise.

South Street, 8th August 1842.

Lord Melbourne presents his humble duty to your Majesty. He thanks your Majesty much for the letter of the 4th. It can hardly be expected that the grief of the French family will, as yet, much diminish, but Lord Melbourne hopes that they are somewhat more composed. He has heard this morning that Lord and Lady Beauvale were at Boulogne on Saturday; they would probably cross yesterday, and will be in London to-day.

Lord Melbourne understands that Lord Beauvale had an interview of three hours with the King of the French. Charles Howard was married this morning, and Lord Melbourne is going to meet Lord and Lady Carlisle and the rest of the family at Baron Parke's58 at dinner. Lord Melbourne thinks that Lord Prudhoe's marriage59 was to be expected.60 Upon looking at the Peerage, he is only fifty years old, and fifty is young enough to marry anybody. The only fault of fifty is that it advances too rapidly on to sixty, which, on the other hand, is too old to marry anybody. It is Lord Melbourne's opinion that if a man does marry either at fifty or sixty, he had much better take a young girl than a woman of more age and experience. Youth is more malleable, more gentle, and has often more respect and compassion for infirmity than middle-age.

Footnote 58: Afterwards Lord Wensleydale.

Footnote 59: To Lady Eleanor Grosvenor.

Footnote 60: Admiral Lord Algernon Percy (1792-1865), President of the Royal Institution, was created in 1816 Baron Prudhoe: in 1847, on the death of his brother, he became fourth Duke of Northumberland.

RESIGNATION OF LORD HILL

Hardwicke Grange,61 9th August 1842.

Lord Hill presents his humble duty to your Majesty, and craves your Majesty's gracious permission to lay before your Majesty his resignation of the Command of your Majesty's Army.

Lord Hill deeply regrets the necessity of taking a step which will deprive him of a charge that has been so long committed to his hands, and for his continuance in which he is indebted to your Majesty's grace and favour; but he has again suffered much from the illness under which he laboured in the early part of the year, and his health has in consequence become so indifferent as to render him unequal to the adequate discharge of the various important duties of his command, which therefore he feels he could not retain with due regard to the interests of your Majesty's Service.

Lord Hill had flattered himself that he should have been able to have laid his application for retirement before your Majesty himself, and personally to have expressed to your Majesty his deep and lasting sense of your Majesty's gracious kindness to him on all occasions. Having, however, left London by the advice of his medical attendants, and being too unwell to undertake a second journey, Lord Hill avails himself of this mode of assuring your Majesty of his unabated zeal for the Service, of his dutiful devotion to your Majesty's person, and of the pain and sorrow with which he relinquishes an appointment that afforded him the honour and advantage of executing your Majesty's commands, and receiving many gracious proofs of your Majesty's support and confidence.

Footnote 61: Lord Hill's country house in Shropshire.

APPOINTMENT OF COMMANDER-IN-CHIEF

Whitehall, 10th August 1842.

Sir Robert Peel presents his humble duty to your Majesty, and begs leave to acquaint your Majesty that he received at a late hour last night the accompanying letter to your Majesty from Lord Hill. From the one which accompanied it, addressed to Sir Robert Peel, he has reason to believe that it conveys to your Majesty the wish of Lord Hill to be relieved, on the ground of ill-health and increasing infirmities, from the Command of your Majesty's Forces.

Sir Robert Peel would humbly submit for your Majesty's consideration whether it might not be a deserved mark of your Majesty's approbation to confer upon Lord Hill the rank of Viscount, with remainder to his nephew Sir Rowland Hill,62 who will succeed Lord Hill in the Barony. Lord Beresford63 and Lord Combermere64 have the rank of Viscounts, and perhaps the long, faithful services of Lord Hill as Commander-in-Chief may appear to your Majesty to entitle him to equal distinction in the Peerage.

Sir Robert Peel has reason to believe that when Lord Hill's retirement shall be known there will be many competitors for the office of Commander-in-Chief.

Sir George Murray,65 Sir Edward Paget,66 Lord Londonderry,67 Lord Combermere, and perhaps Lord Beresford, will severally urge their pretensions.

Sir Robert Peel humbly submits to your Majesty that should the Duke of Wellington be willing to undertake the duties of this important trust, no claims could stand in competition with his, and no selection from the candidates whom he has named would be satisfactory to the Army or public in general.

Sir Robert Peel would therefore humbly recommend to your Majesty that the offer of this appointment should be made to the Duke of Wellington, with the signification of a wish on the part of your Majesty (should your Majesty be pleased to approve of the arrangement), that His Grace should continue a member of the Cabinet, and the organ of the Government, as at present, in the House of Lords.

Footnote 62: Lord Hill died 10th December 1842, and was succeeded in his peerages by Sir Rowland Hill, who died in 1875.

Footnote 63: William Carr Beresford (1768-1854), created Viscount Beresford in 1823 for the victory of Albuera, 1811.

Footnote 64: Sir Stapleton Cotton (1773-1865), created Viscount Combermere for the capture of Bhurtpore.

Footnote 65: Sir George Murray (1772-1846), received a K.C.B. for his services in the Peninsula, M.P. for Perth, and afterwards Commander-in-Chief in Ireland.

Footnote 66: General Sir Edward Paget, G.C.B. (1775-1849), brother of the first Marquis of

Anglesey.

Footnote 67: Prior to being Ambassador at Vienna, Lord Londonderry had distinguished himself in the Peninsula.

THE DUKE ACCEPTS

London, 12th August 1842.

Field-Marshal the Duke of Wellington presents his humble duty to your Majesty. He has been informed by Sir Robert Peel that your Majesty had been graciously pleased to approve of the recommendation submitted by your Majesty's servants that he should be appointed the Commander-in-Chief of your Majesty's Forces.

He is sensible of and grateful for this fresh proof of your Majesty's confidence in him and gracious favour towards him.

He hopes that your Majesty will believe that your Majesty may rely upon his making every effort in his power to promote your Majesty's views for the honour and interest of the country in any situation in which he may be placed.

Which is humbly submitted to your Majesty by your Majesty's most dutiful and devoted Subject and Servant,

Wellington.

Windsor Castle, 12th August 1842.

The Queen has received Lord Hill's letter of the 9th inst., and is much concerned to learn that Lord Hill's health is so indifferent that he thinks it is his duty to resign the important office which he has so long and so honourably held. The Queen can only reluctantly give her consent to this determination, as she regrets to lose Lord Hill's services at the head of her Army. She cannot, however, miss this opportunity of expressing to Lord Hill her entire approbation of his conduct throughout the time he served her. The Prince begs to have his kind regards sent to Lord Hill.

RIOTS IN MANCHESTER

Cabinet Room, Downing Street, 13th August 1842.

Sir Robert Peel presents his humble duty to your Majesty, and is sorry to be under the necessity of troubling your Majesty so suddenly, but he is sure your Majesty will excuse him for making any proposal to your Majesty which the public service may render requisite.68

The accounts received this morning from Manchester with regard to the state of the country in that neighbourhood are very unsatisfactory, and they are confirmed by the personal testimony of magistrates who have arrived in London for the purpose of making representations to your Majesty's servants on the subject.

A Cabinet has just been held, and it is proposed to send a battalion of Guards by the railway this evening. The 16th of August (Tuesday next) is the anniversary of a conflict which took place in Manchester in the year 181969 between the Yeomanry Cavalry and the populace, and it is feared that there may be a great assemblage of persons riotously disposed on that day.

Under these circumstances it appears desirable to your Majesty's confidential advisers that a proclamation should be immediately issued, warning all persons against attendance on tumultuous meetings, and against all acts calculated to disturb the public peace. It is necessary that a Council should be held for the issue of this proclamation, and important that it should arrive in Manchester on Monday.

These considerations have prevented Sir Robert Peel from giving previous notice to your Majesty, and having your Majesty's sanction for the holding of a Council. On account of the urgency of the case, he has requested a sufficient number of Privy Councillors to repair to Windsor this evening, in order that should your Majesty be graciously pleased to hold a Council, the proclamation may be forthwith issued. The members of the Privy Council will be in attendance about half-past six o'clock, as Sir Robert Peel has considered that from that time to half-past seven will probably be the least inconvenient to your Majesty.

He writes this immediately after the breaking up of the Cabinet.

Footnote 68: The disturbances of this month, which originated in a strike for wages in Lancashire, were inflamed by agitators, and rapidly spread through Cheshire, Staffordshire, Warwickshire, and Yorkshire, eventually extending to the populous parts of Scotland and Wales. Several conflicts took place between the populace and the military, and there was much loss of life and property, as well as aggravated distress.

Footnote 69: On 16th August 1819, a great popular demonstration in favour of Parliamentary Reform, presided over by Henry Hunt, the Radical, had taken place in St Peter's Fields, Manchester. A riot ensued, and the Yeomanry charged the populace, with some loss of life. The affair was afterwards known as the Peterloo massacre.

CHARTIST DISTURBANCES

Whitehall, 15th August 1842.

Sir James Graham, with humble duty, begs to lay before your Majesty the enclosed letter from Major-General Sir William Warre70 in command of the Northern District.

From this report it is evident that a strong and salutary moral impression had been produced by the arrival of a reinforcement of 1,400 men in the disturbed district in the short time of six-and-thirty hours after the first requisition for assistance had been sent from Manchester; and the General has now at his disposal a force quite adequate to cope with the vast assemblage of people who are expected to meet to-morrow at Manchester.

Some symptoms of this disposition forcibly to suspend labour have appeared in the West Riding of Yorkshire; but on the whole the accounts, both from Scotland and the disturbed district, which have been received this morning, may be considered favourable. The railroad communications as yet are uninterrupted; no collision has taken place between the troops and the multitude, except at Preston;71 and Sir James Graham is willing to hope that this insurrectionary movement may be suppressed without recourse to extreme measures. Every precaution, however, has been taken, and arrangements are made for augmenting the force under the command of Sir William Warre, if it should become necessary.

The character of these riots has assumed more decidedly a political aspect. It is no longer a strike for higher wages, but the Delegates, who direct the movement, avow that labour shall not be resumed until the people's Charter be granted.72

Sir James Graham will hasten to-morrow to inform your Majesty of the accounts which he may receive.

The above is humbly submitted by your Majesty's dutiful Subject and Servant,

J. R. G. Graham.

Footnote 70: Lieutenant-General Sir William Warre (1784-1853), a distinguished Peninsular officer.

Footnote 71: The mob attacked the military, who fired and killed three or four persons.

Footnote 72: A colossal petition in favour of the Charter had been presented during the Session by Mr T. Duncombe.

SATISFACTORY RESULTS

Whitehall, 18th August 1842.

Sir Robert Peel presents his humble duty to your Majesty, and begs leave to acquaint your Majesty that he returned to London last night.

He has this morning gone through all the letters received from the country, with Sir James Graham, by whom the details of the information will be forwarded to your Majesty.

It appears to Sir Robert Peel that the general tenor of the reports is satisfactory. From Manchester, from Wigan, from Preston, the reports are very good.

The movement is not one caused by distress. The demand for employment has increased, and the price of provisions—and particularly of potatoes, bread, and bacon—has rapidly fallen within the last fortnight or three weeks.

People of property and the Magistrates (notwithstanding their political dissensions) are now acting in harmony, and with more energy.

Orders have been sent to apprehend the Delegates assembled in Manchester, the very moment that the law will warrant their apprehension, and Sir Robert Peel should not be surprised to hear of their committal to Lancaster Castle in the course of to-day.

Every vigilance will be exerted with reference to Cooper[73] (whom your Majesty names) and all other itinerant agitators.

As might be naturally expected, the movements and disorderly spirit spreading from the centre (Manchester) are appearing in remote points; but when peace and confidence are thoroughly restored at Manchester, the example will quickly tell in the circumjacent districts.

Birmingham is tranquil and well-disposed. The accounts from Scotland are favourable.

Footnote 73: A Leicester Chartist, who was afterwards tried for sedition.

PARLIAMENT PROROGUED

South Street, 17th August 1842.

Lord Melbourne presents his humble duty to your Majesty. He is going down to-day to Brocket Hall with Lord and Lady Beauvale. Lord and Lady Palmerston are coming down to-morrow, and Lord and Lady Cowper will probably come over from Panshanger.

Your Majesty read extremely well in the House of Lords on Friday last.[74] Lord Melbourne can judge better of this from the body of the House than he could when he stood close to your Majesty. Nothing can be more clear and distinct, and at the same time more natural and free from effort. Perhaps if your Majesty could read a tone louder it would be as well. Charles Buller, who was amongst the House of Commons, told Lord Melbourne that, where he stood, the voice, although well heard, sounded somewhat weak. But this should not be attempted unless it can be done with perfect ease. Nothing injures reading so much as the attempt to push the organ beyond its natural powers.

Lord Melbourne hopes that these tumults in the manufacturing districts are subsiding, but he cannot conceal from your Majesty that he views them with great alarm—much greater than he generally thinks it prudent to express. He fears that they may last in the form of strike, and turn out much longer than is looked for, as they did in 1832 and 1833.

There is a great mass of discontented feeling in the country arising from the actual state of society. It arises from the distress and destitution which will fall at times upon a great manufacturing population, and from the wild and extravagant opinions which are naturally generated in an advanced and speculative state of society.

This discontent has been aggravated and fermented by the language of every party in the state. Lord Melbourne can exempt no party from this blame, nor hardly any individual except himself. The Tories and Conservatives (not the Leaders, but the larger portion of the party) have done what they could to inflame the public mind upon that most inflammable topic of the Poor Laws. The Times newspaper has been the most forward in this. The Whigs and Radicals have done what they could in the same direction upon the Corn Laws. Mr Attwood75 and another set have worked the question of the Currency, and the whole career of Mr O'Connell in Ireland has been too manifest to be mistaken. It is no wonder if working in this manner altogether they have at last succeeded in driving the country into this which is certainly very near, if not actually a rebellion.

Lord Melbourne earnestly hopes that your Majesty and the Prince, the Prince, and Princess are all well.

Footnote 74: Parliament was prorogued by the Queen in person on 12th August.

Footnote 75: Who represented the Radical views of the Birmingham school.

THE DISTURBED DISTRICTS

Whitehall, 18th August 1842.

Sir James Graham, with humble duty, is happily enabled to state to your Majesty that the accounts from the disturbed districts received this morning are more satisfactory.

In Lancashire a disposition to resume work has been partially evinced; and at Preston, where the most vigorous measures were taken in the first instance, there has hardly been a cessation of employment.

Sir James Graham encloses a letter from the Chief Constable of the County of Lancashire detailing a successful resistance to a fresh attempt on the part of a mob to enter Preston; and he sends also a report from the Mayor of Manchester and from Mr Forster, the Stipendiary Magistrate. Decisive measures will be adopted for the immediate apprehension of the Delegates, not only at Manchester, but in every other quarter where legal evidence can be obtained which will justify their arrest. The law, which clearly sanctions resistance to the entry of these mobs into cities, is now understood by the local authorities. A bolder and firmer spirit is rising among all classes possessing property in defence of their rights against these bands of plunderers, who are the enemies both of law and of property. The prisoners taken in the commission of treasonable felonies are numerous; warrants are issued against others whose persons are known: the supremacy of the law will be promptly vindicated, and Sir James Graham entertains the confident hope that order will be soon restored.

In the Potteries a signal example was made by a handful of your Majesty's troops opposed to a riotous multitude which had burnt houses and spread devastation, and Sir James Graham encloses a letter from Captain Powys giving a description of the occurrence. The effect of this example has been that yesterday throughout this district no rioting took place.

DISTURBANCES IN LONDON

Whitehall, 19th August 1842.

Sir James Graham, with humble duty, begs to announce to your Majesty that the accounts from the North, on the whole, may be considered satisfactory....

Five of the principal Delegates at Manchester have been apprehended. Warrants are out against four others. A very important seizure of papers has been made which discloses a conspiracy, extensive in its ramifications, going back as far as July 1841. It is hoped that these papers, which are still at Manchester, may lead to fresh discoveries. Sir James Graham will send to Manchester to-night an experienced law officer, for the purpose of pursuing the investigation on the spot.

There was a meeting last night in the neighbourhood of London, of a violent character. Sir James Graham had given positive orders to the police not to allow any mob, as night approached, to enter London. Notwithstanding these directions, a mob assembled in Lincoln's Inn Fields about eleven o'clock, and moved through the city to Bethnal Green. Sir James Graham had the troops on the alert, but the multitude dispersed without any serious disturbance.

20th August 1842.

... An attempt to hold a meeting at dusk in the suburbs of London was resisted by the police yesterday evening in pursuance of orders issued by the Government in conjunction with the Lord Major, and the peace of the metropolis was preserved.

The above is humbly submitted by your Majesty's dutiful Subject and Servant,

J. R. G. Graham.

TROUBLE AT THE CAPE

Downing Street, 26th August 1842.

Lord Stanley, with his humble duty, submits for your Majesty's perusal copies of three despatches, received yesterday from the Governor of the Cape of Good Hope, detailing the unfortunate result of an attack made by a small party of your Majesty's troops upon the camp of the insurgent Boers at Natal; and also the copy of a despatch which Lord Stanley has sent in consequence to Sir George Napier,76 which, he trusts, may meet your Majesty's approbation. Lord Stanley would have submitted the draft for your Majesty's approval previous to sending it, had not an opportunity presented itself of sending it off by a fast-sailing private ship which sailed this morning, the intelligence having only been received yesterday. The instructions sent to Sir George Napier, on the 10th of April, but not received when this unfortunate affair took place, were in substance not to attempt the subjugation of these people by direct force, but to warn them that their titles to the land which they occupy would not be recognised by your Majesty, that they would have no title to claim protection from the aggression of the neighbouring tribes, to interdict communication between them and the settled parts of the Colony, and to prevent any intercourse by sea with foreign or British traders. The unfortunate event which has now occurred will render it necessary to take steps, as Sir George Napier has already done, for vindicating the power of your Majesty's Arms; but when that shall have been effected, Lord Stanley would still hope that a considerable number of these misguided men may be induced to return to their allegiance, and to the settled parts of your Majesty's dominions, and he feels confident that in such an event he will be fulfilling your Majesty's wishes in directing that they may be treated with all possible lenity.

All which is humbly submitted by your Majesty's most dutiful Servant and Subject, Stanley.

Footnote 76: Sir George Napier (1784-1855) governed Cape Colony for seven years, and the Boers were extruded from Natal by him.

Bushey House, 7th September 1842.

My dearest Niece,—... Your Mamma's visit gave me great pleasure, and it has been a great treat to me to hear her sing again, and so well, which put me in mind of former happy days. I regret much that she leaves me already this afternoon again, but the strong and powerful magnet which you have left at the Castle draws her back, and I dare not keep her away from such treasures.

I beg you, my dearest Victoria, to give my affectionate love to dear Albert, and to believe me ever most devotedly, your very affectionate Aunt,

Adelaide.

THE QUEEN VISITS SCOTLAND

Taymouth, 77 8th September 1842.

My dearest Uncle,—I make no excuses for not having written, as I know that you will understand that when one is travelling about and seeing so much that is totally new, it is very difficult to find time to write....

Albert has told you already how successfully everything had gone off hitherto, and how much pleased we were with Edinburgh, which is an unique town in its way. We left Dalkeith on Monday, and lunched at Dupplin, Lord Kinnoul's, a pretty place with quite a new house, and which poor Lord Kinnoul displayed so well as to fall head over heels down a steep bank, and was proceeding down another, if Albert had not caught him; I did not see it, but Albert and I have nearly died with laughing at the relation of it. From Dalkeith we went through Perth (which is most beautifully situated on the Tay) to Scone Palace, 78 Lord Mansfield's, where we slept; fine but rather gloomy. Yesterday morning (Tuesday) we left Scone and lunched at Dunkeld, the beginning of the Highlands, in a tent; all the Highlanders in their fine dress, being encamped there, and with their old shields and swords, looked very romantic; they were chiefly Lord Glenlyon's 79 men. He, poor man! is suddenly become totally blind, and it was very melancholy to see him do the honours, not seeing anything. The situation of Dunkeld, down in a valley surrounded by wooded hills, is very, very pretty. From thence we proceeded to this enchanting and princely place; the whole drive here was beautiful. All Lord Breadalbane's80 Highlanders, with himself at their head, and a battalion of the 92nd Highlanders, were drawn up in front of the House. In the evening the grounds were splendidly illuminated, and bonfires burning on the hills; and a number of Highlanders danced reels by torchlight, to the bagpipes, which was very wild and pretty....

Footnote 77: Lord Breadalbane's house. The Queen left London on 29th August for Scotland by sea, reaching Edinburgh on 1st September.

Footnote 78: Scone Abbey was granted to Sir David Murray (afterwards Viscount Stormont) by James VI. of Scotland, whose cup-bearer he was, and whose life he saved.

Footnote 79: Afterwards George, sixth Duke of Atholl (1814-1864).

Footnote 80: John, second Marquis of Breadalbane, K.T. (1796-1862).

DRUMMOND CASTLE

Taymouth, 10th September 1842.

It has been long the Queen's intention to write to Lord Melbourne, but we have seen and done so much, it has been impossible. Everything has gone off so well at Edinburgh, Perth, and elsewhere. This is a princely and most beautiful place, and we have been entertained by Lord Breadalbane in a magnificent way. The Highland Volunteers, two hundred in number (without the officers), keeping guard, are encamped in the park; the whole place was twice splendidly illuminated, and the sport he gave the Prince out shooting was on the largest scale.

The Highlands and the mountains are too beautiful, and we must come back for longer another time. The Queen will finish this letter at Drummond Castle,81 as we leave this in half an hour.

Drummond Castle, 11th.—We arrived here yesterday evening at seven, having had a most beautiful journey. We went with Lord Breadalbane up the Loch Tay (by water) to Ochmore82 (I don't know how it is written), a cottage belonging to Lord Breadalbane, close to Killin. The morning was very fine, and the view indescribably beautiful; the mountains so high, and so wooded close to Killin. It is impossible to say how kind and attentive Lord Breadalbane and poor Lady Breadalbane (who is so wretchedly delicate) were to us. We were so sorry to go away, and might perhaps have managed to stay two days longer at Taymouth, were we not fearful of delaying our sea voyage back too much. However, we mean to visit him for longer another time; the Highlands are so beautiful, and so new to me, that we are most anxious to return there again.

The journey from Killin to Comrie was most beautiful, and through such wild scenery—Glen Ogle, which of course Lord Melbourne knows—and then along Loch Ern. This house is quite a cottage, but the situation is fine, and the garden very beautiful. We leave this on Tuesday for Dalkeith83 where we sleep, and re-embark the next day for England. We greatly admire the extreme beauty of Edinburgh; the situation as well as the town is most striking; and the Prince, who has seen so much, says it is the finest town he ever saw. Scone Palace (where we slept on Tuesday night) is fine, but gloomy; Perth is beautiful.

The Queen hopes Lord Melbourne is very well. The Prince begs to be remembered to him.

Dalkeith is a fine good house, and the park and grounds very pretty.

Windsor Castle, 20th September 1842.

My dearest Uncle,—Pray accept my best thanks for your kind letter of the 15th, which I received on Saturday, the day of our arrival here. Dearest Louise will have told you what I wrote to her. We had a speedy and prosperous voyage home of forty-eight hours, on board a fine large and very fast steamer, the Trident, belonging to the General Steam Navigation Company. We found our dear little Victoria so grown and so improved, and speaking so plain, and become so independent; I think really few children are as forward as she is. She is quite a dear little companion. The Baby is sadly backward, but also grown, and very strong. I am so distressed about dearest Louise's still coughing, but she tells me it is decreasing. Only pray let her give way to her grief; much crying, even if it makes her cough for the moment, can do her no real harm, but stifling and swallowing grief (which she cannot repress) gnaws at the very roots of life and undermines health. Ostend and sea-baths would, I should think, do her good.

I am very glad that you went to see the King of Prussia, and saw so many old friends; Fritz of Mecklenburg84 is, you know, Albert's very dear friend; he is just arrived here.

Alexandrine's brother everybody praises; the whole family are handsome and well brought up.

The Archduke Frederic85 comes here to-morrow for a week's visit. Everybody praises him, and Ferdinand liked him very much; all Archduke Charles's86 sons are said to be very well brought up. How I wish Archduke John87 had come over here!

Now, dearest Uncle, adieu! and pray believe me, always, your most affectionate Niece, Victoria R.

It would be very kind of you if you would tell me if there is a chance of Augustus's marrying Clementine.88 Don't believe I should say a word against it; but I have heard so much about it that I should be really and sincerely glad to know a little of the truth from you.

THE QUEEN'S STEAM YACHT

Whitehall, 22nd September 1842.

Sir Robert Peel presents his humble duty to your Majesty, and begs leave, with reference to your Majesty's note of yesterday, to state to your Majesty that the first act of Sir Robert Peel on his return from Scotland was to write to Lord Haddington89 and strongly urge upon the

Admiralty the necessity of providing a steam yacht for your Majesty's accommodation.

Sir Robert Peel trusts that your Majesty may entirely depend upon being enabled to make any excursions your Majesty may resolve upon in the early part of next summer, in a steam vessel belonging to your Majesty, and suitable in every respect for your Majesty's accommodation.

Sir Robert Peel has had a personal communication with Sir John Barrow,90 one of the Secretaries to the Admiralty, this morning, upon the subject, and Sir Robert Peel has written by this post to Sir George Cockburn,91 who is out of town.

He finds that the Admiralty is now building a large vessel to be worked by steam power, applied by means of a revolving screw instead of paddles. It may be doubtful whether the same degree of velocity can be attained by means of the screw, particularly in a very large vessel. Of this a full trial will be made.

Sir John Barrow assures Sir Robert Peel that he has been on board a steam-boat moved by the screw, and that the working of the engine is scarcely perceptible; that there is none of the tremulous motion which accompanies the beats of the paddles, and that it will be possible to apply an apparatus by means of which the smoke can be consumed, and the disagreeable smell in great measure prevented.

Sir Robert Peel will leave nothing undone to ensure your Majesty's comfort and safety in any future naval excursions that your Majesty may be pleased to make.

Footnote 89: First Lord of the Admiralty.

Footnote 90: Barrow had been made second Secretary in 1804 by Dundas; he was a self-made man, and a most indefatigable traveller, writer, and promoter of Arctic exploration.

Footnote 91: Admiral of the Fleet Sir George Cockburn (1772-1853), First Naval Lord.

QUEEN ISABELLA

27th September 1842.

Lord Aberdeen, with his most humble duty, lays before your Majesty a letter which he has received from Mr Aston, respecting the marriage of the Queen of Spain, and which, after what has already passed, may perhaps cause your Majesty some surprise.

Lord Aberdeen is humbly of opinion that the language hitherto employed by your Majesty's Government upon this subject ought not to undergo any change, and that it ought to be treated entirely as a Spanish question.

Great Britain would naturally regard a marriage with a son of the King of the French as injurious to Spain and menacing to Europe, but would probably not feel it necessary to give such an opinion respecting any other alliance. While this might be plainly stated, and the Spanish Government exhorted to act according to their own independent view of the real interests of the country and of the Queen, Lord Aberdeen would humbly propose that the Regent should be explicitly informed by Mr Aston that he must not expect to receive any assistance from your Majesty's Government in promoting a marriage with a Prince of the Netherlands.

Lord Aberdeen believes that the difficulties in the way of such an alliance will be found to be very great, and especially that the religion of the Prince will present an obstacle which in Spain must be nearly insurmountable.

LORD MELBOURNE ON SCOTLAND

Brocket Hall, 29th September 1842.

Lord Melbourne presents his humble duty to your Majesty, and has to acknowledge your Majesty's letter of the 25th inst., which he had the honour and pleasure of receiving here on the 27th. Lord Melbourne is well aware how much your Majesty's time must have been occupied by the number of visitors at the Castle. We are much rejoiced here that your Majesty saw the Prince and Princess Liechtenstein.92 The latter is a great favourite of Lady Beauvale's, to whom she was always very kind, and who describes her exactly as your Majesty does, as being very "amiable and unassuming," and though one of the first, if not the first lady at Vienna, as not at all partaking of the insolence and hauteur which is by some ascribed to the society of that capital. As a beauty, she is perhaps upon too large a scale, except for those who admire women of all shapes and sizes; but her eyes and brow are very fine, and there is a very peculiarly soft and radiant expression about them. Lord Melbourne had heard of his Sovereignty, but understands that his territory is extremely limited. His possessions as a subject of Austria are worth a good deal more than his German principality.

Lord Melbourne greatly congratulates your Majesty upon the happy progress and termination of the expedition to Scotland. He is very glad of three things—that your Majesty returned by sea, in the steamer, and that the passage was a good one....

The country is indeed most interesting, full of real picturesque beauty and of historical and poetical associations and recollections. There is nothing to detract from it, except the very high opinion that the Scotch themselves entertain of it. Edinburgh is magnificent—situation, buildings, and all—but the boasting of the articles in the newspapers respecting it almost inclined one to deny its superiority. It is also, as your Majesty says, most striking to contemplate in the Clans the remains of feudal times and institutions. It is quite as well, however, particularly for Monarchy, that they are but remains, and that no more of them have been left.

Lord Melbourne thanks your Majesty much for your kind enquiries after his health. He thinks that he is getting better and stronger than he has been, and has a notion of trying a little shooting in October.

Lord Melbourne begs to be respectfully remembered to the Prince.

Footnote 92: Prince Aloysius Joseph of Liechtenstein (1796-1858) and his wife, Princess Françoise-de-Paule, Countess Kinsky.

Windsor Castle, 18th October 1842.

My dearest Uncle,—I only received your kind letter yesterday, for which my best thanks. I am delighted to hear that Louise's cough is decidedly better, and that upon the whole the dear family are well, thank God! Certainly where He sees fit to afflict, He gives strength to bear up!

Louise says Vecto is in great beauty, and the baby magnificent. I wish you could see Pussy now; she is (unberufen) the picture of health, and has just cut her first eye-tooth, without the slightest suffering. We are going to Brighton on the 1st of November for a month; it is the best month there and the worst here. I think I may announce Augusta Cambridge's93 marriage as certain, as I have just received a note from the Duke, which is as follows:—

"Being very anxious to communicate to you as soon as possible an event which concerns deeply my family, I take the liberty of requesting you to let me know on what day and at what hour I may wait upon you."

I shall see him to-morrow, and report the result to Louise on Friday.

I have just taken leave of poor Esterhazy, who has presented his letters of recall. He looked wretched, and Lord Aberdeen told me he is only ill at being obliged to go; he is quite miserable to do so, but the great gentleman at Johannisberg has most ungraciously refused to listen to his entreaties to remain, which is very foolish, as they don't know who to send in his place. I am very sorry to lose him, he is so amiable and agreeable, and I have known him ever since I can remember anybody; he is, besides, equally liked and on equally good terms with both parties here, which was of the greatest importance. It was touching to see him so low and ill and unlike himself.

The accounts of poor dear Alexandrine's eyes continue very bad; she cannot write at all, or go out, or do anything.

Say everything proper from us to the whole family, and pray believe me, always, your devoted Niece,

Victoria R.

Footnote 93: The Princess Augusta of Cambridge, who was married to Frederic William, afterwards Grand Duke of Mecklenburg-Strelitz, in the following June.

HISTORICAL STUDIES

Brocket Hall, 20th October 1842.

Lord Melbourne presents his humble duty to your Majesty, and begs leave respectfully to acknowledge your Majesty's of the 15th inst., which he received here the day before yesterday.

Lord Melbourne is very glad to hear that your Majesty is reading with the Prince. Hallam's work94 certainly requires much consideration and much explanation, but it is a fair, solid, impartial work, formed upon much thought and much reading. St Simon's95 is an excellent work; he has some prejudices, but was a good honest man, and his book is full of useful information. If your Majesty wishes for a book relating to what passed from one hundred to two hundred years ago, Lord Melbourne would strongly recommend the Private Memoirs of the Lord Chancellor Clarendon (Edward Hyde), not the great work, The History of the Rebellion, though that is well worth reading, but the Memoirs, and Bishop Burnet's History of his own time. The reigns of Charles II., James II., and the Revolution are very curious in the latter. During Queen Anne's reign the Bishop was not so much consulted, and his work is therefore not so interesting. If your Majesty wishes to turn your attention to more recent events, Professor Smyth's96 lectures upon Modern History, and particularly upon the French Revolution, seem to Lord Melbourne sound, fair, and comprehensive. Lord Mahon's97 is also a good work, and gives a good account of the reigns of George I. and George II. He has been thought by some in his last volume to have given too favourable a character of the Chevalier, Charles Edward Stuart.

Lord Melbourne is much touched by what your Majesty says of the Princess Royal, and the delight and comfort which your Majesty finds in her, as well as by the whole picture which your

Majesty draws of your domestic happiness. When your Majesty refers to what passed three years ago, your Majesty may be assured that it is with no small pleasure that Lord Melbourne recalls any share which he may have had in that transaction, and congratulates himself as well as your Majesty and the Prince upon results which have been so fortunate both for yourselves and for the country. Lord Melbourne ventures to hope that your Majesty will convey these feelings to the Prince, together with the assurance of his respectful remembrance.

Footnote 94: The Constitutional History, published in 1827.

Footnote 95: Louis Rouffroy, Duc de Saint-Simon, author of the celebrated Mémoires, published 1829-30.

Footnote 96: William Smyth (1765-1849), Regius Professor of Modern History at Cambridge.

Footnote 97: Afterwards fifth Earl Stanhope: the book referred to is his History of England from the Peace of Utrecht to the Peace of Versailles.

WALMER CASTLE

Walmer Castle, 26th October 1842.

My dear Peel,—Arbuthnot has shown me your letter to him respecting this house.

Nothing can be more convenient to me than to place it at Her Majesty's disposition at any time she pleases....

I am only apprehensive that the accommodation in the Castle would scarcely be sufficient for Her Majesty, the Prince, and the Royal children, and such suite as must attend....

It is the most delightful sea-residence to be found anywhere, particularly for children. They can be out all day, on the ramparts and platforms quite dry, and the beautiful gardens and wood are enclosed and sheltered from the severe gales of wind. There are good lodgings at Walmer village and on Walmer beach at no great distance from the Castle, not above half a mile. Believe me, ever, yours most sincerely,

Wellington.

If the Queen should send anybody here, I beg that he will write me a line, that I may have an apartment prepared for him.

LETTER FROM QUEEN ADELAIDE

Canford House, 31st October 1842.

My dearest Niece,—A thousand thanks for your very kind dear letter of yesterday with its enclosures, which I have just received. Your opinion respecting George of Hanover's98 marriage is quite my own, and I regret that the King does not seem to be inclined to settle it and fix a day for the celebration of it. I do not know his reasons against it, for I have not heard from him for a long, long time. I am so sorry to find that the accounts of his health are so indifferent, and fear he is not careful enough.

I am happy to hear that you thought the Cambridge visit went off well, and that the affianced99 looked and seemed happy. I hope it will always be the same, and that the marriage will not be delayed too long. I always had imagined that the Duke of Cambridge was rich and would give a fortune to his daughters, but I have lately heard that it is not the case. I do not know what is the usual marriage portion of an English Princess given by the country. In Germany those portions are called die Prinzessin Teuer.

We received 25,000 Fl. each when we married, and 10,000 Fl. for our trousseaux each.

If the young couple are to live in future with the Grand Duke they will not want any Plate, but if they are to have a separate ménage, then they will want it. I shall find it out by and by. I wonder that the Duchess likes to part with her fine sapphires. I thought the turquoises had been intended for Augusta.

I wish you could see the Convent to which I went the other day. The nuns belong to the Order of the Cistercian Trappists. They are not allowed to speak amongst themselves—what a relief my visit must have been to them!—and they neither eat meat, nor butter, nor eggs—nothing but milk, vegetables and rice. They look healthy, and there were several young rather pretty ones amongst them. One, the best-looking of them all, Sister Marie Josepha, took me affectionately by the hand and said, "I hope the air agrees with you here and that you feel better?" and then she added, "Come again—will you, before you leave this country again?" She told me that she was born in Ireland and had a German grandfather. She seemed to be the favourite amongst them all, for when I bought of their works and asked them to make up my bill, they called Marie Josepha to summon it up, and she said to me, "Do not stay for that; we will send you your things with the bill." Two hours after my visit to them I received my things, with a wreath of flowers besides as their gift to me; on the paper attached to it was written, "To the Queen-Dowager, from the Reverend Mother and her Community."

This old Reverend Mother, the Abbess, was very infirm, and could not get up from her chair, but she spoke very politely and ladylike to me in French. She has been forty years in her present situation, and comes from Bretagne. The chaplain of the Convent is also an old Frenchman, and there are several other French nuns amongst them—one who had been condemned to be guillotined in the Revolution, and was set at liberty just at the moment the execution was to have taken place. I should like to know whether these good nuns resumed again at once their silence when I left them, or whether they were permitted to talk over the events of that day.... Your most affectionately devoted Aunt,

Adelaide.

Footnote 98: Afterwards King George V. of Hanover. He married Princess Marie of Saxe-Altenburg, 18th February 1843.

Footnote 99: Princess Augusta of Cambridge. See p.

LORD MELBOURNE'S ILLNESS

1st November 1842.

... Many thanks for your most kind and amiable letter of the 28th, which I received yesterday. The prospect of the possibility of dearest Louise's spending some time with us quite enchants us, and I hope and trust that you will carry your plan into execution. Our plans, which we only settled last night, are as follows:—the scarlet fever is on the decrease at Brighton, but not sufficiently so to justify our going there immediately; so we therefore intend going to Walmer with the children, but a very reduced suite (as the house is considerably smaller than Claremont), on the 10th, and to stay there till the 22nd inst., when we shall go to Brighton and remain there till the 13th of December. Now if dearest Louise would meet us there then, and perhaps come back with us here for a little while then? Windsor is beautiful in December.

The news of Lord Melbourne, I am thankful to say, are excellent, and he improves rapidly under Dr Holland's care, but his first seizure was very alarming.100 I shall not fail to convey your kind message to this worthy friend of ours.

I am so pleased at your account of Nemours and poor Hélène. Tatane101 is not your favourite, is he?

Lord Douglas's102 marriage with Princess M. of Baden is settled; I shall of course treat her as a Princess of Baden—I can't do otherwise (it is like Aunt Sophie,103 and Princess M. of Würtemberg who married Count Neipperg104)—and him as Lord Douglas, which won't please him.

I wish Clem's marriage was no longer a secret, now that it is settled, as it is (forgive my saying it) really a fashion in our family to have these secrets de la comédie, when one is almost forced to tell a lie about what is true. I own I dislike these secrets; it was so with poor Marie and with Vecto. Now adieu! dearest, kindest Uncle, and believe me, always, your most affectionate Niece,
Victoria R.

Footnote 100: He had a paralytic seizure, and never regained his former health or spirits.

Footnote 101: Duc de Montpensier.

Footnote 102: Afterwards eleventh Duke of Hamilton: he was married to Princess Mary on 23rd February following.

Footnote 103: Sister of the Duchess of Kent and of the King of the Belgians, and the wife of Count Mensdorff.

Footnote 104: Alfred, Count Neipperg, who died in 1865.

THE CROWN JEWELS

Whitehall, 11th November 1842.

Sir Robert Peel presents his humble duty to your Majesty, and begs leave to acquaint your Majesty that he brought under the consideration of your Majesty's servants the questions relating to certain of the Crown Jewels, and the claim upon them preferred by the King of Hanover.105

In the course of the discussion it appeared to Sir Robert Peel that there were still some points in respect to this very embarrassing question which required the grave consideration of legal authorities, and that it would not be prudent to take any step, even that of submitting the case to arbitration, without the highest legal authority.

The submission to arbitration might avoid the evil (and a very great one it would be) of public controversy in a Court of Justice, and of public examination of members of the Royal Family on a matter partly of a domestic nature; but on the other hand, great care must be taken that by submitting the case to the award of arbitrators, even should they be nominated altogether by your Majesty, we do not relinquish any fair advantage for the Crown of England which would have accompanied an appeal to the regularly constituted tribunals of the country.

Your Majesty's Solicitor-General was employed as Counsel for the King of Hanover, and it has been thought therefore advisable to make the reference to the Attorney-General and to the

Queen's Advocate.

Sir Robert Peel has attempted to bring every questionable point in the case submitted to them under the consideration of your Majesty's law advisers, and when their report shall be received he will not fail to lay it before your Majesty.

Sir Robert Peel had a personal interview a few days since with His Royal Highness the Duke of Cambridge, on the subject of a public provision for the Princess Augusta on the occasion of her marriage.106

Sir Robert Peel thought it advisable to enquire from the Duke of Cambridge, as the impression of the public (of which His Royal Highness is quite aware) is that he has a considerable fortune of his own, independently of his annual allowance from Parliament.

PROVISION FOR PRINCESS AUGUSTA

The Duke of Cambridge seemed entirely to share the impressions of Sir Robert Peel that in the present state of the country, and of the public revenue, great caution is requisite in respect to the proposal of a grant of public money as a marriage portion to the Princess Augusta, and that it would be important that in any proposal to be made there should be a general acquiescence on the part of the House of Commons.

As the marriage is not to take place for some time it appears to Sir Robert Peel that it might be advisable to postpone a decision, at least in respect to the particular amount of any provision to be made, till a period nearer to the meeting of Parliament.

A public intimation, or the public notoriety long beforehand of the intention to propose a grant of public money might, in the present temper of the times, interpose additional obstacles in the way of it.

Sir Robert Peel proposes to return to Drayton Manor for a short time, and to leave London to-morrow morning.

Footnote 105: The King claimed them on the ground that part belonged to the Crown of Hanover, and part had been bequeathed to him by Queen Charlotte. The matter was referred to a Commission consisting of Lords Lyndhurst and Langdale, and Chief Justice Tindal. The two former were divided in opinion, and the Chief Justice died before the award was made. It was not till 1857 that a final decision, substantially in favour of Hanover, was given.

Footnote 106: See ante, p. .

SUCCESSES IN CHINA

Downing Street, 23rd November 1842.

Lord Stanley, with his humble duty, has the honour of submitting to your Majesty an original despatch from Lieutenant-General Sir Hugh Gough, received this morning, detailing the triumphant successes which had crowned the exertions of your Majesty's Naval and Military forces in China,107 and of the completely satisfactory result in the execution of a Treaty of Peace with the Emperor of China, upon terms highly honourable to your Majesty and advantageous to this country.

Lord Stanley learns from Lord Fitzgerald that he is also forwarding to your Majesty, by this messenger, the details which the same mail has brought of the complete and triumphant issue of the campaign in Afghanistan.

Lord Stanley trusts that he may be permitted to offer to your Majesty his humble congratulations upon intelligence so glorious to British Arms, and so important to British interests. It is difficult to estimate the moral effect which these victories may produce, not on Asia merely, but throughout Europe also. At the same moment your Majesty has brought to a triumphant issue two gigantic operations, one in the centre of Asia, the other in the heart of the hitherto unapproachable Chinese Empire. In the former, past disasters have been retrieved; a signal victory has been achieved on the very spot memorable for former failure and massacre; the honour of the British Arms has been signally vindicated; the interests of humanity have been consulted by the rescue of the whole of the prisoners; and, after a series of victories, the Governor-General of India is free, without discredit, to enter upon measures of internal improvement, and having established the supremacy of British power, to carry on henceforth a more pacific policy.

In China a termination has been put to the effusion of blood by the signature of a treaty which has placed your Majesty's dominions on a footing never recognised in favour of any foreign Power—a footing of perfect equality with the Chinese Empire; which has obtained large indemnity for the past, and ample security for the future, and which has opened to British enterprise the commerce of China to an extent which it is almost impossible to anticipate. It may interest your Majesty to hear that already enquiries are made in the City for superintendents of ships to trade to Ningpo direct.

Lord Stanley has taken upon himself to give orders in your Majesty's name for firing the Park and Tower guns in honour of these glorious successes. A Gazette extraordinary will be published to-morrow, the voluminous nature of the despatches rendering it necessary to take some time lest an important despatch should be omitted.

All which is humbly submitted by your Majesty's most dutiful Servant and Subject, Stanley.

Footnote 107: Chapoo was taken by Sir Hugh Gough in May: in June the squadron, under Admiral William Parker, entered the waters of the Yang-tze, captured Chin-kiang-fu, and were about to attack Nanking, when the treaty was concluded, embracing among other things a payment by the Chinese of 21,000,000 dollars, the cession of Hong Kong, and the opening of the ports of Canton, Amoy, Foochow, Ningpo, and Shanghai.

VICTORIES IN AFGHANISTAN

India Board, 23rd November 1842.108

Lord Fitzgerald, with his most humble duty to your Majesty, begs leave most humbly to inform your Majesty that the despatches received from the Governor-General of India announce the results of a series of most brilliant exploits by the armies under Major-General Nott and General Pollock in Afghanistan.

Each of those armies has achieved a glorious victory over superior numbers of the enemy.

The city of Ghuznee has been captured, and its formidable fortress utterly razed and destroyed.

The survivors of the British garrison, which had capitulated in the spring of the year, and who had been reduced to slavery, have been redeemed from bondage.

The splendid victory of General Pollock has been obtained over the army commanded by Akbar Khan in person, on the very spot where the greatest disaster had befallen the British Army on their retreat, and where the last gun had been lost.

On the 16th of September, General Pollock entered Cabul with his victorious troops and planted the Colours of your Majesty in the Bala Hissar, on the spot most conspicuous from the city.

An extract from a letter from General Pollock to Lord Ellenborough, dated at Cabul the 21st of September, gives the most gratifying intelligence that all the British prisoners, with the exception of Captain Bygrave, have been rescued from Akbar Khan, and were expected in the British camp on the 22nd of September.

An extract from a letter from General Pollock announcing the redemption of the prisoners is also most humbly submitted to your Majesty, by your Majesty's most dutiful Subject and Servant,

Fitzgerald and Vesci.

Footnote 108: The mail, which informed Ministers of the Chinese success, also brought the news of the capture of Cabul. General Nott (see ante, p.) had by the end of July completed his preparations, and marched upon Ghuznee, having arranged to meet Pollock at Cabul, and having transferred the Scinde command to General England. Nott was before Ghuznee on 5th September, but at daylight on the 6th found it evacuated; the citadel was destroyed by him and the Gates of Somnauth removed, as directed by Lord Ellenborough. Pollock, to whose discretion Ellenborough had entrusted the policy of advancing on Cabul, secured supplies at Gundamuck, and on his advance met the enemy in a strong position in the Jugdulluck Pass and dispersed them; then at Tezeen, on 12th September, he was attacked by Akbar Khan with 20,000 men. The Pass was forced, and the Afghans retired to the Haft Kotal, where they were utterly defeated, close to the scene of Elphinstone's disaster. Nott arrived at Cabul on the day after Pollock.

AFFAIRS OF PORTUGAL

Ardenne, 24th November 1842.

My dearest Victoria,—... I do not think, or I may say I am pretty certain, because I have often seen Donna Maria's letters, they hardly ever speak of politics, except just saying that they are surrounded by such very sad people without honour or honesty. I am sure they are not French at Lisbon beyond the kindly feelings which result from the recollection of Donna Maria's stay at Paris. My constant advice has been to look exclusively to the closest alliance with England, and Ferdinand is now well aware of it; but you know that the Liberal party tried to even harm him by representing him as a mere creature of England. We live in odd times when really one very often thinks people mad; their uncontrouled passions do not develop amiable feelings, but on the contrary everything that is bad and unreasonable....

You are a very affectionate and kind Mamma, which is very praiseworthy; may Heaven preserve your dear little children! Victoria is very clever, and it will give you great pleasure to see the development which takes place with children just at that time of life. What you say of

Ernest is unfortunately but too true; that trick of exaggeration is one of the worst I almost know, and particularly in people in high stations, as one finally knows not what to believe, and it generally ends with people disbelieving all such individuals do say.... Your devoted Uncle,
Leopold R.

Walmer Castle, 25th November 1842.

The Queen wishes Sir Robert to consider, and at an early period to submit to her, his propositions as to how to recompense and how to mark her high approbation of the admirable conduct of all those meritorious persons who have by their strenuous endeavour, brought about the recent brilliant successes in China and Afghanistan.

MILITARY HONOURS

Walmer Castle, 29th November 1842.

Approve of the G.C.B. given to—

* Sir H. Pottinger.
* Sir W. Parker.
* General Nott.
* General Pollock.

Likewise of the proposed pension to Sir R. Sale, and the Baronetcy to Sir Hugh Gough.

Thinks the latter very fit to succeed Sir Jasper Nicols[109] as Commander-in-Chief in India.

Grants with pleasure the permission to her troops engaged in Afghanistan to accept and wear the four medals which the Governor-General has had struck for the Indian Army, and hopes that besides gratifying the troops, it will have the beneficial effect of still further strengthening the good feeling existing between the two armies. Were it not for this impression, the Queen would have thought it more becoming that she herself should have rewarded her troops with a medal than leaving it to the Governor-General.

Footnote 109: Lieut.-General Sir Jasper Nicols (1778-1849), created a K.C.B. for his services at Bhurtpore.

THE GATES OF SOMNAUTH

Simla, 18th October 1842.

Lord Ellenborough, with his most humble duty to your Majesty, humbly offers to your Majesty his congratulation on the entire success which has attended the operations of the Fleet and Army under your Majesty's direction in the Yantze-Kiang,[110] and submits to your Majesty the general order which, on the receipt of the intelligence of that success and of the peace concluded with the Emperor of China upon the terms dictated by your Majesty, he issued to the Army of India.

Your Majesty will have observed that in the letter of the 4th of July to Major-General Nott, that officer was instructed to bring away the gates of the Temple of Somnauth, from the tomb of Mahmood of Ghuznee, and the club of Mahmood also.

The club was no longer upon the tomb, and it seems to be doubtful whether it was taken away by some person of Lord Keane's Army in 1839, or by Shah Sooja, or whether it was hidden in order to prevent its being taken away at that time.

The gates of the Temple of Somnauth have been brought away by Major-General Nott.

These gates were taken to Ghuznee by Sultan Mahmood in the year 1024. The tradition of the Invasion of India by Sultan Mahmood in that year, and of the carrying away of the gates after the destruction of the Temple, is still current in every part of India, and known to every one. So earnest is the desire of the Hindoos and of all who are not Mussulmans to recover the gates of the Temple, that when ten or twelve years ago Runjeet Singh was making arrangements with Shah Sooja for assisting him in the endeavour to recover his throne,111 he wished to make a stipulation that when Shah Sooja recovered his power he should restore the gates to India, and Shah Sooja refused.

Lord Ellenborough transmits for your Majesty's information a copy of the Address he intends to publish on announcing that the gates of the Temple will be restored.112

The progress of the gates from Ferozepore to Somnauth will be one great national triumph, and their restoration to India will endear the Government to the whole people.113

Footnote 110: See ante, p. , note 107.

Footnote 111: See ante, p. .

Footnote 112: "The insult of 800 years," he wrote in this rather theatrical proclamation, "is at last avenged. The gates of the temple of Somnauth, so long the memorial of your humiliation, are become the proudest record of your national glory.... You will yourselves, with all honour, transmit the gates of sandal-wood, through your respective territories, to the restored Temple of Somnauth."

Footnote 113: See post, pp. , , and .

FRANCE AND SPAIN

Windsor Castle, 13th December 1842.

Dearest Uncle,—I have to thank you for two most kind letters of the 5th and 8th. I can report very favourably of the healths of young and old; we are all very flourishing, and have since yesterday perfectly May weather. Clear, dry frost would be wholesome.

Victoire gave me yesterday a much better account of poor little Robert.114

In Portugal affairs seem quieted down, but Ferdinand is imprudent enough to say to Mamma that he would be wretched to lose Dietz (very naturally), and would not be at all sorry to go away. Now, this is folly, and a most dangerous language to hold, as if he entertains this, I fear the Portuguese will some beau matin indulge him in his wishes.

The news from Spain are better, but I must own frankly to you, that we are all disgusted at the French intrigues which have without a doubt been at the bottom of it all, and can, I fear, be traced very close to the Tuileries. Why attempt to ruin a country (which they luckily cannot succeed in) merely out of personal dislike to a man who certainly has proved himself capable of keeping the country quiet, and certainly is by far the most honest Spaniard in existence, whatever crimes or faults the French may choose to bring against him. And what will be the effect of all this? A total dislike and mistrust of France, and a still closer alliance with England. I have spoken thus freely, as a repetition of last year's scenes is too much to remain silent, and as I have ever been privileged to tell you, dearest Uncle, my feelings, and the truth.

Poor Lord Hill's death, though fully expected, will grieve you, as it has grieved us.

I am much amused at what you say about Charles, and shall tell it him, when I write to him.
Believe me, always, your most affectionate Niece,

Victoria R.

Footnote 114: The infant Duc de Chartres.

Windsor Castle, 19th December 1842.

The Queen is very desirous that something should be done for Major Malcolm115 (who was
the bearer of "the news of Victory and Peace"), either by promotion in the Army or by any other
distinction. He is a very intelligent and well-informed officer, and has been employed in China
both in a Civil and Military capacity, and has made, and is going to make again, a long journey at
a very bad time of the year, though suffering severely at this moment from ague.

Footnote 115: In such cases it has been usual to confer some distinction.

Windsor Castle, 26th December 1842.

The Queen thanks Sir Robert for his letter of the 23rd. She thinks that Major Malcolm's going
back to China the bearer of verbal instructions as well as written ones will greatly facilitate the
matter and prevent misunderstandings, which at such a great distance are mostly fatal. The
Queen joins in Sir Robert's opinion, that before coming to a final arrangement it will be most
valuable to have Sir H. Pottinger's opinion upon your present message, and thinks it much the
best that Sir H. should in the meantime be entrusted with the extraordinary full powers for
concluding any provisional arrangements, as she believes that very great confidence may be
placed in him. Lord Stanley's suggestions strike the Queen as very judicious and calculated to
facilitate the future Government of Hong-Kong.

The Queen hopes to hear more from Sir Robert when she sees him here, which she hopes to do
from Monday the 2nd to Wednesday the 4th.

THE SCOTCH CHURCH

Drayton Manor, 26th December 1842.

Sir Robert Peel presents his humble duty to your Majesty, and with reference to enquiries made
by your Majesty when Sir Robert Peel was last at Windsor, on the subject of the Scotch Church
and the proceedings of the last General Assembly, begs leave to acquaint your Majesty that the
Moderator of the Assembly has recently addressed a letter to Sir Robert Peel, requiring an
answer to the demands urged by the General Assembly in a document entitled a Protest and
Declaration of Right.116

The demands of the General Assembly amount to a reversal by Law of the recent decisions of
the Court of Session and of the House of Lords, and to a repeal of the Act of Queen Anne, which
establishes the Right of Patronage in respect to Livings in the Church of Scotland.

That Act by no means gives any such absolute right of appointment to the Crown or other
patrons of Livings, as exists in England. It enables those legally entitled to the patronage to
present a clergyman to the Living, but the Church Courts have the power, on valid objections
being made and duly sustained by the parishioners, to set aside the presentation of the patron,
and to require from him a new nomination.

The Church, however, requires the absolute repeal of the Act of Anne.

An answer to the demands of the Church will now become requisite.

Sir James Graham has been in communication with the law advisers of your Majesty in Scotland upon the legal questions involved in this matter, and will shortly send for your Majesty's consideration the draft of a proposed answer to the General Assembly.117

Footnote 116: The famous Auchterarder case had decided that, notwithstanding the vetoing by the congregation of the nominee of the patron, the Presbytery must take him on trial if qualified by life, learning, and doctrine,—in other words, that the Act of Anne, subjecting the power of the Presbytery to the control of the law courts, was not superseded by the Veto Act, a declaration made by the General Assembly. In the Strathbogie case, a minister had been nominated to Marnock, and 261 out of 300 heads of families had objected to him. The General Assembly having directed the Presbytery to reject him, the civil court held that he must be taken on trial. Seven members of the Presbytery obeyed the civil power, and the General Assembly, on the motion of Dr Chalmers, deposed them and declared their parishes vacant.

Footnote 117: Sir James Graham's letter is printed in the Annual Register for 1843. A petition in answer was drawn by the Assembly and presented to Parliament by Mr Fox Maule. After the debate on it in the Commons, preparations were made throughout Scotland for the secession of the non-intrusionists, as they were called, which event took place on 18th May 1843, when about 500 Ministers, headed by Chalmers, seceded from the Old Kirk, and founded the Free Church.

A SERIOUS CRISIS

Drayton Manor, 30th December 1842.

Sir Robert Peel presents his humble duty to your Majesty, and rejoices to hear that your Majesty approved of the letter which, with your Majesty's sanction, James Graham proposes to write to the Moderator of the General Assembly of the Church of Scotland.

Sir Robert Peel fears that there is too much ground for the apprehensions expressed by your Majesty in respect to future embarrassment arising out of the position of the Church Question in Scotland.

Sir Robert Peel saw yesterday a letter addressed by Dr Abercrombie,118 the eminent physician in Edinburgh, to Sir George Sinclair,119 declaring his conviction that the Secession of Ministers from their Livings would take place to a very great extent—would comprise very many of the Ministers most distinguished for learning and professional character, and would meet with very general support among their congregations.

Sir Robert Peel has little doubt that a serious crisis in the History of the Church of Scotland is at hand, and that the result of it will be greatly to be lamented; but still he could not advise your Majesty to seek to avert it by the acquiescence in demands amounting to the abrogation of important civil rights and to the establishment in Scotland of an ecclesiastical domination independent of all control....

He is very confident that your Majesty will feel that in the present state of the controversy with the Church of Scotland, there is peculiar reason for taking the greatest care that every minister presented to a Crown Living should be not only above exception, but should, if possible, be pre-eminently distinguished for his fitness for a pastoral charge.

Footnote 118: John Abercrombie (1780-1844), one of the chief consulting physicians in Scotland, and a great medical writer. He left the Established Church.

Footnote 119: Sir George Sinclair (1790-1868), M.P. for Caithness-shire, was a supporter of the Anti-Patronage Society, and joined the Free Church.

HISTORICAL READING

Brocket Hall, 30th December 1842.

Lord Melbourne presents his humble duty to your Majesty. He has been much delighted this morning by receiving your Majesty's letter of the 28th. He was the more gratified, as he had begun to be a little annoyed at being such a very long time without hearing from your Majesty.

Lord Mahon has sent Lord Melbourne his book.[120] Lord Melbourne has not yet read it, but he has read the review of it in the Quarterly, which seems to be a sort of abstract or abridgment of the book. The effect of writing it in French has naturally been to direct all attention and criticism from the merits of the work to the faults of the French. People who have read the work speak of it as entertaining, and the times are curious and interesting. The characters engaged in them, striking and remarkable. Lord Melbourne is very glad to hear that Pottinger's conduct is so universally approved. He always appeared to Lord Melbourne to be a man of great ability, resolution and discretion, and Lord Melbourne much rejoices that he has turned out so.

Hallam's opinions Lord Melbourne believes to be in general sound, and such as have been held and approved by the most able and constitutional statesmen in this country.

Lord Melbourne is much rejoiced to hear of the Princess and the Prince of Wales, and also that your Majesty is pursuing your studies quietly, cheerfully, and happily.

Lord Melbourne is very sensible of the interest which the Baron takes in his health and which he warmly reciprocates. There is no man whom he esteems more, nor of whose head and heart he has a better opinion.

We expect here to-morrow the Duchess of Sutherland[121] and Lady Elizabeth Gower,[122] who have been kind enough to propose to pay Lord Melbourne a visit.

Footnote 120: Essai sur la vie du grand Condé, afterwards published in English.

Footnote 121: Formerly Mistress of the Robes.

Footnote 122: Afterwards Duchess of Argyll.

INTRODUCTORY NOTE: TO CHAPTER XII

Repeated debates took place during the year (1843) on the Corn Laws, the agitation against them steadily growing, Mr Cobden coming on one occasion into violent conflict with the Premier. The events of the previous year in Afghanistan were also the subject of constant discussion in Parliament. A movement of some importance took place in Wales in opposition to the increasing number of toll-bars, bands of rioters dressed in women's clothes and known as "Rebecca and her daughters," demolishing the gates and committing acts of greater or less violence. A verse in Genesis (xxiv. 60) fancifully applied gave rise to this name and disguise.

In Scotland the system of private patronage in the Established Kirk had become very unpopular, the Act of Anne in favour of the nomination by lay patrons, and the control given to the Law Courts over the revising action of the Presbytery being ultimately modified by a declaration of the General Assembly known as the Veto Act. But it was decided in what was called the Strathbogie case that the veto was illusory, the disruption of the old Kirk followed, and on 18th May Dr Chalmers and five hundred other ministers seceded from it in order to form the Free Church.

In Ireland the agitation for Repeal was at its height. O'Connell, supported by the Nation newspaper, founded a Repeal Association in Dublin, and monster meetings were held on Sundays on some conspicuous spot of free and historic associations to claim the re-establishment of a Parliament on College Green. It was believed that a quarter of a million people were present on one occasion, and the Government, alarmed at the absolute power wielded by O'Connell over these huge bodies of men, resolved to prohibit the meetings, and somewhat tardily issued a Proclamation against that announced for Clontarf on 8th October. O'Connell accordingly disbanded the meeting, but his action did not please his more zealous supporters, and his ascendency came to an end. The agitation collapsed and the principal actors were arrested.

A military duel fought in the summer of this year, in which a colonel in the Army was shot by his brother-in-law, made the code of honour existing on the subject a burning question, the criminal law of homicide being the same then as now. On Prince Albert's suggestion, the question was taken up by the heads of the Army and Navy, and the Articles of War were in the following year amended so as to admit of an apology and a tender of redress.

The better feeling existing between this country and France enabled the Queen and Prince to visit Louis Philippe at the Château d'Eu.

CHAPTER XII

Windsor Castle, 4th January 1843.

Dearest Uncle,—... We have been very gay; danced into the New Year, and again last night, and were very merry, though but a very small party; young and old danced. Good Lord Melbourne was here from Saturday till this morning, looking very well, and I almost fancied happy old times were returned; but alas! the dream is past! He enquired much after you.

Now adieu! Ever your devoted Niece,

Victoria R.

BETROTHAL OF PRINCE DE JOINVILLE

Claremont, 10th January 1843.

My dearest Uncle,—I am happy to write to you again from this so very dear and comfortable old place, where you will have heard from Louise that we arrived with our dear Pussy on Thursday last. We are all so particularly well, including Pussy, that we intend, to my great delight, to prolong our stay till next Monday. This place has a peculiar charm for us both, and to me it brings back recollections of the happiest days of my otherwise dull childhood—where I experienced such kindness from you, dearest Uncle, which has ever since continued. It is true that my last stay here before I came to the Throne, from November '36 to February '37, was a peculiarly painful and disagreeable one, but somehow or other, I do not think of those times, but only of all the former so happy ones. Victoria plays with my old bricks, etc., and I think you would be pleased to see this and to see her running and jumping in the flower garden, as old— though I fear still little—Victoria of former days used to do. She is very well, and such an amusement to us, that I can't bear to move without her; she is so funny and speaks so well, and in French also, she knows almost everything; she would therefore get on famously with Charlotte....

Might I ask you some questions about Joinville's match,1 which interests me much? First of all, have you heard of his arrival at Rio? Secondly, if the Donna Francesca pleases, is he empowered at once to make the demand, or must he write home first? How nice it would be if the two marriages could take place at once; but I suppose, under any circumstances, that could not be....

Alexandrine is nearly quite recovered; she writes such pretty, affectionate, kind letters, poor dear child, and is so fond of Ernest. I must say I think he seems improved, as he likes to live quietly with her, and speaks of her too with the greatest affection.

Now, my dearest Uncle, let me take my leave, begging you to believe me, always, your devoted Niece,

Victoria R.

Footnote 1: He was married to the Princess Francesca of Brazil on 1st May.

HISTORICAL READING

Brocket Hall, 12th January 1843.

Lord Melbourne presents his humble duty to your Majesty, and thanks your Majesty much for your letter of the 9th inst. which he received yesterday. Every letter that he receives from your

Majesty brings back to his mind the recollection of times, which, though they were clouded with much care and anxiety, were still to Lord Melbourne a period of much happiness and satisfaction....

Hallam has not written a History of the Church, but in all his books there is necessarily much about the Church, and much that is worthy of mention. A short History of the Church is, Lord Melbourne fears, not to be found, the subject is so large and so difficult that it cannot be treated shortly. Dr Short2 has written and published a clever, brief, and distinct summary, but it relates principally to the Church of England, and in order to be fully understood, requires to be read by one who has already some acquaintance with the subject.

The book which your Majesty remembers Lord Melbourne reading is the production of Dr Waddington,3 whom your Majesty, under Lord Melbourne's recommendation, made Dean of Durham, which dignity he now holds. It is a very good book.

Adolphus's4 History is by no means a bad book, and will give your Majesty the facts of the beginning of the reign of George III. well and accurately enough. The Duke of Sussex once told Lord Melbourne that he had asked his father whether Adolphus's account of the beginning of his reign was correct, and that the King had replied that substantially it was so, but that there were some mistakes, and that what had been done by one person was often attributed to another. Adolphus's History will receive some illustration from Horace Walpole's letters of that period....

Lord Melbourne thinks that he is really getting rid of the gout, and gathering strength. He still has some doubt whether he shall be able to go up for the meeting of Parliament. Lord Melbourne begs to renew to your Majesty the warm and respectful assurance of his gratitude and attachment.

Footnote 2: Bishop, then of Sodor and Man, afterwards of St Asaph. His book, a Sketch of the History of the Church of England, was published in 1832.

Footnote 3: George Waddington (1793-1869), Dean of Durham, published in 1833 the History of the Church from the Earliest Ages to the Reformation.

Footnote 4: John Adolphus, barrister, wrote a history of England from 1760 to 1783.

Canford House, Friday, 13th January 1843.

My dearest Niece,—... As you take so kind an interest in our dear Thesy,5 I send you a letter which I have received from her mother-in-law, with an excellent account of her and her infant. Her happiness is a great blessing, and I thank God that she is so well this time. Can you imagine her with two boys? It seems so odd, for it is but a short time since she was here with us. How time flies rapidly. I own I was not a little surprised to find that you are probably the godmother; or is the little boy only to be named after you? I remember well what you said to me when I was asked to be the godmother of the first boy, "that I could not accept it," as I must not take the responsibilities attached to a sponsor with a Roman Catholic child. On that ground alone, and having learned your opinion which sanctioned my own, I refused it then at the risk of offending the dear parents. Now, after all that was said on the subject, if you have accepted the offer of becoming sponsor to this little Victor, YOU, as the Head of the English Church, give to understand that I was wrong in my notions of the duties which our Church imposes upon sponsors, having refused what you accepted. I tell you fairly and openly that it has vexed me, but of course I say this only to yourself, dearest Victoria, and not to any one else, for it does not become me to find fault with what you please to do. But I could not entirely pass it over in silence, and regret that my former refusal must now become doubly annoying to my relations. I beg your pardon for thus frankly stating my feelings to you on a subject which I shall now despatch from my mind, and I trust you will not take it ill, and excuse me for having mentioned it to you alone.... Your most attached and devoted Aunt,

Adelaide.

Footnote 5: Princess Thérèse, daughter of the Prince of Hohenlohe-Schillingsfurst, and wife of Prince Frederick Charles of Hohenlohe-Waldenburg.

Claremont, 15th January 1843.

I am at a loss to comprehend, my dear Aunt, what you mean by saying that you refused being godmother to Thesy's first child, as I had sanctioned your doing so. I never remember even talking to you on the subject, but only heard from Mamma that you had refused doing so—which I was surprised at. I therefore felt no hesitation in accepting the offer of Thesy, particularly as I am already godmother to one of the children of Prince Esterhazy's daughter. I am grieved, dearest Aunt, that this occurrence should annoy you, but I can assure you that I do not remember ever having spoken to you on the subject at all.

GOVERNOR-GENERALSHIP OF CANADA

Downing Street, 19th January 1843.

Lord Stanley, with his humble duty, submits to your Majesty that in pursuance of the permission which your Majesty was pleased to give him personally, he has this day offered to Sir Charles Metcalfe6 the Governor-Generalship of Canada; and Lord Stanley has much satisfaction in adding that the offer has been readily and thankfully accepted. This appointment, Lord Stanley is convinced, is, under the circumstances, the best which could have been made, and he believes not only that it will be generally approved, but that Sir Charles Metcalfe's long experience and tried discretion will afford the best prospect of conducting the affairs of Canada safely and successfully through the present crisis. As Sir Charles Metcalfe will naturally be anxious previous to his embarkation (which, however, will probably not take place for at least six weeks) to have the honour of being presented to your Majesty on his appointment, Lord Stanley hopes he may be honoured by your Majesty's commands as to the time when it may be your Majesty's pleasure to admit him to an audience. Perhaps Sir Charles's attendance after the Council at which your Majesty's Speech on the opening of the Session has to be settled, may give your Majesty as little trouble as any time that could be named.

The above is humbly submitted by your Majesty's most, dutiful Servant and Subject,

Stanley.

Footnote 6: Metcalfe had had a long Indian career, and for a year had been Provisional Governor-General, when he removed the restrictions on the liberty of the Press. He was created a peer in 1845, but never took his seat. He resigned his post at the end of that year, and died soon after.

ASSASSINATION OF MR DRUMMOND

Whitehall, 20th January (1843).

Sir,—I have the painful duty of acquainting your Royal Highness that Mr Drummond, my Private Secretary, was shot at this day about quarter past three o'clock, in the neighbourhood of Charing Cross.7

Two pistols were discharged, the first close to Mr Drummond's back, the second after the assassin had been seized by a policeman.

The ball entered in the back and has been extracted, after passing round the ribs. I have just left Mr Drummond's house. No vital part appears to have been injured, and there is no unfavourable symptom whatever.

The assassin gives his name MacNaghten, and appears to be a Glasgow man.

Two five-pound notes were, I understand, found upon his person, and a receipt for £750 given to Daniel MacNaghten, confirming, therefore, the man's account of his name.

We have not hitherto been able to discover that this man had any alleged grievance or complaint against the Treasury or any public office.

He has been loitering about the public offices for the last fortnight, and being questioned, I understand, some days since, by the Office Keeper of the Council office, said he was a policeman. This, of course, for the purpose of evading further enquiry.

The policeman who apprehended the man, says that he heard the man exclaim after firing the shots: "He or she (the policeman is uncertain which) shall not disturb my peace of mind any more."

These are all the particulars I have heard or learned. I am afraid I have given them to your Royal Highness in a hurried manner. I have thought it better to convey this information to Her Majesty, through the kind intervention of your Royal Highness, than by a direct communication to the Queen.

I have the honour to be, Sir, with sincere respect, your Royal Highness's most faithful and humble Servant,

Robert Peel.

Footnote 7: Edward Drummond had been Private Secretary to Canning, Ripon, and Wellington, as well as to Peel, and was very popular; he was in his fifty-first year. He had just left his uncle's Bank at Charing Cross, when he was shot.

MISTAKEN FOR SIR ROBERT PEEL

Whitehall, 21st January 1843.

Sir Robert Peel begs leave to mention to your Majesty a fact which has not hitherto transpired—and of which he was not aware until he had an interview this morning with Sir James Graham.

On the Inspector Tierney going into the cell of MacNaghten this morning, he said to MacNaghten: "I suppose you are aware who is the person whom you have shot?"

He (MacNaghten) said: "Yes—Sir Robert Peel."

From this it would appear that he had mistaken Mr Drummond for Sir Robert Peel.

The Magistrate thought it better not to have this evidence at present placed on record.

DEATH OF MR DRUMMOND

Whitehall, 25th January 1843.

Sir Robert Peel presents his humble duty to your Majesty, and has the very painful duty to report to your Majesty the fatal consequences of the attack on Mr Drummond.

He breathed his last this morning about half-past ten o'clock.

A very unfavourable change took place last night, and no hopes were entertained after seven o'clock in the evening.

This sad event has had such an effect on Lady Peel, and all the circumstances attending it are so distressing to Sir Robert Peel, that relying upon your Majesty's great kindness, he ventures to express a hope that your Majesty will have the goodness to permit Sir Robert and Lady Peel to remain for the present in London, or should your Majesty desire to see Sir Robert Peel before Wednesday next, to allow him to wait upon your Majesty in the morning of any day which your Majesty may be pleased to name.

He need scarcely assure your Majesty that nothing but such a sad event as that which has occurred would induce him to prefer this request to your Majesty.

Sir Robert Peel encloses such further information as has reached him respecting MacNaghten.

He does not hesitate to send to your Majesty every word of information of the least importance which he receives....

The evidence of his mental delusion is strong, but it must be borne in mind that he was exactly the instrument which others would employ.

Sir Robert Peel has no reason for surmising this to be the case, but the possibility of it ought not and shall not be overlooked.

DEMEANOUR OF MACNAGHTEN

Whitehall, 25th January 1843.

Sir Robert Peel presents his humble duty to your Majesty, and makes no apology for frequently writing to your Majesty on the painful subject in respect to which your Majesty has manifested so deep an interest.

Sir Robert Peel humbly thinks that your Majesty's observations with respect to the clear distinctions in the cases of insanity are most just. It will be most unfortunate indeed if the Law does not attach its severest penalty to a crime so premeditated and so deliberately and savagely perpetrated, as that of MacNaghten.

The Jury are, however, the sole judges on this point, that is to say, it rests with them exclusively, either to find an absolute verdict of guilty of murder, or to acquit on the ground of insanity.

MacNaghten will be charged with the offence of murder, and every effort will be made to bring him to condign punishment.

His counsel will probably endeavour to establish his insanity.

Nothing can be more collected and intelligent in many respects than his conduct in prison. He was conversing with the gaoler, and seemed not disinclined to unburden his mind, when he suddenly stopped and enquired from the gaoler whether such conversations as that which he was holding went beyond the prison walls.

On being informed that no security could be given that they would remain secret, he said he should hold his tongue, but that all would come out by and by.

Sir Robert Peel takes the liberty of enclosing for your Majesty's perusal a note which he has just received from Miss Emily Eden, sister of Lord Auckland, and of Mrs Charles Drummond.

If it should be in your Majesty's power to assign apartments at some future period to Miss Drummond, who lived with her brother Edward, and was mainly dependent upon him, it would be a very great comfort to a lady of the most unexceptionable conduct, and most deeply attached to her poor brother.

Brocket Hall, 25th January 1843.

Lord Melbourne presents his humble duty to your Majesty. He has been much gratified this morning by receiving your Majesty's letter of the 23rd; he has determined upon following your Majesty's advice, and upon not hazarding the throwing himself back by coming up to London and attempting to attend the House of Lords at the commencement of the Session. The assassination of Mr Drummond, for Lord Melbourne fears it must be called so, is indeed a dreadful thing. Lord Melbourne is not surprised, for people are very apt to turn all their wrath and indignation upon the man from whom they actually receive an answer which they do not like, without in the least considering whether he is really responsible for it. Lord Melbourne used often to be himself assailed with threats of personal violence. Sometimes he took notice of them by swearing the peace against those who used them, and having them bound over in sureties. Sometimes he disregarded them, but he does not think it either prudent or justifiable entirely to neglect such intimations. Lord Melbourne does not wonder that this event brings to your Majesty's recollection what has taken place in your own case.

Hallam is, in Lord Melbourne's opinion, right about Ireland. Her advocates are very loud in their outcry, but she has not really much to complain of.

Lord Melbourne was very glad to hear of the marriage of Prince Augustus of Coburg with the Princess Clémentine, as he apprehends that the connection must be very agreeable to your Majesty.

Lord Melbourne begs to be respectfully and affectionately remembered to His Royal Highness.

COMMITTAL OF MACNAGHTEN

Whitehall, 28th January 1843.

Sir James Graham, with humble duty, begs to inform your Majesty, that the prisoner Daniel MacNaghten was fully committed for trial this afternoon. He was not defended before the Magistrates; but in his manner he was quite cool, intelligent, and collected; he asked no questions, but he expressed a wish to have copies of the Depositions.

His trial will probably commence on Friday or Saturday next, and there is reason to believe that, at the request of his relatives in Glasgow, counsel will be retained, and that the plea of insanity will be raised in his defence.8

Every preparation is in progress to meet this vague and dangerous excuse. It will turn out that the pistols were bought at Paisley by MacNaghten on the 6th of August last; and information has reached Sir James Graham, which, he thinks, will prove that MacNaghten is a Chartist, that he has attended political meetings at Glasgow, and that he has taken a violent part in politics. He yesterday saw a Presbyterian clergyman, who prayed with him; who pointed out the atrocity of his crime, the innocence of his victim, the pangs of sorrowing relatives, and who exhorted him to contrition and repentance. Some impression was made at the moment; but his general demeanour is marked by cold reserve and hardness of heart.

Footnote 8: He was defended by four counsel, including Mr Cockburn, afterwards Lord Chief Justice.

THE ROYAL FAMILY AND POLITICS

Brocket Hall, 2nd February 1843.

Lord Melbourne presents his humble duty to your Majesty, and thanks much for the letter of the 30th ult., which he received here yesterday morning. He believes it is more prudent not to go to London, but he greatly regrets that his not doing so will deprive him for so long a time of the honour and pleasure of seeing your Majesty.

The Duke of Sussex acquainted Lord Melbourne and took his opinion before he issued his cards for the dinner. Lord Melbourne does not think that he can have any idea of playing the part to which Lord Erroll alluded. It is better that a dinner should be given somewhere. He having nothing of the kind would look too much like giving up the whole business and disbanding the party. Lord Melbourne entirely agrees with your Majesty as to the political conduct which ought to be pursued by the members of the Royal Family, but he remembers no time in which they have been induced to act with so much prudence and propriety. Your Majesty will see in Adolphus the very prominent share which the Duke of Cumberland,9 the General of Culloden, took in the Party contentions of those days. He was a strong partisan and in a great measure the founder of the Whig party. Lord Melbourne has often heard George IV. converse upon that subject, and he used to contend that it was quite impossible for a Prince of Wales in this country to avoid taking an active part in politics and political contentions. The fact is, that George III. did not discourage this in his own family sufficiently, and the King of Hanover always said that his father had encouraged him in the active part which he took, and which certainly was sufficiently objectionable.

The assassination of Drummond is indeed a horrible event. Lord Melbourne does not see as yet any clear, distinct, and certain evidence of what were the real motives and object of the man. But we shall hear upon his trial what it is that he urges. Your Majesty will, of course, recollect that the Jury acquitted Oxford, and there then was nothing to do but to acquiesce in the verdict. If the Jury should take a similar view of this man's crime, it will be impossible for the Government to do anything to remedy the evil which Lord Melbourne thinks will be caused by such a decision. Lord Melbourne knew Mr Drummond pretty well. He used formerly to be much in Hertfordshire, both at Hatfield and at Gorhambury, and Lord Melbourne has often met him at both places, and thought him with all the rest of the world, a very quiet, gentlemanly, and agreeable man. Lord Melbourne very well remembers the murder of Mr Perceval and Bellingham's trial. Lord

Melbourne was then in the House of Commons, but was not present at the time the crime was perpetrated. There were differences of opinion as to the manner in which Sir James Mansfield conducted the trial. Many thought that he ought to have given more time, which was asked for on the part of the prisoner, in order to search for evidence at Liverpool. But the law which he laid down in his charge is certainly sound, correct, and reasonable. Lord Melbourne is very glad to think that your Majesty has not to go to the House of Lords to-day.

Footnote 9: This Duke died unmarried in 1765, and his nephew, the fourth son of Frederick, Prince of Wales, was created Duke of Cumberland in 1766. He in his turn died without issue, in 1790, and in 1799 the fifth son of George III. (afterwards King of Hanover) received the same title.

THE AMERICAN TREATY

Brocket Hall, 3rd February 1843.

... Lord Melbourne thinks that the Speech was very well and judiciously drawn; the only paragraph which he does not like is that about the American treaty.10 It betrays too great an anxiety for peace, and too much fear of war.11

Footnote 10: See ante, pp. , . The treaty had been negotiated by Lord Ashburton.

Footnote 11: "By the treaty which Her Majesty has concluded with the United States of America, and by the adjustment of those differences which, from their long continuance, had endangered the preservation of peace, Her Majesty trusts that the amicable relations of the two countries have been confirmed."

Laeken, 6th February 1843.

My beloved Victoria,—I am quite of your opinion about balls. Nothing can change what cannot change, and I consider all these things, which have always been a bore to me, as a matter of duty and not otherwise. The duties of station are to be fulfilled like the others, and my first and most pleasant duty is to do all that your Uncle may command or wish. Your Uncle was much shocked by your answer about Miss Meyer,12 whom he considered of uncommon beauty. He is quite in love with her picture, and is very anxious to discover who she is. The other pictures of the book of beauty he abandons to you, and they are certainly worthy of a book of ugliness....
Yours most devotedly,
Louise.

Footnote 12: Eugénie Meyer, step-daughter of Colonel Gurwood, C.B., married the first Viscount Esher, Master of the Rolls. The Queen had written that she did not admire that style of beauty.

KING LEOPOLD AND PEEL

Laeken, 10th February 1843.

My dearest Victoria,—... I am very much gratified by your having shown my hasty scrawl to Sir Robert Peel, and that the sincere expression of a conscientious opinion should have given him pleasure.

It was natural at first that you should not have liked to take him as your Premier; many circumstances united against him. But I must say for you and your family, as well as for

England, it was a great blessing that so firm and honourable a man as Peel should have become the head of your Administration. The State machine breaks often down in consequence of mistakes made forty and fifty years ago; so it was in France where even Louis XIV. had already laid the first foundation for what happened nearly a hundred years afterwards.

I believe, besides, Sir Robert sincerely and warmly attached to you, and as you say with great truth, quite above mere party feeling. Poor Lady Peel must be much affected by what has happened.... Your truly devoted Uncle,

Leopold R.

Brocket Hall, 12th February 1843.

Lord Melbourne presents his humble duty to your Majesty. He received here on Friday last, the 10th, your Majesty's letter of the 8th, which gave him great pleasure, and for which he gratefully thanks your Majesty. Lord Melbourne is getting better, and hopes soon to be nearly as well as he was before this last attack, but he still finds his left hand and arm and his left leg very much affected, and he does not recover his appetite, and worse still, he is very sleepless at night, an evil which he is very little used to, and of which he is very impatient....

Lord Melbourne adheres to all he said about Lord Ashburton and the Treaty, but he thinks more fire than otherwise would have taken place was drawn upon Lord Ashburton by the confident declaration of Stanley that his appointment was generally approved. The contrary is certainly the case. There is much of popular objection to him from his American connection and his supposed strong American interests. Lady Ashburton, with whom he received a large fortune, is a born American. But he is supposed to possess much funded property in that country, and to have almost as strong an interest in its welfare as in that of Great Britain. With all this behind, it is a bad thing to say that his appointment was liable to no suspicion or objection. It seems to Lord Melbourne that what with Ellenborough with the Gates of Ghuznee upon his shoulders,13 and Ashburton with the American Treaty round his neck, the Ministry have nearly as heavy a load upon them as they can stand up under, and Lord Melbourne would not be surprised if they were to lighten themselves of one or the other.

Footnote 13: The Somnauth Proclamation created a good deal of ridicule.

POSITION OF THE PRINCE OF WALES

Brocket Hall, 13th February 1843.

Lord Melbourne presents his humble duty to your Majesty, and has just recollected that in the letter which he wrote yesterday, he omitted to advert to a part of your Majesty's last to which your Majesty may expect some answer. He means the part relating to the character and situation of a Prince of Wales in this country. George IV. was so conscious of having mixed himself most unrestrainedly in politics, and of having taken a very general part in opposition to his father's Government and wishes, that he was naturally anxious to exonerate himself from blame, and to blame it upon the necessity of his position rather than upon his own restless and intermeddling disposition. But Lord Melbourne agrees with your Majesty that his excuse was neither valid nor justifiable, and Lord Melbourne earnestly hopes that your Majesty and the Prince may be successful in training and instructing the young Prince of Wales, and to make him understand correctly his real position and its duties, and to enable him to withstand the temptations and seductions with which he will find himself beset, when he approaches the age of twenty-one. It is true that Sir John made the observation, which Lord Melbourne mentioned to your Majesty, and which you now remember correctly. He made it to Sir James Graham, when he went to talk to him about the offence which William IV. had taken at the Duchess of Kent's marine excursion; and at the receiving of royal salutes. Your Majesty was not very long in the situation of an acknowledged, admitted, and certain Heir Apparent, but still long enough to be aware of the use which those around you were inclined to make of that situation and of the petitions and applications which it naturally produced from others, and therefore to have an idea of the difficulties of it.

Lord Melbourne heartily wishes your Majesty every success in the interesting and important task in which you are engaged of forming the character and disposition of the young Prince.

DOMESTIC HAPPINESS

Canford House, 14th February 1843.

My dearest Niece,—Your delightful letter of Tuesday gave me such pleasure and satisfaction that I must thank you with all my heart for it. Your happiness, and your gratitude for that happiness, is most gratifying to my feelings, having loved you from your infancy almost as much as if you had been my own child. It is therefore happiness to me to hear from yourself those expressions to which you gave vent. I thank God that you have such an excellent husband, so well calculated to make you happy and to assist you in your arduous duties by his advice, as well as his help in sharing your troubles. I pray that your domestic happiness may last uninterruptedly, and that you may enjoy it through a long, long period of many, many years. You cannot say too much of yourself and dear Albert when you write to me, for it is a most interesting subject to my heart, I assure you.

What a shame to have put on darling little Victoria a powdered wig! Poor dear child must have looked very strange with it! Did her brother appear in einer Allonge-Perücke?...

I shall hope to follow you to town early next month, and look forward with great pleasure to seeing you so soon again. Forgive me my horrible scrawl, and with my best love to dearest Albert, believe me, ever, my dearest Victoria, your most affectionate and faithfully devoted Aunt,

Adelaide.

Pray tell your dear mother, with my affectionate love, that I will answer her letter to-morrow.

INTERCHANGE OF VISITS

Windsor Castle, 14th February 1843.

My dearest Uncle,—Many thanks for your kind letter of the 10th, which I received on Sunday. I am only a little wee bit distressed at your writing on the 10th, and not taking any notice of the dearest, happiest day in my life, to which I owe the present great domestic happiness I now enjoy, and which is much greater than I deserve, though certainly my Kensington life for the last six or seven years had been one of great misery and oppression, and I may expect some little retribution, and, indeed, after my accession, there was a great deal of worry. Indeed I am grateful for possessing (really without vanity or flattery or blindness) the most perfect being as a husband in existence, or who ever did exist; and I doubt whether anybody ever did love or respect another as I do my dear Angel! And indeed Providence has ever mercifully protected us, through manifold dangers and trials, and I feel confident will continue to do so, and then let outward storms and trials and sorrows be sent us, and we can bear all....

I could not help smiling at the exactitude about Monday the 19th of June; it is a great happiness to us to think with such certainty (D.V.) of your kind visit, which would suit perfectly. À propos of this, I am anxious to tell you that we are full of hope of paying you in August a little visit, which last year was in so melancholy a way interrupted; but we think that for many reasons it would be better for us to pay you our first visit only at Ostend, and not at Brussels or Laeken; you could lodge us anywhere, and we need then bring but very few people with us—it might also facilitate the meeting with Albert's good old grandmother, who fears to cross the sea, and whose great wish is to behold Albert again—and would not be so difficult (pour la 1ère fois) in many ways. I could, nevertheless, see Bruges and Ghent from thence by help of the railroad, and return the same day to Ostend.

What you say about Peel is very just. Good Lord Melbourne is much better.

I hope soon to hear more about Joinville and Donna Francesca. Now, ever your devoted Niece, Victoria R.

We are all very well (unberufen) and move, to our horror, to town on Friday.

COBDEN'S ATTACK ON PEEL

Whitehall, 18th February (1843).

(Saturday morning.)

Sir Robert Peel presents his humble duty to your Majesty, and begs leave to acquaint your Majesty that the debate was brought to a close this morning about half-past three o'clock. The motion of Lord Howick14 was rejected by a large majority, the number being—

The chief speakers were Mr R. Cobden and Lord John Russell in favour of the motion, Mr Attwood, Lord Francis Egerton, and Sir Robert Peel against it.

In the course of the evening there was much excitement and animated discussion, in consequence of the speech of Mr Cobden, who is the chief patron of the Anti-Corn Law League.

Mr Cobden with great vehemence of manner observed more than once that Sir Robert Peel ought to be held individually responsible for the distress of the country.15

Coupling these expressions with the language frequently held at the meetings of the Anti-Corn Law League, and by the press in connection with it, Sir Robert Peel in replying to Mr Cobden charged him with holding language calculated to excite to personal violence.

Footnote 14: To go into Committee on the depression of the manufacturing industry. The debate turned mainly on the Corn Laws.

Footnote 15: To this attack Peel replied with excessive warmth, amid the frantic cheering of his party, who almost refused to hear Cobden's explanation in reply. Peel, alarmed at the fate of Drummond, thought (or affected to think) that Cobden was singling him out as a fit object for assassination. For years Cobden resented this language of Peel most deeply. "Peel's atrocious conduct towards me ought not to be lost sight of," he wrote in February 1846. A rapprochement was effected by Miss Martineau—see her letter to Peel (Parker, vol. iii. p. 330)—and a reference to the matter by Disraeli in the House of Commons led to satisfactory explanations on both sides.

Buckingham Palace, 18th February 1843.

The Queen, immediately on her arrival yesterday, went to look at the new Chapel, with which she is much pleased, but was extremely disappointed to find it still in such a backward state. As it is of the utmost importance to the Queen to be able to use it very soon, she wishes Lord Lincoln would be so good as to hurry on the work as much as possible; perhaps Lord Lincoln could increase the number of workmen, as there seemed to her to be very few there yesterday.

Footnote 16: Chief Commissioner of Woods and Forests.

FANNY BURNEY'S DIARY

Brocket Hall, 21st February 1843.

Lord Melbourne presents his humble duty to your Majesty. He received safely your Majesty's letter of the 18th inst. Lord Melbourne entreats your Majesty that you never will think for a moment that you can tire him by questions, or that it can be to him anything but a great pleasure to answer them. He will be only too happy if any information that he possesses or can procure can be of the least use or pleasure to your Majesty. Lord Melbourne conceives that your Majesty must be surprised at his complaining of sleeplessness. He is much obliged by the suggestion of the camphor. He mentioned it to the gentleman who attends him, and he said that it was a very good thing, and certainly has a soothing and quieting effect, and that in fact there was some in the draught which Lord Melbourne now takes at night. But Lord Melbourne has taken to going down to dinner with those who are in the house, and sitting up afterwards until near twelve o'clock, and since he has done this he has slept better. We expect the Duke and Duchess of Bedford for two nights on Wednesday next. Lord and Lady Uxbridge and Ella and Constance often come over in the morning and eat their luncheon here, which Lord Melbourne takes very kindly of them. George Byng[17] came the other morning in a waistcoat of Peel's velveteen. Lord Strafford brought the whole piece off the manufacturer, and let George Byng have enough for a waistcoat. It is a dull blue stuff, and the device and inscription not very clear nor easy to make out.[18]

Adolphus is, as Aberdeen says, too rigidly Tory, but there are plenty of narratives of the same period, such as Belsham[19] and others, of whom it may be said with equal truth that they are too Whig....

Lord Melbourne read the Edinburgh on Madame d'Arblay, which is certainly Macaulay's, but thought it unnecessarily severe upon Queen Charlotte, and that it did not do her justice, and also that it rather countenanced too much Miss Burney's dislike to her situation. It appears to Lord Melbourne that Miss Burney was well enough contented to live in the Palace and receive her salary, but that she was surprised and disgusted as soon as she found that she was expected to give up some part of her time to conform to some rules, and to perform some duty. Lord Melbourne is sorry to say that he missed the article on Children's Books,[20] a subject of much importance, and in which he is much interested.

Lord Melbourne has received the engraving of the Princess, and is much pleased by it, and returns many thanks. It is very pretty, very spirited, and as far as Lord Melbourne's recollection, serves him, very like. Lord Melbourne remains, ever, your Majesty's faithful, devoted, and attached Servant.

Footnote 17: Brother-in-law of Lord Uxbridge, and afterwards Earl of Stratford.

Footnote 18: The allusion is to a hoax played on the Premier, by a presentation made to him of a piece of the then novel fabric, velveteen, stamped with a free-trade design. Peel afterwards wrote that he was unaware that the specimen bore "any allusion to any matters which are the subject of public controversy."

Footnote 19: William Belsham (1752-1827) wrote, in twelve volumes, A History of Great Britain to the Conclusion of the Peace of Amiens in 1802.

Footnote 20: In the Quarterly Review, by Lady Eastlake.

Whitehall (4th March 1843).

(Sunday morning.)

Sir Robert Peel presents his humble duty to your Majesty, and begs leave to acquaint your Majesty that the prisoner MacNaghten was acquitted last night, after a trial which lasted two days, upon the ground of insanity.

The fuller account of the evidence which Sir Robert Peel has seen is on the accompanying newspaper.

The only other information which has reached Sir Robert Peel is contained in a note (enclosed) from Mr Maule, the solicitor to the Treasury, who conducted the prosecution. The three Judges21 appear to have concurred in opinion, that the evidence of insanity was so strong as to require a verdict of acquittal—and the Chief Justice advised the Jury to find that verdict without summing up the evidence or delivering any detailed charge upon the facts of the case and the law bearing upon them.

It is a lamentable reflection that a man may be at the same time so insane as to be reckless of his own life and the lives of others, and to be pronounced free from moral responsibility, and yet capable of preparing for the commission of murder with the utmost caution and deliberation, and of taking every step which shall enable him to commit it with certainty.

Footnote 21: Chief Justice Tindal, and Justices Williams and Coleridge.

Whitehall, 10th March 1843.

Sir Robert Peel, with his humble duty to your Majesty, begs leave to acquaint your Majesty that the House of Commons was occupied last night with the attack upon Lord Ellenborough for the Somnauth Proclamation.22

The motion was made by Mr Vernon Smith.23 The resolution proposed condemned the Proclamation as unwise, indecorous and reprehensible. Mr Vernon Smith was followed by Mr Emerson Tennent,24 one of the Secretaries to the Board of Controul.

Mr Macaulay next spoke, and condemned the conduct of Lord Ellenborough in a speech of great bitterness and great ability.

The motion was negatived by a majority of 242 to 157.

The minority included Lord Ashley, Sir Robert Inglis, and six other gentlemen, who generally support your Majesty's servants.

The debate was a very animated one, with a strong infusion of Party zeal.

Footnote 22: See ante, p. .

Footnote 23: Robert Vernon Smith (1800-1873), afterwards President of the Board of Control, created Lord Lyveden in 1859.

Footnote 24: James Emerson (1804-1869), afterwards Sir James Emerson Tennent, M.P. for Belfast, author of Letters from the Ægean, etc.

CRIMINAL INSANITY

Buckingham Palace, 12th March 1843.

The Queen returns the paper of the Lord Chancellor's to Sir Robert Peel with her best thanks.

The law may be perfect, but how is it that whenever a case for its application arises, it proves to be of no avail? We have seen the trials of Oxford and MacNaghten conducted by the ablest lawyers of the day—Lord Denman, Chief Justice Tindal, and Sir Wm. Follett,25—and they allow and advise the Jury to pronounce the verdict of Not Guilty on account of Insanity,—whilst everybody is morally convinced that both malefactors were perfectly conscious and aware of what they did! It appears from this, that the force of the law is entirely put into the Judge's hands, and that it depends merely upon his charge whether the law is to be applied or not. Could not the Legislature lay down that rule which the Lord Chancellor does in his paper, and which Chief Justice Mansfield did in the case of Bellingham; and why could not the Judges be bound to interpret the law in this and no other sense in their charges to the Juries?26

Footnote 25: Solicitor-General. His health gave way in middle life, and he died in 1845.

Footnote 26: In consequence of the manner in which the trial terminated, and the feeling excited in the country, the House of Lords put certain questions on the subject of criminal insanity to the Judges, whose answers have been since considered as establishing the law.

PRINCESS MARY OF BADEN

Foreign Office, 13th March 1843.

Lord Aberdeen presents his humble duty to your Majesty. In obedience to your Majesty's commands he has endeavoured to consider the letter of the Grand Duke of Baden with reference to the position of the Princess Mary27 in this country. Lord Aberdeen does not find in the proceedings of the Conference of Great Powers at Vienna, at Aix la Chapelle, or at Paris, anything which can materially affect the question. The great difficulty with respect to the Princess appears to arise from the fact that in this country the rank and precedence of every person are regulated and fixed by law. Should your Majesty be disposed to deviate from the strict observance of this, although Lord Aberdeen cannot doubt that it would receive a very general acquiescence, it is still possible that the Princess might be exposed to occasional disappointment and mortification....

There is a consideration, to which Lord Aberdeen would humbly advert, which may not altogether be unworthy of your Majesty's notice. Your Majesty does not wish to encourage alliances of this description; and although there may be no danger of their frequent occurrence, it cannot be denied that an additional inducement would exist if Princesses always retained their own rank in this country.

On the whole, Lord Aberdeen would humbly submit to your Majesty that the Princess might be received by your Majesty, in the first instance, with such distinction as was due to her birth— either by a Royal carriage being sent to bring her to your Majesty's presence, or in any manner which your Majesty might command—with the understanding that she should permanently adopt the title and station of her husband. Your Majesty's favour and protection, afforded to her in this character will probably realise all the expectations of the Grand Duke; and, without acknowledging any positive claim or right, your Majesty would secure the gratitude of the Princess.

Footnote 27: The Princess Mary of Baden had recently married the Marquis of Douglas, eldest son of the Duke of Hamilton. See p. .

THE PRINCE TO HOLD LEVÉES

Buckingham Palace, 17th March 1843.

The Queen has spoken again to the Prince about the Levées, who has kindly consented to do what can be of use and convenience to the Queen. There is one circumstance which must be considered and settled, and which the Queen omitted to mention to Sir Robert Peel when she saw him. The chief, indeed the only, object of having these Levées, is to save the Queen the extreme fatigue of the Presentations which would come in such a mass together when the Queen held them herself; the Prince naturally holds the Levées for the Queen, and represents her; could not therefore everybody who was presented to him be made to understand that this would be tantamount to a presentation to the Queen herself? There might perhaps be an objection on the part of people presented to kneel and kiss the Prince's hand. But this could be obviated by merely having the people named to the Prince. The inconvenience would be so great if nobody at all could be presented till late in the season, that something must be devised to get over this difficulty.

LEVÉES

Downing Street, 18th March 1843.

Sir Robert Peel presents his humble duty to your Majesty, and begs leave to submit to your Majesty that should your Majesty determine that the Prince should hold Levées on behalf of your Majesty, the best course will be to announce the intention from the Lord Chamberlain's Office in terms to the following purport:

"His Royal Highness Prince Albert will, by Her Majesty's command, hold a Levée on behalf of Her Majesty on ——

"It is Her Majesty's pleasure that presentations to the Prince at this Levée shall be considered equivalent to presentations to the Queen.

"Addresses to Her Majesty may be presented to Her Majesty through the Secretary of State, or may be reserved until Her Majesty can hold a Levée in person."

Sir Robert Peel humbly submits to your Majesty that it would not be advisable to prohibit by notice in the Gazette subsequent presentations to your Majesty. It will probably answer every purpose to state that they shall be considered equivalent, and when your Majesty shall hold a Levée it may be then notified at the time that second presentations are not necessary.

When the Prince shall hold the Levée, it may be made known at the time, without any formal public notification, that kneeling and the kissing of hands will not be required.

Sir Robert Peel hopes that the effect of holding these Levées may be materially to relieve your Majesty, but it is of course difficult to speak with certainty. He was under the impression that in the reign of Queen Anne, Prince George had occasionally held Levées on the part of the Queen during the Queen's indisposition, but on searching the Gazette of the time he cannot find any record of this.

Claremont, 19th March 1843.

The Queen has received Sir Robert's letter, and quite approves of his suggestions concerning the Levées. The Prince is quite ready to do whatever may be thought right, and the Queen wishes Sir Robert to act upon the plan he has laid before her in his letter of yesterday. Perhaps it would be right before making anything public to consider the question of Drawing-Rooms likewise, which are of such importance to the trades-people of London. It would be painful for the Queen to think that she should be the cause of disappointment and loss to this class of her subjects, particularly at this moment of commercial stagnation. The Queen conceives that it would be the right thing that the same principle laid down for the Levées should be followed with regard to Drawing-Rooms, the Prince holding them for her. The Queen is anxious to have soon Sir Robert's opinion upon this subject. The Queen on looking at the almanac finds that only the two next weeks are available for these purposes before Easter.

Whitehall, 27th March 1843.

Sir Robert Peel presents his humble duty to your Majesty, and hastens to reply to your Majesty's note of this date.

Sir Robert Peel assures your Majesty that he does not think that there is the slightest ground for apprehension on the occasion of the Levée, but Sir Robert Peel will, without the slightest allusion to your Majesty's communication to him, make personal enquiries into the police arrangements, and see that every precaution possible shall be taken.

He begs, however, humbly to assure your Majesty that there never has reached him any indication of a hostile feeling towards the Prince. It could only proceed from some person of deranged intellect, and he thinks it would be almost impossible for such a person to act upon it on the occasion of a Levée.

It may tend to remove or diminish your Majesty's anxiety to know that Sir Robert Peel has walked home every night from the House of Commons, and, notwithstanding frequent menaces and intimations of danger, he has not met with any obstruction.

He earnestly hopes that your Majesty will dismiss from your mind any apprehension, and sincerely believes that your Majesty may do so with entire confidence. But nothing shall be neglected.

THE COMET
Buckingham Palace, 28th March 1843.

My dearest Uncle,—I had the pleasure of receiving your kind letter of the 24th, on Sunday. How lucky you are to have seen the comet!28 It is distinctly to be seen here, and has been seen by many people, but we have till now looked out in vain for it. We shall, however, persevere.

We left dear Claremont with great regret, and since our return have been regaled with regular March winds, which, however, have not kept me from my daily walks. To-day it is finer again.

It is most kind and good of dearest Albert to hold these Levées for me, which will be a great relief for hereafter for me. Besides cela le met dans sa position; he and I must be one, so that I can only be represented by him. I think this, therefore, a good thing for that reason also; and God knows, he, dear angel, deserves to be the highest in everything.

Our Consecration went off extremely well, and the Chapel is delightful, and so convenient. I am sure you will like it.

You will be glad to hear that dear old Eos (who is still at Claremont) is going on most favourably; they attribute this sudden attack to her over-eating (she steals whenever she can get anything), living in too warm rooms, and getting too little exercise since she was in London. Certainly her wind was not in the slightest degree affected by her accident, for in the autumn she coursed better than all the other young dogs, and ran and fetched pheasants, etc., from any distance, and ran about the very evening she was taken so ill, as if nothing was the matter. Evidently part of her lungs must be very sound still; and they say no one's lungs are quite sound. She must be well starved, poor thing, and not allowed to sleep in beds, as she generally does.

Footnote 28: Its appearance gave rise to much discussion among astronomers. On the 17th Sir John Herschel saw its nucleus from Collingwood in Kent, and on the following night a dim nebula only; so it was probably receding with great velocity.

MELBOURNE ON DIET

Brocket Hall, 2nd April 1843.

Lord Melbourne presents his humble duty to your Majesty. He received yesterday morning your Majesty's letter of the 30th ult., for which he sincerely thanks your Majesty. Lord Melbourne is delighted to find that your Majesty was pleased with the bouquet. The daphnes are neither so numerous nor so fine as they were, but there are still enough left to make another bouquet, which Lord Melbourne will take care is sent up by his cart to-morrow, and left at Buckingham Palace. Lord Melbourne is very much touched and obliged by your Majesty's very kind advice, which he will try his utmost to follow, as he himself believes that his health entirely depends upon his keeping up his stomach in good order and free from derangement. He owns that he is very incredulous about the unwholesomeness of dry champagne, and he does not think that the united opinion of the whole College of Physicians and of Surgeons would persuade him upon these points—he cannot think that a "Hohenlohe" glass of dry champagne, i.e. half a schoppen,29 can be prejudicial. Lord and Lady Erroll30 and Lord Auckland and Miss Eden are coming in the course of the week, and they would be much surprised not to get a glass of champagne with their dinner. Lord Melbourne is very glad to learn that the Prince's Levée did well, and feels that His Royal Highness undertaking this duty must be a great relief and assistance to your Majesty. Lord Melbourne hopes to see the Baron here when he comes. The spring still delays and hangs back, but it rains to-day, which Lord Melbourne hopes will bring it on.

Footnote 29: A schoppen is about a pint; it is the same word etymologically as "scoop."

Footnote 30: William George, seventeenth Earl of Erroll, married a sister of the first Earl of Munster.

THE ROYAL CHILDREN

Buckingham Palace, 4th April 1843.

Dearest Uncle,—Many thanks for your very kind letter of the 31st, which I received on Sunday, just as our excellent friend Stockmar made his appearance. He made us very happy by his excellent accounts of you all, including dearest Louise, and the children he says are so grown; Leo being nearly as tall as Louise! En revanche he will, I hope, tell you how prosperous he found us all; and how surprised and pleased he was with the children; he also is struck with Albert junior's likeness to his dearest papa, which everybody is struck with. Indeed, dearest Uncle, I will venture to say that not only no Royal Ménage is to be found equal to ours, but no other ménage is to be compared to ours, nor is any one to be compared, take him altogether, to my dearest Angel!...

Whitehall, 6th April 1843.

Sir Robert Peel presents his humble duty to your Majesty, and has this moment received your Majesty's note.

Sir Robert Peel will immediately make enquiry in the first instance in respect to the correctness of the report of the dinner. The omission of the health of the Prince is certainly very strange—it would be very unusual at any public dinner—but seems quite unaccountable at a dinner given in connection with the interests of one of the Royal Theatres.

The toasts are generally prepared not by the chairman of the meeting, but by a committee; but still the omission of the name of the Prince ought to have occurred at once to the Duke of Cambridge, and there cannot be a doubt that he might have rectified, and ought to have rectified, the omission.

Sir Robert Peel is sure your Majesty will approve of his ascertaining in the first instance the real facts of the case—whether the report be a correct one, and if a correct one, who are the parties by whom the arrangements in respect to the toasts were made.

This being done, Sir Robert Peel will then apply himself to the execution of your Majesty's wishes, in the manner pointed out by your Majesty.

He begs humbly to assure your Majesty that he enters most fully into your Majesty's very natural feelings, and that he shall always have the greatest pleasure in giving effect to your Majesty's wishes in matters of this nature, and in proving himself worthy of the confidence your Majesty is kindly pleased to repose in him.

THE TOAST OF THE PRINCE

Whitehall, 6th April 1843.

Sir Robert Peel, with his humble duty to your Majesty, hastens to make a communication to your Majesty, on the subject of your Majesty's letter of this morning, which he hopes will remove from your Majesty's mind any unfavourable impression with regard to the toasts at the theatrical dinner, or to the conduct of the Duke of Cambridge in reference to them.

Sir Robert Peel, since he addressed your Majesty, has made enquiry from Colonel Wood, the member for Brecon, who was present at the meeting.

In order to have the real statement of the case, Sir Robert Peel did not mention the object of the enquiry. The following were the questions and the answers:—

Q. What were the toasts at the theatrical dinner last night?

Colonel Wood. The first was The Queen and the Prince. The Duke said he thought he could not give the health of the Queen in a manner more satisfactory than by coupling with the name of Her Majesty that of her illustrious Consort.

Colonel Wood said that his impression was that the Duke meant to do that which would be most respectful to the Prince, and that he had in his mind when he united the name of the Prince with that of your Majesty, the circumstances of the Prince having recently held the Levée on behalf of your Majesty.

It might perhaps have been better had His Royal Highness adhered to the usual custom, and proposed the health of the Prince distinctly and separately, but he humbly submits to your Majesty that the intention of His Royal Highness must have been to show respect to the Prince.

The reports of public dinners are frequently incorrect, the reporters being sometimes placed at a great distance from the chairman.

THE KING OF HANOVER

Whitehall, 12th April 1843.

Sir Robert Peel presents his humble duty to your Majesty, and will not fail to forward by the first opportunity the letter to Lord Ellenborough which accompanied your Majesty's note.

In consequence of his conversation yesterday morning with Baron Stockmar, Sir Robert Peel begs to mention to your Majesty that he saw to-day a private letter from Berlin, which mentioned that the King of Hanover had apparently abandoned the intention of visiting England this year, but that on the receipt of some letters from England, which he suspected to be written for the purpose of discouraging his visit, the King suddenly changed his intention and wrote a letter to your Majesty, stating that he had thoughts of such a visit.

It was not stated from whence the letters advising the King to remain on the Continent had proceeded.

This letter also stated that the King of Hanover proposed to waive his rank of Sovereign as far as he possibly could on his arrival in England, and to take his seat in the House of Lords without taking any part in the proceedings.

It added that the King could not, in any event, be in England before the latter end of May or beginning of June, and rather hinted that as his proposed visit was more out of a spirit of contradiction and impatience of obstacles being thrown in the way of it, than from any strong wish on his part to come here, he might probably change his intention and defer his visit, particularly if he should find that there was no particular impediment in the way of it.

Whitehall, 13th April 1843.

Sir Robert Peel presents his humble duty to your Majesty, and begs leave to acquaint your Majesty that the Duke of Cambridge having called on Sir Robert Peel this morning, he took an opportunity of asking His Royal Highness whether he thought the King of Hanover had made up his mind to visit England this year.

The Duke's reply was, as nearly as possible, as follows:—

"Oh yes, the King will certainly come, but I can tell you privately he means to have nothing to do with the House of Lords. He will not make his appearance there. The King has taken his servants for six weeks—that is, engaged their attendance upon him for that time. I know the porter is engaged and the stable servants. The King has written to Her Majesty. His real object in coming is to arrange his private papers, which were left in confusion, and to consult Sir Henry Halford."31

This was all that was material that His Royal Highness said.

Footnote 31: The eminent physician.

THE GATES OF SOMNAUTH

Camp, Delhi, 19th February 1843.

... The gates of the Temple of Somnauth, which have been escorted to Delhi by five hundred cavalry of the protected Sikh States, will be escorted from Delhi to Muttra, and thence to Agra by the same force of cavalry, furnished by the Rajahs of Bhurtpore and Alwar.32

While there has been universally evinced a feeling of gratitude to the British Government for the consideration shown to the people of Hindustan in the restoration of these trophies, there has not occurred a single instance of apparent mortification amongst the Mussulmans. All consider the restoration of the gates to be a national, not a religious, triumph. At no place has more satisfaction been expressed than at Paniput, a town almost exclusively Mussulman, where there exist the remains of the first mosque built by Sultan Mahmood after he had destroyed the city and temples of the Hindoos....

Footnote 32: See ante, p. .

DEATH OF THE DUKE OF SUSSEX

"I desire that on my death my body may be opened, and should the examination present anything useful or interesting to science, I empower my executors to make it public. And I desire to be buried in the public cemetery at Kensal Green in the Parish of Harrow, in the County of Middlesex, and not at Windsor."

Footnote 33: The Duke of Sussex died on 21st April of erysipelas. His first marriage in 1793 to Lady Augusta Murray, daughter of the fourth Earl of Dunmore, was declared void under the Royal Marriage Act. Lady Augusta died in 1830; her daughter married Sir Thomas Wilde, afterwards Lord Truro. The Duke contracted a second marriage with Lady Cecilia Underwood, daughter of the Earl of Arran and widow of Sir George Buggin: she was created Duchess of Inverness in 1840, with remainder to her heirs-male.

Strathfieldsaye, 21st April 1843.

My dear Peel,—I have just now received your letter of this day, and I return the enclosure in the box. It appears to me that the whole case must be considered as hanging together; that is, the desire to be buried at Kensal Green, that of Freemasons to pay Masonic Honours,34 that the body of the Duchess of Inverness should be interred near to his when she dies.

Parties still alive have an interest in the attainment of the two last objects, which are quite incompatible with the interment of a Prince of the Blood, a Knight of the Garter, in St George's Chapel at Windsor.

The Queen's Royal Command might overrule the Duke's desire to be buried at Kensal Green.35 Nobody would complain of or contend against it.

But there will be no end of the complaints of interference by authority on the part of Freemasons, and of those who will take part with the Duchess of Inverness: and it is a curious fact that there are persons in Society who are interested in making out that she was really married to the Duke.36 Against this we must observe that it will be urged that the omission to insist that the interment should take place in the Collegiate Chapel of St George's, Windsor, and thus to set aside the will, lowers the Royal Family in the opinion of the public, and is a concession to Radicalism. But it is my opinion that the reasons will justify that which will be done in conformity with the will.

I confess that I don't like to decide upon cases in such haste; and I cannot consider it necessary that a decision should be made on the course to be taken in respect to the Duke's funeral, on the morrow of the day on which he died.

It would be desirable to know the opinion of the Lord Chancellor, the Archbishop, and others.

I can't think of anything likely to occur, which might alter me: and I'll abide by that which I have above given.

It will be absolutely necessary to take effective measures for the preservation of the peace at this funeral at Kensal Green: and even that the magistrates should superintend the procession of the Freemasons. Believe me, ever yours most sincerely,

Wellington.

Footnote 34: The Duke of Sussex being Grand Master of England, and Master of the Lodge of Antiquity.

Footnote 35: The body lay in state at Kensington, and was eventually buried, as the Duke had desired, in the Kensal Green Cemetery.

Footnote 36: See ante, p. , note 33. The marriage took place, by special licence, at Lady Cecilia's house in Great Cumberland Place.

22nd April 1843.

My dearest Niece,—I am just come back and feel very anxious to know how you are, and beg at the same time to offer to you my most affectionate condolence on the melancholy event which has taken again another member of our family from us. Pray do not trouble yourself with answering this note, but let me hear how you feel, and whether you will like to see me to-morrow or at any time most convenient to you.

I feel deeply our new loss, which recalls all the previous sad losses which we have had so forcibly, and I pray that it may not affect you too much, dearest Victoria, and that you will not suffer from the shock it must have been to you. I was not in the least aware of the danger and near approach of the fatal end, and only yesterday began to feel alarmed by the accounts which I had received.

I have been with the poor Duchess of Inverness on my way to town, and found her as composed as possible under the sad circumstances, and full of gratitude to you and all the family for all the kindness which she had received. I pity her very much. It must be her comfort to have made the last years of the Duke's life happy, and to have been his comfort to the last moment.

I wish you good-night, dearest Niece, and beg you to give my best love to dear Albert, and to believe me most devotedly your most affectionate Aunt,

Adelaide.

BIRTH OF PRINCESS ALICE

Buckingham Palace, 16th May 1843.

My dearest Uncle,—Your kind and dear letter of the 12th has given me great pleasure. I am happy to give you still better accounts of myself.37 I have been out every day since Saturday, and have resumed all my usual habits almost (of course resting often on the sofa, and not having appeared in Society yet), and feel so strong and well; much better (independent of the nerves) than I have been either time. We are most thankful for it. The King of Hanover has never said when he will come, even now, but always threatens that he will....

Our little baby, who I really am proud of, for she is so very forward for her age, is to be called Alice, an old English name, and the other names are to be Maud (another old English name and the same as Matilda) and Mary, as she was born on Aunt Gloucester's birthday. The Sponsors are to be: The King of Hanover,—Ernestus the Pious; poor Princess Sophia Matilda,38 and Feodore, and the christening to be on the 2nd of June. It will be delightful to see you and dearest Louise on the 19th of June, God willing.

Are there any news of Joinville's proceedings at Rio?39 Ever your devoted Niece,

Victoria R.

Footnote 37: Princess Alice was born on 25th April.

Footnote 38: Princess Sophia Matilda of Gloucester.

Footnote 39: He married Princess Francesca, sister of the Emperor of the Brazils and of Queen Donna Maria.

CHRISTENING OF PRINCESS ALICE

India Board, 5th June 1843.

Lord Ripon, with his humble duty to your Majesty, begs to inform your Majesty that despatches have been this day received at the India House from the Governor-General of India and from the Governor of Bombay, announcing the successful issue of a battle, on the 24th of March, between Sir Charles Napier and Meer Shere Mahommed.40 The forces of the latter were completely routed, with the loss of all the guns and several standards.

Ripon.

Footnote 40: Sir Charles Napier, who was in command in Scinde, defeated the army of the Ameers of Upper and Lower Scinde at Meeanee on 17th February, and on the 20th took Hyderabad. On the 24th March he attacked the enemy, who were posted in a strong position on the banks of a tributary of the Indus, and obtained a decisive victory.

Claremont, 6th June 1843.

Dearest Uncle,—I received your kind letter on Sunday, and thank you much for it. I am sorry that you could not take the children to Ardenne, as nothing is so good for children as very frequent change of air, and think you do not let the children do so often enough. Ours do so continually, and are so movable that it gives us no trouble whatever.

Our christening went off very brilliantly, and I wish you could have witnessed it; nothing could be more anständig, and little Alice behaved extremely well. The déjeuner was served in the Gallery, as at dear Pussy's christening, and there being a profusion of flowers on the table, etc., had a beautiful effect.

The King of Hanover arrived just in time to be too late. He is grown very old and excessively thin, and bends a good deal. He is very gracious, for him. Pussy and Bertie (as we call the boy) were not at all afraid of him, fortunately; they appeared after the déjeuner on Friday, and I wish you could have seen them; they behaved so beautifully before that great number of people, and I must say looked very dear, all in white, and very distingués; they were much admired.

We came here on Saturday. The news from Ireland continue to be very alarming. Hoping to hear soon, for certain, when you come, believe me, ever, your devoted Niece,

Victoria R.

I hope you will kindly answer my letter of last Tuesday.

House of Commons, 9th June (1843).

My dear Sir Robert,—The King of Hanover took his seat at twenty minutes past four. He is now on the Woolsack with the Lord Chancellor, the Duke of Wellington, and Lord Strangford; no other Peers are in the House, the time of meeting being five o'clock.

It was not necessary that any other Peers should introduce His Majesty. He merely produced his writ of summons, and went to the table to be sworn. I remain, yours sincerely,

Thomas Fremantle.

Footnote 41: One of the Secretaries of the Treasury: afterwards Lord Cottesloe.

Footnote 42: Forwarded to the Queen by Sir Robert Peel.

IRISH AFFAIRS

Whitehall, 11th June 1843.

(Sunday.)

Sir,—In consequence of the conversation which I had with your Royal Highness on Thursday last on the subject of Ireland, I beg to mention to your Royal Highness that the Cabinet met again to-day at Lord Aberdeen's house.

We had a very long discussion.

The prevailing opinion was that if legislation were proposed,43 that legislation should be as effectual as possible; that there would be no advantage in seeking for new powers unless these powers were commensurate with the full extent of the mischief to be apprehended.

Foreseeing, however, all the difficulties of procuring such powers, and the increased excitement which must follow the demand for them, we were unwilling to come to an immediate decision in favour of recommending new legislation, and resolved therefore to watch the course of events for some time longer, continuing precautionary measures against disturbances of the public peace.

I have not received any material information from Ireland by the post of this day, nor has Sir James Graham.

I have the honour to be, Sir, with sincere respect, your Royal Highness's most faithful and humble Servant,

Robert Peel.

Footnote 43: In consequence of the Repeal agitation, the Ministers had already introduced an Irish Arms Bill, which was carried.

THE REBECCA RIOTS

South Street, 22nd June 1843.

Lord Melbourne presents his humble duty to your Majesty. He was infinitely obliged to your Majesty for coming into the room the other evening when he was with the Prince, and very much delighted to have an opportunity of seeing your Majesty, especially in such good health and spirits.

Lord Melbourne is very glad that your Majesty has seen As you Like It. It is indeed a most gay, lively, and beautiful play. To see or to read it is quite like passing an hour or two in a forest of fairyland. It is so lively, and at the same time so romantic. All depends upon Rosalind, which was an excellent part of Mrs. Jordan. Jaques is also a very particular character and difficult to play.

Lord Melbourne feels himself better, but still weak. He does not like to say much about politics, but he cannot refrain from observing that they seem to him to have permitted these lawless riotings in South Wales44 to go on with success and impunity a great deal too long. When such things begin nobody can say how far they will go or how much they will spread. There are many who expect and predict a general rising against property, and this is invariably the way in which such things begin.

Footnote 44: The agitation against the turnpike system which had broken out in South Wales. See Introductory Note, p. .

Buckingham Palace, 23rd June 1843.

The Queen returns these communications to Sir James Graham, which are of a very unpleasant nature. The Queen trusts that measures of the greatest severity will be taken, as well to suppress the revolutionary spirit as to bring the culprits45 to immediate trial and punishment. The Queen thinks this of the greatest importance with respect to the effect it may have in Ireland, likewise as proving that the Government is willing to show great forbearance, and to trust to the good sense of the people; but that if outrages are committed and it is called upon to act, it is not to be trifled with, but will visit wrong-doers with the utmost severity.

Footnote 45: I.e., the Rebecca rioters.

MILITARY MEDALS

Buckingham Palace, 24th June 1843.

The Queen follows Lord Stanley's recommendation to confer the G.C.B. on Sir Charles Napier with great pleasure, from her high opinion of his late achievements, and she thinks it might be advisable that some of the officers who most contributed to the victories of Meeanee and Hyderabad46 should receive lower grades of the Bath. The Queen is much impressed with the propriety of a medal being given to the troops who fought under Sir Charles Napier, as the armies under Nott, Pollock, and Sale received such distinctions for actions hardly equal to those in Scinde.

Footnote 46: See ante, p. .

Whitehall, 24th June 1843.

Sir James Graham, with humble duty, begs to lay before your Majesty the report received from Carmarthen this morning. The Earl of Cawdor went to Carmarthen this morning.47

Every effort will be made to trace this lawless outbreak to its source, and to bring the principal offenders to justice.

Sir James Graham encloses two Police Reports, which have been received this morning from Dublin. They would seem to indicate some foreign interference, and some hope of foreign assistance mingled with this domestic strife. Several Frenchmen have lately made their appearance in different parts of Ireland.

The above is humbly submitted by your Majesty's dutiful Subject and Servant,

J. R. G. Graham.

Footnote 47: Lord Cawdor was Lord-Lieutenant of Carmarthenshire.

Buckingham Palace, 24th June 1843.

My dear Duchess,—The same right which you feel, and which you had to overcome before you took the final step of tendering your resignation,48 has kept me from sooner acknowledging the receipt of your letter. Under the circumstances which you allude to, it is incumbent upon me to accept of your resignation, but as you throw out yourself a hint that it would be agreeable to you sometimes to perform the duties (which you have hitherto fulfilled), it would give me the greatest gratification if you would let me continue your name on the list of my Ladies of the Bedchamber, and sometimes at your convenience have the pleasure of your society.

I agree with you that for the present your step should not be known, till I shall have had time to find a successor, and I am pleased to think that you will take your waitings, which are at present settled.

With the Prince's kind regards to yourself, and mine to the Duke, believe me, always, yours very affectionately,

Victoria R.

Footnote 48: Of her position as Bedchamber Woman.

DUELLING IN THE ARMY

(July 1843.)

The Queen having attentively perused the proposed General Order for the more efficient repression of the practice of duelling in the Army, approves of the same, but recommends that the Duke of Wellington should submit to the Cabinet the propriety of considering of a general measure applicable to all branches of the Naval and Military Service.49

Footnote 49: An influential anti-duelling association had been formed this year, and subsequently public attention was drawn to the question by a duel on 1st July, at Camden Town, in which Colonel Fawcett was shot by his brother-in-law, Lieutenant Munro, who had reluctantly gone out, after enduring much provocation. Mainly owing to Prince Albert's efforts, the Articles of War were so amended as to put a stop to the practice.

THE SPANISH MARRIAGE

20th July 1843.

My dear Lord Aberdeen,—The Queen and myself have been taken much by surprise by Lord Howard de Walden's despatch marked "most confidential." The opinions of the Portuguese Court must have entirely changed. Although we have not heard anything on the subject, we are fully convinced of the correctness of Lord Howard's statements and of his conjectures. We are both pleased to see the view which he takes, and the good opinion he has of our little cousin. The Queen thinks it right that you should inform Lord Howard that the possibility of a marriage between Prince Leopold50 and the Queen of Spain has been for some time a favourite thought of hers and mine, and that you thought that this combination had some advantages which hardly any other could offer. But that the matter had been and was treated here as one purely and solely Spanish, in which we carefully abstained from interfering with, and that we leave it to work itself out or not by its own merit.

That you wished him to take the same view, but not to lose sight of it, and to report to you whatever he might hear bearing upon the subject. Believe me, etc.,

Albert.

Footnote 50: Son of Prince Ferdinand of Saxe-Coburg, and brother of the King of Portugal. See ante, p. , and post, p. .

Dear Duchess,—I write to inform you that I have named your successor,51 who is to be Lady Douro.52 The great regret I experience at your leaving me is certainly diminished by the arrangement which we have agreed upon together, and which will still afford me the pleasure of having you occasionally about me. I trust that the Duke's health will admit of your taking your waiting in September, but think it right to tell you that we shall probably at that time be making some aquatic excursions in our new yacht, and consequently be from home the greater part of your waiting.

With the Prince's best regards to yourself, and mine to the Duke, believe me, always, yours very affectionately,

Victoria R.

Footnote 51: As Bedchamber Woman.

Footnote 52: Elizabeth, daughter of the eighth Marquis of Tweeddale, afterwards Duchess of Wellington. She died in 1904.

Windsor Castle, 3rd August 1843.

The Queen returns the enclosed papers, and gives her sanction to the bringing in of the Bill for Enrolling and Arming the Out-Pensioners of Chelsea Hospital with great pleasure, as she thinks it a very good measure at the present crisis, calculated to relieve the troops which are rather overworked, and to secure a valuable force to the service of the Government. The Queen hopes that in bringing in the Bill Sir Robert Peel will make as little of it as possible, in order not to make it appear a larger measure than it is.

The Regulations strike the Queen as very judicious, and she has little doubt that they will raise the military spirit in the Pensioners, and will make the measure popular with them, which cannot fail to attach them more to the Crown.

Windsor Castle, 13th August 1843.

The Queen is desirous that whatever is right should be done, but is strongly of opinion that the King of Hanover's threat (for as such it must be regarded) not to leave this country till the affair53 is decided upon, should in no way influence the transaction, as it is quite immaterial whether the King stays longer here or not.

Footnote 53: Of the Crown jewels; ante, p. .

THE SPANISH MARRIAGE

Windsor Castle, 13th August 1843.

The Queen sees with great regret, in Sir Robert Gordon's despatch of 4th August, that Prince Metternich has resumed his favourite scheme of a marriage between the Queen of Spain and a son of Don Carlos, and that King Louis Philippe has almost come to a secret understanding with him upon that point.54 The Queen is as much as ever convinced that instead of tending to pacify Spain this combination cannot fail to call new principles of discord into action, to excite the hopes of a lost and vanquished party for revenge and reacquisition of power, and to carry the civil war into the very interior of the family. The Queen is anxious (should Lord Aberdeen coincide in this view of the subject, as she believes he does) that it should be clearly understood by Sir Robert Gordon, and Prince Metternich.

Footnote 54: Since the Quadruple Alliance (of England, France, Spain, and Portugal) in 1834 to expel Don Carlos and Dom Miguel from the Peninsula, the question of the marriage of Queen Isabella (then aged four) had been a subject of incessant consideration by England and France. The Queen-Mother had suggested to Louis Philippe the marriages of the Queen to the Duc d'Aumale and of the Infanta (her sister) to the Duc de Montpensier: such a proposal, however gratifying to the French King's ambition, would naturally not have been favourably viewed in England; but Guizot promoted warmly the alternative project of a marriage of the Queen to her cousin Don Francisco de Asis, Duke of Cadiz, son of Don Francisco de Paula, the Infanta being still to marry Montpensier. It was believed that, if this marriage of the Queen took place, there would be no issue of it, and Louis Philippe's ambition would be ultimately gratified. To Palmerston's protest against this scheme (before the Melbourne Ministry fell), Guizot replied, "La Reine aura des enfants et ne mourra pas." The other possible candidates for the Queen's hand from the French point of view were Count Montemolin, the son of Don Carlos, the Count de Trapani, son of Francis I., King of the Two Sicilies, and thus brother of Queen Christina, and the Duke of Seville, a brother of the Duke of Cadiz. Other candidates also favoured by the Queen-Mother were (while he was unmarried) Prince Albert's brother, and his cousin Leopold, brother of the King of Portugal; but the French King was bent upon a marriage of the Queen with some descendant of Philip V., and equally determined to prevent the Infanta's marriage either with Leopold or any other Prince not a descendant of Philip V. The view of Prince Albert and of Lord Aberdeen was that it was a matter for the young Queen herself and the Spanish people. See ante, p. .

Foreign Office, 13th August 1843.

Lord Aberdeen, with his most humble duty, begs to assure your Majesty that he will not fail to give his best attention to your Majesty's communication respecting the marriage of the Queen of Spain.

In a recent despatch to Sir Robert Gordon, Lord Aberdeen has repeated the opinion entertained by your Majesty's Government, that the marriage of the Queen with the son of Don Carlos, instead of leading to the conciliation and unison of parties, would be more likely to produce collision and strife, and to increase the existing animosity between the different political factions by which Spain is distracted.

This marriage, however, has always been a favourite project with Austria and the Northern Courts; and it has also been apparently supported by the French Government. It cannot be denied that at first sight there are many considerations by which it may seem to be recommended; but the weight of these can only be duly estimated by the authorities and people of Spain.

The same may be said respecting the marriage of the Queen with any other Spanish Prince, a descendant of Philip V. which, in the opinion of many, would be most agreeable to the feelings and prejudices of the nation. To this project also it appears that the French Government have recently assented.

Lord Aberdeen humbly thinks that the interests of this country and of all Europe are deeply concerned in the exclusion of a French Prince from the possibility of receiving the hand of the Queen; and that it would not be a wise policy to oppose any marriage by which this should be effected, consistently with the free choice of the Queen, and the sanction of the Spanish Government and people. The avowed predilections of Queen Christina, and her increased means of influence recently acquired, render this a matter of considerable anxiety and importance at the present moment.

PARLIAMENTARY OBSTRUCTION

Windsor Castle, 16th August 1843.

The Queen cannot refrain from writing a line to express her indignation at the very unjustifiable manner in which the minority of thirteen members obstructs the progress of business.55 She hopes that every attempt will be made to put an end to what is really indecent conduct. Indeed, how is business to go on at all if such vexatious opposition prevails? At all events, the Queen hopes that Sir Robert will make no kind of concession to these gentlemen, which [could] encourage them to go on in the same way.

The Queen forgot to say this morning that she thinks it would be better that the Investiture of the Thistle should be put off for the present.

Footnote 55: By opposition to the Bill removing doubts as to the admission of Ministers in

Scotland.

Windsor Castle, 22nd August 1843.

The Queen returns these papers to Sir J. Graham, and thinks that this important Memorial[56] should not be decided on without the opinion of the House of Lords; the Queen trusts that everything will be done to secure inviolate the maintenance of the Marriage Act.

Footnote 56: The memorial was that of Sir Augustus d'Este (1794-1848), the son of the union of the Duke of Sussex and Lady Augusta Murray. On 4th April 1793 they were married at Rome by an English clergyman, the ceremony being repeated in the same year at St George's, Hanover Square. The Court of Arches annulled the marriage in 1794, but Sir Augustus now preferred a claim to the peerage. Ultimately the Lords, after consulting the judges, disallowed it.

South Street, 23rd August 1843.

Lord Melbourne presents his humble duty to your Majesty, and thanks your Majesty much for the last note which he had the honour of receiving. Lord Melbourne is much pleased that your Majesty is glad of Wilhelmina Stanhope's marriage,[57] and was very glad to hear that your Majesty had congratulated her and Lady Stanhope upon it, which was very kind, and gave much satisfaction. Lord Dalmeny is an excellent young man, and altogether it is an event much to be rejoiced at, especially as it has been so long delayed, and fears began to be entertained that it would never happen. The Duke and Duchess of Sutherland seem also much pleased with Evelyn's[58] marriage. She is a beautiful girl, and a very nice person in every respect, and everybody must wish her happy. Lord Melbourne has been at Panshanger for two or three days with Uxbridge and Lady Uxbridge, Ella, and Constance. Uxbridge is having continual cricket matches as he used to have, which is a very good thing, making the country gay, and pleasing the people.

Matrimonial affairs, Lord Melbourne is afraid, remain in statu quo.

Lord Melbourne was very glad to hear from Anson yesterday and to learn that he thinks himself getting better. Lord Liverpool had given Lord Melbourne a very poor account of him. Lord Melbourne hopes that your Majesty may have a pleasant tour, but he cannot refrain from earnestly recommending your Majesty to take care about landing and embarking, and not to do it in dangerous places and on awkward coasts. Lord Melbourne is going the day after to-morrow with Lord and Lady Beauvale to Brocket Hall, and from thence on the 29th to Melbourne, to stay about three weeks or a month.

Lord Melbourne congratulates your Majesty upon the near approaching termination of the Session of Parliament, which is always a relief to all parties. Some great measures have been passed. Lord Melbourne wishes your Majesty health and happiness, and begs to be respectfully remembered to the Prince.

Footnote 57: To Lord Dalmeny. En secondes noces, she married the fourth Duke of Cleveland.

Footnote 58: Lady Evelyn Leveson Gower, married, on 4th October, to Charles, Lord Blantyre.

VISIT TO THE CHÂTEAU D'EU

Château d'Eu, 4th September 1843.

My dearest Uncle,—I write to you from this dear place, where we are in the midst of this admirable and truly amiable family, and where we feel quite at home, and as if we were one of them. Our reception by the dear King and Queen has been most kind, and by the people really gratifying.59 Everything is very different to England, particularly the population. Louise has told you all about our doings, and therefore tell you nothing but that I am highly interested and amused. Little Chica (Mdme. Hadjy)60 is a charming, sprightly, lively creature, with immense brown eyes. We leave this the day after to-morrow for Brighton, where the children are, who are extremely well, I hear. Many thanks, dearest Uncle, for your kind letter of the 29th, by which I see that poor Prince Löwenstein61 came to see you; he is Mamma's old friend. As I am in a great hurry, and as I hope, God willing, to see you very soon, I must conclude in haste, and leave all my remarks for another day. Ever your devoted Niece,

Victoria R.

Pray forgive this confused and horrid scrawl.

Footnote 59: The Queen was enthusiastically received at Tréport. On the 2nd there was a great entertainment in the banqueting-room of the Château, and on the 4th a fête champêtre on the Mont d'Orléans in the forest. On the 5th there was a review, and on the 7th the Queen returned to England.

Footnote 60: The Princess of Joinville. See ante, p. . Hadjy is the Prince of Joinville.

Footnote 61: Prince William of Löwenstein (1783-1847).

THE FRENCH VISIT

Melbourne, 6th September 1843.

Lord Melbourne presents his humble duty to your Majesty, and thanks your Majesty much for your letter of the 27th ult., which he received here some days ago. We have been quite dismayed and overwhelmed with the melancholy intelligence of death after death which has followed us. I was much concerned for poor Charles Howard's loss, but we were quite struck down by the melancholy event of poor Mrs W. Cowper.62 She promised to suit us all well, my sister particularly, and to be a great source of happiness and comfort.

Your Majesty is quite right in supposing that Lord Melbourne would at once attribute your Majesty's visit to the Château d'Eu to its right cause—your Majesty's friendship and affection for the French Royal Family, and not to any political object. The principal motive now is to take care that it does not get mixed either in reality or in appearance with politics, and Lord Melbourne cannot conceal from your Majesty that he should lament it much if the result of the visit should turn out to be a treaty upon any European matter, unfavourable to England and favourable to France. Do not let them make any treaty or agreement there. It can be done elsewhere just as well, and without any of the suspicion which is sure to attach to any transaction which takes place there.

Footnote 62: Mr and Mrs William Cowper had only been married on 24th June.

Laeken, 8th September 1843.

My dearest and most beloved Victoria,—I have been highly gratified that you found a moment to write me such a dear letter. I am sure that the personal contact with the family at Eu would interest you, and at the same time remove some impressions on the subject of the King, which are really untrue. Particularly the attempt of representing him like the most astute of men, calculating constantly everything to deceive people.

His vivacity alone would render such a system extremely difficult, and if he appears occasionally to speak too much and to seem to hold a different language to different people, it is a good deal owing to his vivacity and his anxiety to carry conviction to people's mind.

The impression of your visit will besides do wonders in removing the silly irritation which had been got up since 1840, and which might have in the end occasioned serious mischief, and that without being in the least called for, the passions of nations become very inconvenient sometimes for their Governors.... Your devoted Uncle,

Leopold R.

My best love to dearest Albert; he seems to have had the greatest success, and I am very glad of it, as it had some time ago been the fashion to invent all sorts of nonsense.

I left Stockmar extremely hypochondriacal, but I trust not so unwell as he fancied. His son accompanies him to Coburg.

THE QUEEN'S RETURN

On board the Victoria and Albert, in the River,63

21st September 1843.

My dearly beloved Uncle,—I seize the first opportunity of informing you of our excellent passage; we shall be in half-an-hour or three-quarters at Woolwich; it is now half-past ten A.M. The day and night were beautiful, and it is again, very fine to-day. We anchored in Margate Roads at eleven last night, and set off again about five.

Let me thank you and my beloved Louise in both our names again for your great kindness to us, which, believe me, we feel deeply. We were so happy with you, and the stay was so delightful, but so painfully short! It was such a joy for me to be once again under the roof of one who has ever been a father to me! I was very sad after you left us; it seems so strange that all should be over—but the delightful souvenir will ever remain. To leave my dearest Louise too was so painful—and also poor Aunt Julia,64 so immediately after making her acquaintance; pray tell her that, for me. I shall write to Louise to-morrow. You must forgive my hand being so trembling, but we are lighter than usual, which causes the tremulous motion to be so much more felt.

That God may bless and protect you all always is our fervent prayer. Believe me, always, your devoted and grateful Niece and Child,

Victoria R.

Footnote 63: On the 12th the Queen and Prince Albert sailed from Brighton on a visit to King Leopold. They visited Ostend, Bruges, Ghent, Brussels, and Antwerp.

Footnote 64: Sister of the Duchess of Kent, married to the Grand Duke Constantine.

Windsor Castle, 22nd September 1843.

The Queen has received Sir James Graham's letter of the 22nd.65 She has long seen with deep concern the lamentable state of turbulence in South Wales, and has repeatedly urged the necessity of its being put an end to, by vigorous efforts on the part of the Government. The

Queen, therefore, willingly gives her sanction to the issuing of a special Commission for the trial of the offenders and to the issuing of a proclamation. Monday, the 2nd, being the earliest day at which, Sir James says, the necessary Council could be held, will suit the Queen very well; she begs, therefore, that Sir James will cause the Council to meet here on that day at three o'clock.

Footnote 65: The insurrection of the Rebeccaites was assuming a more dangerous form, and at Hendy Gate they committed a cold-blooded act of murder.

MATRIMONIAL PROJECTS

Windsor Castle, 26th September 1843.

My dearest Uncle,—I cannot sufficiently thank you for your two most kind and affectionate letters of the 22nd and 23rd, which gave me the greatest pleasure. How often we think of our dear and delightful visit it is impossible for me to say; indeed, I fear these two never-to-be-forgotten voyages and visits have made me think Windsor and its daily occurrences very dull. But this is very ungrateful for what I have had, which is so much more than I ever dared to hope for. The weather is become colder, and yesterday and the day before were horrid, foggy, raw days; to-day it is finer again....

Feodore and Ernest came to us yesterday, and I find them both very well; Feodore is, I think, grown more serious than she was....

You remember that when we were together we talked of who Aumale could marry; he will only marry a Catholic, and no Spaniard, no Neapolitan, no Austrian, and also no Brazilian, as Louise tells me. Why should not Princess Alexandrine of Bavaria do? It would be a good connection, and you say (though not as pretty as Princess Hildegarde) that she is not ill-looking. Qu'en pensez-vous? Then for Tatane66—a Princess of Saxony would be extremely passlich.

How long does Aunt Julia stay with you?

Albert, I suppose, writes to you, and I, dearest Uncle, remain ever and ever, your most truly devoted and warmly attached Niece,

Victoria R.

We find Pussy amazingly advanced in intellect, but alas! also in naughtiness. I hold up Charlotte as an example of every virtue, which has its effect; for when she is going to be naughty she says: "Dear Ma, what does cousin Charlotte do?"

Footnote 66: Antoine, Duc de Montpensier.

ROYAL VISITORS

Windsor Castle, 3rd October 1843.

My dearest Uncle,—Many, many thanks for your kind letter of the 28th, received on Sunday, which was written from the Camp of Beverloo, which Albert recollects with great pleasure and interest, having amused himself so much there.

I can give you excellent accounts of ourselves. The boy returned from Brighton yesterday, looking really the picture of health, and much embelli; Pussy is in great force, but not to be compared to Charlotte in beauty; and Fatima (alias Alice) is as enormous and flourishing as ever. Dearest Louise seems much pleased with Aunt Julia, which I am glad of, and I rejoice that poor Aunt has had the happiness of making my beloved Louise's acquaintance, for it will be a happy recollection for her in her solitude.

We expect the Grand Duke Michael here this afternoon; he is to stay till Friday. The Michael Woronzows,67 with a son and daughter, are also coming, and we shall be a large party, and are going to dine in the Waterloo Gallery, which makes a very handsome dining-room, and sit after dinner in that beautiful grand Reception Room. How I envy your going to that dear French family! I hope that you will like my favourite Chica. I trust, however, that you will not stay too long away for your good people's sake.

Not being quite sure of your going, I shall direct this to Brussels still.

We went this morning to Kew, visited the old Palace—which is not at all a bad house—the Botanical Gardens, and then my Aunt's.68

The Revolution at Athens69 looks like le commencement de la fin; it was very unanimous.

Now, dearest Uncle, adieu! Ever, your most affectionate Niece,

Victoria R.

Footnote 67: Prince Michael Woronzow (1782-1856) was a plenipotentiary at the Congress of Aix-la-Chapelle (1818), and was in command at the siege of Varna in 1828.

Footnote 68: The Duchess of Cambridge.

Footnote 69: A bloodless revolution had taken place on the 14th of September, partly in consequence of King Otho exercising his patronage in favour of Bavarians rather than Greeks. He now acceded to the popular demands.

THE DUC DE BORDEAUX

Windsor Castle, 9th October 1843.

The Queen has received Lord Aberdeen's two letters. She has been reflecting upon his proposition that Mr Lytton Bulwer70 should be appointed Minister at Madrid, and quite approves it. The Queen trusts that he will try and keep on the best terms with the French Minister there, and that without in any way weakening our interests, the representatives of these two powerful countries will act together. The Queen feels certain that if it is known by our respective Ministers that both Governments wish to act together, and not against one another, that much irritation will be avoided; and that our agents, particularly in distant countries, will understand that they are not fulfilling the wishes of their Sovereign by representing every little incident in the most unfavourable light....

The Queen hopes that Lord Aberdeen will take some early opportunity of employing Mr Aston. Who will replace Mr Bulwer at Paris? his successor ought to be an efficient man, as Lord Cowley71 is rather infirm. The Queen regrets to say that the Duc de Bordeaux72 is coming here; he really must not be received by the Queen, as she fears his reception at Berlin has done no good; and altogether, from what she sees in the papers, she fears there is no good purpose in his coming here.

Footnote 70: Afterwards Lord Dalling.

Footnote 71: Lord Cowley, brother of the Duke of Wellington, and one of four brothers all either raised in or promoted to the peerage, was now seventy years of age. In after-years his son was also Ambassador at Paris.

Footnote 72: Afterwards known as Comte de Chambord, and claiming the French throne as Henri V.: he was grandson of Charles X., and at this time about twenty-three years of age.

Windsor Castle, 13th October 1843.

My dearest Uncle,—It is not my day, but my object in writing is to speak to you about the dear Nemours' visit, which we are so anxious to see accomplished. Louise writes to me about the Duke of Bordeaux coming to England making some difficulty, and I wish therefore to state what we know of the affair. We understand (for of course we have had no direct communication) that the Duc de Bordeaux has embarked at Hamburg for Hull, and intends travelling in Scotland before he visits England, and that incognito and under the name of Comte tel et tel; his being in Scotland when Nemours is in England, and particularly on a visit to us here, could make no difficulty, and even if he were travelling about incognito in England, it could not signify, I think. Moreover, I feel certain that if he knew that I had invited the Nemours and that they were coming over shortly, he would go away, as the Legitimists would not be pleased at Nemours being fêted by me—while their Henry V. was not even noticed or received. I could easily, and indeed have almost done so, make it known generally that I expect the Nemours, and I would say immediately, and he would be sure to get out of the way. I cannot tell you how very anxious we are to see the Nemours; I have been thinking of nothing else, and to lose this great pleasure would be too mortifying. Moreover, as I really and truly do not think it need be, it would be best if the Nemours could come before the 10th of November; which is the latest term when they could come? Now pray, dearest Uncle, do settle this for me; you have no notion how we wish it. I will be sure to let you know what I hear, and if there is anything you could suggest about this, I need not say but that we shall attend to it with pleasure. The Grand Duke Michael will be gone by the end of this month. Ainsi je mets cette chère visite dans vos mains. Ever your devoted Niece,

Victoria R.

Pray, dearest Uncle, let me have an answer by the next post about this, as I am all in a fidget about it.

ARREST OF O'CONNELL

Windsor Castle, 17th October 1843.

My dearest Uncle,—Your kind letter of the 13th I received yesterday, and return you my warmest thanks for it....

By your letter, and by one I received from Victoire yesterday morning, I see every reason to hope that we shall see the dear Nemours, for there will be no difficulty to prevent that poor stupid Duc de Bordeaux from being in London at the time. He is to be informed indirectly that the Nemours are coming at the beginning of next month on a visit to us, in consequence of a pressing invitation of ours; this alone will keep him off, as the contrast would be disagreeable to the Legitimists. Independent of this, his disembarkation at Hull, and proceeding at once to Scotland, seems to indicate his wish to be in private.

The great event of the day is O'Connell's arrest;[73] they have found bail, but the trial will shortly commence. The case against him is very strong, the lawyers say.

Everything is perfectly quiet at Dublin. You will have seen how O'Connell has abused the King; it is all because our visit to Eu has put an end to any hopes of assistance from France, which he pretended there would be, and he now declares for the Duc de Bordeaux!...

You must encourage the dear King and Queen to send over some of the dear family often to us; ils seront reçus a bras ouverts....

We intend to take advantage of Feodore and Ernest's going to the Queen Dowager's to pay a visit to Cambridge, where we have never been; we mean to set off to-morrow week, to sleep at Trinity Lodge that night, and the two following nights at Lord Hardwicke's,74 which is close to Cambridge. These journeys are very popular, and please and interest Albert very much....

Believe me, always, my dearest Uncle, your very affectionate Niece,

Victoria R.

Footnote 73: After the official prohibition on 7th October of the intended Clontarf meeting, O'Connell and others were arrested in Dublin for conspiracy. After giving bail, O'Connell issued an address to the Irish people. The trial was postponed till the following year.

Footnote 74: Wimpole, near Royston, nine miles from Cambridge.

THE DUC DE BORDEAUX

Drayton Manor, 20th October 1843.

Sir,—The enclosed letter75 from Sir James Graham to me (which as your Royal Highness will perceive is entirely of a private character) contains details of a conversation with Baron Neumann which will, I think, be interesting to Her Majesty and to your Royal Highness; and knowing your Royal Highness will consider the communication a confidential one, I prefer sending the letter in extenso to the making of any extracts from it.

I am afraid there is more in the Duc de Bordeaux's visit than the mere gratification of a desire on his part to see again places with which he was familiar in his youth.

If, however, he should be so ill-advised as to make any political demonstration, or to ally himself with any particular party in this country, he would, in my opinion, derive little from it, and there would be the opportunity of giving to the King of the French a new proof of our fidelity to our engagements, and of the steadiness of our friendship towards him and his dynasty.

The great body of the French people would comprehend the object of any such demonstrations on the part of the Duc de Bordeaux, and would, it is to be hoped, see in them an additional motive for union in support of the King, and confidence in the honour and integrity of this country.

I will not fail to inform the Grand Duke of Her Majesty's intended visit to Cambridge, and to suggest to him that it will not be convenient to the Queen to receive him at Windsor before Saturday at the earliest, and probably Monday.

On the day after I spoke to your Royal Highness I gave instructions for enquiries to be made respecting the two properties in the Isle of Wight.76 It is necessary to make such enquiries through some very confidential channel, as a suspicion of the object of them would probably greatly enhance the price.

The party on whom I could entirely rely was out of town, but will return to-morrow, and will immediately find out what he can respecting the properties.

The result shall be made known to the Queen and your Royal Highness without delay.

Will your Royal Highness have the goodness to mention this to Her Majesty?...

I have the honour to be, Sir, with sincere respect, your Royal Highness's most faithful and humble Servant,

Robert Peel.

Footnote 75: Referring to the visit of the Duc de Bordeaux.

Footnote 76: The Queen and the Prince were at this time making enquiries about a suitable residence in the Isle of Wight. The purchase of Osborne resulted.

THE QUEEN'S DECISION

Windsor Castle, 21st October 1843.

My dear Sir Robert,—I return you Sir James Graham's letter. There is a pretty general impression of the Duc de Bordeaux's visit being a got-up thing for various political intrigues. I confess I do not understand the link with Ireland, or at least the importance of his being well received by the Roman Catholics, but am strongly impressed that his presence whether in Scotland, England, or Ireland is for no good, and therefore think it our duty that we should render it difficult for him to protract it. The Queen and myself think that the uncertainty of his being received at Court or not is doing harm, and would much wish, therefore, that it was decidedly stated that the Queen will not receive him. His coming here without ever asking (indeed knowing that it was disliked), as well as the part which Austria and Prussia seem to have taken in the matter, do not strengthen his claim for such a favour. No good can come from the reception, and the King of the French must prefer its not taking place. Let us, therefore, settle that point, and show that we are neither afraid of him nor prepared to be made dupes of.

The Queen is desirous that no official person should treat the Duke with a distinction which is likely to attract unnecessary attention. Believe me, always yours truly,

Albert.

THE DUC DE NEMOURS

Windsor Castle, 24th October 1843.

My dearest Uncle,—I had the happiness of receiving your most kind letter of the 20th yesterday, for which I thank you very much. The good news of the dear Nemours coming is a great happiness to us, and I fervently hope and trust that the Duc de Bordeaux will be kept off, which I fully expect he will. Suppose, however, he could not be, and the Nemours could not come then, would the King not kindly allow them to come later? Even if the Chambers were to be sitting—such a little Ausflug of ten days only could really not be a great inconvenience? Surely if you were to mention this to the dear King, with my affectionate respects, he would grant it. It is besides only in case Bordeaux should come to London, which I really think he will not, if he once knows that the Nemours are coming. And I must add that I think Nemours not coming at all this year, after it had been announced, would have a bad effect, particularly as people here think that some great Powers have instigated Bordeaux's coming here,—and even think that the Roman Catholics and Repealers in Ireland mean to make use of him. Consequently

Nemours not coming at all, should he be prevented from coming at the beginning of November, would not be a good thing politically, independent of the extreme disappointment it would cause us....

The accounts both you and Louise gave me of good Hadjy and Chica give me great pleasure, as I take a lively interest in both, and am very fond of them. We found amongst some very curious old miniatures several of Catherine of Braganza when young (Charles II.'s wife), which are so like Chica;77 it is curious how sometimes you can trace likenesses many generations back....

Pray offer our respects to all. How long do you stay? Ever your devoted niece,

Victoria R.

Footnote 77: The Princess de Joinville was a sister of Queen Maria II. of Portugal, and Queen Catherine of Braganza was daughter of King John IV.

THE DUC DE BORDEAUX

Drumlanrig, 27th October 1843.

Lord Aberdeen, with his humble duty, begs to lay before your Majesty another letter received last night from Lord Morton,78 which gives an account of the visit of the Duc de Bordeaux, and of his further communication with the Duc de Lévis on the projects and views of His Royal Highness.

Lord Aberdeen has ventured to submit this letter to your Majesty, although not intended for your Majesty's perusal, as it gives a pleasing and satisfactory description of the conduct and sentiments of this unfortunate Prince.

In order to explain to your Majesty how Lord Morton, who lives in a very retired manner, should have received a visit from the Duc de Bordeaux, Lord Aberdeen begs to mention that when the family of Charles X. resided at Edinburgh, after the Revolution of July 1830, they received information more than once, from the present Royal Family of France, that certain desperate characters had left Paris for Edinburgh, with the intention of assassinating the Duc de Bordeaux, in order to prevent all possibility of a Restoration. In consequence of this information, it was thought to be dangerous for the Prince to walk or to expose himself in the neighbourhood of Holyrood House. He was frequently driven in a carriage to Lord Morton's,79 where he remained for a few hours, taking exercise in the park, and playing with Lord Morton's children. It is the recollection of this which has led the Prince to make his acknowledgments on the present occasion.

Lord Aberdeen also begs humbly to mention to your Majesty that on his arrival here he found the Duke and Duchess of Buccleuch in expectation of a visit from the Duc de Bordeaux, on his way from Glasgow to Carlisle. Lord Aberdeen informed the Duke and Duchess of the objections which might exist to this visit; but he believes that communications on the subject had already gone too far to render it possible to break it off with any degree of propriety. The great attentions paid by the Duke and his predecessors to the French Royal Family, both during the former and last emigration, sufficient account for this desire on the part of the Prince.

Footnote 78: George Sholto, nineteenth Earl of Morton (1789-1858).

Footnote 79: Dalmahoy, Midlothian.

VISIT TO CAMBRIDGE

Windsor Castle, 31st October 1843.

My dearest Uncle,—I had the pleasure of receiving your dear and kind letter of the 27th yesterday, by which I learn that you are all well and going on the 4th. Forgive me, dearest Uncle, if I say that I am glad that you are at length going back to Belgium, as (though I fully understand from personal experience how delightful it must be to be in the midst of that dear and perfect family) I think these long absences distress your faithful Belgians a little.

We returned on Saturday, highly pleased and interested with our tour,80 though a little done up. I seldom remember more enthusiasm than was shown at Cambridge, and in particular by the Undergraduates. They received my dear Angel, too, with the greatest enthusiasm. This is useful, as these young people will all, in time, have a certain part to play; they are the rising generation, and an event of this kind makes a lasting impression on their minds.

You will have heard from Louise that there is no longer any impediment to the dear Nemours coming, which you may easily conceive gives me the greatest satisfaction. Since then, I have heard that Bordeaux does not intend visiting London till he sees by the papers that the Nemours are gone. I saw a letter from a gentleman, with whom he had been staying, and who says that he is very pleasing and unaffected, and very easily amused, and quite pleased "with missing a few pheasants, and dancing quadrilles in the evening to a pianoforte." Poor fellow! his fate certainly is a melancholy one. He should renounce, buy some property in Germany, and marry, and settle there.

I am glad to hear of Montpensier's arrival, and that my favourite Chica is in your good graces; she is a dear natural child. I am so impatient to see my dear Victoire and good Nemours—who was always a great ally of mine—again!

The Grand Duke came here last night, and goes away after luncheon, and leaves England on Thursday. He is charmed with all he has seen, and I must say is very amiable and civil. He has got a most charming large dog, called Dragon, like a Newfoundland, only brown and white, with the most expressive eyes imaginable and si bien dressé. Prince Alexander of the Netherlands is also coming down to take leave this week. We never had so many visitors.

I am beyond everything interested with that beautiful novel by Rellstab,81 1812, which I know you admire so much. The description of the Russian Campaign is incomparable, and so beautifully written. You quite see everything before you. Have you read his other, Paris und Algier? By the by, have you read Custine's82 book on Russia? They say it is very severe on Russia, and full of hatred to the English.

We found the children very well, and Bertie quite recovered, but poor fat Alice (who, I must say, is becoming very pretty) has had the earache.

Mamma with Feo and Ernest are with the Queen Dowager at Witley Court since Thursday last, and only return next Thursday (the day after to-morrow). Clem seems very happy, and writes that she is happiest when she is tête-à-tête with poor Gusti, which I should not fancy. Ever, dearest Uncle, your devoted Niece,

Victoria R.

BETROTHAL OF THE DUC D'AUMALE

I open my letter, dearest Uncle, to say that I have just seen in a confidential despatch from Lord Cowley that Aumale is authorised to ask for the hand of the daughter of the Prince de Salerno83 (a singular coincidence after what I wrote to you in utter ignorance of this report), and that he was also to find out what the opinions of the Neapolitan Royal Family were respecting an alliance with the Queen of Spain. But tell me, dearest Uncle, if these reports are true? You may rely on my discretion, and I shall not breathe a word of what you may answer me, if you wish the secret to be kept.

Footnote 80: The Royal party went by road from Paddington to Cambridge, and stayed at the Lodge at Trinity; on the following day Prince Albert was made LL.D. The party then went to Wimpole, and visited Bourn (Lord Delawarr's). At the ball which was given at Wimpole, there was a sofa, covered with a piece of drapery given by Louis XIV. to the poet Prior and by him to Lord Oxford, the owner of Wimpole, before its purchase by Lord Chancellor Hardwicke. See Lord Melbourne's letter of 7th November, post, p. .

Footnote 81: Louis Rellstab (1799-1860), a prolific German writer of novels, whose thinly-veiled attacks on public men earned him at one time a sentence of imprisonment.

Footnote 82: The Marquis Astolphe de Custine (1790-1857), author of La Russie en 1839, at this time recently published.

Footnote 83: The Due d'Aumale married in November 1844, Caroline, daughter of the Prince and Princess of Salerno.

INDIAN AFFAIRS

Drayton Manor, 31st October 1843.

Sir Robert Peel presents his humble duty to your Majesty, and begs leave to return to your Majesty the accompanying communication from Lord Ellenborough, and a letter which your Majesty proposes to send to Lord Ellenborough.

In compliance with your Majesty's desire that Sir Robert Peel should inform your Majesty whether he sees anything objectionable in that letter, Sir Robert Peel humbly represents to your Majesty that he does not think it would be advisable for your Majesty personally to express to the Governor-General of India your Majesty's opinion with regard either to the policy of retaining Scinde,84 as being of the greatest importance to the security of the Indian Empire, or as to the completeness of the defence of Sir Charles Napier from the accusations brought against him.

He humbly and most respectfully takes the liberty of submitting to your Majesty, that these being matters of important public concern, the regular and constitutional channel for conveying the opinion of your Majesty with respect to them would be through your Majesty's servants.

In the particular case, indeed, of India, instructions do not proceed from your Majesty's servants, directly signifying your Majesty's pleasure, but are conveyed in despatches to the Governor-General, signed by the three members of the Secret Committee of the Court of Directors.

The Secret Court of Directors—that is, the whole Court acting in secret—have come to a Resolution (in Sir Robert Peel's opinion very unwisely and precipitately) expressing the gravest doubt, on their part, as to the policy and justice of the recent transactions in Scinde.[85]

The Court is aware that your Majesty's servants disapprove of this proceeding on their part, and that they have declined to transmit officially to Lord Ellenborough, through the Secret Committee, the condemnatory Resolution of the Court. One of the grounds on which they deprecated the Resolution was the passing of it in the absence of full and complete information from India, in respect to the policy and to the events which led to the occupation of Scinde.

Under these circumstances, as well on the general Constitutional ground, as with reference to the present state of the public correspondence in regard to Scinde, and the particular relation of the Governor-General to the East India Company, and the Court of Directors, Sir Robert Peel humbly advises your Majesty to forbear from expressing an opinion, in a private communication to the Governor-General, with regard to events in Scinde or to the policy hereafter to be pursued in respect to that country. Sir Robert Peel begs to add that in a private letter by the last mail to Lord Ripon, Lord Ellenborough observes that he is going on very harmoniously with the Members of Council at Calcutta.

Footnote 84: Earlier in the year Lord Ellenborough had appointed Sir Charles Napier Governor of Scinde, and had by Proclamation applied the Slave Trade and Slavery Abolition Acts to Scinde.

Footnote 85: See Parker's Sir Robert Peel, vol. iii. chap. 1.

Melbourne, 7th November 1843.

Lord Melbourne presents his humble duty to your Majesty, and thanks your Majesty much for the letter of the 4th inst., which he has received this morning with great satisfaction. Lord Melbourne hears with great pleasure of the gratification which your Majesty and the Prince received in your visit to Cambridge. Lord Melbourne collects from all the accounts that the proceedings in the Senate House were not only full of loyalty, enthusiasm, and gratitude, but also perfectly decorous, respectful, academic, and free from all those political cries which have recently prevailed so much in the theatre at Oxford on similar occasions.[86] Lord Melbourne hopes he is within [the mark]; if he is it forms a remarkable and advantageous contrast. Lord Melbourne does not know anywhere a better account of Cambridge, its foundations, and the historical recollections of its founders, than is given in Mr. Gray's ode on the installation of the Duke of Grafton, which it would not be amiss to read with the large explanatory notes that are given in the editions of Mason and Mathias.[87]

Lord Melbourne is very partial to Lord Hardwicke, who always is and has been very civil and good-natured to Lord Melbourne, and these are qualities to which Lord Melbourne is not at all indifferent. Wimpole is a curious place. Lord Melbourne is not exactly aware how the Yorkes got hold of it.[88] There is much history and more poetry connected with it. Prior[89] mentions it repeatedly, and always calls the first Lady Harley, the daughter of the Duke of Newcastle, Belphebe.[90] If Hardwicke should have a daughter, he should christen her Belphebe. The Lady Belphebe Yorke would not sound ill....

Footnote 86: See ante, p. .

Footnote 87: Gray, the poet, who had been appointed by the Duke Professor of Modern History, composed an ode (set to music by Randall) for the latter's installation as Chancellor, on 1st July 1769.

Footnote 88: The cultured but indolent Edward, Lord Harley, afterwards Earl of Oxford (son of the great minister), sold Wimpole to Lord Chancellor Hardwicke in 1740 to pay off a debt of £100,000. He had married Lady Henrietta Cavendish Holles, daughter and heiress of John, Duke of Newcastle, who brought him £500,000, most of which he dissipated. Their only child, Margaret, the "noble lovely little Peggy" of Prior, married William Bentinck, second Duke of Portland. Lady Oxford sold to the nation the "Harleian Collection" of manuscripts, now in the British Museum.

Footnote 89: Who died there in 1721.

Footnote 90: Alluding to the rarely printed poem "Colin's Mistakes," where "Bright Ca'ndish Holles Harley" is seen in the glades of Wimpole by the dreamy youth, and mistaken for Gloriana, Belphebe, etc.

PROPOSED VISIT TO PEEL

Whitehall, 9th November 1843.

Sir,—I was greatly gratified by learning on my return to London last night from Witley Court that it is not improbable that Her Majesty and your Royal Highness may confer the high honour of a visit to Drayton Manor towards the conclusion of the present month.

I venture to think, from what I saw of Witley Court, that the arrangement proposed by your Royal Highness will be more convenient to Her Majesty than the staying at Witley Court.

I can assure your Royal Highness that nothing shall be left undone by Lady Peel and me to contribute to the comfort of Her Majesty and your Royal Highness during your occupation of Drayton Manor, and to mark our sense of the kind condescension of Her Majesty and your Royal Highness in making it your abode.

I have the honour to be, Sir, with sincere respect, your Royal Highness's most faithful and humble Servant,

Robert Peel.

TRAVELLING ARRANGEMENTS

Whitehall, Sunday, 12th November 1843.

Sir,—I send to your Royal Highness a little book which is published every month, giving very useful information as to distances, or at least times, on all the railways. Possibly your Royal Highness has this book regularly sent to you.

I think, before Her Majesty promises a visit to Witley Court, there are one or two points worthy of consideration which are in favour of proposing to the Queen Dowager to meet the Queen at Drayton Manor first. The Queen would have to go and to return in the same day. The Queen Dowager might remain either one night or two nights at Drayton. Secondly, the Birmingham and Derby line is not on the same level with the line which goes to Droitwich (eleven miles from Witley Court), and there is a little delay in posting a carriage, or in passing from the lower line of railway to the upper.

Thirdly, there is the passage for Her Majesty, though not through Birmingham as in an ordinary travelling carriage, yet in the immediate outskirts of the town, and this twice in the same day.

The Corporation (which is a completely Radical one) might solicit permission to present an Address to Her Majesty at the station.

There would, I am sure, be nothing but demonstrations of the greatest loyalty and attachment to Her Majesty, but there would probably be a great concourse of people, and some delay, if the Address were received.

Perhaps your Royal Highness will think of these suggestions, which I am induced to offer by the desire to foresee everything which may have a bearing upon the personal comfort of the Queen.

I have the honour to be, Sir, with sincere respect, your Royal Highness's most faithful and humble Servant,

Robert Peel.

THE DUCHESSE DE NEMOURS

Windsor Castle, 14th November 1843.

My dearest, kindest Uncle,—A long and most interesting letter reached me on Sunday, dated 9th and 10th, and I beg to return my warmest thanks for it. The confidence you show me I feel deeply and gratefully, and you may rely on my discretion. Before I touch upon any of the subjects in your letter I will give you news of our visitors. The dear Nemours arrived safely after a good passage on Saturday, well but very tired. They are now quite recovered, and we are too happy to have them here. Nemours looks well, and is very kind and amiable, but I think there is a seriousness since poor Chartres' death which used not to be formerly, though he always was reserved, and that, I think, he is not now. Dearest Victoire is amazingly improved and développée—really quite wonderfully so. We are all so struck by it, by her good sense and by her conversation; and with that she has kept that innocence and gentleness which she always had—and is so lovely, dear sweet child. I must always look at her, and she, dear child, seems so pleased to see me again. I find her grown, but grown very thin, and she has not those bright colours she used to have. All that you say of Bordeaux is just what Nemours says, and what Guizot writes, and what I and also Sir Robert Peel always felt and thought. Aberdeen, with the greatest wish to do all that is kind and right, really thought that B. was only come to amuse himself, and had no idea till now that the feeling in France in all the different parties was so strong. You will have heard by this time that we have decided not to receive B. in any way whatever. It is a pleasure to hear how mildly and sensibly Nemours speaks upon all these subjects, and indeed every subject....

I think you did uncommonly right in what you answered the poor King about the arrêté in favour of the Prussians, and I am very glad you have done so. It will have a good effect here.

Louise will tell you how we celebrated good Bertie's birthday. The children are in great favour with the Nemours.

Pray, dearest Uncle, do not forget to send me the list of Rellstab's works. We think of making another little tour after the dear Nemours' departure, to Drayton (Sir Robert Peel's), Chatsworth, and Belvoir.

We are very sorry to lose dear Feo and Ernest. They are so good and excellent, and she is so brav. Ever, your devoted Niece,

Victoria R.

BIRMINGHAM

[Memorandum enclosed from Sir Robert Peel to Prince Albert, about the political condition of Birmingham, which the Prince was intending to visit.]

The Mayor is a hosier—of extreme political opinions—in fact, a Chartist.

The contest for the office of Mayor was between him and a man of Radical opinions, but Chartism prevailed.

The Mayor has taken a violent part, before his Mayoralty, against Church Rates, and in reference to the state of Ireland.

The Conservative party took no part whatever in the Municipal Elections, and would not vote.

They would, if invited or permitted by the Mayor and Town Council, cordially co-operate with men of opposite opinions in any mark of respect to the Prince.

No probability of any tumult or of any demonstration but one of respect personally towards the Prince, if his visit be clearly and manifestly unconnected with politics.

An immense concourse of people must be expected, not only from Birmingham, but Wolverhampton, Walsall, and all the neighbouring towns, and previous police arrangements must be very carefully made.

There may be a proposal of a collation and of an Address, to be received in the Town Hall.

Should not the Lord Lieutenant (Lord Warwick) have notice?

Is the Mayor to accompany the Prince in the same carriage?91

The Mayor has no carriage.

No communication should be made to any party in Birmingham, except to the municipal authorities, notwithstanding their political bias and extreme opinions.

The late Mayor, Mr James, though a Radical, would have summoned the leading men of different parties.

Doubts as to whether the present Mayor would, or whether he would not, place the whole arrangement in the hands of the party with which he is connected.

This risk must be incurred, as communications to other parties would not be advisable.

Footnote 91: This was the course adopted.

THE DUC DE BORDEAUX

Foreign Office, 1st December 1843.

Lord Aberdeen presents his humble duty to your Majesty. He has not yet received any communication from the Duc de Lévis, notwithstanding he had been led to expect it, from a notice repeatedly conveyed to him to that effect. It seems probable that in consequence of what the Duc de Lévis may have heard, as well as from the course pursued by the friends of the Duc de Bordeaux, Lord Aberdeen may not now see him at all. Should this be the case, Lord Aberdeen is rather inclined to regret it; as although he would formerly have seen him with some reluctance, he would now be glad to have an opportunity of expressing his sentiments very plainly respecting the proceedings of the Prince and his adherents in this country.

Lord Aberdeen understands from Sir Robert Peel that your Majesty would like to be informed of any particulars connected with the Levée lately held by the Duc de Bordeaux. Lord Aberdeen would willingly communicate these particulars, but in reality there is very little to be added to the official accounts contained in the Morning Post, which it is obvious are inserted by authority. He saw M. de Ste Aulaire this morning, who was a good deal excited by what has taken place, and has written very fully to Paris; but he knew nothing more than he had seen in the newspapers.

It may perhaps be worth mentioning to your Majesty that at the presentation of the Address by M. Chateaubriand92 on Friday, the cries of "Vive le Roi!" and "Vive Henri V.!" were so loud as to be distinctly audible in the Square. Lord Aberdeen understands that this enthusiasm has been the cause of serious differences amongst many of those who had come to pay their respects to the Duc de Bordeaux, a large portion of whom are by no means disposed to recognise him as King during the life of the Duc d'Angoulême.93

Lord Aberdeen cannot learn that any other member of the Diplomatic Body has been presented to the Duc de Bordeaux, and does not believe that any such presentation has taken place. Indeed, there appears to be a general disinclination that such should be the case; although some of them feel considerable difficulty in consequence of the relationship existing between their Sovereigns and the Prince.

Footnote 92: François, Vicomte de Chateaubriand (1768-1848), a great supporter of the Bourbons, and made a Peer in 1815. He was Ambassador in London in 1822.

Footnote 93: Eldest son of Charles X.

Chatsworth, 3rd December 1843.

The Queen approves of Lord Stanley's proposed Draft to Sir Charles Metcalfe.94 This question can in no way be settled without giving offence to one part of the country; the Queen, however, hopes that the fixing upon Montreal as the seat of Government will hereafter be considered as fair by impartial minds. Sir Charles continues to show great discretion and firmness in his most arduous and unsatisfactory situation, and deserves much praise and encouragement.

Footnote 94: Governor-General of Canada.

VISIT TO CHATSWORTH

Belvoir Castle, 4th December 1843.

My dearest Uncle,—Being much hurried, I can only write you a few lines to thank you for your kind letter of the 29th, received this morning. You will have heard from Louise the account of our stay at Drayton (which is a very nice house), and of Albert's brilliant reception at Birmingham. We arrived at Chatsworth on Friday, and left it at nine this morning, quite charmed and delighted with everything there. Splendour and comfort are so admirably combined, and the Duke does everything so well. I found many improvements since I was there eleven years ago.

The conservatory is out and out the finest thing imaginable of its kind. It is one mass of glass, 64 feet high, 300 long, and 134 wide.95 The grounds, with all the woods and cascades and fountains, are so beautiful too. The first evening there was a ball, and the next the cascades and fountains were illuminated, which had a beautiful effect. There was a large party there, including many of the Duke's family, the Bedfords, Buccleuchs, the Duke of Wellington, the Normanbys, Lord Melbourne (who is much better), and the Beauvales. We arrived here at half-past two, we perform our journey so delightfully on the railroad, so quickly and easily. It puts me in mind of our dear stay in Belgium, when we stop at the various stations.

Albert is going out hunting to-morrow, which I wish was over, but I am assured that the country is much better than the Windsor country.

The Duc de Bordeaux's proceedings in London are most highly improper.

The Queen Dowager is also here.

We leave this place on Thursday for home, which, I own, I shall be glad of at last. Ever your devoted Niece,

Victoria R.

Footnote 95: It was built by Mr Joseph Paxton, then Superintendent of the Gardens, whose intelligence had attracted the Duke of Devonshire's attention. In 1850 he was the successful competitor for the Great Exhibition building, and was knighted on its completion. He superintended its re-erection at Sydenham, and afterwards became M.P. for Coventry.

Langenburg, 10th December 1843.

My dearest Victoria,—... You ask in your letter about the manner in which my children say their prayers? They say it when in their beds, but not kneeling; how absurd to find that necessary, as if it could have anything to do with making our prayers more acceptable to the Almighty or more holy. How really clever people can have those notions I don't understand. I am sorry it is the case there, where there is so much good and, I am certain, real piety. Dear Pussy learning her letters I should like to see and hear; I am sure she will learn them very quick. Has Bertie not learned some more words and sentences during your absence?...

Your attached and devoted sister,

Feodora.

PRINCE ALBERT WITH THE HOUNDS

Windsor Castle, 12th December 1843.

My dearest Uncle,—I thank you much for your kind letter of the 7th, which I received as usual on Sunday. Louise will be able to tell you how well the remainder of our journey went off, and how well Albert's hunting answered.96 One can hardly credit the absurdity of people here, but Albert's riding so boldly and hard has made such a sensation that it has been written all over the country, and they make much more of it than if he had done some great act!

It rather disgusts one, but still it had done, and does, good, for it has put an end to all impertinent sneering for the future about Albert's riding. This journey has done great good, and my beloved Angel in particular has had the greatest success; for instance, at Birmingham the good his visit has done has been immense, for Albert spoke to all these manufacturers in their own language, which they did not expect, and these poor people have only been accustomed to hear demagogues and Chartists.

We cannot understand how you can think the country about Chatsworth not pretty, for it is (with the exception of the moors) beautiful, wooded hills and valleys and rapid streams. The country round Belvoir I do not admire, but the view from the castle is very fine and extensive, and Albert says puts him so in mind of the Kalenberg....

Pray have you heard anything about Aumale's plans? Dear little Gaston seems much better.

The Duc de Bordeaux has been informed of my and the Government's extreme displeasure at their conduct; they say there shall be no more such displays. He was to leave London yesterday, only to return again for a day, and then to leave England altogether.

With Albert's love, ever, dearest Uncle, your most devoted Niece,

Victoria R.

Footnote 96: The Prince hunted with the Belvoir hounds on the 5th.

AN AMERICAN VIEW OF MONARCHY

Laeken, 15th December 1843.

My dearest Victoria,—I am most happy to see that your journey passed so well, and trust you are not sorry to be again in your very dear and comfortable home, and with your dear children. People are very strange, and their great delight is to find fault with their fellow-creatures; what harm could it have done them if Albert had not hunted at all? and still I have no doubt that his having hunted well and boldly has given more satisfaction than if he had done Heaven knows what praiseworthy deed; ainsi est et sera le monde.

I am glad also that the Birmingham course succeeded so well; the theme had been for some years, particularly amongst manufacturers, that Royalty was useless and ignorant, and that the greatest blessing would be, to manufacture beyond measure, and to have an American form of Government, with an elective head of State.

Fortunately, there has always hitherto been in England a very aristocratic feeling freely accepted by the people, who like it, and show that they like it.... I was much amused, some time ago, by a very rich and influential American from New York assuring me that they stood in great need of a Government which was able to grant protection to property, and that the feeling of many was for Monarchy instead of the misrule of mobs, as they had it, and that he wished very much some branch of the Coburg family might be disposable for such a place. Qu'en dites-vous, is not this flattering?...

There is nothing very remarkable going on, besides I mean to write again on some subjects. Give my best love to Albert, and Pussy, who may remember me perhaps, and I remain, ever, my beloved Victoria, your devoted Uncle,

Leopold R.

Windsor Castle, 19th December 1843.

My dearest Uncle,—Your kind and dear letter of the 15th, written in your true wit and humour, reached me on Sunday and gave me great pleasure. We have had also most wonderfully mild weather, but I think very disagreeable and unseasonable; it always makes me so bilious. The young folks are very flourishing and prosperous—Pussette knowing all her letters, and even beginning to read a little. When I mentioned your birthday to her, she said, "I cried when I saw Uncle Leopold," which was the case, I am sorry to say, the first time she saw you this year....

I don't believe that the white flag on the house at Belgrave Square97 is true. Lord Melbourne and the Beauvales were here for three nights; and it was a pleasure to see Lord Melbourne so much himself again; the first evening he was a good deal excited and talked and laughed as of old; the two other evenings he was in the quite silent mood which he often used to be in formerly, and really quite himself, and there was hardly any strangeness at all. Lady Beauvale is really a very, very, charming person, and so attentive and kind to both her husband and Lord Melbourne. Our little chapel here (which is extremely pretty) is to be consecrated this morning, and Lady Douro comes into Waiting for the first time. To-morrow Mamma gives us a dinner. Poor Lord Lynedoch98 is, I fear, dying, and Lord Grey is so bad he cannot last long.99

Ever your devoted Niece,

Victoria R.

Footnote 97: The house occupied by the Duc de Bordeaux.

Footnote 98: Thomas, Lord Lynedoch, had died the previous day, aged ninety-five. He highly distinguished himself in the Peninsula and in Holland, and received the thanks of Parliament, and a Peerage in 1814.

Footnote 99: He died in July 1845.

THE SPANISH MARRIAGE

Windsor Castle, 28th December 1843.

The Queen has been much amused to see by Sir Robert Gordon's despatch of the 15th, the extreme fright of Prince Metternich at the proposed marriage of Queen Isabel with Count Trapani,100 but she regrets that Sir Robert tried to make excuses for the conduct we have pursued, which the Queen thinks requires no apology.

Footnote 100: See ante, p. , note 55.

Printed by Hazell, Watson & Viney, Ld., London and Aylesbury.

Paper supplied by John Dickinson & Co., Ld., London.

15704575R00223

Printed in Poland
by Amazon Fulfillment
Poland Sp. z o.o., Wrocław